Greenland
& The Arctic

Etain O'Carroll and Mark Elliott

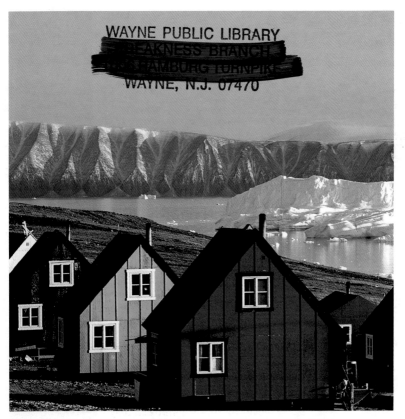

Contents

Arctic Scandinavia p297

Arctic Russia p268

Northwest Greenland p190

East Greenland p203

Disko Bay p169

Southwest Greenland p135

Arctic North America p235

South Greenland p96

Destination Greenland & The Arctic

Put simply, the Arctic is addictive. One trip and you'll be smitten. You'll immediately want to phone your friends, impress your grandchildren and bore your neighbours with your tales of immense blue skies, pure light, endless tundra and gargantuan icebergs. And yet your words will barely do it justice.

It's difficult to explain that overwhelming sense of fear and awe that grips you as you stand on the frozen expanse, far from any man-made object, kilometres from a road, a siren or even a car alarm. The silence just engulfs you. The vastness of the land, the brute force of nature and your insignificance in it all vividly remind you just why you ever yearned to travel.

You can stick to a stay-safe Arctic voyage on a luxury cruise or battle against the elements on a two-month overland trek to the Pole. Either way, you'll learn a new sense of respect both for nature and for the incredible people who make this region their home.

In midafternoon you can stargaze at an endless night sky, watch the playful twists of the aurora borealis and wait for your eyelashes to freeze to your balaclava. You can take off across the tundra by dogsled and get swallowed by kilometres of windswept ice and snow. Or you can wait for summer, when the midnight sun circles overhead and you can hike for weeks without seeing another person.

Life up north will amaze and bewilder you at the same time. Travel here is far from straightforward, but there is simply no other place on earth that will grab your imagination so profoundly, dominate your conversations so obsessively and stay with you in such brilliant detail. No matter what you have to spend to get here, you will be handsomely repaid.

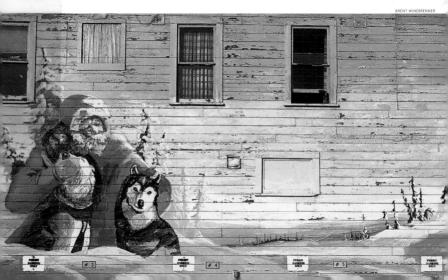

Sea of Okhotsk

RUSSIA

Kamchatka Peninsula

Laptev Sea

Cape Chelyuskin

New Siberian Islands

De Long Islands

Average Summer Minimum Extent of Sea Ice

East Siberian Sea

Arctic Circle

● Anadyr

Wrangel Island

ARCTIC NATIONAL WILDLIFE REFUGE (p254)
Witness the incredible migration of thousands of porcupine caribou

Chukotka Peninsula

Chukchi Sea

Bering Sea

Cape Dezhnev

Bering Strait

● Teller

● Nome

● Kotzebue

Barrow ●

ARCTIC OCEAN

Peary Channel

Parry Island

ALASKA (USA)

Arctic National Wildlife Refuge

Beaufort Sea

Banks Island

McClure Strait

Alaska Peninsula

● Fairbanks

● Fort Yukon

● Anchorage

Aklavik ● ● Inuvik

● Tuktoyaktuk

● Paulatuk

Amundsen Gulf

Franklin Strait

Victoria Island

● Dawson

Arctic Circle

Gulf of Alaska

PACIFIC OCEAN

● Whitehorse

CANADA

● Yellowknife

0 _____ 1000 km
0 _____ 600 mi

SVALBARD (p324)
Take in one of the most accessible High Arctic islands, among the most spectacular spots on earth

NORTH POLE (p270)
Discover that the odyssey to get here – by nuclear icebreaker – is more interesting than arriving

LOFOTEN ISLANDS (p303)
Explore the spectacular scenery, pretty fishing villages and incredible opportunities for outdoor activities

UUMMANNAQ (p191)
Admire dramatic fjords, islands and icebergs by dogsled or by boat under the midnight sun

TASIILAQ (p206)
Be dazzled by wild mountains and ice-choked fjords, and see some of the most traditional settlements in Greenland

AAPPILATTOQ (p133)
Sail through South Greenland's most magnificent fjordland scenery

NANORTALIK (p126)
Stroll around the picture-postcard old town, then get more energetic in the fabulous rock-climbing areas

ILULISSAT (p170)
Stand awestruck by the beauty and force of the most prolific tidewater glacier outside Antarctica

PANGNIRTUNG (p248)
Marvel at the stunning mountain-flanked fjord in the gateway to the incredible Auyuittuq National Park

QASSIARSUK (p104)
Visit a reconstructed Norse longhouse before embarking on some beautiful and relatively gentle wilderness hikes

You'll be entranced by heart-shaped **Uummannaq** (p191), glacial **Hamborgerland** (p158) and the prolific **Ilulissat icefjord** (p176). Activities abound: dogsledding under the midnight sun on **Disko Island** (p186), kayaking the ice-choked fjords around **Tasiilaq** (p206) and joining an Inughuit hunter on a trip to **Inglefield Fjord** (p201). Follow the wilderness trails from **Qassiarsuk** (p104) and **Narsarsuaq** (p97) and visit Norse ruins. For a real treat, gawp at spectacular iceberg-dotted fjords from the bargain-value Alluitsup Paa to Narsarsuaq **helicopter ride** (p123).

GRAEME CORNWALLIS

Photograph the colourful architecture of super-quaint Nanortalik old town (p126)

Meet Greenland's Inuit (p39) – custodians of one of the oldest continuous cultures on earth

DAVID ELSE

Be mesmerised by the incomparably magnificent Aappilattoq (p133)

STEVE HUTTO

ERNEST MANEWAL

Visit the home of the coastal grizzly bear (p254) as you drive Alaska's Dalton Highway

MARK NEWMAN

Admire the majestic caribou (p47),
found throughout Arctic North America

Get up close to a bearded seal – one of the
locals in Svalbard (p324), Norway

DEANNA SWANEY

HIGHLIGHTS Arctic Wildlife

Whales and walruses in the **Chukotka Peninsula** (p290), shaggy muskoxen on **Banks Island** (p244), Porcupine caribou in the **Arctic National Wildlife Refuge** (p254) and grazing reindeer on the road to **Nordkapp** (p319) – the Arctic has no shortage of charismatic residents. You can bag a giant Arctic salmon on the wild rivers of the **Kola Peninsula** (p271), marvel at grizzly bears while canoeing the Porcupine River in the **Yukon** (p241) and sail the seas around **Tuktoyaktuk** (p244) in search of the mysterious beluga whale. Join a spring wildlife tour to **Point Barrow** (p261) and catch a glimpse of the elusive polar bear, and visit the spectacular sea-bird rookeries of the **Lofoten Islands** (p303).

Frozen Landscapes

If it's views you're after, you've come to the right place: marvel at the pure light of **Sirmilik National Park** (p248), the pristine wilderness of **Pallas-Ounastunturi National Park** (p327) and the kilometre-high cliff on the **Akshayuk Pass** (p249). By plane, be dazzled by the **Great Kobuk Sand Dunes** (p262) and the oxbow lakes of the rambling tributaries of the **Lena River** (p289). On the water, admire the turquoise seas around the **Lofoten islands** (p303), the sharp peaks of the Brooks Range as you float down the **Noatak River** (p256), and the **Scandinavian fjords** (p298) from the legendary *Hurtigruten* steamer.

Be awestruck by Ketil's 1400m-high rock slab (p130), Greenland

GRAEME CORNWALLIS

SUSAN RIMERMAN

Feast your eyes on the rugged peaks surrounding dramatic Tombstone Mountain (p242), Canada

Experience the glory of Svalbard (p324), one of the most spectacular destinations on earth

CHRISTIAN ASLU

Getting Started

Nothing quite prepares you for your first trip north and that tingle of expectation as you plot a route, pore over those glossy photos and scare yourself silly with tales of frozen flesh and cavernous ice fissures. Going 'up north' requires a little more planning than most trips, though you'll probably be surprised by the modernity of the facilities available. The time of year you go will impact immensely on the size of your rucksack, of periods of perpetual day or night will determine your activities and the uncertainty of the weather may hamper even the best-laid plans.

WHEN TO GO

Paris in the spring? Don't even think about it – the Arctic is where you really want to be. For that dreamy fantasy of dogsleds, ice fishing and vast blue skies, the Arctic spring brings long days, bearable temperatures, good snow cover and the buzz of a land shaking off a long, dark winter. Depending on latitude, spring is anytime between March and May. The best time for dogsledding and skiing tours is between late March and early May, and most trips to the North Pole take place in April. For the best times to catch a glimpse of the region's animals and birds, see p56.

See the climate charts (p54) for more information.

By June there's perpetual day, winter snow is beginning to melt and the tundra teems with mosquitoes. The mosquito season generally runs from late June to early August, and anyone attached to their sanity should wear long clothing, invest in a head-net (*komarnik* in Russian) and load up on repellent. Summer – July and August – is the peak time for tourists. Maximum daytime temperatures average between 10°C and 18°C in the south and between 5°C and 10°C in the north. It can be wet and windy, though, and coastal fog is common. By late August, nights are getting colder and by mid-September, there's new snow and genuinely cold weather.

The most spectacular displays of the aurora borealis (p31) can be seen from August to mid-November, and mid-February to early April. Areas just south of or around the Arctic Circle are ideal for watching the lights (the northernmost Arctic regions are actually too far north to experience

---

DON'T LEAVE HOME WITHOUT...

Anytime

- Lots of film or a digital camera. If you're travelling in winter/spring a UV lens filter will reduce the glare off snowy surfaces.
- A good dose of patience
- Copies of all documents
- Good hiking boots and gaiters
- Plenty of reading material
- High-protection sunglasses
- Multipurpose pocketknife

In winter/spring

- Thermal underwear
- Warm clothes in multiple layers
- Windproof hat with ear protection
- A good-quality subzero-rated sleeping bag

In summer

- A fleece, hat and gloves
- A giant bottle of insect repellent
- Compass and magnetic deviation tables if you're hiking
- First-aid kit

the best displays). Arctic winters – any time from mid-October to March – are long, harsh and very, very dark. In the far north the sun disappears for months on end, and a perpetual night descends. In the far south, temperatures of -20°C can be expected, but further north it can be -40°C or lower for weeks. However, welcoming the return of the sun after experiencing a winter up north is a truly momentous occasion, with festivals held in every town and village for the light that heralds the coming of spring.

COSTS & MONEY

There's no point denying it: travel up north isn't cheap. The vast distances and severe lack of roads mean that travel costs can easily spiral. Depending on your budget, your best bet is to limit the number of locations you visit and save some money for boat, dogsled or snowmobile trips to 'get out on the land' and experience what it is that makes the area so special.

Greenland

LONELY PLANET INDEX (GREENLAND)

Litre of bottled water Dkr14

Bottle of Carlsberg Dkr14 from supermarkets, Dkr35 to Dkr40 from bars

Souvenir T-shirt Dkr149 to Dkr395

Hot dog Dkr16 to Dkr25

Because of Danish food-import subsidies, eating is not enormously more expensive than in Copenhagen. Better restaurant mains average Dkr160, which seems high if you're arriving from the US or Europe, but cheap if you're coming from Iceland. Accommodation is expensive for the quality you get, with hostel beds averaging Dkr250 and mid-range hotels costing about Dkr600 to Dkr1000 for a double. Transportation is painfully expensive thanks to the vast distances, small passenger numbers and almost total lack of roads. Assuming you're in a fixed location, not taking organised tours and self-catering in hostels, you'll spend between Dkr300 and Dkr400 per day. Visitors staying at hotels and eating in restaurants should plan on spending about Dkr1500 per day.

Arctic North America

HOW MUCH? (GREENLAND)

Mars BarDkr9

Cheapest summertime AUL ferry ride Dkr185

Mid-comfort hotel, double room Dkr800

Dogsledding for a day Dkr1400

100g of dried caribou Dkr40

Prices in Alaska generally increase the further north you go. Organised camp sites cost between US$8 and US$25 per night, while motels generally cost between US$70 and US$90, though they can be much more in out-of-the-way locations. Apart from fast food, eating out will cost you at least US$25, and internal flights to remote destinations cost US$200 to US$500. Backpackers could survive on US$30 a day, but if you're planning to eat out and stay at motels you're looking at about US$130 a day.

Arctic Canada sees few independent visitors and has few road connections. Camping is your only budget accommodation option, and hotels can cost anywhere between C$110 and C$190. Options for eating out are also fairly limited, and in remote locations plan on spending about C$30 on a meal. If you rough it and limit yourself to road travel you could survive on C$50 a day; for more comfort, hotel beds and air transport plan on C$250 a day.

Arctic Russia

In principle, Russia offers the cheapest Arctic options: if you sleep in small-town dosshouses and travel by riverboat or *platskart*-class (third-class) train you could survive on R500 to R800 per day, or R1500 per day staying in nicer city hotels and visiting decent restaurants. However, this style of budget travel will generally show you only the depressing Soviet hub towns. More interesting Arctic regions often lack infrastructure and you may need complex permits and chartered helicopters, which can become much more costly. These factors often make joining an organised tour (from R3000 per day) the only sensible option. Don't underestimate the cost of getting the appropriate visas and permits, which can quickly add up to hundreds of US dollars.

Arctic Scandinavia

Thanks to a good network of camp sites and hostels, travel in Arctic Scandinavia need not be prohibitively expensive. Budget accommodation options will set you back about €30 a night, while guesthouses and hotels cost between €50 and €140 a night. Eating out isn't cheap and will cost about €10 to €25. If you use public transport and self-cater you could squeak by on about €60 a day, but this doesn't allow for much amusement. If you want a little more luxury, plan to take some flights or hire a car, budget on at least €100 a day.

Note that Norway and Sweden have the krone and the krona, respectively, while Finland uses the euro.

TRAVEL LITERATURE

The Arctic has inspired a surprising amount of literature, all of it laced with a peculiar passion for the seemingly desolate landscape.

Arctic Dreams, by Barry Lopez, is a magical evocation of all things Arctic. At once essay, history, nature writing and anthropology, it covers everything from animals, land and people to natural phenomena and explorers.

A classic tale of exploration and discovery, *The Noose of Laurels* by Wally Herbert traces the bitter rivalry between Robert Peary and Frederick Cook in their quest to be first to the North Pole. *The Arctic Grail* by Pierre Berton is an absorbing account of the quest for the Northwest Passage and the North Pole, detailing the drama and the hardships of polar exploration and the contribution of the Inuit.

In *Ice!* Tristan Jones travels across the Arctic by boat with only a one-eyed, three-legged dog for company. He struggles with loneliness, polar bears and possible death with sharp wit and a keen eye.

The classic travelogue *Across Arctic America* by Knud Rasmussen follows Rasmussen's epic voyage across the Arctic on the fifth Thule expedition. It's a mammoth tale with a wealth of ethnographic, cultural and religious observations.

A Year in Lapland: Guest of the Reindeer Herders by Hugh Beach recounts the author's experiences while living with the Sami of Sweden and describes their herding lifestyle and struggles with modern culture and government policy.

Arctic Crossing by Jonathan Waterman is a vivid portrait of extreme conditions, disillusioned communities and incredible landscapes as seen from a kayak on an epic crossing of the Northwest Passage.

Part travelogue, part historical epic, *The Horizontal Everest: Extreme Journeys on Ellesmere Island* by Jerry Kobalenko traces the footsteps of past explorers and their reasons for seeking out this breathtaking but life-threatening island.

INTERNET RESOURCES

You'll need to do a lot of your predeparture planning on the Internet, and there are loads of sites out there just bursting with information.

Alaskan Adventure (www.alaskanadventureguide.com) Community profiles, accommodation options and tour planning for visitors to Alaska.

Arctic News (www.arctic.noaa.gov/news.html) Get up to date on Arctic news, research, issues and events before you leave home.

Greenland Guide (www.greenlandguide.gl) Numerous tourism-related links on transport, tours and events.

TOP TENS
NATIONAL PARKS

The Arctic's national parks protect some of the most pristine and spectacular scenery in the world. Plan a trip to one of these parks for an unforgettable experience.

- Auyuittuq National Park, Canada (p249)
- Gates of the Arctic National Park, Alaska (p256)
- Quttinirpaaq National Park, Canada (p247)
- Northeast Greenland National Park, Greenland (p213)
- Arctic National Wildlife Refuge, Alaska (p254)
- Pallas-Ounastunturi, Finland (p327)
- Sirmilik National Park, Canada (p248)
- Lapland Biosphere Reserve, Russia (p276)
- Abisko National Park, Sweden (p310)
- Wrangel Island, Russia (p293)

ARCTIC VIEWS

The landscape of the Arctic can range from the seriously spectacular to stretches of immense boggy plains. The following views will simply leave you speechless.

- Ilulissat icefjord and its gargantuan bergs, Greenland (p170)
- Thousands of migrating caribou herding in the Arctic National Wildlife Reserve, Alaska (p254)
- Quassik's panorama of spiky mountains, ice islands and fjords, Greenland (p129)
- Kobuk's bizarre desert-like dunes, Alaska (p262)
- Grise Fjord's spectacular peaks and icebergs, Canada (p248)
- The ice fields and jagged peaks of spectacular Svalbard, Norway (p324)
- Narsarmiit village with its jagged rocky backdrop, Greenland (p132)
- The aurora borealis seen from the ice hotel in Jukkasjärvi, Sweden (p309)
- Sivinganeruo Imaa fjord and the whole Aappilattoq fjord system, Greenland (p133)
- Qoornoq ice face and fjord viewed from Mellemlandet, Blue Ice Camp or best of all from an excursion helicopter, Greenland (p102)

ARCTIC ADVENTURES

To really get in touch with the Arctic wilderness, take one of these trips into the great unknown.

- Crack through metre-thick floes on an icebreaker cruise through the Northeast Passage to the North Pole (p270)
- Cycle the Kaiser Route on beautiful Lofoten, Norway (p306)
- Hike the Ikuvik Trail for superb views of Pangnirtung Fjord, Canada (p248)
- Join Inuit seal hunters through the fjords and floes around Cape Farewell, Greenland (p134)
- Follow in the footsteps of explorer Fridtjof Nansen and ski across Greenland's icecap (p216)
- Hike along the Kevo River with its spectacular waterfalls and dramatic gorges, Finland (p319)
- Unwind on lazy riverboat rides up Siberia's vast Ob, Irtysh or Yenisey rivers (p269 and p281)
- Hike through the wilds of Gates of the Arctic National Park, Alaska (p256)
- Go sea kayaking up spectacular fjords from Narsaq (p113) or Nanortalik (p127)
- Walk to the end of the world at Point Barrow, Alaska (p261)

Greenland Tourism (www.greenland.com) Greenland's official tourism site with regional information, tour suggestions and travel tips.
Lonely Planet (www.lonelyplanet.com) Comprehensive travel information and advice.
Nunavut Tourism (www.nunavuttourism.com) Online travel planner for Canada's far north.
Siberia Nomad (www.siberianomad.com) Information on Siberian towns, travel arrangements and tours.
Visit Finland (www.visitfinland.com) Info on route planning, attractions and events in Lapland.
Visit Norway (www.visitnorway.com) Heaps of information on planning a trip to Norway's north.
Visit Sweden (www.visit-sweden.com) Comprehensive information on where to go and what to see in northern Sweden.

The Authors

ETAIN O'CARROLL
Coordinating Author

Stepping off a plane in pitch darkness on a January afternoon, wind chill hitting -60°C and a herd of muskoxen just visible on the far side of the runway, Etain was simultaneously choked by her first breath and smitten by the Arctic. What was supposed to have been a short trip became almost three years 'up north' and an enduring fascination with the extremes of weather, the terrible beauty of the tundra and the wonderful Arctic people. This book allowed her to return north to research the southeast and northwest coasts of Greenland and fantasise over the ultimate travel routes through Arctic North America and Scandinavia.

Etain wrote the introductory Arctic chapters, Disko Bay, Northwest Greenland, East Greenland, Arctic North America Travel Routes, Arctic Scandinavia Travel Routes and part of Southwest Greenland.

My Favourite Trip

A trip up north is always an adventure, but sometimes a combination of landscape, light and timing just makes it extra special. For me, standing fishing by a lake near Kangerlussuaq (p162) at 4am with the sun glowing deep red in the sky, the perfect silence broken by the soft tinkling of candle ice melting and falling into the glassy water was as close to paradise as I imagine I'll ever get – and I don't even like fishing. The other indelible memory of this trip is the first sight of the truly massive, majestically carved icebergs of the Ilulissat icefjord (p170). It left me mesmerised for hours and with enough photographs of icebergs to bore the pants off the most avid of friends.

Ilulissat

Kangerlussuaq

MARK ELLIOTT

Mark Elliott first visited the Arctic in 1982. He has written numerous travel guidebooks and has contributed to a volume of adventure-travel tales. While researching this book he 'enjoyed' some rather overexciting escapades travelling with Greenlandic hunters. In one hair-raising mishap, compacting ice floes closed around his minuscule open boat off Prins Christian Sund. Being stranded for months like Parry or Shackleton was not an option in the uncovered craft. With two Inuit crew friends he finally managed to drag and squeeze the boat across the gathering patchwork of ice and leads, reaching open water late at night. The freezing return trip was lit only by a surreally beautiful, dancing aurora borealis and the fjord's glowing photoplankton.

Mark wrote the remainder of the Greenland chapters and compiled Arctic Russia Travel Routes.

My Favourite Trip

I can't imagine scenery more stunningly impressive than the fjord-lands around Aappilattoq (p133). Wrap up very, very warmly for the boat ride, even on sunny summer days. Start off towards the great tidewater glaciers of Nuup Kangerlua. Whizz back for a quick peek down Prins Christian Sund – the best views are from near its western mouth. Then, ice permitting, loop around Eggers Ø, exploring the spire-tickled southern fjords. I find Cape Farewell (Nunaap Isua/Kap Farvel) exciting more for the *frisson* of passing Greenland's treacherous southernmost point than for the scenery. Afterwards wind up to truly gorgeous Itilleq (Itivdleq), my favourite ex-village site. The most fabulous views are saved for last as you return to Aappilattoq through the jaw-dropping scenery of Sivinganerup Imaa fjord.

Arctic Snapshot

Although dogsleds and *iglos* still exist, life in the Arctic is a far cry from the romanticised notions of most southerners. Today Stone Age traditions collide with modern technology to create a complex society where children chew on whale blubber as they watch satellite TV and hunters learn first-aid skills to qualify as guides.

The fast and furious changes of the past 40 years have brought problems, and in some ways many Arctic villages resemble tough inner-city neighbourhoods. Low standards of education, high unemployment, rampant alcohol abuse and all the associated social problems dog many communities, and across the Arctic suicide rates are high and life expectancy is low. Children witness various kinds of abuse and grow up fast, while many adults find themselves back at school in their forties hoping to make up for lost time.

Despite the social problems, harsh climate, isolation and, in some areas, basic standards of living, the indigenous people of the far north are fiercely committed to their communities and even the young are reluctant to leave. A deep appreciation of the land and the traditional lifestyle, and the huge importance of family connections, far outweigh the lure of the bright city lights to the south.

Unfortunately, this traditional lifestyle is under threat from all sides. Climate change (see p27) is already apparent in the north and threatens the very heart of most communities: warmer weather and bad ice conditions prevent traditional hunting and threaten the habitats of the animals the local people rely on. Arctic scientific research is in an era of unprecedented cooperation, however, and international projects are working feverishly to collect data to accurately predict changes in local climates and the effects on indigenous people.

Meanwhile, oil and gas exploration and the dumping of nuclear waste have left some Arctic areas with severe environmental problems (see p59) and, as pollution from industrialised nations travels north, bioaccumulation of toxic chemicals threatens the health of northern peoples (see p34). An increasing sense of powerlessness in the face of these problems has led to a backlash against badly adapted social systems and government policies set by southern bureaucrats with little understanding of the true concerns of Arctic residents. A real push for self-determination has begun, and the creation of the Inuit homeland, Nunavut, in Canada (see p25) has encouraged other indigenous groups across the north to campaign for similar agreements.

However, with low levels of education and a culture of welfare dependence, it will take years before most communities can look forward to any true financial or political independence. Diversifying the economy and providing meaningful employment for isolated communities without causing irreparable damage to the land remains a real challenge. The people of the far north are renowned for their ingenuity and resilience in the face of difficulty, however. Although no-one may know quite where life is going, the unflinching desire to protect indigenous culture, maintain a meaningful link to the land and make the most of modern innovations is an excellent start.

FAST FACTS

Population: 1.6 million

Region size: 11.3 million sq km

Average unemployment rate: 25%

Temperature differential between winter and summer: 50°C

Depth of Greenland icecap: 3085m

Average deaths by polar bear: 1 in 25 years

Arctic History & Exploration

Since the earliest days of exploration people have attempted to reach the farthest-flung corners of the earth, and for many years the polar regions remained an elusive goal. The vast expanse of the Arctic was *terra incognita* and this was as much a part of its allure as the quest for new shipping routes, financial reward, geographical discovery and personal recognition.

Long before the early explorers headed north, though, the indigenous people of Asia had settled there. New Stone Age artefacts found in the Yana River Valley in Siberia, 500km north of the Arctic Circle, suggest that humans may have been hunting big-game animals in the region 30,000 years ago. When a fall in sea levels at the height of the last Ice Age formed a land bridge between the Russian Far East and North America, the distant ancestors of the Native Americans followed the mammoth herds across to the New World (see p263). Anthropologists believe that a second migration, this time of the ancestors of the Na-Dene people (see p45), occurred 12,000 to 15,000 years ago. The Inuit (see p39) were the last group to migrate east, making their way to Alaska 7000 to 8000 years ago.

The history of the Arctic's indigenous people reflects the harsh and unforgiving landscape in which they choose to live. Life was always a struggle against the elements, but the arrival of the *qablunaq* (white man) created a whole new array of problems. The early explorers had no idea how devastating their contact with local people would be: disease decimated the indigenous populations (see p20) and the influence of their culture began the transformation of the traditional way of life.

The Arctic's extreme weather and environments and newcomers' ignorance of how best to survive them have meant that the history of exploration in the region is pitted with accounts of tragedy and the many expeditions that never returned. Inaccurate maps, cruel temperatures, fluctuations in the extent of sea ice and the arrogant belief by some that rank, class and formal education were more important than practical experience led to the downfall of many.

In the winter, perpetual night severely limited any surveying; in summer, navigation was difficult because the stars were invisible against the midnight sun. The travelling season was short, there was scant knowledge of compass deviation, and sea ice severely constrained movement. Despite the best efforts of countless brave explorers, it was 1948 before the first person stood on the North Pole and 1977 before a surface vessel managed to reach it.

The indigenous people of the north were largely considered savages by explorers, and their knowledge and experience was ignored. However, the Inuit were familiar with vast swaths of land and could draw highly accurate maps. Their dog teams, meat diet and fur clothing could have

DID YOU KNOW?

The word Eskimo means 'eaters of raw meat' and is now considered offensive in some parts of the Arctic.

saved many lives if only the early explorers had deemed them fit for their lofty endeavours. Later explorers who adopted traditional Inuit ways and consulted the local people on travel routes found much greater success.

THE SPECULATIVE PERIOD (TO 1595)

The voyage of the early Greek explorer Pytheas to 'Ultima Thule', as it was known, in about 325 BC, was the first recorded journey to the far north, but exactly how far north he reached is unknown. Later accounts tell the story of the 5th-century Irish monk Saint Brendan, who made the voyage north to Iceland and possibly as far as Newfoundland in a skin boat. At around the same time a Buddhist monk, Hwui Shan, was making his way up Russia's Kamchatka Peninsula and on to Alaska.

Nanook of the North (1922), directed by Robert Flaherty, was the first major anthropological documentary set in the Arctic. It follows Nanook and his family for a year, showing a culture practically untouched by European influence.

The next landmark in Arctic exploration goes to Erik the Red, who was exiled from Iceland in 982 and later founded a settlement in what is now known as Qassiarsuk (see p104) in Greenland. A wealth of Norse ruins covers the area today. At much the same time, the Europeans came into first contact with the Siberian Yup'ik and the first missionaries arrived among the Sami of northern Scandinavia.

For centuries little more was known about the Arctic, and it was 1555 before Oleaus Magnus, the last Catholic Archbishop of Uppsala in Sweden, wrote a detailed account of the area. His monumental publication, *A Description of the Northern Peoples*, is a mixture of fact and fantasy but still served as the chief source of knowledge about Arctic regions for over two centuries.

By the 16th century Spain and Portugal had monopolised the lucrative southern trade routes to the Orient and charged hefty levies for anyone wishing to pass. Rumours of a Northwest Passage to Asia gripped England and in 1576 a group of London merchants employed Martin Frobisher to find the route on their behalf. Over the next three years Frobisher traversed uncharted territory around Greenland and the eastern Canadian Arctic but he failed to find the fabled route.

Between 1585 and 1587, John Davies also attempted to find the elusive trade route; although he too was unsuccessful, he mapped the coast of Greenland, Baffin Island and Labrador, and was the first to keep detailed notes on ice conditions, flora and the indigenous people. He was also the

DID YOU KNOW?

Around 1000 BC the Ancient Greeks named the Arctic after Arktos (the bear) for its position under the Great Bear constellation.

first person to bring attention to the sealing and whaling possibilities in Davis Strait, thereby heralding a new era for both Europeans and the Inuit. Meanwhile, in northern Scandinavia the Sami were beginning to trade with southern Scandinavians and thus to pay taxes. As zealous missionaries flocked north and began a major push to educate the northern people, the Scandinavian monarchies were able to establish and assert political control over the area.

MARINE CARTOGRAPHY (1600–1700)

Most early voyages searched doggedly for the fabled Northwest Passage. Adventurous investors ploughed money into the quest, intent on making a fortune from a successful discovery, while the prospect of fame fuelled explorers' daydreams of discovering new land. However, Arctic charts were a highly inaccurate mix of real and hypothetical lands, and progress was slow.

2400 BC	AD 982
Suspected first arrival of Canadian Inuit peoples in Greenland	Erik the Red sails for Greenland

Although each expedition carried a cartographer and many companies produced their own charts, these were mostly kept secret so as not to give competitors any commercial advantage. The pressure on early cartographers to return home with new maps was immense, yet there was no accurate way to determine longitude and compass variations were unknown. Any land spotted was the subject of an educated guess as to actual location. The season was short, fog was common, and *fata morgana* – realistic mirages on the horizon that occur where there are alternating warm and cold layers of air near the surface of the water – were often taken for land and recorded. It took several hundred years of Arctic exploration before accurate charts were finally published.

Despite the lack of accurate maps, fishermen and whalers had been plying the northern waters for many years. Whalers knew the seas from Novaya Zemlya in the Russian Arctic to Baffin Island in the eastern Canadian Arctic from the late 1500s, and they reported finds of Russian Orthodox graves and wreckage of ships, proving that others had exploited the resources of the area before them. The whalers accumulated great knowledge and experience of Arctic waters during their trips, but this was largely ignored by the gentlemen discoverers, and the whalers had neither the social standing nor the connections to publish details of their discoveries themselves.

More accurate mapping became a reality thanks largely to the Dutch and the voyages of Jan Rijp, Willem Barents and several others searching for a route to China. By the 17th century, exploration and mapping of the Eurasian and American Arctic began to diverge. The wide seaways, open water and fewer islands of the Eurasian Arctic meant that this area became reasonably well mapped more than a century before the American Arctic, where explorers struggled with a patchwork of small, inaccessible islands that were difficult to navigate and often locked in by sea ice.

RUSSIAN EXPANSION (1640–1830)

Russia's long-term campaign to extend its empire and conquer new territory was highly successful, but in the 17th century the northern regions of the country still remained largely unknown. That is, until Russian explorer Semyon Dezhnev rounded the extreme eastern cape of Asia, now Cape Dezhnev (p293), in 1648.

Peter the Great, founder of the Russian navy, became even more intent on expanding his empire after Denmark began the colonisation of Greenland in 1721. He set in motion a series of explorations that culminated in the Great Northern Expedition of 1733–43, led by the Dane Vitus Bering. The expedition was to establish the practicality of the Northeast Passage, an easterly sea route to India and China across the northern Russian coast, and travelled mostly by land using dogsleds to cross the tundra. In 1741 another Russian explorer, Semyon Chelyuskin, reached the most northern point in Asia (later named Cape Chelyuskin) and by 1743 almost the entire Eurasian Arctic coast had been mapped. Only a few outlying archipelagos remained to be discovered. Encouraged by the success of their mission, the Russians then moved on to Alaska, where the tsars ruled until the province was sold to the USA in 1867.

DID YOU KNOW?

In 1867 the United States bought Alaska for $7.2 million, about two cents an acre.

1000	1261
Greenlander Leif Erikson becomes the first 'European' to land in North America	Greenland is annexed by Norway

The Great Northern Expedition produced maps that were detailed and informative but also proved convincingly that the Northeast Passage was not suitable for navigation at that time. The pressure to find an efficient route to China this way relaxed. However, a fortune in furs was brought back from the region and Russian and British traders flocked to the area, exploiting the resources and often cruelly suppressing the local people.

As more regular contact was made with the indigenous people across the Arctic, waves of smallpox, mumps, influenza and chickenpox epidemics formed a sadly familiar pattern, decimating communities and seriously affecting the demographic composition of the region.

THE NORTHWEST PASSAGE (1700–1910)

At the beginning of the 1700s, the central American Arctic was an unknown: whalers had never travelled this far west, and the Russians had never ventured further east than Alaska. Investors were happily accumulating enormous wealth from fur in northern Canada, though, and were less willing to get involved in the more risky business of Arctic exploration. The British Royal Navy, long experienced in naval expeditions, and stuck with a very large and inactive fleet after the end of the Napoleonic Wars, soon got involved instead.

In 1734 the Admiralty set aside £20,000 for the discovery of the Northwest Passage. A year later the invention of the chronometer allowed longitude to be accurately measured for the first time, and a second prize of £5000 was offered to the first past 110°W latitude in an effort to chart the Central Canadian Arctic, an area as yet unexplored. When the Great Northern Expedition failed to open a new sea route, commercial interest in charting the area and discovering the fabled Northwest Passage increased even further. The race was on.

Numerous expeditions set out over the years, but naval insistence on the superiority of rank and the importance of wearing uniform, the refusal to use dogs as a means of transport and the complete lack of interest in Inuit knowledge and experience meant a constant struggle against frostbite, amputation, snow blindness, scurvy and starvation.

One notable explorer of this period was William Scoresby, who had the unusual combination of a Cambridge education and experience as a whaling captain. Although he too failed to find the elusive route across the north, he was noted for his respect for both his crew and the indigenous population. Later explorations that proved highly successful in discovering vast new swaths of the High Arctic, but not the passage itself, were led by William Parry and James Ross.

In 1845 Sir John Franklin's expedition disappeared, and the search for his remains, largely funded by his widow, gripped England. Several dozen search parties scoured the High Arctic for traces of the expedition – it was eventually found on Beechey (p247) and King William islands in the central Canadian Arctic – and in the process produced the first accurate maps of the area. During this time Robert McClure made the first transit of the Northwest Passage by transferring between two boats by sled. It was not until 1903–07 that one ship, *Gjöa*, commanded by Roald Amundsen, made the transit in one vessel. By then the route had been

The journal of the first European woman to spend a winter in the Arctic, *The Distant and Unsurveyed Country*, edited by W Gillies Ross, provides a unique insight into life on a whaling ship and the relationship between the Inuit and Europeans.

DID YOU KNOW?

On one Arctic expedition in 1875, sailors with any old wounds were refused work, as the symptoms of scurvy could reopen them.

Martin Frobisher makes three attempts to find the Northwest Passage

Greenland is claimed by Denmark

deemed commercially unviable, interest had waned and his achievement received little attention.

Today global warming and climate change (see p27) have brought the possibility of a commercially navigable Northwest Passage back into discussion. Predictions of a possible summer-long, ice-free route cutting thousands of kilometres off the journey between Europe and the Orient have shipping magnates planning ahead and military strategists exploring the implications of an ice-free Arctic.

It is interesting to note that at the same time that the Europeans were exploring the Arctic, the Inuit themselves were traversing their own land. In 1856, Qitdlaq, an outlawed shaman in Baffin Island, dreamt of Inuit people living far to the north. He persuaded a group of about 40 people to leave Baffin and try to find them. Half the group turned back mid-way but those that continued eventually arrived in Etah in North Greenland in 1863 where they met a group of local hunters who had managed to survive the Little Ice Age (1450–1850). The climate change had drastically altered the numbers and distribution of animals on which they relied, and the group had lost many of the skills commonly used by the Baffin Islanders. The visitors taught the polar Eskimo how to build and use kayaks, use bows and arrows, hunt caribou and fish for Arctic char.

Meanwhile, in northeast Canada gold had been discovered in the Klondike Basin in the Yukon, and thousands flocked to make their fortunes in the hills. Dawson (see p238) became the 'Paris of the North' and saw an intense but short-lived boom.

Icemen, by Mick Conefrey and Tim Jordan, traces the voyages of explorers from Franklin and the Northwest Passage to the attempts on the Pole, and discusses the importance of the Arctic today and the issues facing its inhabitants.

OCEAN EXPLORATION & NAVIGATION (1860–1930)

By the latter part of the 19th century, only the extreme northern lands, several parts of the High Arctic archipelagos and some isolated islands remained undiscovered. In 1878 a Swedish expedition led by Adolf Nordenskiöld set off aboard the *Vega,* a vessel equipped with a spanking new invention, the steam engine. The voyagers left Stockholm, proceeded round Norway and, after spending one Arctic winter in far eastern Siberia, returned triumphant around Asia and through the Suez canal.

In addition to detailed surveys of the route, the expedition conducted a comprehensive scientific programme. Scientific endeavour was reaching new heights across the globe, and since 1875 Karl Weyprecht, an Austrian army officer and Arctic explorer, had been campaigning for international cooperation and more valid goals in Arctic exploration. By 1882 he had established the first International Polar Year (see the boxed text, p32), persuading 11 countries to set up 12 Arctic stations for a year of scientific observation.

For explorers the focus was now shifting to attaining the North Pole, a dream largely held by the Americans. In 1879 the American polar explorer George De Long took the *Jeannette* through the Bering Strait in an attempt to reach the Pole. The ship got stuck in the pack ice and drifted slowly westwards around Wrangel Island (p293) and the De-Long Islands (named by subsequent search expeditions), where it was crushed and sank on 2 June 1881. Only 13 of the crew of 33 survived.

Three years later Inuit kayaking off southern Greenland found relics of the *Jeannette.* The find generated great interest in the scientific community

For background information on the International Polar Year, visit www .ipy.org.

and gave Fridtjof Nansen an idea. Nansen, who was to become one of the greatest Arctic explorers, commissioned a specially designed polar ship, *Fram* (Norwegian for 'forward'), in 1893 and sailed through the Northeast Passage to a position near the Novosibirskye Ostrova. From here Nansen deliberately sailed north until the *Fram* became surrounded by ice. Over the next three years the drift took her as far north as 85°55.10'N, from where Nansen and his companion Hjalmar Johansen made an attempt for the Pole. They turned back at a new farthest north position of 86°13.10'N but couldn't find the *Fram* because of the continued drift. The pair had a lucky and unplanned rescue from Franz Josef Land the following summer.

The *Fram* voyage brought back vast amounts of scientific observations and proved that a suitably built and equipped ship could withstand the ice. The second voyage of the *Fram*, led by Norwegian explorer Otto Sverdrup between 1898 and 1902, led to the last mapping of the extreme north of the Canadian Arctic.

THE NORTH POLE (1895–1915)

In the two decades after the voyage of the *Fram*, polar exploration took off in a big way. The lands and oceans around both poles were explored, and two expeditions made it to the South Pole in 1911–12.

During this brief but intense period, 17 expeditions attempted to reach the North Pole by sled, balloon, ship and airship. All failed. In 1897 Swede Salomon Andree and two companions attempted to fly a hydrogen balloon, guided by drag ropes, over the Pole. They crashed and perished, their notebooks and undeveloped film lying undiscovered on the remote Svalbard island of Kvitøya until 1930.

Attempts at the Pole set off from many places, and particularly strong – and contentious – claims were made by Frederick Cook in 1908 and Robert Peary in 1909; both are now regarded as fraudulent. The subsequent outbreak of WWI ensured that attempts on the North Pole ceased for over a decade.

THE CONFRONTATION PERIOD (1910–1948)

In 1907 the Russian imperial fleet was defeated by Japan. Military reinforcements coming by way of the Suez Canal had arrived too late, and the loss prompted a survey to investigate the potential of the Northeast Passage's as a strategic waterway. Two specially built coal-fired icebreakers surveyed the Bering Strait region between 1914 and 1915, and then made the journey to Murmansk. Roald Amundsen completed the next transit of the Northeast Passage between 1918 and 1923 aboard the *Maud*. At the same time, 1921–24, Knud Rasmussen's fifth Thule expedition (see p174) was exploring the Arctic from Greenland right across North America.

By 1925 Amundsen had emerged as one of the pioneers of Arctic aviation, attempting to reach the Pole with Lincoln Ellsworth using two aeroplanes. The expedition had to land on pack ice only 2°10', or about 240km, from the Pole because of engine trouble. The following year Amundsen set off from Svalbard (formerly Spitsbergen) in an airship, and on 12 May 1926 he flew over the Pole and continued on to Teller, Alaska, where the 'flying whale' greatly amused the local Inuit. Amundsen had thus become

1908–09	1926
Frederick Cook and then Robert Peary claim to have reached the North Pole – both are eventually discredited	Roald Amundsen flies over the Pole in a dirigible balloon

the leader of the expeditions that first saw both the South Pole and the North Pole.

In 1928 the Committee of the North was established in Russia, and the impact of new economic policies hit the indigenous people hard. Life was collectivised through the organisation of boat crews into seasonal hunting cooperatives, the hunt was monopolised, stocks were decimated and traditional subsistence culture was severely undermined.

Meanwhile, expeditions to establish Arctic research stations on Wrangel Island, Franz Josef Land, Severnaya Zemlya and several mainland sites took place, and in 1932 the Soviet icebreaker *Sibiryakov* made the first transit of the Northeast Passage in one summer. A year later Stalin commissioned a special department, *Glavsevmorput*, to concentrate on opening up the Soviet Arctic.

The number of polar stations vastly increased, and advances in shipping capabilities meant that the Northeast Passage (now known as the Northern Sea Route) became commercially navigable, opening up a trade route for Siberian fur, timber and ore. During this period the use of aviation for exploration rapidly increased. Unfortunately, the characteristic Soviet reluctance to let foreigners know what they were doing has resulted in few of these major explorations being widely known.

Flying expertise improved, long-distance flights became a reality, and in 1937 the first drift station – a scientific camp based on drifting ice – was established from Rudolf Island in the north of Franz Josef Land, its four-person crew making meteorological, hydrographic and other scientific observations. Rudolf Island soon became an important centre for air operations and a refuelling site for Soviet flights.

WWII interrupted nearly all exploratory progress, and the polar station on Franz Josef Land was cut off for almost four years. At the same time, the German navy covertly established manned and automatic weather stations in Greenland, Svalbard and Franz Josef Land to supply meteorological forecasting data for many of its operations.

Finally, in 1948, a Soviet aircraft landed at the Pole, and its occupants, Pavel Senko, Mikhail Somov, Pavel Geordiyenko and Mikhail Ostrekin, became the first to make an undisputed claim to the North Pole.

Ultima Thule, by Jean Malaurie, is a beautifully illustrated book offering a fascinating insight into the history of European and American exploration in the Arctic and its impact on the Inuit.

POST-WAR DEVELOPMENTS

In the 1950s and 1960s forced resettlement of the indigenous people of the north swept through the Arctic, causing huge upheaval and heralding the end of any semblance of a traditional lifestyle for many. Children were sent to formal schools far from home and in many cases they lost the ability to speak their own language.

Huge infrastructural changes also occurred. International politics became deeply set in the Cold War period of confrontation, and with the shortest route between the two main players – the United States and the Soviet Union – lying across the Arctic, it wasn't long before defences went up. US fears of attack by long-range missiles led to the construction, at immense expense, of 63 Distant Early Warning (DEW) stations by 1957. Large airfields for forward-bombing missions were also established on Graham Bell Island in Franz Josef Land and Thule (see p199) in Greenland.

1948	1953
A Soviet aircraft lands at the North Pole – its occupants make the first undisputed claim to have reached it	Greenland becomes a county of Denmark; modernisation drive is in full swing

At the same time, the US was developing nuclear-powered submarines. The first, USS *Nautilus*, made a transit of the Arctic from the Bering Sea under the North Pole to the Greenland Sea in 1958. On 17 March 1959 the USS *Skate* surfaced at the North Pole, and in 1961 the first Soviet submarine did the same. Covert voyages beneath the pack ice then became regular, with constant improvement of cat-and-mouse techniques between nuclear submarines of the Soviet, US and British navies.

Although icebreaker and submarine operations became increasingly common, all were conducted in great secrecy. The Russian Arctic became virtually closed to foreigners, and few Soviet scientists were permitted to visit the research stations, which became essentially military. One exception was for the experiments of the International Geophysical Year in 1957–8, where an unprecedented amount of cooperation in both the Arctic and the Antarctic greatly advanced science.

Unfortunately, the isolation of parts of the Arctic also made it ideal as a test site for nuclear weapons. In 1954 the small civilian population of Novaya Zemlya was unceremoniously removed and a large atomic testing region established instead. The area was used from 1956 to 1989, and 132 bombs were tested. The islands and their coasts have also provided disposal sites for radioactive waste.

Elsewhere in the Soviet Union, Nikita Khrushchev was campaigning for the Northeast Passage to become a route for mass transport. With relations with the West deteriorating rapidly, having a viable sea route to the east became even more important. In 1956 two shipping companies were established to undertake this, and nuclear-powered icebreakers were developed to ply the icy waters.

NORTH POLE ATTAINED

During this period, two notable private expeditions reached the North Pole by surface travel. In 1968 American Ralph Plaisted, with three companions, used snowmobiles to get there, abandoning the machines on the ice and flying out. A year later, Briton Wally Herbert led the first surface crossing of the Arctic Ocean. The four-person team reached the Pole by dogsled while crossing the pack ice from Alaska to Svalbard.

Subsequently, several expeditions have crossed the Arctic on the pack ice and many have made one-way surface journeys, leaving by aircraft. In 1977 the Russian *Arktika* became the first surface vessel to reach the North Pole.

At much the same time, oil was discovered in the Arctic – a factor that changed the face of exploration in the region for ever. The discovery of vast reserves of oil and gas at Prudhoe Bay on North Slope in Alaska and the start of mining operations for lead and zinc in North Baffin and Little Cornwallis islands meant increased infrastructure and flights, the construction of thousands of kilometres of pipeline, and untold amounts of industrial waste, all of which have had negative impacts on Arctic wildlife. Faced with oil and gas development in the Mackenzie Delta, the Inuvialuit formed the Committee of Original People's Entitlement (COPE) in 1969, and in 1971 the Inuit Tapirisat of Canada (ITC) was founded in Ottawa as a voice for Inuit throughout Canada's north. For a people only allowed to vote since the 1960s, the Inuit were beginning to find their political feet.

1962	1979
Canadian Inuit are allowed to vote for the first time	Home rule begins in Greenland

OPEN PERIOD (1990 TO THE PRESENT)

By the late 1980s the cost of maintaining Arctic stations had become unjustifiable for individual nations, and the softening of international politics paved the way for the establishment of the International Arctic Science Committee (IASC) in 1990.

Social and political upheaval in the Soviet Union in 1991 had profound effects on the Arctic in general and the Russian Arctic in particular. DEW line stations closed and military bases in Greenland were handed back to local communities. Tourist traffic began to flow to the North Pole from Russia, and many groups visited the magnificent islands and coasts along the Northern Sea Route. International cooperation and scientific research greatly benefited from the Russian 'openness', and access for foreigners allowed observations of global importance to be made for the first time. In 1994 three icebreakers – the *Yamal* from Russia, the *Louis S St-Laurent* from Canada and the *Polar Sea* from the USA – met at the North Pole in the newfound spirit of cooperation.

However, for the indigenous populations of the Arctic, increased access and influence from industrialised nations hasn't all been beneficial. As Arctic people turn more and more to a Western lifestyle, smaller settlements are abandoned for economic reasons and the indigenous populations struggle to adjust to the new hybrid lifestyle. Dramatic social change and large-scale economic development prompted the Canadian Inuit to press for self-determination – with varying degrees of success. In 1975 the Inuit of northern Quebec signed a land-claim agreement against the backdrop of controversy surrounding hydroelectric development in James Bay. Nine years later the Inuvialuit Final Agreement gave over 90,000 sq kms of the Northwest Territories to the Inuvialuit, together with financial compensation, and gas, petroleum and mineral rights across 13,000 sq kms of land – in return, they had to surrender their right to any further territorial claims.

For more information on the territory of Nunavut, visit www .nunavuttourism.com.

However, it was the creation of Nunavut (Our Land) in April 1999 that was most closely monitored by aboriginal groups from around the world. The agreement handed over one fifth of the land mass of Canada to the indigenous Inuit, making it one of the largest and richest land-claim agreements ever made. It was an enormous leap forward for the area, granting the Inuit subsurface mineral rights on 36,257 sq km of territory. The land chosen contains 80% of Nunavut's known resources of copper, lead, zinc, gold and silver.

In other Arctic areas land claims are still hotly contested, and indigenous people battle for the right to protect areas of vital importance to their traditional culture: in Greenland the people of Qaanaaq fight to return to their original home, which is now being used as a US military airbase (see p200); across Scandinavia the Sami fight for self-determination and protection for their caribou herds (see p44); and the Gwitch'in of the northern Yukon continue to fight the US administration and oil companies to protect the birthing ground of the 152,000-strong Porcupine caribou herd across the border on Alaska's North Slope (see p47).

In Arctic Russia, horrific environmental problems are causing international concern as decommissioned nuclear subs and industrial waste wreak havoc on the land. The situation has become so alarming that an

1977	1985
The *Arktika* becomes the first surface vessel to reach the North Pole	Greenland withdraws from the European Community but remains part of Denmark

international aid package, estimated at US$40 billion, has been pledged to help the Russians clear up the far north.

Read about Ben Saunders' 2004 expedition at www.sercotransArctic .com/home.

As the struggle to protect the traditional lifestyles of the Arctic's indigenous people continues and scientists rush to figure out the puzzle of global warming, the tradition of polar exploration goes on. In 1986 Ann Bancroft became the first woman to travel to the North Pole on foot; in March 2003, Briton Ben Saunders at the age of 25 became the youngest person to make an unsupported return trip to the North Pole. A record-breaking long-distance skier, Saunders has made several trips to the Arctic and in 2004 attempted to become the first person in the world to make a complete crossing of the frozen Arctic Ocean – a journey of nearly 2000km – solo and unsupported. The expedition was a traumatic one, with conditions described as some of the worst on record. Saunders noticed temperatures up to 15°C warmer than on a previous expedition in 2000 and vast, unprecedented areas of thinning ice and open water. Now a campaigner, Saunders continues to raise international awareness of the extent to which climate change is affecting the Arctic.

1999	2003
The Nunavut land claim hands over one fifth of the land mass of Canada to the indigenous Inuit	Ben Saunders (25) becomes the youngest explorer ever to make an unsupported return trip to the Pole

Arctic Research

Although it's sometimes hard to see the connection, scientific research in the Arctic is of paramount importance to the rest of the world. Next time you sit down to dinner with a glass of red wine, spare a thought for that bunch of windswept researchers on the Beaufort Sea looking at climate change. Their findings ultimately influence the types of grapes planted by European winemakers.

The Arctic holds the key to many scientific conundrums, but even with increased cooperation, international projects and better organisation the region remains one of the least studied and least understood on earth.

The first serious Arctic research took place during the first International Polar Year in 1882–3 (see the boxed text, p32), and since then scientists have battled the extreme climate, political boundaries and short season to pursue information that provides clues to life across much of the planet. The establishment of the **International Arctic Science Committee** (IASC; www.iasc.no) in 1990 and the **Arctic Council** (www.arctic-council.org) in 1996 have led to unprecedented international cooperation and coordination of all aspects of Arctic research, with multidisciplinary teams feverishly studying every possible aspect of the environment to better understand the region and its effects on the rest of the world.

CLIMATE CHANGE

At the root of almost all Arctic research is the urgent quest for more knowledge about climate change. The Arctic is seen as an early-warning system for what will happen in the rest of the world, as Arctic ecosystems are extremely sensitive. Already the Inuit are noticing bad sea-ice conditions, that the polar bears appear to be getting thinner, and that summers are warmer. The Sami are reporting changes to reindeer grazing pastures, and people across the Arctic are reporting new species. Predicting the nature of these changes and identifying whether natural cycles or man-made problems are the cause are key areas of research.

Warmer weather will mean that fish stocks will fluctuate, ice and permafrost will thaw, vegetation growth will be disrupted, and migration routes of Arctic animals may change – all of which will affect the traditional lifestyles of indigenous people in remote settlements. Changes in the Arctic will have knock-on effects for the rest of the world, too, as many of the world's wind and water currents are driven by the difference in temperature between the Arctic and hotter parts of the world. The freezing temperatures of the Arctic Ocean during winter create sea ice and cold, salty water that sinks deep and drives ocean circulation. If surface waters grow warmer and ice does not form as well in winter, these processes could be constrained or eliminated, reducing oceanic effects such as the warming influence of the Gulf Stream (see p30) and thus drastically altering the global climate. And as more open water is created, wind speeds pick up and severe coastal erosion becomes likely.

Predicting the effects of global climate change is very difficult, but projects such as the **Arctic Climate Impact Assessment** (ACIA; www.acia.uaf.edu) and the five-year **North Pole Environmental Observatory Program** (http://psc.apl .washington.edu/northpole) have been set up to track long-term changes using an array of automated instruments that collect year-round data on ice thickness, cloud cover, air temperature, ocean currents, water temperature and salinity.

Watching Ice and Weather Our Way, by Conrad Oozeva et al, illustrates the importance of traditional knowledge for researchers investigating climate change in two Yup'ik communities in Alaska.

DID YOU KNOW?

Parts of Russia, Alaska and western Canada have warming trends up to 10 times greater than in other parts of the world.

THE CORE OF THE MATTER IN KANGERLUSSUAQ

As a former military installation, Kangerlussuaq (p162) is a natural site for scientific research and over the years wildlife and climate change have been key areas of study. The Greenland Icecore Program (GRIP), sponsored by a consortium of eight European countries, set up a core-drilling operation at the thickest point on the inland ice, 800km northeast of Kangerlussuaq, and in mid-1992, after four year's work, the operation finally reached bedrock at a depth of 3028.8m. The 5799 ice cores extracted, each measuring 55cm, represent a historical record reaching back thousands of years and have played a key role in climate reconstructions of the Northern Hemisphere.

Further research is being done on the vast peatlands of Siberia, where the permafrost holds ancient stores of carbon and methane. Peatland vegetation doesn't decompose fully, and much of the carbon dioxide taken in by living plants isn't returned to the air. If the permafrost were to thaw, large amounts of methane and carbon dioxide could be released and accelerate the warming process substantially. Already, melting permafrost is destabilising buildings and roads and threatening oil pipelines. Scientists also predict that changes in permafrost could affect migration routes, food chains, wildlife interaction and species composition.

The Day After Tomorrow, directed by Roland Emmerich, graphically shows the catastrophic effects of abrupt climate change.

ICE CORES OF THE GREENLAND ICE SHEET

The Greenland icecap, the largest Arctic glacial mass, holds 10% of the world's total freshwater reserves, and understanding it is fundamental to climate study in the northern hemisphere. To accurately predict future climate change, scientists need to better understand the climate of the past, and two ice cores drilled from the icecap in the 1990s have presented scientists with highly valuable environmental records spanning thousands of years.

Studies of the ancient ice retrieved by the European GRIP (Greenland Ice Core Programme, see the boxed text above) and the US GISP2 (Greenland Ice Sheet Project 2) have provided critical information about past temperatures and precipitation levels, and the composition and properties of ancient atmospheres. Scientists have even been able to estimate historic volcanic activity, sea-ice extent, fires and marine storms.

DID YOU KNOW?

Long-term data from tree rings, ice cores, sediment and lake-bed pollen indicate that the Arctic is warmer now than at any time during the last 10,000 years.

However, the chronology of the oldest and deepest sections of the cores remained uncertain, and the **North Greenland Ice Core Project** (NGRIP; www.glaci ology.gfy.ku.dk/ngrip/hovedside_eng.htm), led by the Danish Research Council, began drilling again in the late '90s. After seven years it reached bedrock at a depth of 3085m and retrieved ice frozen 120,000 years ago. The 10cm cores contain a wealth of information that will provide vital data on the global climate over the entire period.

So far the ice has yielded over 15 new species of ultra-micro bacteria and what appear to be pine needles or leaves in the muddy layers between the ice sheet and the bedrock. If confirmed, it will be the first organic material to be recovered from a deep ice-core drilling project. It could be several million years old.

GLACIOLOGY

Glaciers and ice sheets can be effective indicators of environmental change and are of particular interest to researchers. The **Mass Balance of Arctic Glaciers and Ice Sheets** (MAGICS; www.iasc.no/ProjectCatalogue/magics99.htm) project is assessing the current state of Arctic glaciers and icecaps in order to improve predictions of the effects of climate change on the evolution of polar ice sheets, future rises in sea levels and freshwater input to the sea.

ARCTIC RESEARCH STATIONS & CENTRES

The first Arctic research stations were established in the last decades of the 19th century. Today they offer hi-tech support to international teams across the north.

In Alaska the **Toolik Field Station** (www.uaf.edu/toolik) is a national research facility for the study of biology, geology, hydrology and ecosystems. In Barrow the former Naval Arctic Research Laboratory (UIC-NARL) and the Arctic Research Facility provide venues for research on bowhead whales, fisheries and waterfowl. Also in Barrow, the **National Oceanic and Atmospheric Administration** (www.noaa.gov) operates a key Arctic climate-change research facility. The **University of Alaska Fairbanks** (www.uaf.edu) conducts Arctic and subarctic studies and supports the Geophysical Institute, the **Alaska Satellite Facility** (www.asf.alaska.edu) and the International Arctic Research Center.

In Canada the **Polar Continental Shelf Project** (http://polar.nrcan.gc.ca) runs bases at Resolute Bay and Tuktoyaktuk supporting over 150 scientific groups throughout the Canadian Arctic. The **Nunavut Research Institute** (http://pooka.nunanet.com/~research) centres in Iqaluit and Igloolik focus on linking Inuit traditional knowledge with Western science. The **Aurora Research Institute** (www.nwtresearch.com) in Inuvik is an additional support organisation for long-term data collection.

In Greenland the Danish Polar Centre (DPC) runs the Zackenberg Arctic Field Station. The field station is home to ZERO (Zackenberg Ecological Research Operations), which conducts the world's only integrated long-term monitoring of animals, plants, climate, geology, geomorphology and permafrost. The DPC also supports KISS (Kangerlussuaq International Science Support), a logistics base for researchers that operates year round. In Nuuk the **Greenland Institute of Natural Resources** (www.natur.gl, in Greenlandic) focuses on gathering scientific data on selected species valued by Greenland's society. The Arctic Station, a research base in Qeqertarsuaq, Disko Island, runs all year. It's owned and operated by the University of Copenhagen, which also operates the small field station Sermilik, near Tasiilaq. At the top of the Greenlandic ice sheet the permanent research and monitoring facility Summit is operated by the United States' National Science Foundation.

Ny Ålesund in Svalbard, Norway, is the site of year-round research by the **Norwegian Polar Institute** (http://npiweb.npolar.no/). The Norwegian Institute for Air Research has an atmospheric research station here and the Norwegian Mapping Authority runs a high-precision space geodesy observatory. Other research stations in Norway include the **Svanhovd Environmental Centre** (www.svanhovd.no), which gathers and distributes information about the Barents Region, and the Norwegian Polar Institute headquarters in Tromsø, one of the world's leading polar research centres.

Sweden maintains the **Abisko Scientific Research Station** (www.ans.kiruna.se), which has a long-running meteorological observatory and a focus on plant ecology. In Kiruna the **Swedish Institute of Space Physics** (www.irf.se) conducts an atmospheric research programme in addition to running an environmental satellite data centre and maintaining a climate impacts research centre.

Finland's major Arctic research institute is the **Arctic Centre** (www.arcticcentre.org), which is run by the University of Lapland and based in Rovaniemi. The centre's area of specialisation is the exploration, understanding and communication of the effects of global changes on the societies and environments of the Arctic.

Russia's Academy of Sciences operates the **Kola Science Centre** (www.kolasc.net.ru) in Apatity and the **Murmansk Marine Biological Institute** (www.mmbi.murman.ru). Research on migratory birds is also carried out at the Willem Barents Biological Station on Medusa Bay, while Arctic ecosystems research, environmental monitoring and management are conducted from the Lena-Nordenskiöld Biological Station. In general you need to apply in writing and have some scientific reason for visiting. However, the more remote stations, such as those in Greenland, will usually accept visits arranged through the tourist office. You can arrange guided tours of Svanhold by appointment, and the Arctic Centre's **library** (🕙 10am-5pm Mon-Fri) and information centre (see p314) can be visited.

Currently, there is much debate about whether the Greenland ice sheet has lost or gained mass. Although new snow has been deposited at the summit, ice is melting fast around the edges.

In Norway researchers work inside and underneath the Svartisen Icecap (see p301) in a series of tunnels built by the state power company, which generates hydroelectric power from glacial meltwater. Some of these tunnels provide access to the base of the glacier, offering scientists a unique opportunity to observe a glacier from below. One focus of the team's research has been glacier movement, and scientists have discovered that debris in the ice at the glacier's base creates large amounts of friction, which slows advances. However, glaciers in general are slipping towards the sea faster than expected as meltwater from the surface trickles to the base and lubricates the sheet from below. So far this effect has not been considered in computer models predicting ice sheet response to climate change.

DID YOU KNOW?

Analysis of air bubbles in the ice shows that carbon dioxide concentrations in the atmosphere are now higher than at any time in the last 400,000 years.

SEA ICE RESEARCH

Sea ice is a dominant feature of the Arctic Ocean, and studies of changes to its extent, drift, chemistry and composition are highly important, as they can be early indicators of environmental change. However, increasing losses in the thickness of sea ice are causing serious concerns. Arctic ice has lost as much as 40% of its thickness in the past 50 years, and the area it covers has shrunk more than 25%.

Conditions hit an all-time low in 2002, when sea-ice cover was 15% below the current average. The difference would have covered an area roughly twice the size of Texas. In 2003 ice shelves jutting into the ocean from Greenland's Petermann Glacier were found to be 45m thinner than in the previous year, and the Ward Hunt Ice Shelf on Ellesmere Island, the largest ice shelf in the Arctic, fractured and released all the water from the freshwater lake it dammed. The rare and unusual ecosystems supported by the epishelf lake, and the historic climate information they may have contained, have now been lost.

Sea ice affects the penetration of light into the water and any changes to its extent will affect the productivity of algae and plankton and their part in vital marine systems. Polar bears are also at risk, as they depend on the sea-ice edge as a hunting ground. As the ice disappears, bears cannot find suitable food and must swim longer distances to areas with remaining sea ice, burning up precious energy reserves and lessening the adult bears' sex drive and thereby their ability to reproduce.

DID YOU KNOW?

As ice melts and more soil, rock and open water becomes visible, the planet absorbs more solar radiation and the extra heat accelerates the melting process.

But it's also bad news for the rest of us, as Arctic sea ice is one of the fundamental components of the earth's climate system. Sea ice reflects 80% of solar radiation, whereas open water reflects only 20%. As ice thins, its albedo (reflectivity) is reduced and more solar radiation is absorbed, causing temperature increases in the Arctic Ocean and the Greenland Sea. This may affect the course of the Gulf Stream which in turn could drastically alter climate conditions from the east coast of the United States to Western Europe. Research into sea temperatures in the Fram Strait, which is part of the West Spitsbergen Current, has revealed that waters as deep as 2000m are already showing significant increases in temperature.

Satellites have been used to monitor fluctuations in Arctic sea ice for the past two decades, but with the launch of **IceSat** (Ice, Cloud and land Elevation Satellite; http://icesat.gsfc.nasa.gov) in 2003 data collection made a leap in accuracy. The satellite sends pulses of light to earth 40 times a second, and a telescope collects the reflections and creates maps that can show changes as small as one centimetre a year. The findings are revolutionising the way scientists study ice sheets.

ATMOSPHERIC RESEARCH
Ozone Depletion

Thinning of the stratospheric ozone layer in Arctic areas has been studied since the 1970s, and readings indicate 10% to 40% decreases in some areas. Satellite monitoring has shown that in the Arctic small 'holes' occur at different times during the late winter and early spring. Several research sites have been established throughout the region to better understand the reasons for ozone destruction and to monitor the long-term effects of UV radiation on humans and Arctic ecosystems.

In 2004 a cooperative project involving NASA and scientists from Alfred Wegener Institute for Polar and Marine Research in Potsdam, Germany, released the results of a 12-year study of the relationship between Arctic ozone loss and changes in the temperature of earth's stratosphere. If the upper reaches of the Arctic atmosphere get colder – which is likely to happen as a result of climate change – then the rate of ozone depletion could be three times greater than forecast. Climate models currently vary widely, and the new research should lead to much more accurate simulations of conditions and analysis of data. Current studies by International Arctic Research Center (IARC) Alaska aim to improve large-scale climate models and use them to predict local variations in weather and climate.

DID YOU KNOW?

A temperature rise of 2.7°C would be enough for the Greenland icecap to start melting faster than it can be replaced.

The Polar Vortex

The polar vortex – a massive whirlpool of air above the North Pole – has sped up in recent years, and researchers believe that the increased rate of

---

ATMOSPHERIC RESEARCH – THE AURORA BOREALIS

The Inuit thought they were the souls of the dead, and their shamans called upon them to cure the sick; Scandinavian folklore described them as the final resting place for the spirits of unmarried women; and the Japanese believed that a child conceived under the dancing rays of the aurora borealis would be fortunate in life. Modern science, however, has reduced these romantic notions to a more prosaic explanation.

The magical natural phenomenon that creates the curtains of colour that streak across the northern night sky can be explained as the result of solar wind – a stream of particles from the sun that collides with oxygen and hydrogen atoms in the upper atmosphere. The collisions produce the greens and magentas of the aurora as the earth's magnetic field draws the solar wind particles toward the polar regions. (The website www.northern-lights.no has information about the best times and places to view the aurora, and tips for photographing it.)

An increase in solar flares (sudden releases of magnetic energy from the solar atmosphere) usually means more dramatic displays, but the solar wind also distorts the earth's magnetic field and disrupts high-latitude communications, electric power grids, satellite orbiting and defence systems. Research is focused on predicting such disturbances, largely with what are known as incoherent scatter radar systems.

These systems study disturbances in the earth's magnetic field and upper atmosphere caused by solar winds. Three such systems are operated by seven-nation international group **EISCAT** (www.eiscat.com) in Northern Scandinavia, and the US Stanford Research Institute operates another at Kellyville in Kangerlussuaq (p162).

In Alaska the highly controversial **HAARP** (High-frequency Active Auroral Research Program; www.haarp .alaska.edu) uses a high-power, high-frequency radio transmitter to stimulate a small region of the ionosphere in order to survey the artificial effects produced by radio transmission. However, opponents argue that the transmission can also be used to interfere with radio communication and systems anywhere in the world and could be used to produce severe physiological disruption or disorientation, weather modification and unexpected drag forces on missiles. For more information on the campaign against the facility visit www.earthpulse.com/haarp.

spin is a result of global climate change and may explain some of the dramatic changes now being observed in the Arctic. The winds can break up the ice and force it away from the Pole while also driving warmer water into the Arctic. As leads of open water occur they absorb more solar radiation and accelerate the whole process, which may explain the unprecedented lows in pack ice since 2002.

The Carbon Cycle

Arctic atmospheric research also looks at the role of the carbon cycle – the movement of carbon between the atmosphere, the oceans, living organisms and the earth itself. For decades scientists thought that sea ice prevented the Arctic Ocean from exchanging gas with the atmosphere, creating a carbon sink – or store of carbon – in the icy water. But new research suggests that the opposite is true, radically altering science's understanding of how the Arctic Ocean fits into the world's climate cycles. Understanding the carbon cycle is critical, as rising levels of the gas are responsible for the greenhouse effect. Results show that concentrations of carbon dioxide in the Arctic Ocean alter dramatically at different times of the year, which suggests that in spring and summer it becomes a previously unknown and very significant sink of atmospheric carbon dioxide, but in winter can be a source. The new information will greatly alter the way in which computer simulations project climate changes.

ARCTIC OCEANOGRAPHY

Although the Arctic Ocean is almost landlocked, it plays a fundamental role in the circulation of ocean currents worldwide. This in turn influences the earth's climate system, as water flows out of the Arctic into the northern Atlantic Ocean, whose circulation drives our climate.

Siberian Seas

Regular international research expeditions in the Siberian seas have been possible since the 1990s, and scientists have used the opportunity afforded by increased access to record data on land and ocean ecosystems. In 2004 a research expedition focused on the interconnection of the Pacific, Arctic and Atlantic Oceans, and the effects of fresh water arriving from the estuaries of the Lena, Kolyma and Indigirka Rivers. Studies of coastal erosion and sediment displacement were combined with immediate

---

INTERNATIONAL POLAR YEAR

The first **International Polar Year** (IPY; www.ipy.org), held in 1882–3, was inspired by Karl Weyprecht (see p21), who argued that scientific study rather than exploration should drive polar expeditions. Eleven countries took part, kick-starting a new era of scientific discovery. Fifty years later the second International Polar Year saw 40 nations conducting research, and in 1957–8 the third International Polar Year (also known as the International Geophysical Year) brought together polar researchers from 67 nations.

The fourth International Polar Year will take place in 2007–09 and more than 130 countries are expected to participate. The internationally coordinated campaign will attempt to piece together the puzzle of environmental change at the poles with multidisciplinary and interdisciplinary projects looking at everything from global warming to the depletion of the ozone layer and the thinning of sea ice. It is planned that international projects will not duplicate research activities that are already underway in polar regions; instead, they will include elements from a wide range of scientific disciplines in order to draw more attention to changes taking place around the poles and their effects on the rest of the world.

testing of water samples to record information on everything from pH and chemical levels to temperature and salinity. Changes in salinity can affect ocean circulation and, in turn, global climate. Results will be shared with teams working in Fairbanks and Vladivostok to improve understanding of the ocean's role in global climate change.

Also in 2004, a Russian drift station was deployed off the Novosibirsk Islands in the Arctic Ocean for a two-year project to resume hydro-meteorological monitoring of the Arctic basin, which is vital for the regional economy. It will also allow the physical processes that determine global and regional climatic changes to be studied.

Beaufort Sea

Researchers on the **Beaufort Sea Climate Change** (www.beaufortseaclimatechange.com) project are exploring how changing ocean circulation affects airborne and waterborne contaminants and how climate change is affecting ice cover and the habitats of ice-dependent species such as polar bears and seals. The project also looks at how climate change may affect the now healthy population of beluga whales in the area. Studies of the impact of climate change on fish and marine mammals in the Beaufort Sea, and their adaptation to it, have led to applications as diverse as European coastal and marine management, and assessment of European climate change and its impact on wine production.

Visit http://Arcticcircle .uconn.edu for information on all things Arctic, from scientific research to impacts on local communities.

Sea Bed Sampling

Researchers in Queen Maud Gulf in the Canadian Arctic are taking samples of sediment on the ocean floor as part of an intensive study of the Arctic marine ecosystem. A record of climate change is laid down year by year in the sediment, so researchers can peer at the last 10,000 years. Micro-organisms and fossils in the sediment carry a record of the temperature, salinity and ice content when they were deposited, allowing researchers to document changes to the environment since the time the creatures were alive.

Further north, on the Lomonosov Ridge – an area 250km from the North Pole – the **Arctic Coring Expedition** (ACEX; www.iodp.de) has begun a series of ocean-drilling programmes. Sediment from the top of the ridge is believed to contain a continuous climate record dating back 50 million years, and scientists hope it will provide critical information about how the Arctic Ocean has evolved and how long the Arctic sea ice has been there. Without accurate data on how much ice there was in the past, it's very difficult to model climate change for the future. Research on fossilised algae found on the first expedition in 2004 has shown that temperatures in the ocean were once 20°C, forcing a re-evaluation of the early history of the Arctic Basin.

Census of Marine Life

Another international team is working on recording and listing species living deep in the Arctic Ocean as part of the 10-year **Census of Marine Life** (www.coml.org). It is an urgent task, as species information is essential to discussion of climate change. Research will take place at different levels of the ocean, but one key area is the Canada Basin, a huge and largely unknown submarine hole 3800m deep. The area, immediately north of the Yukon and Alaska, is covered by ice and linked to the Pacific through the Bering Strait, a mere 70m deep. Many species in the extremely cold depths of the Canada Basin never travel to shallower waters and are thought to have been isolated there for millions of years. Another focus will be the diversity of life around the mouths of Canadian and Russian rivers. Russian cooperation is seen as central to the project's success, as sea-bed areas rich in raw materials or used for dumping nuclear waste are frequently off limits to research, for political reasons.

Ocean Circulation

The Age of the Arctic, by Gail Osherenko and Oran R Young, looks at global controversies involving the Arctic, and the conflicts and relationships between the military, industry, environmentalists and indigenous people.

Researchers in the Nansen and Amundsen Basins Observational Systems (NABOS) and Canadian Basins Observational Systems (CABOS) are looking at ocean circulation and water-mass transformation. Major changes in the Arctic Ocean in the past few decades have been linked to extreme amplification of the polar vortex (see p31), but understanding the changes, their links to external climate systems and the processes involved is an ongoing process. Long-term observations are critical to deepening our knowledge in this area and predicting the evolution of the Arctic environment. IARC Alaska has deployed a set of moorings along the shelf slope of the basins, where major transports of water, heat and salt occur.

FRESHWATER STUDIES

About 77% of the earth's fresh water is locked in as polar ice. What happens to it and to the polar oceans is of immense importance to the rest of the world. Some of the world's largest and biologically richest freshwater ecosystems are present in the Arctic and are vital to millions of birds and to the stabilisation of seasonal waterflow from mountain and glacier to sea. Studies of how river systems, wetlands and lowland areas will handle the increased flow of meltwater, combined with more rain instead of snow, are vitally important.

Recent studies have been looking at the role of large river basins in delivering fresh water to the Arctic Ocean. Although the ocean contains only 1% of the world's ocean water, it receives about 11% of world river runoff. In the last 10 years the amount of fresh water flowing into the Arctic Ocean has increased dramatically, possibly as a result of global warming, and scientists fear that this will reduce the ocean's salinity, possibly causing the Gulf Stream to shut down and plunging Europe into a mini Ice Age.

In 2004 studies found that animals in the Mackenzie River Delta in Canada have mercury levels up to four times higher than those of animals living in Lancaster Sound to the east. The Mackenzie is one of the largest river systems in the world, and there's significant industrial development in parts of the watershed. Researchers are hoping to discover if the contaminants are travelling downstream in large quantities or if climate warming and melting permafrost could be responsible.

CHEMICAL POLLUTANTS

Despite its reputation as a pristine wilderness, the Arctic has become highly polluted by chemicals produced in industrialised nations to the south. The Arctic acts as a final 'sink' where pollutants become trapped; the long, dark winters and cold temperatures inhibit the breakdown of chemicals. Air and water currents carry the toxins north, and once there they begin to build up in the food chain, a process known as bioaccumulation.

Animals with a long lifespan and significant proportions of fat for insulation tend to accumulate the chemicals, and both polar bears and humans have been shown to carry unusually high levels of toxins, including dioxins, PCBs and newer compounds like those now used as flame retardants and stainguards. Nearly all Inuit tested in Greenland and more than half of those in Canada have levels of PCBs and mercury exceeding international health guidelines.

MARS ON EARTH

As the most life-friendly extraterrestrial planet, Mars attracts lots of scientific attention, but re-search has always been carried out from a distance. In 1997 NASA began exploring Devon Island, a polar desert in the Canadian Arctic, which is home to a meteorite impact crater 24km in diam-eter. The plan was to learn about Mars by geologic comparison. In 2000 the project expanded into a virtual mission to Mars with the construction of the Mars Arctic Research Station, where scientists began to study geology and microbiology, equipment and robot use, and communica-tions systems while constrained by bulky space-suit simulators. The project enables scientists to develop appropriate field tactics and to test equipment and psychological impact before a real mission. A second station was opened in Utah in 2002 and a third in Iceland in 2004.

Greenland bears the brunt of the world's contaminants because it is in the path of winds from European and North American cities. In 2003 the **Arctic Monitoring and Assessment Programme** (AMAP; www.amap.no) found mercury levels in umbilical-cord blood and breast milk in remote Greenland vil-lages to be 20 to 50 times higher than in urban areas of the United States and Europe.

Scientists are now trying to establish a link between accumulated chemicals and health effects. Many of the toxins are endocrine disrupters, which can impair reproduction, cause developmental or skeletal abnor-malities, weaken immunity and trigger neurological problems. In Canada researchers are also investigating whether pollutants can be blamed for the high number of Inuit women suffering from osteoporosis.

Research in Svalbard in 2004 indicated that polar bears are already showing changes in their hormone and immune systems. High levels of PCBs lead to low levels of antibodies and increased chances of infection, while altered hormone levels could result in a wide range of negative health impacts. Cubs are particularly vulnerable; polar-bear milk is about 30% fat, so any contaminant stores are passed down to the young. In 2000, scientists on Svalbard said that more than 1% of the islands' bears were hermaphroditic, showing the reproductive organs of both sexes.

In the Norwegian Arctic, where pollution from brominated flame retard-ants is concentrated, the bear-cub survival rate is half of that in Canada and Alaska, and sea-bird eggs are contaminated with high levels of PCBs, dioxins and some of the new contaminants. Studies on Bear Island, just to the south of Svalbard, found dead and dying gulls with PCB levels in their brains a hundred times higher than in healthy birds. And it's not just industrial chemicals that are to blame. A Norwegian study in 2003 found that fish in Arctic waters are exposed to an unexpectedly strong cocktail of caffeine and painkillers from local sewers, and samples taken near a psychiatric hospital showed measurable amounts of anti-epileptic drugs and antidepressants.

In May 2004, 151 countries signed the Stockholm Convention on Per-sistent Organic Pollutants, which seeks to phase out the use of 12 of the most dangerous persistent organic pollutants as soon as possible. However, for many, it may be too little too late.

Mars on Earth, by Robert Zubrin, tells the dramatic story of a group of space pioneers who simulated a mission to Mars on Canada's Devon Island.

ARCTIC ECOLOGY

Since 1990 the **International Tundra Experiment** (ITEX; www.itex-science.net) has con-ducted extensive studies in Arctic ecology. The main objective of ITEX is to assess the potential impact of global warming on Arctic and alpine vegetation. The experiment attempts to simulate the climate that may exist in 2050. Results show that in increased temperatures there is evidence of a disintegration of the plant communities on the tundra and, with new plants slow to move into the tundra areas, animal populations using these regions will be at risk. ITEX monitoring and experimental research is ongoing and should provide more long-term understanding of the Arctic botanical processes at work during climate change.

OIL & GAS EXPLORATION

The Arctic is rich in fossil fuels and has long attracted the attention of companies keen to stake a claim to a fortune. However, drilling and mining have proved hugely damaging to the Arctic environment (see p60). In the light of plans for oil and gas development in Canada's Beaufort Sea – a largely untouched expanse of water – scientists are using satellite-based radio tracking to trace marine wildlife in offshore feeding areas and migratory corridors, and local Inuvialuit are working with the **WWF** (www .wwf.org) to identify and reserve key marine areas for conservation. Other recent studies have tested bearded seals, walruses and bowhead whales for petroleum hydrocarbon contamination from crude oil. Meanwhile, huge investments are being made by Denmark, Russia and Canada to survey the Arctic sea bed in an attempt to claim ownership of the area and secure rights to the natural resources in the sea floor, which may be worth millions of dollars.

For excellent links and news on Arctic research and findings, visit www .dpc.dk.

THE FUTURE OF ARCTIC RESEARCH

Never before has Arctic research been so important. Changes to the environment of the far north are now visible to the layperson, and although significant progress has been made in the last decade, climate-change indicators, human-health impacts and ecosystem alterations are increasingly worrying factors.

Umbrella organisations facilitating and organising research projects are key to continued success in this area, as new technologies and more accurate data collection revolutionise scientific understanding of the far north. The International Polar Year 2007–09 (see p32) heralds new research in the area, with international cooperation and improved sharing of regional environmental data, facilities and logistics.

In the meantime the 2005 launch of **CryoSat** (www.esa.int/export/esaLP/cryosat .html), Europe's radar altimetry mission, will mean a leap forward for ice-sheet research, with unprecedented accuracy in measurements helping to determine whether or not our planet's ice masses are thinning due to global warming. **EUMETSAT** (www.eumetsat.de), Europe's first polar orbiting meteorological satellite, is on target for launch at the end of 2005 and will greatly enhance the ability of scientists to monitor the global climate and weather systems. Instruments on board will measure winds and temperature at the surface of the sea and will monitor global ozone distribution, pressure and water vapour in the upper atmosphere.

For the indigenous people of the Arctic, localised studies of climate change and their related impacts on the region's human population are of the utmost importance. What scientists predict the rest of the world will face in the future the indigenous people of the north are experiencing right now. Although the residents of the far north have survived against the odds for thousands of years, they are powerless against the onset of climate change while being the first to feel its effects.

Indigenous Peoples & Cultures of the Arctic

An estimated 650,000 indigenous people have made the great expanse of the Arctic their home. For thousands of years these nomadic tribes survived in almost total isolation before the missionaries, traders, whalers, explorers and colonial governments arrived and slowly tore their world apart.

For many who travel north the modernity of contemporary life for Arctic people is a surprise – supermarkets stock everything from instant noodles to age-defying night creams, housing is modern and satellite TV beams as much dross into Arctic homes as it does elsewhere. However, what is easily forgotten is that these very same people lived a life almost wholly dependent on hunting as a food source until 50 years ago.

The rapid social, cultural and economic change that has swept across the circumpolar north has not been without its problems. When education became compulsory, nomadic life was halted, families became dislocated, children were taken far away to residential schools, and home and family life deteriorated. The skills that were once so important on the land suddenly became redundant, and the consequent loss of identity meant that many once-proud hunters began to drown their feelings of shame and inadequacy in alcohol. For many, self-esteem is still despairing low, and across the Arctic suicide rates are particularly high.

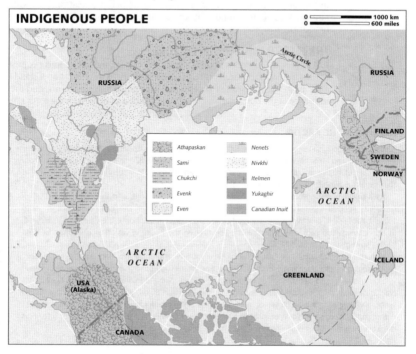

INDIGENOUS PEOPLE

0 — 1000 km
0 — 600 miles

Arctic Circle

RUSSIA

RUSSIA

FINLAND

SWEDEN

NORWAY

Athapaskan	Nenets
Sami	Nivkhi
Chukchi	Itelmen
Evenk	Yukaghir
Even	Canadian Inuit

ARCTIC OCEAN

ARCTIC OCEAN

USA (Alaska)

GREENLAND

ICELAND

CANADA

It was difficult for the indigenous people to assimilate into the Western world, and there is a constant struggle to adapt to the new life while still maintaining aspects of the old. No-one wishes to block out the influence of the south altogether, but so much has changed in such a short space of time that many are lost in the half-world between two cultures, unsure of where they belong. Life is a complicated and contradictory world where women clean and chew caribou or sealskin as they watch American sitcoms and reality TV.

TRADITIONAL CULTURE

The indigenous peoples of the Arctic can all trace similar origins in Central Asia (see p17). These nomadic hunters gradually moved across Canada, eventually reaching Greenland about 4500 years ago. Today distinct groups exist in different areas. In Alaska they are the Inupiat and Yup'ik Inuit, and the Alutiiq (Aleut), while the Athapaskans of the Alaskan interior cross over into the Yukon; in Canada and Greenland they are the Inuit; in Scandinavia the indigenous population is the Sami; and in Arctic Russia indigenous groups include the Chukchi, Even, Evenk, Sami, Nenets, Nivkhi, Itelmen, Yup'ik and Yukaghir.

'nomadic hunters traditionally regarded the environment as simply an extension of their being'

Although each group has evolved its own distinctive culture, all share the same respect for the Arctic environment. Their culture, education and lifestyle depended on it and the nomadic hunters traditionally regarded the environment as simply an extension of their being. Despite the changes in their lifestyle, few local people, even the young and talented, wish to forsake their communities for the bright lights of southern cities. Despite satellite TV beaming in images of the Western world, almost all of those who live in the far north do so because they choose to, because relationships with family are extremely important, and because of the land and what it signifies for the people.

THREATS TO INDIGENOUS CULTURE

Just as they share aspects of their history and culture, the indigenous peoples of the far north face similar threats to their cultures. Low educational standards mean the road to self-determination is pitted with problems, and the influence of the dominant languages and cultures of neighbouring southern

---

ALCOHOL & THE ARCTIC

Alcohol abuse is a huge problem in the far north, and it's readily apparent in most communities at weekends and after payday. The long months of winter darkness, a sense of hopelessness from being caught between cultures, and genetic intolerance due to low supplies of the amino acid that breaks down alcohol have all been blamed.

As a result many communities are now 'dry': no alcohol is sold, and in many cases the ingredients needed to make home brew are also banned. However, this can result in a move to solvent abuse or in creative, but particularly dangerous, batches of home brew appearing instead. In other towns the problem is curtailed by restricting the hours in which alcohol may be sold or the strength of beer available.

Unfortunately, children are often the biggest victims, and child mortality and foetal alcohol syndrome rates are alarmingly high. Violence and domestic abuse influenced by alcohol cause enormous family problems, and for many young people binge-drinking at weekends becomes a way to deal with it all. Sadly, falling asleep in a snowdrift on the way home can mean the loss of limbs, and careering around town on a snowmobile when drunk can often prove to be fatal. Most communities have some form of alcohol treatment programme and support groups for reformed drinkers. However, in remote communities it can be difficult to resist temptation.

populations has meant a gradual but systemic erosion of traditional culture. Oil and gas exploitation (see p60), ozone depletion (see p31) and climate change (see p27) pose enormous threats to traditional lands, livelihoods and cultures. Industrialisation threatens ecosystems and wildlife migration routes, and the accumulation of environmental contaminants – particularly persistent organic pollutants and heavy metals in the food supply – means that the traditional diet is no longer safe to eat (see p34). At the same time, the wholehearted acceptance of processed foods and Western lifestyles means that first-world diseases such as diabetes, obesity, heart problems and cancer are now prevalent among Arctic communities, and alcohol abuse and liver disease are on the increase.

THE INUIT

The Inuit occupy a vast geographical area stretching from Chukotka in the Russian Far East, across Alaska and Canada to the east coast of Greenland. A scant 150,000 people make this area their home, and although different dialects exist, they all speak largely the same language.

The oldest archaeological sites identified as Inuit are in southwest Alaska and the Aleutian Islands and date from around 2000 BC. The Inuit adapted extremely well to the harsh conditions they found themselves in, hunting whale, seal, caribou, muskox and bear for survival. Today, most Inuit hunt to supplement their income only, and commercial fishing, the service industry and oil and mineral extraction have become the main earners in most communities.

LIFESTYLE

Although life in most Inuit towns and settlements resembles that of the Western world, with supermarkets, satellite TV and Internet access, many smaller settlements have few facilities, no running water and a much more traditional and generally impoverished lifestyle.

Wherever you go, however, the veneer of modern life is fairly superficial and tradition influences many daily activities. Family groups are still incredibly important, and in most towns there is a complex network of family relations; often a few extended families make up the whole population. The elderly are taken care of by the extended family and, in line with tradition, children are not disciplined. Children inherit the name and the name soul (see p41) of their ancestors, so disciplining a child shows disrespect for the deceased elder. Children are expected to learn from the repercussions of their mistakes, not from the anger of their parents.

The attachment to the land is also incredibly important, and animals as well as traditional hunters are highly respected. Although commercial whaling and trapping changed the Inuit's relationship with the animals, a powerful respect for nature still exists, and the power of the land to take life is never underestimated.

The economy in most areas has moved from its traditional hunting base into either commercial fishing, as in Greenland, or mining and exploitation of mineral rights, as in Canada and Alaska. However, in some areas, such as the settlements in northern Greenland, and for the Inupiat on Alaska's North Slope and the Yup'ik of southwest Alaska, hunting is still the main form of income. In all others it is a much-needed source of food and the most popular pastime.

In practically all Inuit communities there is a dependence on government subsidies and benefits, and living on welfare is common in modern

'The oldest archaeological sites identified as Inuit...date from around 2000 BC'

Inuit society. Unfortunately, so is a host of social problems ranging from alcohol and solvent abuse to domestic violence and teenage pregnancies. The traditional Inuit tolerance of infidelity has led to a casual attitude to sex and long-term relationships. Sexually transmitted infections are incredibly common, and all sorts of complicated blood ties can bind several families together. However, the situation is open and accepted, and children who are adopted into new families or are born of fleeting relationships are generally fully aware of their true parentage.

Although the culture and lifestyle of the Inuit of North America and Greenland share many characteristics, the majority of Inuit in North America now speak English as a first language. Although the first few years of primary school are taught in a local dialect, language skills are being lost quickly. Dog teams have largely been forsaken for snowmobiles, and it takes a trip to a small outpost to find anyone living a vaguely traditional lifestyle. By contrast, in northern Greenland dog teams are everywhere, Greenlandic is spoken throughout the country and life maintains a less tenuous connection with tradition. However, most Inuit children must leave home to get a high-school education, and homesickness means that many return without graduating.

DID YOU KNOW?

In Greenland dogsleds always have the right of way.

TRADITIONAL CULTURE

In traditional Inuit society, social organisation was built around the immediate kin group, and social obligations to help one's family and to share meat and fish were key cultural principles. Groups were generally small, travelling to favoured hunting and fishing grounds in summer and creating a semipermanent settlement of stone-and-sod houses or a snow-block *iglo* (the Inuit word for house) in winter. Women and men were on an equal footing but there was a sharp division of labour. Men went out to hunt while women cleaned the skins, made clothing, cooked and looked after the children. Today, this distinction is much less apparent, and men and women are treated as equals.

The Inuit depended on the land and its animals for everything, and this relationship with nature was the basis of Inuit culture, spiritual beliefs and religious practices. For the Inuit everything had a spirit, and a complex set of taboos and rituals dictated behaviour on a hunt to ensure that the souls of the animals received proper treatment and respect. Disregarding the rules would mean death, famine or severe misfortune. Traditional myths describe this intricate relationship between humans, animals and the environment, the preparation for a successful hunt, and the appeasement of animal spirits.

Atanarjuat (The Fast Runner), directed by Zacharias Kunuk, is a beautifully shot action thriller recounting the tale of an Inuit blood feud and the supernatural powers of the local shaman.

The shaman, someone who had the knowledge and power to influence and control the spirits, was a prominent figure in all Inuit communities. Shamans acted as intermediaries between humans and animals, and through trances and journeys to the spirit world they could bargain with the animals' guardian for their release to be hunted. The shamans also depended on a variety of helping spirits, usually animals, to carry them silently through the air or aid them to swim effortlessly to the bottom of the sea to perform their duties.

The Inuit commonly believed that a person consisted of three souls: the personal soul, the free soul and the name soul. After death the personal soul travelled either to the underworld – a place overflowing with animals where the souls of dead kin and friends are reunited – or to an upper world of starvation and cold. The free soul, however, could leave the body at will and had to be retrieved by a shaman if it strayed too far and caused illness. At death the name soul was set free until it was called back to reside in the body of a newborn child. While waiting to be reborn these souls combined to form the northern lights. Even today, when an Inuit child receives a name some of the good personal qualities of the deceased are believed to be inherited.

For more information and to view a gallery of work by Canadian Inuit artists, visit www.ccca.ca/inuit.

After a person's death elaborate taboos were observed to appease any malevolent spirits. These spirits were often depicted in the carving of *tupilaks*, and were made by the shaman to cast misfortune and even death on enemies. In Greenland modern *tupilaks* are sold as art and souvenirs (see p86). Some represent polar bears, birds or marine mammals, but most are just hideous imaginary beings. In North America stylistic curvilinear carvings made from soapstone are popular. In Canada communities such as Cape Dorset (see p249) are famous for their master carvers.

DID YOU KNOW?

The blanket toss developed from a traditional method of tossing a hunter into the air to survey the land for distant herds of game.

The best time to see traditional cultural activities or clothing is at community festivals. The arrival of the first light in spring has always been cause for celebration, and many communities hold welcome events for the return of the sun. Later in the year spring festivals feature traditional sports and games, and extended families travel for kilometres to meet at these events. Some of the most popular include the blanket toss, where a large group hold a tarp (traditionally a hide) taut and literally toss another person into the air; traditional competitions of strength and dexterity; and elaborate string games. In the evenings dances are usually held, featuring traditional drum dancing, jigging and throat singing, a guttural performance by two women looking eye to eye.

THE INUIT TODAY

The Inuit today seem caught in a constant battle with outside forces over which they can exert little control. Activities in the industrialised world are having a huge effect on what remains of their traditional culture. Climate change (see p27) is one of the most pressing concerns, as sea-ice conditions are deteriorating quickly and hunters can no longer travel to traditional spring hunting grounds. Couple that with health warnings advising Inuit not to eat their traditional food sources because of bioaccumulation (see p34), and Inuit culture faces a considerable challenge.

Learn how to play traditional Inuit string games at www.isfa .org/arctic.htm.

Despite this, the Inuit have begun to take much more control over their destiny. A growing political awareness has created a heightened sense of group identity and a concerted push for land rights and political self-determination. In 1971 the US Congress passed the Alaska Native Land Claims Settlement Act (ANCSA), giving the indigenous people effective control over one-ninth of the state. The Greenlanders won home rule in 1979, and the Canadian Inuit's homeland of Nunavut (see p25) was created in 1999.

The **Inuit Circumpolar Conference** (ICC; www.inuit.org) was established to give the Inuit a voice in order to tackle environmental threats to their culture, and through it they challenge the policies of governments, multinational corporations and environmental movements, arguing that adequate systems of environmental management and the most appropriate forms of sustainability are only possible if they are based on local knowledge and Inuit cultural values.

For an insight into the political, cultural and economic development of the Canadian Inuit as well as a look at their history and culture, visit www.tapirisat.ca.

In Nunavut, where the Inuit have taken control of their own political future, low levels of education mean a system of positive discrimination is needed to employ local people. Many Inuit welcome the system as a step in the right direction, but others suggest that employing local, but less qualified, public servants could hinder the fledgling territory's progress in the long term.

THE SAMI

The Sami people live in Fennoscandia (more often known as Lapland), a vast swath of northern Norway, Sweden and Finland, and the Kola Peninsula in Russia. Approximately 80,000 people make up this indigenous group and, although they are linguistically related to the Finns, Hungarians and Estonians, the culture and lifestyle are distinctly their own.

DID YOU KNOW?

The name Lapp means 'piece of cloth' or 'patch', and is now considered a derogatory term. The name Sami derives from the people's own name for themselves and is much preferred.

Coastal habitation was established in northern Scandinavia about 10,000 years ago and, as the people moved inland, hunting cultures dependent on elk and wild reindeer developed. Hunting and fishing remained the basis of Sami culture for several hundred years, and it was only in the 1600s that reindeer were domesticated and some Sami began to follow the herds on their annual migration routes. However, not all Sami became nomadic reindeer herders, and today the majority do not use reindeer herding as a main source of income. Despite this, it is reindeer and reindeer herding that have come to define and symbolise Sami culture.

LIFESTYLE

The Sami first encountered southern missionaries in the 11th century, and by the 17th century they were having to fight the loss of traditional reindeer-grazing ground to organised colonisation for farm land. By the 1870s Sami-language newspapers and magazines were being published, and in 1946 the first Sami broadcast was made. Today the Sami are inevitably more westernised than other indigenous groups, and living and social conditions for most Sami today are close to those in the rest of Scandinavia: housing is modern, men and women are treated equally and standards of living are high.

Today those Sami who continue to herd reindeer are firmly in the minority. A constantly shrinking habitat in which to herd, the deterioration of grazing lands due to environmental disturbances, increasing legislation, and an alien capital-intensive focus on producing as much meat as possible have made it difficult for traditional subsistence herders to compete or even survive. Others have embraced new technology and business models, turned to reindeer breeding as opposed to herding, or made use of snowmobiles, ATVs (all-terrain vehicles) and even helicopters to make this traditional way of life profitable in modern society. Most other Sami work in fishing, farming, forestry or mining operations, often combining them with more traditional livelihoods.

Traditional reindeer-herding families have also been affected by policies of 'modernisation' that aimed to raise living standards by settling Sami in permanent communities. Cultural and economic integration, intermarriage with Norwegians, Swedes and Finns, and (in Norway) restrictions on the use of the Sami language have all resulted in a gradual erosion of traditional culture.

Although in core areas the Sami language is in daily use, in coastal regions the pervasive influence of the dominant Scandinavian languages means that Sami is losing ground. Some Sami communities provide both daycare and primary schooling in the native language, but at secondary and tertiary levels access to education in the Sami language is difficult to find.

TRADITIONAL CULTURE

Traditional Sami culture is inexorably linked to reindeer-herding practices and, like the Inuit, the Sami have a very strong bond with the land. They name almost every tree, river, stream, lake, mountain, valley and meadow with names that contain information not only about physical features but also about community history and mythological events. For the Sami many of these places are sacred, and in the past reindeer antlers would have been placed at sacred sites and adorned with gifts. *Seiteh* (sacred stones) were also placed on mountaintops and near lakes and rivers.

For the Sami all elements of nature were imbued with a spirit, and great care and attention went to ensure that spirits were appeased and placated. The Sami *noaidi* (shamans) played a central role in this. Although the *noaidi* acted as diviners and spiritual facilitators of the hunt, their primary role was as healer. With the help of guardian spirits such as fish, birds or reindeer, the spirit of the *noaidi* would travel to hidden spirit worlds either to bargain with the deities to ensure good weather and good hunting or to retrieve a soul that may have wandered from a person's sick body. Although traditional medical carers could treat minor diseases and illnesses, only the *noaidi* had the power to win back a lost soul. Sometimes, depending on the nature of the ailment, the sacrifice of a reindeer, goat or lamb would be offered to the deity or spirit. While many shamans were killed for being in league with the devil during the fervent conversion to Christianity in the 16th and 17th centuries, shamanism survived in some isolated places until the 20th century.

For entertainment the Sami developed a rich oral tradition of storytelling, and an enormous number and variety of legends are part of Sami culture. A particularly distinctive form of this oral literature is the poetry that accompanies the traditional forms of Sami music. Three modes of traditional singing exist: the *joik*, highly personal and deeply felt *a capella* songs which were originally an integral part of Sami shamanism; *Laavloe*, songs with words or lyrics; and *vuelie*, storytelling songs about a person or an event. Although technically incorrect, the word *joik* is often used to describe all of these. All three modes are still used, and in recent years there has been a revival of interest in traditional singing methods.

Traditional drumming, flute playing and bullroaring accompanied the songs. The bullroarer was made from a specially shaped piece of horn or wood that was swung around the head on a string; by varying the length of the string and the speed of the swing the player could create different sounds. Modern *joiks* show the influence of Western rock music, and the most famous Sami singer, Mari Boine of Norway, sings a type of minimalist folk-rock with *joik* roots. *Joiks* and other Sami styles have also been used by non-Sami artists such as Enigma and Jan Garbarek. *Joiks* are often performed in the theatre, and the Sami theatre group Beaivvas, based in Kautokeino, regularly perform them.

Sami festivals are also a good opportunity to see culture in action. The National Sami Day on 6 February is celebrated with traditional games and events, and is a good opportunity to see the Sami in traditional ceremonial dress – embroidered red and blue felt clothing with pearl and ribbon crowns for the women. Although many reindeer herders still dress in traditional

Pathfinder, directed by Nils Gaup, is an Oscar-nominated film about the legend of a young Sami boy whose village is invaded and his quest to outsmart the enemy.

DID YOU KNOW?

Chart hit *Return to Innocence*, by Enigma, features a backing track of Sami *joik* singing.

tasselled hats and brightly coloured tunics, they are definitely not out to be a tourist attraction and don't appreciate being treated as such. The other major Sami festival time is Easter, when the Sami celebrate the end of the dark winter months and the beginning of a pilgrimage north for new pasture. In Kautokeino the celebrations include an annual Reindeer Racing Championship (see p322). It's also a very popular time for weddings.

Sami *duodji* (handicrafts) were originally for domestic use only, but today they are produced in large quantities for the tourist market and provide an important source of income for many families. Men generally work in horn or wood, producing bowls, knives, beads and carvings, while women work in leather, pewter, thread and spruce roots. Contemporary Sami art features strong influences from Sami culture and shamanic symbolism. The outstanding drawings and prints by John Savio, Nils Nilsson Skum, Lars Pirak and Iver Jåks are some of the best to look out for.

For information on the lives, culture and contemporary issues of the Sami people, visit www.sametinget.se, the website of the Swedish Sami Parliament.

THE SAMI TODAY

Although reindeer herding is central to Sami culture, only a minority depend on it today and many of those who do are supported by government subsidies. The expansion of agriculture, the development of mining, tourism, forestry and hydrocarbon projects, and changes in herding and breeding practice have all encroached upon Sami reindeer-herding lands and put further pressure on this way of life.

Across the Sami homeland, environmental problems and resource development are among the biggest issues, and the Sami believe that the only way to protect their traditional livelihoods and culture is to grant them special rights to land and natural resources. However, national governments rarely subscribe to this view, and conflicts over sustainable land use are common. Although the Sami of Finland, Norway and Sweden have their own parliaments to deal with issues relating to their culture and economy, they are severely limited in their powers, especially in relation to determining land rights and resource use. The Sami Council, which represents Sami interests in national, regional and international arenas, is working to protect its people in response to plans by the dominant Norwegian, Swedish, Finnish and Russian nation-states to exploit the vast natural resources of Fennoscandia.

Minor victories came with the EU, Finnish and Norwegian governments' acknowledgments of the Sami as a distinct people, but in Sweden the 20,000 Sami face continuing problems. Although Swedish Sami technically have the right to graze their herds on private land, the law is unclear, and in 1990 three Swedish forestry companies and several private landowners successfully sued five reindeer-herding communities for doing just that. Since then others have also been victims of this legal loophole.

Sami Potatoes, by Mike Robinson and Karim-Aly Kassam, is a testament to the cultural and political strength of the Russian Sami of the Kola Peninsula as they struggle to gain control of their traditional lands.

The Sami of the Kola Peninsula are also demanding self-government and regional autonomy. They have formed their own organisation, the Kola Sami Association, to promote and defend Sami interests and to work for a degree of self-determination, but they face the stiffest challenges of all Sami groups. After the collapse of the Soviet Union and collectivism, few Sami could afford to buy or own a reindeer herd; for those that could, controversies over grazing rights and limited markets for reindeer meat have meant a constant struggle to survive. The Kola Peninsula is also the most industrially developed part of the Russian Arctic and is suffering a severe ecological crisis.

Pollution from mining, commercial fishing and timber production, together with the presence of nuclear submarines and nuclear bomber bases, threatens the entire northern part of Scandinavia and poses great dangers to the Sami communities' economies and health. As a result of industrial activity, about 100,000 hectares of the Kola Peninsula have almost no vegetation, and acid rain is devastating forests. Reindeer pasture is under great threat; lakes and rivers are polluted; land is expropriated by oil, gas, mining and timber companies; and local economies are in danger of collapsing. As the environmental crises force rapid social, economic and cultural change, the future for the Kola Sami looks bleak.

THE ATHAPASKANS

Northern Athapaskan peoples inhabit a huge expanse of coniferous forest both above and below the Arctic Circle that stretches across Alaska, the Yukon and the Northwest Territories, and down into northern British Columbia, Alberta, Saskatchewan and Manitoba. Many northern Athapaskans now call themselves Na Dene, which means 'human beings'.

Since 1997, researchers working in Canada's Yukon have found a host of archaeological sites in the melting snowfields with perfectly preserved artefacts ranging from 800 to 9000 years old. As traditional Athapaskan houses, tents, boats, and hunting and fishing equipment were made from wood and animal hides, they left no trace on the forest floor for contemporary archaeologists to discover. These finds high on the mountains should provide much information on the lifestyle of the people of the northern forests.

'The Athapaskans have lived in harmony with their environment for thousands of years'

LIFESTYLE

The Athapaskans have lived in harmony with their environment for thousands of years, the forests and rivers of Alaska and northern Canada providing them with a rich variety of resources. Traditionally, life in Athapaskan communities revolved around seasonal hunting, gathering and fishing. In smaller remote communities this system has changed little over the years.

Moose and caribou are especially important animals for many communities, and for those on the banks of a river the annual salmon run is the highlight of the year. In traditional times, Athapaskan society was highly mobile; although everyone now lives in settled communities, travelling long distances to hunt or to see friends and family is still an integral part of life. In spring and summer – traditional times for trapping muskrats, hunting caribou and netting salmon – whole villages will virtually empty as families flee the settled life and head to traditional camps where old roles come in to play. Labour is sharply divided between men and women, who each have specific tasks to ensure a successful season and the proper curing of meat or fish. Children grow up with these traditions and learn young how to shoot a gun, skin an animal and prepare hides. For the Athapaskans these sustained periods of life in the bush are the happiest times of year. In autumn the gathering of berries is still an important part of the culture.

During the winter months many women spend their time beading elaborate geometric and floral patterns onto moose hide or caribou skin. Poker games are a favourite for many men. In all respects today Athapaskan women are treated as equals to men, but the influence of traditional roles is still visible. Men chop wood for the fire, look after snowmobiles or dog teams and hunt and fish, while women bead and sew and are the primary caregivers for children.

Athapaskan communities today are generally made up of one tribal band led by a chief and several councillors. Successful land claims have meant that many Athapaskan bands are financially stable and not reliant on government handouts, but many worry that unwise investments mean an unsustainable future for some communities.

As with other northern communities, alcohol and solvent abuse is common, and tribal leaders struggle to contain the associated social problems. Children often have to travel long distances to go to school, and English is used by all but the elders. Despite this, traditions are generally strong, and seasonal hunting and trapping remain priorities in most communities.

TRADITIONAL CULTURE

Traditional Athapaskan culture revolved around the hunting of land mammals such as moose, caribou and bear, and fishing for salmon and northern pike. Social organisation was based on small, mobile kinship groups, and communities generally consisted of several nuclear families, often connected through various relationships and alliances. Regional kinship ties could make up a group or band of several hundred people.

Two Old Women and *Bird Girl & the Man Who Followed the Sun*, by Velma Wallis, retell the legends, life stories and tales of survival of the Gwich'in people, one of 11 Athapaskan groups.

Athapaskan culture has an immensely rich spiritual and cultural heritage. Oral history and mythology describe how landscape features and the moon, sun, wind and stars were originally human beings, whose spirits are now embodied in aspects of the natural world. To this day a fundamental theme in the Athapaskan world view is respect for nature and animals. Traditionally, humans and animals were not clearly distinguished, and stories tell how they often lived in the same communities, even sharing households.

Accounts of Distant Time, a remote and ancient time, describe the origins of the world, the elements and the animals. The Raven is a central figure in these stories; it was he who created the world by banishing the darkness, revealing the daylight and creating the first people. From the Distant Time stories people learn the proper rules and behaviour for interacting with animals and the natural world. If animals are not respected and treated properly, vindictive natural spirits can endanger the whole community. Like other indigenous peoples, the Athapaskans had shamans who called to game in times of starvation, cured the sick, and appeased malevolent spirits.

The Athapaskan respect for animals is perhaps most vividly illustrated by the fact that animals such as bears and wolverines are given funeral rituals after they are killed. Traditionally, after a moose is killed, the hunter punches out the eyeballs so that the moose's spirit can escape and the animal cannot see what is then done to its body.

One of the most famous Athapaskan traditions is the potlatch, a ceremony that honours the dead and the connection between ancestors and the living. The potlatch is also the elaborate, highly ritualised exchange and distribution of gifts, and was often the primary way by which an individual achieved prestige in and beyond their community.

Traditional arts revolve largely around local natural materials. Decorated birch bark containers, porcupine-quill work, moosehair tufting, and beading are the most popular crafts. Intricate beading patterns adorn everything from hair clips to moccasins, jackets, mitts and bags. Contemporary Athapaskan music focuses on the fiddle, and the lively tunes that are now considered traditional resemble a cross between Cajun and Scottish styles.

THE ATHAPASKANS TODAY

Dramatic changes swept through Athapaskan villages over the course of the 20th century. Education delivered through formal schooling, together with policies of modernisation and assimilation into mainstream

American and Canadian society, meant that traditional knowledge and activities were lost. Language skills are now particularly vulnerable: the dominant influence of English and a lack of suitably qualified local teachers to deliver schooling in Athapaskan languages mean that whole generations of children are growing up without learning their native tongue.

For more information on the Arctic National Wildlife Refuge, visit http://arcticcircle.uconn .edu/ANWR/.

However, cultural survival has been made possible through land claims and degrees of self-determination. Some bands have fared particularly well and invested wisely, while others find themselves embroiled in difficulties. However, even successful communities are racked by social problems – as in other Arctic villages, alcoholism, domestic and sexual abuse, suicide, and low educational standards mean that tribal leaders face an enormous set of challenges in the future.

PROTECTING THE PORCUPINE CARIBOU

For more than 30 years the Gwich'in people of the northern Yukon and Alaska have been fighting to protect the calving grounds of the Porcupine caribou herd on which they depend for basic sustenance and cultural survival. Since oil was discovered at Prudhoe Bay on Alaska's North Slope, the prospect of finding more reserves in the neighbouring Arctic National Wildlife Refuge (ANWR) has tantalised the US.

The reserve, however, is one of the most ecologically sensitive areas in the Arctic and is home to the calving grounds of the 152,000-head herd, the world's largest. In Canada these calving grounds are protected within Ivvavik National Park (see p244) and extend into Alaska, where they are part of the Arctic National Wildlife Refuge (see p254). The herd migrates though the tiny Yukon village of Old Crow, where the whole traditional culture revolves around the annual migration. It is the Old Crow residents and a group of hardy environmentalists who have taken on some of the biggest oil companies and the US government.

Their Alaskan neighbours, the North Slope Inupiat, are in favour of drilling, saying that the project could be managed to minimise the impact on the environment. Prudhoe Bay has an average of 400 spills a year, however, and the pollution has destroyed thousands of acres of wildlife habitat and caused declines in wildlife populations. The field is beginning to run dry, though, and for the many Inupiat who rely on oil-related wages as their main source of income, the financial benefit of leasing the oil-rich land to the multinationals is worth the risk. For the Gwich'in subsistence hunters, any development is a threat to their whole culture, and the continued difference of opinion puts the two native communities at odds.

Although the US government estimates that reserves in the ANWR could yield 60,000 barrels of oil a day, environmentalists argue that this figure has never been substantiated and that, even if it were true, it would take over 10 years for the oil to reach the market. They also argue that if Americans could just get three miles per gallon more out of their cars then a million barrels of oil a day would be saved.

In 1995 President Clinton vetoed proposed legislation that would have allowed oil and gas drilling on the Alaskan portion of the calving grounds, but – as environmentalists feared – the Bush administration had different ideas. Despite protestations from the Canadian government, the US plans to go ahead with a 'small' development. However, as the oil is concentrated in pockets, this would also mean a system of roads and airstrips to link sites. If this development goes ahead, one of the world's last great animal migrations could disappear. In 2003, by a narrow margin, US senators voted against opening up the ANWR lands for drilling, but with Bush re-elected to the White House and the majority of members of the House of Representatives supporting a bill to open up the refuge to drilling, the future looks bleak. In January 2005 the newly elected chair of the Senate Energy and Natural Resources Committee, Senator Domenici, made a point of holding an immediate press conference to make public his support for 'responsible' development of the ANWR. At the time of writing, it looked as if pushing through legislation to make this happen was likely to be one of the headlines of 2005.

THE CHUKCHI

The Chukchi live in isolated and remote villages in the northeastern corner of Siberia, in the Chukchi Autonomous Oblast (an administrative territory within the Russian Federation), although small numbers also inhabit the Koryak Autonomous Oblast and Yakutia. The Chukchi call themselves the Lyg Oravetlyan ('the true people'), and are closely related to the Koryak and Itelmen peoples of northeast Siberia. The Russian name Chukchi comes from the Chukchi word *chauchu*, meaning 'rich in reindeer'.

Although a minority of Evens, Koryaks and Yakuts also live in the Chukchi Oblast, all these peoples are far outnumbered by Russian settlers, who were drawn to the region by the development of mining for tin, gold, tungsten, mercury and coal.

LIFESTYLE

Traditionally, the Chukchi have been divided into two groups: the nomadic Reindeer Chukchi, who inhabit the interior and the Chukchi Peninsula, and the Maritime Chukchi, who are settled hunters and fishers living on small peninsulas jutting off the Arctic Ocean and Bering Strait coasts. The groups relied on each other for trade (reindeer skins were traded for whale blubber, sealskins and walrus hides), and were linked through marriage and other forms of alliance.

For more information on the Chukchi people, visit www.chukotka.org.

The Russian policy of forcibly assimilating indigenous people into the political, cultural and economic mainstream of the country caused many problems for the Chukchi and almost eliminated all traditional nomadic and subsistence activities. Reindeer herding was collectivised, the Russian language became essential, and both traditional Chukchi and Russian Orthodox religious ceremonies and festivals were prohibited.

Today the Chukchi are no longer nomadic, reindeer herds are domesticated, and modern technology and scientific breeding techniques have been developed to make the traditional way of life sustainable in modern times. The Maritime Chukchi subsist on a diet of fish and marine mammals; the boat crew, a group of five or six related families who work together to hunt large mammals, is still central to social organisation.

Adapting to this settled life was difficult for many, and unemployment exacerbated the problem. Menial jobs that required no qualifications were all that were open to the Chukchi and, as with many other indigenous communities, excessive alcoholism and high suicide rates became accepted as part of the new life. The change to shop-bought food brought new-world diseases, and the effect of nuclear testing in the Russian far north has been devastating. Today, practically the whole community is ailing. Tuberculosis, cirrhosis of the liver and cancer of the stomach and lungs are common complaints, and child mortality rates are alarmingly high. The indigenous Chukchi population is steadily dropping, and many fear for the future of the nation and its culture.

Most Chukchi children are sent to boarding schools, as educational facilities are not available in all communities. As children return home for school holidays only, several generations have already missed out on the opportunity to learn traditional customs. Russian is spoken at school, in hospitals and in shops, and its influence is pervasive. An increase in mixed marriages, sometimes attributed to Chukchi women hoping for healthier children with a Russian partner, means that Russian has also invaded home life.

However bleak things look for the Chukchi, *perestroika* and *glasnost* ushered in a new era of political freedom and a renewed sense of hope for

Arctic Russia's indigenous people. Topics that had previously been taboo became the object of open discussion, and where once the Chukchi were resigned to their fate they began to hope and fight for a better future. The Chukchi played an active role in the formation of the Russian Association of the Indigenous Peoples of the North, and today small steps have been made to redress the problems in Chukotka. The number of schools teaching Chukot is increasing, Chukot newspapers and fairytales for children are now published, and Chukot radio and TV broadcasts have grown more frequent.

TRADITIONAL CULTURE

Like many other Arctic peoples, the Chukchi believe that the universe is populated with spirits. Everything in the world, be it animate or inanimate, has a life force and shares the same spiritual nature. In traditional Chukchi religion, shamanism was important for healing and divination, and the shaman made journeys to the spirit world to retrieve the wandering souls of the sick.

Chukchi celebrations and rituals revolved around the annual cycle of hunting and harvesting. Traditionally, the Chukchi believed that great spirits – the Reindeer Being and the Master of the Sea – protected the animals they hunted and herded, and supervised their correct ritual treatment after being slaughtered. Mistreatment of the souls of the animals would result in failure in the hunt.

Each Reindeer Chukchi family also has a guardian spirit in the form of a sacred wooden fireboard, which is used to light the fire in the hearth of each home. The fireboard represents the deity of the family fire, which protects the family, the home and the hearth from malevolent spirits. Fire ceremonies play an important part in Chukchi culture: the Supreme Being is said to have pulled the first reindeer out of a sacred fire; the return of reindeer from pasture is celebrated in a fire ceremony; and when Chukchi sacrifice a reindeer, its blood is collected in a ladle and fed to the fire.

Traditional legends and folk tales tell of good and evil, animal spirits, and traditional hunting practice. The bear in particular holds a pre-eminent place in Chukchi mythology, and in Siberia the bear festival is an elaborate form of animal ceremonialism. After a bear has been hunted, a feast is held during which the dead bear is treated as an honoured guest and people ask its forgiveness for slaying it. Rituals, myths and stories surrounding the bear and bear hunting clearly express both the desire of the hunter for the bear and the anxiety that surrounds a kill.

Many of these myths and ceremonies are kept alive by Ergyron (meaning 'dawn'), a Chukchi–Yup'ik theatre company. The company uses traditional forms of dance, song and ceremonial costume-making to bring indigenous legends and ceremonies to life. Recordings of Chukchi and Yup'ik vocal traditions are also available.

Northern Tales: Stories from the Native People of the Arctic and Subarctic Regions, edited by Howard Norman, is a collection of over 100 folk tales from 35 tribes ranging from the Chukchi of northern Siberia to the East Greenland Inuit.

THE CHUKCHI TODAY

The Chukchi suffered terribly under Soviet colonial policy, and since the 1950s massive industrial projects such as mining and resource exploitation have threatened the traditional homeland of the Chukchi and their reindeer-herding economy. Huge numbers of settlers and migrant labourers arrived, the Yup'ik were forcibly settled in Chukchi villages, and life changed irreparably. Although massive incomes were generated by the rich mineral resources of Chukotka, such as coal, gold, tungsten, lead and mercury, the indigenous Chukchi got nothing except a badly polluted environment. Rivers once rich in fish were made barren and pasture for the reindeer was ruined. Consequently, land use and self-determination are the most complex and unresolved issues in the area.

Antler on the Sea, by Anna M Kerttula, looks at contemporary ethnic rivalries between the Yup'ik and the Chukchi of the Russian far east and how traditional customs and beliefs changed the relationship between the two communities.

The Chukchi have been placed in a very vulnerable position and they believe that autonomy and control over their own future are the only ways to ensure their cultural and economic survival. However, any government will face huge challenges. Devastating environmental pollution needs to be addressed, the appropriation of land by oil and gas companies places great strain on herders, indigenous communities are afflicted by a disturbing range of health problems, and local economies have collapsed. Women in particular have borne the brunt of this economic collapse. Many have lost their jobs, or seen their income drop substantially, and childcare facilities have been withdrawn in many communities.

The economic crisis caused by the collapse of the Soviet Union has forced the Maritime Chukchi to turn to traditional subsistence activities. Cut off from western Russia and essential supply lines, they have turned to marine mammal hunting, which has again become vital to eke out extremely short supplies of food. Local hunters who had not harvested whales for many years had no choice but to resume whaling. Although hunting skills had almost disappeared in Chukotka and many had inadequate equipment, help was found through Alaska's North Slope Borough, which initiated a project to assist the Chukchi in relearning traditional activities and skills. Funds have also been used to establish native whale-observing posts along the coast of Chukotka, and the figures recorded should generate a more accurate estimate of whale stock in the area.

The future of the Chukchi is dependent on the revitalisation of whaling and reindeer herding, the strengthening of indigenous organisations, the implementation of local wildlife-management strategies, the development of small-scale community-based business initiatives, and the achievement of a degree of self-determination. However, whole generations have become used to comfortable village life and lack the skills and stamina to return to a traditional lifestyle. Persuading them that this is the way forward may be the biggest challenge that any governing body will face.

The Arctic Environment

Few who experience the fragile beauty of the Arctic are unmoved by it. Whether you visit the dramatic peaks of Alaska and eastern Canada, the magnificent icefjords of Greenland or the vast tracts of flat and frozen tundra that sweep across northern Russia you will be amazed at the diversity of life in this cold and inhospitable land.

In the perpetual darkness of mid-winter it can be a desolate place: frigid winds scream over snow-clad mountains and barren rock. But to experience this and then witness the richness of life and the tenacity of those plants and animals that make this region their home verges on the miraculous.

THE LAND

The Arctic covers a vast geographical area and boasts a wide and diverse array of habitats. The Arctic is not a clearly defined area but, for the purposes of this book, it is the area north of the Arctic Circle (above the latitude of 66°30'). It can also be defined by vegetation, the presence of permafrost or by temperature. It's worth noting that there are two north poles: the geographic north pole (also known as true north) fixed at 90° north latitude, the northernmost point of the earth's axis; and the magnetic north pole, the place where the earth's magnetic field lines point vertically downwards. All compasses point to the magnetic north pole but it is not a static position – between 2001 and 2003 the magnetic north pole moved an average of 41km each year.

At the southern reaches of the Arctic is the taiga, an area of vast spruce and birch forests that are home to a rich variety of life. North of this lies the tundra, a great treeless swath of land that is home to sedges, herbs and dwarf shrubs. The meadows here are often boggy, and they blaze with colour each summer as saxifrage and Arctic poppies bloom in carpets of yellow, red and pink. Further north again is the Arctic Basin, with its frozen sea fringed by a polar desert of bare, shattered bedrock and barren gravel plains. Here you'll find pingos, conical hills that often have a crater lake in the centre, formed by ice expanding in the ground. Throughout the region vast ranges of mountains rise – great jagged spines of rock that have been gouged and carved by glaciers and weathered over the centuries by the wind, ice and rain.

For information on ice in all its forms, see p88.

The Arctic and its Wildlife, by Bryan Sage, describes the Arctic climate, geography and biology, and discusses in detail the ways in which plants, insects, birds and mammals have adapted to and exploited the region.

Arctic North America

Arctic North America makes up a vast tract of land sweeping from Alaska right across Canada to Greenland. The area comprises a diverse range of habitats and is home to a magnificent variety of wildlife. Above the Arctic Circle in Alaska and Canada, vast flat, marshy and lake-ridden boglands dominate the scenery, while just south of this is taiga forest, dotted with thousands of lovely lakes and cut by countless wild rivers.

In Alaska the jagged peaks of the Brookes Range lord over the vast flatlands of North Slope, an area exploited for its oil reserves. Much of Alaska's north is protected by a series of vast national parks (see p58).

On Canada's western border is the mighty Mackenzie River, which flows 1800km from Great Slave Lake in the southeast to the Beaufort Sea near Inuvik. Near its mouth it fans out into one of the world's largest deltas, with hundreds of channels and islands covering an area of 16,000 sq km. The delta is known as one of the world's climate-change hot spots and it has

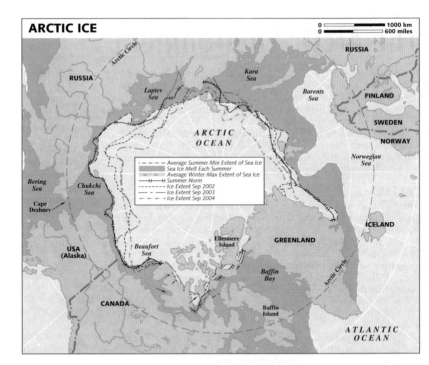

been the subject of many scientific studies over the years. Also in this area, on the eastern coast of Cape Bathurst, are the Smoking Hills (see p244), an area of slow-burning shale fires sustained by pyrite or organic material in the cliffs coming into contact with the air.

Further east is the Canadian Shield, a vast glaciated plain covered with lakes and taiga forests and rich in stores of oil, gas, diamonds and gold. To the north is the vast Arctic Archipelago, made up of enormous islands and vast flat swaths of tundra. In the far east a massive range of mountains rises from the plains, making Baffin and Ellesmere Islands stunningly picturesque. Further east is Greenland; its venerable geology is described on p88.

For a collection of essays by experts on the Arctic environment, visit www.Arctic.noaa.gov /essay.html.

Arctic Russia

The vast expanse of Arctic Russia has long been shrouded in secrecy and has taken on a mysterious allure for many travellers. In physical terms the land is tempered by the last gasp of the North Atlantic Gulf Stream, and low coniferous forest covers much of northwestern Russia. As you move east the trees diminish in size and eventually give way to the tundra that dominates all of northeastern Russia and the various archipelagos.

All the major rivers of northern Russia flow northward into the Arctic Ocean, and in spring the river water melts before the fast ice (sea ice which forms and attaches to the coast) on the northern shore, and vast swamps and marshes flood much of western Siberia.

Five major island groups dominate Russia's north shore and create six seas of the Arctic Ocean. In the far east, the Chukotka Peninsula reaches out and almost touches Alaska's Seward Peninsula (see p292; the Russian island of Big Diomede and Alaska's Little Diomede lie only 3km apart, across the International Dateline), while the vast Kamchatka Peninsula dangles between the Bering Sea and the Sea of Okhotsk (both of which belong to the Pacific Ocean).

Arctic Scandinavia

The northern reaches of Norway, Sweden and Finland lie above the Arctic Circle but have very different land forms. To the west the coast of Arctic Norway is indented with hundreds of fjords flanked by numerous islands and vast, nearly treeless peninsulas. Mountain ranges, some capped with Europe's largest glaciers and ice fields, cover more than half of the land mass, and the only relatively level area is the lake-studded and taiga-forested Finnmarksvidda Plateau, which occupies most of southern Finnmark (Norway's northernmost province).

Svalbard, 1000km north of the mainland, is about the size of Ireland and extends to over 80°N. The islands are gripped in sea ice for most of the year, and much of their interior is covered in glaciers and ice fields.

To the east the Swedish landscape was largely shaped during the most recent glacial periods; as a result, most of the country is covered by thousands of lakes and forests, which are dominated by Norway spruce, Scots pine and birch. In the far north, however, the trees thin out into a taiga landscape. A prominent mountainous spine along the Norwegian border forms a natural frontier between the two countries, with the most dramatic fells rising in Sweden's far northwest.

RESPONSIBLE TRAVEL

Every year thousands of visitors travel north, keen to see the magnificent wilderness that is the Arctic, but the presence of tourists can have a negative impact on the environment. Increased human traffic, whether on foot, by motorised vehicle or by air, disturbs indigenous wildlife, either by frightening them away from breeding or feeding sites, or because creatures like polar bears become used to humans, resulting in encounters that can be lethal (usually for the bears). Arctic vegetation is also extremely sensitive, and a footprint on the tundra or a bog might remain for literally hundreds of years. In addition, visitors need an infrastructure to accommodate them – roads across the permafrost, airstrips, heliports, hotels, camp sites, and imported food and fuel supplies.

In order to minimise your impact and avoid damaging the fragile Arctic ecosystem, follow these rules:

- keep to established paths and roads
- keep a safe distance from wildlife
- question tour companies about their environmental policies and impact
- use environmentally conscious tour operators who employ local people
- remove everything you take on camping and hiking trips
- bury waste products at least 1m deep and remove all tissue paper, as it will take much longer to decompose in cold climates
- show respect for historical sites and do not remove anything from them
- buy locally produced souvenirs and food (souvenirs from Greenland should be accompanied by a CITES permit to ensure they are not made from any part of an endangered species; see p218)
- speak out against careless exploitation and industry in the far north (see www.amap.no, www.wwf.org or www.earthjustice.org for more information)

Further east, Finland is dominated by water: ponds, marshes, bogs, rivers, creeks, rapids, waterfalls and – most prominently – lakes. There are no real mountainous areas; the highest hills, or *tunturi*, are in the far north, adjacent to the highlands of northern Norway and Sweden. The highest point, Halti, in the far northwest, rises to only 1328m. By contrast, Sweden's highest point is Mt. Kebnekaise (2111m) and Norway's is Galdhopiggen (2469m).

CLIMATE

The climate varies enormously across the Arctic; the charts below should help you to prepare for your trip.

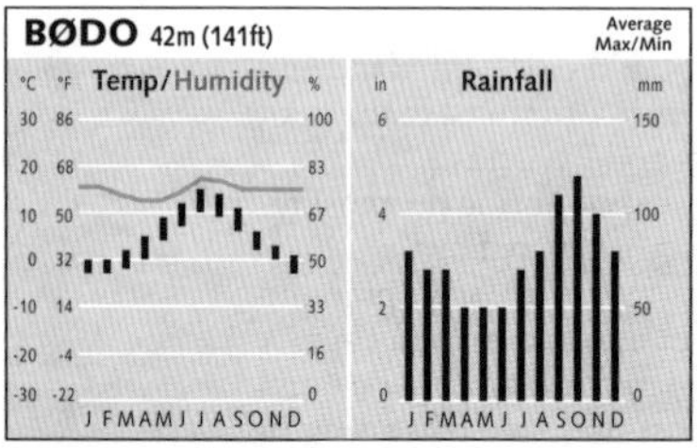

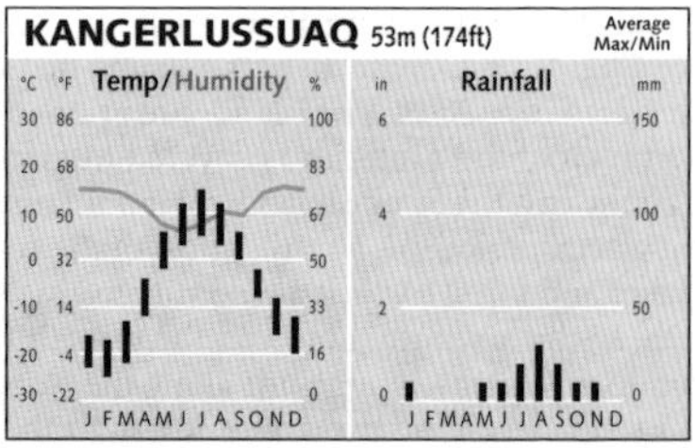

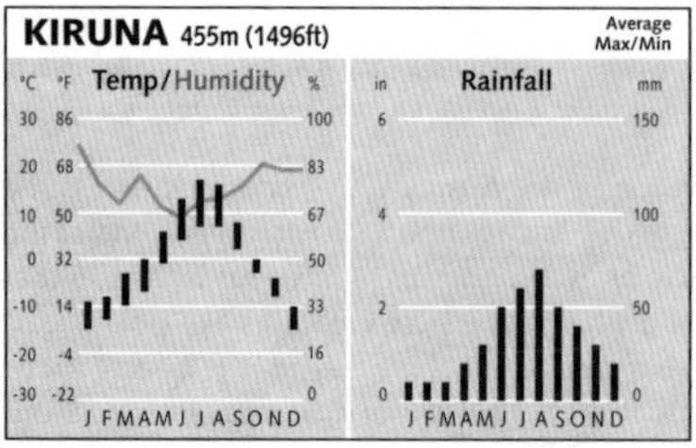

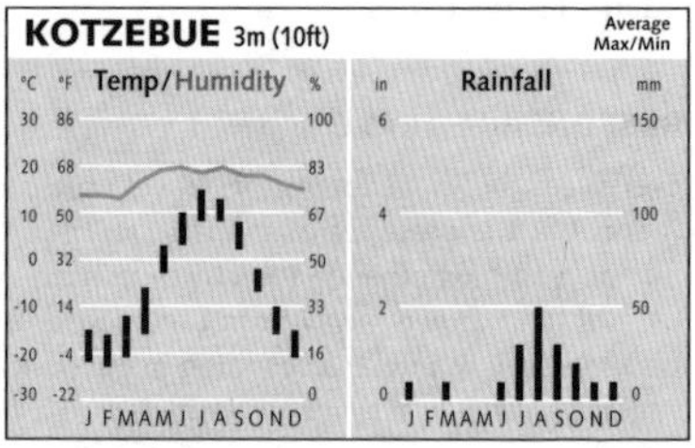

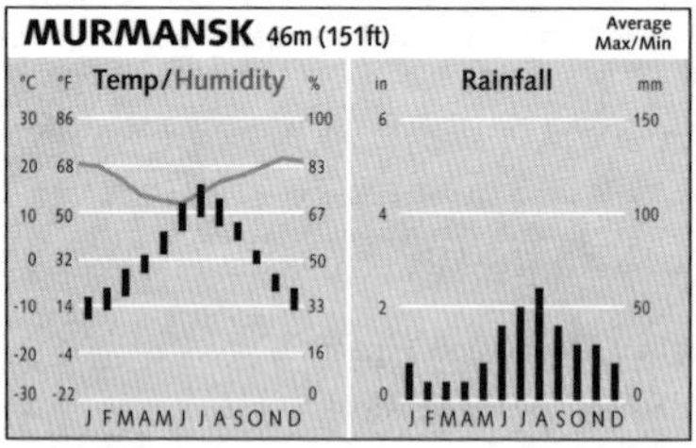

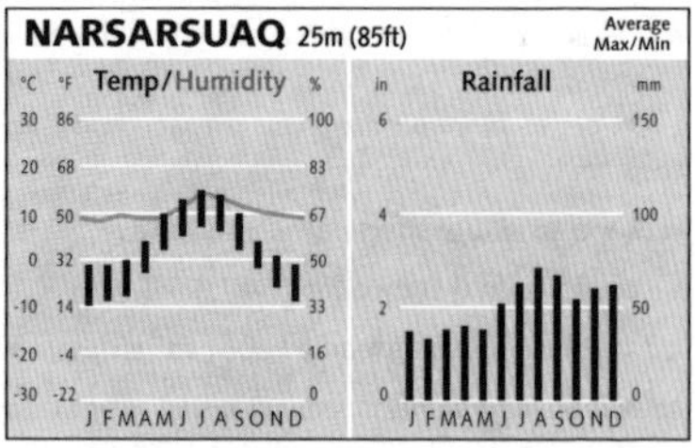

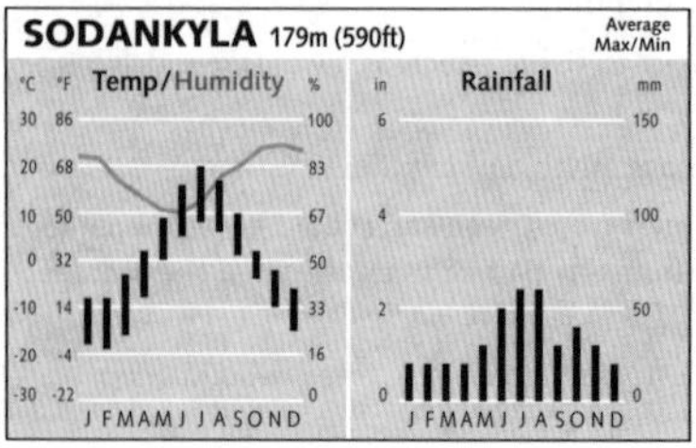

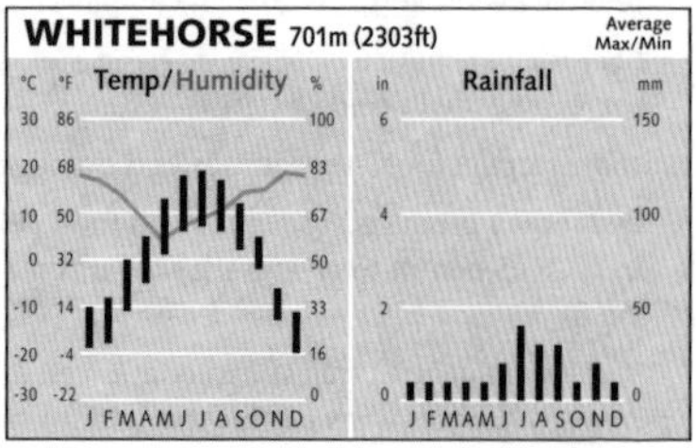

WILDLIFE
Animals
The Arctic is essentially an ocean surrounded by continents and islands, and the moderating effect of the water means that the climate, though severe, is more hospitable to human and animal life than the icelocked Antarctic, and a rich variety of flora and fauna have ingeniously adapted to the cold climate and harsh conditions.

Winter is a dormant time for many kinds of Arctic wildlife, but the brief Arctic spring and summer see everything burst into activity. Millions of migrant birds swarm in from the south to take advantage of the continuous daylight, ample food and wide choice of breeding sites. Large mammals breed and give birth, and the tundra becomes a lush and fertile place for a few short months.

Despite the variety of life in the Arctic, the environment is a fragile one, and it takes very little to destroy its delicate balance. Sudden storms, early winters and unpredictable weather can mean an unsuccessful breeding season, and in industrialised areas the damage caused by pollution might take many centuries to repair.

Details of some Arctic flora and fauna are given in the Environment section of the Greenland Snapshots chapter. A creature not seen in Greenland, but found in the rest of the Arctic, is the grizzly or brown bear *(Ursus horribilis)*, the world's second-largest bear, which can be recognised from its large dorsal hump. Although grizzlies aren't common anywhere, they're often observed in the tundra and taiga regions of Alaska and northwestern Canada, and very fortunate observers may also spot them in Arctic Russia and Scandinavia. For tips on dealing with bear attacks, see p264.

Islands of the Arctic, by Julian Dowdeswell and Michael Hambrey, is a stunning book tracing the environmental and cultural threats to the Arctic.

Another large mammal not found in Greenland is the moose *(Alces alces)*, which is often called an elk in Europe. This is the world's largest deer – an average human would not even reach its shoulder. Moose have a distinctive dewlap, and males have flat, saucer-shaped antlers. Northern Alaska and northwestern Canada are the best places for spotting them in the wild.

One of the most chilling sounds in the Arctic is the howl of a wolf *(Canis lupus)*. Their favourite victims are caribou, and the movements of some wolf packs revolve around the seasonal migrations of caribou herds. Wolves hunt in a highly coordinated way, selecting the older, weaker or incapacitated animals, thereby ensuring the health of their prey stock. Wolves remain widespread in more remote regions of the Arctic, and although casual visitors are unlikely to see a large pack, odd individuals and family groups can be encountered on the islands and mainland of northern Canada and Alaska. A distinct white subspecies inhabits the remotest regions of Canada's Quttinirpaaq National Park on Ellesmere Island (boxed text p247).

DID YOU KNOW?

Scientists predict that polar bears could become extinct within 100 years.

ENDANGERED SPECIES
Many Arctic species are under threat, particularly the magnificent whales that ply the icy waters. The Northern Right Whale *(Eubalaena glacialis)* – so called because it was ideally the right whale to hunt, being large, slow-moving and approachable – was brought to the brink of extinction in the 19th century by the whaling industry and is now one of the world's rarest whales. Researchers believe Northern Right whales number about 300. However, it can still be encountered in Arctic waters, where it appears as a 15m-long black shape with no fin on the smooth back of its thick-set body. Its blow makes a distinctive V.

Other whales under threat include the endangered bowhead whale, which can live for up to 200 years, and grow as large as 20m long. Fortunately,

WILDLIFE WATCHING

Animal	Location	Time of year
Muskox	Kangerlussuaq, Grønnedal, Dempster Hwy, Paulatuk, Aulavik, Arctic National Wildlife Refuge (ANWR), Atigun Pass	year-round
Caribou	Kangerlussuaq, Old Crow, ANWR, Aulavik, Dempster Hwy, Richardson Mountains, Paulatuk, Ivvavik, Iqaluit, Gates of the Arctic, Noatak, Kobuk, Rovaniemi, Inari, Lemmenjoki, Nordkapp, Hammerfest, Kautokeino	spring and autumn
Polar bear	Svalbard, Wrangel Island, Point Barrow, Grise Fjord, ANWR	spring and summer
Whale	Aasiaat, Barrow, Pond Inlet, Tuktoyaktuk, Lofoten, Vesterålen, Narvik	autumn
Grizzly bear	Gates of the Arctic, Dalton Hwy, ANWR, Yukon	summer

it has shown an increase in numbers in the eastern Canadian Arctic in recent years.

Beluga whales are also endangered but have yet to be officially protected. Only in the eastern Beaufort Sea are their numbers considered healthy. In Baffin Bay they are under threat from Greenlandic hunters, and the population in eastern Hudson Bay is very low. Orcas in Alaska have also received special protection, as their numbers there have dwindled to single figures since the 1989 Exxon Valdez oil spill.

For background information and links to numerous related sites, visit the United Nations Environment Programme site: http://arctic .unep.net.

On a brighter note, blue whales, protected since 1965, were seen in Alaskan waters for the first time in 30 years in 2004, prompting hopes that their numbers may be returning to historical levels.

Numbers of Peary caribou, native to northwestern Canada, have dropped by more than 70% in the past 20 years, even though they are not hunted. On Banks Island, one of the worst-affected areas, caribou numbers dropped from about 12,000 in 1972 to about 450 in 1998. Global warming (see p27) is cited as a possible cause. The woodland caribou and wood bison face similar problems.

The imposing Siberian crane *(Grus leucogeranus)* is under threat, as its breeding grounds, migration stopover points and wintering grounds – in Iran, India and China – have all been disturbed by human activities. Only three isolated breeding populations are known, all in northern Siberia. The striking bird has pure white plumage, black wing-tips and red face, beak and legs. In recent years it has become a symbol of Arctic conservation, as great efforts are being made to save it.

In the 1950s and '60s the bald eagle, an impressive and inspiring bird, succumbed to pesticide poisons absorbed mainly through eating dead fish stranded on riverbanks and beaches. This resulted in infertile or thin-shelled eggs and brought the species close to extinction. Though still officially classed as threatened, these magnificent birds with their 1.8m wingspan are slowly recovering in numbers, particularly in Alaska and Canada.

Plants

Arctic vegetation is surprising varied, and in the brief summer months wildflowers can be seen everywhere. By mid-August berries have begun to ripen, and as autumn comes the tundra explodes in a blaze of colour. Above the tree line the open, bare ground of the tundra supports a variety of low-growing vegetation: shrubs, grasses, reeds, sedges, flowering plants, lichens, mosses, liverworts and algae. Plants stay low and spread sideways in order to keep a good grip on the easily eroded soil and to absorb what heat there is.

Flowers you will see in most areas include purple saxifrage *(Saxifraga oppositifolia)*, whose blooms are the first harbingers of spring; moss campion *(Silene acaulis)*, looking like a purple-studded pincushion; mountain avens *(Dryas octopetala)*, with its yellow-and-white single flowers; and various species of gentian *(Gentiana)*, pushing up their incredibly blue trumpets towards the sky.

Lichens set the bare rock of the Arctic ablaze but are incredibly slow-growing – some spread by only 1mm a year, and if conditions are unfavourable they do not spread at all in some years. Some have been estimated to be 4000 years old.

For more on Arctic flora, see p92.

INDIGENOUS CONSERVATION EFFORTS

Indigenous people have always relied on Arctic flora and fauna for survival, and they have been the first to witness the detrimental effects of industrialisation and climate change (see p27). They have also suffered at the hands of regional and federal governments who have appropriated mineral-rich land and returned little, if any, of its wealth to the indigenous people. This environmental injustice and the sight of traditional hunting or herding grounds ruined by industry has turned the native peoples of the north into environmental campaigners and conservationists. Many indigenous people have now been trained to monitor and record species numbers, environmental conditions and changes to flora and fauna. Their observations have become vital for scientists working to predict climate change and preserve the population numbers of many endangered species.

The indigenous people are also fighting hard in many regions to preserve their homelands from industrialisation, oil and gas exploitation or similar developments. In Old Crow in the Yukon the Gwich'in fight for the Porcupine caribou birthing grounds (see the boxed text, p47), the Sami of the polluted Kola Peninsula in Arctic Russia fight for autonomy in their own environment (see p44), the Nenets of the Yamal Peninsula fight to save the summer reindeer-herding pastures from a large gas complex, and the Inuit of Nunavut (see p25) now control both their homeland and the subsurface rights to valuable minerals.

Arctic indigenous people's organisations are now represented and voice their opinions at global talks on the environment. Although the governments of the eight Arctic-rim countries agreed to an Arctic Environmental Protection Strategy in 1991, the problems associated with natural-resource extraction and military activities were deemed too politically sensitive for discussion. Since it is exactly these issues, as well as pollution from other industrialised nations, that pose the greatest threat to the Arctic environment, making the voice of the native people of the far north heard has never been more important.

Arctic National Wildlife Refuge: Seasons of Life and Land, by Subhankar Banerjee, is a beautiful and evocative book, rich in photographs, calling for the preservation of this pristine wilderness.

NATIONAL PARKS

A host of national parks and reserves protects the pristine and fragile Arctic environments of the far north. Those mentioned in the table (see p58) are featured in more detail elsewhere in the book.

Other parks in Norway include Forlandet in Svalbard, which protects the breeding grounds for eider ducks, geese, seals and walrus; lonely and dramatic Rago, with its high mountain peaks divided by plunging valleys and waterfalls; Reisa, which protects the dramatic Reisa Gorge, its lovely waterfalls and its varied wildlife; Saltfjellet-Svartisen, straddling the Arctic Circle and consisting of the upland moors of Saltfjellet and the two vast Svartisen icecaps; the world's most northerly pine forests at Stabbursdalen;

NATIONAL PARKS

National Park	Features	Activities	Best Time to Visit	Page
Alaska				
Gates of the Arctic	glaciated valleys, rugged mountains; caribou, Dall sheep, wolves, bears	hiking, rafting, canoeing	Jun–Sep	256
Kobuk Valley	sand dunes, canyons; caribou, sheefish	rafting, cross-country skiing, trekking	Apr–Sep	262
Noatak	mountain-ringed river basin; caribou, moose, wolves, grizzly bears	rafting, kayaking, trekking	May–Sep	262
Canada				
Aulavik	undulating hills, upland plateaus, steep canyons; Peary caribou, muskoxen	canoeing, trekking, wildlife watching	May–Sep	244
Auyuittuq	jagged mountain peaks, deep valleys, steep-walled ocean fjords, glaciers; caribou, ptarmigan	hiking, climbing	Jun–Sep	249
Quttinirpaaq	glaciers, ice fields; wolves, foxes, muskoxen, caribou	hiking, climbing	May–Sep	247
Vuntut & Ivvavik	boreal forest, low mountains, coastal plains; caribou, grizzly bears, brown bears	canoeing, cross-country skiing, trekking	Apr–Sep	241
Sirmilik	rugged mountains, ice fields, glaciers; sea-bird colonies, whales	hiking, canoeing, climbing	May–Sep	248
Tuktut Nogait	rolling tundra, wild rivers, canyons; caribou, wolves, grizzly bears, muskoxen, raptors	hiking, canoeing	May–Sep	244
Greenland				
Northeast Greenland	vast tundra expanses, icecap, jagged peaks; muskoxen, polar bears, caribou, Arctic wolves, foxes, seals, walruses, whales	hiking, climbing, wildlife watching	Jun–Aug	213
Norway				
Øvre Dividal	spectacular jagged mountains, wide valleys; wolverines, rhododendrons, heather	skiing, hiking	May–Sep	308
Sweden				
Abisko	lakes, gentle mountains, valleys; foxes, reindeer	hiking	May–Sep	310
Finland				
Lemmenjoki	desolate wilderness, rivers, rough Arctic landscape; reindeer, foxes, bears, wolverines	hiking, gold panning, reindeer herding	May–Sep	318
Urho Kekkonen	vast forest, barren wilderness, ravines; foxes, reindeer, hares	hiking	Jun–Sep	317
Pallas-Ounastunturi	fells, forest, peatland; bears, wolverines, lynxes, wolves	hiking, canoeing	May–Sep	327
Russia				
Lapland Biosphere Reserve	tundra, alpine grasslands, marshes, jagged peaks; extensive mammal species & birdlife	hiking, wildlife watching	Jun–Sep	276
Wrangel Island	mountainous peaks, variety of tundra types; polar bears, walruses, grey whales, snow geese, reindeer, snowy owls	hiking, wildlife watching	Jun–Sep	293

Norway's largest national park, Sør Spitsbergen, which protects Spitsbergen's entire southern peninsula; Øvre Anarjåkka, adjoining Finland's wild Lemmenjoki National Park and protecting a vast expanse of birch and pine forests, bogs and lakelands; the boreal forest of Øvre Pasvik, tucked between Finland and Russia, protecting the last habitat of the brown bear in Norway; and tiny Ånderdalen, on the island of Senja, protecting the bogs and coastal pine and birch forests.

In Sweden you'll also find Muddus, which protects Lake Muddusjaure and the surrounding ancient forests and bogs; Padjelanta's high moorland, favoured by grazing reindeer; incredible Sarek with its vast plateaus, glaciers, deep valleys, sharp peaks and large tracts of birch and willow forest; Stora Sjöfallet, dominated by Lake Akkajaure and the lofty Mt Akka; and Vadvetjåkka, Sweden's northernmost national park, protecting a large river delta featuring bogs, lakes, limestone caves and a variety of bird species.

Steven B Young's *To the Arctic: An Introduction to the Far Northern World* is an elegant volume covering the flora and fauna, oceans and ice, and geology and environment of the Arctic.

ENVIRONMENTAL ISSUES

The Arctic environment is extremely fragile, and it takes very little to unbalance the sensitive ecosystems at work there. Global warming (see p27), mineral extraction, the accumulation of pollutants (see p34) and extensive military dumping of nuclear waste all pose enormous threats to the sensitive ecosystem. The low temperatures, limited sunlight, short growing season and slow decomposition of Arctic ecosystems means they are particularly susceptible to pollutants and can take many decades to recover from damage.

While the most dramatic environmental damage is in the Russian north, many other areas are also at risk. Permafrost melt and coastal erosion are already problems for residents of Alaska's northwest. In Norway farmed reindeer have lost 50% of their habitat in 50 years, and wild herds in Canada are steadily declining in numbers, though no-one is quite sure why. Sea ice is thinning, glaciers are melting and pollution is increasing. In many Arctic towns concern about the environment is high, but interest in cleaning up one's own backyard is pretty low: rubbish is dumped everywhere, recycling is limited, and town dumps pile high and often tip into the sea.

Scientists are feverishly studying complex Arctic ecosystems in order to better understand and preserve them. Stricter controls, a separation of research projects from industry funding, and long-term environmental education seem to be the only realistic solutions to the problem. An effective compromise must be made between economic and political interests and environmental and cultural concerns if the vast Arctic wilderness is to see any kind of preservation from the ravages of pollution. To date the absence of any kind of long-term planning and legislation has been the biggest problem of all.

Arctic Russia

Serious environmental problems are readily apparent in the Russian Arctic, where high levels of sulphur dioxide from copper- and nickel-processing plants have destroyed the natural vegetation and caused acid rain, which is devastating forests. Nuclear waste, runoff of industrial chemicals and untreated wastewater leak or are pumped into Siberian rivers and eventually end up in the Arctic Ocean.

The Kola Peninsula in particular is badly affected, as it is the repository of the world's largest amount of radioactive waste. More than 100 decommissioned nuclear submarines now based around the peninsula are ageing fast, and radioactivity levels are spiralling. The testing of nuclear

DID YOU KNOW?
Radioactivity levels in Andreeva Bay on the Kola Peninsula are said to be similar to those in Chernobyl.

ARCTIC WORLD HERITAGE SITES

The extreme and unique environment of the far north has been recognised at the following Unesco World Heritage sites:

- Ilulissat icefjord, Greenland (p170). One of the fastest and most active glaciers in the world.

- Laponian area, Sweden. The largest area in the world with a traditional way of life based on the seasonal livestock movement.

- The Vega Archipelago, Norway. A cluster of dozens of islands with a unique tradition of eider-down harvesting.

- Wrangel Island Reserve, Russia (p293). High levels of biodiversity, including many endangered species.

---

weapons at Novaya Zemlya introduced large quantities of nuclear waste into the environment in the 1960s and '70s, and the scuttling of decommissioned nuclear-powered submarines continues the theme off the coast of the island today.

Russia also plans to redirect two mighty Siberian rivers, the Ob and the Irtysh, hundreds of kilometres to the south in a bid to solve a worsening water shortage. Although the project could help refill the Aral Sea – which has shrunk to a quarter of its former size since 1960 – and offset the increasing amount of fresh water flowing into the Arctic Ocean, it will mainly be used to support the water-guzzling cotton-growing industry in Uzbekistan and Turkmenistan. Critics believe that the project will only cause more social, economic and ecological problems.

For information on environmental threats in Arctic Russia, visit www. carto.eu.org /article2462.html.

In 2003 an international project to clean up the Russian Arctic was announced. Estimated at US$40 billion, the scheme aims to make abandoned military bases safe, explore the use of algae to clean up oil spills and involve indigenous peoples in environmental protection.

Marine Pollution

The Arctic Ocean acts as a sink for long-range pollution such as that caused by heavy metals, PCBs and other persistent organic pollutants, and as the chemicals enter the food chain they quickly accumulate to dangerous levels in the fat of Arctic animals and in the humans who eat them (see p34). This bioaccumulation threatens both the health of the indigenous people and the animal populations of the region. Polar bears have already been found to be increasingly affected by these chemicals; this, combined with thinning sea ice, means that they are now suffering a major threat to their ecosystem and feeding habits.

The Bering Sea is showing advanced effects of pollution and commercialisation, and is suffering from steep declines in marine mammals, fluctuations in sea-bird populations, and the collapse of some crab and fish stocks. As much of the Arctic Ocean is deemed international water, it's hard to pin down where the responsibility for controlling this pollution lies.

The Arctic seas are also under threat from overfishing and oil and gas development. Bottom trawling and dredging has caused considerable damage to the ocean bottom, and cod and haddock are decreasing in numbers despite regulations and controls.

Oil & Gas Exploration

The Arctic holds the world's largest remaining untapped gas reserves and some of its largest undeveloped oil reserves. At Prudhoe Bay in Alaska, dozens of jets and planes land every day, enormous trucks scurry along the gravel roads, and hundreds of oil spills occur every year. Oil companies say they are doing all they can to protect the environment, but in the past some have been fined for illegally disposing of hazardous waste. Oil spills pose a tremendous risk to Arctic ecosystems, as there is no effective method for containing and cleaning up an oil spill in icy water.

Expansion of the hydrocarbon industries in the Arctic region would mean the building of massive infrastructure and, in turn, the opening up of new regions of the Arctic to other kinds of resource exploitation, such as logging, commercial fisheries and mining. In addition to the threat of increased oil spills, repeated seismic surveys and overflights may disturb Arctic wildlife.

The Barents Sea and the Mackenzie River Valley are key locations for development, and Nunavut is keen to get a slice of the action in order to reduce unemployment levels and secure a stronger political voice for the future. In Russia, development of the huge oil and gas deposits on the Arctic shelf is expected to increase oil transport sixfold by 2020.

A significant proportion of these oil reserves lies offshore, though, in the Arctic's fragile and biologically productive shelf seas. Employment and revenue from oil and gas companies are often central to the financial welfare of a nation or community, and the conflicting interests of local and national governments, indigenous-rights groups and environmentalists make the process tense. One government department will encourage oil exploration, whereas another will oppose it. In Norway, revenue from oil exploration supports the state pension plan, and so the Norwegian people are caught between securing their own futures and protecting their treasured environment. In Alaska, where the US government plans to open the protected birthing grounds of the Porcupine caribou herd to oil development, there is ongoing tension between one indigenous group that makes its living from oil-related employment and another across the border in Canada that relies on the herd for its survival (see the boxed text p47).

Global Warming

There is now a consensus among scientists and researchers that the warming trend seen in the far north (see also p27) is not part of a natural blip in the earth's climate but a reaction to man-made pollutants that may well change our environment forever.

The effects of this warming are most keenly felt at the poles, and visible changes to weather patterns are already occurring in the Arctic. These changes aren't just seen in the form of scientific research but are dramatic enough for local laypeople to observe. Thinning sea ice is preventing the annual hunt, melting permafrost is causing roads and buildings to subside, and sandbags are now a normal sight in many Arctic towns to prevent the progression of coastal erosion.

Glaciers are steadily retreating, and the Greenland icecap is beginning to melt. The earth's reflectivity is reduced as more bare land and open water are revealed, and so more sunlight is absorbed and the whole process amplifies itself. It has been predicted that a rise in temperatures of just 2.7°C would begin an irreversible process that would eventually raise global sea levels by 7m.

In more immediate terms, computer modelling has predicted that the Canadian Arctic Archipelago will be virtually ice-free in summer in 20 years, thanks to global warming. This would reduce the journey from England or New York to Beijing by 17,700km but necessitate the construction of navigation posts, harbours and coastal surveillance points. Europe and

DID YOU KNOW?

The elusive Northwest Passage could be virtually ice-free in summer in 20 years.

the US are already pushing for the waters to be deemed international, to take advantage of diluted environmental standards rather than adhering to Canada's stricter regulations.

Whaling & Hunting

Whaling continues to be a contentious issue, and calls for the lifting of the international ban have met with mixed reactions. Marine biologists agree that many species are no longer under threat, but environmentalists argue that some are still in dire need of protection (see p55), and indigenous communities argue that they need income from whaling to reduce their dependency on government benefits. However, campaigners are not swayed by either argument. They say that whaling involves a protracted and painful death for the animals and that the ban should remain firmly in place.

Sealing is another controversial subject in Arctic communities. The media frenzy in the 1980s following the clubbing of young seals appalled most indigenous hunters, who regarded the reports as biased and unfair. Hunters across northern Canada and Greenland who relied on the sale of furs as their main source of income lost their livelihoods overnight. In 2004 Canada increased its quota for seal hunting, to the anger of environmentalists, but Canadian seal numbers are recovering and Renewable Resource officers monitor the situation closely. A greater threat for seals is the commercial fishing industry: it has reduced fish stocks – and consequently seal food – all over the world, and its brightly coloured nets can become death traps for these inquisitive creatures.

Arctic Food & Drink

It's meat, meat and more meat on the Arctic menu, and don't expect any fanfare about it. If you're going to eat traditionally you'll be eating simple fare from the top of the food chain for the duration of your stay.

The nomadic Arctic people were dependent on the animals for their very survival and followed them through the seasons. Although every Arctic town now has a supermarket stocking everything from boil-in-the-bag seal to microwaveable plastic-wrapped burgers, traditional meat fresh from a hunt is of enormous importance and prized above all else.

Depending on where you are, this can range from a choice of whale or seal meat to plenty of fish, caribou or muskox. Although traditional meats and hunting methods may be objectionable to some for sentimental or ideological reasons, this way of life was the only choice for people living in the far north. Even though Western attitudes and values have largely been accepted, hunting is the key to maintaining cultural traditions.

The traditional Arctic diet was very healthy; before Western processed foods were introduced, the area enjoyed the world's lowest rates of cardiovascular disease. Today concerns over bioaccumulation of toxic chemicals in the Arctic food chain (see p34) have prompted health professionals to advise northern peoples to limit their intake of traditional foods.

Visit www.visi.com /~wick/axe/cookbook .html for a selection of traditional recipes from indigenous groups.

STAPLES & SPECIALITIES

Today most Arctic people enjoy a mixed diet of Western food and traditional meats. Although processed foods are expensive and fresh fruit and vegetables are still a luxury, in many places they are readily available.

Traditional Arctic cooking is very simple, with stews and fried meat or fish being the highlight of the menu. Dried fish is popular when travelling and bannock, a simple white pan-fried bread, is common in the native communities of northern Canada and Alaska. The evening meal is usually the main meal of the day, and on special occasions traditional food is always served. In areas where caribou and muskox are plentiful this means a hearty stew or fried meat, accompanied by potatoes and other root vegetables. Fish is a staple across the Arctic. Some, particularly capelin, are dried for the winter, and salmon is normally salted and smoked. Arctic char's firm, delicious meat makes it a favourite, while halibut is softer and subtler in taste. Dried fish, caribou and muskox are eaten as snack foods, particularly when travelling.

Faith, Food, and Family in a Yupik Whaling Community, by Carol Zane Jolles, describes the complex cultural interconnections in a Yup'ik community.

In coastal areas, dark, rich whale meat is also popular, though it's quite salty to the unaccustomed palate. The choice cuts are served as steaks and the others often end up in a stew. Whale blubber (*mattak* or *muktuk*), which is relatively tasteless and difficult to chew, is rich in vitamins and fats that the body uses efficiently to retain heat. Even a thin slice will provide several hours of jaw work. Although it is unlikely that you will be offered any meat from threatened species, it's worth knowing that the beluga, northern right and bowhead whales are considered endangered and these meats should be avoided. Seal is sold at all harbour markets and supermarkets in Greenland and is often available in hotel restaurants across the Arctic. It tastes more fishy than whale does.

DID YOU KNOW?

To make a toast in Greenlandic, use the word *Kasugta*.

A welcome crop of berries and mushrooms supplements traditional Arctic diets, and in late August and early September you'll see locals out on the hillsides gathering huckleberries (small blueberries), crowberries and, in some areas, lowbush cranberries.

Angelica grows in many areas, wild chamomile is abundant, and wild thyme makes an excellent tea and seasoning. In late summer, common harebells *(Campanula greseckiana)* and rosebay willow herb are common in the North Atlantic region, and the sweet, slightly fragrant flowers are delicious. Many varieties of Arctic seaweed are also edible – the slimy species known as sea lettuce is particularly prized.

Food in South Greenland, by Finn Larsen and Rie Oldenburg, gives background information on traditional food sources, and modern recipes in English, Greenlandic and Danish.

A surprising number of mushrooms grow in Arctic areas and several edible varieties exist, though correct identification is essential. The most delicious Arctic mushroom is the slippery jack – a large, chocolate-coloured mushroom with a spongy centre. Reaching its peak in early August, it grows mainly in damp tundra and scrub forest all over the North Atlantic region. In well-drained taiga areas of Alaska and Canada, springtime brings a good crop of morels. These convoluted mushrooms have a strong and delicious flavour, but beware of the false morel, which looks similar but is poisonous.

DRINKS

There are few special drinks indigenous to the Arctic. Tea and coffee are drunk everywhere, and alcohol is often overindulged in, leading to many 'dry' Arctic communities where alcohol is banned. Local *imiaq* (homebrewed beer) often surfaces in these and other areas, but its quality and safety can be pretty dubious – it's often brewed in old oil drums.

VEGETARIANS & VEGANS

Sorry, folks, you're plain out of luck in the Arctic. Diets were traditionally meat based, and not much has changed in terms of cooking or attitude. Other than self-catering you'll have few options. However, most supermarkets, even in small towns, stock a good selection of basic vegetables and fruit, plenty of dried goods such as rice and pasta and the makings of simple vegetarian meals. Even at tourist hotels the menus typically have only three or four dishes, all meat-based. Vegetarianism is unknown to local people, and you'll get a quizzical or just plain blank look when you say *Neqitorneq ajorpunga* ('I don't eat meat') and little assistance in finding something meat-free to eat.

HABITS & CUSTOMS

Getting fed in the Arctic was never a sure thing, so when there was a successful hunt it was time for celebration. Traditionally, the meat was distributed evenly among the families in the village.

DID YOU KNOW?

Traditionally, dog teams were fed before humans, and if there wasn't enough for everyone you just had to go hungry.

Although Western foods are now seen in every household, traditional meat and fish is the favoured fare, and the successful hunter is a respected man. For special occasions extended families gather together and enjoy leisurely meals of several courses. Dried meats are commonly eaten when people are out on the land; on hunts, meat is fried or boiled without much fuss and is often eaten with the hands.

If you're invited to a private home for a *kaffemik* (a Greenlandic coffee party) or other occasion, there are few unusual customs to observe. In all Arctic areas people take their shoes off before entering a house, but apart from that common sense should see you through. Try not to grimace if your food seems unrecognisable. You'll often find offal and bits of animal hair in stews. If you can, avoid picking at your food; however, pulling all the meat off the bone – even with your hands – is seen as a compliment to the cook. If you really can't stomach something, most people will understand. As an outsider you're expected to be less enthusiastic about some things.

Touring the Arctic

To travel in the Arctic you need lots of patience: weather plays havoc with schedules, a broken engine on one flight can mean the cancellation of yours three days later, and local culture is laid back and used to it all – your complaints about bad service or having connections to make will often fall on deaf ears.

Arranging an organised tour is one way to avoid the hassle – or at least it's a way of letting someone else deal with it. In sensitive parts of Russia, joining a tour is often the only easy way to get the necessary travel permits, notably for visiting Chukotka. As part of a tour you won't need to arrange accommodation at every stop or make contact with local ferry companies, airlines or (in Russia) bureaucratic offices who don't answer the phone or have a website in English. The tour companies vet hotels and arrange side trips, and you can just sit back and enjoy the scenery while someone else worries about that missed connection. However, you do lose all independence and any possibility of spontaneity, as tours don't leave any room for changes. You may arrive and realise that you could have done it all yourself for half the price – or that your new companions for the two-week trip are your worst nightmare.

ORGANISED TOURS

The following list (arranged by the company's base location) includes companies that provide sightseeing tours, transport and Arctic cruises for holiday-makers. If you'd prefer more strenuous activity-oriented options, see Adventure Tours, p66. Local outfitters offering regional tours are listed in the destination chapters.

North America

Amazing Cruises & Travel (☎ 973-898 0188; www .amazing-tours.com) Offers two-week cruises to the North Pole from Helsinki (US$15,950), 12-day Greenland and Hudson Bay cruises (US$4295), 14-day tours of Russia's far east and Wrangel Island (US$9850), 19-day Northwest Passage cruises (US$12,150), 14-day cruises of Canada's High Arctic and Greenland (US$8550), and 15-day cruises of Ellesmere Island and Greenland (US$9950).

Borton Overseas (☎ 800-843 0602; www.borton.com /overseas.html-ssi) Outdoor adventure travel in Scandinavia

> ### TRAVEL TO THE NORTH POLE
>
> For travel to the North Pole you can choose from packages such as leisurely cruises aboard nuclear icebreakers, fly-in trips, skiing and dogsledding expeditions, skydiving, and marathon running at the Pole. Routes and possible itineraries for trips to the Pole from North America, Russia and Scandinavia are covered in more detail in the Travel Routes chapters.

and Greenland, including six-day polar safaris in Lapland (US$1470), six-day Arctic adventures in Kangerlussuaq (US$1756), seven-day adventures to Ilulissat (US$2196) and five-day dogsledding tours in Lapland (US$894).

Circumpolar Expeditions (☎ 907-272 9299; www.arctic travel.net/tourprov.htm) Alaska-based agency that organises cruises of the Chukotka coast . Tours cost US$1384 for three days, US$2995 for nine days and US$3495 for 12 days.

Great Canadian Ecoventures (☎ 867-920 7110; www.thelon.com) One-week fly-in canoeing, kayaking and Arctic wildlife photography expeditions with an ecological theme (C$3900 to C$7800).

Mountain Travel Sobek (☎ 888-687 6235; www .mtsobek.com) Operates an 11-day circumnavigation of Svalbard (US$2750 excluding airfares).

Quark Expeditions (☎ 203-656 0499; www.quark expeditions.com) Two-week cruises to the North Pole (US$16,450), two-week cruises to Russia's far east and Wrangel Island (US$9850), 19-day Northwest Passage cruises (US$12,750), and 15-day cruises to Ellesmere Island and Qaanaaq (US$11,450).

Scantours (☎ 800-223 7226; www.scantours.com) Extensive range of short tours in Scandinavia, including an 18-day grand tour (US$4285) and an 11-day North Cape Finnish tour (US$2915).

TCS Expeditions (☎ 800-727 7477; www.tcs-expeditions .com) Runs 17-day cruises through the fjords of Greenland, Scandinavia and Svalbard (US$32,950).

Zegrahm Expeditions (☎ 800-628 8747; www.zeco .com) Two-week cruises from Kamchatka to Nome (US$8290), in Russia's Sea of Okhotsk (US$7690) or circumnavigating Baffin Island (US$12,580).

Russia

North Pole Adventures (www.northpole.ru) Runs week-end trips to the Pole from Moscow (€6000) with opportunities to attend the North Pole ballooning festival or ice-sculpture festival, or go skiing for six days to reach the Pole.

Intourist Ecotours (☎ 95956-4206; www.ecotours -intourist.ru) Offers several unique exploration possibilities in Chukotka; 11-day trips including flights from the UK cost £1199.

South Kola Tours (☎ 81555-74178; www.kolaklub.com /southkola) Small, specialist agency offering mineral-finding, mountain-biking and cultural tours to lesser-known areas of the Kola Peninsula. Four-day snowmobile tours cost US$1557. It also has a friendly Nevada (USA) office.

Scandinavia

Albatros Travel (☎ 3698 0000; www.albatros-travel.com) Operates an 11-day cruise from Nuuk to Upernavik (€3200) and five-day winter tours to Kangerlussuaq (€990 to €1075).

Greenland Travel (☎ 321 205; www.greenland-travel .dk) Greenlandic company offering tours all over Greenland, including boat and dogsledding trips, visits to the inland ice, summer cruises and hiking. Prices range from Dkr4000 for a weekend tour to Kangerlussuaq to Dkr32,000 for multiday dogsledding trips to Thule. The average tour costs Dkr10,000 to Dkr15,000. (See p225 for other Greenland transport options.)

Other
AUSTRALIA
Aurora Expeditions (☎ 02-9252 1033; www.aurora expeditions.com.au) Offers 16-day North Pole cruises (US$15,950), High Arctic cruises to Svalbard, Iceland and Greenland (10 days A$4250, 12 days A$5150), and 17-day trips through Kamchatka (A$8900).

UK
David Oswin Expeditions (☎ 01228-75518; www .expeditions.co.uk) Photographic and adventure holidays in Greenland, including five/six/nine-day dogsled tours (£1292/£1376/£1781) and tailor-made tours.

Saga International Holidays (☎ 0800 096 0801; www.saga.co.uk) Cruising for the over-50s, including 15-day tours along the coast of Norway and on to Svalbard and Iceland (£2369) and 18-day cruises to the Faroes, Iceland and Greenland (£2849).

Wildwings (☎ 0117-984 8040; www.wildwings.co.uk) Booking agent for Arctic cruises including eight-day tours to Svalbard (£1479 to £2485), and two-week trips to Greenland (£2649) and Arctic Canada (£2769).

ADVENTURE TOURS

These tours are generally for those who are prepared to face the elements without any luxuries. Many of the trips require high levels of fitness and stamina, though most of these companies also offer softer options.

North America

ABEC's Alaska Adventures (☎ 877-424 8907; www .abecalaska.com) Good value one- to three-week backpacking expeditions in Noatak, Gates of the Arctic and the Arctic National Wildlife Refuge (ANWR), including an eight-day backpacking trip through the ANWR to witness the caribou migrations (US$2050), 10 days rafting on the Kongakut River (US$3300), eight days kayaking along the Arctic coast (US$2800) and eight-day kayaking or hiking trips to Gates of the Arctic National Park (US$1800).

Adventure Canada (☎ 905-271 4000; www.adventure canada.com) Canadian Arctic specialist offering 11-day cruises across Arctic Canada and Greenland with Inuit artists and culturalists (C$3795); two-week High Arctic cruises between Baffin Island and Greenland, focusing on wildlife and photography or explorers and archaeology (C$3795); and nine-day spring photography trips to the floe edge at Pond Inlet (C$4295).

Alaska Discovery (☎ 800-586-1911; www.akdiscovery .com) Offers eight-day hiking tours (US$3695) and 12-day rafting tours (US$4150) in the ANWR.

Arctic Kingdom (☎ 416-322 7066; www.arctickingdom .com) Runs two-week wildlife-spotting trips to Arctic Bay, one of most prolific areas of wildlife in the Arctic; two-week ice-climbing trips to Pond Inlet; and 10-day trips to Igloolik. Trips include the possibility of scuba diving, ice diving or snowmobiling. Tours cost US$5500 to US$8300. Individual itineraries and custom rock- and ice-climbing expeditions can also be arranged.

Arctic Treks (☎ 907-455 6502; www.arctictreksadventures .com) Adventurous rafting, hiking and fishing wilderness trips in Arctic Alaska's national parks and preserves. Seven- to 10-day trips cost US$2575 to US$3475.

Black Feather Trailhead (☎ 705-746 1372; www.black feather.com) Offers comprehensive canoeing, kayaking and hiking trips across Canada's Yukon and Northwest Territories. Sample trips include a 10-day canoe trip on the Nahanni, Coppermine and Hood Rivers (C$3095); two weeks kayaking in Greenland and the High Arctic (C$3495 to C$4495); and hiking on Ellesmere and Devon Islands, in Auyuittuq National Park and Greenland (two weeks from C$5895). It also does tailor-made trips.

Canadian Arctic Holidays (☎ 877-272 8426; www .canadianarcticholidays.ca) Adventurous outfitter offering one-week ski trips to the North Pole (€16,500), two-week ski tours of Ellesmere Island (C$6500), one-month ski tours from the North Pole to Ward Hunt Island (US$29,900) and eight-day snowmobile polar-bear viewing trips (C$3900).

Global Expedition Adventures (☎ 850-217 9974; www.north-pole-expeditions.com) North Pole specialist offering 11-day skiing expeditions to the North Pole (US$15,000), sky-diving at the North Pole (US$9400) and champagne flights to the Pole (US$8000).

Mountain Spirits (☎ 208-788 2344; www.mountain spirits.com) Organises one-week heliskiing (US$10,000) and ski-touring trips (US$4000) to Maniitsoq in West Greenland. Two-week summer trekking, sea kayaking, fishing and glacier exploration costs US$2500 per week.

ICEBREAKERS – THE NORTH POLE & THE NORTHEAST & NORTHWEST PASSAGES

Once the preserve of those on secretive Cold War missions, travel on a Russian icebreaker is now possible for anyone with enough cash and a sense of adventure. These specially designed ships have reinforced bows and powerful engines that allow them to cut through pack ice by riding up onto the surface of the ice on their rounded keels and then crushing it with their weight. When the ice is particularly thick, the vessel rams its way though. On a North Pole voyage in 1998, one Russian icebreaker encountered a 12m-high pressure ridge in the pack ice that required 28 attempts before the ship was able to break through.

Most icebreakers operating today are diesel powered, though some nuclear-powered vessels, which can stay at sea for longer periods, also operate in the northern seas. The largest of these is the Arktika class: 150m long, 55m tall, and boasting 75,000HP engines. Working icebreakers are used to keep open the Northern Sea Route, a shipping lane that links Russia's northernmost ports. The Canadian and American icebreaker fleets also maintain shipping lanes through ice-choked waters during winter, particularly in connection with the developing oil and gas industries in the Arctic Ocean.

Tourist travel on icebreakers includes cruises to Svalbard, Greenland and the Bering Strait, crossings from Alaska to easternmost Russia, 'circumnavigations' of the Arctic, and the grinding two-week voyage to the North Pole. Accommodation is in the comfortable if relatively basic cabins originally designed for senior officers and crew. Chefs and imported food provide sustenance, and passengers are generally welcome on the bridge. Trips to the Pole cost from about US$15,000 per person for a shared cabin, including some helicopter or Zodiac tours.

Even at this price, attaining the Pole can never be guaranteed. In a heavy ice year not even 75,000HP engines can cut a path to the top of the world. However, few who invest in a shipboard trip to the Arctic are disappointed. You'll still see deeply crevassed glaciers tumble into still, blue-green fjords and desolate mist-swathed islands occupied only by birds and seals. You'll become mesmerised by the great white space and its distances, and spend hours watching your ship plough through 1m-thick ice like a knife through butter – a truly unique experience.

Nahanni Wilderness Adventures (☎ 403-637 3843; www.nahanniwild.com) Runs white-water rafting and canoeing trips; samples are a 21-day trip on the Nahanni River (C$4495) and a two-week canoeing or rafting trip on the Coppermine, Hood and Thelon Rivers (C$4195 to C$5035).
NorthWinds (☎ 867-979 0552; www.northwinds-arctic .com) Runs serious Arctic adventures, such as 30-day kiting (C$14,000) and 28-day dogsledding expeditions in Greenland (C$14,000). Trips to the North Pole include a 60-day skiing expedition and a 52-day skiing and dogsledding trip. Pole trip costs (C$250,000 to C$350,000) are divided among the tour participants. Each tour has a maximum of six participants.
Sourdough Outfitters (☎ 907-692 5252; www.sour doughoutfitters.com) Wilderness trips in Gates of the Arctic and Noatak National Parks, and in the ANWR, including nine-day backpacking, fishing and canoeing trips (US$2700), five-day caribou-viewing trips (US$2595), and 11-day dogsledding trips (US$3995).
Whitney & Smith Legendary Expeditions (☎ 403-678 3052; www.legendaryex.com) Operates guided trips with an emphasis on Inuit culture and Arctic wildlife. Two-week options include Greenland dogsledding and kayaking (C$7300 to C$14,000), hiking and kayaking on Ellesmere Island (C$4995 to C$5995), and kayaking the Thomson River on Banks Island (C$6195).

Russia

K2 (☎ 3812-693075; http://extreme.k2.omsknet.ru/eng) A small but very reliable adventure-travel agency that concentrates on the Altay region but also has projects on the Putorana Plateau. Offers 11-day rafting trips (US$980), 12-day trekking trips (US$845), and 18-day climbing and trekking trips (US$780).
Kola Travel (☎ 287 1311; www.kolatravel.ru) Dutch-run tour agency based in Monchegorsk offering treks into the Lapland biosphere reserve (€245 to €893).
Sakha Tourist Agency (☎ 41122-422652; www.yakutia travel.com) Arranges Lena River tours and homestays in villages right across Sakha including Tiksi.
Tours to Russia (☎ 095-921 8027; www.tourstorussia .com) This Moscow-based company offers 18-day rafting adventures in Chukotka (US$1600).

Scandinavaia

Hvitserk (☎ 2412 6230; www.hvitserk.no) Offers three- and four-week tours across the Greenland icecap on skis or by dogsled (price on application), and two-week expeditions to climb East Greenland's Gunnbjørnsfjeld (€7500) and Mt Vinson.
Nonni Travel (☎ 461 1841; www.nonnitravel.is) Greenland expeditions from Ittoqqortoormiit, including 10-day

dogsledding trips (€2795), 10-day kayaking trips (€4880), two-week kayaking trips from Ammassalik (€3600) and expedition support for trips to the Northeast Greenland National Park.

Pasvik Tours (www.nonnitravel.is) Norwegian agency specialising in cross-border trips into the Kola Peninsula (five-day trips cost from Nkr6500).

Spitsbergen Travel (☎ 7902 6100; www.spitsbergen travel.no) Svalbard travel specialist offering one-week adventure cruises to the northwest (Nkr7100), one-week expedition cruises to the northeast (Nkr18,300), 12-day cruise-and-trekking trips (Nkr16,600), two-week expeditions to Mount Newton (Nkr20,500), four-day winter snowmobile tours (Nkr14,200), five-day winter dogsledding tours (Nkr10,300), and 12-day summer cross-country skiing tours (Nkr16,800).

Svalbard Wildlife Service (☎ 7902 5660; www.wild life.no) In addition to booking a range of day tours from Longyearbyen in Svalbard, this agency operates three-day snowmobile excursions to the east coast (Nkr9200), one-week winter skiing and snowmobiling expeditions to the Atom Mountains (Nkr21,500), one-week summer skiing tours from Longyearbyen to Ny Ålesund (Nkr13,200), eight-day summer hiking trips (Nkr12,800) and four-day kayaking tours (Nkr7350).

Topas Travel (☎ 868 9362; www.greenland-discoverer .com) Minimum-impact tours in Greenland, including a two-week crossing of the icecap (€2600), two-week trekking trips (€1984 to €2532), and 10-day kayaking and dogsledding trips (€2233 to €2600).

Tuning Incoming Agency (☎ 299-981650; www .tuning-greenland.de) Highly recommended ecoconscious sustainable-tourism company offering tailor-made hiking, skiing, kayaking, dogsledding, mountaineering and boat tours in East Greenland with local and international guides.

Ultima Thule (☎ 567 8978; www.ute.is) Organises wilderness sea-kayaking trips through the fjord systems and by the incredible glaciers of East Greenland (US$1690 to US$4100).

Other

FRANCE

Grand Nord Grand Large (☎ 01-40 46 05 14; www .gngl.com, in French) This wonderful French company operates a mind-boggling host of adventure tours focusing on remote locations throughout the far north. Sample trips include one-week wildlife watching in Pangnirtung (€2250), 16-day descents of the Porcupine River (€2195) and 10-day tours of Svalbard (from €2500).

Polar Circle Expeditions (☎ 01-48 08 64 94; www .polarcircle.com) North Pole specialist offering a fly-in champagne trip (US$8000) and a one-week ski-the-last-degree trip (US$10,000).

GERMANY

Polar Travel (☎ 8105-22909; www.polar-travel.de) Runs 18-day trips through remote fjords of East Greenland (€3115), 17-day North Greenland dogsledding expeditions (€6495), 17-day summer expeditions in Thule (€3850), 22-day tours of Kamchatka (€2990), and trips around Svalbard (nine days €3995, 17 days €6995). Those wishing to take part in extreme trips will need to join a shorter trip first as a test of suitability.

NETHERLANDS

Finslapland (☎ 020-6110762) Expert one- to 12-day cross-country skiing treks through the wilds of northern Finland and Russia to meet local Sami people and live off the land (€598 to €1275).

UK

Arctic Experience (☎ 01737-218801; www.arctic -experience.co.uk) Has an extensive list of tours to Arctic Scandinavia and Greenland, including 16-day treks (£2357), 10-day kayaking trips (£2111), 20-day crossings of the Greenland icecap (£2357) and six-day dogsledding trips (£1376). Other tours include wildlife encounters, ice hotel trips, northern lights trips, tailor-made excursions, and rafting, fishing and horse riding in Scandinavia.

Arcturus Expeditions (☎ 01389 830204; www.arcturus expeditions.co.uk) Highly recommended company offering cruises to Svalbard, Greenland, Russia's far east, Wrangel Island, the Northwest Passage, the Canadian High Arctic, Ellesmere Island and Franz Josef Land; dogsledding and skiing trips to Scandinavia, Kamchatka and the North Pole; and walking, trekking and sea-kayaking tours. Sample prices are £1850 for nine days of dogsledding in Lapland, £2950 for a 10-day trip with Inuit hunters in East Greenland and £1990 for a nine-day cruise of north Svalbard.

Tangent Expeditions (☎ 015395 737757; www.tangent -expeditions.co.uk) Mountaineering specialist focusing on lesser-known or unnamed peaks and first ascents. One-week climbing expeditions cost £2950 to £6950 in Greenland, and £3950 to £7750 on Ellesmere and Baffin Islands. The company also runs Greenland icecap crossings (£4950 to £7450), ski-touring and mountaineering expeditions to Svalbard (£3200), last-degree skiing trips to the North Pole (£10,000 to £12,000), and various dogsledding tours.

Greenland

STEVE HUTTON

Destination Greenland

'When you've seen the world there's always Greenland' goes the old travellers' saying. But why wait till then? Greenland is not a cheap destination, but few places combine such magnificent scenery, such clarity of light and such raw power of nature. Vast swaths of beautiful, unfenced wilderness give adventurers unique freedom to wander at will, whether on foot, by ski or by dogsled. With virtually no roads, transportation is expensive, but splurging on helicopter and boat rides is worth every penny. These whisk you over truly magnificent mountainscapes and glaciers or through some of the planet's most spectacular fjords. Greenland also offers world-beating but charmingly uncommercialised opportunities for sea kayaking, rock climbing and salmon fishing.

The world's biggest noncontinental island has the world's sparsest population. Nonetheless, scattered mainly along Greenland's west coast are dozens of photogenic little villages of colourfully painted wooden cottages, plus a few small towns. In the south there's an appealing sprinkling of emerald-lawned sheep farms.

Culturally, the unique blend of Inuit and Danish blood has produced a Greenlandic society all of its own. This sometimes discordant mix of ancient and modern combines seal hunting and dogsledding with Carlsberg and *kaffemiks*. While it has many underlying social problems, Greenland suffers negligible crime, and sensitive visitors with a passionate but unaggressive interest in local ideas will find a fascinatingly rich culture beneath the thick façade of Greenlandic taciturnity.

With an ever-improving network of tourist offices, and comfortable if unflashy mini-hotels and hostels, Greenland is no longer the sole reserve of plutocratic cruise-ship passengers. However you travel, it's wise to schedule a wide safety margin for unpredictable weather. Leave ample time in each destination to unwind, soak up the midnight sun, watch icebergs explode or be dazzled by the magic of the aurora borealis.

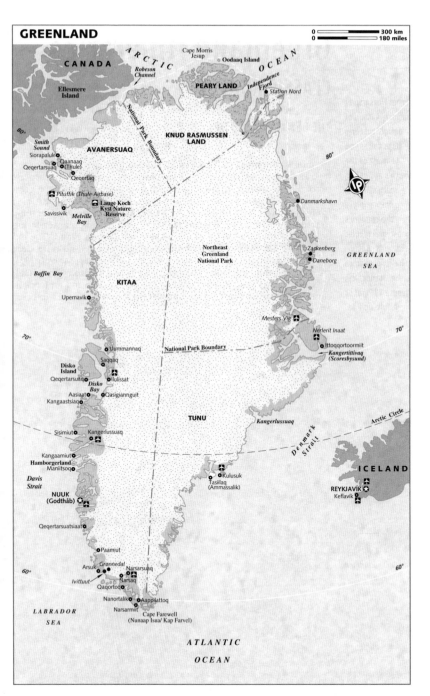

GREENLAND

0 — 300 km
0 — 180 miles

CANADA

ARCTIC OCEAN

Cape Morris Jesup
Oodaaq Island
Robeson Channel
Ellesmere Island
PEARY LAND
Independence Fjord
Station Nord

National Park Boundary

KNUD RASMUSSEN LAND

80°

Smith Sound
Siorapaluk
Qaanaaq (Thule)
Qeqertarsuaq
Qeqertaq
AVANERSUAQ

80°

Danmarkshavn

Pituffik (Thule Airbase)
Lauge Koch Kyst Nature Reserve
Savissivik
Melville Bay

Northeast Greenland National Park

Zackenberg
Daneborg
GREENLAND SEA

Baffin Bay

KITAA

Upernavik

Mesters Vig

70°

Uummannaq
Saqqaq
Disko Island
Qeqertarsuaq
Disko Bay
Aasiaat
Kangaastsiaq
Ilulissat
Qasigiannguit

National Park Boundary

70°

Nerlerit Inaat
Ittoqqortoormiit
Kangertittivaq (Scoresbysund)

Sisimiut
Kangerlussuaq

TUNU

Kangerlussuaq

Arctic Circle

Kangaamiut
Hamborgerland
Maniitsoq
Davis Strait

Denmark Strait

ICELAND

Kulusuk
Tasiilaq (Ammassalik)

REYKJAVÍK
Keflavík

NUUK (Godthåb)

Qeqertarsuatsiaat

Paamiut

60°

Arsuk
Grønnedal
Narsarsuaq
Ivittuut
Narsaq
Qaqortoq
Nanortalik
Narsarmiit
Aappilattoq
Cape Farewell (Nunaap Isua/ Kap Farvel)

60°

LABRADOR SEA

ATLANTIC OCEAN

Greenland Itineraries
CLASSIC ROUTES

From Narsarsuaq airport, 420km of delightful ferry hops takes you to most of the south's appealing main villages, culminating in the country's most spectacular fjordlands. Return by helicopter from either Nanortalik (some 115km) or Alluitsup Paa.

THE BEAUTIFUL SOUTH
Four to five weeks / Narsarsuaq, Narsaq & Nanortalik

In summer **Narsarsuaq** (p97) is a handy international arrival point, where treks, boat transfers and lovely excursions are conveniently easy to arrange. Prettier **Narsaq** (p109) offers much more local culture and a great museum. Boat hops are reasonably frequent to cultured **Qaqortoq** (p114) from where you can visit the classic **Hvalsey Norse ruins** (p120). Continue to traditionally minded **Alluitsup Paa** (p121), with its tempting sea-facing hotel and fairly easy access to Greenland's hot-springs island. The old harbour of **Nanortalik** (p126) is heart-burstingly quaint, and on a clear day the surrounding fjords, especially approaching **Aappilattoq** (p133), are indescribably gorgeous. The helicopter ride back from Nanortalik to Narsarsuaq is magnificent too. If you've got the time and money left, continue north by coastal ferry and be awed by even bigger icebergs around Disko Bay.

DISKO BAY   10 days / Aasiaat to Disko Island via Qasigiannguit & Ilulissat

Iceberg-studded Disko Bay is the stuff that armchair travellers' dreams are made of; see it from the deck of a coastal ferry and you'll never forget it. First stop is the quiet fishing town of **Aasiaat** (p183), located on the outer edge of a beautiful archipelago. Continue on to the brightly coloured village of **Qasigiannguit** (p181), an excellent destination for hikers, whale-watchers and history buffs. Nearby **Ilulissat** (p170) has become the centre of Greenland's tourist industry with its magnificent icefjord, the most prolific tidewater glacier outside Antarctica. From here you can day trip to the icecap, heli-tour over the glaciers or lose yourself in the splendid isolation of the untouched landscape. Top it all off with a trip to see the bizarre landscapes of **Disko Island** (p186), where you can hike and dogsled under the midnight sun.

A 220km ferry ride around bergy Disko Bay from the sleepy fishing villages of Aasiaat and Qasigiannguit to the gargantuan icebergs of Ilulissat and extraordinary landscapes of Disko Island in a 10-day odyssey you'll never forget.

GREENLAND

DISKO
ISLAND

Qeqertarsuaq

Ilulissat

DISKO
BAY

Qasigiannguit

Aasiaat

TAILORED TRIPS

Greenland is way off the beaten track – if you're self-sufficient, disappearing into utterly untouched wilderness is simple. Destinations are dependent upon your interests and the time available; fierce travel costs often preclude linking many different destinations, so this section offers thematic attractions rather than a single route.

HIKING, CLIMBING & DOGSLEDDING

The **Sisimiut to Kangerlussuaq trek** (boxed text, p163) is the classic multiday camping trek, with easy access at either end and pristine wilderness in between, but others start from **Hvalsey** (p120), **Igaliku Kujalleq** (see p125), **Igaliku** (see p109), **Narsaq** (p109) and **Kapisillit** (p154). For shorter, easier hikes, great starting points are **Narsarsuaq** (p97) and nearby **Qassiarsuk** (p104), from where you can walk from hostel to hostel.

If you want to take it up a notch and get climbing, head to the area around Nanortalik, where kilometre-high granite cliff faces rising above **Tasermiut Fjord** (p130) and **Torsukattak fjord** (p133) form a unique climbers' paradise. Inaccessible **east-coast mountains** (p211) are the Arctic's highest, but many first ascents are possible on equally stunning ranges near Tasiilaq and Ittoqqortoormiit.

And if you're dog-tired after all this activity, dogsled rides are possible almost anywhere above the Arctic Circle. **Uummannaq** (p191) and **Ittoqqortoormiit** (p211) are top spots to try. Sledding is also very popular at **Ilulissat** (p170) and **Sisimiut** (p158), where the route to Kangerlussuaq offers a great, accessible experience for the hardy.

TAKE TO THE WATER

Classic rivers and lakes for world-class salmon and Arctic-char fishing abound in the areas around **Nuuk** (p144) and **Kangerlussuaq** (p162), though conditions are rough and generally require expensive boat charters and/or lots of walking to access (see p215).

Greenland's fjords offer fabulous if sometimes treacherous sea-kayaking for experienced, self-reliant paddlers (see p217). A great compromise between beauty and relative simplicity of organisation is the **Narsaq to Narsarsuaq route** (see p113).

To take things at a more sedate pace, go on a lazy boat trip. Superb possibilities include the weekly public ferry ride along the fabulous **Torsukattak fjord** between Aappilattoq and Narsarmiit (see p132), whale-watching tours from **Aasiaat** (p185) or **Nuuk** (p149), and stunningly impressive glacier approaches from **Ilulissat** (p173), **Grønnedal** (p139), **Nanortalik** (p130) or **Narsarsuaq** (p102).

GREENLAND'S PAST: GHOST TOWNS, RUINS & MUSEUMS

Norse and Inuit ruins are historically intriguing, but in most cases all you'll see is a faint undulation of turf. Only at **Hvalsey** (p120) and (reconstructed) at **Qassiarsuk** (p104) will non-archaeologists really get much of a visual impression. Dozens of settlements have been abandoned, of which the most evocative, best preserved and most historically meaningful is **Ivittuut** (p138).

Otherwise, to get a real feel for the past, head to the museums. Greenland's best are housed within preserved historical buildings, as in **Nuuk** (p144), **Nanortalik** (p126), **Paamiut** (p141) and, most charmingly, in **Narsaq** (p109). **Upernavik museum** (p196) is also a real surprise.

ASTOUNDING VIEWS

For many people it's all about the icebergs, and if you're one of them you won't be disappointed. **Ilulissat Kangerlua** (p176) produces the biggest, most impressive bergs. Less prolific but extremely scenic icefjords are relatively accessible on excursions from **Narsarsuaq** (p97), **Upernavik** (p196) and **Kapisillit** (p154).

Of all the jaw-droppingly marvellous fjords, the most incredible are in the area around **Aappilattoq** (p133) and **Nanortalik** (p126) in the far south.

Greenlandic villages are colourful and often very picturesque. **Uummannaq** (p191) is particularly appealing thanks to its stunning setting on a heart-shaped outcrop of rock and, like Aappilattoq, has a fabulous setting. **Nanortalik**, **Upernavik**, **Qaqortoq** (p114), **Sisimiut** (p158) and **Nuuk** (p144) all have photogenic old-town areas behind newer surroundings.

Greenland Snapshots

After much wrangling, the USA's lease on the Thule Air Base (see the boxed text 'Plutonium Peril in Pituffik', p200) was renewed in summer 2004. It was a unique historic moment for Greenland, not because of the agreement itself but because then US Secretary of State Colin Powell came all the way to tiny Igaliku to sign it. In the 25 years since Home Rule, this was the first time that Greenland's foreign policy had not been entirely conducted from Copenhagen.

This was great news for Greenland's Home Rule government, which is desperately keen to move towards independence. But it's in a deep quandary, as Greenland is totally economically dependent on a massive budget subsidy from Denmark. At some Dkr3,000,000,000 that's almost US$10,000 per year for every man, woman and child, or around one third of GDP. Infuriatingly for the nationalists, it's hard to see the Danish largesse as anything other than well intentioned. That doesn't prevent quite unsubstantiated rumours circulating that somehow Denmark is siphoning off secret profits from something…but what?

National priorities are firmly aimed at balancing the books to allow an eventual political disengagement. Nobody's arguing for a return to traditional Inuit subsistence hunting; the idea is to squeeze money out of the ice, and the biggest hope is oil and mineral extraction. Production costs are prohibitively high, but rocketing petroleum and gold prices since the Bush and Blair 'War on Terror' began have made some developments look more viable. A new gold mine near Nanortalik was officially inaugurated in 2004 and it sent its first production to be made into wedding rings for the Danish Crown Prince and his Australian bride. (Perhaps paradoxically, most Greenlanders are intensely fond of the Danish royals.)

Greenland is also pushing for increased energy self-sufficiency. The country's greatest waterfall, Qorlortorsuaq (p125), is to be sacrificed for hydro power. The routing of Greenland's power lines across previously pristine fjords to Narsaq remains controversial, as the most economically logical pylon routes traverse the greatest Greenland Norse ruins (at Hvalsey, see p120).

For now, nearly 90% of exports are based on shrimps, crabs and fish, while local village economies depend on seal hunting. Foreign criticism of Greenland's laissez-faire hunting and fishing policy is seen as culturally insensitive interference.

Greenland's domestic economy works to a rather Soviet-style model, with central planning, state-owned shops, no private land ownership and heavily subsidised jobs. Arguably it has to be that way. Many villages have effectively lost their *raison d'être* since cod stocks collapsed in the 1980s, and even with huge subsidies the ships and planes needed to keep them supplied are painfully expensive. Air and ferry timetables are major political issues. The money spent on building the new Qaanaaq airport could have given everyone in that village free helicopter tickets for life to the existing Pituffik airport.

In big towns housing remains a dominant issue. While municipalities such as Paamiut have ample spare housing, others (especially Nuuk) are overflowing as people come to seek opportunities in the 'big city'. Demand has pushed Nuuk house prices to double those in Copenhagen – way above most people's wildest possibilities. Meanwhile many residents are stuck in a poverty trap. A rental apartment often comes with a job. This creates great inflexibility of labour. Changing jobs could mean losing your home, and bosses are loath to fire even the most incompetent worker if that would make them homeless when it's -20°C.

Like many postcolonial nations, Greenland has a language dilemma. Moving towards all-Greenlandic schools might sound sensible. However, without Danish (or another foreign language) few students are likely to get further education. And that, some locals fear, threatens to sentence Greenlanders to a future as second-class citizens in a globalising world.

Always the conundrum returns: how and whether to escape from Denmark. Most Greenlanders admit that they could have done much worse than to have the Danes in charge. Denmark's relatively enlightened attitude toward traditional native cultures has spared them much of the outright exploitation and plunder that many other colonies suffered. Instead, Denmark provided schools, hospitals and even the odd kilometre of road. But having been half-killed with Danish kindness, how will Greenland do on its own? It may take some years to find out.

HISTORY
Inuit History

Greenland's predominant population group is known simply as the Inuit ('people'). Though out of favour and faintly pejorative, the term Eskimo ('eaters of raw meat') is still used in some historical references (see the boxed text, p40). Originating in Siberia, different proto-Inuit peoples reached Greenland in various waves via Alaska and Canada.

Archaeologists have divided these peoples into several historical 'cultures' based on their tool technologies. The cultures are named after the places where evidence was first discovered: Independence (Independence Sound in Peary Land), Saqqaq (on Disko Bay), Dorset (Cape Dorset in Nunavut, Canada) and Thule (now Pituffik). Our conception of each, possibly interconnected, culture is very hazy but develops with every new archaeological find and improvement in carbon dating.

The first known group, Independence I, probably arrived from Canada's Ellesmere Island in around 2400 BC. Perhaps no more than 500 souls in total, these nomadic hunters somehow eked out a meagre existence at the frontier of human endurance for several centuries before apparently dying out between 1800 and 1600 BC.

Discoveries at Qeqertasussuk (near Qasigiannguit, p181) suggest the west-coast Saqqaq culture may have been concurrent. It was certainly much more widely spread and lasted around 1000 years. The Dorset culture probably derived from the Saqqaq or a second Independence culture. It was more technologically advanced and more communally based than its predecessors. Dorset people carved weapons and artistic pieces from bone and ivory, and used sleds to transport belongings. Learning to extract oil from whale and seal blubber meant that they could heat their way through colder climatic cycles. However, their apparent insistence on inflexible design rules suggests a strong resistance to innovation. Thus when the Thule culture arrived from Canada around the 11th century with harpoons, dogsleds and *qajaq* (kayak) technology, the Dorset ways were rapidly swept aside. Within 150 years the Thule, ancestors of most present Greenlandic Inuit, had spread all over north Greenland's coasts, absorbing or supplanting other cultures.

A cooling climatic shift in the 12th century pushed the Thule ever further south, increasingly fragmenting into a number of subcultures. By the time east- and west-coast subgroups met at Greenland's southern tip in the 19th century their languages had become almost mutually unintelligible.

The Greenland Research Centre website (www .sila.dk/History/) makes the fascinating if arcane subject of Inuit history readily accessible through a hyperlinked timeline.

The Norse Arrive

Curiously, just as the Thule Inuit started arriving in Northwest Greenland, Viking Norsemen were beginning to colonise the south. They weren't nearly as well prepared for Greenland's climatic hardships and within 500 years they had all mysteriously disappeared. Nonetheless, their haunting history gives a strange appeal to the extremely minimal ruins that you'll find dotted all over southern Greenland. Some of the most worth seeing are at Hvalsey (p120), Herjolfsnæs (p132) and Anavik (p155).

According to the sometimes contradictory Norse sagas, the first European to discover Greenland was Gunnbjörn Ulfsson, an Iceland-bound Norwegian who got blown off course in AD 930. Unimpressed with Gunnbjörn's Skerries (now named for him, near present-day Tasiilaq), he did a quick about-turn and retreated to Iceland.

Vikings regularly wallowed in vicious family blood feuds involving generations of revenge killings. However, such killings were not sanctioned, and killers would typically be exiled. In 978, the land reported by Gunnbjörn seemed to offer a desperate last hope to one such exile, the unsavoury Snæbjörn Galti. However, icy Blåserk Fjord near Tasiilaq proved a bad place to lodge. Holed up by the snow all winter, his party swiftly degenerated into murderous quarrels and virtually exterminated itself.

This didn't put off later exile Eiríkur Rauðe Þorvaldsson, who's generally remembered in English as Erik the Red for his russet hair and florid face. He and his father had already been forced to flee Norway after a rather bloody revenge killing. They settled in northwest Iceland. But in 982 Erik was again convicted of outlawry when he avenged the killing of two of his slaves, who had vandalised a neighbour's property.

Like his predecessors, Erik and his retinue fled to Greenland. They made landfall at Blåserk, but considering the place unlucky after Snæbjörn's fiasco, they continued down the coast. After rounding Cape Farewell (Nunaap Isua/Kap Farvel), they settled in for the winter on an island that Erik modestly named Eiríksey (Erik's Isle). The following summer they continued farther up Erik's Fjord (now Tunulliarfik), where they found tolerable country with animal-rearing potential. On the best plot Erik set up a farm that he called Brattahlíð. This name (meaning 'Steep Hillside'), along with local archaeological discoveries, has led some to identify Narsaq (p109) as the site of this original Brattahlíð. Undoubtedly Narsaq has the requisite steep, sloping pasture, but the majority of historians still place Brattahlíð at the head of the fjord on the site of modern Qassiarsuk (p104).

In 985 Erik returned to Iceland. There he pulled off one of the greatest masterstrokes in the history of marketing, calling the new country Grænaland (Green Land) to make it sound attractive. His reports of a land rich, fruitful and ripe for settlement encouraged 25 shiploads of prospective colonists to join him on the return journey. Ice and storms en route destroyed many ships, and others turned back when they saw the less-than-green reality of their new home. But 14 boatloads settled, and with their pick of virtually virgin land the colonists found conditions better than expected. Soon farmsteads dotted the fjord systems as far south as Herjolfsnaes (near modern Narsarmiit). Southern Greenland became known as the Eastern Settlement (Østerbygd) as more recent colonists settled new lands in the fjords behind modern Nuuk (the Vesterbygd or Western Settlement).

Christianity & Cooling

Fired with pioneer zeal and equipped with Viking ships, the first wave of Greenland Norse travelled widely, hunting ever further north and exploring the seas to the west. Erik the Red's son, Leif Eriksson, is famously credited

Berkeley Online Medieval Library (http://sunsite.berkeley.edu/OMACL/) has hundreds of searchable pages of Norse sagas.

DID YOU KNOW?

In North America the Norse would visit Labrador (Markland), Baffin Island (Helluland) and Newfoundland (Vinland), but they rarely stayed for long. Their settlement at L'Anse Aux Meadows lasted just three years before being abandoned following tensions with *skrælings* (Native Americans).

as being the first 'European' to visit North America, in 1000. Meanwhile, Leif and his mother, Þjóðhildur, converted to Christianity. Þjóðhildur demanded that Erik build her a church at their farm and refused to sleep with her pagan husband until he agreed. Spreading to create some 300 farms, the Norse community successfully bred sheep, cattle and pigs and soon became piously Catholic. They petitioned Norwegian king Sigurd Jorsalafare to establish a Greenland bishopric. The lavish gifts of walrus tusks, whalebone and two polar-bear cubs accompanying this request apparently did the trick. A Swedish monk called Arnald was nominated as bishop in 1124, and by the time he arrived in 1126 a red-sandstone church awaited him at Gardar (now Igaliku). Perhaps the colonists were later to rue their pro-church enthusiasm. While bishops proved useful at settling local disputes, they also exacted considerable tithes and taxes and could fine troublemakers by requisitioning their stock or land. By the time Greenland was annexed by Norway in 1261, most of the land had been thus appropriated by the church. Also, a lack of wood (as there were no trees, Siberian driftwood was the only source of timber) meant that building or repairing boats was tough. This reduced mobility to head north to hunt or trade with the Inuit, who were themselves spreading steadily southward.

By the terms of a 13th-century trade monopoly, two Norwegian ships were supposed to visit annually with supplies. In turn they would carry skins, narwhal tusks, locally made wool and other Greenlandic trade goods to Europe. Unfortunately, a notable cooling climate trend late in the 13th century made conditions increasingly tough for shipping and colonists alike. The colder Western Settlement was eventually abandoned around 1350; even in the warmer Eastern Settlement animals died and sheep needed their wool much longer, ruining the cloth industry. As ice choked the seas, navigation became increasingly hazardous. In 1380 the Norwegian supply ship sank. Worse, in 1392 the Hanseatic League (a powerful commercial confederation of North German port city–states) destroyed the port of Bergen, through which all Greenland trade was conducted.

Left with no link to the outside world, Greenland was effectively forgotten. And, as the value of walrus tusks had dwindled, Europe had little commercial incentive to restore contact. At some point in the 15th century the Greenland Norse simply vanished.

What Happened to the Norse?

There is no archaeological proof to suggest a massive epidemic or murderous raids by Inuit or *skræling* (Native American) tribes. Various theories include a scourge of caterpillars that destroyed the grazing lands, emigration to North America or absorption into the Inuit community. Wildest of all is the idea that the Norse people were kidnapped by pirates in the 1470s and sold as slaves at Tenerife. One particularly far-fetched version claims that the kidnappers had been sent to extract long-overdue tithes owed to Pope Sixtus IV, who was at that time on a spending spree sponsoring the Sistine Palace in Rome.

The last confirmed report of the Norse communities was given by an Icelander who attended a wedding at Hvalsey in 1408. Fascinating new research by Gavin Menzies suggests that China's brief era of exploration may have included voyages to Greenland during a sudden warm spell in 1422 or 1423. Perhaps the Chinese were the mysterious barbarians obliquely referred to by Pope Nicholas in a belated 1448 epistle telling Irish bishops of Greenland's reported ravaging 25 years earlier. However, it's unlikely that the fact-finding, trade-minded Chinese would have been aggressive towards

DID YOU KNOW?

Imported walrus ivory had been used extensively in Europe's early-medieval ecclesiastical art. However, the 15th century's improving Mediterranean trade made elephant ivory available more cheaply.

Although fictional, Jane Smiley's *The Greenlanders* is a magnificent epic offering better insights than any history book into the brutally harsh day-to-day life of the 14th-century Norse colonists.

locals. Sadly, all official Chinese records of that period were destroyed by later isolationist dynasties.

The disappearance of the Greenland Norse colonies remains one of history's great mysteries.

New European Interest

The lure of cheaper spices awoke late-16th-century Europe from Dark Age isolation as a race developed to find trade routes to the Orient. This included the hunt for a possible Northwest Passage past Greenland and around the unmapped, icebound north coasts of America (see p18). Famous attempts included those of Frobisher (1575), Hudson (1607) and Baffin (1615), but the trips of John Davis (from 1585) were most significant in mapping Greenland's west coast. Davis established a rapport with local Inuit and wrote the first ethnographic, geographical and biological studies of the island.

The latter part of the 17th century saw another mini ice age, but this didn't dissuade a new breed of European visitor. From the 1670s whalers – mostly Scottish, Dutch and Basque – arrived in ever-increasing numbers. Though they mainly lived on board, they inevitably indulged in some romantic dalliances and limited trade with the local Inuit, who were anxious to acquire knives; previously the only source of iron had been meteorite scrapings. In return, the Europeans valued narwhal ivory – spiral tusks which had long been considered to be the horns of unicorns and were considered a potent aid to virility. The whalers came to know the coasts much more intimately than the adventurers ever would, but their centuries of hunting would eventually spell disaster for marine mammal stocks.

Christianity & Trade Monopoly

With a 1605 expedition King Christian IV claimed Greenland for Denmark – a claim unsuccessfully disputed by Norway as recently as 1924. The first attempt at renewed European colonisation was over a century later, in 1721, when pastor Hans Egede received permission to establish a trading post and Lutheran mission. Egede's original plan was to find the lost Norse colonies. Convinced that Norse descendants had survived but reverted to paganism, he was determined to reclaim their souls for Christ. Finding no sign of any Norsemen, however, he decided that saving Inuit souls might be worth a go instead. In 1728 he founded Godthåb ('Good Hope') which, with the arrival of a competing Moravian mission in 1733, immediately became the centre for converting native Greenlanders to Christianity. The former missions now form the most attractive core of old Nuuk.

Before Christianity, Inuit hell was freezing cold, various easily angered spirits needed to be appeased by *angakok* (shamans), and everything from seals to rocks to icebergs had an immortal soul. Using trade as an encouragement, Christian missionaries set out to undermine these 'superstitions'. The church outlawed the shaman's drum and urged couples to form nuclear families. People had formerly lived communally, sharing food, tasks and even wives. Long term the attack on this lifestyle is considered to have dangerously fractured social cohesion, undermining organisations like the *umiaq* women's boat teams and the very practical sharing of food.

In 1774 Denmark imposed a trade monopoly administered by the Royal Greenland Trade Department (KGH), whose locally run successor still manages the ubiquitous Pilersuisoq stores. Over time the locals discovered a taste for KGH's addictive luxuries such as coffee and tobacco. This in turn encouraged a move away from nomadic subsistence hunting and a greater tendency to settle semipermanently near trade posts. Meanwhile,

1421: The Year China Discovered the World, by Gavin Menzies, is a superb read that gives a controversial new angle on the medieval history of Greenland and indeed the whole world. Check the associated website: www.1421.tv.

Give Me My Father's Body, by Kenn Harper, eloquently retells the extraordinary tale of Minik, one of six Inuit taken to New York by Robert Peary in 1897. The trip proved far from a holiday and Minik was horrified to discover his dead father as an exhibit in the Museum of Natural History.

Greenland remained closed to non-Danish shipping and trade right up until WWII. The only exception was for Faroese fishermen, who were permitted to develop their own village (Faeringehavn/Kangerluarsoruseq, now abandoned) in the early 20th century. They also established isolated, normally uninhabited boat stations from which they caught cod in Viking-style *inaati* skiffs that would be walled into shelters in winter. One derelict *inaati* boat remains sadly forgotten amid rubbish in Paamiut.

Further Exploration

The 1815 Battle of Waterloo ended Europe's exhausting Napoleonic wars, but victorious Britain suddenly found itself with thousands of under-employed military officers. To keep their oversized Navy busy the British Admiralty encouraged a new age of exploration, and the race resumed to find the fabled Northwest Passage (see p20). Once this was achieved (by Robert McClure in 1854) the race mutated into a competition to achieve 'furthest north'.

One of the best-known if not best-loved Arctic explorers was the American Robert Peary. Ruthlessly single-minded in his passion to reach the North Pole, he infamously part-funded his expeditions by 'stealing' the 37-tonne Savissivik meteorite (north Greenland's main historical source of iron) and by bringing back living 'human specimens' to the US, hoping to impress his sponsor, Morris Jesup. Peary claimed to have reached the Pole in 1909, at the cost of eight expeditions and eight toes (to frostbite), but it's generally accepted that he didn't actually make it (see p22). The northernmost lobe of Greenland is nonetheless named after him, and his descendents still live around Qaanaaq.

A quite different breed of explorer was the Norwegian Fridtjof Nansen. He is remembered as the first European to cross Greenland's inland ice (in 1888) but he also developed theories of Arctic ice drift (see p21).

Greenland's greatest home-grown explorer was Knud Rasmussen (see the boxed text, p174), born in 1879 at Ilulissat. Unique amongst ethnographers of the era, he lived among the most remote Inuit tribes, many of whom had previously had little or no contact from outside. Speaking their languages fluently, he recorded their stories, beliefs and shamanic rituals and lived as a native. His extensive reports remain a unique record of societies that have now disappeared forever. Rasmussen remains something of a national hero, and his 1936 film *Paolo's Wedding*, using an original cast of Inuit playing themselves, is a unique document; it's available on video from Nuuk's museum.

World War II & the 1950s Social Revolution

In 1940 Hitler occupied Denmark. In early 1941, even before it officially joined the war, the USA set up air bases at Søndre Strømfjord (Kanger-lussuaq), Thule (Pituffik) and Narsarsuaq. At Green Valley (Grønnedal) they built a naval base to protect the intensely strategic Ivittuut cryolite mine (see the boxed text, p138) and bartered the cryolite they needed for aluminium production for Greenland's basic imports. Meanwhile, on Greenland's east coast a thrilling if tiny-scale battle raged for control of the weather stations (see the boxed text, p212).

Apart from its trading stations and Christianising missions, Denmark had largely left the traditional Inuit lifestyle alone before the war. However, a mixture of wartime American openness and post-war idealism resulted in a massive social shake-up. In what later backfired as perceived cultural imperialism, Denmark set out to offer Greenlanders full Danish citizenship. In 1953 Greenland became a county of Denmark, and soon locals were being

DID YOU KNOW?

Greenland's northernmost cape was named by Peary for his sponsor, Morris Jesup, a railway magnate turned philanthropist who was a major benefactor of the American Museum of Natural History and a co-founder of the YMCA movement.

The Sledge Patrol, by David Howarth, grippingly retells the tale of the WWII East Greenland skirmish. Behind some gratuitous anti-Nazi moralising lies a deeply human story of hunters' lives and the bewitching spiritual power of the Arctic.

Siulleq Photo-gallery (www.arktiskebilleder.dk/siulleq) has thousands of fascinating historical and recent photos listed alphabetically (in Danish) by place (sted), person and theme (emne).

moved out of their insalubrious turf huts and rehoused in comfortable but alien apartment blocks built in the ugly modernist styles of the day. In the now infamous G60 policy, many smaller villages were considered impossible to supply or to 'properly modernise', so their populations were shipped off to regional centres where a bright new future appeared to beckon with new jobs in the booming cod factories.

In retrospect the project seems to have been doomed to failure. Subsistence hunters were totally unaccustomed to town life. Many felt disconnected from their land and rapidly turned to drink. Things became even worse in the 1980s, when the changing climate caused the cod to simply swim off elsewhere. Overnight the factory jobs disappeared and unemployment was added to the growing social discontent.

Recent History

In a 1972 referendum Denmark decided to join the European Economic Community (the forerunner of the EU). But in Greenland the referendum vote was heavily against joining. Greenlanders feared opening their territorial waters to European trawlers. Sure enough, before long there was almost uncontrolled fishing, particularly by German and British fleets. To most locals this looked like daylight robbery, especially as they themselves officially now had to ask Brussels for 'permission' to fish their own seas. Angry Greenlanders noticed that another Danish dependency, the Faroe Islands, had managed to avoid a similar fate. The Faroes, which had had its own home-rule government since 1946, had quietly remained outside the EU. Pressure thus built for Greenland to start running its own domestic affairs, too. In 1979 the 'county council' of Greenland was replaced by a Home Rule government. The KGH, which had run trade activities for centuries, was replaced by Kalaallit Niuerfiat (the ubiquitous KNI) to handle supplies and infrastructure. Greenland retained two representatives in the Danish parliament and (initially) one in Strasbourg's European Parliament. The latter, Finn Lynge, was later given the task of easing Greenland out of Europe after a second referendum in 1983 that was much more closely fought. To general relief, new fisheries agreements were introduced, and Greenland left the EEC in 1985 while remaining part of Denmark.

Nanoq (http://dk.nanoq .gl) is the official website of Greenland's Home Rule government.

In the 1980s there was a backlash of anti-Danish feeling. Schools moved increasingly towards using Greenlandic rather than Danish, and there was very occasional violence against 'colonisers'. Tensions have calmed since, but there remain murmured hopes of eventual independence. However, so long as Greenland's rather Soviet-style economy remains dependent on Danish subsidies the prospect seems unrealistic.

THE CULTURE
The National Psyche

DID YOU KNOW?

Kalaallit Niuerfiat (www .kni.gl) runs the ubiquitous Pilersuisoq chain of supermarkets, duty-free airport shops and general stores that are the lifeline of small rural villages.

Inuit people tend to be emotional and live very much in the moment. Such spontaneity is a wonderful spiritual gift but is rarely an advantage in a materialistic world. 'If there's cash let's spend it' is a common Inuit mindset. On payday tools lie where they're dropped once the cash arrives. The Danish-minded Greenlanders who actually budget and count their money can end up rich…and resented. In reality most modern Greenlanders by blood and by culture are a mix of Inuit and Danish. Locals may hunt reindeer or seal by day and return home to surf the web, or they may carve traditional-style *tupilak* (p86) yet go to church on Sunday. A curious blending of values has occurred, but since the two thought systems are often almost diametrically opposed there's bound to be a certain tension

RESPONSIBLE TRAVEL

'In Greenland you're as unlikely to meet an unfriendly man as to meet a friendly bear' goes the local maxim. You're equally unlikely to find someone who's talkative (unless they're drunk). The lack of emphasis on talk means that even at parties and on festive occasions there might be a marked lack of conversation. Europeans often find this uncomfortable, mistaking it for shyness, rudeness or standoffishness. In return, Inuit people often consider Europeans annoyingly loud, brash, boisterous and chatty. Yet Inuit emotions are generally near the surface, expressed through body language that you should learn to read. People love to laugh, and chuckles are common at occasions which can seem very inappropriate to Westerners. Be aware that smiles don't always mean pleasure and need to be interpreted. The Inuit often raise their eyebrows to say yes and squint to say no without making any verbal communication at all.

Only children are openly inquisitive. Even in small villages that rarely see foreigners, local adults might appear to ignore you (though doubtless the rumour mill will be running overtime). To get into village life it's thus really important to have at least one advance contact. Once you have made a local friend and gained some respect you'll usually find you get 'passed on', and the cultural experience becomes ever richer and easier. Homestays are a great first step for meeting people.

in the psyche. As they've effectively been dragged from subsistence hunting to citizenship of a developed modern country in just 50 years, it's hardly surprising that many Greenlanders suffer a certain philosophical confusion and a vague, often indefinable feeling of loss. This is worst in the bigger towns, where the distancing from nature is most marked. The void is frequently filled with alcohol, sex, extraordinarily expensive hashish or – rather less frequently – religious piety. Today there's a growing societal divide. On one side are those who are content to blame historical mistakes for their present despondent inactivity; on the other is a new forward-thinking generation of Greenlanders who accept that the past is gone and it's up to them to improve the future.

TRADITIONAL INUIT PHILOSOPHY

Harmony and balance between the environment and its inhabitants is a traditional goal. Rocks, fish, vegetation, animals and even abstracts such as moods and misfortunes were all attributed to independent souls in shamanistic Inuit belief systems (for more, see p39). The traditional Inuit attitude is to love, fear and respect nature on its own terms – to simply accept both its kindness and its wrath without wanting to conquer or change it. There is no sentimentality about the death of animals, who are considered to give up their lives to sustain human life, just as sometimes humans sacrifice themselves in the hunt. Common to any people living at high latitudes, there's a high incidence of depression during the long, dark winters. Greenlanders call this *perlerorneq* (the burden). Violent or other abnormal behaviour is often blamed on it, but people don't try to explain it away or make excuses. Rather, they accept it as part of life.

Miss Smilla's Feeling for Snow, by Peter Høeg, is a fine examination of ambivalent loyalties in the part-Danish, part-Greenlandic heroine, who's far from loveable. A movie version has some great photography but loses the book's gripping psychological depth.

Lifestyle

Greenlandic society offers a curious mixture of images. A smartly dressed woman holds a Burberry handbag and dried fish in the same manicured hand. A motor is left running in a parked car in a village that's so small you could walk anywhere. Homes are left unlocked so guests can let themselves in. The eternal coffee pot or thermos is filled yet again. Friends greet each other then sit comfortably in silence. Beside the flapping bedsheets, seal ribs hang to dry from washing lines in city apartment blocks.

DID YOU KNOW?

Perlerorneq, the Greenlandic term for Seasonal Affective Disorder, is also the local word for rabies.

TOP GREENLANDIC INUIT EXPERIENCES

- Riding a dogsled
- Falling in love with the land
- Learning to pronounce the 'll' sound without embarrassment
- Knowing when to leave a *kaffemik* at the appropriate moment

- Seeing the traditional costumes worn on the first day of school
- Appreciating silence in company without discomfort
- Seeing the other side of the whaling debate
- Eating *kivioq* without gagging

Children

One thing you'll soon notice is that Greenlandic children seem to have a remarkable degree of independence. This is partly because an Inuit child is considered to be born with a complete personality that is preordained as a direct gift from the ancestors. Punishing a child might show dissatisfaction or ingratitude for those gifts. Sadly, in modern Greenland, children's independence is often less philosophically driven. Especially at weekends you'll often find children who stay on the streets all night, not to celebrate inherited magic but out of general neglect, or perhaps to avoid a beating from drunken parents who have drowned their traditions in alcohol.

Education

Grønlands Statistik (www.statgreen.gl/english/) has all the figures you might need on demographics, geography and economy.

In principle Greenland has the same educational standards as the rest of Denmark. However, a shortage of qualified Greenlandic teachers means that many educators are still Danish expatriates, sometimes helped out by untrained Danish assistants.

There are primary schools even in small villages, but for secondary education most rural kids have to move away from home. There's a choice between high school or various vocational schools such as the marine training college in Paamiut and the catering school in Narsaq. Nuuk has colleges for business, teacher-training and nursing. Nuuk's University of Greenland has around 100 full-time students, though many more study in Denmark.

Population

DID YOU KNOW?

Greenland has the world's lowest population density (0.026 humans per sq km). Even sparsely inhabited Australia is 100 times more crowded, Macau 700,000 times more so.

The vast majority of the tiny population lives on or near the west coast. In the south, villages are sometimes interspersed with sheep farms, so occasionally you can walk between population centres without camping en route. Further north, villages are even sparser. Almost every village has at least one English-speaking teacher. The ethnic Danish tend to be concentrated in the bigger towns.

Sport

In 2002 Nuuk co-hosted the **Arctic Games** (www.awg.gl), a sort of Olympics for polar competitors. Included are several Inuit sports that originated as training exercises for hunting and *qajaq* (kayak) competence. Examples include various balance games, snow-stake throwing, target high-kicking (*aratsiaq* with one leg, *akratcheak* with two), and *aksaraq* (finger pulling). The latter is somewhat reminiscent of arm-wrestling and is popular in local pubs.

Skiing, especially Nordic (cross country) is popular. Sisimiut's 160km **Arctic Circle Race** (www.acr.gl), held every April, is considered the world's toughest such competition; see p160.

Other popular international sports are handball, table tennis, badminton, kayaking and, less predictably, tae kwon do. Nuuk organises its own **marathon** (www.arctic-marathon.gl). Most Greenlandic villages have a rough football pitch with enough gravel to dissuade diving for free kicks. Geographical distances make a regular football league far too expensive, so instead teams meet up for an annual tournament in late August. Details vary each year, but the 2005 tournament will be held in Uummannaq from 17 to 24 August. No tickets are required – the pitches aren't fenced.

Qajaqsite (http://home .att.net/~jimcoburn/) has a step-by-step guide to building your own Greenland-style *qajaq*.

The **Sports Confederation of Greenland** (www.gif.gl) has applied to FIFA mooting Greenland's future eligibility for World Cup soccer qualifiers.

At around -8°C in mid-April, a world championship of **Ice Golf** (www.golf onice.com) is played at Uummannaq (p191). Compared to normal golf, the balls are softer (and red, to show up in the snow), the fairways are shorter and the holes are bigger. Nonetheless, the basic rules are the same, with 'whites' instead of greens around the pin.

DID YOU KNOW?

Greenlander Hans Pavia Lind was Denmark's 2004 Olympic hope in archery. Sorry, no medals.

Multiculturalism

Traditionally, Greenland's harsh environment has encouraged a reflex of communal self-help: survival means overcoming petty human differences. Social acceptance is based on one's actions and attitudes rather than one's origins, as discovered by Togolese writer Tété-Michel Kpomassie (in *An African in Greenland*).

However, in the last 60 years large numbers of foreigners, mostly Danes, settled rather less sensitively, as part of Denmark's well-intentioned but socially destructive colonial paternalism. Society became not so much multicultural as bicultural. Following Home Rule, a few Inuit Greenlanders vented belated, subdued anger with attacks on Danes, some of whom returned to Denmark. Attacks have almost entirely petered out now, though sections of both cultures remain somewhat unreconciled. Notably, many Danes are contemptuous of the perceived Inuit lack of work ethic and predilection for alcohol bingeing. Meanwhile, some Inuit eye Danish commercialism with suspicion and grumble that Danes still seem to get most of the best jobs.

This Cold Heaven, by Gretel Ehrlich, poetically evokes the unique mix of action, stasis, ecstasy and terror of travelling in rural-most Greenland. A superb travel companion.

Still, Greenlanders of Danish, Inuit and mixed origin share a bond of objective, philosophical realism, and they mock incoming Danes and foreigners alike for their unrealistic belief in clocks, appointments and deadlines.

RELIGION

Greenland is at least nominally Christian. The Norse settlers were Catholics but, burdened by sometimes crippling tithes to bishops and popes, they died out without trace. Today's form of Christianity is a rather morose Lutheranism. As in Denmark, pastors still wear the vaguely Jacobean-style ruff collars. Perhaps these were still fashionable in the early-18th century when the religion arrived with Hans Egede. Conversion was as much by trade incentives as faith. Pre-Christian Inuit beliefs had attributed souls to everything, living or inanimate. Spirits of weather and sea were especially powerful and needed to be constantly placated by *angakok* (shamans). The souls of hunted animals needed to be thanked and not taken for granted. To avoid disasters there were numerous talismans, protective amulets and complex taboos. Accepting the Christian God proved reasonably convenient as a cure-all. However, the Bible didn't catch on so well. Inuit society has always been experiential, and talk is relatively minimal. In such a context John's Gospel's assertion that 'In the beginning was the Word…and the Word was God' sounds entirely farcical. While Inuit society was always superstitious, sex was not a hang-up. Until a generation or two ago isolated

DID YOU KNOW?

Church interiors are painted metaphorical colours: blue (sky), white (snow) and yellow-gold (sun). Altars popularly display the seven-stemmed candelabra (*menorah*) honouring Jesus' origins.

communities welcomed (rare) male visitors by inviting them to widen the gene pool. Don't expect that nowadays. While travellers still tell apocryphal tales of such 'welcomes', taking up such an offer now could land you in serious troubled: it's more likely to be an alcoholic aberration than a cultural celebration.

Most churches are beautifully maintained, but on Sunday morning the traditional 10am service often has more lighted candles than worshippers. Almost all churches hang a model ship from the rafters to remember those lost at sea. At Qoornoq (p154) it's an *umiaq* (women's boat).

ARTS

Greenland's artists are abuzz with the counterpoint of ancient and modern and patchily galvanised by the political dilemma of neocolonialism. The land is living art, suffused by dazzling light or mysterious fog and spiritually haunted by an unfathomable vastness. It's hard not to be inspired. Perhaps that's why a land with a population smaller than many European county towns has such a remarkable wealth of artistic expression, both traditional and international-minded. See www.arcticartsales.com for photos of the traditional-style artworks and carvings.

Art & Craft
TRADITIONAL ART

Aana (http://aana.net) is an as-yet underused but developing inter-disciplinary organisation for local artists.

Carving is the most archetypal Greenlandic art form. Artists use soapstone, antlers, bones, narwhal tusks or walrus ivory to make jewellery, animal models and grotesque little figurines known as *tupilak*. Originally *tupilak* were spiritual creations used like voodoo dolls or jujus to cast misfortune and even death on enemies. One had to use extreme caution, for if the victim's powers were greater than the assailant's then the spell could backfire and harm its maker. *Tupilak* gradually took physical form, and these days the figures are purely artistic creations. Celebrated contemporary *tupilak* carvers include Aron and Cecilie Kleist, whose work you'll see in occasional museum exhibitions.

Carving has taken a wonderful modern twist in Qaqortoq (p114), where the town's ubiquitous boulders are gradually being transformed into sculptures by a team of artists. Julius Jakobsen of Arsuk (p139) has carved official gifts for Danish royalty.

Fur is traditionally seen as a functional item, but there is great artistry in the various processes of shaping and working the material, whether for drums, bags, clothes or increasingly for souvenir knick-knacks.

Be aware when buying animal products, including carvings, that some may not be exported and others require permits (see p218).

QAJAQ & UMIAQ

The *qajaq*, forerunner of the kayak, originally developed as an Inuit hunting boat. Longer and narrower than modern recreational kayaks, the traditional *qajaq* was constructed with a driftwood or whalebone frame, covered with tightly stretched sealskin and waterproofed with animal fat. It was ideal for hunting walruses, seals, polar bears and whales, as it could be rolled over and then righted by the occupant without taking on water.

Accompanying groups of women would follow the *qajaqs* in a larger, open boat called an *umiaq* (women's boat), which could transport cargo and bring home the hunters' kills. Traditional skin boats haven't been in common day-to-day use since the 1950s. However, several towns now have *qajaq* clubs to preserve construction and handling skills. They'll often perform shows when a cruise ship is in port (and has paid for it!).

Beadwork is the pastime of many retired women. While the tiny *saparn-gaq* beads they use are often garishly coloured, there's no doubting the care and intricacy of the best work. Such beadwork is used in great quantity for the surprisingly heavy *nuilarmiut* shoulder-and-neck piece of traditional Greenlandic women's clothing.

FINE ART
The queen of 20th-century Greenlandic art is Aka Høegh. Her work is varied, vivid and expressive and turns up everywhere from book illustrations to panels on coastal ferries. A former director of the Greenland National Museum, Jens Rosing is an author and artist whose illustrations add a distinctive poignant depth to his storytelling. Up-and-coming artists include Anne-Birthe Hove, who makes imaginative text-image lithographs. Buuti Pedersen (www.buuti.com) produces many rather scrappy watercolour landscapes, but her oils of polar-bear couples wrestling (or cuddling?) are iconic and appealing. For the 25th anniversary of Home Rule in 2004, Asmund Havsteen-Mikkelsen and film-maker Inuk Silis Høegh produced a provocative if amusingly tongue-in-cheek installation piece for Copenhagen's Nordatlantens Brygge gallery (www.bryggen.dk). Amid prison-camp décor and martial music it announced Greenland's invasion of the world, ice weapons set to stun global warming and new Inuit names to replace Denmark's 'unpronounceable' European ones. Very thought-provoking.

The best places in Greenland to see contemporary art are the Qaqortoq Museum (p115), the Home Rule building in Nuuk (p148), Katuaq Cultural Centre (p148) and (for sale) at the small Nitz Gallery in Nuuk (p152).

Last Places – A Journey in the North (1981), by Lawrence Millman, is alternately snide and amusing; the author's Brysonesque reports of being sexually harassed by geriatric Greenlandic women seem improbable…until you visit the same pubs.

Literature
ORAL TRADITION
Traditionally the words and songs of shamans had special powers, so stories were carefully passed down through generations with little alteration right up until the early 20th century. Although most of these have been lost from the contemporary Inuit memory, many songs, poems and stories were collected by Danish Governor HJ Rink in the 1860s and explorer Knud Rasmussen between 1914 and 1924. Much like Aesop's fables, many conveyed lessons or suggested appropriate codes of behaviour but were also poetically full of anthropomorphism and wild, easily angered spirits.

WRITTEN TRADITION
Although literature is a relatively recent addition to Greenlandic culture, writing is a popular pastime and the Greenlandic Society of Authors has around 100 members.

Desperately little Greenlandic writing has been translated into English. One selection of 11 snippets (written or recorded between 1922 and 1982) is included in Michael Fortescue's sampler *From the Writings of the Greenlanders* (1990). The sampler also includes the original Greenlandic text and an extensive glossary, but it's less interesting as literature than as a set of anthropological snapshots or as a Greenlandic language learning tool.

Some works written and illustrated by Jens Rosing are locally available in English; others are published in Canada by Penumbra Press (www.penumbrapress.com).

Sacred Text Archive (www.sacred-texts.com/nam/inu) posts whole books by Rink and Rasmussen, including texts about *tupilak, angakok* and feared *kivigtok* (*qivittoq;* outcasts).

Music & Dance
Despite its tiny population, Greenland has a very active music industry. Though most home-grown bands are part time, many release their own CDs, which normally sell for Dkr145 in department stores and at a few

tourist offices. Greenlandic music is neither traditionally Inuit nor 'world music'. Indeed it developed its distinctive 'Vaigat-style' Hawaiian twang from American recordings popularised during WWII. Today's styles mix country-and-western riffs, folksy reels and fairly mainstream pop sounds. For archetypal chuntering polkas and accordions, listen to Rosa Willie and Tuukkakkormiut. For pub-style singalongs, get Lallaati's *As-anninnileraarut* or Martin Løvstrøm's *Soormi Taava*. Mainstream Julie Berthelsen is a Greenlander who's made it big in Denmark singing could-be-anywhere ballads in English. More interesting Pamyua are funky, multitalented artists now based in Alaska; they mix jazz, reggae and even a hint of throat singing. Rasmus Lyberth is the beloved 'old man' of Greenlandic pop. His early songs counterpoint a longing for traditional values with the desire to hang on to the benefits of 1960s Danish liberalism. Malik Høegh is considered Greenland's John Lennon. He started with the classic 1970s protest group Sumé, though his recent work sounds more influenced by Radiohead than Dylan or the Beatles. Greenlandic rap is currently ascendant. Reversing traditional rapper roles, teenage sensation Prussic rage against their parents' alcoholism and drug use. You'll see their name popularly graffitied around the less salubrious apartment blocks.

ULO (http://iserit.greennet.gl/ulomusic/) is the site of Greenland's main Sisimiut-based record label. It features disc reviews in a variety of languages, sometimes English.

On weekend evenings most bigger towns have live music in at least one of the pubs for dancing and raucous singalongs. One weekend in early September Aasiaat gathers several bands at once and calls the event a **rock festival** (www.nipiaa.gl).

There are some anachronistic attempts to revive shaman drumsongs, but if you're invited to listen to 'traditional' local singers the chances are they'll sing hymns. These may be beautifully harmonised a cappella or accompanied by harmonium, but they're almost always old-church dirges. Despite a few distinctive foot-scrape movements, Greenlandic dance is mostly an adaptation of reels learnt from Scottish and Dutch whalers in the 18th century.

ENVIRONMENT
The Land

The Age of the Earth, by G Brent Dalrymple, is ideal if you're wondering how rocks' ages can be calculated or simply want to brush up on your Rubidium-Strontium isotope methodologies.

Over 50 times bigger than mainland Denmark, Greenland is the world's biggest noncontinental island. Measured from north to south, the mainland is over 2500km long. Oodaaq Island, a tiny scrap of rock off the north coast of mainland Greenland, is the world's most northerly land at 83°40'N. Yet Cape Farewell (Nunaap Isua/Kap Farvel), the southernmost tip, is on the same latitude as the Shetland Islands. While the northern limits have midnight sun for nearly three months each summer and long weeks of polar night in winter, the far south experiences several hours of real daylight even in December.

At their nearest points, Greenland and Canada's Ellesmere Island are only 26km apart. Iceland is only 300km southeast across the Denmark Strait, but geologically it couldn't be more different. Iceland's dynamic volcanoes produce the world's youngest minerals, while Greenland has the oldest rocks yet discovered. Gneiss samples from Akilia Island and Isukasia (both around Nuuk) are reckoned to be over 3.8 billion years old. The earth itself is only approaching its 4.6 billionth birthday.

The Ice

Ice in all its multifarious forms gives Greenland's glorious scenery a very special photogenic extra. Some 79% of Greenland's massive 2,175,600-sq-km surface area is beneath an icecap that's up to 3km thick. This ice-age remnant is so heavy that Greenland's interior has sunk into an immense concave basin depressed just below sea level. Were the ice to melt, the water produced would raise world sea levels by around 7m, submerging coastal cities from London to LA. Scarily, global warming makes this doomsday scenario less than impossible over future centuries. The ice's creation took millennia of compacted snowfall. Most of its dripping noses are 'dead glaciers', meaning they melt into rivers. Much more impressive for visitors, however, are tidewater glaciers where the inland ice comes right to the sea or fjord and calves chunks of ice directly into the water. When such chunks are really massive they're called icebergs (though, technically, for the chunk to qualify as an iceberg over 5m of it should show above the waterline). Smaller chunks are known as bergy bits or, when less than a metre shows, as growlers.

Greenland's most productive tidewater glaciers produce fabulous icefjords packed with icebergs, most impressively near Ilulissat (a Unesco-recognised site).

Icebergs contain considerable quantities of pressurised air bubbles so, especially on hot summer afternoons, they can quite literally explode. The result is myriad shards and fragments of brash ice, which float around the bizarre spiky remnant of the central iceberg. Partial melting can also make big icebergs suddenly roll over. While impressive to watch, this can cause a tidal wave that's very dangerous to small boats and kayaks, and to anyone on a nearby shore: don't camp on bergy beaches.

Greenland Iceberg Paradise (www.geocities.com /Yosemite/Rapids/4233) has enthusiastic explanations of all things icy, including how Greenland ice cores are used to research climate-change history.

SEA ICE

A completely different source of ice is frozen sea water. First frazil ice forms; it's made up of small plate-shaped crystals suspended in viscous water. These later coagulate to make a soup known as grease ice because of the matte finish it gives to the sea's surface. This can become slush or spongy lumps called shuga, solidify into a thin crust called nilas, or form vaguely circular platelets called pancake ice. Finally the floating sea ice may thicken to as much as 3m. This pack ice is always in motion and often breaks up into flat-topped plates called floes. The channels of open water between floes are known as leads.

In spring the ice floes start drifting south down Greenland's east coast, rounding the southern tip, then swinging north up the west coast where in early summer they can block harbours and fjords entirely. Some ice floes can be several kilometres across. Curiously, icebergs can move in completely different directions to the main ice floes, as their bulks are in much deeper water.

DID YOU KNOW?

Even in the middle of pack ice there are patches of open water called polynyas where upwellings of warm water prevent the formation of ice at all.

NAVIGATING IN ICE

Every few days the Danish Meteorological Service (DMI) produces estimates of ice-floe densities with scores out of 10 according to the proportion of ice to open water when viewed from the air. Scores of 10/10 mean consolidated pack ice, which is effectively solid. Close ice (DMI code A) scores 7/10 or 8/10 and is dangerous to navigate without an icebreaker, though it's possible with a small motorboat and a gung-ho disregard for personal security. Tides, currents and wind can cause it to close up and trap you. Open pack ice (code B, scores 4/10 to 6/10) can be pushed aside by boats and is thus navigable if conditions are calm. For little motorboats the very low-density ice can be dangerous due to the smallest growlers, which can be virtually colourless but still big enough to cause serious damage if struck at high speed. Things can change very rapidly, so look at previous maps as well to see the trends.

DMI (www.dmi.dk/dmi /index/gronland/iskort .htm) has online ice maps: click Ugekort for all Greenland, Kort1 for the southern tip and Kort2 for the inhabited area of East Greenland.

Wildlife
ANIMALS

Due to the harsh conditions, Greenland's Arctic wildlife is necessarily sparse. Very distinctive are shaggy, handlebar-horned muskoxen (*umim-maq/muskus okse*). They look like woolly bison, though bizarrely they're actually related to goats. Vegetarian and fairly passive unless closely approached, they were traditionally seen as walking steaks by hungry Inuit hunters. In western Greenland they were hunted to extinction. However, a few individuals specially shipped over from the east were reintroduced and now form considerable populations that are very easy to spot around Kangerlussuaq (see p162) and Grønnedal (p136). In September virtually every Greenlander takes time off work to hunt for elk-like caribou (*tuttu/rensdyr*) and reindeer. These are now considered to be too common for the environment's carrying capacity.

Arctic foxes (*terianniaq*) are white in winter for snow camouflage, but their coats turn blue-grey in summer. They're liable to nibble your camp provisions if you don't stash your food securely. Beware of foxes that look too tame – they may have rabies.

Polar bears (*nanoq/isbørn*) are brilliantly adapted creatures with natural sunglasses: a second, inner eyelid to protect their vision from snow blindness as well as from water when swimming. Most live far from human habitation in Greenland's northeast. Even in Nanortalik, whose name means 'the place of bears', you're not really likely to see any. You'd probably have more success spotting polar bears in either Svalbard, Grise Fjord (Canada) or Point Barrow (Alaska). Just a handful every year float south on drift ice, where they're welcomed to the human realm with both barrels, their skins being made into traditional trousers. Magnificent as they look, polar bears are far from amicable. However, they're so used to scaring the daylights out of anything they encounter, they'll probably be taken aback if you stand your ground. So don't run away if cornered – your best hope is to act aggressively annoyed. One famous field archaeologist defended himself for decades armed only with a lot of bravado and a trumpet.

Mouse-like lemmings make burrows in the soil, which can trip unwary hikers in the Northeast Greenland National Park. Their famous Monty Pythonesque mass suicides are actually caused when overpopulation sends thousands in search of food; some get pushed over cliffs by the force of those coming behind them.

White Arctic Hares (*ukaleq*) are sometimes seen by hikers; the hares freeze instantaneously in confusion before bounding off to rejoin Alice in Wonderland.

Whales & Walruses

Limited quota-based whale hunting continues (p93) and whales (*arfeq/hval*) are probably more common in Pacific waters). Still, from Greenland's coastal ferries visitors regularly see smaller minke whales (*tikaagullik*) and dramatic humpback whales (*qipoqqaq*), especially in September. The latter typically blow out about eight spurts of their very bad breath before breaching spectacularly and diving, tail up. There are special whale-watching trips from Nuuk (p149) and notably Aasiaat (p183). Killer whales (*aarluk/orka*) are among the most common in Arctic waters and sometimes tease boats with nerve-racking swim-pasts.

A narwhal (*qilalugaq qernertaq*) is an extraordinary marine mammal known for the incredible spiral tusk on its snout. Technically, this is a distended tooth, but when first brought to medieval Europe it was considered proof that unicorns existed. In those days tusks were worth 20 times their

A Nature and Wildlife Guide to Greenland (2004), by Benny Génsbøl, is a very practical illustrated identification guide covering Greenland's most common birds, animals, fish and flowers. It's sold in tourist offices.

DID YOU KNOW?

Caribou skins are reckoned to have the best insulation per weight ratio of any material, artificial or natural.

DID YOU KNOW?

Its pallid, cadaverous appearance gave the narwhal its name, meaning 'corpse whale' in old Norse.

weight in gold, and narwhals were thus heavily hunted. Today the best time to spot one is during the summer in Inglefield Fjord near Qaanaaq and in the Davis Strait.

Greenland's beluga are white whales, not caviar-producing sturgeon. They are considered to have the tastiest *mattak* (skin), but their numbers have reduced by two thirds in the last 20 years and they have virtually disappeared from waters south of Maniitsoq.

Walruses were once fairly common and they posed a real threat to *qajaqs*. However, they were hunted close to extinction for meat and their distinctively goofy, carveable fangs. Although they have been globally protected since 1972, limited hunting by Greenlanders is still permitted, and sightings are consequently rare except when they're basking on a few remote beaches of the very hard-to-reach Northeast Greenland National Park.

Zoom Whales (www .enchantedlearning.com /subjects/whales) is a delightful introduction to whales that's designed for schoolkids but great for any age group.

Seals

From boats you'll often spot seals *(puisit)* bobbing up inquisitively. Commonest are ringed seals *(natseq)* and harp seals *(aataaq)*, which lounge on ice floes, giving them their Latin name *Pagophilus groenlandicus* (Greenland's ice-lover). Rarer are bearded seals *(ussuk)*, whose skin was once prized for use as rope, and hooded seals *(natsersuaq)*, whose males inflate a curious red facial bladder when excited. Seals are at the heart of the rural Greenlandic economy. Global anti-fur sentiment caused by the perceived inhumanity of cub-clubbing in Newfoundland resulted in plummeting demand for sealskins in the 1990s. The resultant rock-bottom prices caused unintended financial devastation in Greenlandic communities. This was particularly galling as, traditionally, all parts of the animal were eaten or used, including the blubber, which made lamp oil. Nonetheless, a recent price rebound means hunters currently receive Dkr285 per pelt, so long as it's the right quality and pattern. So, increasingly, the meat is becoming just a partly used by-product. Present hunting levels are reckoned to be within the carrying capacity of the species, though whether these statistics include 'lost' kills is unclear. Most of the 'sustainably harvested' skins are salted and sent to the Great Greenland tannery in Qaqortoq (see p117).

Fish

Fish are abundant in both fresh water and salt water, though commercially valuable cod *(saarullik)*, Atlantic halibut *(nataarnaq)* and scallops have been drastically overfished. The lakes and streams abound with Arctic char *(eqaluk)*, a colourful type of trout (see p215). There are also fine Atlantic salmon *(kapisilik)* and tasty red fish *(suluppaagaq)*. Deepwater shrimps and snow crabs are commercially important but rarely served fresh. Relatively plentiful Greenland halibut *(qaleralik)* is smoked and exported.

DID YOU KNOW?

Confusingly for anglers, in Greenlandic Danish both Arctic char and Atlantic salmon are known by the same term, *laks*.

Birds

Greenland is not an exceptional bird-watching destination, but 52 bird species traditionally breed on or near the shores and around 150 species migrate through. The small Grønne Ejland isles in Disko Bay have Greenland's highest level of bird diversity – visit from Aasiaat or Ilulissat. The commonest urban sightings are northern wheatears *(kussak/stenpikker)*, redpoll *(orpimmiutaq/gråsisken)*, black-and-white sparrow-like snow buntings *(qupannaaq/snespurv)*, and noisy jet-black ravens *(tulugaq/ravn)*, which watch hikers quizzically.

Common sea birds include Iceland gulls (*naajaannaq/hvidvinget måge*), glaucous gulls (*naajarujussuaq/gråmåge*), terns (*imeqqutaalaq/havterne*), skuas (*isunngaq/kjove*) and kittiwakes (*taateraaq/ride*). From Disko Bay

Birds of Greenland (Atuakkiorfik) is a locally sold ornithological guide that has slightly more recognisable pictures than the *Nature and Wildlife Guide*, so it's a better choice if you're exclusively interested in bird-watching.

north, fulmars *(qaqulluk/mallemuk)* are common and fairly tame, and localised populations of puffin *(qilanngaq/lunde)* breed around Upernavik. In the hills, highly edible ptarmigans *(aqisseq/fjeldrype)* look like stretch-necked chickens and turn white in winter. In higher wetland areas red-necked phalarope *(naluumasortaq/odinshane)* nest from early June. Arriving snow geese *(kangoq/snegås)* herald spring in the north.

You might mistake dovekies (little auks; *appaaraq/søkonge)* for small penguins until they take falteringly to the air (real penguins are only found in the southern hemisphere). Millions of Brünnich's guillemots (common murres; *appa/polarlomvie)* once brought the cliffs north of Disko Bay raucously to life, but the species has been decimated by hunting, egg collecting and fishing nets, which act as traps. Confusingly, in Greenlandic Danish they're usually called *alk*, which more correctly applies to razorbills *(apparlluk)*. Black guillemots *(serfaq/tejst)* are more often seen but have smaller breeding colonies. The common eider duck *(aavooq/ederfugl)* is not common any more; indeed it's locally endangered.

IBGL (http://groups .yahoo.com/group/ibgl) is an English-language open forum for Greenland bird observations.

Small populations of impressive white-tailed eagles *(nattoralik)* are fairly regularly spotted along the west coast south of Nuuk, notably around Paamiut and Arsuk. Rarer birds of prey include peregrine falcons *(kiinaaleeraq/vandrefalk)* and gyrfalcons *(kissaviarsuk/jagtfalk)*, which shriek distinctively. Snowy owls *(uppik/sneugle)* are limited to remote northeastern Greenland.

PLANTS

Arctic vegetation is fairly limited and typically stunted. Dwarf willow and birch that are mere centimetres high might be decades or even centuries old. In just a few very sheltered areas they grow into bushes or small trees, which Greenlanders consider an attraction. Common in villages are limpid, yellow-petalled Arctic poppies *(sungaartorsuaq/fjeld-valmue)*, and wide varieties of buttercups, cinquefoils, dandelions and hawkweeds all add a golden dazzle to grassy areas. These contrast photogenically with the ubiquitous clumps of edible, violet-blue Arctic harebell *(tikiusaaq/blåklokke)*. Perhaps the most dramatic blooms belong to Greenland's national flower, the broad-leaved fireweed *(niviarsiaq/storblomstret gederams)*, which emerges purple and proud from gravelly scree.

Mountainsides are made eminently more climbable thanks to tightly woven carpets of crowberries *(paarnaqutit/sortebær)* and Arctic bilberries *(kigutaarnat nagguii/møsebølle)*, commonly translated into local English as blackberries and blueberries respectively. Their fruits are edible and their tiny leaves redden the hillsides to a glorious autumnal russet in late September. Boggy areas are easy to spot from their vivid deep-green mosses and from tufty-headed cotton grass *(ukaliusaq/polar-kæruld)*. Of five orchid types supposedly present, all are rare, with *leucorchis albida* the easiest to find – look beneath eagle nesting sites.

Environmental Issues

At first glance, Greenland may seem a pristine realm of nature. However, the country is dealing with many problems caused by citizens of other nations. These include centuries of overhunting and overfishing, which notably decimated whale stocks. As elsewhere in the Arctic, the build-up of toxins from global marine pollution (see p34) has been concentrated higher up the food chain and thus has most affected bear and seal meat, the traditional mainstays of the Inuit diet. Most horrifyingly, in August 2000 the US finally admitted that a plane that crashed 30 years earlier into a bay near Thule (Pituffik) 'lost' a US hydrogen bomb. Whoops, cancer worries.

Locally, whales and sea mammals are legally caught subject to very strict quotas. Other nominally 'sustainable' hunting is less controlled and some 'traditional' pursuits have overstretched resources – notably egg-collecting, which has had a devastating effect on bird populations in certain areas. Nonetheless, with hunting such a key part of Inuit culture, any implied criticism is taken very much to heart. Greenpeace and other activist groups remain widely despised for their anti–seal fur campaigns. A pair of must-read books encapsulate the culture-versus-protection arguments. Finn Lynge's *Arctic Wars, Animal Rights, Endangered Peoples* (1992) sturdily upholds the Greenlanders' rights to respectful, traditional hunting and lambasts the incongruities of interfering, urban-minded animal-rights groups. However, in *A Farewell to Greenland*, Kjeld Hansen counters with a scathing attack on Greenland's laissez-faire attitudes to animal protection. Read both.

Meanwhile, relatively plentiful Arctic wildlife survives largely unpestered within the remote Northeast Greenland National Park, the world's biggest. This covers around a quarter of the nation, but it's very remote and access is tough (see p213).

Proact Greenland (www .proact-campaigns.net /greenland/) has a partial online text of *A Farewell to Greenland* and plenty of discussion on Greenland's environmental issues.

FOOD & DRINK
Restaurants & Cafés
Greenland has relatively few restaurants. Most are in hotels and offer international-style cuisine with some local ingredients. Restaurant meals aren't cheap (they average Dkr200 to Dkr300), but many are worth the money. Indeed Nipisa in Nuuk (p151) offers world-class cuisine that would impress critics in Paris or New York. Cheaper cafeterias offer acceptable and hearty but unmemorable meals-of-the-day with meat, boiled potatoes and frozen vegetables. Side salads are sometimes available, but vegetarian options are few and far between. Fast food generally means a grill-bar specialising in hot dogs (*pølser*). A few places offer pseudo-Oriental cuisine or pizza. There's a good Thai restaurant in Nuuk. The term café can mean anything from pub to fast-food stand, but there are a couple of real cafés in Nuuk with decent espresso coffee.

Self-Catering
As most hostels have equipped kitchens, economy-conscious travellers can survive relatively cheaply on supermarket food and fresh fish or seal meat bought from markets (*kalaaliaraq/brædtet*). Considering that almost everything else is imported, the variety of groceries is amazing, especially in the big Pisiffik and Brugsen supermarkets (in bigger towns only). Supplies of fresh vegetables can be sporadic, especially in smaller shops; they might have pineapples and mangoes yet have no more onions till the next supply boat arrives. Prices seem high to many Europeans but are comparable to those in Scandinavia and low compared with Iceland. Supermarkets usually have an associated bakery supplying fresh bread, pastries and biscuits.

KNI's Pilersuisoq shops have village branches where prices are usually no different from those in the towns, but stocks can be limited. 'Kiosks' open late to sell candy and a small selection of groceries at up to 50% above Pilersuisoq prices.

Fishers and seal hunters nibble eternally on tasteless, jaw-crackingly hard *Ngguteeqqat* ship's biscuits.

Traditional Foods
Traditional Greenlandic fare is dominated by meat, especially whale and seal. Before rejecting these foods for sentimental or ideological reasons, remember that Inuit subsistence culture has lived harmoniously hunting

these animals for millennia. It was European commercial whaling that caused the collapse in cetacean numbers. Today, all whale catches are regulated by strict quotas. Fresh whale steaks cost around Dkr50 per kilogram. The best raw whaleskin *(mattak)* comes from beluga or narwhal, taking on a slightly nutty, mushroom-like flavour when cooked.

There's no quota on hunting harp seals, whose populations are counted in millions. Originally people killed no more than they could use, but rising skin prices have inspired liberal interpretations of the tradition, and in hunting villages seal meat is so plentiful that it's given away. In towns seal meat costs around Dkr30 per kilogram from the harbour markets. Cook it by boiling chunks in water for an hour or more. The cooked meat has a deep, chocolate-brown colour. Back-joint meat is soft and tender. Cuts edged with a centimetre of blubber taste rather like lamb chops: excellent when straight from the pot but slightly sickening if kept.

In September virtually everyone takes time off work to hunt caribou *(tuttu)*, which yield superb steaks and very tasty leg-meat (rarely sold). Muskox *(umimmak)* meat is generally tender and gristle-free. Greenlandic lamb is perhaps the most fragrant anywhere due to the sheep's diet of flowers and berries. However, sheep are expensive to feed through the harsh winters and thus local lamb ironically costs more than frozen imports from New Zealand. Delicious Greenlandic smoked lamb tastes rather like *jamon* or prosciutto but is hard to find.

Arctic char and trout *(eqaluk)*, salmon *(kapisillit)*, capelin *(ammassat)* and cod all appear at fish markets, sometimes dried, smoked or pressed with herbs for a similar culinary effect. Although shrimps and snow crabs are a mainstay of many village economies, most are frozen for export and are remarkably difficult to find fresh.

North Greenlanders once survived by eating dovekies (penguin-like small birds). Stuffed in hollowed-out seal carcasses and left to rot, they form *kivioq*, Greenland's most unappetising speciality. It was food poisoning from bad *kivioq* that killed explorer Knud Rasmussen. Traditional egg-collecting has decimated bird cliffs and is now much less common.

Many of the wild foods described below are served with local meals.

> 'North Greenlanders once survived by eating dovekies. Stuffed in hollowed-out seal carcasses and left to rot, they form *kivioq*, Greenland's most unappetising speciality'

Wild Foods

In summer you can supplement your diet with some of Greenland's abundant wild foods. From August to early September the bush is carpeted with black crowberries *(paarnaqutit/sortebaer)*, which are a popular addition to ice cream. Tarter, tastier Arctic bilberries *(kigutaarnat naggui/møsebølle)* are commonly known as blueberries.

All over South Greenland, but especially around ruins and deserted villages, you'll find ball-headed Garden Angelica *(kuanneq/fjeld-kvan)*, which makes great pickles and jams. Tiny leaves of low-lying wild thyme *(tupaarnat/skotsk timian)* make excellent tea as well as seasoning, but although abundant in grassland slopes the plant is only easy to spot in July or August, when it produces little clusters of pink-red flowerlets. In late summer you'll see abundant growths of Arctic harebells, known locally as *tiiusaaq/Grønlandsk blåklokke*. Though it seems odd, you can pick off and eat the violet-blue, bell-shaped flower heads. An excellent alternative to salad, these taste like fragrant mangetouts. Check inside for flies before eating, and consume immediately.

Common all over southern Greenland in summer, the delicious birch bolate (slippery jack) mushroom has a smooth golden-brown dome and distinctive spongy underside. No Greenlandic mushroom of that type is poisonous, though check older specimens for little worms.

Fishing also provides nourishment, and you don't even need a rod – just a hook and line will do in some places, where pan-sized Arctic char will snap at anything. Fishing legally requires a licence (Dkr75/200/500 per day/week/month; see p215).

At low tide, blue mussels are common in sheltered bays. They're excellent steamed or fried with butter and garlic, though chew carefully as they often contain miniature pearls. Avoid collecting shellfish near towns, where they may be tainted by sewage.

Drinks
NON-ALCOHOLIC DRINKS
Tap water is almost always drinkable. Giardia does not occur, so one can generally drink stream water while hiking, except around animal farms.

Coffee is a social institution and is almost constantly on offer wherever one goes. The *kaffemik*, a coffee morning with cakes and possibly other food, is the archetypal Greenlandic get-together. In villages the whole population might be invited to celebrate a birthday, christening or school-entrance day. Sitting in silence isn't considered bad form – indeed it shows comfortable sociability. However, it's polite to leave after one's second cuppa, especially if other guests have arrived.

Tea is also popular. Urban Greenlanders are increasingly discerning in their blend selection when supply allows.

ALCOHOL
Most beer sold is 4.6% Carlsberg or Tuborg. Either usually retails at Dkr14 for a 330ml bottle in shops (plus Dkr2 deposit), or Dkr25 to Dkr40 in pubs. Stronger beers can cost as much as double.

Wine is popular, and a surprising international range is available. Supermarket prices start at around Dkr70 for a 750ml bottle of drinkable plonk; since much of that price is transportation cost, though, an extra Dkr20 can net you a much better bottle. Vintage port can cost as little as Dkr200 – when it turns up.

Stronger alcohol is fiercely expensive. You'd be wise to buy some duty free on arrival even if you don't drink: it's a prized gift and a delight to share. If you're going to splash out on a bar cocktail, try the symbolic and potently warming Kalaallit Kaffiat (Greenland Coffee). This takes Kahlua, whiskey and fresh coffee and adds whipped cream as metaphorical ice. Then Grand Marnier is heated over a flame, set alight and poured from a height onto the cream. The blue flames represent the aurora borealis (northern lights).

Alcoholism is a serious and very obvious problem. This becomes all too apparent in bigger towns on weekends, especially payday Friday nights. To limit the problem, alcoholic drinks may only be sold in shops from noon to 6pm on weekdays and from 11am to 1pm on Saturday.

South Greenland

HIGHLIGHTS

- Sail with seal hunters through some of the world's most awesome fjords around **Aappilattoq** (p133)

- Unwind in photogenic do-nothing villages **Alluitsoq** (p124), **Narsarmiit** (p132) and **Alluitsup Paa** (p121)

- Hike the beautiful but easy trail between **Tasiusaq** and **Nunataaq** (p106)

- Stroll the picturesque old-town cores of **Qaqortoq** (p114) and **Nanortalik** (p126)

- Head for the inland ice from **Narsarsuaq** (p97), whether on foot, by helicopter or by boat into berg-packed Qooroq Icefjord

- Hire kayaks to explore the dramatic fjords around **Nanortalik** (p126) and **Narsaq** (p109)

- Discover how Norse settlers lived at the long-house reconstruction in **Qassiarsuk** (p104)

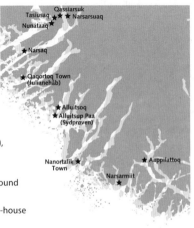

Blissfully scenic South Greenland is far more than a touristic also-ran to the big ice of Disko Bay. The bergs may be smaller, but the mountains are much more impressive, coming to an astonishing scenic climax in the far south. Archaeology buffs might also enjoy the widespread if rather indistinct Norse ruins.

The region's gateway, Narsarsuaq, lacks cultural appeal but is very well organised for easy day hikes and lovely short-hop excursions. The region's other settlements are all colourfully quaint, yet each is visually distinct. Relatively verdant Narsaq is pretty, very 'real', and graciously free of flies and mosquitoes. Along with bucolic Igaliku and historically fascinating Qassiarsuk, Narsaq is easily combined with Narsarsuaq for lower-budget short stays. Qaqortoq is the south's biggest town and a relatively vibrant cultural centre. Like loveable Nanortalik it has a small but delightfully photogenic old-town area. Nanortalik's sub-settlements are scattered among some of the world's most fabulous fjords with surreally spindly peaks and magnificently sheer granite cliffs. The scenery might well rate as the most memorable you'll ever see. In this area Nanortalik and Alluitsup Paa have the best accommodation, Narsarmiit has the most dramatic backdrop, and charming Aappilattoq enjoys an incomparable position commanding the very finest fjordlands.

All of the south's destinations are very well worth a visit, but it's most satisfying to leave the far south to last so that you progress from the subtle loveliness of Narsaq to the overpowering raw grandeur of ice-choked Aappilattoq. Try to allow much more time than you think you'll need, as everything depends on the fickle weather. Bring a few books to read on those inevitable foggy days.

NARSARSUAQ, IGALIKU & THE NARSAQ PENINSULA

NARSARSUAQ

pop 190

Not really a village but rather more than an airport, Narsarsuaq is the gateway to southern Greenland. The name means 'big plain'. Big by Greenlandic standards, perhaps, but don't expect Kansas. Indeed most of the flat area is filled by the airport's runway, alongside which Narsarsuaq settlement forms a rather haphazard scattering of buildings, hemmed in by the long scraggy Signalhøjen hill to its direct east. The architecture is functional but the setting is pleasant, with icebergs visible from the port and a very distant horizon of spiky peaks beyond the icecap. With the inland ice relatively acces-

sible (on foot), a nearby calving glacier to seek out (by boat or helicopter) and plenty of hikes and boat excursions to enjoy, Narsarsuaq makes an excellent, well-organised gateway to Greenland.

History

In April 1941, after the WWII invasion of Denmark by Nazi forces, the USA agreed to create temporary supply bases in Greenland. The previously uninhabited Narsarsuaq Delta became Bluie West One base practically overnight, months before the USA officially entered the war. A way station for transatlantic bombers, by 1945 it had become Greenland's largest settlement with a population of 12,000 and all the trappings of a small US town.

Contrary to the original agreement with Denmark, the base was not decommissioned after the war, and it continued well into the Cold War era. Usage of the base's hospital during the Korean War remains the focus of

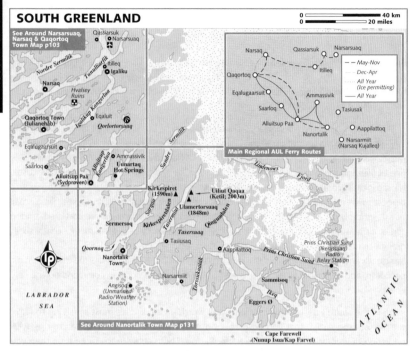

much controversy (see the boxed text, p99). A plan of science-fiction proportions to construct a road over the icecap to Kangerlussuaq was eventually defeated by reality.

The hospital and much of the remaining base closed in 1958. Although a Norwegian company quadrupled its investment on salvage rights to the site, the area remained littered with intriguing debris for decades afterwards. The airfield turned civilian, and has since become Greenland's second international airport and a reconnaissance base for Greenland's DMI Ice Patrol (see p88).

Orientation

Blue Ice Café and the youth hostel sell the region's three hiking maps *Narsarsuaq*, *Narsaq* and *Qaqortoq* (each Dkr80), various Saga maps, and a more general Eastern Settlement map (Dkr40) with notes on the most important Norse ruins.

Information

EMERGENCY

Clinic (☎ 665211; airport bldg)
Police (☎ 665222)

LAUNDRY

Washing machines in the youth hostel cost Dkr30 per load including powder.

LEFT LUGGAGE

Lockers at the airport cost Dkr5 per 24 hours (maximum is 72 hours). Guests can leave bags at the youth hostel without charge.

MONEY

Considering that this is one of Greenland's main gateway cities, it's surprising and inconvenient that there is no bank, bureau de change or ATM.

Airport Administration office (☎ 665266; B30; 10am-2pm Mon-Thu, 10am-noon Fri) Gives credit-card cash advances and changes foreign cash with no commission. Rates at the post office are better for larger amounts.

Hotel Narsarsuaq Exchanges cash and travellers cheques and gives cash advances on credit cards if you know the PIN. However, the supply of cash is finite and first call goes to guests.

Pilersuisoq supermarket It won't change money, but if you buy something using a credit card you can get cash back free of commission.

POST

Post office (airport; ☺ 2-3pm Mon-Thu, 11am-3pm Wed & Fri) Sells stamps and fishing licenses. (Stamps are also available from the youth hostel.) Changes foreign cash at sensible rates but with a Dkr30 commission.

TOURIST INFORMATION

Blue Ice Café (☎ 497371; www.blueice.gl; ☺ 9am-6pm Jun-Sep) Acts as a helpful tourist office as well as selling Blue Ice tours. A great library of Greenland-relevant books to browse and no pressure to buy. A useful range of maps and equipment plus everything from postcards to camping gas, to local honey and reindeer jerky.

Hotel Narsarsuaq Arctic Adventure representatives in the lobby (7-7.30pm only) are knowledgeable but often overworked.

Tourist Information Desk (airport) Staffed by a Blue Ice representative when international planes arrive.

Dangers & Annoyances

Prevent kamikaze flies dive-bombing your ears and eyes by buying a head-net at Blue Ice Café or from the Hotel Narsarsuaq.

Sights

The real attractions lie outside the settlement itself (see Around Narsarsuaq, p102, Qassiarsuk, p104, and Igaliku, p108). However, there are a few oddments around town to keep you occupied.

Narsarsuaq Museum (admission Dkr20; ☺ 10am-6pm summer), accessed through the Blue Ice Café, is extensive and worth a visit. Displays take you through a variety of historical exhibits on the Norse, sheep farming and the US presence in South Greenland.

Opposite the airport terminal is the **Viking Millennium Stone**, an egg-shaped boulder inscribed with runes and an inscrutable Viking face design. It marks the visit of Queen Margrethe of Denmark in 2000 for the 1000th anniversary of Leif Erikson's American adventure. The anniversary's frolics and feasting are still fresh in local memories. Fixed to a rocky bluff behind the little playground, a bronze **Naomi Uemura plaque** commemorates the Japanese explorer extraordinaire. Uemura, who climbed Everest, dogsledded solo to the North Pole and crossed Greenland's inland ice north to south, looks distinctly uncomfortable to have been memorialized wearing a jacket and tie.

Crowned by a radio tower and forgotten war-era wooden poles, 240m **Signalhøjen** (Signal Hill) makes a handy quick hike for views

across the airport and fjord. The main gravel track winds up from behind the Pilersuisoq store. A sometimes boggy alternative footpath skirts the reservoir behind the Youth Hostel.

Hospital Valley, some 3km north of the Hotel Narsarsuaq, was the site of the controversial US military hospital **Bluie West One** (see boxed text, above) but the only remaining structures are a lone fireplace and chimney and a few concrete foundations.

Activities

Narsarsuaq is a good place from which to organise regional multiday hiking or kayaking trips, even if you eventually start from Igaliku, Qassiarsuk or Narsaq. Enquire with Blue Ice about mooted winter snowmobile trips. The very taxing five-day **Greenland Adventure Race** (www.gar.gl; ☺ late Aug) is an 'Ironman' competition, where entrants run, cycle and kayak a punishing loop via Narsaq and Qaqortoq.

Tours

Blue Ice (☎ 497 371; www.blueice.gl; Blue Ice Café; ☺ summer) is the mini-empire of multilingual

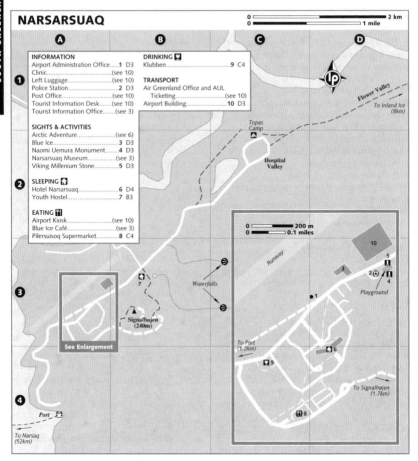

NARSARSUAQ

0 — 2 km
0 — 1 mile

INFORMATION
Airport Administration Office.....**1** D3
Clinic.................................(see 10)
Left Luggage......................(see 10)
Police Station.........................**2** D3
Post Office..........................(see 10)
Tourist Information Desk........(see 10)
Tourist Information Office.......(see 3)

SIGHTS & ACTIVITIES
Arctic Adventure.....................(see 6)
Blue Ice...................................**3** D3
Naomi Uemura Monument.......**4** D3
Narsarsuaq Museum...............(see 3)
Viking Millennium Stone.........**5** D3

SLEEPING 🛏
Hotel Narsarsuaq.....................**6** D4
Youth Hostel............................**7** B3

EATING 🍴
Airport Kiosk..........................(see 10)
Blue Ice Café.........................(see 3)
Pilersuisoq Supermarket..........**8** C4

DRINKING 🍷
Klubben.................................**9** C4

TRANSPORT
Air Greenland Office and AUL
  Ticketing..........................(see 10)
Airport Building....................**10** D3

Flower Valley
To Inland Ice (8km)

Topas Camp

Hospital Valley

0 — 200 m
0 — 0.1 miles

Runway

Waterfalls

Signalhøjen (240m)

See Enlargement

10
5
3
2
4
1
Playground

To Port (1.2km)

9

6

To Signalhøjen (1.7km)

8

Port

To Narsaq (52km)

Jacky Simoud, and offers almost every service visitors might need including tours, transfers, the info-office café and youth hostel. Nowhere in the south is better organised to deal with independent travellers looking for summer-excursion ideas, and there's a fairly good chance of finding enough fellow travellers to ensure that a trip's minimum quota is attained. If you email your reservation several months ahead you might be able to get a guaranteed departure date for the excursion of your choice. For Qassiarsuk, transfers (Dkr120) and tours (Dkr450) run almost daily; tours to Qooroq Icefjord (Dkr450) and Igaliku (Dkr900) run a couple of times most weeks, but the brilliant helicopter trips to the icecap and Mellemlandet

(Dkr1600) rarely reach the (varying) minimum passenger quota.

Arctic Adventure (☎ 665 240; www.arctic-adventure
.dk; Hotel Narsarsuaq Lobby ⏰ 7-7.30pm) runs various guided day trips, designed mainly for booked clients. It often works jointly with Blue Ice.

Sleeping

There are two places to stay. Should both be full you may have to resort to camping, so book ahead.

Youth Hostel (☎ 665 221; www.blueice.gl/hostel
.htm; PO Box 58; adult/child Dkr200/100; ⏰ Jun–mid-Sep) This neat single-storey building sits all alone about 600m north of the airport, backed by a small mountain attractively ribboned with waterfalls. Dorms and showers are clean and

very well kept. The big sitting and dining room has a library of interesting books and is one of the best places in Greenland to meet fellow travellers; both they and the staff here are a great source of hiking and travel information. There's a well-equipped kitchen, and laundry facilities are available (Dkr30 per load). Accommodation prices assume that you'll bring your own sleeping bag, but you can hire one for Dkr50 per night. To camp in the yard costs Dkr100 per person including hostel facilities, but the ground is rock hard. From mid-September to May the hostel might open by arrangement for groups. At any time booking well ahead is strongly recommended. Nonguests may use the showers or the kitchen for Dkr30 each.

Hotel Narsarsuaq (☎ 665 253; www.glv.gl/hoteller /default.asp; PO Box 504; dm Dkr265, s/d Dkr995/1195, with private bath Dkr645/795) Built originally for those in transit through the airport, this functional hotel feels rather like a retirement home. The downstairs rooms with en suite are comfortable and recently renovated. Pairs of cheaper rooms share a bathroom and are a little more tatty, with curiously acrid dry air. Prices include breakfast. The dorms are not worth bothering with unless the youth hostel is full or closed.

Wild camping is possible in Hospital Valley, though the nicest area is taken up by an organised Topas/Blue Ice tour camp, complete with wigwam-style meeting tent. More appealing camping places are found further towards the inland ice.

Eating

Hotel Narsarsuaq (mains Dkr185; ☼ 6-9.30pm) Upstairs is this semi-smart dining room with candles but rucked carpets. Its small selection of international dishes includes salmon with shellfish and chive hollandaise sauce. On Friday nights try the special Greenlandic fish platter. Whatever the official closing time you'd be wise to arrive before 7.30pm. The unpretentious ground-floor **cafeteria** (mains Dkr50-129; ☼ 6.30am-7.45pm) has school-style meals, but the Dkr60 set dinner is relatively generous.

Blue Ice Café (☼ 9am-6pm 15 Jun–15 Sep) While this is predominantly an information office, there's ice cream and coffee (from a machine) that you can consume at leisure while reading the books. When weather and mosquitoes oblige there's a sunny patio outside beside the airport's boundary fence.

When flights are expected, a counter in the airport's waiting lounge serves hot dogs (Dkr17 to Dkr20), open sandwiches (Dkr16) and apples (Dkr4). The central **Pilersuisoq supermarket** (☼ 10am-5.30pm Mon-Fri, 10am-1pm Sat) has a typical selection of produce, clothing and ammunition.

Drinking

The town's only **bar** (Hotel Narsarsuaq upstairs; beers Dkr39; ☼ 7pm-midnight Sat-Thu, 7pm-1am Fri) is dull and uninspiring, with sparse wooden tables and a dartboard. On Thursday to Saturday before 10pm, happy-hour beers cost Dkr27. Klubben (the Club), not far from the supermarket, has a very local get-together party roughly every second Saturday in summer.

Getting There & Away
AIR

Weather permitting, **Air Greenland** (☎ 665 288; Narsarsuaq Airport; www.airgreenland.com; ☼ 7am-3pm Mon-Fri) has flights from Copenhagen (Dkr2813, 4½ hours) at least once a week, three times weekly in summer. Flights between Narsarsuaq and Kangerlussuaq (Dkr3398, two hours) are sometimes laid on if Narsarsuaq's Copenhagen service is not operating. From June to early September **Air Iceland** (☎ 354-570 3030; www.airiceland.is) flies in twice a week from Reykjavík (not Keflavik) for around US$400 (€340; half price if booked well ahead). The latter flight uses an **Atlantic Airlines** (www.atlantic .fo) aeroplane continuing from the Faroe Islands, but you'd have to buy two separate tickets to make a through trip.

Almost all domestic flights run on Monday, Wednesday and/or Friday, including shuttle flights to Nuuk (Dkr2408, 1½ hours) by Dash-7 aircraft, and helicopter hops to Narsaq (Dkr612, 15 minutes) and Qaqortoq (Dkr847, 20 minutes). Helicopters to Nanortalik (Dkr1392) fly direct on Friday mornings, but via Narsaq, Qaqortoq and Alluitsup Paa for the same price on Wednesday, giving you lots of fabulous extra views for the money. On Monday and Wednesday helicopters serve Kangilinnguit/Grønnedal (Dkr1892, 50 minutes) and Paamiut (Dkr3252, 1¾ hours), returning the same day.

Be aware that all timetables change very frequently according to politics, weather and demand. KNR-TV teletext page 400 has the day's departure details.

BOAT

AUL tickets are available through **Air Greenland** (☎ 665 288; Narsarsuaq Airport; ☑ 7am-3pm Mon-Fri), which charges an outrageous Dkr75 ticketing fee. Tickets bought onboard only incur a Dkr50 surcharge, but as ferries are often full in summer most travellers grudgingly stump up the extra to book ahead.

From May to November the *Najaaraq Ittuk* runs between Narsarsuaq and Qaqortoq (Dkr215 to Dkr265, 4½ hours) twice weekly via Qassiarsuk (Dkr150 to Dkr185), Itilleq (Dkr150 to Dkr185) and Narsaq (Dkr150 to Dkr185). In summer it usually makes more sense to use a Blue Ice boat transfer to reach Qassiarsuk (Dkr200) and Itilleq (Dkr250).

From mid-June to August the coastal ferry *Sarfaq Ittuk* extends its route to Narsarsuaq, allowing weekly connections to Ilulissat (couchette/two-bed cabin Dkr3080/5115, 77 hours) via Aasiaat (Dkr2845/4750, 72 hours), Sisimiut (Dkr2395/3940, 59 hours), Kangaamiut (Dkr2125/3470, 52 hours), Maniitsoq (Dkr1995/3250, 48 hours), Nuuk (Dkr1700/2580, 37 hours), Paamiut (Dkr1045/1615, 23 hours) and Arsuk (Dkr840/1245, 15 hours).

From December to April you'll have to go by plane.

Getting Around

Free shuttles meet booked hostel or hotel guests from incoming flights and ferries. Hospital Valley is only about 40 minutes on foot, but hotel guests are given a free ride on request; hostel guests pay Dkr15. In either case, book some hours ahead. The Blue Ice Café hires mountain bikes (Dkr30/75/100 per hour/half-day/day), though they are of minimal use as the nicest routes (beyond Hospital Valley) are not really suitable for cycling. Blue Ice also hires single/double sea kayaks to experienced paddlers from Dkr400/500 per day or Dkr2000/2500 per week.

AROUND NARSARSUAQ
Towards the Inland Ice

By far the most popular day hike from Narsarsuaq starts from the asphalt loop of Hospital Valley. An obvious gravel track leads up into pretty **Flower Valley** (Narsarsuaq Valley) then descends more steeply through unusually tall bushes towards a wide, flat hayfield ringed by rocky cliffs. Cross a plank bridge, then follow the stream's west bank, passing an impressive three-strand cascade that pours off the Mellemlandet massif. The hayfield soon gives way to moraine. Jump the outflow of a pond where the path almost meets the main river. Thereafter wind over a rocky headland, curving around until you meet a straggly waterfall.

Up to this point the walking is easy and the views delightfully varied. Beyond, the milky-blue river curves away through a chasm that's impossible to walk through. To continue towards the inland ice you'll need to be fit and reasonably confident, as immediately after the waterfall you have to climb straight up beside it. The path is fairly obvious when you look for it and has thick blue nylon ropes to help you pull yourself up. However, in wet conditions it can be scary. Some older tourists reckon it's too much for them and criticise agencies that sell the walk as a guided excursion without suitable warnings.

After gaining around 300m altitude, you arrive on the stark but lovely pond-dappled **Iceview Plateau**. A prehistoric-looking lake is flanked by tundra and glacier-scraped boulders. Various viewpoints look down onto the grey-white crocodile skin of the inland ice. Except for all the flies, it's delightful (bring a head-net). To walk on the ice you'll need to descend again on a steep but fairly straightforward path from Iceview Plateau. It's traditional to bring a hip-flask of whisky to drink a hikers' toast chilled by 10,000-year-old ice cubes that you chisel off. This isn't quite as easy as it sounds, as much of the ice here is black with glacial debris.

The walk from Narsarsuaq to Iceview Plateau and back typically takes between five and six hours. To reach the ice face, add around 1½ hours down and back. Getting a ride to Hospital Valley saves you over half an hour each way. Guided hikes (Dkr400 with packed lunch) are available, but the route is pretty easy to follow without such help.

Qooroq Icefjord

Some 200,000 tons of ice a day calve off the spectacular face of Qoorqut Sermiat (also called Qooqqup Sermia) glacier into berg-choked Qooroq Icefjord. You will catch a glimpse of the fjord's mouth from any boat to Itilleq, Narsaq or Qaqortoq. To weave between the bergs towards the ice face, join Blue Ice's popular icefjord boat trips (Dkr450, three hours). These usually run twice weekly in summer. The money is well worth it if you

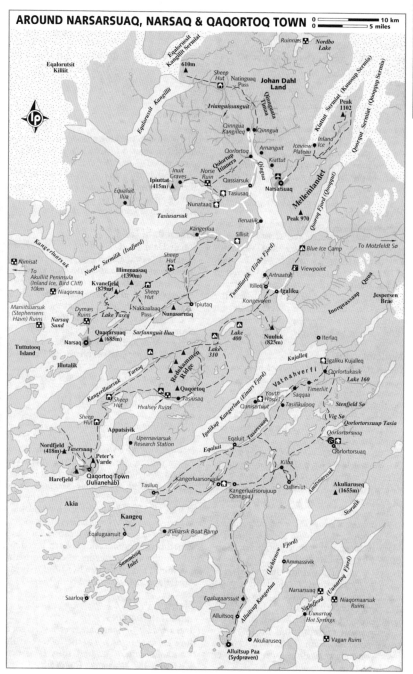

AROUND NARSARSUAQ, NARSAQ & QAQORTOQ TOWN

0 — 10 km
0 — 5 miles

can get deep into the fjord. However, after prolonged southwesterly winds the surface ice can get so densely packed that boats won't get far at all. Ask carefully about conditions before you book.

To see the ice face from above you could hike strenuously across Mellemlandet (see below). Alternatively, you could take a helicopter excursion from Narsarsuaq. In perfect visibility these are well worth the hefty Dkr1600 cost, but flights are often cancelled due to bad weather or lack of customers.

Blue Ice Camp is an idyllic camping spot overlooking the fjord's mouth near Itilleq (see p107).

Motzfeldt Sø

East of Qooroq Icefjord, a wide, incredibly barren valley of ferric-red scree leads to a large, elbow-shaped lake called Motzfeldt Sø. It's constricted by towering 1600m-high sides, though the total lack of vegetation makes the scale difficult to grasp. Lifeless and bare except for its two gently calving glaciers, its atmosphere is otherworldly and forbidding. It's very tough to reach or explore except by helicopter fly-through.

Mellemlandet

Mellemlandet is a huge slab of bog-pocked uplands paralleling the Narsarsuaq Valley. Its central ridge rises to over 1100m towards the northern tip. Further south there are quite fabulous 360 degree views from **Peak 970**, east of Narsarsuaq. With perfect weather, Qooroq-bound helicopter excursions land here for a few photogenic minutes. Walking up from Narsarsuaq, however, is considerably tougher than one might expect. It's quite easy to get disorientated, and sudden white-outs could prove perilous as there are various small cliff ledges to avoid.

A somewhat easier Mellemlandet alternative is to hike directly up from the Iceview Plateau. Most of the route is jolly bog-hopping with occasional hidden streams to jump. However, to enjoy the prized view down to the Qoorqut Sermiat ice face you'll need to cross the large stream between lakes 475 and 505. Hiking maps show a path going straight across. However, its uneven sides mean that jumping this stream is only really possible in one direction. Coming back, you may struggle and get rather wet; it's dangerous if you slip.

If you're equipped to camp at least one night you could walk north right along the ridge to see the forking of two glaciers from Peak 1102. Super views are somewhat spoilt by abominable clouds of flies and mosquitoes in the warm months (until the first frosts of late August).

Qinngua

pop 4

Maps and old trekking guides suggest hiking from Narsarsuaq to Qassiarsuk via a sheep farm called Qinngua. It's poor advice. The route is relatively dull by regional standards, the hikers' hut at Qinngua is now a private house, and you'll need tractor rides to cross rivers both at Qinngua and near Narsarsuaq.

Johan Dahl Land

Johan Dahl Land is a huge, rugged massif north of Narsarsuaq. Empty and extremely harsh even for very experienced hikers, it still somehow attracts a trickle of hard-core masochists seeking utter isolation. Most hikers who've walked here admit that the relatively underwhelming views don't often justify the effort and danger. One possible exception is a viewpoint high above Ruinnæs ruin site overlooking **Nordbo lake** and glacier. Descending Qinnguata Timaa to Qinngua is every bit as terrifying as the map would suggest.

QASSIARSUK (BRATTAHLÍÐ)

pop 60

Just 15 minutes by boat from Narsarsuaq, Qassiarsuk is a prettily situated fjordside village offering lovely, easy walks, a wealth of Norse ruins and a unique reconstruction of a Norse longhouse. Except perhaps in Narsaq (see p109), it's widely accepted to be the site of Brattahlíð, the place Erik the Red (Eiríkur Rauðe) chose for his farmstead, having scouted much of South Greenland in 982. Today's village dates from a successful 1920s experiment to reintroduce sheep-breeding. Most inhabitants are descended from the founding Frederiksen family, who also spread operations to Tasiusaq and Nunataaq.

Sights

BRATTAHLÍÐ RUINS

It takes a lot of imagination or a very good tour guide to bring life to the 1000-year-old Brattahlíð ruins. The best story is associated with the **Þjóðhildur's Church Site**, a tiny,

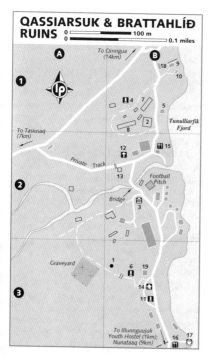

QASSIARSUK & BRATTAHLÍÐ RUINS

0 — 100 m
0 — 0.1 miles

easy-to-miss squared horseshoe of slightly raised turf. Archaeologists believe that the first Christian church in the New World was built here in summer AD 1000. It's named for the Erik the Red's wife, who was a zealous convert to Christianity. When Þjóðhildur's heathen hubby remained obstinately unstirred by her faith, she tried to convert him by less subtle means – refusing sex until he got himself baptised. Erik never relented. However he compromised somewhat by permitting her to build a church, provided it was out of sight of his farm.

The church moved and was enlarged several times. The most obvious **Norse ruin** (still only two stones high) is thought to have been the fourth church site, probably dating from around AD 1300. Other ruins represent foundations of a **manor house** (purportedly on the site of Erik and Þjóðhildur's pad), along with several indistinct cattle and sheep byres, dykes and ditches.

RECONSTRUCTIONS

A highlight of Qassiarsuk is the turf-covered **reconstructed longhouse** built and furnished to

a 10th-century Viking design. Norse sleeping arrangements were fascinating. The master and his wife got a special closeable sleeping box. (Þjóðhildur locked Erik out of his while waiting for her church.) Young girls safeguarded their virginity by sleeping on a separate upper storey. Everyone else dossed down communally, but overlord and slave classes would sleep on opposite sides, with the former enjoying the luxury of walls insulated by wood. Driftwood timber was a great luxury too good to burn, so day-to-day fuel was a dried mix of straw and cow-pats. Feeble lighting was provided by seal-blubber lamps, which can't have smelt great. A stream would probably have flowed beneath the house, forming a self-flushing privy. Notice how little storage space there is – people had virtually no private possessions.

A simple 2.5m by 4m rectangular building within an enclosure is a **reconstruction of Þjóðhildur's Church**. The altar-cloth was made from local wool using the loom displayed in the longhouse. The lovely driftwood cross above is by celebrated artist Aka Høegh.

An **Inuit turf hut** has been reconstructed fairly authentically from an 1870s design. It's accurate except for the door, which is an anachronism to allow easy tourist access. Originally, residents would have entered by crawling along the long snout of tunnel so that the hut could stay warm using only seal-blubber lamps and the body heat of some 15 souls squeezed in together.

A look inside the reconstructed buildings costs Dkr40. When there's no tourist group around you'll need to get the key from **Birgit** (☎ 243116; B1002), who lives in the small red house above. Birgit speaks English.

OTHER SIGHTS

Standing proud on a small hill above the Old Youth Hostel is a 3m tall, firm-jawed Viking figure armed with axe, sword and cross. This fine bronze represents **Leif Eriksson** (Erik the Red's son), credited as the first 'European' to have set foot on American soil, in 1000AD. It was erected on that event's millennium in July 2000 at a great celebration attended by Denmark's Queen Margrethe. The statue is actually a recast of a 1962 original made by August Werner for the Seattle World's Fair.

West of the statue are the graveyard, a rock-top cross and an abandoned **antique tractor**. Near the bridge, the **Frederiksen Plaque** commemorates Otto Frederiksen, the sheep breeder who refounded Qassiarsuk on 30 July 1924. That day remains a village festival celebrated in Frederiksen's original, tumble-down pioneer cottage, which stands behind the plaque. White with green trim, it also houses a cutely minimalist **museum** of shepherding life. It's usually left unlocked, even when nobody's there.

The current 1936 **village church** has a one-bell campanile and an attractively decorated interior. When it's locked, the key is available from the **Kommunia** (☎ 665026; B918; ⏲ 8.30am-4pm Mon, 8am-4pm Tue, 8am-2pm Fri). Church paintings are by Hans Lynge, who also made the modest 1982 **Viking Millennium monument** that stands near the Old Youth Hostel.

The 1970 **Havsteen-Mikkelsen Sculpture** is a collection of stylised bronze shapes bolted to a rocky bluff. Erik and Þjóðhildur cuddle beneath astral and religious symbols. A dragon-head Viking boat prow rises towards a dangle-hatted 14th-century horseman. To the right, abstract squares represent the village ruins beneath an eagle symbolising death.

Sleeping & Eating

There are two hostels, both with communal kitchens.

Illunniguujuk Youth Hostel (☎ 665093, mobile 497 185; ekcf@greennet.gl; dm without/with sheets Dkr195/295)

This welcoming house is 1km south of the dock. There's no sign, but it's within the last farm compound, entered where the tractor road turns inland for Nunataaq. Beds are in small, cosy rooms, and there's an indoor toilet, but the shower is hidden away in a basement. Fjord views are especially lovely at sunset from the rather cramped room No 2. At the time of research, extra bedrooms were being added in the cellar of an adjacent building.

Old Youth Hostel (☎ /fax 665010; dm Dkr165) Now Spanish run, this unmarked faded yellow building has basic cell-like rooms. However, it's wonderfully central, handy for the dock and a great place to meet fellow hikers. There are kayaks and mountain bikes to rent, and outside there's good grass for **camping** (Dkr70 incl use of hostel facilities).

Quiet, appealing wild camping opportunities are available about 2km out of the village towards Nunataaq.

Brattahlíð Café serves coffee (Dkr10), hot dogs (Dkr20) and ice creams (Dkr15 to Dkr20), but only opens sporadically when there are enough tourists around. **Pilersuisoq** (⏲ 9am-4pm Mon-Fri, 9am-1pm Sat, 11am-1pm Sun) is the grocery shop beside the dock.

Getting There & Away

Blue Ice boat transfers to or from Narsarsuaq cost Dkr120 per person either way, which is cheaper than AUL ferries. With some bargaining, Qassiarsuk fishermen might run you across for a similar price. Arctic Adventure's guided tour is more extensive but much more pricey. As long as passengers have booked, the AUL ferry *Najaaraq Ittuk* stops by twice weekly (May to November) heading for Qaqortoq (Dkr245, four hours) via Narsaq (Dkr150 to Dkr185) and Itilleq (Dkr150 to Dkr185). By arrangement Blue Ice Itilleq–Narsarsuaq transfers can drop off or pick up passengers in Qassiarsuk (Dkr250 per person). For the classic trek to Narsaq, see p113.

AROUND QASSIARSUK
Tasiusaq & Nunataaq
pop 10 & 5

Hiking from Qassiarsuk to either of these two little sheep stations is joyously easy, as each is on an attractive but well-worn tractor road. The approach to three-house Nunataaq is longer but more beautiful. Tasiusaq has a more open aspect and offers more exploration potential. Completing a delightful loop, the unmarked path between the two is fairly easy by Greenland standards and offers absolutely delightful views over the ice-dotted Tasiusaq inlet.

From Tasiusaq it's about an hour's hike north to the **Qorlortup Itinnera river**, which has there are nice fishing and camping possibilities. A small bridge gets you across to a metre-high **Norse ruin** first excavated in 1838. It's reasonably straightforward to continue around Tasiusaq Bay towards **Ipiuttat**, a 415m knob of peninsula with some Inuit graves. A few minutes before reaching the graves you could instead branch right and climb a saddle to the northwest. This path isn't obvious, but with the 1:100,000 hiking map it's easy to guess an approximate route. As you emerge on the far side there are memorable views across a berg-encrusted fjord towards the inner ice prongs of Eqalorutsit Killiit glacier.

SLEEPING
Both hamlets have hostels. Both are family homes, but neither is permanently occupied and in summer hiking tour groups sometimes book both places – thus booking ahead is strongly advised. Ask a local to help you call via radio-phone Qaqortoq ☎ 131.

Nunataaq Youth Hostel (☎ Nunataaq 43; house 814B; adult/child Dkr165/82.50) Now painted bright blue, this is a sweet family cottage with 12 beds, an indoor toilet, kitchen and shower booth. The wooden balcony offers distant glacier views somewhat diminished by tractors and a fuel hut in the foreground. The cutely old-fashioned sitting room even has a harmonium.

Tasiusaq Youth Hostel (☎ Tasiusaq 18; adult/child Dkr180/90; ☺ Jun-Sep) Variable dorm rooms and one pleasant double share a kitchen and ecofriendly solar-powered shower. The toilet is accessed from outside via the balcony. In winter, while the owners hibernate in Narsaq, they take bookings (in Danish) on ☎ 497775 or jfoutfitter@greennet.gl.

GETTING THERE & AWAY
The full 22km loop from Qassiarsuk and back is easily walked in a day, but it's well worth staying at one of the farm hostels and exploring further. Qassiarsuk to Tasiusaq (7km) is less than two hours' walk. A much longer alternative way to hike back from Tasiusaq

is to follow the Qorlortup Itinnera river up and descend to the Narsarsuaq fjord near Qorlortoq. There's a nice waterfall en route and an easy track on the final section.

With notice, the youth hostels can generally arrange a 4WD transfer to or from Qassiarsuk for around Dkr250 per car. The tracks are possible by mountain bike, but the Tasiusaq–Nunataaq path isn't. The longer, steeper track to Nunataaq (10km) is the more attractive.

IGALIKU & ITILLEQ
This port-and-village combination makes a great day trip from Narsarsuaq, a launching point for hikes or simply a nice area to unwind.

Itilleq
pop 16
Gateway to Igaliku, tiny Itilleq ('The Crossing Place' or 'isthmus') is not a village but a very diffuse collection of relatively luxuriant hayfields and scattered sheep farms. A lonely green hut north of Itilleq's cove beach is the waiting room for AUL boats. These stop between Narsaq and Qassiarsuk/Narsarsuaq twice weekly in either direction, from May to November only. Blue Ice offers boat transfers (Dkr250) to Itilleq from Narsarsuaq, though a minimum of eight passengers is usually required. The misleadingly regal name for the 3km gravel road to Igaliku is Kongvegen ('King's Way'), which dates from the 1921 visit of Danish monarch Christian X. Blue Ice has a beautifully situated **Blue Ice camp** at Narsarsuk, about 6km northeast of Itilleq with views of Qooroq Icefjord. However, access is easier by boat (Dkr250 from Narsarsuaq) or on foot from Igaliku.

Igaliku (Igaliko)
pop 60
In Igaliku, Greenland really does appear idyllically green. Cottages are scattered about the base of a grassy amphitheatre on a hypnotically calm bay. Icebergs are rare here, but the milky-blue waters are surreally beautiful, trimmed by a horizon of mountains that remain snow-dappled throughout summer. Artists and Home Rule ministers alike have summer houses here. Even US Secretary of State Colin Powell (as he then was) dropped by in 2004, though not to pick

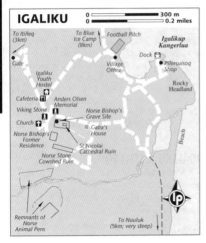

IGALIKU

0 — 300 m
0 — 0.2 miles

the plentiful summer flowers (see the boxed text, p200). Igaliku is most famous for the ruins of Garðar, once the religious heart of 12th-century Norse Greenland. But it's the soothing setting and lilting bucolic charm that you're more likely to remember.

RUINS

Norse ruins dot the village. Sites of old stone enclosures and ancient irrigation dykes are meticulously marked on the Garðar archaeological plan, which is inset on the *Eastern Settlement* tourist map. However, in reality only three building foundations are easily discernible in the long grass. A guided tour (offered from Narsarsuaq by both Blue Ice and Arctic Adventure) might help fire your imagination.

In 1124 Greenland became its own bishopric. Within the two years it took for the first bishop to arrive from Scandinavia, the colonists had erected **St Nicolai Cathedral** for him in Garðar (Igaliku). By Norse Greenlandic standards it was elaborate. Windows used rough glass rather than stretched animal stomachs, the interior was decorated with soapstone carvings and a large bell called the faithful to worship.

Don't expect to see any of this. For centuries the building was gradually dismantled, the dressed stones being used for more practical purposes in homes and sheds. Today all that remains are a few hewn boulders in the buttercups, piled up at one point to give the impression of a doorway.

Beneath the cathedral site archaeologists have found 25 walrus and five narwhal skulls, which may have been charms held over from pre-Christian times. In 1926 a remarkable grave was excavated beside the ruins. For decades it was thought to be that of Garðar's third bishop, Jan Smyrill (though this is now disputed). The skeleton was adorned with a fine episcopal ring and held a walrus-tusk crosier. A missing foot and sheered-off cranium led conspiracy theorists to smell murder. Archaeologists suspect careless gravediggers.

Directly southwest of the cathedral's perimeter, the **bishop's former residence** is now little more than a rhubarb patch. South of this is a long former **stone cowshed** with relatively well-preserved walls and an intact rock-lintel doorway. The cathedral needed plenty of barns: Norse colonists paid ever heavier tithes, taxes and fines to the bishop, who merrily confiscated fields and received bequests until the church became Greenland's main landowner.

OTHER SIGHTS

Close to the main ruins are two memorials: a recently sculpted **Viking Stone** and a plaque to **Anders Olsen**, the Norwegian colonist who founded modern Igaliku in 1783. The squat modern **church** is made of typical Igaliku sandstone, which has a distinctive mottled-pink surface that looks almost edible.

It's pleasant to stroll the rocky headland near the Pilersuisoq shop or hop across the minuscule stream to stare at the mesmerising water from the grey-pebble beach. With vastly more energy, hikers could fight their way up the steep northwest ridge of **Nuuluk** to its lumpsome 823m summit. For the less masochistic, however, the views are perfectly lovely if you just stroll for 10 minutes up the pass along the Kongevejen road towards Itilleq.

SLEEPING & EATING

Igaliku Youth Hostel (☎ 642510; fax 666151; house 971B; dm adult/child Dkr175/90, with sheets Dkr350/175) Neat bunks share a sparkling indoor bathroom and a sitting room that doubles as an acupuncture studio. Attached is the town's pleasant, peach-walled **cafeteria** (lunch Dkr115, dinner Dkr150; ☺ 8am-10pm), where meals are only available if you order a few hours ahead. Pancakes and beer (Dkr35) are quicker.

CLASSIC TREKS 1: IGALIKU–QAQORTOQ

South Greenland is relatively popular for multiday camping hikes, though even along the three most celebrated routes (see the two other Classic Treks boxed texts, p113 and p125) you'll only see a handful of hikers at any one time and there are virtually no way-markers. Good maps are essential.

The Igaliku–Qaqortoq hike takes four to seven days (five is usual). It offers a great wilderness experience and an attractive palate of views, it links two readily accessible settlements, and there's the added thrill of stumbling across Norse ruins at Hvalsey (p120). However, the section between Hvalsey and Qaqortoq is less appealing. It's an awkward and rather tiresome slog that you'd be best to skip. This is easily achieved heading towards Igaliku by joining the Qaqortoq tourist office's Hvalsey-bound boat tour (one-way tickets are available for hikers). The boat ride saves you a day and a half and means you'll only need to buy one map (the 1:100,000 *Narsaq Hiking Map*).

Groceries are sold at **Pilersuisoq** (☎ 666144; ⏰ 10am-4pm Mon-Fri, 10am-1pm Sat, 1-3pm Sun), beside the jetty. The annual village festival on 31 July is joyously alcoholic.

GETTING THERE & AWAY

On a few winter loops, AUL ferries from Qaqortoq call at Igaliku. However, in summer boat access is via Itilleq (p107), from which you need to walk 3km on a sloping but easygoing gravel road. The benches along the way have great views that provide a fine excuse for frequent rest stops. Hitchhiking with very occasional tractors or 4WD vehicles is possible for an agreed fare.

Local speedboat rides to Igaliku Kujalleq in Vatnahverfi (p125) can cost as little as Dkr100 per person, but Dkr250 to Dkr600 is more typical. Ask Gaba, the hostel owner.

NARSAQ

pop 1708

Narsaq's pretty cottages sprawl colourfully across grassy undulations beneath the abrupt twin peaks of Qaqqarsuaq and Tasiigaaq. Narsaq is one of the friendliest towns in Greenland, has a brilliant museum and offers plenty of undertapped tourist potential for hiking, kayaking or day-tripping by boat. The town also has several cottage industries.

History

The area is dotted with Norse ruins and, according to a controversial theory, Narsaq rather than Qassiarsuk is considered by some historians to be the site of Erik the Red's original Brattahlíð camp. The present settlement was founded in 1830 as Nordprøven, though it only gained town status in 1959. The shrimp-processing plant was originally opened in 1952 and partly supplied with labour by forcibly evacuating the village of Niaqornaq, on the northern shore of Nordre Sermilik Fjord. It now also doubles as a slaughterhouse for the region's sheep, which (while alive) do a miraculous job of keeping the area free of flies and mosquitoes. A local company collects icebergs to make designer ice cubes for export.

Information

Hospital (☎ 661211; Aaninnguit)

Laundry (Block E) In the pink-ended apartment block across from the hospital. Buy Dkr100 *Vaskekort* prepaid cards at Brugsen supermarket.

Police (☎ 661222; Niels Bohr's Plads)

Post office (☎ 661255; ⏰ 9am-3pm Mon-Fri) Has ATMs, changes money (cash only), sells Tusass SIM-cards, and is an agent for AUL ferry tickets.

Public library (Kong Frederik IXs vej; ⏰ 7-8pm Mon, 3-5.30pm & 7-8.30pm Tue & Thu, closed Jun & Jul) Internet access.

Tourist office (☎ 661325; www.2narsaq.gl; Sondervej B157; ⏰ 10am-4pm Mon-Fri, 10am-1pm summer weekends) Incredibly obliging staff give away town maps, sell regional maps and have a well-stocked gift shop with mini café. Internet planned. Offers some transfers and limited excursions and can make arrangements for special interests.

Sights

NARSAQ MUSEUM

The buildings of historic Nordprøven trading station now house the delightful, very visual **Narsaq Museum** (☎ 661659, mobile 497859; www.narsaq-museum.org; Kirkevej B84; adult/student/senior Dkr25/free/free; ⏰ 1-4pm Jun-Sep or by appointment).

Start your visit in the 1928 main building, marked A-34 on its roof for WWII identification. Here are various historical and cultural exhibits, a great little gift shop and, upstairs, a fine exhibition of traditional *qajaq*s (kayaks)

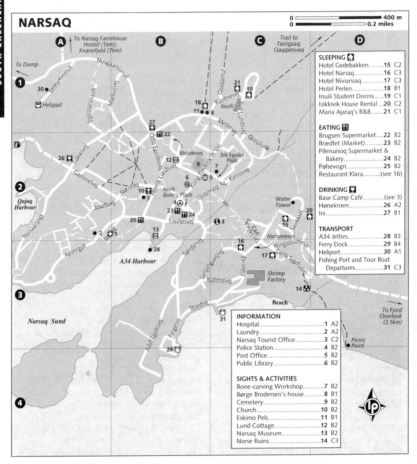

NARSAQ

and hunting techniques. When you've finished, museum staff can open up the various other houses. A former blubber store contains a geological collection. An 1830s house (Narsaq's oldest) has an interesting display of printing presses and etchings from *Sujumut*, once South Greenland's main newspaper, which was printed here. There's also recent work by local artists, talented and otherwise. Upstairs is a very sweet one-room recreation of a 1950s shop, displaying everything from aged tinned apricots to scythe handles to wooden hoops for the tops of *qajaqs*. In a similar vein, a neighbouring low-roofed house from 1908 has been furnished with 1950s utensils, pinups of Jesus and Marilyn Monroe, and a wood-and-sealskin bed.

The appealing **Lund Cottage** (Henrik Lundsvej) is only accessible if the main museum can spare the staff to walk across town and open it for you. Henrik Lund (1875–1948) was a priest, painter and poet whose song 'Nunarput' has since become Greenland's national anthem. Outside the red-and-green cottage, amid wildflowers, his bust sports a Lutheran priest's ruff, and his bronze lips have turned blue – from graffiti, not Arctic cold.

NORSE RUINS
Narsaq's most significant **Norse ruin** is the oldest in Greenland to have been positively carbon-dated to the 14th century. And as it was abandoned relatively early (rather than being continuously redeveloped, as at Qas-

siarsuk), the longhouse ruin has helped give archaeologists a better idea of how the early Norse lived. Some historians even suggest that this, not Qassiarsuk, was the original site of Erik the Red's Brattahlíð. The site itself is marked by a slightly raised turf rectangle amid the buttercups. To get there, descend past house B909 through a gap in the wire fence and follow red-painted stones.

More Norse sites lie beneath the town's **cemetery**. A visitor to the town in 1894 noted that much of early Narsaq had been constructed using stones from this site. A fireplace, cooking pot and several stone tools were uncovered by gravediggers in the 1990s, but the sensitive nature of the location prevents further excavation.

Viewpoints

Striking twin peaks Tasiigaaq and Qaqqarsuaq form Narsaq's dominant geographical feature. A punishingly steep path climbs to the 400m-high saddle between the two. A longer but gentler option is to climb **Tasiigaaq** (450m) from the north, starting near the Farmhouse Hostel. **Qaqqarsuaq** (685m) is a tougher proposition but gives fabulous fjord views towards the dramatic saw-toothed ridge of **Redekammen** (Killavaat, 'the Comb').

A34 harbour looks attractive from many angles. There are nice port views from the Hotel Niviarsiaq and from a rough picnic spot 10 minutes' walk south of the Norse ruins. **Qajaq Harbour** is loveliest at sunset. On moonless nights from early August, the aurora borealis (northern lights) can dance impressively: a suitably dark viewing point is down the unasphalted track behind the Hønekroen pub.

Other Sights

Narsaq has a relative wealth of craft industries. Most places allow you to wander in for free, though you may feel more comfortable and better informed visiting as part of a tourist office **town walking tour** (Dkr150; ☾ weekday afternoons), which also takes you to the museum and gets you inside the distinctive 1927 red-and-white timber **church** (☾ 9.30am Sun). A sporadically operating **bone-carving workshop** lurks in a scrappy low-rise hut west of the church. More interesting is **Eskimo Pels** (☎ 661001; www.eskimopels.gl; Mestervej; admission free; ☾ 8am-4pm Mon-Fri), a small factory where local women turn sealskins into designer bags and

---

> ### TUTTUPIT, BLOOD OF THE REINDEER
>
> A young Sami girl called Tuttu (meaning 'reindeer') found herself expecting an illegitimate child. Afraid to admit her pregnancy, she fled to the mountains to give birth secretly. There the blood of her placenta seeped into the ground, imbuing the rocks below with spiritual powers. This, according to Sami legend, is the origin of tuttupit (tugtupite, 'reindeer blood'), a rare soft mineral ($Na_4AlBeSi_4O_{12}Cl$) valued by certain New Age cultures. The most common form has garish pink and red flashes. However, the stone is at its most impressive under ultraviolet light, when it glows with magical fluorescent greens and reds. Apart from tiny finds at Mt St Hilaire (Canada), tuttupit is found only on the Kola Peninsula (Russia), where the legend evolved, and on the mountains behind Narsaq. There's no commercial mining, but walkers occasionally find samples on Kvanefjeld or near Lake Taseq. Vivid red examples make highly valuable gemstones.

---

clothes. There's a decent gift shop attached. Both the wool workshop and the excellent ceramics workshop are presently closed but might re-open.

Narsaq is especially famous for its unique minerals, notably the curious semiprecious pink Tuttupit (Tugtupite; see the boxed text above). The easiest way to see (and possibly buy) examples is to visit the impressive mineral collection of charming **Børge Brodersen** (☎ 661062, mobile 226932; www.narsaq.dk/bb; Mestervej B866; admission free). It's in his private house, but anyone can ring on the doorbell and ask to have a look. **Peter Lindberg** (☎ 661518, mobile 497152; www.grstones.com) also sells local gems, mainly via the Internet. Norwegian-born **Harry Andersen** (☎ 661149, mobile 227523) offers motorboat rides to **Crystal Cove** (Dkr250 per person, three hours return) to let enthusiasts chip at clear calcite from a fjord-facing cliff. You might try searching for your own Tuttupit on **Kvanefjeld** (see p114).

Sleeping
BUDGET

Maria Ajaraq's B&B (☎ 661168; Kantinevej B990; per person Dkr200) This cosy, very real home has three guest rooms and a commanding perched position near the Inuili culinary college. There's a good shared bathroom, and the breakfast is extensive. Maria speaks no English, so contact her taxi-driver daughter, Theodora (☎ 249694), who can collect you for free on arrival.

Isikkivik House Rental (☎ 662080; www.silamut .com; first day Dkr800, subsequent days Dkr400) Paul and Monica Cohen's tiny, super-cute cottage has a delightful picture window, a balcony and a multilingual bookshelf. Perched at the top of the village, you get wonderful views as far as the icecap. The bed is a very small double squeezed into a cupboard room – romantic or cramped? You decide. The little kitchen has running water, but there's no shower and the toilet is a Greenland-style bag-and-box affair.

Hotel Niviarsiaq (Gl Sygehusvej B503; dm without/ with sheets Dkr250/350) This house-hotel with a fairly well-equipped kitchen now hires out beds youth-hostel style. Two rooms plus the wide terrace have lovely views over the harbour area. Shower and toilet are communal, and there's a washing machine (Dkr20) and a TV/dining room. Arrange bookings and keys through Hotel Narsaq.

Narsaq Farmhouse Hostel (☎ 661049, 572073; helgioutfitter@greennet.gl; dm/d Dkr160/420; ⊙ May-Sep) Beautifully situated 2km northeast of the town centre on the Kvanefjeld track, this former mink farm faces a photogenic curve of bergy seascape. However, the interior is rather tatty and haphazardly laid out. There's a shower in between beds downstairs in the main building. Double rooms are in hut structures with box toilets and no running water. Fishing equipment and two bicycles (Dkr75 per day) are available for hire. You may camp outside and use the hostel facilities for Dkr100. It's beside the Kvanefjeld track. Turn off the asphalt, first right after the heliport.

There are some lovely wild camping spots around the bay beyond the Dyrnæs fence.

MID-RANGE
Hotel Narsaq (☎ 661290; hotelniv@greennet.gl; www .hotel-narsaq.com; Sarqanguaqvej B819; s Dkr800-950, tw Dkr1050-1150) The town has several little hotels, all run by 'Hotel Mama' Dorthe and family. The Hotel Narsaq has the newest, smartest rooms and acts as reception desk for the others. Cheaper rooms share good but communal showers and toilets.

Hotel Perlen (s/d/tr Dkr750/1150/1450) Bland but neat and tidy twins have TV and bathroom. The singles are a big step down: clean, but cramped like university cells with shower booth but shared toilets. Bathrobes and duvet are provided. There's a fair-sized, functional sitting/dining room and kitchen.

Hotel Gedebakken (tw Dkr1250) The hotel's one-room 'apartments' with mini-kitchenette are pleasant enough but very overpriced. Sheets are provided.

Inuili Student Dorms (s/d Dkr750/1150; ⊙ Jul) Bathrooms are shared between pairs of hospital-style rooms. You could rent both for Dkr1600, but that's still overpriced. At the time of writing, management was due to change in 2005; details are available from the tourist office.

Eating
Restaurant Klara (☎ 497728; Hotel Narsaq, Sarqann-guaqvej B819; mains Dkr170-200; ⊙ 6-8.30pm) Comfortably smart yet reasonably cosy, Narsaq's only restaurant serves extremely generous snowcrab starters, succulent reindeer steaks and a small range of other wholesome, well-cooked local delicacies including minke whale and muskox. Book ahead.

Pølsevognen (Louisevej; snacks Dkr12-40; ⊙ 11am-6.30pm) This hot-dog wagon parked outside the Timimut Shop puts out plastic tables so you can eat your chips (small/big Dkr12/17) while overlooking A34 harbour.

If you don't want the seats, the same fast food is 30% cheaper from a stand in the **Pilersuisoq Bakery** (Niaqornarssangmut B842; ⊙ 7am-5pm Mon-Fri, 7am-1pm Sat, 8am-noon Sun), attached to the **Pilersuisoq supermarket** (Niels Bohr's Plads; ⊙ 9am-6pm Mon-Fri, 9am-1pm Sat, 10am-4pm Sun). **Brugsen supermarket** (Mestervej B1230; ⊙ 9am-6pm) is slightly better stocked.

Several kiosks open later, and there's a small **brædtet** (market; Niels Bohr's Plads; ⊙ Mon-Sat) for fresh fish, seal, whale meat and seasonal berries.

Drinking
Base Camp Café (☎ 661325; Sondervej B157; ⊙ 10am-4pm Mon-Fri, 10am-1pm summer weekends) This is simply the appealing, sunny terrace of the tourist office, where you can get a coffee (Dkr5), soft drink (Dkr15) or chocolate bar.

Hønekroen (☎ 661002; Tobiasvej; ⊙ 9pm-3am Thu-Sat) This converted chicken farm is now an extensive bar, billiard hall and dance joint with live music after midnight Friday and Saturday. Low ceilings, dim lights and occasional volleys of beer bottles give it a deliciously disreputable edge, but it's certainly the liveliest place in town. Beer prices rise progressively from Dkr25 to Dkr30 to Dkr35 according to the time.

Ini (☎ 661360; Kantinevej; beers Dkr25-30; ⊙ 9pm-1am Mon-Thu, 9pm-2am Fri-Sat) Fundamentally similar to Hønekroen, but quieter, slightly smaller and marginally less daunting to enter despite a total lack of signs.

Shopping

The craft workshops all sell their wares, as does the tourist office and the museum gift shop, which also has a very useful selection of books. The tourist office also stocks a few hiking maps.

Getting There & Away

AIR

At least once on Monday, Thursday and Friday and up to four times on Wednesday, **Air Greenland** (☎ 661488) choppers buzz across to Narsarsuaq (Dkr571, 15 minutes). On the same days there are hops to Qaqortoq either direct (Dkr351, 10 minutes) or via Narsarsuaq (Dkr533). The helicopter from Narsarsuaq to Grønnedal and Paamiut sometimes stops in Narsaq en route.

BOAT

The weekly Nuuk-bound coastal ferry *Sarfaq Ittuk* calls at Narsaq. Prices are slightly less than from Qaqortoq, with journey times 4½ hours longer from mid-June to August but 2½ hours shorter the rest of the year. Twice weekly the *Najaaraq Ittuk* runs to Qaqortoq (Dkr150 to Dkr185, 1½ hours). Between May and November it also links Narsaq to Itilleq, Qassiarsuk and Narsarsuaq (Dkr150 to Dkr185, 2¾ hours).

You can arrange various boat transfers and charters through **Harry Andersen** (☎ 661149, mobile 227523), who's a great English-speaking storyteller. For two to four people reckon on Dkr600 per person to Qassiarsuk and Itilleq, and Dkr650 to Hvalsey Ruins and Qaqortoq. With a group of eight you'll usually pay less per person by booking through **Blue Ice** (☎ 497 371; www.blueice.gl; Narsarsuaq), eg Dkr400 to Narsarsuaq or Qaqortoq.

To take things really slowly, practised paddlers should consider heading for Narsar-

---

CLASSIC TREKS 2: NARSAQ–QASSIARSUK

Of the three classic multiday hikes, Narsaq–Qassiarsuk has arguably the most dramatic scenery. It's typical to take four to five days, and there's a choice of routes. Use the Narsaq 1:100,000 scale map. By far the hardest part is a nerve-racking descent on lifeless red scree from Lake Taseq to a lovely camp site near Sarfannguit Ilua, though the views of Redekammen Ridge en route are a great reward. You can cut out this stage by taking a speedboat from Narsaq to the trout-rich lake at the head of Sarfannguit Ilua (around Dkr150 per person for a minimum of three people). From here, despite some annoying scrub, the path is pretty straightforward and becomes a decent tractor path near Sillisit, where there's a small **youth hostel** (☎ 131-Radio 'Sillisit 29').

---

suaq by sea kayak. This is usually easier than kayaking from Narsarsuaq, due to prevailing winds. Blue Ice and Narsaq tourist office cooperate, making one-way rentals possible.

Getting Around

The tourist office runs transfers towards Kvanefjeld (Dkr125) and to Dyrnæs (Dkr100) for a minimum of two passengers. Taxis cost Dkr16 per km in town. Drivers include **Theo** (☎ 496161), **Otto** (☎ 496449) and **Ole** (☎ 497600). Theo speaks English. Bicycles can be hired from **Helgi Jonasson** (☎ 572073; Farmhouse Hostel; per day Dkr75).

AROUND NARSAQ
Dyrnæs

North of Narsaq a grand, U-shaped valley opens up splendidly to the east. Meanwhile, icebergs crack and burst fitfully in a photo-perfect bay to the west. Near the head of the bay is the Norse site of **Dyrnæs**, 300m off the Kvanefjeld track where it turns inland just 20 minutes' walk beyond the Farmhouse Hostel. In the 11th century, Dyrnæs was the Eastern Settlement's richest homestead, as the wily landowner refused to pass on church tithes. He figured, correctly enough, that the pope would not find it economic to send agents all the way there to collect Peter's Pence. The Dyrnæs church foundations are now just a scattering of lichen-covered stones, but the setting is delightful. The homestead's little spring still flows, and several smaller ruins lie hidden in the grass awaiting archaeologists, who last visited in 1932. A very congenial walk continues around the headland on sheep-mown grass between great, sometimes spiky boulders west of the Dyrnæs site fence.

Kvanefjeld & Illimmaasaq

The splendid U-shaped valley behind Dyrnæs passes through the rich hayfields of a sheep farm (noisy dogs) with a decent gravel track rising inexorably towards the dark, glacier-braided peak of Illimmaasaq (1390m). This is flanked to the west by scenically unremarkable but geologically fascinating Kvanefjeld (879m). Together they form the heart of a massive volcanic structure. Instead of continuing its eruption cycle, it solidified slowly over millions of years, creating some 200 minerals, including uranium ores and the almost unique gemstone Tuttupit (see boxed text, p111). The track deteriorates some 7km from Narsaq (as far as a 4WD can go), then wiggles up hairpins to the concrete-sealed tunnel of a former uranium mine. This was used by eminent nuclear physicist Niels Bohr to supply his research laboratory, but fortunately it proved uneconomic to develop for commercial extraction. This didn't stop smugglers trying to waltz off with seven barrels of uranium ore in the mid-1980s. Fortunately, they were stopped by the police. The mine is now definitively closed, but you shouldn't drink the possibly radioactive water from the nearby stream.

Occasional red markings from here help you find the steep footpath up onto the top of Kvanefjeld. Even if you don't find any interesting gemstones, there are some spectacular views north onto berg-packed fjords and the distant inland ice.

Alternatively, veer east from the main Kvanefjeld track to the large 518m-high **Lake Taseq**, from which you could continue a multiday hike to Qassiarsuk via Sillisit (see boxed text, p113).

GETTING THERE & AWAY

If you want a head start, the tourist office will take you 7km towards Kvanefjeld for Dkr125 per person one way (minimum of two passengers). This makes for a much nicer day hike, and returning downhill you face the attractively ice-dotted bay all the way to Dyrnæs.

Fjord Trips

If you think global warming is just a theory, join one of the popular visits across Ikersuaq (Bredefjord) towards the **Akulliit Peninsula**. A nose of inland ice to its west still halfheartedly calves into the water, and boats drop you at a convenient jetty to let you touch the heavily fissured glacier. However, this ice face is only a shadow of its 1980s self, when it was reportedly over 100m tall and very active. The ice on the peninsula's eastern side is 'dead' – it no longer reaches the water. Nonetheless, the scene is more picturesque thanks to an almost sheer beige granite cliff with minimal ledges that offer nesting sites for thousands of Iceland gulls.

Some boat trips stop on the way back at Nimisat to see an **old Inuit settlement** that was only finally abandoned in the 1960s. Skulls are visible in the rough graves. There are more **Inuit ruins** at Maniitsuarsuk (Stephensens Havn), on mosquito-blighted Tuttutooq Island. House sites date from 1350 to 1800, giving archaeologists a vivid impression of Inuit house development across the centuries, though perhaps the greatest attraction for tourists is the lovely view of Narsaq's mountain backdrop on the return voyage.

A four-hour speedboat charter to see all of the above from Narsaq costs Dkr550 per person for two or more people. Tourist boats from both Narsaq and Qaqortoq do a similar trip for around Dkr800, but these move more slowly, which can get rather dull. The ride is pleasant enough and the icebergs attractive, but the fjord-sides are somewhat monotonous and nowhere near as scenic those around Nanortalik.

On a very calm day you could buzz out by speedboat from Narsaq to the much more active **Qalerallit glacier** for about Dkr1000 per person. The scenery en route is similar.

QAQORTOQ REGION

QAQORTOQ TOWN (JULIANEHÅB)
pop 3100

Pronouncing Qaqortoq is a conundrum for the tonsils. Don't attempt it with your mouth full. South Greenland's most populous town, this is an artistic and visually distinctive place. Behind a charming old town square, Qaqortoq's brightly coloured buildings huddle closely together, clinging to a rugged, steep-sided amphitheatre. This starkly rocky backdrop is an interesting contrast to the soft, open greenery of nearby Narsaq.

History

Founded by Norwegian trader Anders Olsen in 1775, Qaqortoq was originally named Julianehåb after Queen Juliane Marie of Denmark. Local fishermen started to thrive on the cod trade, especially after WWI. While most of the world was in depression in the 1930s, Qaqortoq was enjoying a remarkable boom. The town's loveliest buildings date from this era, as does the cute little fountain, which for years was the only one in Greenland. Qaqortoq also boasted Greenland's first piped water and its first bathhouse. Thanks to its having a venue (the town's 1937 village hall, still standing), it became something of a local cultural centre, too. It remains a centre for expressive innovation, most obvious through the wonderful Stone and Man sculptures, which have turned urban boulders into living art. Meanwhile, the cod have disappeared, but Qaqortoq survives economically as a regional service hub, and it has Greenland's only industrial tannery.

Information
BOOKSHOPS

The museum shop stocks a superb selection of tourist-oriented books. The upstairs section of Pisiffik supermarket sells postcards, CDs and just a few books in English.

EMERGENCIES
Hospital (☎ 642211; Maaliakasiup Av B909)
Police (☎ 642222; Torvet B134)

INTERNET ACCESS
Net Café Nanok (☎ 642121; per min/hr Dkr1/50; ☺ 3-10pm Mon-Fri, noon-11pm Sat, noon-10pm Sun) Two Internet terminals lurk behind the game computers in this easy-to-miss little dive behind the Nanoq Bar.

LAUNDRY
Laundry Errorsisarfik (Ground fl, Block J, JH Lytzensvej; ☺ 9am-7pm) Lurking in the second of four six-storey apartment blocks, the machines operate using washcards (minimum Dkr50) bought from the Brugseneeraq Minimarket.

MONEY
Grønlandsbanken (☺ 10am-3pm Mon-Fri) Changes cash/travellers cheques for commissions of Dkr30/75. ATMs operate 6am to 6pm.

POST
Post office (Anders Olsenvej B998; ☺ 9am-3pm Mon-Fri, payphone access 7am-7pm)

TOURIST INFORMATION
Tourist office (☎ 642444; www.qaq.gl; Torvevej B68; ☺ 10am-5pm Mon-Fri, 10am-1pm Sat-Sun) Books homestay B&Bs, college hostel beds and outlying farmhouse accommodation, and organises several tours and excursions. The sizeable gift shop sells hiking maps and souvenirs. Internet (per 30 minutes Dkr50) and good free town maps are available.

Sights & Activities
QAQORTOQ MUSEUM
Qaqortoq Museum (☎ 641080; geny@qaqortoq.gl; Torvevej B29; admission Dkr10; ☺ 10am-noon Mon-Fri & 1-4pm daily Jun-Sep) is housed in a tar-blackened 1804 building that was once the Julianehåb colony manager's house. Today its most unique features are right up on the top floor. Beautifully restored, with churchlike décor and curious 1930s swing-out sink stands, these were once the town's guestrooms. The red room was explorer Knud Rasmussen's base when he was preparing his later expeditions. The blue room hosted famous American aviator Charles Lindbergh when he was scouting sites for a Pan Am stopover airport. Seventy years later Qaqortoq's still dreaming of an airport.

The museum's ground-floor displays include local artefacts including an extraordinary gut anorak. Much of the space is used for a gallery of recent artwork that is possibly the best in Greenland. There's also a very tempting multilingual bookshop. There's a recreated turf house in the attractively overgrown garden (opened on request). Its interior is given a 'lived-in' feel with boots left to dry over a traditional blubber lamp.

TORVET & THE OLD TOWN
Tiny **Torvet** (the old town square) is a picture-book collection of sweet timber cottages around a famous if dinky little three-dolphin **fountain**. When there's enough wind to scatter the clouds of flies, benches here are a very popular place to meet or relax. It's especially cute at twilight, with candles glowing warmly

QAQORTOQ TOWN (JULIANEHÅB)

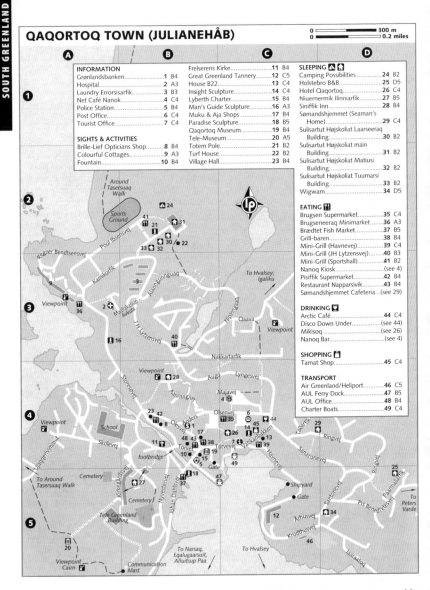

INFORMATION	
Grønlandsbanken	1 B4
Hospital	2 A3
Laundry Errorsisarfik	3 B3
Net Café Nanok	4 C4
Police Station	5 B4
Post Office	6 C4
Tourist Office	7 C4

SIGHTS & ACTIVITIES	
Brille-Lief Opticians Shop	8 B4
Colourful Cottages	9 A3
Fountain	10 B4

Frelserens Kirke	11 B4
Great Greenland Tannery	12 C5
House B22	13 C4
Insight Sculpture	14 C4
Lyberth Charter	15 B4
Man's Guide Sculpture	16 A3
Muku & Aja Shops	17 B4
Paradise Sculpture	18 B5
Qaqortoq Museum	19 B4
Tele-Museum	20 A5
Totem Pole	21 B2
Turf House	22 B2
Village Hall	23 B4

SLEEPING	
Camping Possibilities	24 B2
Holstebro B&B	25 C4
Hotel Qaqortoq	26 C4
Niuernermik Ilinniarfik	27 B5
Siniffik Inn	28 B4
Sømandshjemmet (Seaman's	
Home)	29 C4
Sulisartut Højskoliat Laarseeraq	
Building	30 B2
Sulisartut Højskoliat main	
Building	31 B2
Sulisartut Højskoliat Matiusi	
Building	32 B2
Sulisartut Højskoliat Tuumarsi	
Building	33 B2
Wigwam	34 D5

EATING	
Brugsen Supermarket	35 C4
Brugseneeraq Minimarket	36 A3
Brædtet Fish Market	37 B5
Grill-baren	38 B4
Mini-Grill (Havnevej)	39 C4
Mini-Grill (JH Lytzensvej)	40 B3
Mini-Grill (Sportshall)	41 B2
Nanoq Kiosk	(see 4)
Pisiffik Supermarket	42 B4
Restaurant Napparsivik	43 B4
Sømandshjemmet Cafeteria	(see 29)

DRINKING	
Arctic Café	44 C4
Disco Down Under	(see 44)
Mikisoq	(see 26)
Nanoq Bar	(see 4)

SHOPPING	
Tamat Shop	45 C4

TRANSPORT	
Air Greenland/Heliport	46 C5
AUL Ferry Dock	47 B5
AUL Office	48 B4
Charter Boats	49 C4

in the windows of Restaurant Napparsivik, a converted 1880 cooperage. Sadly overshadowed by the port chimney, the cute 1859 cottage housing **Lyberth Charter** (☎ 493352; Torvet B27) was the former Fortanderkabshuset (elders' council chamber). Red with green stairs, it retains the bronze 'colony bell' that once announced the start of work each morning. The

copper ship's lantern is a more recent addition, like the fake saloon doors. The present shop sells hunting and fishing equipment, offers boat charters, and displays a poster from the owner's days as a Danish guitar hero.

Set back a bit, **Muku & Aja Shops** (Olesvej B61) occupies an 1871 former blacksmith's workshop. It has wooden shingle roof, thick stone walls, arched windows and a small cannon aimed at the Torvet.

OTHER HISTORIC BUILDINGS

Beautiful **Frelserens Kirke** (Saviour's Church) was prefabricated in Norway in 1826, but the ship delivering it got wrecked at Frederikshåb (now Paamiut) and only in 1832 was the miraculously salvaged timber erected on its current site. A lifebelt displayed inside is the only piece ever found from the wrecked *Hans Hedtoft*, Greenland's *Titanic*, which sank on its maiden voyage in 1959. Former Home Rule Premier Jonathon Motzfeldt was once vicar in this church.

When climbing **Vatikanbakken** (Vatican Hill), notice the attractive timber **House B22** (Vatikanbakken B22). This was once home to a KGH trader who, legend relates, was something of a *bon-vivant* playboy. Indeed on occasions he was found to be 'as drunk as a pope', hence the ironic name for the road on which he lived.

West of the Pisiffik supermarket is the 1937 **village hall** (Qaqortup Katersertarfia; Storesøvej B100; ☾ sporadic) with its neoclassical interior, stage and upper balustrade. To the east, the sweet little **Brille-Lief Opticians Shop** (www.brille lief.gl; Storesøvej B26) is made of pink Igaliku sandstone and was originally built as Greenland's first public bathhouse (1931). It sells lovely postcards as well as spectacles.

STONE & MAN SCULPTURES

Ubiquitous local artist Aka Høegh had the superb idea of turning Qaqortoq's sometimes oppressive grey rock surfaces into a living sculpture gallery of curious faces, animals and abstracts. Several international artists have contributed since 1993, helping to keep ideas fresh. Many of the best are carved into the cliff that parallels Torvevej, notably behind the tourist office, where you'll find Aka Høegh's appealing **Insight** smiley faces. Beside the brædtet, Jun Ichi Inoue's **Paradise** is a disembodied stone breast which makes a curious foreground for colourful harbour photos. To find out what **Man's Guide** is, walk up Storesøvej beyond house B228. The Qaqortoq Museum shop sells a guide map (Dkr20) featuring all 31 works.

TELE-MUSEUM

On weekend afternoons it's well worth visiting the **Tele-Museum** (admission free; ☾ 1-4pm Sat & Sun). It traces Greenland's role in the development of transatlantic communications and has such mechanical curiosities as 1900 telephone switching table which, although already archaic in Denmark, was sent for use in Nuuk in the 1950s. Most interesting are the timelines, which put regional history in context decade by decade. Hosted in the 1925 building of a former radio station, the museum has splendid views across town from its minuscule café room. For Dkr10 per person (minimum of eight people) you can arrange a private viewing – ask at Qaqortoq Museum.

TANNERY

The **Great Greenland Tannery** (www.great-greenland .gl; tours Dkr50; ☾ 3.30pm Mon-Fri) prepares sealskins for export and turns some into designer fashion items. A surprisingly interesting one-hour tour (organised exclusively through the tourist office) explains all about the tanning processes. Whatever your emotional feelings about fur (and in Qaqortoq you'd best appear to approve), remember that the industry is a crucial economic lifeline for both Qaqortoq and rural Greenlanders. Traditionally, the skins are just a by-product of seals hunted for food. Whatever guides may tell you, that's not always the case nowadays, judging from trips the authors have made with Greenlandic hunters. But without the skin trade several small hunting villages would lose their distinctive Inuit way of life and might simply die out altogether.

VIEWPOINTS

Qaqortoq has many great and varied viewpoints. The port itself is very colourful. For a magnificent townscape there are two good perches off Qaava and wonderful panoramas from a **viewpoint cairn** near the communication tower. That hill was used for centuries to spot arriving supply boats, and graffiti around the cairn goes back to at least 1835. The balcony of the Siniffik Inn is great for lovely sunset views across Lake Tasersuaq. Alternatively, wander around the peninsula, where Regner Bendtsensvej ends in an unasphalted row of sweet, colourful cottages in great contrast to the ugly apartment blocks of Poul Ibsensvej.

For a superb view across the fjords to the rounded pyramid peaks east of Qaqortoq, walk a few minutes steeply uphill from the far end of Prs Benediktesvej. Pick a route between the highest houses and walk from cairn to cairn. The highest and most spectacular of these viewpoints is known as **Peters Varde**.

OTHER SIGHTS

The sizeable if somewhat austere **Lake Tasersuaq** is a popular place for a half-day's walk (start from behind the sports ground). The rather derelict **turf house** near the Sulisartut Højskoliat is not original but was built as a student project. There's a curious wooden **totem pole** nearby.

Tours

From mid-June to late August the tourist office has guaranteed-departure tours to Hvalsey (p120; Dkr450, three times weekly), Uunartoq hot springs (p123; Dkr850, twice weekly), and the Akulliit Peninsula inland ice (p114; Dkr800). Town tours (Dkr150, minimum two people) and tannery tours leave the tourist office almost daily in summer. For details, see www.qaq.gl.

Sleeping

Although there appear to be numerous options, Qaqortoq's accommodation tends to fill fast, and reservations are highly recommended. The tourist office is expanding a list of possible B&Bs.

Siniffik Inn (☎ 642728; www.siniffik-inn.dk; qaqsana@greennet.gl; Aaninngivit B-242; dm Dkr225) Looking out over the lake, this delightful red-and-yellow wooden youth hostel has an appealing terrace and a delightful lounge area with games and music system. The kitchen is extensive and a great place to meet fellow travellers, but the four- and six-bunk rooms could get very cramped indeed if full. At the time of research, a much-needed extra bathroom complex was planned. Breakfast (included) is served by the owner's charming family.

Hotel Qaqortoq (☎ 642282; www.hotel-qaqortoq.gl; s/tw Dkr885/1095) Perched on the hill overlooking the harbour, this is a neat two-storey, wooden affair with an airy, plant-filled atrium. The small, rather overpriced motel-style rooms lead off lugubriously lit corridors, and the potentially pleasant harbour views are filtered through disappointingly narrow windows. Rates include breakfast. Occasionally you can get weekend specials with two nights' stay and at least one meal for Dkr1395 if you book online.

Niuernermik Ilinniarfik (s Dkr200; ♥ Jul) Although only available in late June and July, these student rooms in wonderfully equipped six-room houses represent excellent value. Each six-room unit shares two bathrooms, a kitchen and laundry facilities. Don't waste your time contacting the college, as all tourist sub-letting is handled through the Qaqortoq tourist office. Book ahead.

Sulisartut Højskoliat (Folk Workers High School; ☎ 642466; www.suliartut.gl) There are a wide variety of room types in four separate units (listed below), though vacancies are often relatively sparse. Whichever room type you want, you'll first need to visit the large main building, where **reception** (♥ 8am-4pm; other times call ☎ 493490 to organise room keys) also sells postcards and some of the last available copies of Birgitte Hertling's *Greenlandic for Travellers* (Dkr110). The main building's cafeteria (it's best to order ahead if you're not on full-board) and free Internet room are available to all guests.

Sulisartut Højskoliat main building (s/d full board Dkr675/1100) Upstairs are new, functionally appointed en-suite rooms with a small communal kitchen.

Sulisartut Højskoliat Laarseeraq building (s/tw Dkr550-950/1100-1450) Here there are bigger VIP rooms with TV, plus some standard rooms with shared bathrooms. As with the main building, all rooms come hotel style with bed linen and include three meals a day.

Sulisartut Højskoliat Tuumarsi building (2-/3-bed apt Dkr 750/1000) The apartments here are self-catering and are often full.

Sulisartut Højskoliat Matiusi building (dm Dkr165) By far the cheapest Sulisartut Højskoliat option, with slightly tatty but perfectly reasonable two-bunk dormitories sharing a decent shower, a small kitchen and a Dkr20 token-operated washing machine.

Sømandshjemmet (Seamen's Home; ☎ 642239; www.soemandshjem.gl; Ringvej; s/tw/tr Dkr695/920/1135) Prices listed are for pleasant if functional rooms with desks and private bathrooms with a small tub. Smaller rooms with shared bathrooms (s/tw Dkr555/765) can be pretty cramped, and the second bed is a foldout sofa. The communal sitting room has a library of (Danish) books and a piano. As with all seamen's homes, alcohol is prohibited.

Wigwam (☎ 642182; vvstekni@greennet.gl; Santorievej B300; s/tw Dkr650/750) This neat little red cottage that overlooks the helipad is available for short-term rentals. Add Dkr285 per extra person. The owners are based down the road at No 276.

Holstebro B&B (☎ 641725; kattaisbo@hotmail.com; Paarmaliarfik B816; r per person Dkr175) The Isbosethsen house offers a self-contained two-bed apartment downstairs. It's set in a luxuriant garden eccentrically decorated with animal horns and a Manneken Pis statue.

There's no official camping site, but there are possible pitches beyond the sports hall, behind the Sulisartut Højskoliat, if you can deal with Qaqortoq's ubiquitous flies.

Eating

Restaurant Napparsivik (☎ 643067; Torvet; mains Dkr198-225; 6-9.30pm Mon-Sat, group lunches by arrangement) In one of the loveliest beamed cottages on the old town square, this atmospheric eatery has tasteful art, wooden floors and a shiny copper serving bar. Dishes on the short menu use local fish and meat, very appetizingly served and garnished. On warm, sunny afternoons coffee (Dkr20) and cappuccino (Dkr28) are served outside.

Hotel Qaqortoq Restaurant (☎ 642282; mains Dkr190) Although closed at the time of research, the Hotel Qaqortoq restaurant has now found a chef whose new menu includes whale meat and Greenlandic lamb.

Sømandshjemmet Cafeteria (☎ 642239; Ringvej; mains Dkr45-55; 7am-7.30pm Mon-Sat, 8am-7.30pm Sun) A good-value Danish-style meal of the day is available 11.45am to 1pm and 5.30pm to 7.30pm (even the 'small' (Dkr45) serving is very generous). Open sandwiches and fast-food snacks are served throughout the day, and a pay-per-item breakfast is available before 10am.

Grill-baren (Torvevej B578; burgers Dkr25-48; 6am-7pm Mon-Sat, noon-7pm Sun) The biggest of several fast-food outlets, Grill-baren doubles as a slot-machine gambling room, though there's a small area of outdoor tables to eat your hot dogs should the flies abate. There are other daytime Mini-Grills on JH Lytzensvej, by the waterside on Havnevej and operating sporadically within the sports hall on Poul Ibsensvej.

Self-catering options:

Brædtet (market; Johan Dahlsvej B928) Fresh fish and seal meat.

Brugsen supermarket (☎ 642285; Anders Olsensvej B852; 9am-6pm Mon-Thu, 9am-7pm Fri, 10am-2pm Sat, 11am-3pm Sun)

Brugseneeraq minimarket (Storesøvej; 7am-8pm Mon-Fri, 9am-8pm Sat)

Nanoq Kiosk (Nipinngaaq B695; 3-10pm Mon-Thu, noon-11pm Fri-Sat, noon-10pm Sun) Open late, but pricey.

Pisiffik supermarket (☎ 647000; Storesøvej B135; 8am-6pm Mon-Fri, 8am-1pm Sat)

Drinking

Arctic Café (☎ 648080; Augo Lyngesvej B278; beers Dkr35; noon-midnight Mon-Sat) Don't expect coffee and cakes at Qaqortoq's primary drinking venue. It's easily recognised by the yellow VW crashing imaginatively out through an upper wall. In the afternoon the glassed-in terrace beyond the billiard tables can be invitingly warm and sunny. While occasionally boisterous, especially on Wednesday, Friday and Saturday band nights, this is a friendly place that can be hard to leave. Downstairs the **Disco Down Under** (10pm-3am Fri-Sat) attracts under-30s to a could-be-anywhere barrage of electronic dance rhythms, though it only gets busy after 1am.

Nanoq Bar (9pm-3am Fri) Older soaks seek late-night solace at this rougher-edged billiard bar.

Mikisoq (Hotel Qaqortoq; 5-11pm Mon-Fri, noon-midnight Sat, noon-11pm Sun) The fairly cosy bar of the Hotel Qaqortoq attempts to be something of a British-style pub.

Shopping

For souvenirs, visit the tourist office or museum shops. All-important antifly head-nets sell for Dkr28 at **Tamat Shop** (☎ 642576; Vatikanbakken B205; 10am-5.30pm Mon-Fri, 10am-1pm Sat). For local CDs (Dkr145), look upstairs within Pisiffik supermarket.

Getting There & Away

The **AUL office** (☎ 642240; bktjju@aul.gl; Torvet B23; 10am-3pm Mon-Fri) sells ferry tickets from an old cottage in the historical area. **Air Greenland** (☎ 642188; 11am-1pm Mon & Fri, 8am-4pm Tue & Thu) has a ticket window at the heliport.

AIR

From Qaqortoq there are sublimely beautiful helicopter connections twice weekly to Nanortalik (Dkr1071, 25 to 40 minutes) and Alluitsup Paa (Dkr611, 15 to 55 minutes), and three or four days a week to Narsarsuaq (Dkr806, 20 minutes) and Narsaq (Dkr315, 10 minutes). For Paamiut (Dkr3876, 1½ hours) via Grønnedal (Dkr2666, 40 minutes) it's quite illogically cheaper to depart from Narsarsuaq.

BOAT

Coastal ferries operate year round to Sisimiut (Dkr1600 to Dkr2130, 54 hours) via Kangaamiut (Dkr1395 to Dkr1860, 47 hours), Maniitsoq (Dkr1295 to Dkr1730, 43 hours), Nuuk (Dkr1075 to Dkr1435, 30 to 32½ hours), Paamiut (Dkr590 to Dkr780, 18 hours) and Arsuk (Dkr430 to Dkr575, 10 hours). The route extends to Aasiaat (Dkr1995 to Dkr2580, 67 hours) and Ilulissat (Dkr2110 to Dkr2815, 72 hours) from mid-May until Christmas.

The *Najaaraq Ittuk* serves Nanortalik (Dkr260 to Dkr350), taking 4¾ hours direct, 5½ hours via Eqalugaarsuit (Dkr150 to Dkr185) or 6¾ hours via Ammassivik (Dkr195 to Dkr245), stopping on any routing at Alluitsup Paa (Dkr160 to Dkr215). From May to November the *Najaaraq Ittuk* also makes two weekly runs to Narsarsuaq (Dkr215 to Dkr265, 4½ hours) via Qassiarsuk (Dkr150 to Dkr185) and Itilleq (Dkr150 to Dkr185), and visits Narsaq (Dkr150 to Dkr185, 2¼ hours) year round. In winter only the *Aleqa Ittuk* makes sporadic runs to Igaliku and Narsaq.

Getting Around

Qaqortoq's local transport system consists of a single rickety minibus that runs eccentric 20-minute loops around town for Dkr10 regardless of distance. Supposedly the service is continuous, but in reality it's pretty sporadic. Many locals use **taxis** (☎ 641111, 642888 or 641414), though anywhere is walkable.

AROUND QAQORTOQ TOWN
Hvalsey (Hvalsø, Qaqortukukooq)

Stone structures at Hvalsey are the only Norse ruins in all of Greenland that casual visitors would easily identify as former buildings. The relatively large **church ruin** (16m by 8m) even has window holes and door lintels in place. The **Great Hall** also has fine, metre-thick stone walls. Directly above the modern jetty is a notable circular **horse fold** enclosure, and nearby is the presumed **grave of Thorkel Farserk**, the cousin and follower of Erik the Red who founded Hvalsey in around 985. Totally alone beneath starkly imposing triangular peaks, the ruins elicit a strange sense of timeless awe, except when occasionally mobbed by cruise-ship escapees. Locals believe the site deserves Unesco World Heritage status.

Hvalsey was the venue for the last confirmed events before the mysterious disappearance of the Norse colonies. These were a 1408 wedding and the 1407 execution of a certain Kolgrim, burned at the stake for sorcery. Kolgrim's real 'crime' was seducing a daughter of the local sheriff. The booklet *Hvalsø – the Church and the Magnate's Farm*, by Joel Berglund, tells the full stories. It's available in English for Dkr35 at Narsaq Museum. In Qaqortoq Danish-language versions only are currently in stock.

Controversy currently surrounds the placing of future pylons to carry power to Narsaq from the planned Qorlortorsuaq power station. The most economic solution would string high-tension electricity wires right across the site, but that would ruin Hvalsey's pristine appeal.

Be aware that the site has no toilet facilities, no gift shops and no signs of modern life except for the jetty. There is no accommodation here or at Tasiusaq sheep farm, 2km east. If you're camping, please do so outside the demarcated ruins area.

GETTING THERE & AWAY

The approach by boat shows Hvalsey at its most impressive, backed by the reclining 1059m triangular rock face of Qaqor-

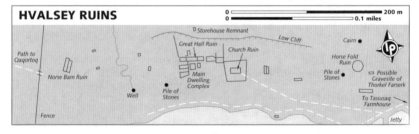

HVALSEY RUINS

0 — 200 m
0 — 0.1 miles

Storehouse Remnant
Great Hall Ruin
Church Ruin
Low Cliff
Cairn
Path to Qaqortoq
Horse Fold Ruin
Main Dwelling Complex
Pile of Stones
Possible Gravesite of Thorkel Farserk
Norse Barn Ruin
Well
Pile of Stones
To Tasiusaq Farmhouse
Fence
Jetty

tukuluup Qaqqaa. Qaqortoq tourist office runs regular half-day boat tours to Hvalsey via **Upernaviarsuk**, a passingly interesting agricultural research station. Charter-boat prices depend on comfort and engine size. Various Qaqortoq boat operators ask from around Dkr300 per person return, with a minimum charge of Dkr1000 to Dkr1500. Contact **Motzfeldt Rentals** (☎ 641045, mobile 493116), **Ole Peter Kleist** (☎ 494615) or **Peter Lyberth** (Lyberth Charter; ☎ 493352; per person Dkr480, minimum Dkr1450). An interesting alternative is to visit by speedboat from Narsaq (Dkr650 per person) and get dropped off at Qaqortoq on the way back.

Hvalsey is the ideal starting point for the classic three- or four-day hike to Igaliku. Use the 1:100,000 Narsaq hiking map. By contrast, walking between Hvalsey and Qaqortoq (1½ days) is miserably slow going through entangling vegetation and annoying boulder fields, rewarded by comparatively uninteresting views.

Eqalugaarsuit
pop 130

Relatively easy to reach yet completely off the tourist radar, this fleetingly picturesque, umbrella-shaped village protrudes from the southern underbelly of scraggy Kangeq Island. In two hours you can climb the steeply scooped valley behind the village following an impressive but often dry cascade. On top is a hummocky plateau peaking at 454m with various fine panoramas of the fjords and distant mountainscape horizons.

The **hotel** (Dkr200 per person) is actually a typical one-up, two-down cottage with equipped kitchen, box toilet and tap (but no shower). Booking is easiest through Qaqortoq tourist office, though key-holder **Kristine Poulsen** (☎ 649703; B593) does speak a few words of English. For Dkr75 extra you can share a family dinner at her house, which is opposite the village's bone-carving workshop.

Kristine can also help you find a local fishermen to take you up the fjord towards Kangerluarsorujuk (see p125) for as little as Dkr300. En route the most interesting stop is at **Itilliarsik**, where the long southern peninsula narrows to a mere 200m. An ingenious (though currently broken) system of winches and ramps has been built here to drag small boats across. This would save some 30km of rough seas on the journey to Alluitsup Paa.

AUL's *Najaaraq Ittuk* stops once a week in Eqalugaarsuit between Qaqortoq (Dkr185, one hour) and Alluitsup Paa (Dkr185, two hours). From May to August only, current timetables allow you to make a one-night return trip from Qaqortoq, leaving Wednesday afternoon and returning Thursday midday.

ALLUITSUP PAA & VATNAHVERFI

Between Igaliku and Alluitsup Paa, the Vatnahverfi Peninsula has fish-filled lakes, a fairly mild climate, and relatively gentle moors and fells. These appeal to hikers (see the boxed text 'Classic Treks 3', p125) much as they did to the early Norse settlers whose ruins dot the region, many of them unexcavated. For a gentler experience simply relax in Alluitsup Paa and take small boat trips, perhaps staying the night at one of the several lonely sheep-farms that offer homestays. Most of the latter are single-family affairs, so call ahead in case everyone's away.

ALLUITSUP PAA (SYDPRØVEN)
pop 510

Alluitsup Paa combines the appeal of a relatively traditional hunting-and-fishing village with some wonderful accommodation that's unique in South Greenland for its seafront open-air balconies. Colourful cottages are sprinkled across a series of low, rocky gullies and pretty harbour inlets that are somewhat reminiscent of Cornwall. It's the logical base for visiting the Uunartoq hot springs.

Information
Internet café (☎ 619204; per 30 min/hr Dkr25/35; ☼ 1-6pm & 7-11pm)
Laundry (☼ 9am-7pm Mon-Fri) It's much more convenient and no more expensive to use the hotels' Dkr30 wash-and-dry service.
Post office (☼ 10am-2pm Mon-Fri) Gives credit-card cash advances and sells AUL ferry tickets.
Tourist office Planned but not yet operational in the old stone salt-house in front of the Hotel Qaannivik. At the time of research a full-time, multilingual summer guide was mooted to be available from 2005.

Sights
Across the small, historical harbour area or from your balcony at the Seaside Whale

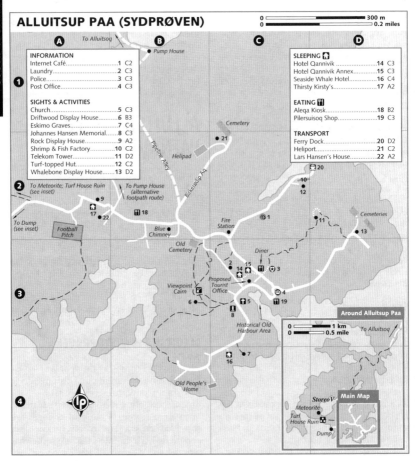

ALLUITSUP PAA (SYDPRØVEN)

0 ——————— 300 m
0 ——————— 0.2 miles

To Alluitsoq

● Pump House

INFORMATION
Internet Café...........................1 C2
Laundry.................................2 C3
Police...................................3 C3
Post Office............................4 C3

SIGHTS & ACTIVITIES
Church..................................5 C3
Driftwood Display House.........6 B3
Eskimo Graves......................7 C4
Johannes Hansen Memorial......8 C3
Rock Display House................9 A2
Shrimp & Fish Factory...........10 C2
Telekom Tower......................11 D2
Turf-topped Hut....................12 C2
Whalebone Display House......13 D2

SLEEPING 🛏
Hotel Qannivik......................14 C3
Hotel Qannivik Annex............15 C3
Seaside Whale Hotel..............16 C4
Thirsty Kirsty's.....................17 A2

EATING 🍴
Aleqa Kiosk.........................18 B2
Pilersuisoq Shop...................19 C3

TRANSPORT
Ferry Dock............................20 D2
Heliport................................21 C2
Lars Hansen's House..............22 A2

Cemetery

Pipeline Alley

Helipad

Birkedalip Aqq

To Meteorite; Turf House Ruin
(see inset)

To Pump House
(alternative
footpath route)

To Dump
(see inset)

Football
Pitch

Blue ●
Chimney

Fire
Station

Cemeteries

Old
Cemetery

Diner

Viewpoint
Cairn

Proposed
Tourist
Office

Historical Old
Harbour Area

Around Alluitsup Paa

0 ——————— 1 km
0 ——————— 0.5 mile

To Alluitsoq

Old People's
Home

Storeø

Meteorite
Turf
House Ruin

Dump

Main Map

Hotel you could happily gaze for days towards the powerful horizon of Sermersoq Island. There, waves of dramatic grey granite cliffs turn a magical rose-pink at sunset, appear to snarl diabolically in wild sudden storms and make a great backdrop for the opera house–sized icebergs that queue up in the bay like oil tankers awaiting a docking berth.

Climb to **viewpoint cairn** or the **telekom tower** for easy panoramas, and notice three **houses** (coincidentally all yellow) with outdoor displays of wave-smoothed rocks, driftwood and whalebones respectively. Opposite the **Johannes Hansen Memorial**, try to peep inside the 1926 red timber **church** (🕙 10am Sun), which has a lovely interior with wooden colon-

naded upper galleries. The new tourist office will be able to get you in and organise someone to play the harmonium for you. It'll also arrange tours of the brand new **shrimp-and-fish factory**, culminating in an appropriate fish dinner. The curious wooden **turf-topped hut** behind was a primitive cold store for an earlier factory almost a century ago. The easiest-to-find **Inuit graves** are the pair beside a house just east of the Seaside Whale Hotel. Ten minutes' walk around the south shore of Storeø (Big Lake) there's a grassy **turf-house ruin** where the lake drains into the sea. This was for centuries an Inuit hunting camp. From here cross the stepping stones and walk less than 100m further along the lakeside to find a red-tinged, metre-tall **meteorite** that rings metallically when struck with the stone that sits on top and marks it. Although only 15 paces from the water, it's easy to miss amongst other lichen-mottled rocks.

Sleeping

Seaside Whale Hotel (☎ 619209; ekjaer.boegeholt@ greennet.gl; s/d/tw Dkr925/1175/1175; ✗) Three lovely sea-facing rooms share a long terrace above the mesmerising sea-battered rocks. Views are brilliant, and the rooms combine a bright professional elegance with some artistically personal touches. A small toilet-and-shower room is attached, and there's coffee making paraphernalia. Breakfast (at the sister Hotel Qaannivik) is included. There are also two bigger family apartments with a kitchen but no view. All rooms are nonsmoking. The same charming owners run the **Hotel Qaannivik** (s/d/tw Dkr675-725/925/925), a poorly marked cream building in the old-harbour historic area. The four rooms share two bathrooms, and rates include buffet breakfast with freshly baked muesli-bread. The nearby **Annex** (dm Dkr350) is a very comfortable mini hostel with three triple-bedded rooms sharing a bathroom and fully equipped kitchen.

Thirsty Kirsty's (☎ 619146; kkran@greennet.gl; blue house B985; Dkr200) If and when she's in residence Kirsten Løgstrup offers sleeping-bag space and her bohemian spare room with its distinctive botanical features. Nicknamed 'Thirsty Kirsty', Kirsten is an eccentrically philosophical former teacher and crane-driver with plenty of stories to tell in English, German or Danish and many useful local contacts. Expect the unexpected, and bring a bottle or 10.

Eating & Drinking

Hotel Qaannivik Restaurant (☎ 619199; room 6; dinner Dkr125; ☼ 7.30-9.30am, noon-1pm, 6-7pm) This attractively appointed place has standing candelabra, wood and rattan furniture, and Greenlandic costume designs. You should book in advance for the set lunch (Dkr70 to Dkr95) and filling home-cooked dinner of the day.

The small fast-food diner was not operating at the time of research. The mid-sized **Pilersuisoq Shop** (☼ 9am-4.30pm Mon-Thu, 9am-5pm Fri, 9am-1pm Sat) does mini-pizzas (Dkr15) and plain hot dogs (Dkr10). The tiny **Aleqa Kiosk** (1-6pm daily & 7-9pm Mon-Fri) sells crisps and candles.

The **bar** (beers Dkr40; ☼ 9pm-3am Fri) below the Hotel Qaannivik is a typical bare-bones local affair. Space is limited, so revellers tend to spill outside and dance beneath the aurora. On a good night it can be super-friendly, and fights rarely result in much bloodshed.

Getting There & Away

Twice weekly helicopters fly to and from Nanortalik (Dkr611), Narsarsuaq (Dkr1220) and Qaqortoq (Dkr635). There's no Air Greenland ticket office, but Karen Kjær from the Hotel Qaannivik doubles as heliport manager and can arrange bookings.

The *Najaaraq Ittuk* ferry calls in three times weekly in each direction between Qaqortoq (Dkr210) and Nanortalik (Dkr185). Once a week the Qaqortoq service stops in Eqalugaarsuit. A different day the Nanortalik boat goes via Ammassivik.

The hotels and new tourist office will be able to alert you to group trips to Uunartoq and beyond. It may be cheaper to contact boat owners directly, though prices and availability can vary wildly. Teachers **Lars Hansen** (☎ 619138; house B933) and **Johannes Rosing** (☎ 619280) offer particularly reasonable rates but are often too busy. Lars speaks English.

AROUND ALLUITSUP PAA
Uunartoq Island & Fjord

Near the west coast of Uunartoq Island, Greenland's best and most accessible hot springs bubble gently at between 34°C and 38°C. That's not incredibly hot, but it's warm enough to laze happily in a couple of outdoor pools watching icebergs float by surreally a few hundred metres beyond. Apart from a small changing hut there are no facilities, just wild flowers and, on summer weekends, groups of picnicking or camping locals. The springs have been known since the Norse period, when they were considered medicinally valuable and belonged to a Benedictine convent at **Narsarsuaq** (not the airport but an isolated ruin across the fjord). That site's excavation in the 1930s was interrupted by WWII – Karen at Alluitsup Paa's Hotel Qaannivik can tell you the full romantic story.

On the island's southeast coast are the relatively extensive **Qerrortuut Inuit ruins**, 26 house sites that were inhabited in the late 18th and early 19th centuries. In the 1920s a set of naturally mummified human remains was discovered here amid remnants of carved wooden toys and personal artefacts. They're now in the Harvard University collection.

There are dozens of other indistinct ruins to explore on the nearby mainland shores of Uunartoq Fjord, notably at **Niaqornaarsuk**, once a Norse sheep farm and manor house.

GETTING THERE & AWAY

From Alluitsup Paa, you can charter motorboats to drop you at Uunartoq Island and pick you up at a specified time. Typical costs per person are in the Dkr300 to Dkr500 range (minimum Dkr1000) for the return trip, which can include Alluitsoq (Lichtenau), though price variation is considerable. At weekends you might be able to hitch a ride with local families, but the atmosphere is better midweek, when you have the place to yourself. Twice monthly in summer there are tour boats from Qaqortoq (Dkr850 per person, eight hours return) organised by the Qaqortoq tourist office. Once a week in summer Blue Ice in Narsarsuaq (p99) offers a Dkr2000 day-return excursion including Narsarsuaq–Alluitsup Paa helicopter transfers. It's feasible to arrange a charter boat from Nanortalik.

Alluitsoq (Lichtenau)

pop 2

At first sight Alluitsoq looks like a picture-postcard fishing village. The little cupola-topped wooden church in a sea of buttercups is well kept with fresh candles. Rhubarb and potato patches are backed by clapboard homes and stone-and-timber sheep barns. The harbour arc of grey-white sand is ringed by golf-course-green turf. However, closer inspection reveals that almost every house is empty. It wasn't always this way. Founded in 1774 as the Moravian mission settlement of Lichtenau, this was once, incredibly, the biggest village in Greenland. In 1814 it was the birthplace of Samuel Petrus Kleinschmidt, who produced the first Greenlandic translation of the Bible. However, the mission was closed down in 1900 and the village withered away. Today there's just a single old couple in residence, though there are plans to develop the site as a holiday-camp village. Primarily the clientele would be Danish union members and their families, but spare capacity would likely be available to drop-in tourists.

Walking from Alluitsup Paa (about 5km, two hours) is pleasant, but the just-discernible path is easy to lose at several points. Follow the pipeline footpath north out of Alluitsup Paa and walk around the west side of the first lake, crossing the stream near a small red pumphouse. A slight double-back may be required to loop anticlockwise round the bluff blocking the narrow isthmus that makes Alluitsup Paa virtually an island. Once across this isthmus, climb somewhat but return as soon as possible to the coastal path, which becomes increasingly clear as you approach Alluitsoq. It's easier still to take a boat from Alluitsup Paa (Dkr100 to Dkr200) and then walk back. From Alluitsoq you could walk on to Igaliku Kujalleq (p125) in several days via Kilua, near Qorlortorsuaq (opposite).

Alluitsup Kangerlua (Lichtenau Fjord)

Across the fjord from Alluitsup Paa on a spear-tip of peninsula is minuscule **Akuliaruseq**, a two-house village with its own little church. **Ammassivik** (Sletten) is a big enough village to have a shop and school. It's very attractively situated, especially when viewed across the fjord from the southwest. There's some decent short-distance hiking if you can stand the thick clouds of summer midges. Accommodation is possible at **House No 907** (per person Dkr150). As well as a twin bedroom, it has a big lounge furnished with sofa beds. There's a box toilet and a kitchen with a wonderfully old-fashioned wrought-iron stove, but there's no running water. Keys are available from **Vera Lund** (☎ 617360; house B934) who lives between the Pilersuisoq shop and the little school with its glass pyramid roof. She speaks only Greenlandic.

As you move further north the fjordsides get steeper, with several long, narrow ribbons of waterfall. Although the views are not as awesome as those around Aappilattoq (p133), a boat ride past the glacier-gouged Akuliarusersuaq (1655m) is very scenic.

A 15-minute stroll inland from its picturesque harbour inlet, appealing Qallimiut consists of just six houses, four barns and a cute little church with a working harmonium. The scattered village occupies a lovely position overlooking fjord and lake across potato patches and rolling hayfields that are sandwiched between rock-and-moss ridges. There are half-hearted plans to develop one of the empty houses as tourist accommodation. In Kilua, about 5km further inland by tractor road around the lake, **Hans Nielsen** (☎ 619712) can arrange accommodation for hikers walking the main Vatnahverfi trek. Note that Hans doesn't speak English.

The fjord's northwestern spur squeezes through the narrow, forbiddingly steep-sided Amitsuarsuk fjord, which dead-ends at the Qorlortorsuaq jetty. From here, **Qorlortorsuaq** is a leisurely 3km walk inland along a tractor road through bucolic, emerald-green meadowlands and around a shallow lake. Long before you arrive you'll see the handful of houses impressively overshadowed by the dramatic gushing of Greenland's biggest waterfall. But not for long. Sadly, these 75 vertical metres of roaring pure energy will soon disappear into the pipes of a new hydro power station. But even then it should be worth climbing to the lip of the upper Qorlortorssuup Tasia feeder lake for lovely, dizzying views back across the meadows towards Akuliarusersuaq Mountain. The lonely, well-equipped homestead 900m south of the falls will be available for rent to tourists or workers once **Elias Nielsen** (☎ 619603) completes his new farmhouse. At the time of research, this was expected to be sometime in 2005, with beds expected to cost Dkr80 to Dkr150.

GETTING THERE & AWAY
Once a week in either direction an AUL ferry follows the Nanortalik–Ammassivik–Alluitsup Paa–Qaqortoq route. Beyond Ammassivik there's no public transport. Chartering a decent motorboat from Alluitsup Paa to Qorlortorsuaq via Ammassivik and Qallimiut can cost anything from Dkr800 to Dkr2500, so ask around carefully. Very occasional tour boats charge Dkr1000 per person on the same route. Boat rides direct to Qorlortorsuaq from Alluitsup Paa should become easier to arrange once the power-station building commences in earnest. From Qorlortorsuaq it's possible to walk to Igaliku Kujalleq in one long day, starting up the west side of Qorlortorssuup Tasia from the Qorlortorsuaq power station/falls. Maps are essential.

CENTRAL VATNAHVERFI
Igaliku Kujalleq (Søndre Igaliku)
Igaliku Kujalleq is built on the historic Norse site of **Unðir Höföi**. Relatively substantial church ruins remain near the dock and

---

> **CLASSIC TREKS 3: VATNAHVERFI**
>
> Use the 1:100,000 Qaqortoq and Narsaq hiking maps to navigate the charming web of multi-day walking possibilities. Try avoiding lower valleys that can be clogged by annoyingly thick bushes. The classic route goes from Igaliku Kujalleq via Qorlortorsuaq and Kilua (near Qallimiut), eventually emerging at Alluitsup Paa (p121) or Kangerluarsorujuk (below), but there are many variants. Well-respected **Topas** (www.greenland-discoverer.com) organises two-week group treks sleeping in sheep farms and huts, including one of their own near Jespersen Bræ glacier.

the two-house **youth hostel** (☎ 666913, mobile 492270; soffiannguaq@yahoo.dk; dm Dkr175). The hostel is often unstaffed, as English-speaking owner Sofianguak Kristiansen lives 5km away at Qorlortukasik.

The hostel can provide meals including a big brunch/breakfast (Dkr150/75). It also hires out bicycles (Dkr150 per day) on which you could pedal a track that winds round several lakes to Timerliit, Saqqaa, Tasilikulooq and Qanisartuut, where there's another **hostel** (☎ 649412; qanisartuut@greennet.gl; dm Dkr225).

Either hostel can arrange boat transfers to and from Igaliku or Narsaq for around Dkr600. Some hikers walk from Igaliku to Iterlak and get picked up there. However, this trek is overrated, saves no money and involves wading at least one very cold river en route. Rivers between Iterlak and Igaliku Kujalleq are too wide to ford unless you trek well up towards Jespersen Bræ glacier.

Kangerluarsorujuk
The grassy bowl around Kangerluarsorujuk farm is rendered photogenic by the curious 'graveyard' of stray icebergs caught near the dead end of the long, straight Kangerluarsorujuk fjord. The super-friendly Nielsen family speak good English and rent a cosy **hut** (☎ 649415; kang27@greennet.gl; dm Dkr225) with kitchenette that could sleep up to four squeezed together. It's serenaded by a stream rich in Arctic char. Costs include breakfast and showers in the homely main farmhouse, where the yard is adorned by geological curiosities. Pick-ups from Qaqortoq or Eqalugaarsuit cost Dkr600. Arranging your own ride from Eqalugaarsuit may cost less.

Simplest of myriad possible hikes is a pleasant 2km stroll by tractor road to the hospitable if rather ramshackle Kangerluarsorujuk Qinngua farm (no accommodation). Avoid walking alongside Ammassiviup Tasia lake – the going is annoyingly tough due to bushes and many mosquitoes.

NANORTALIK REGION

If you visit only one area of Greenland, the Nanortalik region makes a superb choice, provided the weather and the ice situation oblige. If you're touring extensively in South Greenland, save the Nanortalik area as the finale or you may find everywhere else a slight anticlimax.

NANORTALIK TOWN

pop 1540

Nanortalik town colourfully fills a fairly flat but eccentrically edged peninsula on a moorland island that rises to two chunky heights with great viewpoints. The town's historic southern quarter retains oodles of charm and offers sea views peppered with islands and icebergs. Leave as much time as possible to visit the surrounding fjords, which are backed with astonishingly spiky granite spires.

History

The Norse name for Nanortalik Island was Hrakbjarnarey (Bear Hunt Island), and doubtless it was a hunting ground used by both Norse and Inuit people, though details are scanty. In 1797 a permanent trading and supply depot was set up by Julianehåb traders at Sissaritoq (see p129). The population shifted to Nanortalik's present location in 1830 to make use of the better harbour facilities. The region's main export was whale blubber and seal products, seals being particularly attracted to the ice floes that crowd the local fjords in early summer. However, in the 20th century declining demand for seal products resulted in the abandonment of many outlying settlements. The summer ice that had been a boon to seal hunters made Nanortalik much less viable as a fishing base.

Information

Hospital (☎ 613211; Isua)

Internet café (Jujuqaat Aqq) Upstairs in a blue cube building above the music studios; computers are set up,

but at the time of research there was nobody to run the place.

Laundry (Chemnitzip B480/2; ☺ 8am-8pm) Buy wash cards from Brugsen supermarket.

Police (☎ 613 222; Roskildip Aqq)

Post office (☺ 9am-3pm Mon-Fri) Behind the tourist office. Changes cash (but not travellers cheques) with a Dkr30 commission. Two ATMs.

Tourist office (☎ /fax 613633; mobile 490298; nanortalik@greennet.gl; Lundip B128; Postboks 43, DK-3922 Nanortalik; ☺ 8am-noon & 1-4pm Mon-Fri, 9am-noon Sat & Sun) The ever-helpful Niels does all in his power to help and is often able to juggle boat charters to match tourists and climbing groups, saving both a lot of money. The tourist office doubles as AUL booking office and contact point for the town's hostels. It rents climbing and fishing gear and kayaks, and has ADSL Internet (per 15 minutes Dkr25). The extensive shop sells maps, camping gas, souvenirs and Greenlandic music CDs. You can exchange US dollars, UK pounds and euros without commission but at a poorer rate than in the post office. Credit cards are accepted. For cash advances the 3.75% charge is passed on.

Sights

OLD HARBOUR AREA

Nanortalik's old harbour area is incredibly picturesque. With red picket fences, carpets of yellow flowers and painted timber cottages it looks like a film-set New England fishing village that's been given a pantomime mountain backdrop. It's well worth strolling around several times at different tides and times of day to enjoy it in a variety of light conditions. Beside a set of mini cannons you can climb stairs up the curious egg-shaped **flag-mast rock** for a bird's-eye view. The most striking building is the distinctive 1916 **church** with its white, rocket-shaped façade. Nearby is the large **face boulder** that locals consider bears a likeness to national hero Knud Rasmussen. To see why, sit on the bench 40m south of the church and look over your left shoulder. The dockside building marked A14 on its roof (as a WWII aerial identifier) is a **sealskin processing workshop** where you might see pelts being salted and scrubbed. Nuuk St ends near the tiny youth hostel cottage on a little peninsula with lawns and fine sea views.

MUSEUM

Most of the other lovely harbour-area buildings date from the 19th century and are now elements in the multifaceted **town museum**

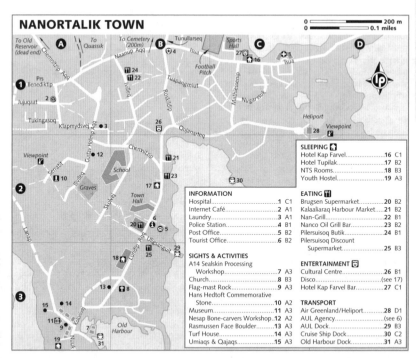

NANORTALIK TOWN

SLEEPING
Hotel Kap Farvel	16 C1
Hotel Tupilak	17 B2
NTS Rooms	18 B3
Youth Hostel	19 A3

INFORMATION
Hospital	1 C1
Internet Café	2 A1
Laundry	3 A1
Police Station	4 B1
Post Office	5 B2
Tourist Office	6 B2

EATING
Brugsen Supermarket	20 B2
Kalaaliaraq Harbour Market	21 B2
Nan-Grill	22 B1
Nanco Oil Grill Bar	23 B2
Pilersuisoq Butik	24 B1
Pilersuisoq Discount Supermarket	25 B3

SIGHTS & ACTIVITIES
A14 Sealskin Processing Workshop	7 A3
Church	8 B3
Flag-mast Rock	9 A3
Hans Hedtoft Commemorative Stone	10 A2
Museum	11 A3
Nesap Bone-carvers Workshop	12 A2
Rasmussen Face Boulder	13 A3
Turf House	14 A3
Umiaqs & Qajaqs	15 A3

ENTERTAINMENT
Cultural Centre	26 B1
Disco	(see 17)
Hotel Kap Farvel Bar	27 C1

TRANSPORT
Air Greenland/Heliport	28 D1
AUL Agency	(see 6)
AUL Dock	29 B3
Cruise Ship Dock	30 C2
Old Harbour Dock	31 A3

(☎ 613406; nanortalik.museum@greennet.gl; Kiffat B7; admission free; ☙ 1-4pm Sun-Thu Jun-Sep, Tue, Thu & Sun Oct-May).

The green shingle-fronted building with attached bell was once the general store. Next door an 1852 blubber house exhibits *qajaqs* and hunting paraphernalia, while the 1839 oil-boiling house has somewhat gruesome vats, big cauldrons, presses and winches. Along Kiffat Aqq is the **museum office** (B7), hidden at the back of which are displayed costumes and a mid-20th-century room. In an 1840 house beyond is a collection of radio equipment and a small **geological display** (house B18). The museum **bakery** (B6) is said to date from 1860, but the ovens are fairly recent. There's also an **old cooperage** (B122), stables and a reconstructed turf hut with its walls plastered in old newspapers. Near the waterside is another **turf hut** (partly built, showing construction methods) and some sealskin tents. There are often several *qajaq* and *umiaq* boats on drying stands nearby.

On request, the museum will open specially for groups, but it then charges Dkr25 per person.

OTHER SIGHTS

If you don't want to climb Quassik there are several places within town to get some lovely, effortless views. For the magnificently jagged horizon of Sermersoq, stand behind the Hotel Kap Farvel or on the view rock just southeast of the heliport. For seaward views, sit on the youth hostel lawn or stroll up to the radio mast on Serratit. The **commemorative stone** at this point is for the *Hans Hedtoft* shipwreck; the ship went down off Cape Farewell in 1959 with no survivors.

It's possible if not mind-blowingly interesting to visit the **Nesap bone-carvers' workshop** (☎ 613540; Gustav Holmip Aqq B176; ☙ irregular).

Activities

In this region, climbers have an unparalleled choice of vertical rock walls and granite spikes to get their clips into. Many peaks are as yet unclimbed, and even the most popular 'standard' routes are mostly for very advanced trad-climbers. Comparisons are with Patagonia, Norway's Lofoten islands and El Cap in Yosemite. This would be the ultimate place for base jumping. Check out the photos on www.nanortalik.gl. Niels at Nanortalik tourist office is reckoned to be one of the most climber-friendly tourist officers on the planet. He keeps collections of expedition reports, and can offer detailed assistance if you're organising transport and provisions shipments.

Nanortalik Island and Tasermiut Fjord are spectacular places for sea kayaking. The tourist office hires out kayaks (per day/week/fortnight Dkr400/2000/3500), but only to experienced paddlers: the fjords have sheer-sided sections with no available sheltering beaches, so this is not a place for beginners.

Sleeping

Nanortalik has a good accommodation selection for so small a place but nowhere has a reception desk, so book ahead. You'll be met on arrival and given a key.

Hotel Kap Farvel (☎ 613294; www.kapfarvel.gl; Isua B304; s/d from Dkr625/1000, with bathroom s/tw Dkr900/1125) The better rooms with en-suite bathroom might not be five star, but they're among the best appointed in Greenland. Bed linen and lamps are stylish; coffee, tea and a kettle are provided; and there's a welcome marzipan when you arrive. Views across the fjord to craggy Sermersoq are truly idyllic. Curiously, the building itself looks less than appealing, and there's no obvious entrance so dropping in unannounced is not a good idea. There are smaller, older rooms with shared bathrooms, but in that lower price bracket you'd be better off in NTS. The hotel website advertises dormitories, but that refers to the **Hotel Tupilak** (dm/tw Dkr250/500), which despite the name is now run as a hostel. It's a little less cosy than the old youth hostel but much more spacious, and it has a worn but welcoming sitting room looking out towards the harbour. Several 'dorms' have only two bunks and can be rented as rooms. There's a decent kitchen, and guests have free use of the sauna. Arrange bookings and keys through the tourist office.

Youth Hostel (Nuuk; dm Dkr195) This delightful eight-bed cottage seems to have been built for Lilliput. There's a sweet, well-equipped little kitchen and communal sitting room, a shower and a Greenland box-toilet. Just outside, a picnic table has fine sea views. Organise bookings and keys through the tourist office. Camping on the lawn outside with use of the hostel facilities costs Dkr100.

NTS rooms (☎ 613386; nicoh@greennet.gl; Lundip B254; s/d/tr Dkr550/700/900) These very neat and clean, if somewhat impersonal, furnished mini apartments are near the church. Each has a table, an equipped kitchen and a fairly large shower room. Triples have an extra sitting room.

Eating

Hotel Kap Farvel Restaurant (☎ 613294; mains Dkr105-190; ⏰ 7.15-9.30am, noon-1.30pm & 6-8pm) This highly recommended restaurant is fairly reckoned to be one of the best in rural Greenland. Celebrated chef Per Grenå cooks local ingredients with a delicious modern twist. The excellent vegetarian alternative is much more than a token garnish. There's a Dkr85 multi-item lunch deal, and the very filling Dkr125 two-course set dinner is superb value. Reserve a few hours ahead so that the appropriate fresh supplies can be purchased.

Nan-Grill (☎ 613580; Ivilleq B1344; ⏰ 11am-8pm Sun-Thu, 11am-9pm Fri-Sat) The grill has the standard hot-dog and burger selection.

Nanco Oil Grill Bar (☎ 613210; Lundip; snacks Dkr16-56; ⏰ 8am-4pm Mon-Fri) Served from a side room in the petrol station, the same standard selection is advertised with disarming honesty as 'Junk Food'.

SELF-CATERING

Brugsen supermarket (Lundip B376; ⏰ 9am-5.30pm Mon-Thu, 8am-6pm Fri, 9am-1pm Sat) Includes a bakery counter, open from 7am.

Kalaaliaraq Harbour market (⏰ variable, Mon-Sat) Sells whatever may have been recently caught or picked, from seal ribs to berries to potatoes.

Pilersuisoq Butik (⏰ 9am-7pm)

Pilersuisoq discount supermarket (⏰ 9am-6pm Mon-Fri, 9am-1pm Sat)

Entertainment

At the side of the Hotel Kap Farvel there's a pleasant if sometimes rowdy **bar** (⏰ 6pm-midnight Mon-Sat; beers Dkr39). There are fairly frequent bingo nights at the **cultural centre** (Lundip). You could listen at the door of the church when the talented town choir practices (early most evenings), and on special occasions (eg when cruise ships pay for it) you can see *qajaq*, *umiaq* and folk-dancing demonstrations performed by children in costume. Dancing is more perfunctory at the disreputable Hotel Tupilak **disco** (⏰ 8pm-3am Fri), which produces plenty of broken glass.

Getting There & Away

The tourist office doubles as the **AUL agency** (☎ 613633). **Air Greenland** (☎ 613288; Qujanarteq 1371; ☼ 8am-4pm Mon-Fri, 7am-5pm Wed) is within the heliport.

AIR

Fog willing, Air Greenland has Wednesday and Friday helicopter shuttles to Alluitsup Paa (Dkr570), Qaqortoq (Dkr995), Narsaq (Dkr1426) and Narsarsuaq (Dkr1295). Each ride is spectacular and well worth the money.

BOAT

The *Najaaraq Ittuk* sails up to three times weekly between Nanortalik and Qaqortoq (Dkr350, 4¾ to 6½ hours) via Alluitsup Paa (Dkr200). Once weekly in each direction there's a stop in Ammassivik (Dkr235); on a different run there's a stop in Saarloq (Dkr260) and Eqalugaarsuit (Dkr275). The highlight of a trip from Qaqortoq is the section between Alluitsup Paa and Nanortalik, passing between forbiddingly tall mountain walls down Sermersuup Sarqaa sound.

Once a week between mid-November and April the tiny *Ketil* goes to Aappilattoq (Dkr225, 3½ hours), returning the same day. This is an unmissable voyage of quite exceptional scenic wonders, but weather and ice conditions mean it is often cancelled.

Getting Around

The tourist office hires out the enclosed 12-seat *Ketil* (Dkr1320 per hour when moving, Dkr550 waiting time), can help match you with fellow travellers to spread the costs of boat charters, and occasionally arranges excursions of its own. Other boats are not officially licensed for passengers. Nonetheless, you can arrange your own (uninsured) rides with local fishers. Reckon on around Dkr3000 to Kirkespirdalen, Dkr5500 to the end of Tasermiut Fjord and Dkr7500 to Prins Christian Sund (ice permitting) for up to eight passengers. A useful first contact is **Niko Hansen** (☎ 613386; NTS rooms).

NANORTALIK ISLAND

Nanortalik is on a manageably sized island that offers several excellent part-day hikes. Each route is best started by walking north up Tunullaritseq St from Nanortalik town's tiny police station, passing the fairly photogenic cemetery and then bearing left on Isaf-jordurip Aqq, a doglegged street that looks like a colourful suburban afterthought. Some 150m beyond the end of the asphalt, having passed some gravel pits, the main tractor track swings west past a shallow lake and continues towards Qaqqarsuasik and various east-coast ruins. Alternatively, continue north on a small but fairly obvious footpath that rises steadily through berries and later follows a small stream to ascend Quassik.

East Coast Ruins

Of several inconspicuous Norse and Inuit ruins, the most extensive is **Sissarissoq**. The original site of Nanortalik (1770–1830), it once had a shop, a manager's residence and blubber-storage facilities as depicted on the signboard (Danish and Greenlandic only). Today the remnants of stone-and-peat dwellings in a thick patch of buttercups are easily spotted by heading for the white cross on a coastal rock less than 10 minutes' easy walk southwest of the Vandsø reservoir where the tractor track ends. Another 10 minutes beyond, past a dyke and a **yin-and-yang mosaic**, romantic visitors use the rounded white pebbles from **Pukitsut beach** to spell out eternal valentine initials on the bog grass. As you walk back towards Nanortalik you may spot the site of the **Nanertaliutaa ruins** amid more buttercups on the first headland northwest of the Vandsø Reservoir. The small, listing basalt pillar here is known as the **Bear Stone**. It's a lintel from one of the ruins and supposedly got its name when it was used by a spoilt Inuit boy to tie up a pet polar-bear cub.

Quassik (Ravnefjeldet)

It takes just over an hour to climb 308m Quassik (Ravens' Mountain) for sublime 360-degree views encompassing the eccentric spires of Sermersoq island. There are glimpses of Kirkespiret's raised rocky finger and Tasiusaq Bay, plus the lovely iceberg-spangled island seascapes to the south. The walk is pretty easy with only one very short steep section and a few boggy patches, but allow plenty of time to gaze from each of the three subpeaks. True to its name, guardian ravens will be watching you.

Qaqqarsuasik (Storfjeldet)

If you want to go higher, it's not too difficult to climb the island's highest massif, Qaqqarsuasik (Storfjeldet), though there are no marked paths. Beware, though, that the southern summit (559m) has an especially naughty tendency to suddenly vanish into fog. Accordingly, be very cautious when walking here, as the peak's western flank drops away almost vertically as sea cliffs. View-seeking locals generally stick to the northerly subpeak **Apussigaajivitseq** (482m).

AROUND NANORTALIK TOWN

There are numerous opportunities for spectacular boat rides in the region's fjords, notably to Tasermiut (see below) and in the Aappilattoq area (see p133). By kayak or motor launch you might consider heading up Qoornoq sound to **Umiiviarsuk Island**, where there are a number of hunters' cabins on the north tip. Further up the same impressive waterway at the pointy southern tip of Amitsoq Island are the ruins of an abandoned **graphite mine**, where the rocks shimmer with an iridescent film of carbon grease. Amid scraps of rusting extraction equipment are several hazardously decaying mine tunnels. **Kirkespirdalen**, a valley named for the spindly vertical protrusion of Kirkespiret (1590m), is Greenland's Klondike, with burly Canadian labourers and massive lorries working a new **gold mine**. The mine is not yet open to tourists, but in the future Nanortalik tourist office hopes to arrange excursions, including panning for your own golden souvenir. It's possible to hike across to Tasermiut Fjord from here, or to continue a boat tour to the hot springs at Uunartoq Island (p123).

Tasermiut (Ketils Fjord)

Grand and beautiful, Tasermiut winds some 70km northeast from Nanortalik to the nose of a tidewater glacier. The fjord's landscapes are a symphony of grandly chiselled mountains interspersed with relatively lush U-shaped valleys. These are backed with yet more clusters of dangerously oversharpened mountains that seem drawn from a Tolkien fantasy. The drama starts as you round the nose of **Jakobinerhuen** (634m), a bare-stone peak resembling two canoodling walruses. Commanding a scenic mountain-ringed bay, the fjord's only village is picturesque little **Tasiusaq** (population 100). Beyond the photogenic **Nuugaarsuk Peninsula** (with its sheep farm and school summer camp), Greenlanders are excited to see that rarest of phenomena: trees. A few diminutive pines grow beyond

the Kuussuaq river, outlet of Lake Tasersuaq, behind which Qinnguadalen approximates a small forest.

Further up the fjord, Tasermiut's top attractions are the towering finger of **Kirkespiret** (1590m), the gleaming vertical rock-faces of **Ulamertorsuaq** (1830m to 1858m, 'Uli' to climbers) and **Nalumaasortoq** (2045m, 'Nami'), plus the rocky horn of **Ketil** (2003m) with its 1400m granite wall. Beyond lies the green, mosquito-rich valley of **Klosterdalen**, site of a Norse-era Augustinian monastery, of which some very limited ruins remain.

The fjord ends in another flurry of photogenic peaks and a pair of massive, retreating glaciers. Sermitsiaq has already recoiled into its valley, but Sermeq still reaches the fjord. With a small boat you can land and touch the ice, which slopes up in a cracked, slow-motion cascade to over 1300m, pegged by two rocky *nunatak* fangs.

HIKING

There's a 1:100,000 scale Tasermiut hiking map, but don't be fooled – most of the walking in this region is extremely taxing, with some difficult or downright dangerous river crossings and lots of bushwhacking through overzealous shrubby growth. Nonetheless, with such gorgeous surroundings you may find it all worth the struggle. A relatively easy short hike is the bouncy bog-hop between Tasiusaq and Nuugaarsuk. For all other routes take careful advice before setting off.

SLEEPING

Take a tent. Tasiusaq has no formal accommodation, though **Peter Andreasen** (Green house) reportedly offers homestays. Nanortalik school's Nuugaarsuk camp-hostel is beautifully situated, but it's so rundown with graffiti on its walls that at the time of writing management was refusing to accommodate tourists. It's still worth enquiring, and repairs are mooted. Climbers typically strike a base camp at the mouth of the unnamed valley some 5km south of Klosterdalen, allowing convenient attacks on both Uli and Ketil.

GETTING THERE & AWAY

On Wednesday evenings the *Ketil* mini-ferry makes a quick return dash from Nanortalik to Tasiusaq (Dkr185, one hour each way). That trip makes a very scenic excursion, but to see the most dramatic granite peaks you'll

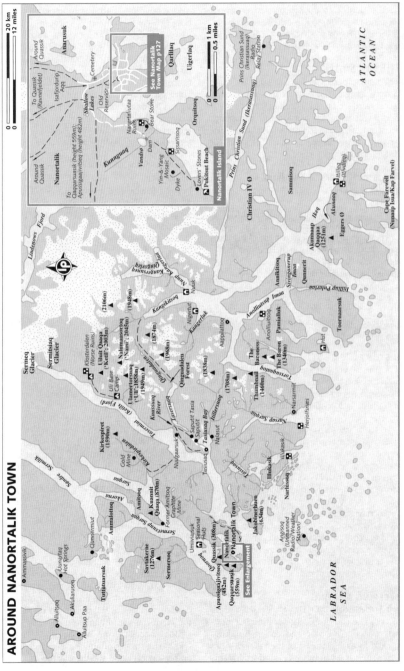

AROUND NANORTALIK TOWN

Enlargement (inset)

See Nanortalik Town Map p127

To Quassik (Ravnefeldet)

Isafjordurp Aqq

Around Quassik

Cemetery

Shadow Lakes

Old Reservoir

Anarusuk

Nanortalik

Around Quassik

To Qaqqarsuasik (height 559m); Apusiigaajiivitseq (height 482m)

Kunnguaq

Nangertaluttaa Ruins

Bear Stone

Dam

Vandso

Yin-&-Yang Mosaic

Dyke

Lovers' Stones

Pukitsut Beach

Sissarsisoq

Orpuitsoq

Qarlilaq

Uigerluaq

Nanortalik Island

Main map

Serneq Glacier

Sermitsiaq Glacier

Sondre Sermilik

Lindenows Fjord

Klosterdalen (Norse Ruins)

Uluit Qaqa 'Ketil' (2003m)

2106m

1948m

Nalumasortoq 'Nami' 2045m

Kangikitsoq

Kangersuneq Qingordleq

Nuuk Kangerlua

Nuuk

Uli Base Camp

Ulamertorsuaq 'Uli' 1858m

1949m

Tasermiut (Ketils Fjord)

Kaussuaq River

Kirkespiret (1590m)

Gold Mine

Kitsigsutarken

Nuulgaarsuk

Tasersuit

Saputit Tasia

Saputit

Tasiusaq Bay

Tasiusaq

Nalasut

1874m

1968m

Qooroq

Qimguadalen Forest

1838m

Hillernaq

1708m

The Baroness

The Baron (1340m)

Thumbnail (1466m)

Torssukatak

Anniliuttup Imaa

Pamialuk

Sivingenerup Imaa

Qunnerit

Toormaarsuk

Anniliutoq

Hut

Narsarmit

Narsaq Sarqaa

Herjolfsnes

Sondre Sermilik

Alorna

Amitsoq

Kuannit Qaqa (870m)

Former Amitsoq Graphite Mine

Sernersuup Sarqaa

Umivarsuk

Seasonal Huts

Savtakerne (1276m)

Qooroq Quassik

Nanortalik

Nanortalik Town

See Enlargement

Jakobinerhuen

Ilukasik

Illukasik

Festisissut

Narttusoq

Ammassivik

Uunafaq Hot Springs

Qimermiut

Ammalortoq

Sermersoq

Apusiigaajiivitseq (482m)

Qaqqarsuasik (559m)

Angisoq (Unmanned Radio/Weather Station)

Christian IV O

Prins Christian Sund (Herrasussuaq)

Prins Christian Sund (Ikerasassuaq)

Sammisoq

Akunnaap Qaqqaa (125m)

Ikeq

Akunaaq

Itilleq 'the valley'

Eggers O

Cape Farewell (Nunap Isua/Kap Farvel)

ATLANTIC OCEAN

Tutfiutuarsuk

Alluitsoq

Ammassivik

Alluitsup Paa

Akularuseq

Illuitsup Saqqa Relay Station

LABRADOR SEA

0   20 km
0   12 miles

0   1 km
0   0.5 miles

need to join a group trip or charter a boat (around Dkr5500) to Klosterdalen or beyond. If there's nobody to share with, consider riding the *Ketil* to Aappilattoq instead.

THE FAR SOUTH

The landscapes east of Nanortalik are quite simply some of the most beautiful on earth. Access and facilities are limited, but the wonderful villages of Aappilattoq and Narsarmiit are stunning places to unwind, and the fjords beyond are unforgettably beautiful when not hidden by fog or blocked by ice.

Narsarmiit (Narsaq Kujalleq/ Frederiksdal)

pop 127

Greenland's southernmost settlement, Narsarmiit has a glorious northwestern backdrop of rocky spires best viewed by walking 2km east along a narrow asphalt lane out to the lighthouse and then looking back. Although the village is less convenient than Aappilattoq as a base for reaching the very finest fjords, the accommodation options are better, and there are a fine **church**, a **sealskin workshop** (☎ 618561) and various short-distance hiking opportunities.

HISTORY

The present village dates from an 1824 Moravian mission that was named Frederiksdal to honour King Frederik VI. Materials for the delightful 1826 church with its perfect little central bell cupola were transported all the way from Qaqortoq in *umiaq* skin boats. Even more extraordinary were the shopping-spree trips made by east-coast families, who would paddle down from Tasiilaq to buy a gun or a few fish hooks from Frederiksdal's store; the return trip might take three to five *years*. Since WWII the village has hosted a radio navigation station. Until the 1980s it was Greenland's node on the Canada to Iceland telecommunications cable, and today it relays crucial signals between aeroplanes and the transatlantic air-traffic control centre in Gander Newfoundland.

SLEEPING & EATING

Tele-Frederiksdal (☎ 618539; kef@tele.gl; s/d/tw Dkr450/ 450/450) The communication station is a modest collection of blue and cream buildings tucked away 500m east of the village. It has three slightly worn but very comfortably fur-nished buildings. Each has equipped kitchen, hot shower, flush toilet, TV room and up to four bedrooms. The biggest also has a billiard table and a super-cute bar, though you must bring your own drinks. Knud and Jaspur speak great English. Note that, while tourists are welcome, reservations can't be 100% guaranteed: the accommodation is designed primarily for visiting technicians, who may arrive suddenly if emergency repairs are required. In such cases your best shot is the **service house** (☎ 618577; sleeping space Dkr125). What you get there is a fold-out couch or floor space in the village meeting room, entered through the public laundry. Camping is best beyond the helipad towards the lighthouse, where the infuriating flies aren't as bad and several streams provide good fresh water. **Pilersuisoq store** (☼ 9am-4pm Mon-Fri, 9am-noon Sat) stocks limited food supplies. Seal meat is available in such abundance that, if you have a knife and a bag, you can often help yourself from a freshly skinned carcass left on rocks by the harbour.

Herjolfsnæs

Across the dramatic Narsap Sarqaa fjord from Narsarmiit lies the windswept Norse site of Herjolfsnæs. It was established by Icelandic merchant Herjólf Bårdsen, who arrived with Erik the Red in 985. Unlike other fjord-head Norse stock-rearing settlements, this was primarily a trading station and would have been the de facto entry and exit point for all medieval commerce between Greenland and Iceland/Norway, hence its relative wealth. Between two arcs of unusually sandy beach, the most visible ruins are of the 13th-century parish church, with piled, cut stones up to a metre high and equally thick. There's also a distinct turf-walled hall close to the concrete shell of a failed 1960s sheep farm. An information-board map shows several more ruins, and there are yet more an hour's walk away at Sandhavn, where much of the settlement's Norse population probably lived.

Archaeologists discovered some of the oldest garments ever found intact preserved in the permafrost beneath the Herjolfsnæs churchyard site. Replicas are on display at the Nanortalik and Narsaq museums.

Boat access from Narsarmiit (around Dkr200 return, 10 minutes each way) depends on reasonably good weather, as the mooring points are guarded by dangerous submerged rocks. A reliable, good-humoured boatman with decent spoken English is **Kristian Kvist** (white cottage B785).

Aappilattoq
pop 160

Superbly photogenic Aappilattoq (Augpilagtoq) sits on a perfect natural harbour, a cleft pyramidal rock face soaring above it. The village surveys an astounding panorama of fjords and bare, spiky peaks. It's so hemmed in by cliffs as to make hiking beyond the lovely rock-knob viewpoints virtually impossible, but its situation is ideal for boat trips into Greenland's most beautiful inland waterways (ice permitting). Unbelievably untouched by tourism, the village economy revolves around seal hunting. If you're not squeamish, and have extremely warm clothing and nerves of steel, the cheapest and most thrilling way to visit the area is by joining a seal hunt. But do be aware just how vulnerable those open, single-engine hunting boats are to the ever-shifting ice and how minimal your chances of rescue are should you have a problem!

Even if you don't stay in Aappilattoq, the ride there and back from Narsarmiit or Nanortalik is an absolute must if you have the opportunity and the good weather to enjoy it.

SLEEPING & EATING

Homestays are somewhat awkward to arrange, but councillor **Lars Isaksen** (☎ 617605) sometimes accepts individual travellers to sleep on his sofa (Dkr150), and he might feed you too. He speaks no English, but his home is a delightful village archetype, and his son-in-law Anthon is an active hunter with a sturdy if uncovered speedboat.

The village service house is the yellow building No1438 in front of the school. For 200Dkr you could sleep on the bare mattress or the foldout sofa in its communal TV room. You'll need to clear this with caretaker Titus Amalie (red house No 1436 on the small ridge directly south of the service house), but as he has no phone it's wise to send messages ahead via the school (☎ 617625).

Although there's precious little flat space, camping is possible and rather idyllic in several flat, mossy depressions that you'll find as you climb the rocky domes beyond the

very makeshift circle of bollards that form the heliport.

Pilersuisoq store (☼ 9am-4pm Mon-Fri, 9am-noon Sat) is surprisingly well stocked for so small a village. Fish is sporadically sold at the portside.

Around Aappilattoq

The grandeur of the region's scenery is extraordinary and worthy of several day trips if you can manage to afford and arrange them. The easiest taster and indeed one of the finest boat rides anywhere is along **Torsukattak** (Torssuqaataq). Crammed with towering granite cliffs, this fjord squeezes all the spiky splendour of Tasermiut (see p130) into a third of the distance. Better still, the spectacle is relatively cheap to gawp at thanks to the public AUL ferry, which passes through between Narsarmiit and Aappilattoq. It's surely the most spectacular passenger ride anywhere. The majestic granite walls of Torsukattak and **Pamialluk Island** have obvious appeal to climbers: the 1340m spire nicknamed the **Baron** was first climbed in 2004, the nearby **Baroness** wall (600m) is increasingly popular, and the 1460m **Thumbnail** is reckoned to be the world's highest sea cliff.

Northeast of Aappilattoq it's a relatively quick flit up **Nuup Kangerlua** to two splendid tidewater glaciers, which have awesome ice walls that calve regularly into the fjord. **Prins Christian Sund** (Ikerasassuaq) is a channel over 60km long with more glacier noses, several fine waterfalls and a parade of half a dozen rounded tipped peaks lining the southern flank of its most picturesque western end. It gets less impressive further east, where there's a permanent radio station but no village. Some cruise ships promise routes through Prins Christian Sund, but this can never be assured as in some years the fjord never entirely clears of ice and passage might prove impossible.

Possibly the most spectacular fjord in all of Greenland is the superlative **Sivinganerup Imaa** south of Aappilattoq, running east between veritable cathedrals of rocky spires. Twin islands **Qunnerit** and **Toornaarsuk** are joined here by a land bridge so insignificant that one can take a Zodiac dinghy across at high tide into **Itilliup Pulariaa**, a fjord so dark, narrow and high sided that it's positively eerie. The grandeur continues on **Eggers Ø** island, where **Akunaaq Inlet** leads to an idyllic if fly-blighted trout stream and frames the surreally sharp needle peak of **Akunnaap Qaqqaa** (1251m). At **Itilleq** (Itivdleq) there's a four-bunk heated hunters' hut (free but often full) at the base of an enchanting abandoned village. Here you'll find well-preserved turf walls, overgrown angelica gardens and a big cross at a fjord lookout. An easy 15-minute stroll past some Inuit graves and up a hummocky rock bluff brings you marvellous panoramas over the **Ikeq fjord** and east across otherworldly lakes to the island's spindly mountain spine.

Pudding-shaped **Cape Farewell** (Nunaap Isua/Kap Farvel) is a pale, barren rocky outcrop that's considered Greenland's southernmost point (though this status ignores Uummannarsuaq and several islets). Icebergs and Cape Farewell's infamous currents sank the *Hans Hedtoft*, Greenland's *Titanic*, in 1959. For scenery the cape isn't inordinately spectacular, but seals are common and views improve dramatically if you venture up the inlets in Eggers Ø's deeply indented southern coast.

Getting There & Away

Once a week (currently Wednesday), weather conditions permitting, the 12-seat mini-ferry *Ketil* sails out and back from Nanortalik to Aappilattoq (Dkr225, 3½ hours) via Narsarmiit (Dkr185, 1¾ hours). It's a fabulous ride but, especially in May and June, ice can block the route completely and a helicopter service might be substituted (Dkr450 to Narsarmiit).

A chartered open boat along Torsukattak (going between Aappilattoq and Narsarmiit) usually costs Dkr400 to Dkr700. Friendly Aappilattoq hunter and boat-owner **Themo Bejaminsen** (☎ 617666) speaks some words of English and can get you almost anywhere that the ice allows for a negotiated fee.

Southwest Greenland

CONTENTS

SOUTHWEST GREENLAND

HIGHLIGHTS

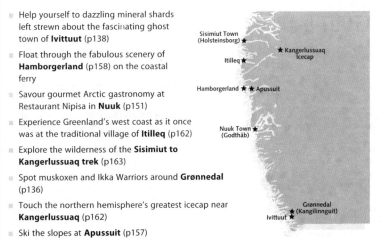

- Help yourself to dazzling mineral shards left strewn about the fascinating ghost town of **Ivittuut** (p138)
- Float through the fabulous scenery of **Hamborgerland** (p158) on the coastal ferry
- Savour gourmet Arctic gastronomy at Restaurant Nipisa in **Nuuk** (p151)
- Experience Greenland's west coast as it once was at the traditional village of **Itilleq** (p162)
- Explore the wilderness of the **Sisimiut to Kangerlussuaq trek** (p163)
- Spot muskoxen and Ikka Warriors around **Grønnedal** (p136)
- Touch the northern hemisphere's greatest icecap near **Kangerlussuaq** (p162)
- Ski the slopes at **Apussuit** (p157)

Sisimiut Town (Holsteinsborg) ★
★ Kangerlussuaq Icecap
Itilleq ★
Hamborgerland ★ ★ Apussuit
Nuuk Town ★ (Godthåb)
Grønnedal ★ (Kangilinnguit)
Ivittuut ★

Southwest Greenland has its share of attractive scenery, great whale-watching spots, lovely fjords, and some of the world's most underestimated sport-fishing opportunities. However, the widely spread villages make transport relatively expensive, so many tourists simply pass through the region en route to Disko Bay, having arrived in Kangerlussuaq, Greenland's main international airport. Kangerlussuaq itself may not be especially beautiful, but it offers easy access to wildlife and the icecap, and some superb wilderness hiking. A popular long-distance trek links Kangerlussuaq to Sisimiut, which is above the Arctic Circle and is thus the southernmost west-coast town to offer dogsledding. Skiing is a possibility in several centres across the region, most notably at Apussuit, near Maniitsoq.

The nation's much-maligned capital, Nuuk, is not a primary tourist attraction, but behind its unaesthetic slab-block buildings lie a photogenic old-town area and a fine museum. Nuuk also has the country's best selection of restaurants, cafés and bars. It commands an impressive if very spread out fjord system, though rain and fog often obscure the views. South of Nuuk, Paamiut and Arsuk are quietly famous for carving crafts, and a few rare white-tailed eagles attract the occasional ornithologist. Tourists are even rarer. Ivittuut, once Greenland's most economically important settlement, is now a fascinating ghost town. It offers appealing mineral-collecting opportunities if you can afford to reach it. To do so, you could start at nearby naval base Grønnedal, the main settlement on the lovely Arsuk-Ikka fjord system. With a fine waterfall, a tidewater glacier and the unique underwater Ikka Warriors, this area could be a considerable tourist attraction were it more easily accessible. As at Kangerlussuaq, Grønnedal is an ideal place to spot those extraordinarily shaggy walking rugs known as muskoxen.

GRØNNEDAL, IVITTUUT & ARSUK

One of Greenland's least-known touristic gems, the lovely Arsuk-Ikka fjord system nonetheless has many attractions. It has a fascinating ghost town, offers unparalleled opportunities for amateur mineralogists and is home to muskoxen, white-tailed eagles and the unique Ikka Warriors. The short-distance hiking options are excellent, and accommodation is a relative bargain.

Maps show three towns. Arsuk is served by the coastal ferry but sometimes gets cut off by rough waves. Ivittuut was (and on paper still is) the main local municipality, but Ivittuut town itself is no longer inhabited and confusingly the municipality office (Ivittuut Kommunia) is physically in Grønnedal, 5km away. Grønnedal's position would make an ideal tourist hub. However, it is fundamentally a naval base, not a town, and that means you need permission before you turn up. Getting this permission is usually straightforward, but make sure you arrange everything well in advance through Ivittuut Kommunia.

GRØNNEDAL (KANGILINNGUIT)
pop 154

Grønnedal (Kangilinnguit by Greenlandic translation) was founded as 'Green Valley' by the American navy during the Second World War to protect the highly strategic cryolite quarry at nearby Ivittuut (see p138). Since 1951 it has been the main Danish naval base in Greenland, focussed mainly on fishery protection, coastguard and rescue work. Neatly arranged wooden buildings are colourfully painted, there are no tank traps or fences and the friendly atmosphere is way more relaxed than you might

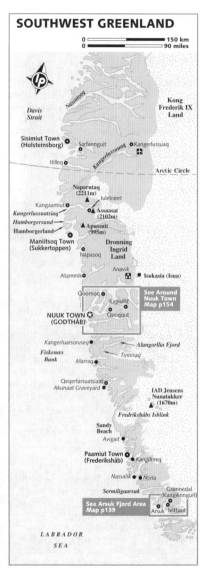

SOUTHWEST GREENLAND

[Map of Southwest Greenland showing locations including Davis Strait, Sisimiut Town (Holsteinsborg), Itilleq, Sarfannguit, Kangerlussuaq, Kong Frederik IX Land, Arctic Circle, Naparutaq (2211m), Juletræet, Kangaamiut, Assaasat (2102m), Kangerlussuatsiaq, Hamborgersund, Hamborgerland, Apussuit (995m), Maniitsoq Town (Sukkertoppen), Napasoq, Dronning Ingrid Land, Atammik, Anavik, Isukasia (Isua), Qoornoq, Kapisillit, See Around Nuuk Town Map p154, NUUK TOWN (GODTHÅB), Qooqqut, Kangerluarsoruseq, Fiskenæs Bank, Alangorllia Fjord, Tinnisaq, Marraq, Qeqertarsuatsiaat, Akunaat Graveyard, IAD Jensens Nunatakker (1670m), Fredrikshåbs Isblink, Sandy Beach, Avigait, Paamiut Town (Frederikshåb), Kangilineq, Nassalik, Neria, Sermiligaarsuk, Grønnedal (Kangilinnguit), See Arsuk Fjord Area Map p139, Arsuk, Ivittuut, LABRADOR SEA]

0 ——— 150 km
0 ——— 90 miles

See Around Nuuk Town Map p154

See Arsuk Fjord Area Map p139

expect from a military outpost. If you take time and make friends here you may be able to hitch boat rides or even borrow somebody's kayak. If not, there are plenty of tempting short hikes nearby. Grønnedal's fjordside setting is especially lovely when golden sunsets blaze behind distinctive Mt Kugnat.

Information

At **Ivittuut Kommunia** (☎ 691077; sp@ivikom.ki.gl), contact Sonja Peary well in advance for all tourist information, accommodation and arrangements.

There are no bank or exchange facilities.

Sleeping

Contact Ivittuut Kommunia. If space allows they'll reserve you a place either in Ivittuut ghost town (see p138) or better still in the comfortable on-base **'hotel'** (B126; s/tw Dkr250/500), which is primarily designed for servicemen's guests. Neat, unfussy rooms off college-style corridors have private toilet and shower and share a very pleasant kitchen and sitting room. Sheets and towels are included. Walkers may use the Kommunia's basic rural huts (or at Arnaqqivassat a caravan that's been specially helicoptered in). There's no charge, but you should book ahead.

Eating

If you're classified as an official guest of the Grønnedal base, you'll be allowed to use the excellent-value **Kostforplejning canteen** (meals Dkr20-65; ☯ 7-8am, noon & 5.30pm sharp Mon-Thu, 7-8am, noon & 6.30pm Fri, 9-10am & 5.30pm Sat & Sun), the **Kostudsalg grocery shop** (☯ 3-5pm Mon, 2-4pm Wed & Fri) and the friendly **Nanoq Bar** (Konstabel Klub; beers Dkr16; ☯ 7pm-close Mon-Sat, 2-4pm Sun). There's no alternative shopping, so nonguests need to bring all supplies from Arsuk or beyond.

Getting There & Away

AIR

Kangilinnguit (code JGR), as Air Greenland calls Grønnedal, is on the viciously expensive Paamiut–Qaqortoq–Narsaq–Narsarsuaq helicopter route. Perversely, fares from Narsarsuaq (Dkr2042, 1½ hours) are cheaper than from Qaqortoq (Dkr2666, 40 minutes) or Narsaq (Dkr2431, 90 minutes). Some Paamiut flights (Dkr1726, 40 minutes) continue to Nuuk (Dkr4937, 2½ hours), but flying via Narsarsuaq (6½ hours) costs less (Dkr4409).

BOAT

The official rate for a boat transfer to Arsuk starts at Dkr1800, but it's not usually too hard to find someone who will take you for around Dkr600 if the weather is perfect. In unfavourable winds the ride can be totally impossible. For around Dkr2000 day-trip charters are possible on the Ivittuut Kommunia boat (maximum capacity 12).

AROUND GRØNNEDAL
Ivittuut (Ivigtut)

This well-maintained ghost town is built around an 80m-deep cryolite quarry. It's now filled with water but was once the single most important hole in Greenland (see the boxed text, below). Cryolite supplies ran out in 1987, and by 2001 the last families and even the town hall had relocated to Grønnedal.

The town is a dream for stone collectors. Over 90 types of mineral occur within a square kilometre. Rock fragments from the quarry workings lie all over town and make it very easy to find superb quartz and cryolite specimens embedded with glittery galena or shimmering gold-brown flakes of siderite. Every August there are residential hands-on courses on gem-finding, polishing and general geology. A large yellow house is slowly being converted into a **geological museum**, though don't expect much before around 2007. Of the other surviving buildings, the most delightful is a little gingerbread-style pavilion above a former tennis court. Known as the **Norwegian Tea House**, this was originally part of Norway's stand at the 1889 Paris World's Fair, making it a little brother to the Eiffel Tower. Behind is a poignant old graveyard, with white markers for men and black for women.

The large white mansion surveying the quarry hole is nicknamed the **Castle** and was once the manager's luxurious home. Now it's getting spookily derelict. The large red building nearby housed the staff canteen, and the kitchens still look useable.

SLEEPING & EATING

Two well-kept former houses and a converted former clinic now make up a seasonal but unstaffed **hotel** (s/d Dkr250/500; ☻ Jun-Sep). Each has electricity, a kitchen, shared bathrooms and flush toilets. Bring food with you unless you have other arrangements with the Ivittuut Kommunia, where the keys are kept.

GETTING THERE & AWAY

By arrangement (and snow permitting), someone from the Kommunia can drive you from Grønnedal to Ivittuut and back for Dkr100 per person including commentary. Otherwise it's a pleasant, easy walk, 5km each way along a fjordside gravel road.

Ikka Fjord

Ikka Fjord culminates in a perfect, high-sided U-shaped valley called Ikka Bund. Here, Inuit legends claim that an ancient force of invaders crashed through the ice and were petrified into stalagmite-like stone pillars. Up to 20m tall, the tops of these underwater **Ikka Warriors** reach within a metre or two of the fjord's surface. Though not always easy to locate, they are visible from a boat at low tide using a viewing periscope. Young pillars are composed of a unique 'living mineral' named Ikaite. Geologists discovered

---

CRYOLITE

Opaquely white, the mineral cryolite is known as *orsugiak* to Inuit fishers. They once used it to weight their fishing nets, as it's easy to drill holes in and doesn't dissolve in water. Cryolite means 'frost-stone' in Greek, but its value comes when it's hot. It had been used since 1853 for making soda for glass making and textile colouring, but in the 1890s someone noticed that adding cryolite to aluminium ore made it melt at half the normal temperature. This may sound an arcane scientific fact, but it was a revolution. Today, light, malleable aluminium metal is everywhere from aeroplanes to pans to 'tin' foil. It's made by electrolysing molten ore and, without cryolite, melting that ore was impracticably expensive. As the world's biggest source of cryolite, Ivittuut was made very wealthy by the discovery. The workers' dormitories came to be nicknamed 'millionaires' alley'. Between 1922 and 1956 the town even minted its own coins (examples are on display in the Ivittuut Kommunia office in Grønnedal). Cryolite's importance peaked in WWII. With aluminium essential for fighter planes and Denmark occupied by Nazi Germany, the US military rushed to safeguard the Ivittuut mine. America commandeered cryolite for the Allied war effort and in return supplied Greenland with basic food, clothing and essential imports. By the 1980s, however, a synthetic cryolite alternative had become available. With the natural source almost exhausted, the Ivittuut mine closed altogether in 1987.

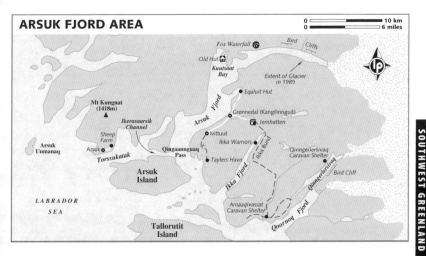

ARSUK FJORD AREA

0 — 10 km
0 — 6 miles

Fox Waterfall · *Bird Cliffs*
Old Hut
Kuutsaat Bay
Extent of Glacier in 1985
Eqaluit Hut
Mt Kungnat (1418m) ▲
Ikerasaarsik Channel
Grønnedal (Kangilinnguit)
Jernhatten
Sheep Farm
Ivittuut
Ikka Warriors
Arsuk Fjord
Arsuk Uumanaq
Arsuk ○
Torssukatak
Qingaannguaq Pass
Qinngerlersivaq Caravan Shelter
Taylers Havn
Arsuk Island
Ikka Fjord
Ikka Bund
Bird Cliff
Qiongerlersivaq
LABRADOR SEA
Arnaaqivassat Caravan Shelter
Qoornoq Fjord
Tallorutit Island

SOUTHWEST GREENLAND

that, when removed from the sea, this simply disintegrates into sand and a puddle of water. Older pillars, however, are stabilised by algae that excrete layers of chalky calcium carbonate, allowing mature examples like the one displayed in Ivittuut Kommunia in Grønnedal to be removed whole.

A lovely boat stop between Ikka and Grønnedal is **Taylers Havn**, an idyllic natural harbour where the pebble beaches are littered with mussels. It's named for one of the 19th-century geologists who explored the area on behalf of the cryolite barons. It's possible if rather taxing to trek back to Ivittuut from here across the 310m Qingaannguaq pass.

Arsuk Fjord

The attractive fjord culminates in an impressive, occasionally calving tidewater glacier with an ice cliff over 50m high. Although it's possible to get right up to the ice by kayak, it's strongly advised that you stay at least three times the height of the ice away from it at all times. Attractions en route include lovely **Kuutsaat Bay** (Ellerslie Havn) and the **Fox Waterfall**, named for Ivittuut's original cryolite-carrying clipper ship. When in full flow, these three-stage falls can be extremely impressive. An important **bird cliff** on the north shore towards the ice face is most active in spring, but close approaches are not allowed.

Hiking

A 1:75,000 Ivittuut hiking map (Dkr55) is sometimes available in Grønnedal. Easy but very rewarding is the 1½-hour jaunt up **Jernhatten**, which offers breathtaking panoramas over Ikka Fjord and the rugged ice-streaked mountains behind. From the base, where the road turns 90 degrees, a very clear track winds up as far as a red hut at around 400m altitude (walk unconfrontationally around any muskoxen that might block your way). From the hut, climb steeply beside the small stream, keeping right of a double lake. Jernhatten is the small, fairly unimposing rise behind. You could continue down to Ikka Bund, but without a boat you won't see the warriors.

Eqaluit is another short, simple stroll away. There's a hut if you want to stay overnight and there are excellent fishing opportunities for Arctic char.

ARSUK

pop 155

Sweet little Arsuk, founded in 1805, is primarily useful as the ferry stop for Grønnedal and Ivittuut. Once, however, during the 1970s cod boom, it was one of the world's richest villages (per capita). Tales of BMWs and Mercedes are exaggerated, but there were indeed cars on the few hundred metres of paved roads. Perhaps this explains the strange misnomers of the town's two 'motels'.

Information

Post office (☎ 685044; 🕑 9am-3pm Mon-Fri) Upstairs within the Pilersuisoq supermarket. Sells AUL tickets and can photocopy a town map for you.

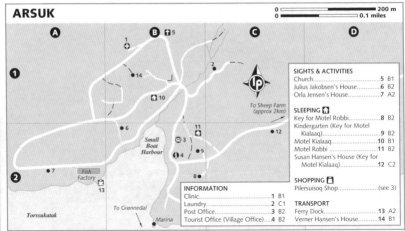

ARSUK

SIGHTS & ACTIVITIES	
Church.................................5 B1	
Julius Jakobsen's House..............6 B2	
Orla Jensen's House..................7 A2	
SLEEPING	
Key for Motel Robbi..................8 B2	
Kindergarten (Key for Motel	
Kialaaq)...........................9 B2	
Motel Kialaaq......................10 B1	
Motel Robbi........................11 B2	
Susan Hansen's House (Key for	
Motel Kialaaq)...................12 C2	
SHOPPING	
Pilersuisoq Shop...............(see 3)	
TRANSPORT	
Ferry Dock.........................13 A2	
Verner Hansen's House..............14 B1	
INFORMATION	
Clinic...............................1 B1	
Laundry.............................2 C1	
Post Office..........................3 B2	
Tourist Office (Village Office)....4 B2	

Tourist office (☎ 685022; pemi@paamiut.gl; ⏰ 10am-2pm Mon-Fri) Just a non-English-speaking gentleman in the village office with out-of-date Danish-language brochures. **www.arsuk.gl/tak.htm** Takes you to the relevant section of the (Danish-language) Arsuk Fjord website.

Sights

Arsuk's cute timber **church** (built 1930) has a double roof of grey-green shingles and a little black spire. Of several artists, the best known is the charming **Julius Jakobsen** (B186), who made a famous cryolite bear that was presented to Queen Margrethe of Denmark in 2001. During his 75th birthday *kaffemik*, the queen popped in to his Arsuk home to say thank you! Julius' work is in great demand (there's a long waiting list), but his wife's top-quality beadwork may be for sale. **Orla Jensen's house** (B865) has one of the loveliest bay views in town. Orla grinds, mounts and sells local minerals, including rare black Nuumiit, and also smokes trout and salmon.

Walk east beyond the sheep farm for a good chance to spot eagles.

In the west of town, curious **Arsuk Uumanaq** island looks like the profile of Charles de Gaulle when viewed from offshore.

Sleeping

Two unoccupied houses offer rooms with equipped kitchen, sitting room and rudimentary shower. Both inexplicably call themselves 'motels'. The nicer is the lime-green **Motel Kialaaq** (B237; s/tw Dkr350/700), with flush toilet

and an airy lounge. Discounts for groups of six or more should be discussed with owner **Susan Hanssen** (☎ 685188; B825), who works at the kindergarten.

Deep green **Motel Robi** (B508; s/tw Dkr250/450) is nicer than the ragged porch settee and crumbling chimney suggest, though the shower is ropy and there's a Greenland-style box toilet. Get the key from B512.

Getting There & Away

Northbound coastal ferries stop in weekly en route to Disko Bay via Paamiut (Dkr330, 6½ hours) and Nuuk (Dkr980, 24 hours). Southbound they head for Narsaq (Dkr410, eight hours) and Qaqortoq (Dkr575, 11 hours), but in midsummer they stop in Qaqortoq (nine hours) first and extend the route to Narsarsuaq (Dkr840, 16 hours). In early summer ice can cause severe delays.

For a boat transfer to Ivittuut or Grønnedal, try **Verner Hansen** (☎ 685007, 576565; B761; no English).

PAAMIUT REGION

With a strong craft tradition, wildlife to watch and numerous abandoned villages to explore, the Paamiut region could be a treasure trove for tourists. However, the main town lacks the photogenic charm of other southern Greenland towns and transport is relatively awkward, so very few visitors ever take the trouble to stop.

PAAMIUT TOWN (FREDERIKSHÅB)

pop 2000

Lacking in sea views, Paamiut is a somewhat nondescript mix of colourful cottages and glum apartment blocks on a modest plain edged with rocky hills. The offshore waters are relatively good for watching humpback whales in September, and the region is ideal for spotting white-tailed eagles. Local outfitter Birger Knudsen is a particularly knowledgeable guide if you can find a moment when he's free. Don't worry about outdated rumours circulated elsewhere in Greenland that Paamiut is lawless or dangerous. Though it's somewhat economically depressed and has its share of drunken rascals, the sheer lack of visitors makes Paamiut a relatively easy place to make local friends.

History

Established in 1742 as Frederikshåb, Paamiut became the regional KGH fur-trading colony and was known for its whale products and soapstone artists. Until WWII the village was little more than the current museum district with a few harbourside warehouses and a sprinkling of turf homes opposite. Everything changed with the 1950s cod boom. Paamiut expanded, local villages were closed and people moved en masse into the town's new apartment blocks. The population was slated to grow to 10,000 by 1990. However, cod stocks evaporated virtually overnight in 1989. The fish factory, Paamiut's main employer, stalled. Suddenly the town had major unemployment problems, and the population dwindled. However, after several false restarts there's a certain newfound optimism with a 2004 refit of the fish factory to process snowcrabs. The town also hosts Greenland's maritime training school, a handicrafts co-operative and the country's only candle factory.

Information

Note that there is no public Internet access in Paamiut.

Birger Knudsen (☎ /fax 681019; PO Box 84, DK-3940 Paamiut) An outfitter with an exceptional depth of local knowledge, Birger knows where to find a wealth of local wildlife, is a mine of interesting historical titbits, and can arrange reasonably priced boat excursions, mountaineering trips and local accommodation including getaway fjordside cabins.

Hospital (☎ 681211; Poul Ibsensvej)

Police (☎ 681222; Augo Lygnip Aq)

Post office (☎ 681255; Poul Ibsensvej 1; ☽ 8.45am-3pm Mon-Fri) Two ATMs inside.

Tourist office (☎ 681673) Within the museum. Has free town maps and sells 1:250,000 regional ones (Dkr50). Organises choir shows and kayaking displays for rare cruise-ship arrivals, but doesn't offer regular excursions for independent travellers. Staff changes frequently.

Sights

A circle of five historic stone-and-timber buildings around a turf-ringed former wellhouse constitute **Paamiut Museum** (☎ 681673; fax 681854; admission free; ☽ 10am-noon & 1-3pm Mon-Fri, 1-4pm Sun). The 1839 former **governor's residence** (B10) contains the main museum exhibition hall and tourist office. The **old trading post** (B55) has bubble-tar doors, a cooperage and a geological collection upstairs. Downstairs the whaling exhibits include a very rare sealskin diving suit, a reproduction of an original sold in 1913 and now in St Petersburg. Other buildings such as the 1878 **goat house** (B19) have no exhibits, but the **Carpenters' House** (B17) still has the little bell that would ring to announce work availability. The **former post office** (B38) is used by Alcoholics Anonymous.

The original Inuit settlement was beside the current **Candle Factory** (Naneruusiorfik; Titkit B15; ☽ 8am-noon & 1-4pm Mon-Fri), and one **turf house** has been reconstructed (get the key from the museum). The preserved 1948 fishing boat **Dina** beside it was the first of its type during the cod boom and was owned by controversial local godfather Anthon Petersen.

Fredenskirche (Othorssussuup Av B83), Paamiut's colourful 1909 church, has a Norwegian-style Hansel-and-Gretel façade. Incredibly the church was 'stretched' by 6m in the 1980s: try to spot the added two-window section. To visit the interior, enquire at the **priest's office** (Poul Ibsensvej B86; ☽ 10am-1pm Mon-Fri), which is a relatively grand red mansion across the footbridge. The neighbouring scraggy park has a **whalebone gateway** and a children's slide imaginatively formed around a sculpture of a harpoon and *ulo* (flensing knife).

Paamiut is known for its craftspeople, especially soapstone carvers. The **carvers' co-operative** (☽ irregular) occupies a small room of a nicely renovated 1930s trade warehouse (upstairs on the left opposite the toilets). **Ujaloq Gift Shop** (☎ 681329; Qunnemut B622; 10am-5pm Mon-Fri) has an attached sealskin workshop and sells decently priced souvenirs.

SOUTHWEST GREENLAND

SOUTHWEST GREENLAND

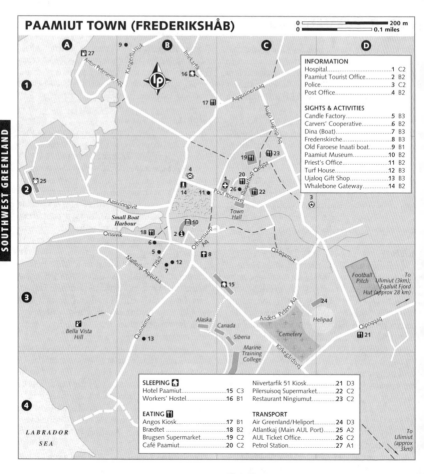

PAAMIUT TOWN (FREDERIKSHÅB)

0 — 200 m
0 — 0.1 miles

INFORMATION	
Hospital	1 C2
Paamiut Tourist Office	2 B2
Police	3 C2
Post Office	4 B2

SIGHTS & ACTIVITIES	
Candle Factory	5 B3
Carvers' Cooperative	6 B2
Dina (Boat)	7 B3
Fredenskirche	8 B3
Old Faroese Inaati boat	9 B1
Paamiut Museum	10 B2
Priest's Office	11 B2
Turf House	12 B3
Ujaloq Gift Shop	13 B3
Whalebone Gateway	14 B2

SLEEPING	
Hotel Paamiut	15 C3
Workers' Hostel	16 B1

EATING	
Angos Kiosk	17 B1
Brædtet	18 B2
Brugsen Supermarket	19 C2
Café Paamiut	20 C2

Niivertarfik 51 Kiosk	21 D3
Pilersuisoq Supermarket	22 C2
Restaurant Ningiumut	23 C2

TRANSPORT	
Air Greenland/Heliport	24 D3
Atlantkaj (Main AUL Port)	25 A2
AUL Ticket Office	26 C2
Petrol Station	27 A1

Bella Vista hill is topped by a wooden lookout point, reconstructed from a late-19th-century original. Views are extensive.

Within sight of the main Atlantkaj port is the rusting shipwreck **Greenland Star**. Its demise was so suspiciously convenient for the crew's escape that the Dkr32,000,000 insurance was never paid out. Within three days the hulk had been comprehensively looted.

With a guide, a very pleasant walk southwest of town (one hour each way) winds through bogs and rocky hills and past rocky inlets to the peaceful **Ulimiut Inuit ruins**. The ruins themselves are just raised turfs beneath thicker grass, but the bay and promontory make a lovely picnic or camp site.

Sleeping

Hotel Paamiut (☎ 681798; fax 681328; B346 Kirkegårds-vej; s/d/tw Dkr794/998/998) The hotel is a long unmarked red building. Use the central door and go upstairs to seek out the unstoppably talkative manager. In galloping, flawless English he seems to be simultaneously understudying for *Fawlty Towers* and *The Shining*. Most rooms are overpriced: tatty, slightly musty and with communal bathroom. However, for the same price there are also three bungalows with kitchen and bathroom. One is significantly nicer than the others, and if the hotel is empty (it often is) you might get it to yourself for Dkr794 per person. Rates include breakfast in the underused restaurant, where guests (only) can take a dinner of the day (Dkr68) if they order by noon. There's a surprisingly well-stocked (and well-fortified) wine cellar.

There's no other formal accommodation. However, **Birger Knudsen** (☎ /fax 681019) might manage to find you a homestay or arrange beds in the passably comfortable three-room **worker's hostel** (B298 Imekarfik; s/tw Dkr200/400) owned by **Betoncentral** (☎ 681160; frhbeton@greennet.gl; Imekarfik 10).

Eating

Restaurant Ningiumut (☎ 681299; B287 Illokafiup Kerka; beers Dkr40; ☉ 10.30am-1.30pm & 9pm-midnight Mon-Thu, 10am-2pm & 7pm-3am Fri, 9pm-3am Sat) Behind a somewhat quaint façade, this is a run-of-the-mill Greenlandic beerhouse. However, at lunchtimes it serves open sandwiches (Dkr20) and a set hot meal (Dkr32) that's filling if gastronomically forgettable.

Café Paamiut (☎ 681779; B580 Illokafiup Kerka; snacks Dkr14-36; ☉ 9am-6.30pm Mon-Fri, 9am-1pm Sat, noon-4pm Sun) Brightly painted walls and local naive art make the Café Paamiut relatively pleasant by fast-food standards. It serves burgers and hot dogs.

Facing off in the town centre are two well-stocked supermarkets: **Brugsen** (B764 Illokafiup Kerka; ☉ 9am-6pm Mon-Fri, 9.30am-2pm Sat-Sun) and **Pilersuisoq** (B953 Illokafiup Kerka; ☉ 7am-5.30pm Mon-Thu, 7am-6pm Fri, 7am-1pm Sat-Sun). Both have bakery counters. The **brædtet** at the old harbour sells fresh fish. Of several overpriced kiosks the best are **Angos** (B439 Avkusinertaak; ☉ 10am-9pm) and **Niivertarfik 51** (B946 Qipoqqaq; ☉ 10am-11pm Sun-Thu, 10am-midnight Fri-Sat), beyond the heliport.

Getting There & Away

AIR

Air Greenland (☎ 681288; Heliport; ☉ 9am-3pm Mon-Fri) has helicopters on Monday and Wednesday to and from Narsarsuaq (Dkr2042) via Grønnedal/Kangilinnguit (Dkr1726), Qaqortoq (Dkr3252, 1¾ hours) and Narsaq. On Wednesday helicopters connect to Nuuk (Dkr3211, 1½ hours).

BOAT

Weekly in each direction, AUL's *Sarpik Ittuk* calls for 30 minutes at Paamiut's Atlantkaj dock en route between Qaqortoq (Dkr780, 19 hours) and Nuuk (Dkr725, 17 hours). That's just enough time to run and glimpse the façades of the church and the museum buildings, at least in midsummer (in other seasons boats arrive when it's too dark). Tickets are sold at **AUL** (☎ 681799; B580 Illokafiup Kerka; ☉ 9am-3pm Mon-Fri), beside Café Paamiut.

Getting Around

For a taxi call ☎ 576427 (mobile) or 498298. There's no tourist boat for hire, but most residents have a speedboat. Reliable, English-speaking boat owners include **Ottorak Møller** (☎ 498124) and the ever-resourceful **Birger Knudsen** (☎ 681019).

AROUND PAAMIUT TOWN

Paamiut sits at the mouth of **Kuannersooq** (Kvanefjord), a long multi-armed fjord that reaches inland toward several dramatic tidewater glaciers. **Nerutussoq's** three-branched fjord system is fairly picturesque, and there are a couple of cabins. **Avigait** (closed 1984) and **Nassalik** (closed 1973) are ghost villages with houses still maintained as summer retreats. **Kangilineq**, more accessible from Paamiut, has two houses, a stone church and a turf house. South of the eternally ice-filled **Sermilik fjord** is **Neria**, with four little homes.

Two hours by speedboat north of Paamiut is the 20km-wide **Frederikshåbs Isblink glacier**. It doesn't reach the sea, but its grey-black summer ice looms above an outwash plain highly rated by caribou hunters. There's a wide curve of sandy beach where you might find whalebones.

Hiking

Paamiut is not ideal for long-distance hiking, and even those walks that are reasonably easy are hampered by the lack of a 1:100,000 map. Beware of following *Trekking in Greenland*'s suggestions for a long route circling up to the inland ice near Nunatarssuaq hill (730m): the Qordlortoq river is usually impassable here, and helicopter rescues are very expensive.

The only standard hiking route takes you to a hut at the head of the short **Eqaluit fjord** (about eight hours). Start by bearing east from the end of the asphalt on Qipoqqaq (the street running east from the south edge of Paamiut's heliport). Keep south of the big radio mast, then veer north around the biggest lakes rather than following the waterpipe south. Occasional red path-markers aren't always obvious.

PAAMIUT TO NUUK

Running between Paamiut and Nuuk the coastal ferry's only stop is **Qeqertarsuatsiaat** (Fiskenæsset). It's a small seal-hunting village rising unspectacularly on the northern tip of a large, relatively low-lying island. On the same island is the ghost village of **Akunaat**, founded by German missionaries as Lichtenfels, of which only a graveyard remains. To see anything else in this section you'll need a private charter boat.

About 60km north of Qeqertarsuatsiaat, the abandoned WWII **Marraq airfield** site is still discernible thanks to a few oil drums and an old jeep. Another 12km northeast the narrow Amitsuarssussuaq channel leads into the extremely impressive **Alangorllia fjord**. The soaring southern wall rises almost vertically to around 1500m and is sliced through with glaciers, while the north shore is roamed by plentiful reindeer. The fjord is almost closed off by a constriction called Tinissaaq, where tidal water-level changes leave icebergs curiously stranded and can produce fearsome currents and waterfall-like sluices. It's only passable by small boats at mid-tide.

About 50km before Nuuk, the once-picturesque village of **Kangerluarsoruseq** (Færingehavn) is now abandoned and looted. The Danish name means 'Faroese harbour', as it was here that cod fishers from the Faroe Islands were granted permission to reside from 1900, setting up small cod-boat stations all along the coast. Færingehavn became a major cod-processing centre, and locals from Paamiut would at times consider it worth sailing all the way there to get better prices for their catch. In 1989 the cod disappeared and the village died.

NUUK REGION

NUUK TOWN (GODTHÅB)

pop16,200

Nuuk is Greenland's capital and by far its biggest, most cosmopolitan town. It commands a grand fjord system and is backed by a splendid panorama of mountains. From carefully chosen angles the town can look picturesque, and if you haven't seen anywhere else in Greenland you may find it almost quaint. But if you've been travelling around the country it's easy to get depressed by Nuuk's decaying heart of long-slab apart-ment blocks and its rather pervasive sense of economic apartheid. You'd do better to start than to end a trip here.

History

Nuuk was home to 12 Greenlandic families in 1728 when missionary Hans Egede moved in and officially founded the trading-post village as Godthåb. Egede is now revered as the 'Greenland Apostle', yet his insistence on nuclear families caused enormous social change, the impact of which can still be traced today. One Greenlandic leader, Ulaajuk, dismayed at his people's growing materialism and dependence on mission trade goods, moved them away from Nuuk. Then in 1736 a smallpox epidemic decimated the remaining population. Hans Egede's wife, Gertrude Rask, was among the dead, and Egede himself returned to Denmark. Nonetheless, he left his sons to carry on his work, and their missions continued to attract people to Godthåb. During WWII the town became the administrative centre of Greenland. It boomed from the 1950s, when Denmark made a well-intentioned but retrospectively questionable attempt to launch Greenland into the 'modern' world. The giant, ugly housing blocks were initially a great opportunity for locals to escape the discomfort and sometimes unhealthy conditions of their turf homes. However, as elsewhere, the estates soon dislocated people from their culture and became centres of social discontent.

Orientation

Nuuk has two main lobes. The centre's architecturally functional commercial area is a V formed by Aqqusinersuaq and partly pedestrianised Imaneq. To the west (Kolonihavn) and south (university district) you'll find older homes with some real Greenlandic charm, but to the direct north and east are rows of spirit-crushing housing blocks.

Nuuk's second lobe, further to the north-east, contains the mostly residential Nuussuaq and Equalugalinnguit suburbs. Directly to the east but accessed by a long horseshoe of road is Nuuk airport, some 5km from the centre. Roads currently end at the disconnected new Qinngorput estate 2km beyond.

MAPS

The tourist office's excellent free city maps are also available in hotels including the

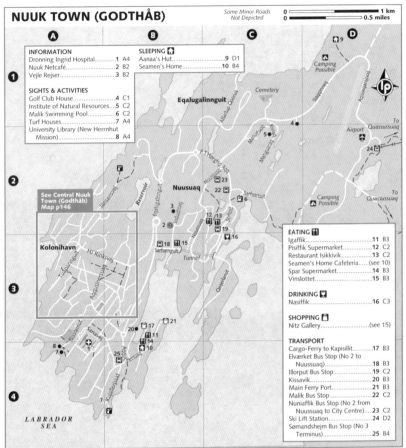

NUUK TOWN (GODTHÅB)

Some Minor Roads Not Depicted

INFORMATION	
Dronning Ingrid Hospital	1 A4
Nuuk Netcafé	2 B2
Vejle Rejser	3 B2

SIGHTS & ACTIVITIES	
Golf Club House	4 C1
Institute of Natural Resources	5 C2
Malik Swimming Pool	6 C2
Turf Houses	7 A4
University Library (New Herrnhut Mission)	8 A4

SLEEPING	
Aanaa's Hut	9 D1
Seamen's Home	10 B4

EATING	
Igaffik	11 B3
Pisiffik Supermarket	12 C2
Restaurant Isikkivik	13 C2
Seamen's Home Cafeteria	(see 10)
Spar Supermarket	14 B3
Vinslottet	15 B3

DRINKING	
Nasiffik	16 C3

SHOPPING	
Nitz Gallery	(see 15)

TRANSPORT	
Cargo-Ferry to Kapisillit	17 B3
Elværket Bus Stop (No 2 to Nuussuaq)	18 B3
Illorput Bus Stop	19 C2
Kissavik	20 B3
Main Ferry Port	21 B3
Malik Bus Stop	22 C2
Nuniaffik Bus Stop (No 2 from Nuussuaq to City Centre)	23 C2
Ski Lift Station	24 D2
Sømandshjem Bus Stop (No 3 Terminus)	25 B4

SOUTHWEST GREENLAND

Seamen's Home, handy for those arriving by boat. The 1:75,000 *Hiking Map West Greenland – Nuuk* is sold at the tourist office for Dkr80, but be aware that Nuuk's road system has been extended considerably since its publication. The useful 1:250,000 *Vesterbygden* map (Dkr70) takes the Saga Nuuk Fjord map and adds historical and archaeological details on the reverse.

Information
BOOKSHOPS
Atuagkat Boghandel (Map p146; ☎ 321737; atuagkat@greennet.gl; Imaneq 9; ⏱ 10am-5.30pm Mon-Thu, 10am-6pm Fri, 10am-1pm Sat) Greenland's largest bookshop has a limited but extremely well-chosen selection of books in English dealing with Greenlandic history, culture, economy,

politics and natural history. Maps, and a few guidebooks and postcards, are also available. Mail order available.
Atuakkiorfik (Map p146; ☎ 322122; Hans Egedesvej 3; ⏱ 8am-4pm Mon-Fri) Greenland's main publisher. The office is most useful to buy Dkr4 postcards and the *Birds in Greenland* guide (Dkr135).

EMERGENCY
Ambulance (☎ 344112)
Dronning Ingrid Hospital (Map p145; ☎ 323312; Tjalfesvej B1826)
Police (Map p146; ☎ 321448; PH Lundsteensvej 1)

INTERNET ACCESS
Hotel Hans Egede (Map p146; per quarter/half/full hr Dkr25/45/80; ⏱ 7am-10pm) Two computers in a foyer booth. Daily rate Dkr200.

SOUTHWEST GREENLAND

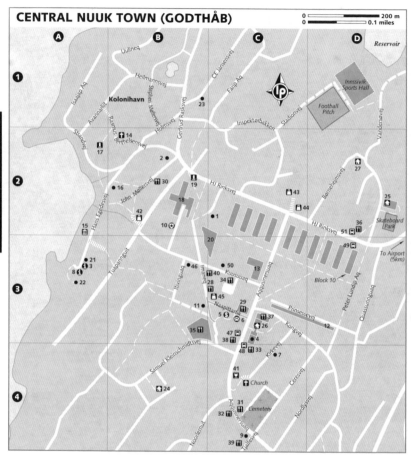

CENTRAL NUUK TOWN (GODTHÅB)

Nuuk Netcafé (Map p145; Comby; ☎ 342677; www.nnc
.gl; Industrivej 31; per half/full hr Dkr30/45; ☺ 4pm-midnight
Mon-Thu, 4pm-1am Fri, noon-1am Sat, noon-midnight Sun)
Public & National Library (Map p146; Nunatta Atua-
gaateqarfia; ☎ 321156; Centervej; ☺ 10am-7pm Mon &
Wed, noon-7pm Tue & Thu, 10am-5pm Fri, 10am-2pm Sat)
Half-hour slots are free at four Internet computers, but you
often need to sign up a day in advance. Ten-minute slots on
one other computer are available on a queue basis.

MONEY & POST
Grønlandsbanken (Map p146; Naapittarfik; ☺ 10am-
3pm Mon-Fri) Charges Dkr75 to change travellers cheques.
Expect long queues for the ATMs (open 6am to 6pm) at
weekends.
Main Post Office (Map p146; ☎ 321855; Aqqusinersuaq
4; ☺ 10am-3pm Mon-Fri, 10am-1pm Sat) Two ATMs inside.

TOURIST INFORMATION
Greenland Tourism (Map p146; ☎ 342820;
www.greenland.com) Occupies the same building as Nuuk
Tourism.
Nuuk Tourism (Map p146; ☎ 322700; www.nuuk
-tourism.gl; Hans Egedesvej 29; ☺ 10am-4pm Mon-Fri
year-round & noon-4pm Sat & Sun Jun-Aug) Excellent free
city maps, good souvenir shop and useful brochures. Its extensive range of tours are the easiest way to see the fjord
without your own contacts, but maximum and minimum
quotas apply so enquire well ahead. Staff are well meaning
but sometimes poorly informed and uncreative at offering
alternative suggestions and ideas.
Pikkori Sports (Map p146; ☎ 321888; butik@pikkori.gl;
Aqqusinersuaq 16; ☺ 10am-5.30pm Mon-Thu, 10am-6pm
Fri, 10am-1pm Sat) Morten Heilmann, the very knowledgeable manager, can offer valuable advice on where to hike,

mountain-bike or fish and can help you make contact with local boat owners and sports groups.

TRAVEL AGENCIES

Greenland Travel (Map p146; ☎ 321205; nuuk@ greenland-travel.gl; Hotel Hans Egede building; ⏱ 10am-4.30pm Mon-Thu, 10am-4pm Fri)

Vejle Rejser (Map p145; ☎ 322899; www.vejle-rejser.gl; 43 Industrivej)

Sights

The city's main sights can be comfortably visited in a day, but you might want to allow several days more to find a boat to take you around the fjord or to wait for suitably co-operative hiking weather.

KOLONIHAVN

From certain angles, especially walking north from the museum, you could almost believe you were in an old-Greenlandic village. This is **Kolonihavn** (Map p146), the photogenic historic quarter of Nuuk, albeit still surveyed by concrete housing developments. On some summer weekends and evenings, you might catch a *qajaq* (traditional kayak) off the museum jetty. At any time, keep watching the sea, as humpback whales just might breach offshore as you pass.

The central focus of the area is a cliff-top **statue of Hans Egede** in a typical Danish preacher's ruff. On the strangely sparse area below is the simple 1849 **Frelsers Kirke** (Church of Our Saviour; Rasmus Berhelsensvej 2). The sturdy 1728 **Hans Egede House** (Hans Egedesvej 15) is the oldest in Greenland and has a pretty vegetable

garden. Originally home to Nuuk's missionary founder, it's now the venue for official government receptions. Several other historic buildings and monuments dot the area. Nuuk city's coat of arms features the fine 1907 **Teacher Training College** (Seminarium; CE Jansenvej B144) backed by the horned silhouette of **Sermitsiaq** (1210m), a tent-shaped island peak. The latter is attractively viewed from several parts of town, notably the rocky knoll at the northern end of CE Jansenvej.

GREENLAND NATIONAL MUSEUM

The spacious, well-presented **Greenland National Museum** (Map p146; ☎ 322611; www.natmus. gl; Hans Egedesvej 8-12; admission free; ⏱ 1-4pm Tue-Sun Oct-Apr, 10am-4pm Tue-Sun May-Sep) is based in an extended 1936 warehouse. Its better exhibits include an interesting section on 1950s social change and a geological room emphasising that the world's oldest rocks (3.8 billion years old) come from the Nuuk region. However, the unmissable climax is the mummy room. Here a trio of mummified 15th-century women and a very spooky six-month-old child stare blindly out from their dimly lit display cases. Their fur clothes and *kammiks* (traditional boots) are intricately sewn and embroidered, but their cause of death remains uncertain. Found at Qilakitsoq near Uummannaq, they made the cover of *National Geographic* and are an eerily unforgettable sight.

Several other nearby buildings also fall under the museum's protection, including a restocked **cooper's workshop**. A display of

blubber vats & presses is accompanied by brief notes on the train-oil industry that only died out in 1963.

SANTA CLAUS POST HOUSE
Entered from within the tourist office, the appealing little **Santa Claus Post House** (Map p146; Hans Egedesvej 29) is a Victorian-style mailroom with Christmassy décor and framed curiosities like a 1946 letter from Ireland to 'Santy Claus, Greenland'. The mail desk is used in December to write and send Christmas greetings cards from Father Christmas. You can order one for the child of your choice: pay for and address it at the tourist-office counter. Some of the Dkr25 charge goes to help local charities.

Hidden around the far side of the building is a gigantic red **Santa Mailbox**, which rates as one of Nuuk's more photogenic sights. It's full of letters sent to Santa, Greenland, all of which get answered by…well, Santa of course.

Close by is **Kittat** (Map p146; ☎ 325557; Hans Egedesvej 29; ⏰ 10am-noon & 1-4pm Mon-Thu, 10am-2pm Fri), a low-key fur workshop that specialises in making traditional style costumes and *kammiks*. Anyone can peep inside at the small, functional flensing and sewing rooms. The skin-drying racks are outside. Along with the museum and a carver's co-operative, this is where you'd end up on the tourist office's rather pricey Dkr198 'handicraft tour'.

UNIVERSITY LIBRARY
The **University Library** (Map p145; www.ilisimatusarfik.gl; Herrnhutvej B7) was established in 1747 as the New Herrnhut Mission (House of Moravian Brethren), originally set up by a trio of missionaries who arrived soon after Hans Egede. It's a most attractive red wooden building topped with bell-shaped campanile and set behind a forest of white, wooden grave posts. In the grass leading down towards a peaceful pebble beach are several ruins of old turf houses. The sea views are very pleasant.

CITY CENTRE
The spacious **Katuaq Cultural Centre** (Map p146; Kulturip Illorsua Katu; ☎ 323300; www.katuaq.gl; Imaneq; ⏰ varies) is by far Nuuk's finest piece of modern architecture, a sinuous wooden wave edged in glass. It houses the Greenland Art School, the NAPA Nordic Institute and a reading library as well as hosting exhibitions,

conferences, concerts, a cinema and Nuuk's best café.

Nearby are the art-decked corridors of the **Home Rule Government** (Map p146; www.nanoq.gl; ⏰ 8am-4pm Mon-Thu). Except on Fridays when it's in session, you are free to poke your head into the little **parliament chamber** (upstairs, room 66), though it's polite to ask first at the parliament secretary's office (room 62). There's not much to see, but a visit is more interesting accompanied by the political explanations of a guide (Dkr198, tours through the tourist office).

Outside parliament is Nuuk's most imaginative statue, a wonderfully grotesque two-headed bronze representing **Kassassuk**, a tormented mythical orphan child who fought back against the forces of evil. The sculpture is misattributed to Samuel Kleinschmidt (it's actually by Simon Kristoffersen) in an otherwise useful tourist pamphlet, *Memorials in Nuuk*, which brings a little life to Nuuk's many other rather less distinguished plaques and monuments.

The **City Hall** (Map p146; Nuup Kommunia; ☎ 347004; Kuussuaq 2; ⏰ 10am-3pm Mon-Thu, 10am-noon Fri) is not architecturally distinguished, but it's worth looking inside to see the impressive 1998 tapestry of Inuit life. Curiously, it includes a vignette about missionary Hans Egede.

Graffiti-daubed **Block P** (Map p146; Prinsessevej) is Nuuk's biggest housing monstrosity. It's so depressing that it's almost an attraction in itself. Only five storeys high but 64 apartments long, it houses over 1% of Greenland's population under one roof.

INSTITUTE OF NATURAL RESOURCES
At the north edge of town near the sweet little golf course is the **Institute of Natural Resources** (Map p145; Kivioq), in a pair of glass-nosed wooden-slab buildings that look passingly photogenic in low evening light. A tourist-office tour (Dkr198, one hour) takes you inside on certain working-day afternoons.

AURORA BOREALIS (NORTHERN LIGHTS)
Despite the distraction of city lights, even in Greenland's 'big city' it's quite possible to see the aurora borealis from unlit areas of town.

Activities
CLIMBING
Nuuk region's basaltic cliffs are less suitable for climbing than Nanortalik's granite, but in

spring the ice-climbing is promising and you can hire equipment from the tourist office.

FISHING
The world's sports fishermen are just discovering that certain trout and salmon beats around Nuuk are almost as good as on the celebrated Kola Peninsula (Russia) and with slightly fewer of those pesky midges. However, there are virtually no facilities. Access to some of the best sites on the Akia (Nordlandet) Peninsula and up the Qussuk inlet of the Nuup Kangerlua fjord requires expensive boat charters, wild camping and occasionally arduous hiking. Nuuk Tourism hires equipment and has extensive information. Greenland Tourism has helped some fishers find boat transfers.

GOLF
There's a small golf club out towards the airport. Locals claim it's one of the world's hardest, and lost balls abound.

HIKING
Rising east across a bay from the city is the stark rocky mass of **Ukkusissat** (Store Malene). Although it looks scarily steep, the three- to five-hour climb is not too difficult when you summit from the north. Start the hike from the new Qinngorput suburb, reached on one of the extended-route No 3 buses (five daily, Monday to Friday only). From there follow the power lines northeast past an attractive lake to a mountain saddle at around 400m. Here you double back to the twin summits (761m and 772m). Views are superb over Nuuk, its landmark island peak Sermitsiaq (1210m), the vast Akia (Nordlandet) Peninsula and the battalions of mountain peaks that line the grand fjord system. The white needle-shaped mountain in the middle distance is 1616m Qingaq. The big glacier across the water to your south is Teqqiinngallip.

Less energetic hikers can enjoy views nearly as lovely for much less effort or danger by climbing 443m **Quassussuaq** (Lile Malene). The most obvious of several possible routes follows very close to the line of the ski-lift from behind the airport. It takes a little over an hour to get up, much less descending.

Be aware that on either of these mountains the rock gets very slippery after rain, and clouds descend very suddenly, obliterating visibility. If conditions seem inclement you'd

be much safer walking the valley between them known as **Paradisdalen**. It has traditionally been considered a clockwise loop but is now more sensibly approached as a northbound arc using the Qinngorput bus outbound. Return along the coast to the north end of the airport runway and hitchhike or take bus No 3 back into town.

KAYAKING
Adventure Sula (☎ 245671; www.sula.gl; PO Box 378, 3900 Nuuk) offers guided sea-kayaking trips at weekends or on evenings, rents equipment to experienced paddlers, and has occasional training courses and longer expeditions.

SKIING
From January to May, two ski-lifts behind the airport charge Dkr50 per day to tow you up Quassussuaq (Lile Malene) for alpine skiing. You can hire skis, boots and poles for Dkr150 to Dkr200 per set per day. Older equipment is cheaper rented from the tourist office. Snowmobiles are not officially available for rent, but (uninsured) paid-for rides are easy enough to arrange if you ask around.

SWIMMING
Nuuk's splendid new **Malik Pool** (Map p145; ☎ 342600; Sarfaarsuit 4; adult/child Dkr45/35; ☺ 6-8am, noon-4pm & 6-8pm Mon-Fri, 6am-6pm Sat & Sun) offers indoor swimming but is better for splashing about while enjoying lovely bay views through the cleverly designed glass walls. In midsummer it's open all day from 6am till 9pm. Take bus No 2.

WHALE WATCHING
From Nuuk's university area, or from the public ferries, you are reasonably likely to see whales. To improve your chances you could join one of Nuuk Tourism's four-hour **whale-watching trips** (Dkr550), which operate most evenings from 15 June to 15 September, fewer in the off season. Trips start at 4pm if a minimum of four people have signed up. You don't go particularly far out into the bay, and some visitors report that the equivalent trip in Aasiaat is more inspiring, but much will depend on your boat captain.

Tours
The tourist office organises numerous other day tours; check the calendar on www.nuuk-tourism.dk. Booking is wise, as all have

minimum and maximum group sizes. Popular options include a hike around Ukkusissat (Dkr595, six hours), themed city tours (Dkr198, two hours), and various fjord cruises (see Nuup Kangerlua, p154). The interesting 1½-hour **Home Rule tour** (Dkr198; ☾ 11am Mon & Thu) explains government functions and shows you the administrative offices, the city council building and Parliament Hall.

Festivals & Events

In midsummer there's the **Nuuk Marathon** (www.arctic-marathon.gl) and a small arts and music festival. The **Snow Sculpture Festival** (www.snow.gl; ☾ Mar) is open to artists from around the world. It's supposedly annual but was cancelled in 2004 for lack of snow!

Sleeping

Note that Hotel Nuuk currently only lets whole floors (to institutions) and that Hotel Godthåb is a restaurant complex, not a hotel at all.

BUDGET

The tourist office lists around a dozen B&B homestays for Dkr325 per adult. Off season you may be in the centre, but in summer you'll probably be further out – not necessarily a bad thing, especially if you're planning to go walking. Having a host family also makes it easier to find a friend of a friend to take you sailing on the fjord.

Godthåbshallen Youth Hostel (Map p146; Sportshallen Sleep-in; ☎ 321654; Vandsøvej 2; dm Dkr110) In an ageing sports centre behind Nuuk's most unappealing housing estates, Nuuk's youth hostel has 17 beds, a kitchen and a dining table all in one big room. That's fine (if a little eerie) when you're alone. But when it's full with schoolchildren or athletic groups it can get very cramped, and the single shared shower soon runs out of hot water. Friendly manager Jens is generally in the front office between 8am and 4pm, but you're better off booking via the tourist office and collecting the key on arrival (from the airport or Seamen's Home). Use the white door at the rear.

Aanaa's Hut (Map p145; Siaqqinneq; hut Dkr625) In principle it's a fantastic idea to sleep in a reconstructed traditional Greenlandic turf hut. However, while the structure's lonely coastal setting and fjord panorama are delightful, the price is high considering there's no toilet

whatsoever and the only water for washing or cooking is a dribble of nearby stream. It only makes financial sense if you squeeze in half a dozen good friends to sleep on the floors and cuddle together on the traditional *Illeq* bed. Aanaa (literally 'grandmother') can prepare coffee and cakes (Dkr40) and Greenlandic meals (Dkr80) on request. Organise bookings through the tourist office.

There's no organised camping, but wild camping is possible along the north coast, close to Aanaa's Hut off the airport road. Grassy areas around the university look appealing, but these form a protected archaeological zone and camping is not permitted. Nuuk Tourism can hire you camping gear including a (large) tent for Dkr150 per night or Dkr650 per week. There's a Dkr1000 deposit. Several sports shops sell tents, boots and backpacks.

MID-RANGE & TOP END

Centerbo Mini-Apartments (Map p146; Samuel Kleinschmidtsvej 11; s/d Dkr595/795) Centerbo offers relatively reasonably priced rooms, each with hotplate, sink, fridge and shower-toilet unit. The bed is a small, foldout double. There's no reception, and all arrangements are handled by **Nuuk Kontor & Bogføring** (☎ /fax323901; Kirkevej 1; ☾ 8am-4pm Mon-Fri), a local book-keeping company that also deals with simple hut lets in the Eqaluit Paarliit valley (Dkr700 to Dkr800 per week, access by boat, then hiking).

Nordbo Hotel Apartments (Map p146; ☎ 326644; nordbo@greennet.gl; Vandsøvej 13; s/d/apt Dkr650/850-950/1250) Another short-term rental unit close to the youth hostel.

Seamen's Home (Map p145; Sømandshjem; ☎ 321029; nuuk@soemandshjem.gl; Marinevej 3; s Dkr735-945, d & tw 1050-1245) Near the main port; most of the rooms are now fairly smartly upgraded with private bathrooms. The best are brand new, but cheaper ones are pretty cramped. The very cheapest Dkr595 singles have communal toilet and showers.

Hotel Hans Egede (Map p146; ☎ 324222; www.hhe.gl; Aqqusinersuaq 1-5; s/d/ste Dkr1185/1485/1600-2600) Nuuk's self-proclaimed 'international' hotel is a blue-and-white slab of glass and concrete right in the town centre. All rooms have private bath, TV/video and mini-bar. 'Polar class' rooms cost an extra Dkr210 for better views. A few single rooms cost a reduced Dkr795 because they're beside the noisy elevator shafts.

Eating

Nuuk offers the best variety of dining in Greenland, but it's wise to reserve at least a day or two ahead for the better places.

RESTAURANTS

Restaurant Nipisa (Map p146; ☎ /fax 321210; www.nip isa.com; Aqqusinersuaq 6; mains Dkr200-220; ⏰ noon-2pm, 6-10.30pm Mon-Sat) Above the Maximut Pub, this smart but relaxed restaurant creates extraordinary gastronomic magic using superb fresh local ingredients. Dishes are artistic creations to be savoured at considerable length. The daily-changing set dinner (Dkr275/295 for two/three courses) might sound expensive but is actually a bargain for a world-class culinary experience that's heightened yet further if you accept the waiter's wine suggestions, which complement the flavours magnificently. Booking for dinner is almost essential, maybe a week ahead for weekends. Lunches (Dkr50 to Dkr80) are relatively simple.

Charoen Porn (Map p146; ☎ 325759; Aqqusinersuaq 5; mains Dkr80-120; ⏰ 6-10pm Tue-Sun) Behind uninviting metal doors, warm soft lighting and oriental embroideries welcome you into Greenland's best and most genuine Thai restaurant. Very generous portions of Thom Kha soup (Dkr89) are delicious but very mildly spiced despite being labelled 'hot'.

Restaurant Isikkivik (Map p145; ☎ 327667; Satiarfiaq 26; mains Dkr45-130; ⏰ 9am-11pm Mon-Sat, 10am-11pm Sun) This good-value eatery is out in Nuussuaq with views across the marina. The dining room may not be lavish, but it's surprisingly pleasant for its odd position above a mini-market. Enter from Salliarnaq (the road behind). The reliably filling Dkr45 meal of the day is available from 11.30am and from 5.30pm as stocks last. Pizzas and steaks are also on offer. From central Nuuk take bus No 2 to the Illorput (marina) stop.

A Hereford Beefstouw (Map p146; ☎ 324222; www .a-h-b.dk/nuuk; Hotel Hans Egede, top floor; mains Dkr79-259; ⏰ 6-10.30pm) The Nuuk branch of a relatively upmarket Danish steakhouse chain manages to give some atmosphere to an inherently characterless room by creative use of space breaks, chunky wooden furniture and flickering oil lamps. The limited salad bar costs an extra Dkr46, or Dkr88 if used as a complete meal in itself (including baked potato). The adjoining room with paintings and starched tablecloths is the upmarket **Gertrud Rask Spisehus** (☎ 324222; mains Dkr180-210;

⏰ 6-10pm Mon-Sat), where you may feel uncomfortable without a jacket or dress. Creative daily menus cost Dkr325/350 for three/four courses.

Hotel Godthåb (Map p146; ☎ 348042; Imaneq; full meals Dkr148; ⏰ 6-10pm Thu, 7.30-10pm Fri-Sat) This family-atmosphere carvery has an interior of fake shopfronts that segues strangely into a period drawing-room area. Both sections have heavy new beams, happily mismatched pseudo-Victorian prints and photos of the *Hindenburg*. Thursday night there's a Mongolian barbecue. Friday and Saturday evening you get carved meats, garnishes and a half bottle of wine for the same price. After 10pm there's a DJ and bar till 3am.

CAFÉS

Café Tuap (Map p146; ☎ 323300; Katuaq; coffees Dkr15-100, mains Dkr45-85; ⏰ noon-11pm Sat & Sun, 11am-11pm Mon-Fri) This stylishly minimalist gallery-café is within the light-suffused atrium of the Katuaq Cultural Centre. Lunches including reindeer and muskox steak or filled baked potatoes are served until 3pm. Otherwise, come here for real cappuccinos or a genuine Greenlandic coffee (*Kalaallit kaffiat*, Dkr100); see p95.

Torve Caféen (Map p146; ☎ 322000; Hotel Nuuk; coffees Dkr10-15, mains Dkr79-259; ⏰ 6pm-10.30pm) Good coffee and delicious slices of cake (Dkr20) are served in a screened-off area of hotel foyer illuminated by a video of a log fire.

QUICK EATS

Café Crazy Daisy (Map p146; ☎ 323636, 9; ⏰ 8am-10pm) This diner-style place has a range of fast food (Dkr16 to Dkr50) but also serves cooked breakfasts (Dkr28 to Dkr56), fish, steaks, pizza and chicken, plus a menu of Chinese and Thai cuisine (Dkr55 to Dkr87) served through the dragon portal at the back.

Igaffik (Map p145; ☎ 322480; Qasapi; meals Dkr38; ⏰ 8am-8pm) The no-nonsense canteen of Nuuk Transport serves a good-value Dkr38 set lunch (11.30am to 1.30pm) and dinner (5pm to 7pm), or snacks at other times. It's upstairs via a narrow atrium in a warehouse-style building off the trawler wharf.

Seamen's Home cafeteria (Map p145; ☎ 321029; Marinevej 3; meals Dkr50-55 ⏰ 5.30am-8pm) The basic but tasty hot meals and good breakfast buffet are open to nonresidents.

Bella's Pizza (Map p146; ☎ 314031; pizzas 49-70; ⏰ 11am-8pm Mon-Sat) This itinerant former kebab wagon is usually parked outside Unik gift shop (Imaneq 29). It bakes remarkably good takeaway pizzas; Dkr15 to Dkr20 slices are available at lunchtime. Try the garlic-charged Firenze.

Dupond & Dupont (Map p146; ☎ 348060; www.hhe .gl/ghb/dupond.htm; Hotel Godthåb complex; ⏰ 11.30am-10pm daily; 11.30am-2am some Sat & Sun) Here there's fast food that you order McDonald's style but can eat while sitting down in the nicer bowling-alley bar next door.

Other less interesting central options:

Café Mik (Map p146; ☎ 321506; Spindlersbakke 2B; ⏰ 8am-5pm Mon-Fri, 10am-6pm Sat & Sun) Sandwiches and burgers.

Grill & Pizza Bar (Map p146; Kuussuaq; pittas Dkr31-39; ⏰ 11am-10pm) At Trolles petrol station.

SELF-CATERING

Pisiffik supermarket (Map p146; Aqqusinersuaq 1; ⏰ 9am-8pm Mon-Sat, 10am-8pm Sun) A good selection of wines and food. There's a smaller **Nuussuaq branch** (Map p145; Saqqaa; ⏰ 7am-8pm Mon-Sat, 8am-8pm Sun) with a small fish market alongside.

Brugsen supermarket (Map p146; Aqqusinersuaq 2; ⏰ 9am-7pm Mon-Fri, 9am-6pm Sat, 11am-6pm Sun) is also well stocked with a separate **bakery** (⏰ 6.30am-6pm Mon-Thu, 6.30am-7pm Fri, 6.30-4pm Sat & Sun) next door.

Other options:

Brædtet (Map p146; John Møllersvej, Kolonihavn) Great selection of fresh fish.

Nukøb (HJ Rinksvej; ⏰ 7.30am-midnight Mon-Sat, 11am-midnight Sun) Handy mini-market for the youth hostel. Open late, but rather expensive.

Spar Tjalfesvej (Map p146; ⏰ 7am-7pm Mon-Fri, 8am-7pm Sat & Sun); Qasapi (Map p145; ⏰ 8am-6.30pm Mon-Sat) Supermarket.

Vinslottet (Map p145; ☎ 311850; www.vinslottet.gl; Industrivej 2D; ⏰ 9am-6pm Mon-Fri, 9am-1pm Sat) Nuuk's best wine shop, with a small delicatessen.

Drinking

As anywhere in Greenland, Nuuk's pubs can be fun, rough or both. Visiting in a 'gang' may provoke trouble in some places.

Kristinemut (Map p146; Aqqusinersuaq 7; beers Dkr38; ⏰ noon-midnight Sun-Thu, noon-3am Fri-Sat) Wild-west themed with wagon-wheel ceilings, this was Greenland's first pub, made (in)famous in Lawrence Millman's book *Last Places*. It remains an understandably popular, appealingly raucous place to drink and dance, with Dkr25 happy-hour beers before 8pm. There's

a live band every night from around 9pm. Attached is the electro-throbbing **Afterdark Rock Bar** (⏰ 9pm-midnight Thu, 9pm-3am Fri-Sat), attracting a young crowd of late-night partiers.

Takuss (Map p146; Hotel Godthåb Complex; beers Dkr38; ⏰ 4pm-midnight Sun-Thu, 4pm-3am Fri-Sat) Skis and kayaks decorate this brass-railed pub and dance floor. If you order food (basic mains Dkr49 to Dkr79, from 5.30pm to 8pm) you can get two beers for Dkr55. Some reports claim that the very local crowd is aggressively anti-Danish, but the authors found the atmosphere to be very friendly. Housed in a back room of the same complex, **Daddy's** (beers Dkr42; ⏰ noon-midnight) has billiard tables, darts and padded leather seats.

Skyline Bar (Map p146; ☎ 324222; Hotel Hans Egede, top floor; beers Dkr42; ⏰ 5pm-midnight Sun-Thu, 5pm-3am Fri-Sat) This is Nuuk's safest bar, but not its most character-filled. In daylight there's a curious view between the bottles of the bar out across the town centre, but after dark the ultraviolet glow is less appealing. There's a pianist some nights.

Nasiffik (Map p145; ☎ 329190; beers Dkr35, meals Dkr30-40; ⏰ noon-midnight Sun-Thu, 8am-3am Fri-Sat) Although calling itself a restaurant, this is really more of a café-bar where most of the clientele are drinkers enjoying the pleasant marinaside location in Nuussuaq. Snacks are served, and there's a good-value meal of the day from 5pm till 7pm.

Entertainment

The one-screen **cinema** (Map p146; ☎ 323300; Katuaq Cultural Centre; www.katuaq.gl) shows a marvellously eclectic range of films in various languages and of various eras, generally with two or three screenings daily from Dkr50.

Bowl For Sjov (Map p146; ☎ 348080; Hotel Godthåb complex; ⏰ noon-10pm Sun-Thu, noon-1am Fri-Sat) Tenpin bowling costs Dkr80 per lane for 55 minutes Monday to Thursday. You'll pay Dkr150 Friday to Sunday and Dkr300 after 10pm. Shoe hire is Dkr10 extra.

Shopping

Nitz Gallery (Map p146; ☎ 312929; Industrivej 2D; ⏰ noon-6pm Mon-Fri, 10am-2pm Sat) Framing shop with a small but unrivalled collection of original lithographs and prints by both new and established stars of Greenlandic modern art.

Pikkori Sports (Map p146; ☎ 321888; butik@pikkori .gl; Aqqusinersuaq 16) Sells camping, hiking, fishing and skiing equipment plus all-important anti-mosquito head-nets (Dkr40 to Dkr45). Knowledgeable and extremely obliging staff can offer exploration tips and contacts.

Outlets for craftwork, carvings and furs:

Anori Art (Map p146; ☎/fax 327874; anori@greennet.gl; Indaleeqqap Aqqutaa 14)

Arktis Gaveshop (Map p146; ☎ 324944; HJ Rinksvej 23)

Kattaana Gifts (Map p146; HJ Rinksvej 33)

Unik (Map p146; ☎ 324096; unik@unik.gl; Imaneq 29) Small range of Greenlandic jewellery and furs, along with teas and Danish chocolates.

Getting There & Away
AIR
Controversy currently surrounds a possible airport extension. Many feel it would be wastefully expensive, as even the proposed new 1800m runway wouldn't handle the big Airbuses that **Air Greenland** (☎ 343434; Airport; ☺ 9am-3pm Mon-Fri, 10am-2pm Sat) currently uses on Copenhagen–Kangerlussuaq runs. Meanwhile, Dash 7 planes link Nuuk on weekdays to Maniitsoq (Dkr1021, 40 minutes), Narsarsuaq (Dkr2408, 1½ hours) and via Kangerlussuaq (Dkr1696, 55 minutes) to Ilulissat (Dkr1611 to Dkr2971, 2¼ hours) or Sisimiut (Dkr1666 to Dkr2574, 1½ to 2¼ hours). Weekly helicopters fly to Paamiut (Dkr3211, 80 minutes).

BOAT
The **AUL office** (Map p146; ☎ 349934; bktgoh@aul.gl; Kuussuaq; ☺ 9am-3pm Mon-Fri) is easy to miss at the side of the Bang & Olufsen shop. Southbound weekly ferries link Nuuk and Qaqortoq (Dkr1075 to Dkr1435, 30 to 32½ hours) via Paamiut (Dkr540 to Dkr725, 15 hours), Arsuk (Dkr735 to Dkr985, 23 hours) and Narsaq (Dkr1050 to Dkr1400), going on to Narsarsuaq (Dkr1700 to Dkr2580, 37 hours) in summer. Northbound one or two weekly ferries visit Maniitsoq (Dkr355 to Dkr475, 8½ hours), Kangaamiut (Dkr460 to Dkr610, 12¼ hours), Sisimiut (Dkr660 to Dkr880, 19 hours), Aasiaat (Dkr1020 to Dkr1355, 32 hours), Qeqertarsuaq (Dkr1075 to Dkr1435, 36 hours) and Ilulissat (Dkr1175 to Dkr1505, 42 hours). Mid-June to mid-November the *Sarpik Ittuk* continues to Uummannaq (Dkr1610 to Dkr2145, 2½ days) and, until mid-August, to Upernavik (Dkr2715, 3¼ days).

AUL also sells passenger tickets for the cargo boat *Angaju Ittuk* to Kapisillit (1 September to 14 June/summer Dkr215/270, six hours).

Getting Around
City-bus timetables *(Køreplaner)* are downloadable in local languages on www.nuup bussii.gl. Hourly bus No 3 runs from the airport into town (7.01am to 6.01pm weekdays only), reaching the youth hostel (Nukøb stop) in just 10 minutes and then winding through the city centre towards the Seaman's Home. However, the other way takes 40 minutes, with various suburban detours and a clockwise loop around Nuussuaq before continuing past Aanaa's Hut. Five 'extended No 3' services continue beyond the airport to Qinngorput. Bus No 2 is much more frequent (daily every 15 minutes from 6.20am till around 9pm, then half-hourly till midnight). Its convoluted suburban loops are most useful for linking the centre with Nuussuaq marina.

All taxis use a **central switchboard** (☎ 363636). To or from the airport costs about Dkr120 (metered).

At the time of research **NUIF** (Map p146; ☎ 347341; Kuussuaq 17; ☺ 10am-4pm Mon-Fri) was planning a free bicycle-ride service. Pikkori Sports hires mountain bikes for Dkr100 to Dkr150 per day.

BOAT RIDES
With some persistence and patience it should be possible to find a day's motorboat charter from Dkr1500 to Dkr5000 plus petrol, depending on distance covered. To find contacts, ask at Pikkori Sports or Greenland Tourism, or contact **Jes ('Yes') Burghart** (☎ 553 492; blaaside@greennet.gl; PO Box 18, 3900 Nuuk), who speaks fluent English. His biggest boat is a converted trawler, the 74ft *Kissavik* (www .kissavik.com), which has bunks to sleep 12 on minicruises. Reckon on Dkr8500 per day for up to six hours' sailing, and add Dkr400 per extra sailing hour.

You can always try asking around the marina or the trawler-port area, both of which have dozens of motorboats moored.

AROUND NUUK TOWN
Nuuk becomes a whole lot more appealing if you find boat access to its surrounding wonders. The intricate waterways of the **Akia (Nordlandet) Peninsula** are renowned for superb fishing. The fjordsides of **Ameralik Kangerlua (Lysefjord)** are famed for reindeer hunting, while steep-sided **Buksefjorden** culminates at a hydro-power station from

which a clear, easy track leads up to the vast Kangerlluarssunguup Taserssua lake. However, most tourists stick to the three parallel fjords of the grand Nuup Kangerlua (Godthåbsfjord) system.

Nuup Kangerlua

Of the three main choices, **Qornup Suvdula** is the most photogenic fjord, especially where a glacier cascades down the side of 1616m Mt Qingaq on Qeqertarsuaq Island. Gently attractive **Qooqqut** (Qorqut) has new hut accommodation currently under construction, and the Tingmianguit Inlet is well reputed among anglers for red fish. Qooqqut is also the starting point for classic two- to three-day hikes to low-key **Kapisillit** (Kapisigdlit). Unassuming Kapisillit is the area's only village to maintain 'hotels' or a shop and is a great base for other regional hikes. In an easy day return from Kapisillit you could walk around the bay and across the narrow isthmus to look into iceberg-packed Kangersuneq Fjord. With several days you can explore the head of Ameralla Fjord and **Austmannadalen** (East Man Valley), where cele-

brated Norwegian explorer Fridtjof Nansen descended from the icecap in 1888, having completed the first east–west crossing of Greenland. At Nansen's Teltplads he cunningly refashioned one of his tents into a boat and managed to row it all the way to Nuuk. If you're approaching Kapisillit by boat, notice 1220m **Pisigsarfik** above some desultory Norse ruins. Legend relates that Norse and Inuit rivals once held a fateful archery competition from the top of this cliff, shooting at a reindeer-skin target below. The loser had to jump and his people vacate their land. The Inuit won. Nobody saw the Norse again.

If you don't plan to hike and simply want an attractive Nuuk day trip by motor boat, don't bother with Kapisillit as **Qoornoq** village is more immediately picturesque. Although some houses are ruined, Qoornoq's sweet little church has been beautifully restored, complete with model *umiaq* hung from the rafters.

Sermitsiaq Island (Sadelø) is impressive from afar, but the grandeur is not necessarily improved by taking a boat trip closer, and the

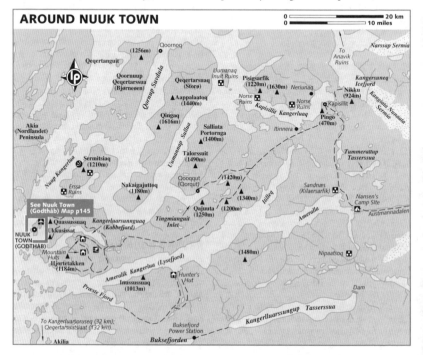

AROUND NUUK TOWN

touted waterfall on its northwestern flank runs almost dry later in the summer.

The whole Godthåbsfjord region was once the Norse Western Settlement (Vesterbygd) of 90 widely spread farms that prospered in the 11th century but died out by 1350. The biggest was **Sandnæs** (Kilaersarfik) at the head of Ameralik Kangerlua (Lyserfjord). Today, however, the only Norse ruin to bear a building-like form is at **Anavik** (Ujaragassuit), accessible on a helicopter excursion with Nuuk Tourism (Dkr2600). This tour continues even further down the south hook of impressively berg-packed Kangersuneq fjord, and stops off at both the inland ice and Kapisillit.

To the northeast of Anavik but hard to access is **Isukasia** (Isua supercrustal belt), well known to geologists as the source of the oldest rocks ever discovered on earth (3.8 billion years).

Sleeping & Eating

Two houses in Kapisillit function as mini-hotels.

Paarnat Cottage ('Boatel'; ☎ 359659; B285; dm/s/d Dkr180/225/400) This easy-to-spot bright-green cottage has a terrace offering panoramic views of the port and fjord system. The key is available from Kaaleeraq Ringsted (B1878), whose son Berthel speaks a smattering of English.

Barakki (☎ 359653; B1008; s/d Dkr200/300) Much less appealing than Paarnat, with basic cell-like rooms in a red hut off the path to Nuussuaq.

Nuuk Tourism can book either house. Neither place has running water, but you can get a shower (Dkr10) and do laundry (Dkr20) at the bright yellow **service house** (8am-4pm Mon- Fri, 9am-2pm Sat).

Kapisillit's small **Pilersuisoq store** (9am-4pm Mon-Thu, 9am-5pm Fri, 9am-noon Sat) sells limited food supplies.

Getting There & Away

The only public transport is AUL's *Angaju Ittuk* cargo boat (Dkr215 to Dkr270, six hours) sailing three to five times monthly between Nuuk and Kapisillit. Mid-June to mid-September, with a minimum of six people, Nuuk Tourism runs day trips to Kapisillit (Dkr12000 including lunch, twice weekly), around Sermitsiaq (Dkr810, Sunday) and to the icefjord (Dkr1200). Ask

about the multiday trips, too. For more flexibility, chartering an unlicensed, uninsured boat is possible for around Dkr6000 per day through personal contacts. Or, like Fridtjof Nansen, build your own! Walking between Kapisillit and Nuuk typically takes around five days, though the record is 21 hours by a drunken local heading for a party.

KONGSGAARDEN

pop 0

An indefinable distance from Nuuk is the world-famous workshop enterprise of **Kongsgaarden**, a colourful virtual house rumoured to be bundled full of consumer goods. Incredibly, these are given away absolutely free on a seasonal basis, especially in late December. As a result, Claus the manager receives more mail than anyone else in the whole of Greenland. Given the recent unreliability of reindeer-sleigh services, Kongsgaarden is only accessible by web (www.santa.gl). At the time of research, the entire business was planning to move back to the ancient Castle Royal at Greenland's northernmost tip in 2005.

MANIITSOQ REGION

MANIITSOQ TOWN (SUKKERTOPPEN)

pop 2883

Dramatic Maniitsoq blankets a series of rocky outcrops squeezed into a basin littered with islands and backed by cliff walls, canyons and low, rugged hills. It's traditionally known as 'the Venice of Greenland'; the analogy is pretty farfetched, but the wooden bridges and staircases that connect the rocky outcrops and leads of water do give it a very picturesque aspect.

Although Maniitsoq itself is pretty sleepy, the deep narrow fjords and high mountains that surround the town make the region ideal for kayaking, hiking and skiing. Tourism is just getting off the ground in the area, and the local economy relies mostly on services and some fishing and hunting. The discovery of deposits of niobium and uranium nearby may change all that in the future.

The town's Danish name, Sukkertoppen (Sugar Loaf), came from the towering peak that dominated its original location 65km north of here, now the site of the present-day village of Kangaamiut.

Information

Grønlandsbanken (Langeskov-ip Aqq 4) There's an ATM in the lobby.

Hospital (☎ 813211)

Police (☎ 813222)

Post & telephone office (A W Nielsen-ip Aqq 3) The post office is in the Pisiffik supermarket.

Tourist office (☎ 813100; mantour@greennet.gl; Illunnguit B56; ☿ 9am-4pm Mon-Fri)

Sights

Start your trip with a visit to the excellent **Maniitsoq Museum** (☎ 813100; admission free; ☿ 9am-4pm Mon-Fri year-round & noon-2pm Sun Jun-Aug), housed in a series of picturesque historic buildings constructed in 1874 and originally used to house a bakery, a blacksmith's shop and work sheds. The museum displays artefacts dating from Saqqaq times right up to the early 20th century. Another section is devoted to local art and features the work of Kangaamiut artist Jens Kreutzmann.

Maniitsoq's **old church**, built in 1864, is of historical interest, but its 1981 replacement is also worth a look. The altar and font at the **new church** are made of beautiful rough-cut stone, the altarpiece has a driftwood cross created by Greenlandic artist Aka Høegh, and the altar itself is carpeted with sealskin.

Activities

Maniitsoq Island offers good hiking opportunities through its labyrinth of narrow gorges. Although it looks small on the map, it's a full-day hike to the northern tip of the island. Most of the valley floors are rather soggy, claustrophobic and plagued by mosquitoes, but the landscape of criss-crossing gorges, which is probably unique in the world, makes it worthwhile.

A good destination is Pattefjeld (570m); it takes about three hours each way, but it's hard to resist exploring several of the beautiful valleys and gorges en route. The most direct (and nicest) route is via Blomsterdalen, then over Kig Pass and down Langedal – the going is pretty easy. The southern slope of Pattefjeld is a nearly vertical granite wall. To reach the summit, cross Borgmester Pass and keep bearing right; the way to the top will be clear, although there's a lot of scree near the summit. Ask at the tourist office for the 1:75,0000 *Hiking Map West Greenland – Maniitsoq* (Dkr80).

For cross-country skiing (late January to April), Maniitsoq Island has around 100km of tracks and 500 sq km of terrain. See also opposite. You can hire skis from the tourist office for Dkr100 per day.

Maniitsoq is an excellent area for kayaking, but at the time of writing there were no kayaks for hire in town. The tourist office hopes to have kayaks and canoes available for hire by summer 2005 for Dkr150 to Dkr200 per day.

Tours

The tourist office can organise several tours including a 2½-hour city tour (Dkr165); a half-day kayaking trip to Ataa fjord or Sarfat (Dkr395); a half-day sea-angling trip to Ammaqqoq (Dkr750); a half-day boat trip to Sermilinnguaq and Ikkamiut to see abandoned settlements and hanging glaciers (Dkr550); a half-day whale-watching trip (Dkr550); a day trip to Ikkamiut and Hamborgerland (Dkr895); and a variation of this last trip that includes a visit to the 2000m cliffs of Kangerlussuatsiaq, the Taateraat Sermiat Glacier and Mt Atter (Dkr1795).

See p66 for details of skiing tours around Maniitsoq organised by US-based Mountain Spirits.

Sleeping & Eating

The best place to camp is about 2km from town, near the airport and close to a lake. Alternatively, you can camp at the museum and use the toilets and water supply there.

Unnuisarfik (☎ 812047; unnuisarfik@greennet.gl; Annersuaq B626; r Dkr375; ✂) The unmarked youth hostel has excellent-value, spacious modern rooms, and a large kitchen and living area. It's about 1km west of the centre, towards the airport, but a pick-up can be arranged.

Seamen's Home (☎ 813535; maniitsoq@soemands hjem.gl; Ivissuat 3; s without bathroom Dkr555, s/d with bathroom Dkr695/920; ✂ ⛫) The spacious modern rooms at this friendly place are a good bet and right in the centre of town. Although the décor is corporate style and functional, the rooms are good value and each has an ADSL connection. The cafeteria (mains Dkr18 to Dkr60) serves decent but predictable food such as burgers, chips, hot dogs and spaghetti.

Hotel Maniitsoq (☎ 813035; www.hotelmaniitsoq.gl; Ajoqinnguup Aqq B1150; s/d Dkr900/1300; ✂ ⛫) Atop a hill overlooking the harbour, this place has comfortable rooms with TV, telephone, minibar and tea/coffee bar. There's also an annexe, just north of the town centre on Ortooqqap, with a guest kitchen; rooms here cost Dkr495/745, excluding breakfast. The restaurant (one/two courses Dkr295/335) is the best in town, with good food and great views of the harbour. It serves a range of traditional and Danish dishes.

Café Puisi (☎ 812228; Jenseralaap 15; mains Dkr40-70; ⛭ 10am-9pm) The food at this place can be a bit hit and miss, but it's a good place to meet the locals. The menu consists of the usual burgers, chips and sandwiches as well as a good selection of Thai dishes.

For self-caterers the best selection is at **Pisiffik** (AW Nielsensip Aqq; ⛭ 9am-6pm Mon-Fri, 9am-1pm Sat), with a fine bakery, or **Brugsen** (Johs Rosingsvej; ⛭ 9am-6pm Mon-Fri, 9am-1pm Sat, 11am-4pm Sun). A brædtet at the harbour sometimes sells caribou meat in August.

Getting There & Away
AIR
Air Greenland (☎ 813759) has five weekly flights to Kangerlussuaq (Dkr1351, 1½ hours) via Sisimiut (Dkr1021, 40 minutes) and Nuuk (Dkr921, 30 minutes).

BOAT
The big **AUL** (☎ 813346; bktjsu@aul.gl) ferries call in weekly in either direction between Nuuk (Dkr475, 11½ hours), Kangaamiut (Dkr250, 3¼ hours), Sisimiut (Dkr525, 10 hours) and Ilulissat (Dkr1205, 37½ hours). The ferries normally stop for 30 minutes, but the landing is around 1km south of town, so you have no chance to look around.

AROUND MANIITSOQ TOWN
Apussuit
From April to July, alpine skiing is possible on the 995m-high ice field of Apussuit, on the mainland 30km northeast of Maniitsoq. In spring good powder on the slopes, dramatic landscapes and the possibility of skiing right down to sea level make it one of the top heliski destinations in the world.

Apussuit is accessible by taking a boat to Tasiusaq Bay, about 20km from Maniitsoq. It's 10km from there to base camp, or you can go further up the fjord for a steeper 4km-long route to the base camp; it's accessible on skis or snowmobiles early in the season and on foot later in summer.

Base camp, 931m above sea level, accommodates around 30 people and has cooking facilities, toilets, showers and a sauna. Costs are based on group use, and accommodation is priced at Dkr5000 for up to 12 people per night. Boat transfer from Maniitsoq costs Dkr2500 one way for the group. To hire a snowmobile you'll pay Dkr350 per hour, and skis cost Dkr100 per day.

The main cross-country route goes 5km southeast from base camp towards South Peak (995m). The difficult run down the southern slope of Apussuit drops 200m in 1600m.

Kangerlussuatsiaq

Magnificent Kangerlussuatsiaq (Evigheds-fjorden, or Eternity Fjord) has sheer cliff walls 2000m high and numerous glaciers along its length. It's one of Greenland's finest mountaineering and ski-touring areas. Recommended Maniitsoq outfitter **Adam Lyberth** (☎ 812225; adamoutfitter@greennet.gl) can transfer climbers to the Juletræet base camp below 2102m Assaasat and advise on routes. West Greenland's highest peak, Naparutaq (2211m), looms above the northern side of the fjord. The new *Hiking Map West Greenland – Evighedsfjorden* gives an excellent overview of the possibilities.

Hamborgerland

The dramatic island of Hamborgerland, also known as Sermersuut, to the north of Maniitsoq, is one of the most spectacular sights on the west coast of Greenland: an island of sheer and jagged granite spires, tangled glaciers and utterly forbidding terrain. Hamborgersund, the channel between the island and the mainland, is surprisingly well sheltered and normally remains calm. In fine weather the big ferries pass through Hamborgersund between Maniitsoq and Sisimiut, allowing excellent viewing. Don't miss it! To land on the island, you must charter a boat or take a tour from Maniitsoq.

SISIMIUT REGION

SISIMIUT TOWN (HOLSTEINSBORG)
pop 5247

Nestled between rocky peaks on either side of a wide valley, the bustling town of Sisimiut is an excellent base for travellers. It's the second-largest town in the country, with excellent facilities, and yet it still manages to feel like a small fishing village. The town lies 75km north of the Arctic Circle and is Greenland's northernmost year-round ice-free port, with a colourful harbour and better weather than most other parts of the west coast.

The surrounding countryside is ideal for hiking, skiing and dogsledding as well as trips to vast fjords and abandoned settlements. Sisimiut is also home to the most northerly PADI dive centre in the world.

History

Lying amid rich whaling grounds at the southern extent of walrus habitat, Sisimiut was originally an Inuit centre and also functioned as a trading place between the people of northern and southern Greenland. Dutch whalers and traders arrived in the 17th century, and conflict ensued when Danish missionary Hans Egede established a joint mission and competing whaling station at Nipisat. It wasn't until 1756 that the Danish successfully set up a mission, Ukiivik, 40km north of present-day Sisimiut. They named it Holsteinsborg, and in 1764 the settlement and some of its original buildings were shifted to its present site.

Although civil construction continued, the 19th century was characterised by plagues that decimated the local population. Late in the 19th century the whaling industry began to decline, and by the early 20th century it had been replaced with fishing and shrimping. Population growth resumed, and by the mid-1950s Sisimiut had transformed from a traditional hunting and fishing community into the shrimping centre of Greenland. It now processes around 10,000 tonnes of shrimp annually and is a thriving education centre.

Information

Grønlandsbanken (Kaaleeqqap Aqq 4)
Hospital (☎ 864211)
Laundry Tuapannguanut (☒ 8am-8pm Mon-Fri) Buy a laundry card from Brugsen or Pisiffik for Dkr100 (allows four washes).
Police (☎ 864222)
Post office (☎ 866855; Kaaleeqqap Aqq 6)
Sisimiut Atuagaarniarfik (☎ 865590; Aqqusinersuaq 33; ☒ 9am-5.30pm Mon-Fri, to 1pm Sat) Sells souvenir coffee-table books and a few English-language books on Greenlandic topics.
Sisimiut Library (☎ 865023; Guutaap Aqq 5; ☒ 10am-noon & 1-6pm Mon & Thu, 10am-4pm Tue & Wed) One computer with Internet access.
Tourist office (☎ 864848; Jukkorsuup Aqq 6; ☒ 10am-5pm Mon-Fri, 10am-2pm & 6-9pm Sat Jun-Sep, 9am-4pm Mon-Fri Oct-May)

www.info-sisimiut.gl The town tourist site, with comprehensive information on everything from accommodation to tours.

Sights

A whale-jawbone arch marks the entrance to Sisimiut's **old town**, a clutter of brightly coloured buildings dating from the mid-18th to the mid-19th centuries. For some background head to the **museum** (☎ 862550; Jukkorsuup Aqq 7; adult/child Dkr25/10; ☻ 2-5pm Tue-Sun Jun-Aug), which is housed in the Gammelhuset (Old House), dating from 1725, and the old general shop (1825). The museum displays the usual Greenlandic gamut of settlement history, hunting and fishing boats, tools and relics, and local art. It's also where

you'll find the key for the blue **Bethel Church**, Greenland's oldest church, which was consecrated in 1775. The **red church** on the hill was built by Bojsen-Møller in 1926 and extended to its present size in 1984.

Opposite the museum, the building that is now the tourist office was originally the vicarage. Behind it are two stone buildings; one was a blacksmiths' workshop and the other a hospital, laundry, post office and jail.

Beside the harbour are several **stone warehouses** built in the 1860s and extended to two storeys in the 20th century – the bottom storeys are made of stone and the upper of timber. One originally housed a cooperage, and the others were used for the extraction and storage of fish and whale oil.

SOUTHWEST GREENLAND

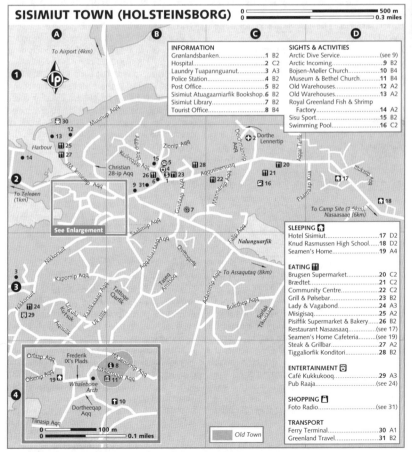

SISIMIUT TOWN (HOLSTEINSBORG)

0 — 500 m
0 — 0.3 miles

INFORMATION
Grønlandsbanken.....................1 B2
Hospital.....................2 C2
Laundry Tuapannguanut.....................3 A3
Police Station.....................4 B2
Post Office.....................5 B2
Sisimiut Atuagaarniarfik Bookshop.6 B2
Sisimiut Library.....................7 B2
Tourist Office.....................8 B4

SIGHTS & ACTIVITIES
Arctic Dive Service.....................(see 9)
Arctic Incoming.....................9 B2
Bojsen-Møller Church.....................10 B4
Museum & Bethel Church.....................11 B4
Old Warehouses.....................12 A2
Old Warehouses.....................13 A2
Royal Greenland Fish & Shrimp
Factory.....................14 A2
Sisu Sport.....................15 B2
Swimming Pool.....................16 C2

SLEEPING
Hotel Sisimiut.....................17 D2
Knud Rasmussen High School.....18 D2
Seamen's Home.....................19 A4

EATING
Brugsen Supermarket.....................20 C2
Brædtet.....................21 C2
Community Centre.....................22 C2
Grill & Pølsebar.....................23 B2
Lady & Vagabond.....................24 A3
Misigisaq.....................25 A2
Pisiffik Supermarket & Bakery.....26 B2
Restaurant Nasaasaaq.....................(see 17)
Seamen's Home Cafeteria.....................(see 19)
Steak & Grillbar.....................27 A2
Tiggaliorfik Konditori.....................28 B2

ENTERTAINMENT
Café Kukkukooq.....................29 A3
Pub Raaja.....................(see 24)

SHOPPING
Foto Radio.....................(see 31)

TRANSPORT
Ferry Terminal.....................30 A1
Greenland Travel.....................31 B2

Old Town

About 1km west of the harbour, **Teleøen** is worth a visit to see ruins from the Saqqaq culture, graves, whale-meat storage houses and an old telegraph station. There are also some offshore islets where locals keep their dogs in summer. To get there, cross the bridge near the head of Sisimiut harbour and go through the gate on the left, just before the oil tanks. The walk takes about two hours return. Ask the tourist office for a free map and guide to the remains.

Activities

DIVING

The northernmost dive school in the world, **Arctic Dive Service** (☎ 527733; info@arcticdive.com; Aqqusinersuaq 23) offers PADI courses up to assistant-instructor level. A six-day open-water course, including a dry-suit course, costs Dkr5995. The dry-suit course alone costs Dkr1995.

The water temperature in summer is 3°C to 4°C, and visibility is usually 5m to 25m. For one boat dive, including equipment hire, you'll pay Dkr600; four dives over two days will cost Dkr1695.

HIKING

There are a number of good walks from Sisimiut; the following are two of the most popular, but the tourist office can help with other suggestions. The best map to use is the *Hiking Map West Greenland – Sisimiut* (Dkr75).

The 784m peak Nasaasaaq (Kællingehætten) dominates the view inland from Sisimiut. The climb to the top is quite steep, and the return trip will take an entire day. Route-finding on this mountain isn't particularly easy, and the weather is changeable; even experienced trekkers may want to hire a local guide.

Begin by heading east past the old heliport and the lake to the east of town, then climb the ravine north of the massif, bearing right at the top onto the level area below the summit. From there, turn east and follow the clear route directly up to the summit; at one very steep bit there are ropes to assist you. The summit is marked with a large cairn.

Another option is the long day hike that will take you to a view of the abandoned village of Assaqutaq, which lies on an offshore island. The route is well marked with cairns and orange blazes, but visibility is often poor. It begins at Nalunguarfik (Spejdersøen, or Scout Lake) in town and heads south to the shore of Amerloq Fjord, following the bizarrely eroded and marshy southern slopes of Nasaasaaq.

Halfway along is a deposit of garnet-bearing rock, which is known as Sisimit, and beyond are a couple of abandoned Inuit whaling settlements. Return the way you came or, if your orientation skills are exceptional, you can return the other way around Nasaasaaq.

SKIING

In winter a ski-lift supported by the local ski club operates at the foot of Nasaasaaq. It's usually open from February to April, and lift tickets cost Dkr50/100 per half/full day (Dkr200 for annual membership).

Sisu Sport (☎ 865501; www.sisu.gl; Kaaleeqqap Aqq 10) does ski and snowboard hire (including boots) for Dkr100/500 per day/week.

The three-day **Arctic Circle Race** (☎ 866830; www.acr.gl) is one of the toughest ski races in the world. It follows a 160km circular route around the mountains east of Sisimiut and usually takes place during the first week of April. Two nights are spent camping on the tundra, and dog teams follow skiers for safety reasons.

SWIMMING

Sisimiut's amazing and popular heated open-air **swimming pool** (☎ 865983; admission adult/child Dkr25/10; ☉ noon-6pm & 7-10pm Mon-Fri, noon-10pm Sat, 1-10pm Sun) is about 500m east of the bank, off Aqqusinersuaq.

Tours

Two main companies operate a huge variety of tours in Sisimiut, though all can be booked through the tourist office. Most tours have minimum participation numbers and operate weekly or even less frequently, so booking is advised.

Arctic Incoming (☎ 865595; incoming@greenland -travel.gl; Aqqusinersuaq 23) offers a half-day boat trip to Sarfannquaq and Itilleq (Dr495); a two-hour cultural history excursion to Teleøen (Dkr175); an easy four-hour hiking trip to Anker's House including Greenlandic food (Dkr375); a one-hour *kaffemik* with a Greenlandic family (Dkr125); and six-hour hikes to Nasaasaaq (Dkr525).

Inuit Outfitting (☎ 865367; ingemann.m.m@green net.gl) offers full-day combined boat and hiking trips to Assaqutaq (Dkr890) and Kangerluarsuk Fjord (Dkr925); half-day fishing trips (Dkr500); a three-day family muskox and fishing safari (Dkr4590); a six-hour hike to Nasaasaaq (Dkr275) and a half-day whale safari (Dkr500).

The above companies and several other outfitters offer dogsledding tours between December and January. A two- to three-hour trip will cost about Dkr425, a five-hour trip about Dkr625. Trips to the head of Kangerluarsuk Fjord (seven to eight hours) cost Dkr11250. To travel to Kangerlussuaq by dogsled takes three days and costs about Dkr5000. The truly die-hard can organise a 730km, three-week trip across the inland ice to Isortoq on the east coast for Dkr136,600. Ask at the tourist office for details.

You can also tour the **Royal Greenland Fish & Shrimp Factory** (☎ 864088; Umiarsualivimmut 25) for free, if it's not too busy – try between 9am and 4pm on weekdays.

Sleeping

The recommended free camp site is 2.5km east of town; there are toilets, and the river water is OK. There are several mountain huts on Kangerluarsuk Ungalleq and along the Kangerlussuaq to Sisimiut trek; ask at the tourist office for details.

Knud Rasmussen High School (☎ 864032; knud@ greennet.gl; Aqqusinersuaq 99; s without bathroom Dkr300, s/d with bathroom Dkr400/600; ☯ Jun-Aug) During the summer months the high school lets its modern, renovated student residence as a hostel. Rooms are fairly functional but comfortable. Breakfast isn't included, but kitchen facilities are available.

Seamen's Home (☎ 864150; sisimiut@soemandsh jem.gl; Frederik IX's Plads 5; s without bathroom Dkr555, s/d with bathroom 695/920; ✗) The freshly renovated and extremely comfortable Seaman's Home has bright, contemporary rooms with good bathrooms, a TV and a phone. Someone will pick you up from the airport if you let them know when you're going to arrive.

Hotel Sisimiut (☎ 864840; hotsisi@greennet.gl; Aqqusinersuaq 86; s/d Dkr895/1250; ✗ 💻) Newly renovated but still looking like something from the '70s, the functional corporate-style rooms at the town's hotel are very comfortable but

lack a little soul. Two-room self-catering flats cost Dkr1250.

Eating

Misigisaq (☎ 863888; JM Jensenip Aqq BV1064; mains Dkr75-125; ☯ noon-midnight Sun-Thu, noon-3am Fri & Sat) The Arctic meets the Far East at this Chinese restaurant, which is renowned in West Greenland for its superb food. Typical Chinese décor and bustling atmosphere form the backdrop to an extensive menu made up entirely of Greenlandic traditional foods cooked in Oriental style.

Restaurant Nasaasaaq (☎ 864700; Hotel Sisimiut, Aqqusinersuaq 86; lunch Dkr110, dinner mains Dkr185, three-course dinner Dkr298; ☯ noon-1.30pm & 6-9pm) Excellent, contemporary cuisine is available in the corporate surroundings of the hotel restaurant. The menu features a good choice of Danish and international food as well as Greenlandic specialities (Dkr150, order one day in advance). There's also a dance floor and live music.

Community Centre (☎ 865740; Aqqusinersuaq; dishes Dkr50; ☯ noon-1.30pm Fri, 6-7pm Wed Aug-June) For a brush with true Greenlandic food, cooked and served by the locals for the locals, head for the community buffet, where you can sample real Greenlandic fare – including whale, seal, muskox, caribou and fish – for down-to-earth prices.

Lady & Vagabond (☎ 864889; Nikkorsuit; mains Dkr60-140; ☯ 6-9pm Wed-Sun) Low lighting and dark décor are supposed to make this place look intimate, but it falls a little short of the mark. The food is good if predictable, however, with a decent selection of pasta, pizza and some vaguely Italian meat dishes on offer.

Other options:

Grill & Pølsebar (Ane Sofiap Aqq 1; mains Dkr35-50)

Seamen's Home cafeteria (Seamen's Home; meals Dkr45-55) Snacks, fast food, simple meals and cakes.

Steak & Grillbar (JM Jensenip Aqq B1299; mains Dkr35-50) This and the Grill & Pølsebar have hot dogs, burgers and chips.

SELF-CATERING

Sisimiut has a **brædtet** (Aqqusinersuaq 54), and it also has **Brugsen** (Aqqusinersuaq 52) and **Pisiffik** (Kaaleeqqap Aqq) supermarkets (the Pisiffik supermarket has a bakery). Located off the main road is Tiggaliorfik Konditori, which is a wonderful independent bakery and pastry shop.

SOUTHWEST GREENLAND

Entertainment

The local folk-dance troupe performs irregularly but can be requested for group visits – ask at the tourist office for details.

Sisimiut's two pubs are side by side, so if you don't like the look of one you can always go next door. **Café Kukkukooq** (☎ 665813; Nikkorsuit) is slightly the better of the two, with a more dignified atmosphere come closing time. **Pub Raaja** (☎ 864549) is the locals' bar and can get a bit rowdy at weekends.

Shopping

Arctic Incoming (☎ 865595; Aqqusinersuaq 23) sells a good selection of local crafts and carvings. For film, cameras and batteries, try **Foto Radio** (☎ 865610; Aqquisinersuaq).

Getting There & Away

AIR

Air Greenland (☎ 85199) flies six times weekly from Sisimiut to Kangerlussuaq (Dkr836, 30 minutes), Nuuk (Dkr1666, 1½ hours) via Maniitsoq (Dkr1021, 40 minutes), and Ilulissat via Kangerlussuaq and Aasiaat (Dkr2414).

BOAT

There's no AUL office in town, but you can buy tickets at **Greenland Travel** (☎ 865747; Aqqusinersuaq 23).

The three big ferries call in once weekly in either direction most of the year. There are connections to Aasiaat (Dkr610, 13 hours), Qasigiannguit (Dkr765, 23 hours), Ilulissat (Dkr820, 25 hours), Maniitsoq (Dkr525, 10 hours) and Nuuk (Dkr880, 22 hours).

An AUL cargo boat sails to Sarfannguit/Itilleq on Sunday (Dkr415). Book through Greenland Travel.

Getting Around

Regular town buses cost Dkr10 per ride. The **airport bus** (☎ 527390) costs adult/child Dkr25/10 and will drop you wherever you're staying. A **taxi** (☎ 865533) will cost you about Dkr100.

The charter boat *M/S Mimi* carries up to 12 people and is available for day trips or longer excursions to outlying areas and. It can be chartered for Dkr5000 per day; contact the tourist office for bookings.

Sisu Sport (☎ 865501; www.sisu.gl; Kaaleeqqap Aqq 10) hires mountain bikes for Dkr100 per day.

ITILLEQ

pop 127

This tiny and very traditional village lies on an island sheltered from the sea about 45km due south of Sisimiut. It's worth a visit if you want to escape from other travellers and experience west-coast Greenland as it once was. The only accommodation option is to camp – you can get provisions at the Pilersuisoq shop. It's a fantastic boat trip to get there. For details, see above.

The Kangerlussuaq tourist office (see p164) offers trips to Itilleq including boat transfer down the fjord followed by a 9km hike across Itialinguaq pass and a boat pickup on the far side to take you to Itilleq. You can overnight there, try out some deep-sea fishing and get a feel for village life before being transferred back to Kangerlussuaq. Prices are by arrangement.

SARFANNGUIT

pop 104

The village of Sarfannguit is easily reached on foot from the high route of the Kangerlussuaq to Sisimiut trek, or on a rather long detour from the low route. It's also often used as a starting or ending point for the Kangerlussuaq to Sisimiut trek, as it allows you to cut off the section between Sisimiut and the Nerumaaq Valley, which is the most difficult bit of the hike.

Sarfannguit, which is dotted with ancient Inuit ruins, has a community service house with beds for Dkr100 and a Pilersuisoq shop (with post and telephone services), where you can restock with basic supplies for the onward journey. Locals operate a free ferry service across Sarfannguit Channel (the village is on an island).

The village can also be reached by RAB cargo boat (see above).

KANGERLUSSUAQ (SØNDRE STRØMFJORD)

pop 490

Plonked at the head of Greenland's third-longest fjord, Kangerlussuaq looks and very much feels like an ex–military base. It's a surreal kind of place, spread out over a wide area and lacking any soul or Greenlandic feel. However, it's what is outside the town that is worth visiting. The icecap is accessible by road, it's the end of the fabulous trek from Sisimiut, and it's the best place in

SISIMIUT TO KANGERLUSSUAQ TREK

Greenland's most popular long-distance trek, the 150km-long hike between Sisimiut and Kangerlussuaq is one of the great walks of the world, offering you easy access at either end and pristine wilderness in between.

The trek takes between 10 and 14 days and requires careful planning, but anyone who can read maps well and is not daunted by the prospect of at least 10 days' walking can probably handle it. The trip can be done in both directions, but if you start in Sisimiut you'll be able to stock up on supplies and tackle the more challenging terrain and the possibility of less favourable weather while your legs are still fresh. You should notify the tourist offices at either end of the route of your intentions and be sure to promptly report your safe arrival.

Although there are technically two routes, a high route and a low route, the former is discouraged as it passes through sensitive caribou grounds and is more technically challenging. The walk description and the map in this book are intended as a rough guide only. All hikers need the three essential 1:100,000 hiking maps *West Greenland – Kangerlussuaq*, *Pingu* and *Sisimiut*, which show the route in detail.

Note that the compass deviation in this area was approximately 34°23'W in 2004 and is decreasing by approximately 0°31' every four years. Visit www.ngdc.noaa.gov/seg/geomag/jsp /Declination.jsp for the current compass declination.

To get information and advice on what to bring, details of the routes, terrain and weather conditions, and what kinds of things to expect, contact the Sisimiut tourist office or the Kangerlussuaq tourist office.

The Low Route

Leave Sisimiut on the trail to Nasaasaaq and head into the valley that lies immediately north of the mountain. Follow the southern bank of the river that flows down the valley and cross the pass at the top. Then make your descent along the eastern bank of the river that traces its way down the other side. Follow the dogsled track over the Qerrottusup Majoria pass, where you'll find a hiker's hut, and then descend the slope to the head of Kangerluarsuk Tulleq.

Follow the valley leading away from the fjord up to a pass near Peak 427. Just north of here a stream flows down to Hut Lake. Midway between the fjord and Hut Lake there's a mountain hut open to hikers. When you reach the lake traverse along the northern shore. On a hillock at the eastern end is an eight-person hut.

Hut Lake is part of a chain of lakes that you should follow westward along their southern shores. At the western end of Lake 290 you'll ascend to the highest point on the trek (400m) on Iluliumanersuup Portornga. The route then cuts south and follows a stream through the marshy valley Itinneq towards the enormous Lake Tasersuaq. About 2km from the western end of Tasersuaq you'll find a new hiker's hut.

The route continues south of the lake to the extended arm of Kangerluatsiarsuaq Bay. Follow another stream from here to the vast Lake Amitsorsuaq. Near the western end of the lake there's a big 30-person hut with canoes that can be borrowed (free) for paddling around the lake. From here it takes a day along the southern shore of Amitsorsuaq to an eight-person hut at the eastern tip of the lake.

Bear east and north along the arc-like southern shore of the large Lake Qarlissuit, and continue east past a chain of lakes and then north along the northwestern shore of the large elongated lake immediately to the south of Hundesø (marked Limnæsø on the hiking map). Pass around the southern shore of Hundesø and you'll soon come to a gravel track that leads down past Kellyville radar facility. From here it's just 2km east to Kangerlussuaq Harbour.

Greenland to observe native wildlife, with large herds of muskoxen and caribou surrounding the town and Arctic fox slinking over the hills.

Kangerlussuaq lies just north of the Arctic Circle and, thanks to its inland position, the climate is one of the most stable – and extreme – in Greenland, with temperatures ranging from -50°C in winter to 28°C in the 24-hour summer daylight.

History

Kangerlussuaq was never an Inuit settlement but a seasonal hunting and camping ground. The nearest major Inuit habitation was 90km away at Arnangarnup Qoorua, or Paradisdalen, where extensive ruins have been found; it's now a protected historic site and nature reserve.

After the German occupation of Denmark in April 1941, a defence treaty between the USA, the Greenland governor and the Danish ambassador handed the security of Greenland over to the US military. The stable climate made the long and narrow Søndre Strømfjord an ideal location for the US base Bluie West Eight, and in October of that year a military airfield and a host of personnel barracks were constructed overnight. During the war it became the main waystation for bombers and cargo carriers flying between North America and Europe, and at the height of WWII over 8000 military personnel were stationed here.

In 1950 the defence treaty expired and the base was handed back to Denmark. However, the continuing Cold War threat prompted a renewed agreement, and Bluie West Eight returned to US military operations a year later. From 1958 the Americans set up four DEW-line (Distant Early Warning line) radar bases in Greenland to provide early warning of a possible Soviet attack, and Sondrestrom became the main supply base for the stations.

After the Soviet Union collapsed and the 'communist threat' dematerialised, both the DEW-line and the air base became redundant. The DEW stations were closed in 1990 and 1991, and on 30 September 1992 the base was closed. The following day the base came under the control of the Greenland Home Rule government and was officially renamed Kangerlussuaq.

For information about the scientific research currently being carried out in Kangerlussuaq, see p28.

Information

There's no bank, but you can change money and travellers cheques and get a cash advance on credit cards at Hotel Kangerlussuaq.

Old Camp Hostel (Internet access per 15 mins Dkr40)
Police (☎ 841222)
Post office (☎ 841155) In the airport complex.
Tourist office (☎ 841648; www.kangtour.gl; airport terminal; ☯ 9am-5pm Mon-Fri, to 2pm Sat) At weekends you can get information at the Old Camp Hostel.
www.arcticchar.dk This Danish site has details on river and deep-sea fishing around Kangerlussuaq.
www.greenland-icecap.com Information on crossing the Greenland icecap from Kangerlussuaq.
www.kangtour.gl General tourist information about the Kangerlussuaq area.

Sights

In the former base commander's office on the old Sondrestrom US air base (south of the runway) there's a **museum** (adult/child Dkr35/15; ☯ 10am-3pm Mon-Fri, 2-5pm Sun) dedicated to the history of Søndre Strømfjord/Kangerlussuaq. Exhibits also include meteorology, the recovering of aircraft wrecks and glaciology. A free shuttle bus runs from Hotel Kangerlussuaq (the main building at the airport terminal, see p166) every half-hour.

Kellyville, inland from the harbour and overlooking Lake Helen, is home to the operations of the **Stanford Research Institute**. It's currently conducting ionosphere research, with emphasis on the aurora borealis (see the boxed text, p31). Ask at the tourist office if you'd like to arrange to visit the facility.

Activities

Kangerlussuaq is the Arctic equivalent of Club Med, thanks to the American military, which left behind a host of recreational facilities – including a gymnasium, a bowling alley, an indoor swimming pool and an 18-hole golf course!

A round at the sandy **Sondie Arctic Desert Golf Club**, 4km east of the airport, costs Dkr100, including club and golf-ball hire. Pay at the tourist office. You'll need to take a **taxi** (☎ 237507) to get there.

The indoor **swimming pool** (admission Dkr40; ☯ 2-10pm Mon-Fri, noon-6pm Sat & Sun) also has a

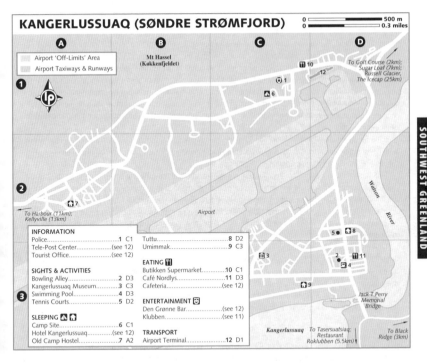

KANGERLUSSUAQ (SØNDRE STRØMFJORD)

0 _____ 500 m
0 _____ 0.3 miles

INFORMATION
Police..1 C1
Tele-Post Center...................(see 12)
Tourist Office........................(see 12)

SIGHTS & ACTIVITIES
Bowling Alley............................2 D3
Kangerlussuaq Museum............3 C3
Swimming Pool...........................4 D3
Tennis Courts.............................5 D2

SLEEPING
Camp Site...................................6 C1
Hotel Kangerlussuaq...............(see 12)
Old Camp Hostel.......................7 A2

Tuttu..8 D2
Umimmak...................................9 C3

EATING
Butikken Supermarket.............10 C1
Café Nordlys.............................11 D3
Cafeteria..................................(see 12)

ENTERTAINMENT
Den Grønne Bar......................(see 12)
Klubben...................................(see 11)

TRANSPORT
Airport Terminal......................12 D1

SOUTHWEST GREENLAND

gymnasium, complete with bodybuilding equipment and squash court. The **bowling alley** (5-10pm Mon-Thu, 12.30-6pm Sat & Sun), next to the swimming pool, hosts an open bowling tournament on Saturday.

Festivals & Events

In October the **Polar Circle Marathon** (www.polar-circle-marathon.com) takes place in Kangerlussuaq. The course covers a range of challenging terrain, including a section across several glacial tongues. On 8 October 2005 the event will be upgraded to the first Adventure Marathon World Championship, including tougher terrain and a 3000m ascent on the icecap.

Tours

Kangerlussuaq's tourist office (one of Greenland's busiest) has come up with enough tour possibilities to keep you occupied for days. Some must be booked at least a day in advance.

Tours include a 1½-hour muskox safari (Dkr175); a 3½-hour trip to the Russell Glacier or the inland ice (Dkr475), which

includes plenty of opportunities to see wildlife; a variation of this last tour that includes a barbecue (Dkr650); and a one-day boat trip on the fjord (Dkr695), an excellent opportunity for trout fishing. You'll need to buy a licence (one week Dkr200) at the post office.

Dogsledding tours run from December to April (Dkr895/3050, half day/overnight). Other winter tours include trips to view the aurora borealis (northern lights; Dkr3000, two hours) and ice-fishing expeditions on the frozen fjord (Dkr500, four hours).

See p160 for information about dogsledding expeditions between Kangerlussuaq and Sisimiut.

Sleeping

There's a free camp site west of the airport, but it only has a cold-water tap; toilets are at the airport terminal.

Old Camp Hostel (☎ 841648; kangtour@greennet.gl; beds Dkr275, family cabins Dkr1200;) The Kangerlussuaq tourist office runs the flash and nicely renovated hostel, 2km west of the

SOUTHWEST GREENLAND

KANGERLUSSUAQ WILDLIFE

The hills around Kangerlussuaq are the best place to see and photograph Greenlandic wildlife. Twenty-seven muskoxen introduced to Kangerlussuaq in the early 1960s thrived in the area and have increased to a population of more than 5000 animals. In 1986, several muskoxen were transplanted from Kangerlussuaq to Pituffik, and later some were also taken to Ivittuut in South Greenland, to Nunavik in the Upernavik region, and to Naternaq between Aasiaat and Qasigiannguit. Muskoxen from Kangerlussuaq have also extended their range south into the Nuuk region. Subsistence hunters are permitted to take an increasing quota of about 1500 muskoxen per year.

Late September is the season for love on the muskox calendar, and it's awesome to watch and hear amorous and headstrong males doing horn-to-horn combat for eligible females. The calves are born early in spring.

The best viewing spots for muskoxen are east and southeast of the airport. If you want good photos, a telephoto lens is essential. A cornered or irritated muskox can become extremely aggressive, though, so don't approach within about 35m or there could be real problems. If the animal begins to snort or rub the side of its face, you're too close, and it's preparing an attack. Be prepared: go to www.dpc.dk/wildlife and read the page entitled, 'Encounters with Wildlife in Greenland'.

There are also about 5000 caribou in the Kangerlussuaq area. This figure is down from an all-time high of 40,000 in the 1970s. The decline has been attributed to a shortage of the animals' favourite meal, lichen (reindeer moss). The best places to see caribou are found northeast of the airport.

Kangerlussuaq is also prime territory for spotting Arctic foxes, Arctic hares, ptarmigans, gyrfalcons, peregrine falcons and smaller birds.

---

airport terminal. The comfortable rooms only have two beds, there are good kitchens and living areas, and the price includes breakfast, linen and transfer to and from the airport.

Hotel Kangerlussuaq (☎ 841180; kangbook@glv.gl; s/d Dkr645/795, with bathroom Dkr995/1195; ☒ ▯) This hotel, built in the 1960s, comprises three buildings and has large, comfortable rooms with corporate-style décor. The Umimmak (muskox) and Tuttu (caribou) annexes are 1km south of the airport and are a little less comfortable than the main building.

Ice Hotel (s/d Dkr495/795) From the middle of December to the middle of April, Hotel Kangerlussuaq operates an ice hotel with two large central *iglo* connected by tunnel to six smaller double-room *iglo* that are kept at -12°C. Beds are on huge ice blocks, with mattresses, muskox skins and good sleeping bags. Guests have access to showers, and rooms in the main hotel if they can't stand the cold.

Eating

Restaurant Roklubben (☎ 841996; 1/2/3 courses Dkr188/219/239; ☽ noon-4pm & 6pm-midnight) In a scenic location on the shore of Lake Fergusson, Restaurant Roklubben serves the best food in town, with muskox, caribou and Arctic char served in innovative modern dishes. A free shuttle bus runs from Old Camp Hostel every night.

Hotel Kangerlussuaq restaurant (☎ 841180; mains Dkr162-208; ☽ 6-9.30pm) This rather soulless place overlooking the runway does a decent à la carte menu featuring plenty of muskox, caribou, halibut and lamb, but service is a bit sloppy.

Cafeteria (☎ 841180; snacks & mains Dkr18-52; ☽ 6.30am-8.30pm) If you find comfort in familiarity you'll be relieved to discover that the airport cafeteria resembles its namesakes anywhere in the world. Its menu consists of cheap and predictable food ranging from burgers, fish and chips, and spaghetti Bolognese to dried-up sandwiches.

Café Nordlys (☎ 841440; Kangerlussuaq Entertainment Centre; mains Dkr50-100; 5pm-midnight Tue-Thu & Sun, to 3am Fri & Sat) A dimly lit grill bar straight out of the American Midwest, this place serves up hearty portions of respectable chicken, steaks, pasta and pizza and has plenty of loud music and snooker to help you work off the calories.

You can get a limited supply of groceries at Butikken, opposite the airport terminal.

Drinking

Den Grønne Bar (☎ 841180; ☼ 9am-1pm Mon-Sat, 5pm-midnight daily) Huge windows overlook the runway at the bright and modern Grønne Bar, located at the airport terminal. During happy hour, from 5pm to 6pm, the drinks are half price.

Klubben (☎ 841180; Kangerlussuaq Entertainment Centre; ☼ 6pm-midnight Sun-Thu, 9pm-3am Fri & Sat) Another remnant from the American occupation, this lively place is dimly lit and ideal for an evening's heavy smoking and propping up the bar.

Ice Bar (Ice Hotel; ☼ 7.30-10pm) For a cool drinking experience, the Ice Hotel also has its own bar, charging Dkr55 for drinks in a glass made of ice.

Getting There & Away

AIR

Air Greenland (☎ 841288) uses Kangerlussuaq as its main Greenland terminal. It has five weekly flights to Copenhagen (Dkr3900 return, 4½ hours), eight weekly flights to Ilulissat (Dkr1578, 45 minutes), six weekly flights to Aasiaat (Dkr1223, 45 minutes), Sisimiut (Dkr836, 30 minutes) and Maniitsoq (Dkr1351, 1½ hours), eight weekly flights to Nuuk (Dkr1738, 55 minutes), and two weekly flights to Kulusuk (Dkr3173, 1¾ hours).

BOAT

Kangerlussuaq is well off the beaten path for regular ferry lines, but cruise ships visit in summer. If you have the opportunity to sail, don't miss it. The outermost 50km of the fjord, constricted between high glacier-ravaged peaks, is nothing short of awesome.

Getting Around

Blue town buses cover the road between the youth hostel and the Umimmak building. They depart approximately hourly between 5.15am and 7pm from Monday to Friday (Dkr20).

The tourist office hires cars/scooters/bikes for Dkr900/375/100 per day. Kangerlussuaq has the longest road system in Greenland, with sandy, pebbly tracks leading to all areas. It's slow going on a bicycle.

AROUND KANGERLUSSUAQ
Hiking

Although the Kangerlussuaq to Sisimiut trek is the star hiking route, Kangerlussuaq offers numerous other hikes, and if that's your emphasis you could spend an entire holiday exploring this area. *Walks Around Kangerlussuaq* (Dkr25), by Peter Fich, includes a map and is sold by the tourist office. The following are just several of the many possibilities.

BLACK RIDGE

A road out of Kangerlussuaq heads in a southerly direction and then crosses the Watson River by means of the Jack T Perry Memorial Bridge (he drowned in 1976 while trying to ford the river). Turn left after the bridge and follow the road to Black Ridge (1½ hours), where there's a great view of the outwash plain south of the airport. You may also see muskoxen on the ridge, especially near the curious salt lake Store Saltsjø, which is three hours' walk from the airport.

SUGAR LOAF

Sugar Loaf, east of the golf course, makes an easy 16km return hike from town. A gravel road leads up to the former radio installation, providing a great view of the airport and the glaciers spilling down from the inland ice.

RUSSELL GLACIER

The straightforward and easy three- or four-day return expedition to Russell Glacier can be done on the bumpy track or along the sandy plain of the valley floor. The impressive Russell Glacier is active and it's advancing 25m each year. Don't approach the 80m ice cliffs too closely, since the glacier frequently gives birth to some whopping chunks of ice. Temperatures on the glacier and inland ice can be up to 10°C cooler than in Kangerlussuaq, so bring warm clothes and a windbreaker. The tourist office can arrange a one-way 4WD transfer for up to five people (including luggage) from Kangerlussuaq. The cost is Dkr800.

AMMALORTUP NUNAA

For a complete feeling of getting away from it all and some wonderful views, head off from Restaurant Roklubben on Lake Fergusson and walk east along the northern lakeshore. Then ascend the ravine beneath the southern slopes of Tasersuatsiaap Kinginnera (630m) and follow the lake-studded pass down to Orsuarnissarajuttoq.

Continue southeast along the southern shore of the lake. From the southeastern end of the lake, head southeast over a minor pass before descending steeply to the beautiful large lake known as Ammalortoq. If you use the lakeshore as your base camp, this area will be good for a couple of days' exploring. Departing from Kangerlussuaq, allow two or three days for this hike.

STEVE HUTTON

Beached icebergs near Nanortalik, Greenland (p126)

GRAEME CORNWALLIS

Greenland's Pamialluk Island (p133), viewed from an AUL ferry

Ulamertorsuaq's vertical rock face (p130), Greenland

DEANNA SWANEY

RICH PROHASKA

Qaqortoq's Stone and Man art (p117), Greenland

Greenlandic coast near Paamiut (p141)

DEANNA SWANEY

Russell Glacier (p167), Greenland

STEVE HUTTON

Townscape of Sisimiut (p158), Greenland

STEVE H

Disko Bay

CONTENTS

DISKO BAY

HIGHLIGHTS

- Sit mesmerised by the natural force and beauty of **Ilulissat Kangerlua** (p176), the northern hemisphere's most prolific glacier
- Dogsled under the midnight sun on **Disko Island** (p186)
- Catch a gig at the **Aasiaat Rock Festival** (p185)
- Discover the roots of Greenland's past at **Qasigiannguit** (p181)
- Spend a night on a glacier at **Icecamp Eqi** (p180)

Many visitors to Greenland make a beeline for iceberg-studded Disko Bay, and more specifically to Ilulissat, the centre of the country's tourist industry. The town is home to star attraction Ilulissat Kangerlua (Jakobshavn Icefjord), the northern hemisphere's most prolific tidewater glacier. The massive ice-choked expanse it creates disgorges gargantuan icebergs – some weighing up to seven million tonnes – into Disko Bay, a truly stunning sight. Consequently, Ilulissat is well set up for travellers, but at times is overwhelmed by them.

The town's tourist agencies offer a huge variety of tours to and around the local glaciers, to wilderness camps and to outlying villages. For a real taste of the High Arctic, a trip to these smaller, less frequently visited settlements is highly recommended. These outposts see few visitors and offer an authentic look at life in the area. Alternatively, you could visit out of season and see Ilulissat in winter or early spring.

Out in Disko Bay lies the largest and newest of Greenland's islands, Disko Island. The bizarre geological landscape of the island makes for excellent hiking, and its relatively remote location means you'll have most trails entirely to yourself. Inland, the island has its own icecap, offering a chance to go dogsledding throughout the summer months.

For visitors heading north on the ferry, the Disko Bay area offers the first glimpse of the true north. At 300km north of the Arctic Circle you can expect perpetual day from late May to mid-July, and many visitors sleep restlessly as the sun circles day after day without setting. In winter the area is in darkness for six weeks and is normally the marker for the southern extent of the pack ice.

ILULISSAT REGION

ILULISSAT TOWN (JAKOBSHAVN)
pop 4470

This is it. This is why you came to Greenland and spent all that money. Ilulissat is one of those places so spectacular that it just makes everything else pale in comparison. Within walking distance of town you will be confronted with icebergs of such gargantuan proportions that they are truly incomprehensible – and you don't even have to take an expensive helicopter trip to see them.

The town is situated at the mouth of a 40km icefjord that produces 20 million tons of ice per day (equal to the volume of water used by New York city in an entire year), and the chunks that break off can produce tidal waves up to 10m high.

Ilulissat is Greenland's third-largest town and its most popular tourist destination, often overwhelmed with visitors between early July and mid-August. It's scruffy and unkempt and has a disorderly spirit that's noticeably absent in the tidier towns farther south, but the facilities are good and competition to pull in the tourist dollars is strong.

Six thousand sled dogs also call Ilulissat home, and their howling can keep the whole town awake at night. Do not approach them, however; they're not pets and can bite.

History

From 4000 to 3500 years ago, the Ilulissat area was inhabited by the Saqqaq and Dorset cultures. The abandoned village of Sermermiut, beside the icefjord, dates back perhaps 3500 years and is one of over 120 archaeological sites in the Ilulissat district. When the Norwegian missionary Poul Egede arrived in 1737, Sermermiut was the largest Inuit village in Greenland, with 200 people living in 20 or more houses.

The first Europeans to visit Ilulissat were the Norse, who sailed up the coast to hunt

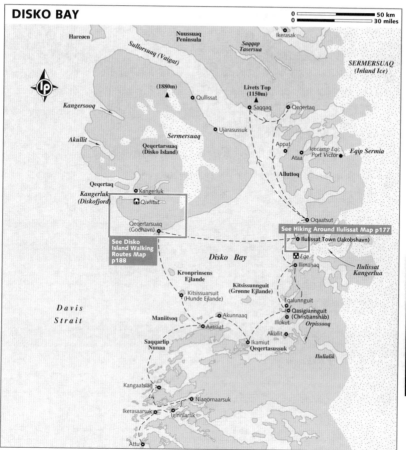

DISKO BAY

0 ——————— 50 km
0 ——————— 30 miles

Hareøen

Nuussuaq
Peninsula

Ikerasak

Sullorsuaq (Vaigat)

Saqqap
Tasersua

SERMERSUAQ
(Inland Ice)

Kangersooq

(1880m) ▲

Qullissat

Livets Top
(1150m) ▲

Saqqaq

Qeqertaq

Ujarasussuk

Akullit

Sermersuaq

Qeqertarsuaq
(Disko Island)

Appat

Ataa

Icecamp Eqi;
Port Victor

Eqip Sermia

Alluttoq

Qeqertaq

Kangerluk

Kangerluk
(Diskofjord)

Qivittut

Qeqertarsuaq
(Godhavn)

Oqaatsut

See Hiking Around Ilulissat Map p177

Ilulissat Town (Jakobshavn)

**See Disko
Island Walking
Routes Map
p188**

Eqe

Disko Bay

Ilimanaq

Ilulissat
Kangerlua

Kronprinsens
Ejlande

Kitsissunnguit
(Grønne Ejlande)

Egalunnguit

Davis
Strait

Kitsissuarsuit
(Hunde Ejlande)

Maniitsoq

Akunnaaq

Qasigiannguit
(Christianshåb)

Illokut

Orpissooq

Aasiaat

Ikamiut
Qeqertasussuk

Saqqarlip
Nunaa

Iluilalik

Kangaatsiaq

Niaqornaarsuk

Ikerasaarsuk

Iginniarfik

Attu

DISKO BAY

seals and walruses. The next contact wasn't until the late 17th century, when Dutch whalers arrived and established trade with the Inuit. Some of the outsiders cheated the locals so much that the Dutch government placed the mistreatment of Greenlanders in the same category as piracy, with the same stiff penalties!

In 1780 the Danish king decided that monopoly trade would be appropriate for Greenland, and the nuisance Dutch whalers were ousted in the only naval battle ever fought in Greenland, just outside the town's present harbour.

Poul Egede officially founded Ilulissat in 1741, intending to use it as a summer mission and trading centre. The mission was so successful that it attracted increasing numbers of local Inuit, and by 1782 Ilulissat had grown into a colony and later became the metropolis and service centre of Disko Bay. Today tourism, fishing and shrimping are the mainstays of the local economy.

Information

Greenland Tours Elke Meissner (☎ 944411; www.visitgreenland.com/gtem; Kussangajannguaq B450; ☒ 9am-6pm)

Greenland Travel (☎ 943246; Kussangajaannguaq 7; ☒ 10am-4.30pm Mon-Thu, 10am-4pm Fri)

Grønlandsbanken (☎ 947700; Kussangajannguaq 7)

Hospital (☎ 943211)

Ilulissat Tourist Service (☎ 944322; www.its.gl;

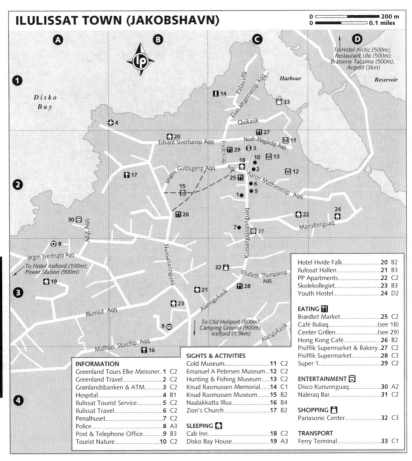

ILULISSAT TOWN (JAKOBSHAVN)

To Hotel Arctic (500m); Restaurant Ulo (500m); Brasserie Tacanna (500m); Airport (3km)

Disko Bay

Harbour

Reservoir

Quikasik

INFORMATION
Greenland Tours Elke Meissner..**1** C2
Greenland Travel.....................**2** C2
Grønlandsbanken & ATM..........**3** C2
Hospital.................................**4** B1
Ilulissat Tourist Service............**5** C2
Ilulissat Travel.......................**6** C2
Penalhuset.............................**7** C2
Police...................................**8** A3
Post & Telephone Office...........**9** B3
Tourist Nature.......................**10** C2

SIGHTS & ACTIVITIES
Cold Museum.........................**11** C2
Emanuel A Petersen Museum....**12** C2
Hunting & Fishing Museum......**13** C2
Knud Rasmussen Memorial......**14** C1
Knud Rasmussen Museum........**15** B2
Naalakkatta Illua...................**16** B4
Zion's Church........................**17** B2

SLEEPING
Cab Inn................................**18** C2
Disko Bay House.....................**19** A3

Hotel Hvide Falk....................**20** B2
Ilulissat Hallen......................**21** B3
PP Apartments.......................**22** C2
Skolekollegiet........................**23** B3
Youth Hostel.........................**24** D2

EATING
Brædtet Market......................**25** C2
Café Iluliaq.........................(see 18)
Center Grillen.......................(see 29)
Hong Kong Café.....................**26** B2
Pisiffik Supermarket & Bakery..**27** C2
Pisiffik Supermarket...............**28** C3
Super 1................................**29** C2

ENTERTAINMENT
Disco Kununnguaq..................**30** A2
Naleraq Bar..........................**31** C2

SHOPPING
Panasonic Center...................**32** C3

TRANSPORT
Ferry Terminal.......................**33** C1

Kussangajannguaq 11; 9am-6pm) Internet access for Dkr40 per half-hour.

Ilulissat Travel (944300; www.ilulissattravel.gl; Aron Mathiesenip Aqq 2ab; 9am-6pm)

Penalhuset (944925; Kussangajannguaq; noon-5pm Mon-Fri, 10am-1pm Sat) Stocks a selection of English-language books and a good choice of postcards.

Police (943222)

Post office (943655; Alanngukasik; 10am-4pm Mon-Fri)

Tourist Nature (944420; touna@greennet.gl; Kussangajannguaq 5; 9am-6pm)

Sights
KNUD RASMUSSEN MUSEUM

The lovely red house that once served as the town vicarage was also the birthplace of Greenland's favourite son, Knud Rasmussen (see p174). It now houses the town **museum** (943643; www.ilumus.gl; Nuisariannguaq 9; admission Dkr25; 10am-5pm Apr-Oct), dedicated to the Arctic explorer, anthropologist and author whose typically Greenlandic philosophy of life was summed up in his oft-quoted utterance 'Give me winter, give me dogs, and you can have the rest'.

One room is devoted to his expeditions and anthropological and linguistic studies across the North American Arctic. Other exhibits deal with Greenlandic traditions, early Danish life in Greenland, and ancient Inuit artefacts and history. There is also an exhibition on the development of Ilulissat and a large collection of photographs of the town.

EMANUEL A PETERSEN ART MUSEUM

Greenlandic landscapes are on view at the **Emanuel A Petersen Art Museum** (☎ 944443; Aaron Mathiesenip Aqq 7; admission Dkr25; ☺ 10am-4pm Tue-Sun), where most of the works are by the eponymous Danish artist. Petersen (1894–1948) was a prolific painter, and during his career he made several trips to Greenland to paint its extraordinary landscape and light. Through numerous exhibitions around Europe and his illustrations in *Greenland in Pictures*, published in 1928, he introduced the magic of the Arctic to the rest of Europe. When he died he left an extraordinary collection of paintings of early-20th-century Greenland, 66 of which are exhibited here.

HUNTING & FISHING MUSEUM

The newly renovated **Hunting & Fishing Museum** (☎ 944484; off Noah Møgårdip Aqq; admission free) emphasises the hunting and fishing traditions of the polar Inuit, and contains both traditional and modern tools, implements and conveyances, as well as a wooden dory. There are no set opening hours, but during business hours there's usually someone at the door; if not, ask for the key at the Knud Rasmussen Museum.

Nearby is the **Cold Museum**, housed in Ilulissat's oldest building, the tarred 'black warehouse' that dates from Ilulissat's commercial whaling days. It houses a collection of tools and machinery from the old trading settlement. Ask at the Hunting & Fishing Museum for the key.

CHURCHES

The missionary Jørgen Jørgensen Sverdrup managed to instil such religious fervour into his Ilulissat flock in the late 18th century that they set about raising the funds to build their own church. From 1777 to 1779 the Greenlandic residents of Ilulissat and nearby Oqaatsut collected 59 whales and 157 barrels of whale oil. Combined with the contribution of 25 whales and 52 barrels of oil from the Danish inhabitants, they managed to cover the costs of **Zion's Church**, a striking edifice constructed of heavy timbers. Inside the church a lovely votive ship hangs from the ceiling, and above the altar is a copy of the famous *Christus* by Bertel Thorvaldsen.

The church is only open on Sunday; at other times, visits must be arranged through the Ilulissat Tourist Service.

Ilulissat's other church, **Naalakkatta Illua** (the house of Our Lord), was originally constructed at the coal-mining village Qullissat, on Disko Island, but when the coal ran out in 1972 the settlement was abandoned, and the following year the church was moved to Ilulissat. Whoever did the job apparently took quite literally Christ's admonition that his church be built upon a rock.

Festivals & Events

In mid-April each year Ilulissat celebrates the **Arctic Palerfik**, a three-day family dogsledding trip along the icefjord. Over 200 people generally take part, with as many as 1200 dogs making the trek. It's a fantastic way to meet the locals as well as a magnificent trip.

Ilulissat hosts the **Arctic Midnight Orienteering Festival** (http://iog.ilulissat.gl) each July. The event has challenging 5km, 10km, 15km and 20km courses across rough terrain. Races are held in the midnight sun, with courses of varying degrees of difficulty set out through the magnificent local scenery.

Tours

The four tourist offices, which are a combination of tourist office and travel agency, and Greenland Travel offer a bewildering number of tours. Each has its own speciality, and although you may sign up for a tour with one agency it may well be run by one of the others.

Many of the tours are offered by all the agencies, including two-hour guided town walks or walks to Sermermiut (Dkr150 to Dkr175); four- to five-hour guided walks to the icefjord (Dkr295 to Dkr325); boat trips to the icefjord (day/night Dkr400/450); and five-hour boat trips to Oqaatsut or Ilimanaq (both Dkr700). Day trips to the tidewater glacier Eqip Sermia and Port Victor (see p180) cost Dkr1395, including lunch.

Tourist Nature (☎ 944420; touna@greennet.gl; Kussangajannguaq 5; ☺ 9am-6pm) runs a two-day trip to Ataa (see p179), including lunch at Oqaatsut, accommodation in Ataa, a traditional Greenlandic dinner and a trip to Eqi glacier (Dkr2895). A three-day version includes a full-day hike to the icecap at Eqi (Dkr3795). It also runs a combined boat and hiking trip to Ilimanaq, passing the icefjord en route (day/evening Dkr1095/1195), and six-hour fishing trips for groups of six to 10 people (Dkr850 per person).

DISKO BAY

KNUD RASMUSSEN

By far the most famous, and the most loved, of Greenland's explorers, Knud Rasmussen is Ilulissat's most celebrated son, born in the old vicarage on 7 June 1879. Kunuunnguaq, 'little Knud', as he became known, was the son of the local pastor and was of Danish, Norwegian and Greenlandic descent.

After completing school in Copenhagen, Knud tried his hand at a variety of careers, including opera singing and medicine, but it was his talent as a writer that earned him a place on the Danish Literary Expedition to Northwest Greenland in 1902. The result was his first book, *The New People*, about the traditional polar Inuit of the Melville Bay area. From 1906 to 1908 Knud joined the Ethnographical Expedition, which attempted to find the route travelled by early migrants to Greenland from Canada's Ellesmere Island.

Smitten by life in the far north, Knud and fellow Arctic enthusiast Peter Freuchen (who later wrote the book *Arctic Adventure*, which detailed many of their exploits together), established a trading company in Qaanaaq (Thule), with the objective of funding subsequent expeditions. Freuchen wrote: 'Rasmussen was something of a dandy and always carried a pair of scissors for cutting his hair and beard. Even in the most biting cold, he washed his face every day with walrus blubber and his footwear was the most beautiful in the Arctic.'

Their joint business was successful and, between 1912 and 1919, Knud conducted four more expeditions to Greenland. The experience gained from these trips led to what he hoped would be the fulfilment of his dreams: tracing the migration of the Inuit peoples from Siberia all the way to Greenland. The fifth Thule expedition set out in 1921 to gather ethnographical, archaeological, geographical and natural-history data from Greenland right across the North American Arctic. Knud visited all the Inuit communities in Arctic Canada and Alaska, collecting myths, legends and linguistic studies; he would have continued across Arctic Russia but was deported by the Soviet authorities.

The result of this trip was *The 5th Thule Expedition – The Danish Ethnographical Expedition to Arctic America*, which detailed linguistic and cultural differences between the Inuit groups across the region. It was also the basis for Rasmussen's best-known book, *Across Arctic America*. These projects earned him an honorary doctorate from Copenhagen University.

Subsequently, the sixth and seventh Thule expeditions travelled to Greenland's east coast. Knud also tried his hand at film direction, with the making of *Palos Brudefærd* (Palo's Wedding) in the summer of 1933 in Ammassalik (now Tasiilaq). Sadly, during the filming he contracted food poisoning from pickled auks and died shortly afterwards, on 21 December 1933.

Ilulissat Tourist Service (☎ 944322; www.its.gl; Kussangajannguaq 11; ⏰ 9am-6pm) offers a two-day hike to the cabin Himmelhytten (Dkr1775), two-hour twin-otter tours to the inland ice (Dkr2495) and a 30-minute helicopter or Twin Otter tour over the icefjord (Dkr995). At the time of research it was planning to offer diving from summer 2005.

Ilulissat Travel (☎ 944300; www.ilulissattravel.gl; Aron Mathiesenip Aqq 2ab; ⏰ 9am-6pm) can arrange dinner with a local family (Dkr250); 30-/45-minute helicopter tours over the icefjord (Dkr1595/1895); an overnight stay in tents at the edge of the icefjord (Dkr4500); a two-day trip to Eqi (Dkr2390); and a guided day hike to Oqaatsut with return by boat (Dkr695). At the time of writing Ilulissat Travel was planning to have boat trips around Disko Bay four days a week from summer 2005.

Greenland Tours Elke Meissner (☎ 944411; www.visitgreenland.com/gtem; Kussangajannguaq B450; ⏰ 9am-6pm) offers 20-minute helicopter tours to the icefjord (Dkr1695), and a flight to Lyngmarksbræen on Disko Island, with one hour of summer dogsledding (from Dkr21,000 for seven people plus Dkr750 per person for dogsledding).

Dogsledding tours, most of which run between November and April, are extremely popular and run by all agencies. They range from a quick spin around town (Dkr700, two hours) to a six-hour trip to Oqaatsut (Dkr1195 to Dkr1400). Ilulissat Travel operates tours to its Café Roofless Hut, 1½ hours' sled ride from town. From March to April longer trips are possible (two/three/four days Dkr2850/4350/6150), with overnight stays in a hunting hut or *iglo*. The Ilulissat Tourist

Service offers multiweek trips to Uumman-naq, Upernavik and Qaanaaq for real tough nuts; prices are by agreement.

In winter you'd be advised to hire some proper fur clothing if you're planning on doing any dogsledding. Daily/weekly hire costs are Dkr200/1400 from Ilulissat Travel and Ilulissat Tourist Service.

Sleeping
BUDGET
B&B accommodation (Dkr375) in private homes in town or outlying villages can be arranged by any of the tourist offices.

Camping facilities (☎ 944300; info@iluslissattravel .gl; tent/person Dkr50/60) including hot showers, a kitchen and toilets have been set up at the old heliport. Make sure you put all food in the kitchen, as wandering dogs may make a meal of your tent otherwise. You can sleep in a large communal tent for Dkr150.

It's also possible to hike out of town and find a suitable spot just about anywhere, but camping is prohibited in the Sermermiut Valley. The Ilulissat Tourist Service hires tents (per day/week Dkr150/875), sleeping bags rated to -40°C (Dkr50/250) and stoves (Dkr15/75).

Youth Hostel (☎ 943377; www.ilulissathostel.dk; Marralinnguaq 47-49; dm Dkr245 Jun-Sep, Dkr295 Oct-May; ✗) Functional twin rooms are available at the large and friendly hostel close to the centre of town. There's a kitchen, TV room and laundry (Dkr20) and plenty of outdoor seating space.

Ilulissat Hallen (☎ 943459; Alanngukasik 2; dm Dkr150) Very basic 12-bed dorms are available at the sports hall. There are simple cooking facilities and a communal TV room. Bookings can be made through Ilulissat Tourist Service.

Skolekollegiet (Dkr255-295) This sleeping option is sleeping-bag accommodation at the school dormitories; book through Ilulissat Tourist Service.

MID-RANGE
Hotel Icefiord (☎ 944480; www.hotelicefiord.gl; Jørgen Sverdrup-ip Aqq 10; s/d Dkr745/990; ✗) Pleasant, motel-style accommodation with good views over the bay is available at this new hotel. The modern, simply designed rooms all have coffee-/tea-making facilities, en suite and TV. Two self-catering rooms (single/double Dkr855/1150) are also available.

Cab Inn (☎ 942242; cab-inn@icecaphotels.gl; Frederi-ciap Aqq 5; s/d Dkr500/800) Simple but comfortable modern rooms with en suite are available right in the centre of town at this small hotel. The rooms are pretty small, and noise from the bar can be a problem at weekends.

Other options available through any of the tourist offices:

Disko Bay House (s/d Dkr525/575) Comfortable rooms with kitchenette and shared bathrooms.

PP Apartments (Dkr650) Self-contained units or full house rental (Dkr700-1000).

TOP END
Hotel Arctic (☎ 944153; www.hotel-arctic.gl; Mittarfim-mut Aqq B1128; s/d from Dkr995/1365; ✗ 💻 ; wheelchair access) Well removed from traffic and noise, this swish hotel occupies an isolated promontory north of town with a view over the bay and icebergs. The stylish rooms are some of the best in Greenland, and there are even a few surreal aluminium *iglos* (Dkr150 extra) as annexe accommodation. There are also a sauna, a solarium and a small gym.

Hotel Hvide Falk (☎ 943343; hotel.h.falk@greennet .gl; Edvard Sivertsenip Aqq 18; s/d Dkr985/1320; ✗ 💻) Showing its age a little, this hotel doesn't offer nearly as much as the competition, and rooms on the first floor are in need of a makeover. Ask for a room on the new second floor, where modern design, flatscreen TVs and great views await you.

Eating
RESTAURANTS & CAFÉS
Café Iluliaq (Fredericiap Aqq 5; mains Dk46-125) Bright, modern and buzzing, this little place with plenty of outdoor seating has sandwiches, burgers and salads, more substantial meaty mains, and some excellent Thai food.

Brasserie Takanna (☎ 944153; Hotel Arctic; mains Dkr55-148; 6-10pm) Giant windows flood light into the hotel brasserie, where you can fill up on a good selection of light meals ranging from pasta or nachos to fish of the day.

Restaurant Ulo (☎ 944153; Hotel Arctic; mains Dkr72-210, 2-course dinner Dkr235) The fine-dining restaurant at the Hotel Arctic offers innovative, international fusion cuisine and wonderful views over the ice-filled bay. Greenlandic barbeques (Dkr295) are held on the terrace on Saturday from late June to late August.

Hotel Hvide Falk restaurant (Edvard Sivertsenip Aqq 18; 2-/3-course dinner Dkr195/228, mains Dkr85-170) Big windows provide an excellent view of

DISKO BAY

the ice-choked bay and a distraction from the dated décor at this hotel restaurant. The summer Greenlandic buffet (Monday and Thursday, Dkr198) is the real highlight, with a chance to sample polar bear, seal, muskox, caribou and local fish. On other nights the menu offers contemporary European cooking, and the Thai restaurant has a good range of excellent dishes (four courses Dkr189, mains Dkr85 to Dkr135).

QUICK EATS
For hot dogs, snacks or coffee, try **Center Grillen** (Fredericiap Aqq; dishes Dkr30-55), or the basic **Hong Kong Café** (Nuissariannguaq; mains Dkr35-65), which serves burgers, fish and some mediocre Chinese dishes.

SELF-CATERING
The best supermarkets are the **Pisiffik stores** (9am-6pm Mon-Fri, 9am-1pm Sat) on Alanngukasik and Noah Møgårdip Aqq; otherwise, try **Super 1** (Ilulissat Center Marked; 8am-9pm).

The *brædtet* is in the centre.

Entertainment
The best bets for quiet entertainment are the hotel bars. The Falkereden pub at Hotel Hvide Falk has a billiard table and good views over the ice. It sometimes has live music and it sells bar snacks (Dkr39). Pub Tuukkaq at Cab Inn has a disco with happy hour from 10pm to 11pm.

The **Naleraq Bar** (Kussangajaannguaq 23; cloakroom Dkr10-20) hosts Greenlandic bands, and offers either disco or live music and dancing nightly. Both it and the Disco Kununnguaq can get a bit rough at weekends.

Shopping
The tourist offices (except Ilulissat Travel) sell foreign-language books on Greenland, and local art and carvings. Camera supplies and processing (Dkr89) are available from the **Panasonic Center** (944601; Alanngukasik).

Getting There & Away
Greenland Travel (943246; Kussangajaannguaq 7; 10am-4.30pm Mon-Thu, 10am-4pm Fri) has AUL, Air Alpha and Air Greenland information.

AIR
Air Alpha (943004) has direct helicopter flights to Qasigiannguit (one way Dkr945, six per week) and Qeqertarsuaq (Dkr945,

12 per week). Since schedules can change daily, be sure to check in advance, even if you have a confirmed booking.

Air Greenland (943988) flies eight times weekly to Kangerlussuaq (Dkr1578, 45 minutes) and Nuuk (Dkr2971, two hours), six times weekly to Sisimiut (Dkr2414, two hours), twice weekly to Qaarsut (Dkr1046, 40 minutes), three times weekly to Upernavik (Dkr3286, 1½ hours), and twice weekly to Qaanaaq (Dkr4296, 3¾ hours).

BOAT
Ilulissat is served by ferry three times weekly from Nuuk (Dkr1565, 42 hours), once or twice weekly from Qeqertarsuaq (Dkr290, five hours), twice weekly from Uummannaq (Dkr740, 16 hours) and once weekly from Upernavik (Dkr1150, 33 hours). Two local AUL ferries chug around Disko Bay, connecting Ilulissat with Oqaatsut (Dkr185, one hour), Saqqaq (Dkr260, 7¼ hours), Qeqertaq (Dkr265, 8¼ hours), Ilimanaq (Dkr185, one hour), Qasigiannguit (Dkr200, three hours), Aasiaat (Dkr310, nine hours) and other places.

Ilulissat Tourist Service also offers boat transfer to Oqaatsut (one way Dkr350) and Eqi (Dkr647), from Eqi to Ataa (Dkr250), and from Ataa to Ilulissat (Dkr624).

Getting Around
There's no airport bus. A **taxi** (944944) will cost between Dkr70 and Dkr100.

The Ilulissat **town bus** (Dkr10; 7.30am-10pm Mon-Fri) operates like a communal taxi and has no fixed route or timetable.

Bike hire costs Dkr100 per day from Ilulissat Travel.

AROUND ILULISSAT TOWN
Ilulissat Kangerlua
One of the most awesome sights in Greenland and indeed the world, Ilulissat Kangerlua (Jakobshavn Icefjord) is one of the most active glaciers on the planet. Icebergs the size of small towns lie grounded at the mouth of the fjord, glistening majestically and emitting thunderous claps as they crack and fissure. The sight is guaranteed to leave an indelible impression on even the most jaded of tourists. In 2004 the icefjord was designated a Unesco World Heritage site.

The icefjord is also unique in that you don't need to take an expensive helicopter

HIKING AROUND ILULISSAT

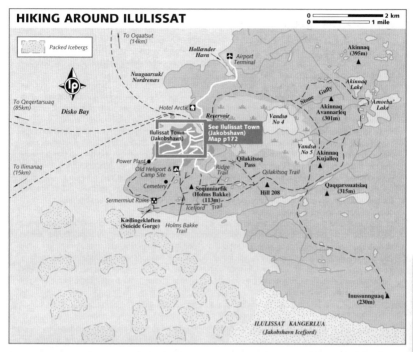

0 ——————— 2 km
0 ——————— 1 mile

Packed Icebergs

To Oqaatsut
(14km)

Holländer
Havn

Airport
Terminal

Akinnaq
(395m)

Nuugaarsuk/
Nordrenæs

Akinnaq
Lake

To Qeqertarsuaq
(85km)

Disko Bay

Hotel Arctic

Reservoir

Stone Gully

Akinnaq
Avannarleq
(301m)

'Amoeba'
Lake

See Ilulissat Town
(Jakobshavn)
Map p172

Vandsø
No 4

Ilulissat Town
(Jakobshavn)

Vandsø
No 5

Akinnaq
Kujalleq

To Ilimanaq
(15km)

Power Plant

Old Heliport &
Camp Site

Ridge
Trail

Qilakitsoq
Pass

Qilakitsoq Trail

Cemetery

Seqinniarfik
(Holms Bakke)
(113m)

Hill 208

Qaqqarssuatsiaq
(315m)

Sermermiut Ruins

Icefjord Trail

Kællingekløften
(Suicide Gorge)

Holms Bakke
Trail

Inussunnguaq
(230m)

ILULISSAT KANGERLUA
(Jakobshavn Icefjord)

DISKO BAY

flight or boat trip to see it – it's just a short walk from town. Head for the old heliport, 1km from Ilulissat, and follow the clearly defined path to the shore. The actual walk will only take about 20 minutes, but give yourself the whole day as you'll spend much of it sitting mesmerised by the spectacular views.

You can continue east along the shoreline to Seqinniarfik or as far as Inussussuaq, or return via the partially marked coastal route (see Hiking, below, for details).

Hiking

Local hiking clubs have marked a series of walking routes with blazed cairns. The best map is the 1:100,000 *Hiking Map West Greenland – Ilulissat*. The compass declination in this region is about 36.1°W.

SERMERMIUT

The easiest and most popular walk from Ilulissat will take you to the ruins of Sermermiut, Ilulissat Kangerlua and 113m-high Seqinniarfik (Holms Bakke), where the entire town of Ilulissat gathers on 13 January to welcome the sun back after its six-week sojourn below the horizon.

Begin along the obvious track from the old heliport, 1km south of town, which passes through a valley and then descends gently to the shore. In a prominent grassy patch lie the remains of Sermermiut, an Inuit winter settlement that was first inhabited around 3500 years ago.

The peninsula jutting into the icefjord near Sermermiut has many inviting benches overlooking the mouth of the fjord. At the base of the peninsula is Kællingekløften, also called Suicide Gorge, after the cliff at its southern end. In times past, older people who were tired of life or becoming a burden on their families would come here to jump to their deaths in the icy waters below.

If you follow the well-marked track up the icefjord (taking either the Ridge Trail, which goes via Seqinniarfik, or the Icefjord Trail), you'll reach a narrow lake; head inland above its western shore and you'll strike the Qilakitsoq track back to Ilulissat via Qilakitsoq Pass. Alternatively, head across the stream and towards the shore

---

UNDERSTANDING ILULISSAT KANGERLUA

Ilulissat Kangerlua (Jakobshavn Icefjord) is the world's most prolific glacier outside Antarctica, and has been studied for over 250 years in order to develop our understanding of climate change and icecap glaciology. In the last 15 years the glacier has been slowly retreating; it has receded by more than 5km in the last two years.

At its face the glacier measures 5km wide, but only about 80m rises above the surface. Over a kilometre more of continuous ice lurks below the waterline. The glacier annually calves over 35 cubic kilometres of ice – that's about 20 million tonnes per day (enough to supply New York with water for a year) and about a tenth of all icebergs floating in Greenlandic waters.

The sea at the glacier face is 1500m deep, but the largest bergs, seven-eighths of which typically float beneath the surface, actually rest on the bottom. A 260m-deep underwater moraine lies across the mouth of the fjord, 40km away, and the ice backs up behind it until the pressure rises enough to either break up the icebergs or shove them out to sea. Consequently, the fjord is so choked with floating ice that liquid water isn't in evidence at all. It can take up to two years for the largest icebergs to reach the mouth of the fjord, and they may lie stranded in the bay for up to another year. They then move north with the currents before heading down the east coast of Baffin Island towards Newfoundland (both in Canada).

A trip around the icebergs stranded at sea is a truly amazing experience. The bergs you'll see are of two main types: those with a jagged, contorted surface have just broken off the glacier and drifted out to sea; those with a smooth surface have turned over on the way, and what you are seeing is the bottom of the glacier smoothed by years of grinding against the surface. You'll also see streaks of clear or blue ice in the bergs – this is where a crack has been filled with meltwater that has refrozen. The ice in the bay that comes from these cracks is translucent 'black' ice rather than white ice.

(about one hour) to stand at the edge of the choked icefjord.

An alternative way from Sermermiut back to town follows a marked route northward, which parallels the coast 50m to 75m above water level. If you keep following the coast you'll wind up at the power station (look for the tastefully painted stacks), immediately west of Ilulissat.

Don't go onto any of the small gravel beaches in the area; a sudden rolling iceberg or collapsing chunk of ice can create a tidal wave up to 10m high, sweeping anyone on low-lying ground to their death.

VANDSØEN

The five-hour circuit across the Ilulissat plain, past the five Vandsøen lakes, makes a pleasant and easy day hike, but the ground does get soggy in places. The area is noted for its rare flowers in July and August.

Begin by crossing the bridge above the harbour and continue on to the reservoir, where you turn east and follow its southern shore. Cross the river connecting the reservoir with the next lake upstream, then bear east and follow the highest ground available past three small ponds (Vandsøen Nos 1, 2 and 3) to Vandsø No 4.

After descending to Vandsø No 5, continue along the eastern shore to the lake's southern end. Follow the obvious track south over the hill and past a long, narrow lake. Walk west, above its northern shore, then bear north around hill 208 – or climb it for a nice view across the Vandsøen and the Ilulissat plains. Here you can follow the trail up and over Qilakitsoq Pass, which leads straight back to Ilulissat, or take the more scenic route down to Ilulissat Kangerlua to meet up with the icefjord or ridge tracks back to town.

AKINNAQ

A more challenging loop hike will take you to the mysterious-looking Akinnaq region east of the airport. Follow the Vandsøen route as far as Vandsø No 4, then cross the inflow stream, which streaks down a broad gully of shining slickrock. If you ascend the western slope of this gully you'll reach a wild and eerie landscape of boulders, peaks and small lakes.

If you follow the prominent ridge due east, you'll reach the largish craterlike Lake Akinnaq; from its western shore it's an easy scramble up Akinnaq peak (395m), which offers a view north to Oqaatsut and southwest back to Ilulissat. Keep to high ground as you pass south of Lake Akinnaq, then descend slightly to an amoeba-like lake immediately to the southeast and cross its outflow stream, which tumbles over a series of miniature, terrace-like waterfalls.

Here the going gets a bit tougher, as you must traverse the slope southward against the lay of the land, which means constant ascents and descents over steep humpback rocks. If you're tempted downhill toward the west, you'll reach the eastern bank of Vandsø No 5 and thus rejoin the Vandsøen route. However, if you keep to the high ground, you'll eventually descend into the deep gashlike valley between Akinnaq Kujalleq and the area's most prominent peak, Qaaqarssuatsiaq. This valley is dominated by a long, narrow lake. If you follow the low ridge above its northern shore, you'll eventually meet the Qilakitsoq track.

Oqaatsut (Rodebay)

pop 52

After the heady delights and tourist clamour of Ilulissat, a visit to the lethargic village of Oqaatsut (The Cormorants) seems like a lifetime away. Just 20km north of Ilulissat, this tiny place has only a handful of vehicles, and sled dogs outnumber villagers four to one. Fishing and hunting are still the main focus of community life, and at low tide you can pick mussels off the beach.

The surrounding area has a rich collection of overgrown turf-hut sites, testament to the enduring presence of the settlement. The town, which is named after the bird colony that inhabits the nearby cliffs, first operated as a trading post for 18th-century Dutch whalers, who bestowed its Dutch name, which means 'bay of rest'. The original blubber house, cooperage and storehouse are still in use, and at the harbour you can see a large iron pot for storing whale oil and a hoist used to pull whales up on shore.

Oqaatsut makes a convenient destination for a two-day return hike from Ilulissat. Follow the dogsled track north from the airport to Bredebugt and follow the shoreline right around the bay to the lake Kangerluarsup Tasia Qalleq. Bear northwest to the northern end of the Qarajaq Cove to reconnect with the sled track into Oqaatsut. The hike takes six to nine hours one way.

You can camp on any flat ground around town other than on historic remains. The best place is on the plain south of town before the descent to the cemetery. Showers and toilets are available at the community service house, and you can collect drinking water from the shed by the bay.

Greenland Tours Elke Meissner (see p174) offers accommodation in the restored trading company buildings (Dkr250). The cosy old shop has eight beds, and the rustic cooperage can accommodate up to six people. **Restaurant H8** (☎ 948585; lunch/dinner Dkr150/160), a simple outfit in the former warehouse, is the only place to eat in town. The menu features anything from halibut, whale and seal to caribou and muskox.

The village also has a **Pisiffik shop** (☯ 9am-noon & 1-4pm Mon-Fri, 9am-1pm Sat).

GETTING THERE & AWAY

AUL's *Aviaq Ittuk* calls twice weekly on its way from Ilulissat (Dkr185, one hour) to Saqqaq (Dkr235, five hours).

Otherwise, Greenland Tours Elke Meissner offers transfers from Ilulissat (one way/return Dkr350/550), and also runs a guided day trip from Ilulissat for Dkr750. Travel on to Icecamp Eqi (Dkr350) can also be arranged.

Ataa

If you feel like getting away from it all, the abandoned settlement of Ataa, 60km north of Ilulissat, is now a wilderness camp among the tumbledown remains of the village. Excellent kayaking, canoeing and fishing are available on nearby Lake Tasersuaq.

You can stay at the **Smilla Holiday Centre cabins** (☎ 944420; touna@greennet.gl; camping Dkr45, unmade bunk Dkr165, s/d Dkr295/390), used in the film *Miss Smilla's Feeling for Snow*. The camp is run by the Ilulissat-based Tourist Nature (see p173), which can organise a complete trip including boat transfer, accommodation, meals and use of kayaks for Dkr775 per day. It also offers hiking and sailing tours (from Dkr85), seal safaris (Dkr300), guided hikes (Dkr115) and treks to the icecap at Eqi (Dkr695). Kayak, canoe and windsurf hire costs Dkr275, and fishing equipment can be hired for Dkr250. All-in weekend packages including transfer, accommodation and full board cost Dkr2395. Boat transfer from Ilulissat costs Dkr1250 return.

DISKO BAY

Port Victor & Icecamp Eqi

For easy access to the inland ice, a trip to Port Victor, about 60km north of Ilulissat, takes you to within 3km of the massive tidewater glacier Eqip Sermia. The area was used as a base by French polar expeditions from 1948 to 1953, and the derelict basecamp hut is still standing.

Uphill from the original base is Icecamp Eqi, run by Ilulissat Travel (see p174). The camp has fantastic views over the sea and ice. Its excellent wilderness hotel has ensuite cabins each with its own terrace. The group also runs Café Victor, where meals cost from Dkr150. A day trip to Eqi including lunch at Café Victor costs Dkr1395, and an overnight stay costs Dkr2390 (Dkr995 per extra night).

Campers can arrive by boat (one-way Dkr647), stay several nights for free and leave another day. It's well worth the money.

Ilimanaq (Claushavn)

pop 90

Little has changed in Ilimanaq since the community was founded in the 18th century. The original houses still stand, and even today there are no cars in the village. Life revolves around the cycles of nature, and fishing is the mainstay of the economy. From mid-June to early September there are good chances of spotting whales in the waters off Ilimanaq, which are also a great spot for sea-kayaking.

Although there's no formal accommodation option, you can camp anywhere or the tourist offices in Ilulissat may be able to help you find B&B accommodation.

ILULISSAT KANGERLUA HIKE

For a look at ice-choked Ilulissat Kangerlua from a southern perspective, make a day hike north along the coast to Aappaluttuarssuk. En route you can visit the three ancient ruined settlements Iglumiut, Avannarliit (Nordre Huse) and Eqe.

If you have more time and don't want to return the way you came, walk east along the shore for a couple of kilometres (with great views of the fjord all the way) and turn inland over the pass to Tasersuaq Qalleq. Follow the western shore of the lake south to the next lake, Tasersuaq Alleq, then turn due west and return to Ilimanaq by climbing directly over the mountain.

You can also walk between the two Tasersuaq lakes and cross over to the convoluted Tasiusaq Bay, which is cut off from Disko Bay by the icefjord itself.

ILIMANAQ TO QASIGIANNGUIT TREK

A relatively easy four-day trek covers the 35km from Ilimanaq to Qasigiannguit. The landscape may not be overwhelming, but the hike isn't difficult. The best available map is Greenland Tourism's *Hiking Map West Greenland – Qasigiannguit*.

Start by walking south along the coast to meet the marked dogsled track. From the broad open area marked Narsarsuaq you can continue south along the uninteresting dogsled route or head east towards hill 320. Skirt this hill to the north and east, then turn south and climb up to the pass. When you're immediately west of hill 430, turn southwest, and keep going until you reach the small lake immediately west of hill 420. Follow its outlet river down to the western shore of Qinguata Tasia and cross the isthmus.

After climbing partially up the other side you'll reach the head of a long, narrow lake. Follow its eastern shore to the end, then bear east and then south around the eastern slope of Salleq (marked 'Sagdleq'). Near the southern end of Salleq, follow the western shoreline of Sallup Tasia. At the end of this lake, strike west toward the outflow of lake 90, which may only be crossed at low tide. Once you're safely across, follow the western shore of this lake down the valley into Qasigiannguit (see p181).

GETTING THERE & AWAY

The AUL boat *Aviaq Ittuk* stops at Ilimanaq once a week on its journey between Ilulissat (Dkr185, one hour) and Qasigiannguit (Dkr185, 1¾ hours).

SAQQAQ

pop 177

One of the nicest villages on Disko Bay, Saqqaq is a friendly place set in relatively lush surroundings on the southern coast of the vast Nuussuaq Peninsula. The cluster of brightly coloured houses is framed by the backdrop of **Livets Top** (1150m) to the northeast.

Archaeological excavations west of the settlement revealed the existence of the Inuit culture, later named the Saqqaq culture, that inhabited this area between 2900 and 4400 years ago. Today the village survives mainly on income from its meat- and fish-processing plant.

The **village church**, built in 1908, is particularly photogenic. Also worth a visit is **Hannibal's House**, the former home of Danish Greenlander Hannibal Fencker, who served as the trading-station manager and was dedicated to improving local living conditions. He supplied Saqqaq's electrical generator, grew vegetables in the 24-hour Arctic daylight, reared village orphans and promoted secondary education for villagers. Although he died in 1986, his big red house and greenhouse garden – the world's most northerly – remains a tourist attraction of sorts.

There's plenty of hiking on the great Nuussuaq Peninsula. Use the 1:250,000 *Saga Map Nuussuaq*. To warm up, make the taxing day hike to the summit of 1150m Livets Top, immediately northeast of Saqqaq. It provides incredible views of the area. The finest destination, though, is the unforgettable emerald-coloured lake Saqqap Tasersua, which slices through the heart of the peninsula. The return walk takes five days. Saqqaq is also a common starting or finishing point for the demanding 10-day trek across the peninsula to Kuusuup Nuua, near Uummannaq. It's better to do the trip from north to south, as transport is easier from Saqqaq.

If you'd like to stay in Saqqaq you may be able to arrange accommodation at the communal service house or with local families. The communal service house has benches and floor space people can sleep on if necessary, but no phone number. A small community shop stocks basic food items.

The *Aviaq Ittuk* calls to Saqqaq twice weekly on its rounds through Disko Bay and to Ilulissat (Dkr260, 6¼ hours).

QASIGIANNGUIT (CHRISTIANSHÅB)

pop 1340

The bright houses of Qasigiannguit adorn the rocky shores at the foot of a steep escarpment in Southern Disko Bay. The rounded hills and valleys surrounding the town, and the regular *föhn* (warm, dry winds that flow off a mountain slope) that bring warm, clear weather in summer, make it an excellent spot for hiking. The area also has a wealth of historic interest, with house sites, meat caches and hunting blinds easily visible. Despite this the town receives few visitors and remains a sleepy kind of place where the locals are genuinely glad to see you.

From July to October whales visit the waters around Qasigiannguit and often come close to shore; they're easily visible from the hotel terrace.

History

The Qasigiannguit area has been inhabited for over 4500 years, and remnants of the Saqqaq, Thule and Dorset cultures have been found here. The earliest evidence yet discovered of habitation in Greenland is the skeleton of a Saqqaq woman who lived around 3800 years ago on the nearby island of Qeqertasussuk. Excavations on the island revealed some of Greenland's oldest and best-preserved remains, most of which are now displayed at the town museum.

The town was founded in 1734, but flooding and icy winds from the east made the original site unfavourable, and in 1764 the town was moved across the bay.

Qasigiannguit briefly operated as a military post to protect Danish whaling interests from Dutch 'intruders', and it experienced a minor trade war between Denmark and Holland in the mid-18th century. When the rich offshore shrimping grounds were discovered in the early 1950s the town numbered just 245 people, but the construction of the shrimp-processing plant in 1952 soon saw the town grow. Today halibut fishing and processing is the mainstay of the local economy.

Information

Hospital (☎ 911211; Takuuk Peqqissaavik)

Police (☎ 911222; Poul Hansensvej 23)

Post office (☎ 911355; Poul Hansensvej 5) Has two ATMs and the AUL office.

Tourist office (☎ 911081; discobay@icecaphotels.gl) At the Disco Bay Hotel and only open whenever someone's around. It's primarily concerned with tours and hotel guests.

Sights

The **Qasigiannguit Museum** (☎ 911477; www.museum.gl/qasigiannguit; Poul Egedesvej 24; admission free; ☼ 1-5pm Mon-Fri & Sun) has an excellent collection of finds dating from the Saqqaq culture to the present Inuit culture. Fantastically well-preserved items recovered from excavations in Qeqertasussuk have a permanent home in the museum and give a detailed picture of life in Greenland's earliest Stone Age culture. Artefacts from the site are evidence

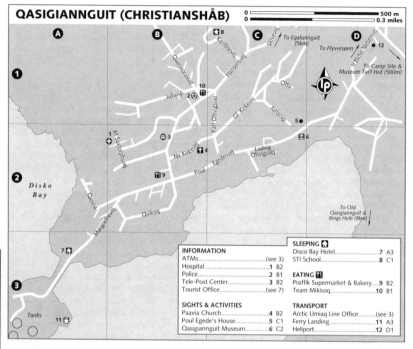

QASIGIANNGUIT (CHRISTIANSHÅB)

INFORMATION
ATMs..............................(see 3)
Hospital...........................1 B2
Police.............................2 B1
Tele-Post Center..................3 B2
Tourist Office...................(see 7)

SIGHTS & ACTIVITIES
Paavia Church.....................4 B2
Poul Egede's House................5 C1
Qasigiannguit Museum..............6 C2

SLEEPING
Disco Bay Hotel...................7 A3
STI School........................8 C1

EATING
Pisiffik Supermarket & Bakery.....9 B2
Team Mikisoq.....................10 B1

TRANSPORT
Arctic Umiaq Line Office........(see 3)
Ferry Landing....................11 A3
Heliport.........................12 D1

that society of that period was far more advanced than previously assumed. The finds include a large collection of tools and the northernmost discovery of the now extinct great auk. There are also natural-history displays and exhibits of hunters' clothing.

Next to the museum is **Poul Egede's house** (built 1734), Greenland's oldest wooden building. The structure was moved to its present location in 1806, and was used as a shop and provisions store until 1990.

Also worth a visit is the **Paavia Church** (Nv Kirkevej), built 1969. The nave symbolises an *umiaq*, and the altarpiece is a glass mosaic decorated with a huge cross and golden sun surrounded by a polar bear, whales, fish, a kayak, an *umiaq*, and the pagan spirits scurrying from the light of Christianity.

Activities
HIKING
Qasigiannguit is an excellent area for hiking, with gentle hills and lush summer vegetation. The new (1:100,000) *Hiking Map West Greenland – Qasigiannguit* shows the various hiking routes in the area.

Worthwhile day hikes, marked with painted blazes, will take you 5km north to Eqalunnguit (1½ hours), a beautiful place favoured by locals for fishing trips, or 8km south to Illukut (Bryggerhusbugten; 2½ hours), where Old Qasigiannguit was founded in 1734. The colonial governor's house and several other log buildings, meat caches, hunting shelters and kitchen middens are along the coast.

About 20 minutes' walk to the south, over a low pass, is the cave Bings Hule, which was the site where ancient shamans were initiated. Ironically, it was named after the first missionary to the colony, who used it as a quiet retreat. From the cave, continue south and east, around the back of the ridge, for a straightforward climb to the summit of Qaaqarsuaq (456m). It affords a stunning view over Disko Bay and takes three to four hours.

The walk between Qasigiannguit and Ilimanaq (p180) takes about four days. For more information on hiking around Qasigiannguit and details of multiday hikes, visit www.sydforisfjorden.dk.

Tours

During summer the tourist office organises two-hour guided town tours (Dkr120); two-hour *kaffemiks* (Dkr100); a four-hour midnight tour to Qaaqarsuaq (Dkr450); a four-hour boat trip to the old whaling station (Dkr575); a full-day boat journey out to Grønne Ejland, a group of islands rich in archaeological remains and home to one of the world's largest Arctic-tern colonies (Dkr695); and a full-day boat trip out to Garnet Bay, a garnet-encrusted cliff, and Akulliit, an abandoned settlement (Dkr965).

The winter programme from December to April includes three- to four-hour dog-sledding trips (Dkr700), a two-hour aurora borealis viewing trip by dogsled (Dkr765), and half or full day ice-fishing trips (prices by agreement).

Many tours have minimum participation numbers, so book ahead if possible so that the tourist office can try to gather a group.

Sleeping & Eating

The best free camp site can be found east of the heliport and football pitch, where there's a toilet hut and piped water. The tourist office can book B&B with local families (Dkr275) or rooms at the STI School (Dkr275).

Museum turf hut (☎ 911477; lm@qaskom.ki.gl; per day/week Dkr150/800) For an authentic Greenland experience you can stay at this traditional turf hut with its plank beds and simple décor. It has no heating or running water but is surprisingly warm and bright.

Disco Bay Hotel (☎ 911081; discobay@icecaphotels .gl; Margrethevej 34; s/d Dkr850/1150) Large, comfortable rooms with en suite are available at this modern hotel overlooking the sea. The bright and airy restaurant serves decent European food and some Greenlandic specialities, though on quiet days only the daily special (Dkr55) is available.

Other eating options:

Pilersuisoq (Poul Hansensvej 1) Local supermarket and bakery.

Team Mikisoq (☎ 911100; Qaarsorasaat 11; mains Dkr20-45) The local grill bar.

Getting There & Away

AIR

In summer you can fly by helicopter to/from Ilulissat four times weekly (Dkr945) and to Qeqertarsuaq (Dkr945) three times weekly.

FROZEN ASSETS

Most visitors to Disko Bay come to see its world-famous icebergs, but the 'bergy bits' of Disko Bay ice – that is, the semi-trailer-sized chunks – are towed into harbours, chipped into cubes and exported to Japan and Europe to chill drinks. That scotch you order in a Tokyo pub may contain 25,000-year-old cubes from the frozen heart of Greenland's icecap, and the air that fizzes out as they melt has been trapped since long before anyone ever heard of smog alerts.

BOAT

Two of the big **AUL** (☎ 911546; bktjch@aul.gl) ferries sail in once weekly on their runs between Nuuk (Dkr1505, 46½ hours) and Ilulissat (Dkr200, three hours) or Uummannaq (Dkr825, 20 hours). The smaller ferry calls in three times weekly and calls at all local settlements, including Aasiaat (Dkr225, 8½ hours), Ilulissat and Qeqertarsuaq (Dkr305, five hours).

AROUND QASIGIANNGUIT
Akullit

The abandoned village of Akullit provides a serene and silent antidote to modern living. The former settlement is now used as a hunting camp and summer base for locals, but you can stay in the restored school building (Dkr250) in August and September. It's pretty basic but has a decent kitchen. Bookings can be made through Qasigiannguit's tourist office, which also offers boat trips to the area.

SOUTHERN DISKO BAY

AASIAAT (EGEDESMINDE)
pop 3130

Located on an island on the outer edge of a beautiful archipelago, Greenland's fourth-largest community is a sleepy fishing town surrounded by low hills and rocky islets. This relatively flat area at the southern entrance to Disko Bay lacks the dramatic peaks of other coastal towns, but makes a good base for whale watching, kayaking and gentle hiking during the summer months and for cross-country skiing in spring.

DISKO BAY

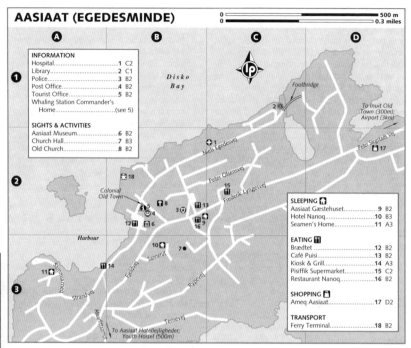

AASIAAT (EGEDESMINDE)

INFORMATION
Hospital.................................1 C2
Library...................................2 C1
Police....................................3 B2
Post Office.............................4 B2
Tourist Office.........................5 B2
Whaling Station Commander's
   Home.............................(see 5)

SIGHTS & ACTIVITIES
Aasiaat Museum.....................6 B2
Church Hall.............................7 B3
Old Church.............................8 B2

SLEEPING
Aasiaat Gæstehuset................9 B2
Hotel Nanoq.........................10 B3
Seamen's Home....................11 A3

EATING
Brædtet 12 B2
Café Puisi.............................13 B2
Kiosk & Grill..........................14 A3
Pisiffik Supermarket..............15 C2
Restaurant Nanoq.................16 B2

SHOPPING
Ameq Aasiaat......................17 D2

TRANSPORT
Ferry Terminal......................18 B2

Aasiaat means 'the spiders', but it's probably a derivation of Aasiat, 'the gathering place'.

History

The original site of Aasiaat, immediately south of the present town, had long been locally called Eqaluksuit, but when Niels Egede founded a settlement there in 1759 he renamed it Egedesminde in honour of his father, Hans. It was out of the way as a trading post, so in 1763 it was shifted to its present location.

Prosperous trading alternated with repeated smallpox epidemics, and the population was decimated four times by the disease. At one point only 21 people remained alive. During WWII a small American base was established near the mouth of Aasiaat's harbour, but when the base shut down the town's fortunes stagnated, and for years primitive methods of fish salting and shrimp processing carried the meagre economy. In the mid-1980s an efficient fish- and shrimp-processing plant was established, and today Aasiaat prospers once again.

Information

Hospital (☎ 891092; Niels Egedesvej 47)
Library (☎ 892463; Niels Egedesvej; ☺ noon-3.30pm, 7-8.30pm) Allows a half-hour of free Internet access.
Police (☎ 892222; Fredrick Lyngesvej 9)
Post office(☎ 891555; Niels Egedes Plads1)
Tourist office (☎ 892540; aasiaat.tourist@greennet.gl; Niels Egedesvej 6; ☺ 9am-4pm Mon-Fri, 10am-1pm Sat)

Sights & Activities

Start your visit with a trip to the small **Aasiaat Museum** (☎ 892597; Niels Egedesveg; admission Dkr20; ☺ 1-4pm Mon-Fri, 1-3pm Sun). The collection includes an interesting array of carvings, archaeological finds, old photos, birds and a turf house outside.

Aasiaat's older buildings are clustered around the harbour area in the **colonial old town**. Perhaps the nicest is the whaling station commander's multistorey home, constructed in 1778 and relocated to Aasiaat when the station was abandoned in 1826. There's also the **old trading manager's home** (which now houses the tourist office), the **old church** and a monument to Niels Egede, Aasiaat's founding father.

The **church hall**, on a hill overlooking the town, has a sizeable collection of paintings by well-known Danish painter Per Kirkeby. Across the bridge east of the centre is the picturesque traditional hunters' community in the **Inuit old town**.

The terrain around Aasiaat is relatively flat and ordinary for hiking, but the 10-sq-km island is easily explored. The low hills behind town offer some fine views across the archipelago and make an excellent area for cross-country skiing between March and April.

Festivals & Events

During the last week of August or the first week of September the town hosts the four-day **Aasiaat Rock Festival** (www.nipiaa.gl), featuring mainly Greenlandic bands alongside a clutch of groups from Scandinavia, Italy and the UK. A festival pass for access to all gigs costs Dkr400.

Tours

The tourist office offers several day tours, but most have minimum participation numbers, so you'll need to organise a group or cough up the full tour price. Options include three-hour whale-watching cruises from June to September (Dkr550); six-hour whale-watching trips with visits to abandoned settlements (Dkr870); a town walk with a visit to a local family for a *kaffemik* and tasting of traditional Greenlandic food (Dkr150); a three-day boat and trekking trip to see muskox and caribou, followed by kayaking to a glacier (Dr6895); and two-/eight-day kayaking trips (Dkr1800/8225). In winter two-/three-hour dogsledding or snowmobile trips cost Dkr650/850 and a three-day dogsledding trip costs Dkr5795. Shark fishing may also be a possibility; ask at the tourist office for information. For more details, visit www.greenland-guide.gl/aasiaat-tourist.

Sleeping

Camping is possible anywhere in the rocky tundra knolls behind town. There are also numerous hunters' huts around the archipelago that are open to hikers. The tourist office can organise B&B for Dkr375 per person per night.

Youth Hostel (☎ 892195; vinther@greennet.gl; dm Dkr250; ✗) The basic but functional youth hostel is a bit of a hike from the airport and sits at the western end of the lake, about 700m south of the tourist office. It has a large kitchen, shared facilities and a laundry.

Seamen's Home (☎ 892711; Sammiarneq 9; aasia at@soemandshjem.gl; s/d Dkr450/650, with bath Dkr695/920; ✗) Situated by the harbour, this place has a good choice of newly renovated rooms with TV. The older rooms with shared facilities are a little shabby, though.

Hotel Nanoq (☎ 892121; hotel-aasiaat@iss.gl; Sannerut 8; s/d Dkr795/975; ✗) Perched on a hill overlooking town, the hotel offers spacious rooms with en suite, TV, telephone, video and minibar. The décor is comfortable but fairly functional.

Other options:

Aasiaat Hotellejligheder (☎ 892195; vinther@ greennet.gl; apt Dkr695-1295) Comfortable three-bedroom apartments with modern décor, large rooms and cooking facilities.

Aasiaat Gæstehuset (☎ 892233; fax 892232; Frederik Lyngesvej 16; s/d Dkr500/600) Simple rooms with bathroom.

Eating

Seamen's Home cafeteria (Seamen's Home, Sammiarneq 9; mains Dkr50; ✆ 7am-10pm) Popular with local fishers, this place is a good option for simple but excellent-value meals. Meat and two veg supplement the fast-food options, and the daily specials are usually a good bet.

Café Puisi (☎ 891112; Pollersvej 12; mains Dkr40-70; ✆ 9am-9pm Mon-Fri, 11am-8pm Sat & Sun) Basic but cosy, this simple little café serves up a choice of burgers, chips and sandwiches as well as a good selection of mediocre Thai dishes.

Restaurant Nanoq (☎ 892121; Frederik Lyngesvef; mains Dkr90-150; ✆ 6pm-midnight) Not exactly a happening spot, this is the only restaurant in town, and you need to let them know a day in advance that you'd like to eat! Fortunately, the food is pretty good, but most people come to drink as it's also the only bar in town.

Other eating options include the **Kiosk & Grill** (dishes Dkr20-40), which sells greasy burgers and hot dogs, and (for self-caterers) the Pisiffik supermarket and the brædtet.

Shopping

The local leathercraft shop and handicrafts centre **Ameq Aasiaat** (☎ 892797; Peter Siegstadsvej 4; ✆ 9am-5pm Mon-Fri) focuses on traditional tanning, drying, sewing and embroidery skills. There's also a small sealskin processing plant.

DISKO BAY

Getting There & Away

AIR

Air Greenland (☎ 892787) flies every day except Sunday to Ilulissat (Dkr671, 25 minutes) and Kangerlussuaq (Dkr1223, 45 minutes). Helicopter connections are available at Ilulissat for Qasigiannguit.

BOAT

AUL (☎ 891644; bktjeg@aul.gl) ferries call in at Aasiaat once weekly en route between Nuuk (Dkr1355, 33½ hours) and Ilulissat (Dkr310, nine hours), with stops at Qeqertarsuaq (Dkr225, 3½ hours) and at Qasigiannguit (Dkr225, 8½ hours). Two other local services run to all the other district settlements, including Ilimanaq (Dkr245, seven hours) and Kitsissuarsuit (Dkr185, 1¼ hours).

AROUND AASIAAT
Kitsissuarsuit (Hunde Ejlande)
pop 110

For a glimpse of life in an isolated settlement, a trip to tiny Kitsissuarsuit, on an island 21km northwest of Aasiaat, is a good idea. Although there are no sights of specific interest, the settlement is renowned for its traditional arts, particularly the crafting of *qajaqs* and *umiaqs* and decoration of leather products. Ask at the tourist office in Aasiaat about accommodation with local families. The ferry sails between Aasiaat and Kitsissuarsuit twice weekly (Dkr185, 1¼) in summer.

KANGAATSIAQ
pop 670

Kangaatsiaq was only founded in January 1985, though the settlement itself is much older. Fishing and seal hunting are still very important to the local people, and the evidence is all over town: drying racks for fish, stretched sealskins, and the sounds and smells of hundreds of sled dogs. East of town a 150km fjord system makes a wonderful destination for exploration by boat or canoe.

There are few facilities, but **tourist information** (☎ 871077; www.kangaatsiaq.gl) is available through Kangaatsiaq Kommunia. It can organise five- to 18-day kayaking, dogsledding and camping tours around the district (five days Dkr4500).

The Kommunia can also provide accommodation at municipally owned hostel **The**

Lodge (Dkr200), with space for six people. More comfortable accommodation can be found with local families for Dkr395. Contact **Hans Aronsen** (☎ 232734; kalloq@yahoo.dk), **Severine Inusugtoq** (☎ 871354; siiva2@greennet.gl) or **Allan Glasdam** (☎ 871032; glasdam@greennet.gl). Choices for food are limited to the local grill bar or the Pilersuisoq shop.

The big ferries call at Kangaatsiaq en route between Nuuk (Dkr1280, 33 hours) and Ilulissat (Dkr395, 15 hours), and a smaller vessel sails four times weekly between Kangaatsiaq and other southern Disko Bay villages including Aasiaat (Dkr185, 1¼ hours). A six-hour stopover in Kangaatsiaq is possible on Tuesday and Thursday.

DISKO ISLAND

Greenland's largest and newest island combines spectacular rock formations with dramatic scenery, an interior icecap, several warm springs (with water 3°C to 10°C), unexpected flora and a galloping glacier that moves up to 100m a day. Despite this, the island sees few visitors and is a haven of calm. Those who make it this far will be rewarded with wonderful hiking opportunities and the chance to go dogsledding under the midnight sun, with fantastic views over Disko Bay and the massive icebergs below.

Apart from Qeqertarsuaq, tiny Kangerluk (Diskofjord), 30km to the northwest, is the island's only other permanent habitation.

QEQERTARSUAQ (GODHAVN)
pop 998

Set against a backdrop of magnificent basalt mountains and spectacular rock formations, Qeqertarsuaq is the only significant town on the island. Although there's little to see in the town itself, the water-absorbing porous basalt hills make the area lush with vegetation, clusters of stranded icebergs glisten majestically offshore, and there are excellent hiking opportunities nearby.

History

Godhavn, the Danish name of Qeqertarsuaq town, means simply 'good harbour', and the protected waters of the bay meant that European whalers settled here long before a formal trading post was established in 1773. Trade flourished, and the town remained the most important community north of Nuuk until 1950. However, as other Disko Bay communities began to prosper, Qeqertarsuaq sank quickly into its present obscure position. Today hunting and fishing are the primary sources of income for the local people.

Information

Hospital (☎ 921090; Adam Mølgård-ip Aqq)
Kommunia (☎ 921277; Oqaluffiup)
Police (☎ 921222; Piitarsuup Aqq 16)
Post office (☎ 921055; Holten Møllerip Aqq 3C)
Qeqertarsuaq Tourist Service (☎ 921628; www
.qeqertarsuaq.gl; Adam Mølgård-ip Aqq B82; ⏱ 10am-
4pm Mon-Sat Jun-Aug, 10am-3pm Mon-Fri Sep-May)

Sights

The **Qeqertarsuaq Museum** (☎ 921153; Juaanng-uup Aqq 2; adult/child Dkr10/free; ⏱ 10am-2pm Mon-Fri, 10am-4pm Sat), in the beautiful former inspector's house at the harbour, has exhibitions on the town's history, including the colonial and whaling period; the Arctic Research Station; and Greenlandic Christmas customs. The museum also houses a col-

lection of works by Jakob Danielsen, local artist and hunter.

Just by the town bakery there's a traditional **turf house**, which has been left intact but is uninhabited.

Qeqertarsuaq's unique and odd-looking octagonal **church** was designed by Danish architect Bojsen-Møller in 1915. Known to the locals as 'God's little inkpot', the bell-tower resembles a storybook wishing well. Occasionally, locals will dress in traditional clothes for Sunday services at 10am, but this is not a tourist attraction.

The **Arctic Research Station** was founded by the University of Copenhagen in 1906. Today it carries out field work and holds classes for university students; its library, opened in 1966, contains the largest collection of Arctic studies in Greenland. Visits must be organised in advance. Contact the station through its secretariat in Copenhagen. Information about who to contact is on the website www .nat.ku.dk/as/indexuk.htm. Alternatively, you could try the tourist office when you arrive – it's practically impossible to contact by email or phone.

DISKO BAY

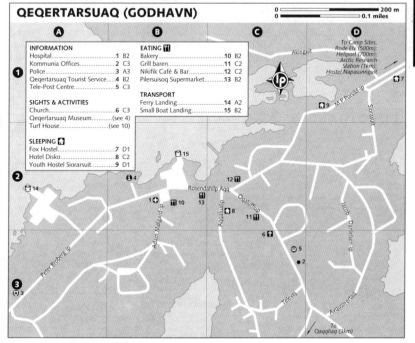

QEQERTARSUAQ (GODHAVN)

0 ——— 200 m
0 ——— 0.1 miles

INFORMATION	
Hospital	1 B2
Kommunia Offices	2 C3
Police	3 A3
Qeqertarsuaq Tourist Service	4 B2
Tele-Post Centre	5 C3

SIGHTS & ACTIVITIES	
Church	6 C3
Qeqertarsuaq Museum	(see 4)
Turf House	(see 10)

SLEEPING 🛏	
Fox Hostel	7 D1
Hotel Disko	8 C2
Youth Hostel Siorarsuit	9 D1

EATING 🍴	
Bakery	10 B2
Grill baren	11 C2
Nikifik Café & Bar	12 C2
Pilersuisoq Supermarket	13 B2

TRANSPORT	
Ferry Landing	14 A2
Small Boat Landing	15 A2

To Camp Sites,
Rode Elv (500m);
Heliport (700m);
Arctic Research
Station (1km);
Hostel Napasunnguit

Behind the station one of the island's warm springs allows three species of orchids and the carnivorous butterwort to grow, but the plants are extremely fragile and should not be touched.

At **Qaqqaliaq**, or Udkiggen (The Lookout), the southernmost tip of Disko Island, stands a red-and-white tower that was used by early whalers as a lookout. Its frame was constructed of four whale jawbones and looks like an American football planted in the headland. Whenever a whale was spotted, a cannon was fired to alert the fleet and set the hunt in action. Qaqqaliaq is about a 30-minute walk from the village and is still the best spot for whale watching.

Tours

The tourist office organises dogsledding trips in summer on Lyngmarksbræen, high above the village. Getting there requires reasonable fitness, as you must hike to the base hut, which can take between three and four hours. At the hut you'll meet the dogs and handlers for a 1½-hour tour (Dkr750) by dogsled with fantastic views of Ilulissat and the icebergs. Staying overnight in the hut costs Dkr1350 including meals.

Short guided hikes (one to three hours) to Kuannit, Qaqqaliaq, Blæsedalen or the Arctic Research Station cost Dkr175. The tourist office also organises Greenlandic barbecues (Dkr225), and in bad weather you can try your hand at making your own souvenirs with free use of the tools at the community workshop. You just need to pay for some antler to work on.

Winter dogsledding varies from two hours (Dkr600 including lunch) to a three-day visit to Kangerluk (Dkr3990 including meals and accommodation).

Sleeping & Eating

There are lots of dry, level camp sites across the bridge over the Rode Elv, and northward along its banks, with dry toilet facilities and water from the river. You can shower at any of the hostels for Dkr20. The tourist office can also arrange B&B accommodation with local families for Dkr300.

Fox Hostel (☎ 921273; autobyg@greennet.gl; MH Porsildip Aqqutaa 11; s/d Dkr500/700) This large house can be rented as one unit (three/six people Dkr1500/2200) or by individuals. Accommodation is in twin rooms or small dorms. There's a large kitchen with washing machine and a TV/video room for guests' use.

Hostel Napasunnguit (☎ 921628; qeq.tourism@ greennet.gl; Kuussuunnguup Aqqutaa 13 - 160; dm Dkr195) This basic hostel is located in the old meteorological institute out of town and has a few double rooms and a larger dormitory as well as good kitchen facilities and a common room.

Youth Hostel Siorarsuit (☎ 921026; julianeb@ greennet.gl; PH Rosendahlip Aqqutaa; dm Dkr195, with linen Dkr295) Located close to a black-sand beach, this simple hostel has single, double and twin rooms, a dormitory and a large living/dining area.

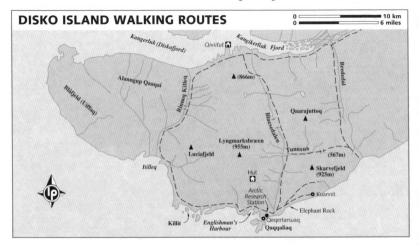

DISKO ISLAND WALKING ROUTES

0 ———— 10 km
0 ———— 6 miles

Kangerluk (Diskofjord) Qiviitut Kangikerllak Fjord

Alanngup Qaaqai

Blåfjeld (Uilfaq)

Rinneq Killeq

▲ (866m)

Brededal

Qaarajuttoq ▲

Blæsedalen

Lyngmarksbræen (955m)
Luciafjeld ▲   ▲

Tunusua ▲ (567m)

Itilleq

Hut

Arctic Research Station

Skarvefjeld ▲ (925m)

Kuannit

Elephant Rock

Killit   Englishman's Harbour   Qeqertarsuaq   Qaqqaliaq

Hotel Disko (☎ 921310; qalut@greennet.gl; Aqqaluaiip Aqq 3; s/d Dkr650/950; ✗) Small, standard rooms with an en suite and TV are available at the town hotel, and guests are welcome to use the hotel kitchen themselves.

Nikifik Café & Bar (☎ 921450; Rosendahlip Aqq 9; mains Dkr50-65; ✆ Mon-Sat) The only real choice for food in town is the dimly lit Nikifik bar, which serves a decent but uninspired array of fish and meat dishes. On some Friday and Saturday nights there is live music.

Other eating options:

Bakery (Adam Mølgård-ip Aqq) Bread and pricey sandwiches.

Grill baren (Oqaluffiup Aqq 4) The usual greasy burgers and hot dogs.

Pilersuisoq supermarket (PH Rosendahlip Aqq 2)

Getting There & Away

Air Alpha (☎ 943004) helicopters fly to/from Ilulissat (Dkr945) 12 times each week and Qasigiannguit (Dkr945) up to four times each week.

AUL ferries serve Qeqertarsuaq weekly, offering direct connections to/from Aasiaat (Dkr225, 4½ hours) and to/from Qasigiannguit (Dkr305, five hours).

AROUND DISKO ISLAND
Hiking

Disko Island is a vast and uncompromising wilderness, measuring 120km from north to south and the same from east to west. Trekking is limited to the most accessible areas on the southern peninsula near Qeqertarsuaq. In summer travelling any further into the interior would amount to expedition-level trekking. However, in winter it's possible to do it relatively easily by dogsled. Unfortunately, there's no way to reach the glacier in Kuanersuit Valley. The best map is the Greenland Tourism 1:100,000 sheet *Qeqertarsuaq*.

KUANNIT

A fine 6km walk east from Qeqertarsuaq follows the beautiful coastline to Kuannit (Angelica), where there's an impressive outcrop of basalt columns to spark the imagination.

About halfway along the route is the formation known as Elephant Rock – looking west, you can see the ears, head and trunk of an elephant on the shore. It's impossible to continue further east from Kuannit because the cliffs drop right into the sea. Nor can you travel further east by walking around Skarvefjeld, as the route is blocked by a gaping ravine.

SKARVEFJELD

From Qeqertarsuaq it's a straightforward climb to the summit of Skarvefjeld (925m) which is visible from Blæsedalen. Follow the southwestern ridge up the mountain to the truncated summit. It's important to go in clear weather, as parts of the route are frequently obscured by fog.

ITILLEQ & KANGERLUK LOOP

This is another excellent walk, which requires five days or more. The coastline west of Qeqertarsuaq is relatively easy walking, but at times you'll have to divert up the slope and away from the shore. From the pleasant beach at Killit, which was once the site of a Dutch whaling station, follow the steep but negotiable coastline northward to Itilleq, then turn inland and ascend through the broad and easy pass Itinneq Killeq. Watch for the well-formed basalt columns on Luciafjeld, east of the valley.

After descending to the coast at Kangerluk Fjord (Diskofjord), turn east and follow the shore to the mouth of Blæsedalen, from where it's a long but manageable route over the pass back to Qeqertarsuaq. The valley's eastern side is easiest, but the river crossing is difficult.

Another route takes you from the terminal moraine at Blæsedalen's mouth. Walk east along the shore of Diskofjord to the head of Kangikerllak Fjord and then ascend the Brededal Valley until you reach the Tunusua Valley. From the mouth of the Tunusua Valley turn west and climb up it to cross the 567m-high pass back to Blæsedalen, then follow this valley southward to Qeqertarsuaq. This adds about two days to the total hike.

DISKO BAY

Northwest Greenland

HIGHLIGHTS

- Dogsled through the dramatic fjords of **Uummannaq** (p193)
- Visit the site of the discovery of the **Qilakitsoq** mummies (p195)
- Traipse around the historic buildings of **Upernavik** (p196)
- Take a trip with a traditional hunter in **Qaanaaq** district (p200)
- Visit the traditional communities of **Siorapaluk** (p201) or **Inglefield Fjord** (p201)

Extreme distance and costs have long kept Northwest Greenland one of the least visited areas of the country, and the ensuing isolation has meant that it remains one of the least developed and least westernised areas of Greenland. It was less than 150 years ago that the last group of Baffin Islanders migrated to this area, and 40 years ago hunting was still the full-time occupation of most locals.

In the far north and in smaller communities many families still depend on hunting as their main source of income, and a ban on hunting and fishing by snowmobile or motorboat means that the dogsled and the kayak are still the primary means of transport for traditional hunters. The authenticity of it all hits you with the smell of dogs, drying fish and stretched skins wafting through the air. However, junk food, alcohol, snowmobiles, mobile phones, speedboats and prefab housing are increasingly encroaching on that traditional way of life.

Gloriously scenic Uummannaq, to the south of the region, is the only area with any kind of tourist industry, and even this means just a trickle of travellers and a few organised tours. Further north, life proceeds at a slower pace, and a successful trip will depend on your ability to make contacts with local people and get access to the vast beauty that lies beyond the towns.

UUMMANNAQ DISTRICT

UUMMANNAQ ISLAND
pop 1350

Fly or sail into Uummannaq (Heart-shaped) on a clear day and you'll be smitten. The towering red gneiss peak that dominates the tiny island lords over the colourful village below, where houses cling precariously to the steep rocky shore and a network of wooden steps plays snakes and ladders with the winding roads.

Uummannaq Island sits at 70°N latitude, 600km north of the Arctic Circle, and it's famed as Greenland's sunniest spot. It is also one of the driest places in the country: mineral-rich desert landscapes dominate the nearby islands, creating a surreal image when set against the surrounding iceberg-littered fjord. Elsewhere in the region are soaring cliffs sweeping down to the sea, home to thousands of nesting sea birds.

In winter, darkness descends for two months, but spring ushers in excellent conditions for dogsledding, and in April the

town hosts the ice golf world championships (www.golfonice.com), where there are icebergs instead of bunkers.

History

Uummannaq has been a seasonally inhabited hunting ground for several millennia and found fame as a whaling district in the 17th century. The first permanent settlement, however, was founded on the Nuussuaq Peninsula in 1758 and shifted to the present site in 1763. Over the years it developed into a sealing district and service centre for the mines around outlying Maarmorilik and Qaarsut. Today shrimp-processing and halibut fishing sustain the local economy.

Information

The Tele-Post Center has two ATMs in the lobby.

Arctic Umiaq Line (AUL) office (☎ 951246; bktumd@aul.gl; ☻ 9am-3pm Mon-Fri)

Police (☎ 951222)

Uummannaq Tourist Service (☎ 951518; uummannaq@icecaphotels.gl) At Hotel Uummannaq; hotel guests and tour groups are their definite priority.

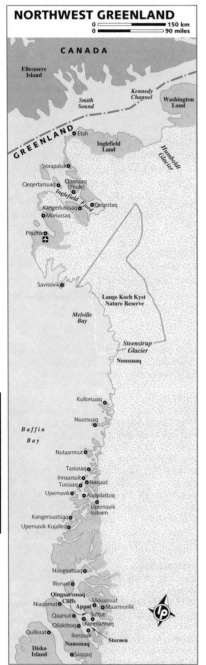

NORTHWEST GREENLAND

Sights

UUMMANNAQ MUSEUM

The excellent **Uummannaq Museum** (☎ 954461; Alfred Berthelsen-ip Aqq B9B; admission Dkr20; ✆ 9am-3pm Mon-Fri, noon-3pm Sat) is one of Greenland's better town museums and houses a diverse collection featuring displays on the Qilakitsoq mummies (p195), the whaling era, the former marble quarry at Maarmorilik, and Greenlandic history and archaeology. There's also a display on the ill-fated 1930–31 inland ice expedition of German scientist Alfred Wegener, famous for his theory of continental drift.

The northern end of the building was constructed in 1880 as a home for the Royal Greenland Trade Department clerk. It was enlarged nine years later and converted into a hospital, with further additions made in 1921. The nearby yellow houses were built in 1907, one as the vicarage and the other as the doctor's residence.

Before leaving the museum ask for the keys to the church and turf huts down the road. You'll most likely get a guided tour.

CHURCH, TURF HUTS & BLUBBER HOUSE

The town's striking granite **church** (Kussangajaannguaq), consecrated in 1935, seems a fitting creation for the rocky community: the granite was quarried from the wall just north of the church. Look out for the faces carved into the boulder above the church clock and on the font. To get a good view over the harbour and bay, climb up the bell tower.

Near the church, three traditional **turf huts** are preserved as national historical buildings. They're surprisingly bright and spacious inside. The largest, constructed in 1925, once housed two families, while another of the same year was inhabited until 1982. The third dates from 1949, when it served as a potato-storage shed.

Opposite the turf huts is the yellow washed stone **Blubber House**, built in 1860 as a whale-oil warehouse. Because of the strong smell, the blubber wasn't actually boiled down there, but at a train oil factory; its scattered **remains** can still be seen about 1km north of the harbour, near the heliport.

Activities

HIKING

Uummannaq sits on a small, precipitous island with limited walking opportunities, but

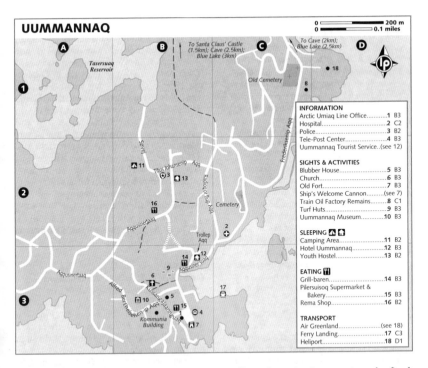

UUMMANNAQ

0 ———————— 200 m
0 ———————— 0.1 miles

Tasersuaq Reservoir

To Santa Claus' Castle
(1.5km); Cave (2.5km);
Blue Lake (3km)

To Cave (2km);
Blue Lake (2.5km)

Old Cemetery

Frederiksenip Aqq

Sayeĸ

Titus Johansenip Aqq

Radioq.ʀ'nup Aqq

Aqqusinertaaq

Cemetery

Trollep Aqq

Aqqusinertaaq

Alfred Berthelsenip Aqq

Ulamip Aqq

Kangilineq Aqq

Kommunia Building

INFORMATION
Arctic Umiaq Line Office............1 B3
Hospital......................................2 C2
Police...3 B2
Tele-Post Center.......................4 B3
Uummannaq Tourist Service..(see 12)

SIGHTS & ACTIVITIES
Blubber House.............................5 B3
Church..6 B3
Old Fort......................................7 B3
Ship's Welcome Cannon.........(see 7)
Train Oil Factory Remains........8 C1
Turf Huts....................................9 B3
Uummannaq Museum...............10 B3

SLEEPING
Camping Area...........................11 B2
Hotel Uummannaq....................12 B3
Youth Hostel.............................13 B2

EATING
Grill-baren................................14 B3
Pilersuisoq Supermarket &
  Bakery.................................15 B3
Rema Shop...............................16 B2

TRANSPORT
Air Greenland.......................(see 18)
Ferry Landing..........................17 C3
Heliport...................................18 D1

the 1170m mountain that acts as a backdrop to the town is one of the most unusual and colourful sights in the Arctic. It changes dramatically from moment to moment as the light plays across the stripy granite, swapping dull cloud-wrapped grey for pastel rose and carrot orange. The mountain and the entire island are composed of a geological formation known as basement gneiss – granite that has been metamorphosed by intense pressure and heat into wild black, white and rose swirls and stripes. Several expeditions have made it to the top via the north ridge, but it's a serious rock climb. Most visitors are content to tramp around the base.

The easiest hike is to **Santa Claus' Castle** (see the boxed text p194), a traditional turf hut less than an hour's walk from town. The trail begins from the centre of town near the reservoir and is marked with yellow boulders. From the castle a steep walk takes you to a **cave** known locally as 'the troll's grotto' and on to the small **Blue Lake**. The trail is marked with cairns and red-painted stones but can be difficult to follow. At Blue Lake you are almost at the far end of the island, where

you'll get fantastic views out into the fjord. The return walk should take no more than a leisurely three to four hours.

DOGSLEDDING
Uummannaq is an excellent spot for dogsledding trips with local seal hunters, who guide tourists during the slack hunting period from mid-March to May. The frozen sea provides a level sledding surface between the far-flung villages of the district, and accommodation can be arranged at community halls (Dkr200 per person) or with local families (Dkr275 to Dkr375). Typical costs start at Dkr2000 per person per day for a dogsledding trip, including accommodation (food is extra). However, it's only Dkr800 to Qaarsut and back (five hours). In the sledding season, dogsled races are held around the district and provide a festive atmosphere and a chance to see the professionals at work.

Tours
Friendly local guide **Lucia Ludvigsen** (☎ 951421; luusi_uummannarmiu@hotmail.com) organises recommended boat trips to the hunting and fishing

---

SANTA CLAUS' CASTLE

Santa's a busy man but he manages to maintain homes all around the Arctic. The Finns have him living in Rovaniemi, Icelanders say he's resident in Vopnafjörður, the Swedes put him somewhere around Kiruna and Alaskans claim he hails from the village of North Pole near Fairbanks. Even the Turks have a claim on him, maintaining that St Nicholas was a native of their fair country.

It comes as no surprise, then, that Danes and Greenlanders cite his official address as Spraglebugten, DK-3961 Uummannaq. His 'royal castle' is in fact a traditional turf hut, built for a Danish children's TV programme, *The Christmas Calendar*. Beware, however, that Santa may not be home, though he kindly leaves his key with the tourist office when he goes on tour. There are several stone graves near the hut and some 19th-century inscriptions on the rocks near the shore.

---

village of Ikerasak (Dkr500, six hours); the Qilakitsoq Inuit ruins and mummy cave (Dkr400, four hours); and through grand fjords to Maarmorilik (Dkr600, nine hours). Prices are per person based on three people joining the tour. In winter, long-line fishing trips (Dkr250 per hour) and dogsledding tours to local settlements (price by agreement) are possible. She can also arrange an evening visit to a local family to see traditional crafts and try on typical winter fur clothing (Dkr100), and can organise accommodation in local settlements (Dkr275). Another local outfitter, **Karl Markussen** (☎ 23292; kmoutfitter@greennet.gl), can arrange similar trips.

Trips by the **Uummannaq Tourist Service** (☎ 951518; uummannaq@icecaphotels.gl) all require a minimum number of participants and so can be hard to arrange. You'll get the hard sell about their full-day boat tour (Dkr1100), though. The trip goes through iceberg-filled waters to Qilakitsoq, and then along the Nuussuaq Peninsula, on to the desert landscape of Storøen and the 1000m cliffs at Qingaarssuaq – a breeding ground for thousands of fulmars – before heading home via the small settlement of Sattut. It's pricey but very informative and well worth the cost.

Other tours include a half-day trip to one of the smaller settlements (Dkr550); a full-day boat trip to Great Qarajaq, one of the fastest moving glaciers in the world (Dkr1200); a half-day boat trip to Qilakitsoq (Dkr450); a half-day whale-watching trip (Dkr635); a hike to Santa Claus' Castle (Dkr190); a two-hour midnight boat trip (Dkr350); and an evening glacier tour and barbecue (Dkr700). In winter the tourist service offers half-day dogsled tours (Dkr700) and tours to local settlements (three/four days Dkr9400/10,500). They can also arrange accommodation in local settlements (Dkr375) throughout the year.

If you want to see narwhal (4m-long mottled whales with tusks up to 2m long), you're advised to visit in late October or November.

Sleeping

Youth Hostel (☎ 951518; Aqqusinertaaq; dm Dkr325; ☯ mid-Jun–Jul) Basic but expensive dorm accommodation can be had at the makeshift youth hostel near the police station. The place has little character, but there is a kitchen. Bookings should be made through the tourist service.

Hotel Uummannaq (☎ 951518; uummannaq@icecahotels.gl; Trollep Aqq B1342; s/d Dkr850/1150; ☒) Excellent-quality but fairly basic modern rooms are available at the hotel, but you've no guarantee you'll get one with a view or anything other than mediocre service. The hotel restaurant (mains Dkr148 to Dkr168) is about the only place to eat in town, but outside the peak season it only offers the two-course menu of the day (Dkr168). If you're staying at the hotel the full-board option (Dkr250 extra) is a good deal.

The island is made of solid rock, but 50m west of the reservoir, near the police station, there are a few level, grassy spots suitable for camping. There are also acceptable sites around Santa Claus' Castle.

The tourist office can arrange B&B accommodation (Dkr375) and fully equipped house or apartment rental (single/double Dkr550/775). You can stay in the town's traditional turf huts (Dkr250) by contacting the museum in advance.

Eating

Lucia Ludvigsen (☎ 951421; meals Dkr100) To sample some typical Greenlandic food, contact this local guide the day before and you can savour seal, whale, caribou, halibut or other local fish cooked in the traditional way at a typical family home.

You'll find groceries and a good bakery at the Pilersuisoq supermarket and a more limited selection at Rema. **Grill-baren** (Aqqusinersuaq B799A; meals Dkr40-55) has burgers, fries and hot dogs.

Getting There & Away

To get to any of the district's seven villages or Kuusuup Nuua (for the trek to Saqqaq, see p180), you'll need to fly (Dkr445), charter a boat (Dkr1800 per hour) or organise a tour. The most affordable charters are offered by Lucia Ludvigsen (see Tours, p193).

AIR

Air Greenland (☎ 951289; Frederiksenip Aqq B1515), which is based at the heliport, flies to Ilulissat (Dkr1572, 1½ hours) and on to Kangerlussuaq (Dkr2847, 2½ hours) twice weekly via Qaarsut (Dkr526, 10 minutes). Helicopter flights run on weekdays from the district villages from Uummannaq (Dkr445) and daily except Wednesday and Sunday to Qaarsut (Dkr445).

BOAT

AUL ferries serve Uummannaq once weekly on their run from Nuuk (Dkr2145, 60 hours) via Ilulissat (Dkr740, 16 hours). The trip to Upernavik costs Dkr800 (15 hours), but the ferry arrives in the middle of the night. For information on midnight culture tours of Upernavik see p198.

AROUND UUMMANNAQ

Qaarsut

pop 240

Tiny, untouched and rarely visited, Qaarsut sits in a broad, level valley on the Nuussuaq Peninsula, 21km west of Uummannaq. All flights to Uummannaq include a transfer to helicopter in Qaarsut, but few visitors make it outside the airport terminal. This is a shame, as the traditional village gives a good insight into life in small northern Greenland settlements without requiring visitors to cough up for an expensive side trip.

A coal mine operated in Qaarsut until 1924, but today the village subsists on seal hunting and fishing. Local women have formed a small **cooperative** (⏱ 10am-4pm Mon-Fri) where they sew sealskin into traditional boots, gloves and coats.

QILAKITSOQ

Sometime in the late 15th century a group of eight Inuit were buried with some care in the now abandoned village of Qilakitsoq (Where the Sky is Low) near Uummannaq. As was customary, they were dressed in their winter clothes for the long, cold journey to the land of the dead and were provided with the tools needed to survive in the afterlife. There was nothing unusual about their burial except that the grave was placed high above the village away from the others and, thanks to their location, the bodies were unintentionally preserved – dry air, low ground temperature and an overhanging rock protected the graves from wind, water, sunlight and snow.

Although the older villagers at Uummannaq claimed they knew of the existence of the grave for years, it was two ptarmigan hunters, Hans and Jokum Grønvold, who rediscovered the site in 1972, photographed it and reported their find to government authorities. It was 1977, when Claus Andreasen took over the director's post at Greenland's National Museum, before any attention was paid to the site, but then Qilakitsoq was catapulted to international fame. The eight bodies and their clothing were almost perfectly preserved and were by far the most significant archaeological find in the Arctic. There were six adults in the group, all women; one of them had a brain tumour. With them were a six-month-old baby, and a four-year-old boy who apparently had Down's syndrome. In February 1985 *National Geographic* did a cover story on the mummies and the subsequent research, and suddenly people everywhere were captivated by the haunting face of the six-month-old boy who had lived and died in 15th-century Greenland.

You can see several of the mummies on display at the National Museum in Nuuk (see p147) and the tourist office in Uummannaq sells the booklet *Qilakitsoq – 15th Century Greenlandic Mummies*. You can visit the abandoned village and the site of the find from Uummannaq. Ruins of houses from several different periods are visible, and there are 33 other graves, some with visible skulls and bones inside.

SHIP'S WELCOME

It's an Uummannaq tradition to heartily welcome the first ship to sail into the harbour each spring. Lookouts are posted on Nasiffik hill, west of town, and when they call out 'Umiarssuaq!' (Ship!) the entire village gathers on the hill to await the arrival. From the fort hill, south of the harbour, three old cannons are fired in welcome not only to the ship but also to springtime. The cannons are fired again for the departure of the season's last ship, but with considerably less fanfare.

B&B (Dkr275-375) can be arranged in Uummannaq and there's a Pilersuisoq shop, for supplies.

Air Greenland (☎ 957699) flies helicopters daily except Wednesday and Sunday to and from Uummannaq (Dkr545). Lucia Ludvigsen and the Uummannaq Tourist Service organise charter trips for visits to Qaarsut's sandy beach and for climbing or hiking around the distinct cone-shaped peak, Qilertinnguit (1977m).

UPERNAVIK DISTRICT

UPERNAVIK TOWN

pop 1200

Historic Upernavik sits on one of a series of tiny islands facing the open sea. It's a scruffy little place, but it's also home to a host of historic buildings and one of the country's most fascinating museums. Boat trips to the surrounding areas offer views of the inland ice reaching down to the sea, fantastic bird cliffs and a variety of archaeological sites.

The town is the most northerly ferry terminal in Greenland and nearly 800km north of the Arctic Circle. Even though the sun does not set from mid-May to early August, average summer temperatures still hover at a chilly 5°C.

History

All known Greenlandic cultures must have migrated though the Upernavik area to reach southern Greenland, and the district is littered with archaeological sites. In 1772 Upernavik town was founded, but the colony was abandoned several times by the Danes.

In 1826 trade was firmly established and by 1833 a mission had also been founded. In the early 1980s fishing took off, and despite its northerly location the town is now much more a fishing than a hunting society. To experience a more traditional lifestyle you need to travel to the smaller settlements, which give a real glimpse of life in times past.

Information

Hospital (☎ 961211)
Police (☎ 961222)
Tele-Post Center (Napparsimaviup Aqq B656) There's an ATM inside this post office, but it does not accept American Express cards.
Tourist office (☎ 961700; turist@greennet.gl; Niuertup Ottup Aqq B-12; ⊙ 9am-4pm Mon-Fri) In the museum building.

Sights

UPERNAVIK HISTORICAL DISTRICT

The entire historical district of the village has been designated a conservation area. Upernavik's **museum** (☎ 961085; www.iserit.green net.gl/inussuk; Niuertup Ottup Aqq B-12; admission Dkr25; ⊙ 2-4pm Tue-Fri, 2-5pm Sun) is Greenland's oldest, and the collection is housed in a series of beautifully restored buildings.

The **colony manager's former home**, brought to the site in 1831 from near Aasiaat, is host to a late–13th-century rune stone found in 1824, bearing evidence of a visit to the district by three Norse hunters. There's also a collection of images from Greenland mythology by Danish artist Gitz Johansen (1897–1977), carved *tupilaks* (figures traditionally used by Greenlandic shamans), and finds from local archaeological sites.

The **old shop**, built in 1864, holds a fascinating original *qajaq* ensemble (see p86) complete with a harpoon, a throwing stick, a bird skewer, a knife and a seal-stomach float (to prevent seals diving after being hit or sinking after being killed). You'll also see an ethnographic collection including tools for hunting, household implements, traditional costumes and exhibits on traditional hunting and fishing methods.

In the **old church**, built in 1839, you can see the former meeting rooms of the district council. Greenlandic furniture is on display, as well as chandeliers, ashtrays and match holders made from brass salvaged from a 1921 shipwreck. The council guest book contains the signatures and drawings

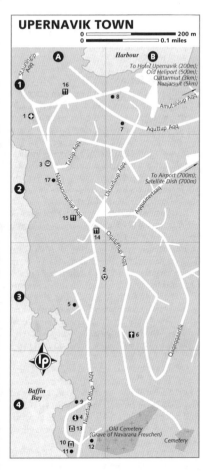

which was taken from the old church (now the museum), and the pulpit and kneeling altar, which are decorated with pearl and embroidered sealskin. The *Madonna and Child* altarpiece was made by Danish artist Mathias Fersløv Dalager (1770–1842).

Due to the permanently frozen ground, the graves in Upernavik's **cemetery** are raised and covered with rock and concrete. Incredible floral memorials adorn the graves, and downhill from the main cemetery you'll find the grave of Navarana Freuchen, the wife of Peter Freuchen; she died in 1921 on the fifth Thule expedition with polar explorer Knud Rasmussen (see p174).

Hiking

Tiny Upernavik Island doesn't offer the most challenging terrain for hiking. However, even a short hike to the satellite dish or the airport terminal will give you views of surrounding islands, the 130m-high Umiasuussuk (Women's Boat Mountain) to the east, and the icefjord and inland ice to the northeast.

For a longer hike, start at the old heliport and follow the coast north for about 2km until you hit a gashlike valley that slices across the island. Rather than taking the steep descent into the valley, follow it across to the far side of the island, where you'll get an overview of the extensive ruins of **Qattarmiut village** and a couple of nice lakes. The slope to the valley floor is much more gentle on this side. The steep northern slopes of the valley reveal some brilliantly coloured mineral deposits.

of numerous Arctic explorers and scientists. It was used as the guest book at the museum after the council disbanded in 1950.

Other historic buildings in the area (but closed to the public) include the **old rectory** (1863), the **old school** (1911) and the **old bakery and cooperage** (1848), which is now used as a studio for visiting artists-in-residence. South of the centre, you can see the **Blubber House**, which dates from 1912. Down by the harbour are the **historic KNI office**, built in 1936, and the **Jorgensen Warehouse**, which was in use from 1929.

OTHER ATTRACTIONS

The new **church**, which dates from 1926, was renovated in 1990. Take a look at the crucifix,

From here you can either follow the waterpipes from the lake back to the airport or head to **Naajarsuit**, the northern tip of the island, where you'll find an ancient landscape of twisting bands of folded granite, feldspar and gneiss inlaid with tiny garnets. There are some very steep slopes of loose rock down to the sea at this end of the island, so be wary about your footing.

A leisurely walk to Qattarmiut and back will take about two hours; add another hour or so if you plan to go to Naajarsuit.

Tours

Organised tourism in Upernavik is still in its infancy, and your best bet is to contact the tourist office in advance. It can help put you in contact with local hunters who may be able to take you on boat trips during the summer months. The average cost is Dkr300 per hour for the whole boat.

On a half-day or full-day trip you can visit the Upernavik Isstrøm (Upernavik Icefjord), where the inland ice meets the sea and breaks off into some of the largest icebergs in the northern hemisphere. Unlike at the icefjord at Ilulissat, you can travel to the face of the glacier and see it calve. Longer trips can also take in the bird cliffs at Apparsuit, one of the world's largest bird colonies. There you can see thousands of fulmars and, at other locations nearby, guillemots, great northern divers, puffins and cormorants.

Three-hour archaeological trips are also possible, guided by Eskimologist Bo Albrechtsen, leader of Upernavik museum. A typical trip will visit two sites where evidence of different eras of the Thule culture can be found (Dkr1200 per boat).

Keen fishers may be interested in a trip to sheltered Eqallugaasuit (Sea Trout Bay), for fishing (in July and August) and to see trees of up to 1.5m, a rarity at this northern latitude.

The Upernavik district is also good for kayaking, and although you cannot rent kayaks the tourist office is happy to give advice on routes, safety and logistics.

In winter the tourist office organises dog-sledding tours in the district. For a three-hour trip you'll pay about Dkr500; a full-day tour will cost Dkr1200. Ice conditions have been bad in recent years, so you'd be well advised to contact the tourist office in advance if you'd like to plan a longer trip.

Hotel Upernavik (see Sleeping & Eating, following) owns a three-berth boat that can be chartered for trips or tours (prices by arrangement).

Sleeping & Eating

The hills and valleys north of town offer lots of free scenic camp sites, but flat areas can be quite soggy. Ask at the tourist office for information on the best locations.

The tourist office can arrange B&B accommodation (Dkr300) in private homes, but you must book in advance. It's a good way of meeting a local family and getting an insight into life in the town. Payment should be made at the tourist office.

Hotel Upernavik (☎ 962279; www.hotel-upernavik .gl; Mittarfiup Aqq B748; s/d Dkr895/1295; ✗) You'll find modern but fairly basic, comfortable rooms at this small hotel by the harbour. The price includes breakfast and pick-up at the airport. There's a kitchen for guests' use, and the restaurant serves decent meals for Dkr75, though it has all the character of a hospital canteen and only opens when there are guests around. There's live local music in the bar downstairs every weekend (Dkr20 to Dkr40). Note that you can't pay by credit card here.

Grill-baren (Ukuarluup Aqq; meals Dkr25-45; ☯ 10am-10pm) The only other option for food in town, the grill-bar serves a good variety of fast food from burgers and kebabs to pizzas and hot dogs. The building is unmarked, but you'll recognise the smell and the gaggle of teenagers hanging around outside.

Other eating options are the **Pilersuisoq supermarket and bakery** (Umiarsualiviup Aqq B143) and LT's kiosk, which stays open after hours and on weekends and sells hot dogs and chips for Dkr35.

Getting There & Away

AIR

Air Greenland (☎ 961148) has three weekly flights between Ilulissat (Dkr3286) and Upernavik and on to Qaanaaq (Dkr1226, 1¾ hours). Helicopters fly to each of the district settlements twice a week (Dkr525).

BOAT

AUL (☎ 961044; bktjuv@aul.gl; Napparsimaviup Aqq B676) runs ferries once weekly from Nuuk (Dkr275, 75 hours) to Upernavik from mid-June to mid-August, calling at Uummannaq

(Dkr800, 15 hours), Ilulissat (Dkr1150, 20 hours) and Sisimiut (Dkr1970, 54 hours). Although the ferry arrives in the middle of the night and only has a short stop, the tourist office runs a 'Culture Night' (Dkr100) for passengers. A guide will meet you at the harbour and show you the town and the museum before you return to the ship in time to sail south. Contact the tourist office in advance to let them know you'd like to take part.

With lots of time and money, you can charter a boat up through icy Melville Bay to Savissivik and Qaanaaq. Ask the tourist office for information.

AROUND UPERNAVIK TOWN

Although Upernavik district is only slightly smaller than Great Britain, it has just 2965 inhabitants. Of the 10 outlying settlements, those without fish-processing plants (Kangersuatsiaq, Nuussuaq and Upernavik Kujalleq) remain the most traditional and can make fascinating destinations for travellers. In these villages life still revolves around the seal and polar-bear hunt. In spring and autumn respectively, narwhal and belugas are frequent visitors, and both are still hunted from kayaks at the northern end of the district in Melville Bay.

The northern part of Upernavik district has very different vegetation from the southern part; it has only sparse ground cover and some very scenic but barren mountains. The most northerly and largest settlement of the district, **Kullorsuaq** (The Devil's Thumb), at the southern end of Melville Bay and 300km from Upernavik, has a striking rock pinnacle rising from the town, just like a thumb.

In the south the fishing village of **Aappilattoq** is located at the mouth of Upernavik Isstrøm, and boat trips in the area visit the calving glacier.

For a unique perspective on village life you can visit the smaller settlements and stay overnight. The tourist office in Upernavik can help arrange accommodation at local service houses (community washing facilities) and make contact with hunters in the settlements who could take you on local tours. Although it is possible to charter boats to most settlements, the heavily subsidised Air Greenland helicopter fares (Dkr525) are good value for once. A flat-fare system

operates, and so you pay the same cost to travel to Aappilattoq, just 23km away, as you do to Kullorsuaq, 300km away.

QAANAAQ (THULE) DISTRICT

Ultima Thule. Even the name sounds exotic. Fourth-century geographer Pytheas coined the term 'the furthest north', and for centuries afterwards Europeans had no idea what this enigmatic area looked like. But long before they postulated on its appearance the first waves of Inuit migration were occurring from the west, and this gateway to Greenland remained open for centuries: the last migration took place only 130 years ago. Today the modern Thule Inuit refer to themselves not just as Inuit, but Inughuit (pronounced inu'hhui'), the 'great people'.

The vast Qaanaaq district is among the northernmost inhabited places on earth. It's also one of the least populated, with only about 1000 people living in its 297,000 sq km. Life here is the closest you'll find to the traditional Inuit lifestyle: hunting is still the main source of income, and restrictions on the use of snowmobiles and motor boats for hunting mean that dogsleds, kayaks and harpoons remain in daily use. However, the area has not stood still, and prefab housing, junk food, alcohol and mobile phones are also part of everyday life.

The area is also the last bastion of the US military in Greenland, and the US base at Pituffik remains a thorny issue for all politicians and an open sore for the local people (see p200).

Visits to Qaanaaq are far from cheap but afford a glimpse of a lifestyle that has changed very little in modern times. Here, many of the traditions of the past are held as firmly as they were thousands of years ago. If you're merely interested in attaining a new 'furthest north', parts of Norway's Svalbard (p324) are farther north and cheaper to visit.

QAANAAQ TOWN (THULE)

pop 650

On 17 February each year the first sunrise turns the skies of Qaanaaq pink, orange and red after a prolonged stint of polar night.

NORTHWEST GREENLAND

PLUTONIUM PERIL IN PITUFFIK

The Thule Air Base is a serious bone of contention in international relations between Greenland, Denmark and the USA. The greatest controversy involves the US B-52 bomber that crashed near Thule in January 1968 and was later revealed to have been carrying four hydrogen bombs with nuclear detonation devices.

A two-month clean-up operation followed; of the 1000 people who worked on it, over 100 have since died, half of them from cancer. In 1988, health problems prompted 166 workers to file a joint complaint, but it took until 1995 before it was even confirmed that the plane did indeed carry 6kg of plutonium. The Danish government paid US$9000 tax-free compensation to each of the 1500 Danish and Greenlandic workers and residents of the base area. However, in August 2000 it was revealed that only three hydrogen bombs were recovered – meaning that the fourth is still in Greenland. Both the Americans and Danes have admitted that between 500g and 1.8kg of plutonium was never recovered. The results of environmental-impact studies in the area remain secret.

Meanwhile, local hunters complain of finding muskoxen with deformed hooves and seals with no hair. This, coupled with continued ill-feeling over the forced relocation of their community, means that many Greenlanders feel strongly that the base should be closed down. However, the lease was renewed in 2004, and the USA is planning to upgrade the base as part of its controversial Star Wars national missile defence system, saying it is of strategic importance.

For the local Inuit the campaign to allow them to return to their traditional territory continues. In 2003 the Danish Supreme Court ruled that the people of Qaanaaq did not have the right to return to their original home. They have now taken their case to the European Court of Human Rights, where they hope to see the issue resolved by 2006.

This far north, life runs on a different beat, and the small community of Qaanaaq has attracted explorers and adventurers for hundreds of years. Knud Rasmussen established his expedition base here, and Robert Peary came back repeatedly until he claimed to have reached the North Pole in 1909, with the assistance of many local hunters. Although the town has few specific attractions, the surrounding landscape, traditional lifestyle and the possibility for visits to outlying settlements make it a worthwhile trip for the modern adventurer.

Qaanaaq was moved 200km north to its present location in 1953 after being displaced by the expanding US airbase at Pituffik.

Information

There's nowhere to change money in town, but the general store accepts Visa, MasterCard, Eurocard and Dankort.

Police (☎ 971022)
Post Greenland (☎ 971044)
Tourist office (☎ 971473; www.turistqaanaaq.gl; ☻ 11am-1pm Mon-Fri)

Sights

A good starting point for any tour of the area is Qaanaaq's **museum** (☎ 971126; admission free; ☻ 1-3pm Sun), housed in the former home of famed polar explorer Knud Rasmussen (see p174). Displays include items relating to his work, archaeological finds from around the district, and tools and clothing used by the Inuit.

You can see busts of the famous Minik (see p80) and his family in the assembly hall in the Kommunia.

Activities

In April and May dogsledding is the most popular local activity, but cross-country skiing trips are also possible. During summer, boat trips, fishing and hiking are popular, and the inland ice is only a two- to three-hour hike away.

Tours

Tours can be arranged through the tourist office, Hotel Qaanaaq (see opposite) or outfitter **Finn Hansen** (☎ 971148; finnhansen@greennet .gl). Prices have been standardised and range between Dkr1000 and Dkr1400 per day. On multiday trips, overnight stays may be in local houses at a settlement, in a hunters' hut, or in a tent.

A two- to three-hour dogsledding trip will take you close to huge icebergs frozen into

STEVE HUTTON

Sled dogs, Ilulissat (p170), Greenland

Disko Bay's Qasigiannguit (p181), Greenland

GRAEME CORNWALLIS

Ilulissat Kangerlua (p176), the icefjord south of Ilulissat, Greenland

DEANNA SWANEY

Children in Greenlandic national clothing, Uummannaq (p191)

Upernavik cemetery (p197), Greenland

Uummannaq's church and harbour (p192), Greenland

the sea and is a great way to decide whether to participate in a longer trip and to try out skin clothing. A full-day trip goes to the large abandoned island of Qeqertarsuaq (Herbert Island). Seals are hunted here during winter and spring, and you may see narwhal in late spring. Nearby islands are home to millions of little auks (small round diving birds), who also arrive in late spring.

Longer trips can be made to settlements around Qaanaaq or to hunting grounds. It is a full-day trip to Siorapaluk (see below), and one-week trips are available to Moriusaq and Savissivik, tiny settlements south of Qaanaaq that are totally dependent on hunting from the sea. Guides will hunt on these trips if the opportunity arises, and if they need to feed their dogs. Depending on ice conditions, a route partially over the ice-cap may be taken.

Trips to Etah to see muskoxen, reindeer, and archaeological remains are also possible.

Sleeping & Eating

The tourist office rents a small two-bed **cabin** (per person Dkr200) with kitchen, shower and toilet. Accommodation in private homes (Dkr200 to Dkr300) and rentals of other rooms can also be arranged, both in Qaanaaq and in smaller settlements.

The basic **Hotel Qaanaaq** (☎ 971234; hansje@ greennet.gl; s/d Dkr575) has a handful of simple rooms with shared bathroom but can arrange accommodation elsewhere if it happens to be fully booked. The restaurant serves lunch for Dkr45 and dinner for Dkr85.

The Pilersuisoq supermarket has a bakery and hot-dog counter and sells pretty much anything you might need. Stocks can get low in late spring and early summer before new supplies arrive by ship.

Shopping

Artistic talent runs especially high in Qaan-aaq and it's an excellent place to look for traditional Inuit art. **Ultima Thule** (☎ 971473) markets genuine and original artwork and crafts typical of the district.

Getting There & Away

AIR

Air Greenland has flights every Tuesday and Thursday between Qaanaaq and Ilulis-sat (Dkr4296, 3¾ hours) via Upernavik (Dkr1226, 1¾ hours).

Siorapaluk, Moriusaq and Savissivik are accessible by helicopter (Dkr525 one way).

BOAT

From Qaanaaq, you can charter private boats in the summer or dogsleds in the spring to the other Qaanaaq district villages of Savis-sivik, Siorapaluk, Qeqertaq and Moriusaq. Expect to pay about Dkr1000 to Dkr1400 per day.

You can also charter boats to Upernavik from Qaanaaq, but it's very expensive. Quark Expeditions (see p65) runs cruises that call at Qaanaaq.

AROUND QAANAAQ TOWN
Inglefield Fjord

The vast Inglefield Fjord east of Qaanaaq has several active glaciers, which calve huge icebergs during the summer, and there are many sites of Thule-culture dugout houses. At the head of the fjord is Qeqertaq, a small village home to about 10 families. Motor-boats are not permitted in the area, and restrictions on all travel are enforced in summer months, when the waters become a sanctuary for breeding narwhal. The narwhal are the main prey for local hunters, who use traditional kayaks and harpoons. The area around Qaanaaq is the only place in the world where the traditional skill of hunt-ing narwhal by kayak and harpoon is still alive.

Contact the tourist office well in advance if you would like to visit either Inglefield or Qeqertarsuaq to see narwhal. You will need a lot of luck to catch sight of these beautiful creatures if you're travelling in any kind of motorboat, as the sound frightens them into a deep dive.

SIORAPALUK
pop 90

Siorapaluk is the northernmost natural settlement in the world (Longyearbyen and Ny Ålesund in Norway's Svalbard began as coal-mining centres, and Alert on Canada's Ellesmere Island is a military post), and it remains a bastion of tradi-tion. Most of Siorapaluk's residents still survive by fishing for halibut and hunting seals, narwhal, walruses, birds and polar bears, and in summer many people return to traditional hunting camps in the fjords with their families.

Two glaciers pour down into the head of the fjord, and the cliffs around the town are home to millions of little auks (diving birds) that migrate here to breed. The hills above the settlement abound in Arctic hare and Arctic fox, and north of Siorapaluk there are caribou and muskox hunting grounds as well as many archaeological sites.

The town has a church, school, general store and skin workshop, and has electricity but no running water. A guesthouse may be rented, or accommodation in private homes can be arranged through the tourist office in Qaanaaq (Dkr200 to Dkr300 per person).

You can reach Siorapaluk from Qaanaaq by dogsled, private boat or helicopter (Dkr525). The dogsled trip between Qaanaaq and Siorapaluk is about 60km and takes six to eight hours. Depending on the ice conditions, it's sometimes possible to dogsled well into June.

East Greenland

HIGHLIGHTS

■ Stay overnight at **Kulusuk** (p204) and appreciate traditional culture without the crowds

■ Visit the immense **Northeast Greenland National Park** (p213)

■ Kayak the ice-choked fjords around **Tasiilaq** (p208)

■ Make a **first ascent** of an isolated peak (p211)

■ Take part in the gruelling **Arctic Team Challenge** (p209)

Northeast Greenland National Park ★

Tasiilaq (Ammassalik) ★★ Kulusuk

A land apart, known to Greenlanders as Tunu or Tunua (the Back Side), the isolated east coast of Greenland has developed differently from the rest of the country in cultural and linguistic terms. Today it remains one of the most traditional areas of Greenland. The communities here are less developed, and in many ways the lifestyle reflects a past long lost in other parts of the country. Villagers are still dependent on subsistence hunting and fishing, and development is still very low key. Although tourism is big business around Tasiilaq, the area seems doggedly unchanged by it.

East Greenland is also home to some of the most spectacular scenery in the country, with stunning peaks and dramatic fjords providing ample opportunities for first ascents, fantastic hiking and spectacular kayaking. Tasiilaq is the most popular base for any of these activities and is easily accessible from Iceland. A handful of respected outfitters supply everything from route advice to essential equipment. Recreational hikers can take in a variety of day hikes or opt for more strenuous multiday walks through the incredible scenery. Serious hikers and mountaineers have the option of scaling one of the local peaks or heading up to the icecap for a polar odyssey.

Further north is the vast wilderness of the Northeast Greenland National Park, the world's largest national park, which protects almost half of East Greenland. It's one of the most remote areas of Greenland, permits are required and access is cruelly expensive. However, the pristine wilderness, unscaled peaks and abundant wildlife make it a once-in-a-lifetime experience.

History

The east coast of Greenland has always been isolated. Although there is evidence that both the Independence I (p77) and Saqqaq cultures had settlements near the present site of Ittoqqortoormiit, they lasted only briefly. In the 15th and 16th centuries a second wave of migration from the Thule area occurred, but by 1800 Ammassalik was the only settlement that hadn't been abandoned.

Europeans, too, seemed to have little luck in the area. The first European settler to East Greenland was Gunnbjörn, a lost sailor who washed up in 930, named the offshore islets he'd found Gunnbjörn's Skerries, and moved on posthaste. Europeans most likely sailed up the east coast on hunting or exploratory expeditions over many years, but it was 1884 before any contact was made with local Inuit. At this point the Danish Umiaq expedition came across 416 Inuit near the site of present-day Tasiilaq, and 10 years later the first Royal Greenland Trade Department post was established on Ammassalik Island.

KULUSUK (KAP DAN)

pop 310

Spectacularly situated on the craggy slopes of an ice-filled bay, Kulusuk is a stunning place surrounded by dramatic peaks and rocky outcrops. The village maintains a very traditional way of life; most people survive on subsistence hunting of seals and polar bears, few houses have running water, and dog teams far outnumber snowmobiles.

Kulusuk is, however, one of the most popular destinations in Greenland and is just a two-hour flight from Reykjavík, making it possible for day-trippers to drop in out of the sky and overwhelm the village for a few hours. To experience real life here, stay overnight and explore when the day-trippers have left.

Sights & Activities

There are few specific sites of interest in town, but the spectacular setting and brightly coloured traditional houses more than make up for this. The poignant and photogenic

EAST GREENLAND

0 — 300 km
0 — 180 miles

LINCOLN
SEA

WANDEL
SEA

Cape Morris
Jesup
Oodaaq Qeqertaa
Kaffeklubben Ø
Independence
Fjord
Princess
Margrethe
Island

ARCTIC
OCEAN

Peary Land
Station
Nord

Jørgen Brønlund
Fjord
Mylius
Erichsen
Land
Havgård
Island
Knud Rasmussen
Land
Kronprins
Christian Land

GREENLAND
SEA

Kong
Frederik VIII
Land
Île de France

Dronning
Louise Land
Danmarkshavn
Koldewey
Store

Zackenburg
Shannon

Northeast
Greenland National Park

Daneborg
Clavering Island
Hold with Hope
Kong
Christian
Land
Ymer Island
Peninsula
Petermanns
Bjerg
(2940m)
Suess
Land
Geographical
Society Island
Traill Ø
Mesters Vig
Kong Oscar
Fjord
Stauning
Alps
Jameson
Land
Nerlerit Inaat
Ittoqqortoormiit
Milne Land
Kangertittivaq

Gunnbjørns
Fjeld
(3730m)
▲

Kong Christian
IX Land
Kangerlussuaq
Mont Forel
(3360m)
Aputiteeq
Arctic Circle

Denmark Strait

See Around
Tasiilaq Map p210
Kulusuk
Tasiilaq
(Ammassalik)

Kong
Frederik
VI Kyst
Timmiarmiut
Ikermiut
Qulleq

Lindenows Fjord
Prins Christian Sund
(Ikerasassuaq)
Cape Farewell
(Nunaap Isua/Kap Farvel)

ATLANTIC
OCEAN

National Park Boundary

old cemetery has rows of simple white crosses overlooking the ice-filled bay and backdrop of craggy peaks.

Informal *qajaq* demonstrations and drum dance performances are put on for day-trippers on the bluff behind the church, and all visitors are welcome to attend. It's a bit of a tourist trap, but if you're on a short visit it's a good chance to catch a bit of culture.

You can hike up any of the rocky outcrops that surround the town for a stunning view over the village and bay. Alternatively, head straight up the hill south of the airport to an eerie mountain lake. It's easy to ascend the first peak on the ridge, and you may see ptarmigan and Arctic fox.

Qalorujoorneq (676m) is the highest peak on the island, but its steep, wet snowy slopes aren't easy to climb.

Tours

From June to September Hotel Kulusuk (see Sleeping & Eating, following) offers a two-hour cruise to the tidewater glacier on the island of Apusiaajik (Dkr295); a three-hour boat tour to Tasiilaq (Dkr595); a walking tour of Kulusuk village (Dkr75); and a two-hour mountain-jeep tour to Isikajia Mountain (335m; Dkr210). In winter it also offers 2½-hour/half-day/full-day dogsledding trips (Dkr395/595/995) and a superjeep snow tour (Dkr295, two hours).

Local outfitter **Fred Kilime** (☎ 986801; kilimeoutfitter@greennet.gl) can also arrange tailor-made hiking, dogsledding and skiing trips, while **Johann Brandsson** (☎ 986888; kulusuk@greennet.gl) organises sailing and dogsledding tours.

For kayaking tours in this area, try **Ultima Thule Expeditions** (www.ute.is), which offers trips (six/eight/12 days US$1690/2390/2790) around the spectacular local glaciers and fjords.

Air Iceland (☎ 986978; www.airiceland.is) day tours from Reykjavik to Kulusuk cost Ikr40,300/29,900 in high/low season. The trips include a return flight, a guided tour of Kulusuk village, and the dance and *qajaq* demonstrations. Add on a half-hour of dogsledding on the Apusiaajik Glacier, and the cost rises to Ikr55,500/45,500.

Sleeping & Eating

Camping is possible about 1.5km southwest of the airport, but there are no facilities.

Kulusuk Youth Hostel (☎ 986888; kulusuk@greennet.gl; dm Dkr150) Established within a traditional

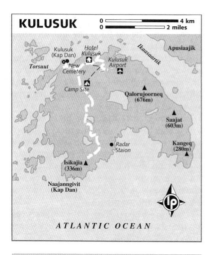

KULUSUK

ATLANTIC OCEAN

DAY-TRIPPING IN KULUSUK

Staunchly traditional Kulusuk can see up to 150 day-trippers six days a week in summer, and though the income this provides is welcome, their influence isn't always so benign. Although the village looks poor, this is because the local people choose to follow traditional ways in some respects; despite the lack of running water, many have satellite TV, mobile phones and home computers.

In the past, well-meaning visitors have given sweets, money or pens to Greenlandic children, but this patronising behaviour upsets parents and demeans the children by inspiring them to ask subsequent visitors for more of the same. Please resist the temptation to play Santa Claus, and let traditional life survive as the locals see fit.

Greenlandic house, this basic hostel has open-plan rooms and no running water. It has a good kitchen and satellite TV. Check in and get directions at the souvenir shop in the centre of town.

Hotel Kulusuk (☎ 986993; www.arcticwonder.com; s/d Dkr890/1085; ☒) This fine hotel has comfortable, modern rooms with en suite, TV, kettle and phone. Most also have good views over the bay. If you fancy just dropping in for a meal, breakfast will cost you Dkr75; lunch and dinner cost Dkr165.

The village shop has a range of groceries for self-caterers.

Shopping

East Greenlandic carvings, beadwork and other gifts are of consistently high quality and are generally much cheaper than on the west coast. In Kulusuk some curios are sold by relaxed street vendors when tour groups pass through, and you'll normally pick up something for less than you would in Tasiilaq.

Kulusuk Art & Souvenirs (☎ 986888) sells a good selection of *tupilaks*, sealskin bags, caribou horn, jewellery and postcards.

Getting There & Away

AIR

Kulusuk's airport is chaotic, as most flights arrive and depart within an hour of each other and the tiny terminal building can't handle the crowds: you'll have to fight your way to the check-in desks.

From mid-May until mid-September, **Air Iceland** (☎ 986978; www.airiceland.is) has flights between Reykjavík and Kulusuk (from Ikr30,000 return) every day except Sunday. There are two to four flights weekly the rest of the year. For more details, see p227.

Twice a week **Air Greenland** (☎ 986926; www.airgreenland.gl) flies from Kulusuk to Kangerlussuaq (Dkr3173, 1¾ hours), where you can connect to other domestic flights.

Air Alpha (☎ 981313; www.airalpha.com) helicopters shuttle passengers between Kulusuk and Tasiilaq (one way Dkr545) from about 10am to 3pm or as the need arises. These flights can't be pre-booked, but they run until every passenger has been transferred.

BOAT

Ice conditions permitting, the Royal Arctic Line cargo boat connects Tasiilaq and Kulusuk (one way Dkr205, two hours) once weekly. If you're travelling with others it's worth enquiring about chartering a boat from a local hunter to take you to Tasiilaq, as the cost can be as little as half that of the helicopter. Alternatively, call your hotel in Tasiilaq, as they often transport guests on tours by boat and may be able to accommodate you.

TASIILAQ (AMMASSALIK)

pop 1800

Set on the steeply sloping shores of placid Kong Oscars Havn, Tasiilaq is the largest community on Greenland's east coast and the administrative centre for Ammassalik district. Noticeably more developed than Kulusuk (it has paved roads and a large supermarket), it is still a very laid-back place, with most of its people still hunting and fishing for personal food supplies.

While the town itself is in a beautiful setting, the local area is an outdoor adventurer's dream landscape, with fantastic kayaking, mountaineering and hiking on the craggy peaks, giant glaciers and ice-clogged waters that surround the town. To come here and not make an effort to get out on the water or into the wilderness would be a real shame.

Information

Ammassalik Tourist Office website (www.greenland guide.gl/ammassalik) Regional guide with information on accommodation, excursions and travel.

Destination East Greenland (www.eastgreenland.com) The official tourism site for East Greenland.

Hospital (☎ 981211)

Neriusaaq Bookshop (☎ 981018; Nappartsimavimmut; ☷ 2-6pm & 7.30-10pm) Stocks souvenir books, maps and some English-language reading material. It also has a pay phone, a public fax service and one Internet terminal (per minute Dkr1).

Netcafé (☎ 249210; per half-hr Dkr30) Has a whole bank of computers and opens in the evenings only, usually from 3pm or 4pm until 8pm or 10pm.

Police (☎ 981448)

Post Office (☎ 981055) Has two ATMs inside.

Tourist office (☎ 981543; tourism@ammassalik.gl; ☷ 9am-5pm Mon-Fri, noon-4pm Sat)

Sights

Start your tour of the town at the **Tasiilaq Museum** (☎ 981311; admission free; ☷ 10am-noon & 1-4pm Mon-Fri, noon-4pm Sun), housed in the old church (built in 1908). It has a wonderful collection of exhibits on the history and culture of East Greenland, including the largest mask collection in the country, some stunning old photos, beadwork, traditional costumes and carvings.

The pentagonal **new church** (☎ 981292; ☷ 10am-4pm Mon-Fri, 8am-noon Sun) was built in 1985 and has an unusual steeple. Inside there's traditional and modern Greenlandic art and a model *umiaq* votive light.

Tasiilaq's oldest building, the **Citadel**, opposite the tourist office, was constructed in 1894 as the home of the first Danish missionary and his wife, who shared it with a trade manager, a carpenter and a sailor. The next

oldest building is the **Missionaries' House**, built in 1895 as a home for Danish missionaries. It also served as an impromptu church, school and hospital.

The original imposing **Trade Manager's House** dated from the 1920s, but it was destroyed by fire in the late 1950s and rebuilt shortly afterwards. In 1932 and 1933 Knud Rasmussen occupied the attic while filming *Palos Brudefærd* (Palo's Wedding; see p174).

Not so old, but still interesting, is the turf-roofed building known as the **Potato House**. It is a copy of a Greenlandic peat house, which traditionally would have housed between 15 and 25 people. The Potato House, however, was originally built in the mid–20th century for dry storage of vegetables and is still used to store potatoes.

Activities

In winter a small ski lift operates just south of town above the prominent football pitch. Narsuuliartarpiip (Flower Valley) offers excellent cross-country skiing, and ski mountaineering in the surrounding area is usually excellent, with deep powder snow. Hotel guests can hire Nordic skis from Hotel Angmagssalik for Dkr50 per day. The Red House (see Sleeping & Eating, following) hires every type of ski imaginable and can supply all the equipment you will need for a ski tour, including tents, radios, stoves, fuel and food supplies, for Dkr400 per day.

For information on hiking and mountaineering in the area, see p210.

Tours

The only contact you really need in Tasiilaq is Robert Peroni at the Red House. His **Tuning Agency** (☎ 981650; www.eastgreenland.de) arranges socially and ecologically conscious tourism, and works hard to provide jobs and opportunities for local people and preserve the identity of East Greenland and its inhabitants. For low-impact and ethically sound tours or expeditions, this is where you should go.

The company creates tailor-made tours depending on the participant's wishes, skills and experience, and can provide everything from route advice to equipment, radios, fuel and food supplies. Guided hiking trips cost between Dkr100 and Dkr480, two- to three-hour whale-watching trips cost Dkr450, and boat transport to any starting point for a trip costs Dkr800 (the same by dogsled in winter).

EAST GREENLAND

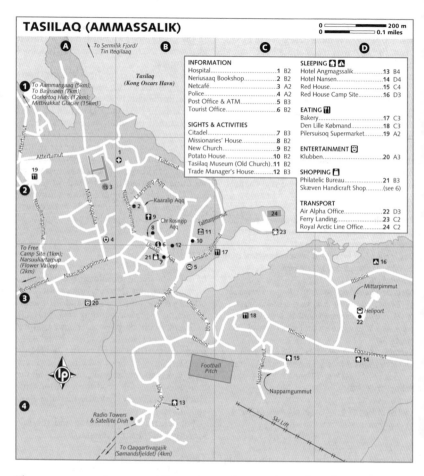

TASIILAQ (AMMASSALIK)

0 ————— 200 m
0 ————— 0.1 miles

INFORMATION
Hospital.....................................1 B2
Neriusaaq Bookshop..................2 B2
Netcafé.....................................3 A2
Police.......................................4 A2
Post Office & ATM....................5 B3
Tourist Office............................6 B3

SIGHTS & ACTIVITIES
Citadel......................................7 B3
Missionaries' House...................8 B2
New Church..............................9 B2
Potato House...........................10 B2
Tasiilaq Museum (Old Church)..11 B3
Trade Manager's House..........12 B3

SLEEPING 🏠 🏕
Hotel Angmagssalik.................13 B4
Hotel Nansen..........................14 D4
Red House...............................15 C4
Red House Camp Site..............16 D3

EATING 🍴
Bakery.....................................17 C3
Den Lille Købmand....................18 B3
Pilersuisoq Supermarket...........19 A2

ENTERTAINMENT 🎭
Klubben...................................20 A3

SHOPPING 🛍
Philatelic Bureau.....................21 B3
Skæven Handicraft Shop.......(see 6)

TRANSPORT
Air Alpha Office.......................22 D3
Ferry Landing...........................23 C2
Royal Arctic Line Office...........24 C2

The company can also arrange tailor-made hunting and dogsledding expeditions (price by agreement) and expeditions on the icecap (from five days to two weeks). It also hires kayaks and skis. For further information on kayaking tours in this area, see p205.

From 1 March to 15 May, Hotel Angmagssalik runs half-day dogsledding trips (Dkr545); one-day trips to Ikateq (Dkr985); and half-/full-day snowmobile tours (Dkr795/985). Nordic ski trips with dogsled support are around Dkr500, including equipment hire. All trips require at least two participants. In summer the hotel offers an iceberg cruise (Dkr295) and five-hour cruises to Ikateq village (Dkr495). Helicopter tours to 900m-high Mittivakkat glacier (Dkr1005) take 10

minutes each way, but allow 30 minutes on the icecap.

Hotel Nansen operates tours from June to September, including a two- to three-day trip to the Tasiilaq mountain hut (Tasiilap Kuua; Dkr3000, three people minimum) at the edge of Kaarali Glacier. This strenuous four- to six-hour hike is suitable for experienced hikers only. Day trips to Polhems Fjeld (Dkr500, three people minimum) include a strenuous three- to five-hour hike to the 1003m summit, which offers incredible views of the icecap and Ammassalik Fjord.

Robert Christensen (☎ 981052) will hire out snowmobiles for Dkr1000 per day, or Dkr250 per hour with driver.

EAST GREENLAND

For boat charter or help finding a local to take you dogsledding or snowmobiling, contact the tourist office.

Festivals & Events
Every July Tasiilaq hosts the **Arctic Team Challenge** (www.atc.gl), a five-day combined stage and expedition race that takes four-person teams over a distance of about 250km and a total elevation of about 9000m of peaks in a series of challenges that include mountain trekking, glacier trekking, icefjord paddling and mountain biking. Only the hardy and seriously fit need apply!

Sleeping & Eating
The best free camp sites are in Narsuuliartarpiip, beginning 1km upstream from Klubben; security may be a problem. The Red House has an organised **camp site** (☎ 981650; Dkr60) near the heliport. The camp site has water and toilets.

Red House (☎ 981650; tuning@greennet.gl; s/d Dkr320/640; ✗ ▣) By far the best value, choice and experience in town, the Red House provides simple but comfortable accommodation in an incredibly friendly house with a fantastic atmosphere. You can also opt for hostel-style beds for Dkr240, and there's a kitchen for self-catering. The restaurant serves excellent traditional food, and nonguests are welcome. Breakfast costs Dkr70, lunch Dkr80 and a four-course traditional Greenlandic dinner Dkr180. For visits to smaller settlements, Red House can arrange accommodation with local families (Dkr150 to Dkr200); it's a fabulous opportunity to experience Greenlandic life first-hand.

Hotel Nansen (☎ 982101; www.hotelnansen.dk; s/d Dkr420/630; ✗ ▣) This bright, comfortable place has functional but comfortable modern rooms and a lovely high-ceilinged restaurant with wonderful views. All rooms have shared bathroom, and there's a kitchen for self-caterers. Rather strangely, the restaurant serves Thai food only (lunch/dinner Dkr90/140).

Hotel Angmagssalik (☎ 981293; arcwon@greennet .gl; s/d Dkr890/1050; ✗) Perched on a rocky outcrop above the town, this large and somewhat soulless hotel offers comfortable rooms and great views, though noise from the bar can be a problem. Rooms with shared bathroom cost Dkr495/695. The restaurant serves a buffet lunch and set dinner for Dkr165.

Self-caterers can resort to the bakery by the harbour, the giant Pilersuisoq supermarket and the after-hours kiosk **Den Lille Købmand** (☒ 11am-8pm).

Entertainment
The pub-disco **Klubben** (☎ 981299; admission Dkr65; ☒ 8-11pm Wed & Thu, to 3am Fri, to 1am Sat) is the best local action spot but may be some way off your idea of a good night out. If you can wangle an invitation from a member, you can get in free.

Both hotels operate rowdy and very sad bars where some locals attempt to drown their sorrows with bucketloads of alcohol until they are unceremoniously kicked out by the management. You'll do yourself and the community no favours by adding to the circus.

Shopping
Skæven handicraft shop (☎ 981543; ☒ 9am-5pm Mon-Fri, noon-4pm Sat) shares a building with the tourist office and stocks a good range of carvings, slippers, jewellery and mitts. Greenland's **Philatelic Bureau** (☎ 981075; www.stamps.gl) is based in Tasiilaq; you'll need to call to make an appointment.

Getting There & Around
AIR
All air access to Tasiilaq is via Kulusuk; the 15-minute **Air Alpha** (☎ 981689) shuttle between Kulusuk and Tasiilaq costs Dkr545. When ice conditions prevent the Royal Arctic Line supply boats from getting through, helicopter transport (all fares Dkr545) is also available to locations around Tasiilaq, including Isortoq, Tiniteqilaaq, Sermiligaaq and Kuummiut. For Air Greenland and Air Iceland tickets, contact Hotel Angmagssalik.

Helicopters may be chartered through Air Alpha for Dkr16,500 per hour.

BOAT
Royal Arctic Line (☎ 981888; ☒ 8am-noon & 1-4pm Mon-Fri) boats carry 12 passengers and travel once weekly between Tasiilaq and Kuummiut (one way Dkr260, 3½ hours), Kulusuk (Dkr205, two hours), Isortoq (Dkr310, five hours), Sermiligaaq (Dkr330, 5½ hours) and Tiniteqilaaq (Dkr270, four hours), stopping for an hour in each village. Ice conditions normally permit them to start running in early July, and the service continues until

routes are no longer passable. You should buy your ticket a day in advance if possible.

AROUND TASIILAQ
Hiking

This region is home to numerous adventurous routes and is truly one of the planet's most spectacular places. The Tasiilaq tourist office sells the excellent 1:100,000 *Hiking Map East Greenland – Tasiilaq* (Dkr300) with a book describing local routes; it also sells a 1:250,000 map (Dkr75). As there's a slight chance of encountering bears, seek local advice before striking out on a longer hike.

NARSUULIARTARPIIP

The easiest day-hike close to town is the excursion up Narsuuliartarpiip (Flower Valley/Blomsterdalen) past the cemetery and along the river. The walk has gentle gradients and a host of Arctic flora on display.

QAQQARTIVAGAJIK (SØMANDSFJELDET)

From the radio towers and satellite dish it's a stiff but straightforward climb up 679m-high Qaqqartivagajik (Sømandsfjeldet). Fit hikers can do the return trip in three hours, but lesser mortals need more time. On clear days, the summit view encompasses Tasiilaq, Kong Oscars Havn, the inland ice and the wild iceberg- and floe-studded coastline – a truly spectacular sight.

BASISSØEN & AAMMANGAAQ LOOP

For a longer hike, there's a compact four-person mountain hut near the shore of Basissøen, northwest of Tasiilaq. Follow the shore northwest from town and cross the footbridge over the large stream that defines the first major valley. Basissøen lies in the next valley, north of the 641m-high peak Aammangaaq (Præstefjeldet). To reach the small hut, you must ford the river. You're now on the route known as the Sermilikvejen. The hut, which isn't exactly obvious, is embedded in the hillside about 20m above the lake.

From the hut, continue past a smaller lake, then up and over the low pass to lake 168 (Icy Lake). Cross the river and follow the lakeshore eastward. You'll reach an abrupt drop where Icy Lake drains into a convoluted

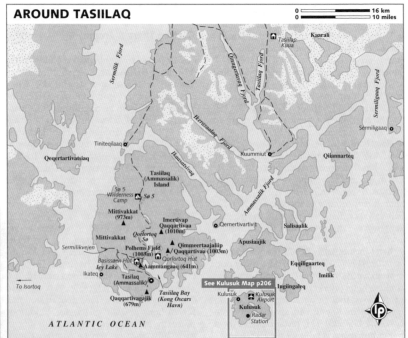

AROUND TASIILAQ

0 — 16 km
0 — 10 miles

tangle of turquoise lakes with a dramatic waterfall that can be heard as a roar from several kilometres away. From here, it's easy going down the slope back to the bridge. This loop takes about seven hours from Tasiilaq.

You can also climb Aammangaaq from the south by going straight up the hillside above the bridge. The top is a bit steep, sandy and slabby. It takes three hours going up and 1½ hours coming down.

AAMMAQQAAQ & THE SØEN

Begin as you would for the Aammangaaq loop, but instead of heading up to Basissøen keep following the shore. Ford the river, and after rounding the northern head of Tasiilaq Bay (Kong Oscars Havn) cross the base of the Aammaqqaaq Peninsula; the free Qorlortoq hut lies over a largish river on the eastern side of the peninsula.

If you continue upstream past the waterfall, you'll reach the enormous Sø 1 (Qorlortoq Sø). Follow the western shore right around to the inflowing stream at its northern end, then turn north and keep climbing up the same valley, always keeping to the western side, past three more lakes, Sø 2, Sø 3 and Sø 4. At the southeastern corner of the fifth lake, Sø 5, is a wilderness camp established by the Tasiilaq tourist office. It consists of three mountain huts and an area for camping; huts cost Dkr300/1500 per day/week.

It's a full-day hike from Tasiilaq.

LONGER HIKES

Longer hiking possibilities include the challenging but classic hike across Dødemandsdalen to Sermilik Fjord. This and a range of other routes are depicted and described in the 1:100,000 *Hiking Map East Greenland – Tasiilaq*.

Mountaineering

A number of guides and tours are available for mountaineering in the area. **Robert Peroni** (☎ 981650; tuning@greennet.gl) at the Red House in Tasiilaq has over 30 years' experience as an accredited mountain guide and has led about 50 worldwide expeditions. He organises accommodation, expedition support (including transport), equipment rental (tents, cooking equipment, GPS, satellite phones, radios, kayaks, skis, pulks, ice axes, crampons, ropes and all the technical-climbing 'ironmongery'), permits, fuel and food. His company can also supply guides qualified with UIAGM (Union Internationale des Associations de Guides de Montagne – the highest professional award in mountaineering).

Hans Christian Florian runs **Mount Forel Expedition Support** (☎ 981320; florian@greennet.gl), a guide service that assists in organising expeditions. He handles permits, fuel and insurance logistics, and organises helicopter and dogsled transport. He can also organise climbs on the highest local peak, 3360m-high Mt Forel, as well as a number of unnamed first ascents and the popular inland ice crossing between Isortoq and Kangerlussuaq. Budget on spending about Dkr750 per day for guided climbs.

Tangent Expeditions International (www.tangent -expeditions.co.uk) organises climbs of Greenland's highest peak, 3730m-high Gunnbjørnsfjeld, including a chartered ski-plane from Akureyri (Iceland), a guide, equipment, food and fuel. The trip costs around £4500 per person (minimum five people). You can also add climbs of the nearby Qaaqaq Kershaw (The Dome; 3700m) or Qaaqaq Johnson (The Cone; 3700m).

TASIILAP KUUA

The mountain hut at Tasiilap Kuua, perched dramatically at the edge of a glacier tongue at 750m, makes an ideal retreat and a base for climbing and mountain hiking. Beds cost Dkr125, and there is access to cooking facilities, but you must bring your own food and sleeping bag. It's accessible by speedboat charter from Tasiilaq for Dkr500 per person. Alternatively, you can take the Royal Arctic Line cargo boat to Kuummiut and arrange a charter from there. It can also be reached by helicopter. For arrangements, contact the keyholder, **Hans Christian Florian** (☎ 981320), in Tasiilaq.

ITTOQQORTOORMIIT (SCORESBYSUND VILLAGE)

pop 500

The world's longest and widest fjord, Kangertittivaq (Scoresbysund) was named for Scottish whaler William Scoresby, who visited in 1822. Near its mouth, Ittoqqortoormiit (Big House) village occupies an area rich in muskoxen, seals and polar bears. It's exaggeratedly nicknamed the Arctic Riviera because its climate is slightly less unstable than elsewhere. But don't expect Cannes.

Ittoqqortoormiit is the only real village for hundreds of kilometres around and sports a neat little red-painted wooden church and a small **museum** (info@ittkom.gl). The main attractions, however, are dogsledding, wonderful fjord-kayaking, and people-watching. Local residents are true Greenlandic hunters, mostly descended from Ammassalik (Tasiilaq) emigrants who sailed north in September 1925.

Facilities remain very limited, and if you arrive without local contacts and a planned itinerary you can't be sure of easily finding guides, kayaks or other necessary equipment. **Nonni Travel** (☎ 461 1841; www.nonnitravel.is) is helpful in making arrangements, and offers dogsledding adventures in Liverpoolland and kayaking tours round Milne Land. **Arcturus** (www.arcturusexpeditions.co.uk) offers sea kayaking around Scoresbysund Fjord's Sydkap and Bear Islands (12 days for £3890, including flights).

Note that plentiful polar bears in this area are more than happy to have a human brunch. Hiking without a rifle is hazardous.

Ittoqqortoormiit time is two hours ahead of the rest of East Greenland and one hour behind Iceland.

Information
Danish Polar Centre (DPC; ☎ 3288 0100; www.dpc.dk)
Ittoqqortoormiit Municipality (www.ittoqqortoormiit .gl/) Has plenty of photos and information on its website.
Post office (☎ 911044; ⏲ 10am-2pm Mon-Thu, 10am-3pm Fri)
Tourist office (☎ 991280; fax 991290; c/o Nonni Travel)

Sleeping & Eating
The seven-room **Ittoqqortoormiit Guesthouse** (☎ 991018; www.simonsen-holtz.dk/; s/d Dkr325/450) is simple but reasonably comfortable with an equipped shared kitchen and communal bathrooms. There's a four-person **house** (per week Dkr3000) to rent 7km south by snowmobile at Kap Tobin hamlet. There's a **Pilersuisoq shop** (☎ 991044) and a Sumaar Kiosk. Camping isn't allowed in the village and would be unwise further afield due to polar bears.

Getting There & Away
All access is via Nerlerit Inaat (Constable Point). The Pilersuisoq shop is the Air Alpha agent in Ittoqqortoormiit.

AROUND ITTOQQORTOORMIIT
This area is great for **mountaineering**. Greenland's highest peak is Gunnbjørnsfjeld (3730m), between Tasiilaq and Ittoqqortoormiit. Fly-in, fly-out ascents are among the trips offered by **Tangent Expeditions** (☎ 1539 737757; www.tangent-expeditions.co.uk) and **Hvitserk** (www.hvitserk.no). For other companies, see p68 and p67. These companies also run expeditions into obscure areas of the Northeast Greenland National Park, giving you a crack at previously unclimbed peaks in the Stauning Alps and Dronning Louise Land. It's best to have some cross-country skiing ability, but most routes are fairly straightforward for experienced mountaineers.

Nerlerit Inaat (Constable Point)
The happy by-product of failed oil-drilling tests was the construction of Nerlerit Inaat

---

THE SIRIUS SLEDGE PATROL

Before satellites, East Greenland's weather stations were essential for predicting Atlantic storms. During WWII this information suddenly attained immense strategic value for transatlantic supply shipping and bomber flights. With Denmark occupied by Germany and no army of its own, Greenland set up a tiny volunteer force to watch for enemy incursions along the 1600km of almost uninhabited east coast. A thrilling mini war ensued, in which a 19-strong German contingent tried to set up their own base on Ella Island. Sniffed out by the barely armed volunteers, the Germans counterattacked and burnt the allied weather station at Eskimoness (now Daneborg).

After the war Denmark's military formalised the East Greenland force, which became the Sirius Sledge Patrol. Such dogsled patrols still watch the coast today, doubling as wardens of the Northeast Greenland National Park.

Patrol members are selected from elite officers of the Danish army and work in pairs. Their harsh two-year stints take them between extraordinarily isolated hunting huts in temperatures that can dip to -50°C. Denmark's Crown Prince Frederik gained enormous local respect for serving on the patrol in 2000.

(Constable Point) airport. There's no village, but the **airport hostel** (☎ 993 850; dm DKr260) and cafeteria operate for stranded or waiting passengers. **Air Iceland** (www.airiceland.is) has triangular services starting in Reykjavík (Iceland). On summer Wednesdays and winter Saturdays it flies first to Constable Point (as the place is designated on the airline's website), then to Kulusuk and then back to Reykjavík (Ikr15,000 to Ikr30,000 each leg). On summer Saturdays and winter Wednesdays the direction reverses. In mid-winter there's only one loop weekly. To reach Ittoqqortoormiit, **Air Alpha** (☎ 993858; www.airalpha.com/greenland.aspx) runs helicopter shuttles (Dkr545) as many times as is necessary to transfer all the passengers from the Air Iceland flight. Air Alpha also operates charter flights to Northeast Greenland National Park for scientists and mountaineers.

In spring you can dogsled the 50km to Ittoqqortoormiit in eight to 10 hours.

Northeast Greenland National Park

Greenland's only national park is also the world's largest, encompassing some 972,000 sq km. That's the entire northeastern quarter of Greenland. Most of the park is icecap and mountaintops, but coastal tundra provides a haven for muskoxen and polar bears, while dramatic fjords shelter walruses and whales. There are no tourist facilities whatsoever. Getting anywhere near it is a full-blown expedition, so only the most determined mountaineers and Arctic researchers tend to make it. Carrying a rifle is obligatory, and you'll require permits issued by the Danish Polar Centre (DPC; see opposite. Apply by December of the year prior to your intended visit. **Arcturus** (www.arcturusexpeditions.co.uk) offers various specialised expeditions.

Access is by Air Alpha charters from Nerlerit Inaat (Constable Point) or direct from Iceland. Monthly **twin-otter flights** (www.dpc.dk/Res&Log/ProjectPlanner/Platforms/Dkhavn.html) supply Danmarkshavn meteorological base via **Zackenberg** (www.zackenberg.dk), where accommodation is available for approved scientists. More scientific facilities are available at Station Nord, 933km from the pole. Apply through the DPC.

Greenland Directory

CONTENTS

ACCOMMODATION

A general overview of accommodation types is given below; more specific details are outlined in reviews in the destination chapters. Where a settlement has many options these are generally grouped by price band (budget then mid-range) and, within those categories, by value for money. Booking ahead is always recommended – not just in summer when availability is tight, but at any time, since many options are unmanned and the owners will need to meet you on arrival to provide keys. Some accommodation operates only in the summer (generally mid-June to early September). There's not usually any seasonal price variation, and rates are generally fixed and non-negotiable.

B&B/Homestays

Homestays offer wonderful insights into family life. While it may be possible to or-ganise your own by asking around, certain tourist offices (notably those in Narsaq, Nuuk, Uummannaq and Upernavik) offer organised B&B schemes. Be aware that none are full-time businesses: they won't operate if the house owner is away or has family staying over. Typical rates are Dkr200 to Dkr325 with breakfast for your own room, or Dkr150 to sleep on a couch.

Camping

With no private land ownership, Greenland has very few restrictions on camping, though you should not camp near water-supply reservoirs or within 20m of histori-cal ruins. Several hostels allow you to camp outside and use their showers and kitchen for around half the price of a bed.

Arctic ecosystems are fragile, and camp-fires are not permitted. There's little chance of finding any wood for one anyway.

Canisters of camping gas are available in small quantities from just a few tourist offices (including those in Narsarsuaq and Nanorta-lik). Methylated spirits (denatured alcohol) is sold in local supermarkets as *Borup Hush-oldnings Spirit 93%*. Petrol *(bensin)* is cheap

---

PRACTICALITIES

- Greenland uses European-style **electric-al plugs**, which have two round pins. The supply is 220V to 240V at 50Hz.

- Trilingual **Suluk**, the semi-annual Air Greenland in-flight magazine, is free from airline offices as well as on aircraft.

- Radio Greenland (KNR) broadcasts a town-by-town **weather forecast** in Eng-lish at 9.10am on summer weekdays.

- **Tipping** is not required in restaurants or in taxis.

- Some **TV films** are in English but sub-titled in Danish (locals joke that Green-landic words are too long!). Teletext page 400 has useful travel and airport information.

- Greenland uses the **metric** system (see the inside front cover for conversions).

at around Dkr2.50 per litre but tends to be very dirty-burning. White spirit (Coleman fuel or Shellite) is known locally as *rense bensin* or *lampeolie* and is sold by some tourist offices, shops and petrol stations. Paraffin (kerosene) stoves can use *lugtfri* petroleum, available from hardware stores and certain supermarkets.

Hotels

Most Greenlandic towns have at least one hotel. Bigger hotels tend to be functionally comfortable if architecturally drab. Many offer older basic rooms with shared bathroom for around Dkr650/950 single/double, and smarter renovated rooms with private toilet and shower unit, towels, TV, kettle and instant coffee for around Dkr900/1200. Smaller hotels don't have reception desks, so booking ahead is often essential. You'll generally be met on arrival. Certain villages use the term 'hotel' rather optimistically to describe an empty house in which you can rent a room for around Dkr200 to Dkr500.

Huts

Dotted about the fjords are a wide variety of cabins and huts. Some are private, and others are run by the local municipality for use by passing hunters and fishermen or for shepherds during round-ups. The public huts are generally unlocked and available for anyone if there's space. In a few cases – for example, around Grønnedal – you should prearrange things and occasionally you'll pay a small fee. Conditions vary from almost uninhabitable to well maintained with oil heaters and bunks. They're often to be found on the sites of otherwise abandoned villages.

School Hostels

During the summer holidays (effectively July), some colleges allow travellers to rent student rooms. Standards vary considerably, but typically you'll have to make arrangements through the local tourism authorities. Prices are roughly the same as for youth hostels. Several schools also have rather basic camping huts in the countryside, which may occasionally allow you refuge.

Seamen's Homes (Sømandshjem)

Five larger Greenlandic towns have a seamen's home – see www.soemandshjem.gl.

Historically, these were created as missions of the Danish Lutheran church to provide clean, safe lodging for transiting sailors and fisherfolk. Although still Christian-oriented, with regulations against alcohol and carousing, in price and quality they are increasingly hard to distinguish from other hotels. All have Danish-style cafeterias where you can usually fill up for around Dkr60.

Service Houses (Servishuset)

As a last resort, certain small villages with no formal accommodation allow visitors to stay in the community's service house. These typically contain a meeting room, a public laundry and showers provided primarily for locals whose houses have no running water. For a youth-hostel style fee you may get a fold-out couch, mattress or rough floor mat. There's zero privacy and minimal comfort. Arrangements can be hit-and-miss, and English is rarely spoken.

Youth Hostels (Vandrehjem)

Many settlements maintain a youth hostel. Some are run by tourist offices, travel agencies or private individuals, but none is affiliated with Hostelling International. Almost all have well-equipped kitchens and communal showers with (sometimes limited) hot water. You'll be expected to bring your own sleeping bag, though sheets are occasionally available, expensively, for hire. There are no curfews; indeed, some hostels are unmanned, and you might simply be given the key on arrival at the airport or port. Prices range from Dkr110 to Dkr325, but Dkr200 is typical.

ACTIVITIES
Fishing

Greenland offers great opportunities to fish for *kapisillik* (salmon) and especially *eqaluk* (Arctic char). The char *(salvelinus alpinus)* is a salmonid fish, and is possibly the ancestor of the trout. Some are resident in lakes, while others battle their way up fast-flowing streams from the fjords to their regular autumn spawning in freshwater lakes and the headwaters of rivers. These fish can weigh up to 8kg. Some 2½ hours by boat from Kangerlussuaq followed by two hours' bushwhacking is a waterfall on the torrential Robinson River (Angujartorfiup), where big char remarkably manage to leap their way up around 8m of cascades. The river provides world-class fly and spinner fishing. More details are available from **Kangerlussuaq Tourism** (www.kangtour.gl) – see p164. Hundreds of kilometres of promising but largely unexplored water is found around Nuuk on the vast Nordlandet Peninsula (p149), and on rivers entering the Godthåbsfjord.

To reach the very best fishing rivers you will usually have to pay boat charters, camp, and trek often considerable distances. However, if you just want to feed yourself it's possible to incorporate char fishing with walking holidays in central and southern Greenland. In certain ponds and rivers, catching a meal is so easy that just a string with an unbaited hook will suffice.

Note that Greenland's char, though abundant, are vulnerable. Anglers should use debarbed hooks and practise catch-and-release for those fish they don't plan to eat.

Some supermarkets and sports stores carry limited supplies of fishing tackle. Non-resident anglers are legally required to buy a fishing licence. These cost Dkr75/200/500 per day/week/month. Application forms are available from tourist offices but the fee should be paid in a post office.

Hiking & Trekking

Greenland offers some of the world's most marvellous trekking for those seeking a total wilderness experience. Except for a few farm tracks in South Greenland, almost all walking is on entirely unmarked routes. On a bright, sunny day it's an incredible feeling of liberty to go bog-hopping at will across glorious moorlands or to wind your own course across gnarled rocky passes. The views are magnificent and the purity of light is magical. There's a mind-blowingly profound silence, broken only by ravens, trickling streams or the reverberating thuds of exploding icebergs.

However, weather can change extremely fast. Once the fog comes down, a jolly afternoon stroll can become a nightmarishly dangerous series of stumbles, so come prepared with at least basic survival gear. In reduced visibility or heavy rain it's easy to get lost, injured or both. Even in good weather you'll need to be adept at reading landscapes. Thick, low-lying vegetation hides ankle-cracking crevasses. Rocks become slippery when wet. Mossy bogs and hidden waterholes abound, and it may be necessary to take long, strenuous routes over lofty ridges or tough boulder fields to avoid dangerous stream crossings. A twisted ankle is unpleasant anywhere, but in Greenland it could prove fatal if you're hiking alone and unequipped – after all, no other hikers are likely to wander past in the next week or month.

The requisite 1:100,000 or 1:75,000 hiking maps are sold locally and are generally very accurate. However, they are not detailed enough to show every minor 10m-high cliff. Most importantly, be aware that dotted lines show 'proposed routes', not clear paths. In some cases these are perfectly navigable; in others they appear to have been simply dreamt up by the cartographer. Even along popular routes the terrain can become suddenly impassable, requiring long detours. Note that all maps show the (very considerable) local deviation between magnetic and geographical north (see p51).

There are trek notes on the backs of the maps, on the www.greenland.com website and in Torbjoern Ydegaard's very dated guidebook *Trekking in Greenland*. Although they are often helpful, occasionally these can be dangerously wrong or no longer applicable, especially regarding the whereabouts of huts and shelters. Always ask local advice before setting out. In recent years, several trekkers have gone missing in Greenland and have never been found. These warnings aren't designed to put you off trekking – there is no better way to appreciate the wilderness – but outdoor skills and careful preparation are important.

Trekkers, even day hikers, should tell someone about their plans and estimated time of return. Do remember to inform them when your trip is complete: rescue helicopters cost around Dkr60,000 per hour, and it's the missing hiker who pays. Forgetting to report arrivals or changed itineraries could very quickly make you poor. Note that crossing the inland ice requires a special permit and compulsory search-and-rescue insurance from the **Danish Polar Centre** (DPC; www.dpc.dk).

Icecap Crossings

Very experienced cross-country skiers can emulate Fridtjof Nansen and join one of the annual expeditions across the inland ice organised by **Tangent Expeditions** (www.tangent-exped itions.co.uk) and **Hvitserk** (www.hvitserk.no). With just white infinity ahead for three exhausting weeks, some claim it's meditation, others that it's wanton masochism. Some crossings are accompanied by dogsled; on others you drag your own supplies.

If you cross the icecap in the far south the chore is much shorter (though still very tough going) and can be combined with trekking through more appealing landscapes. One such tour is offered by **Topas** (www.greenland-discoverer.com).

Icecap Visits

If you just want to touch rather than cross the icecap, that's much easier: hike from Narsarsuaq (p97), cycle from Kangerlussuaq (p162) or boat in from Narsaq (p109) or Tasermiut Fjord (p130).

Kayaking

Greenlandic *qajaq* are the precursors of modern kayaks, and few places in the world are more mindbogglingly beautiful for sea-kayaking than Greenland's inner fjords. Though many people prefer to ship their own, it's increasingly possible to hire equipment locally, typically from tourist offices. However, if you've never paddled before this is not the place to start: renters want an assurance that you're reasonably experienced.

When kayaking, it's important to keep close to land. Good maps and charts are essential, given the sudden sea-fog whiteouts. Rolling icebergs present real dangers, and the tidal wave created can wash your boat and tent off a beach if you don't pull up high enough when camping.

If that hasn't deterred you, great accessible areas to paddle include Tasermiut Fjord (p130), Nuup Kangerlua (p154) and the sheltered sounds around Aasiaat (p183). The Ilulissat area is also superb but seriously bergy. One-way drop-off rentals mean the lovely route from Narsaq (p109) to Narsarsuaq is especially popular.

Mountaineering

Dramatic East Greenland has mountains that are almost as high as the Alps and much more extensive. Many peaks remain unclimbed. Major mountaineering areas are around Tasiilaq (see p206) and in the Stauning Alps (see p212). The **DPC** (☎ 3288 0100; www.dpc.dk) must sanction any mountaineering ventures. This combined with the extreme isolation of the main climbing peaks means that mountaineering expeditions are generally best organised as part of a specialist tour.

Rock Climbing

Unlike mountaineers, rock climbers don't need official DPC clearance. For tradclimbers, Greenland's southern tip is a remarkable paradise of nearly pristine vertical granite. Walls and spires, many still unclimbed, rival those of Yosemite or Patagonia, yet are unusually accessible once you have a boat. Shipping in a couple of Zodiac dinghies will pay off if your group plans to stay a long time; otherwise, reaching different walls will require boat transfers. These must be prearranged, which will reduce your flexibility to attempt new challenges. Niels at the Nanortalik tourist office (p126) is widely acclaimed for his assistance with and understanding of climbers' needs, and can help by receiving your pre-sent gear. Kangerlussuatsiaq (Evighedsfjorden), accessed from Maniitsoq (p155), also has superb climbing.

Many Greenland expedition reports are kept by the **British Mountaineering Council** (www.thebmc.co.uk), and basic trip summaries and planning advice are available online.

Rock Collecting

The world's oldest rocks can be found around Nuuk, and some pretty unique minerals can be sought, notably Tuttupit near Narsaq (p109) and Cryolite's at Ivittuut (p138). Collectors may legally keep samples that are smaller than a fist, but see Legal Matters, p220 for related regulations.

Skiing

Cross-country skiing is possible nearly anywhere in winter, though spring temperatures are less forbidding. For downhill alpine skiing, small ski lifts operate at Grønnedal, Nuuk, Sisimiut and Tasiilaq in spring. Apussuit, near Maniitsoq, offers excellent heliskiing from April to July, but it's predictably expensive. The three-day **Arctic Circle Race** (www.acr.gl) is one of the world's toughest ski races.

Sky Gazing

Especially in the south, Greenland offers great opportunities to enjoy the spectacular aurora borealis (northern lights) from August to April. Walk beyond the areas of street lighting on dark, moonless nights and look above you towards the north.

ADDRESSES

Houses in Greenland generally have building ('B') numbers. As in Japanese towns, these are assigned chronologically, not according to their position along the road. However, some Greenlandic towns use both this system and street numbers in parallel. Thus Egedesvej B146 and Egedesvej 2 could be the same address. Egedesvej 4 would probably be next door, but Egedesvej B148 could be across town. The 'B' number is typically marked with a white-on-blue signplate; the street number (if there is one) with a black-on-yellow one. In smaller settlements the roads are not named.

BUSINESS HOURS

Typical business hours for banks and post offices are 9am to 3pm Monday to Friday. Standard shop hours in Nuuk are 10am to 5.30pm Monday to Thursday, 10am to 6pm on Friday and 10am to 1pm on Saturday. Town supermarkets open from at least 9am to 5.30pm Monday to Friday, and 9am to 1pm Saturday. Some open on Sundays as well. Bakery sections tend to open earlier, often around 7am. Village Pilersuisoq grocery shops generally close by 4pm. A few 'butik' or 'kiosk' shops selling groceries and sweets stay open till 10pm or midnight to cater to those desperate enough to pay mark-ups of up to 50%. By law, alcohol cannot be sold in shops after 6pm on weekdays or after 1pm on Saturday.

CHILDREN

Travelling with children in Greenland is not common, though many hotels can provide extra beds for kids. Most villages have a playground, and in Nuuk there's a floodlit skateboard park outside the youth hostel. Some Westerners might be disturbed by the very laissez-faire attitude of local parents who leave kids to amuse themselves all day entirely without supervision in potentially hazardous environments.

Disposable nappies and powdered baby milk are available in even the smallest village store.

Lonely Planet's *Travel with Children* is a good source of generally applicable trip-planning advice.

CUSTOMS

Travellers over 18 may import 1L of spirits (over 22% alcohol by volume) or 2L of fortified wine (15% to 22% alcohol), 2.25L of wine (under 15% alcohol) and 2L of beer duty free. Anyone over 17 may bring in 250g of tobacco, and 200 cigarette papers or 200 prerolled cigarettes. All travellers are allowed up to Dkr1000 worth of cosmetics and a maximum of 2kg of confectionery. There are various other limits on importing food and drink. Live animals, revolvers and automatic weapons are prohibited, though hunting rifles can be brought in if the airline gives permission.

Any bones or carvings from fin, sperm, blue and humpback whales may not be exported; neither may stuffed white-tailed eagles or even their feathers.

Souvenirs made of West Greenlandic minke whale, beluga whale, narwhal, polar bear, wolf and walrus products may be exported but only with a CITES (Convention on International Trade in Endangered Species of Wild Fauna and Flora) permit. Most relevant shops have such permits prepared. However, if you buy privately you'll need to get local approval or send the item to the **Department of Environment & Nature** (☎ 345050; PO Box 1614, DK-3900 Nuuk) and hope it gets back to you before you depart.

You don't need permits to export seal, caribou and reindeer products, but be sure to check your home country's import regulations; for example, the USA prohibits imports of marine-mammal products, including seal furs.

Anything made before 1940 is considered to be a cultural artefact and requires an export permit from the national museum in Nuuk.

DANGERS & ANNOYANCES

Theft is rare, and violent crime mostly results from family feuds or broken relationships, both of which are highly unlikely to affect most short-term visitors. However, alcohol-fuelled fights, including volleys of beer bottles, are not uncommon in and around pubs, especially on pay-day Friday nights. Drunks can be scarily prone to inexplicable and violent mood swings, so be sensitive in bars and don't stay too late. Rampant sexually transmitted diseases (in 2002 gonorrhoea was more common than flu) should make you cautious about accepting the more intimate forms of Greenlandic hospitality.

Otherwise, most of the dangers found in Greenland come from nature. The perils are only severe if you're not properly prepared or if you ignore local advice. It's crucial to remember just how isolated you are. Twisting an ankle when hiking in the countryside could become a major catastrophe if nobody knows where you are: there's virtually no hope of anyone just wandering by. The conditions are extremely fickle, and you should be well prepared for cold and wet weather. Fog can descend suddenly, so while hiking you'd be wise to keep a stock of food and a survival bag in case you get caught and can't find your way back.

'If you don't fear the sea, you won't last a year in Greenland,' say local fisherfolk. If people tell you that the sea is too rough to go out, believe them. Even if it means missing a key excursion, it's not wise to push a reluctant boatman to make an unsafe journey. Small boats are easily swamped in strong winds, and the seas are so cold that your chances of swimming even a short distance to shore would be tiny. Flotation suits give you a few extra minutes to contemplate death should your boat sink. Even if you do make it to land, the chances of being rescued before you become hypothermic are minimal. There is a lifeboat-style rescue service, but it comprises only four boats for all of Greenland. Even helicopter rescues can take several hours – as well as tens of thousands of dollars – to reach you.

Polar bears are very rare and they generally avoid humans. Where they are a hazard locals will advise you to carry a gun and might lend you one. If you're cornered by a bear when unarmed, try to keep your cool (see p90).

Be careful how you store food when camping, to avoid attracting foxes.

Major summer annoyances are clouds of mosquitoes, midges and mini-flies, which seek out eardrums, shoot up nostrils and make kamikaze attacks on eyeballs. They're at their worst in July, especially on wilderness hikes, when a head-net is virtually essential. Head-nets are widely sold for around Dkr40, some designs working best when worn over a baseball-style cap. Insects are curiously absent in sheep-farming areas, and fortunately few seem to come indoors. At night you'll rarely be bothered, and by mid-September most have disappeared.

DISABLED TRAVELLERS

Greenland is likely to be a challenge to disabled or infirm travellers. Except in Nuuk, lifts (elevators) are virtually unknown. In many towns stairways abound and streets are by no means always paved. Getting aboard ferries, planes and helicopters usually involves steps, and boarding smaller boats can involve some minor acrobatics. For the less able a cruise is often the favoured option. However, even on certain expensive excursions from cruise ships, some passengers have expressed surprise at the need to walk sometimes considerable distances as well as at the total absence of public toilets in remote areas. Don't expect bushes, either!

EMBASSIES

Greenland is represented abroad by Danish embassies and consulates. Consult www.um.dk/en for a full listing. There are no embassies in Greenland, though Finland, Iceland, the Netherlands, Norway and Sweden each have honorary consuls in Nuuk.

FESTIVALS & EVENTS

Celebrations and sighs of relief mark the end of northern Greenland's polar night, when the sun finally returns after its sojourn below the horizon. This occurs in mid-January in Ilulissat, in early February in Upernavik and in late February in Qaanaaq. Around Easter, villages north of the Arctic Circle hold dogsled races accompanied by general festivities.

Aasivik (Summer Settlement) was once a gathering of disparate Inuit groups meeting up in the warm summer months to trade, meet friends and tell stories. It was revived in modern guise in 1976 as two alcohol-free weeks of 'fresh air and fresh thought', a social and political gathering protesting against 'missionary culture' and encouraging traditional theatre, drum dances and folk music. Over the years it became more like a pop festival and eventually petered out altogether. However, a revival is likely in July 2006, its 30th anniversary.

In summer some South Greenland towns and villages hold a sort of sheep rodeo that includes shearing, herding and other ovine-related competitions. In early August, the first day at school is a big event. New scholars are formally introduced to academic life, shaking hands with the head teacher while being cheered on by their families in the school grounds. Many people wear national dress and throw fistfuls of coins into the crowd.

HOLIDAYS

July is the main holiday season, with long days and temperatures at their warmest. However, transport and hotels fill up, flies and mosquitoes are at their peak, and the weather is not ideal. Late August is colder, but it's more appealing overall. In September many Greenlanders take time off to hunt reindeer.

Public Holidays

Public holidays observed in Greenland:
New Year's Day 1 January
Epiphany 6 January
Easter Maundy Thursday, Good Friday and Easter Monday (March or April)
Labour Day 1 May
Common Prayer's Day Four weeks after Good Friday
Ascension Six weeks after Maundy Thursday
Whitmonday Seven weeks after Easter Monday
National Day, Ullortuneq (Longest Day) 21 June
Christmas Eve 24 December
Christmas Day 25 December
Boxing Day 26 December
New Year's Eve 31 December (afternoon only)

INSURANCE

Although it's part of Denmark, Greenland is not covered by the European E111 mutual-health-insurance scheme. Arrange your own cover. Travel insurance covering delays, missed connections and incomplete holidays is particularly advisable, as the weather simply can't be relied upon. Check that your policy covers any kayaking, climbing or hiking activities that you might plan.

Visitors from the Americas should also carefully check the small print on their fly-me-home coverage. Many policies (even those tailored for expensive cruises) only cover evacuation flights that head in the direction of home. However, to reach the Americas from Greenland you must almost inevitably fly first to Copenhagen or Iceland and then double back. That's not your fault, but it breaks the rules and can thus result in a very expensive exclusion. See also p330 for further information about health insurance.

INTERNET ACCESS

Almost every town has had an Internet club at some point during recent years. However, few such ventures proved profitable and many closed forthwith. Public Internet access remains hit-and-miss and will generally cost a hefty Dkr40 to Dkr100 per hour. Richer locals increasingly have their own computers connected to the web for a tiny fraction of that cost. Schools and libraries are often online and sometimes allow free public use.

Accessing the Internet using a laptop is hopeless unless you subscribe to the local ISP, which is called **Greennet** (☎ 341255; www .greennet.gl, not in English).

LAUNDRY

Some hostels have washing machines. There are usually laundry services in hotels, but these are sometimes scarily expensive. In small villages public washing machines (Dkr20 per load) and dryers (Dkr10) are found in the service house (see p215), and you can buy individual tokens. In bigger towns they lurk in unpleasant housing blocks and you'll need a *Vaskekort til Vaskeriet* (a prepaid magnetic strip-card giving you Dkr50 or Dkr100 of wash-or-dry credit, which is generally more than you'll need as a passing traveller). Inconveniently, the cards are almost never sold on site, so you'll usually have to go to the nearest Brugsen supermarket to buy one. To save money, bring some soap powder and do your laundry by hand.

LEGAL MATTERS

It's forbidden to disturb historic or prehistoric sites by camping or removing stones. Finds of potential archaeological interest should be reported to the **National Museum** (☎ 322611) in Nuuk (p147), which also has sole authority to grant export licences for cultural artefacts, including anything made before 1940.

As part of the effort to conserve Greenland's wildlife, the export of certain animal products is controlled or completely banned (see Customs, p218).

Tourists need permits for hunting and fishing (see p216). For mountaineering expeditions, visits to the icecap (p216) or permits for the Northeast Greenland National Park (p213), apply well ahead to the **DPC** (☎ 3288 0100; www.dpc.dk; Strandgade 100, DK-1401 Copenhagen, Denmark).

Soft drugs, including marijuana, are illegal, and although locals seem to indulge in the latter with relative impunity, users do occasionally get arrested.

Police are generally low key and friendly. The prison system is perhaps the world's most liberal (see the boxed text, below).

MAPS

Saga Maps products cover Greenland's coastal areas with reasonable 1:250,000-scale topographical clarity for around Dkr80 per sheet. They are ideal for general travellers, although their use of old spellings and place names can be confusing. There's a discount for regional sets. Three special tourist sheets for the Eastern Settlement (far south), Western Settlement (Nuuk Fjord area) and Ammassalik Area (east coast) add historical information and some archaeological plans of the main Norse ruin sites.

If you're planning on going hiking you'll need Greenland Tourism's more detailed 1:75,000 or 1:100,000 trekking maps (see p216).

The relevant maps are almost always available for sale from local tourist offices. Virtually all are stocked by a shop in Kangerlussuaq Airport and by Nuuk's

bookshop **Atuagkat Boghandel** (☎ 321737; www .atuagkat.gl). Atuagkat Boghandel also offers mail order. Although its online ordering system is scarily lacking in confirmation messages or cancellation possibilities, maps arrive safely, and the postage charge (which is not quoted on the site) is only Dkr16 per map.

MONEY
Currency

Greenland's currency is the same as Denmark's: the generally stable Danish krone (Dkr), which is equal to 100øre. Exchange rates are listed inside the front cover of this book. As there is no coin smaller than 25øre, cash registers automatically round totals up or down. Thus if an item is Dkr9.95 you'll save a tiny sum by buying three at once. For costs, see p10.

Exchanging Money

Travellers cheques are a poor idea in Greenland. You'll pay a Dkr75 commission to change them, and even then that's usually only possible at Grønlandsbanken in Nuuk, Qaqortoq, Maniitsoq, Sisimiut and Ilulissat. Changing cash (euros, US dollars and other major currencies) is cheaper (Dkr30), and where there's no bank it's generally possible in post offices. Even in the smallest branches, confused clerks can eventually manage this after a flurry of telephone calls. Still, it's wise to carry plenty of krone with you.

ATMs

With most common credit or debit cards you can withdraw money using ATMs at banks and a few bigger post offices. However, most are inside, and even hole-in-the-wall ATMs generally close between 6pm and 6am.

NAUGHTY BOY

The cheapest hotel in Greenland is Nuuk prison. While the most dangerous criminals are exported to Denmark's 'real jails', most other offenders are generally locked up only at night. By day many hold down jobs, make unescorted shopping trips and – most remarkably – even go on the annual reindeer hunt. That's right: they're given a gun. Well, as long as they're not drunk. This apparently lenient system makes more sense in Greenland, where there's effectively nowhere to run and so little incentive to escape. However, some provincial businesses dread Christmas, when prisoners come home for the holidays. Festive raids to steal alcohol can cost store owners much more in repairing the structural damage than in losing the value of the stolen booze.

Credit Cards

Major credit cards are accepted at better restaurants, hotels and shops, and at most tourist offices. Supermarkets and Pilersuisoq shops usually say that they take credit cards, and they can give cash back with purchases, but in smaller settlements the card-readers are frequently out of order, so you should have back-up cash.

POST

The postal rates for airmail postcards and letters weighing less than 20g are Dkr5 within Greenland and Dkr5.50 to most other countries. When sending mail poste restante, include the postcodes (DK-3920 for Qaqortoq, DK-3900 for Nuuk, DK-3952 Ilulissat for Disko Bay and DK-3913 Tasiilaq for East Greenland). It will help to speed things along if you add 'via Denmark' at the end of the address.

SHOPPING

Archetypal Greenlandic souvenirs are the work of local craftspeople. They include beadwork, seal-fur items and carvings, notably *tupilak*-style figures (p86). Fine local jewellery is made from local ivory, bone, antler and silver-set gemstones. Unusual Greenlandic gems include rare pink Tuttupit, which comes from Narsaq (see p109), and black Nuumiit, nicknamed the 'Greenland opal', which comes from around Nuuk. Virtually every town has a craft shop – they're often found within hotels or tourist offices. Paamiut has some of the cheapest crafts and is exaggeratedly famous for soapstone carvings. *Tupilaks* are generally better value in East Greenland. Nuuk and Qaqortoq are best for modern art. Before you buy any such souvenirs, refer to the information listed under Customs, p218.

CDs of Greenlandic music (p87) make interesting cultural souvenirs.

TELEPHONE

Greenland's country code is ☎ 299. There are no area codes, even for mobile telephones. To access an international line (including a line to Denmark), dial ☎ 00, followed by the desired country code, the area code and the telephone number. The directory assistance number is ☎ 118, and each call costs Dkr3.

Mobile, Satellite & Radio Telephones

Your mobile-phone company is unlikely to offer roaming service in Greenland. However, if it does the costs can prove to be exorbitant, so be sure to check with them before you go. The best idea is to bring your GSM telephone and buy a Tusass pay-as-you-go SIM card. For Dkr400 you get a local Greenlandic number and Dkr100 of call credit. Dial ☎ 801010 to check your credit balance. However, GSM phones only work in towns and major settlements or within direct sight of them for a range of approximately 30km. Satellite phones can be rented if you're planning a major expedition. Boats, hunters and even a few hostels beyond telephone range use VHF radios. To be put through, dial ☎ 130 (Aasiaat/Disko), ☎ 131 (Qaqortoq/South), or ☎ 132 (Ammassalik/East). Then give the recipient's radio-code name or number.

Call Costs

One-minute calls to Europe or North America cost Dkr2.04/2.79 from a private line/Tusass mobile. For calls to most other countries you'll pay Dkr2.89/3.64, but it's vastly more expensive to various Pacific islands, North Korea, Cuba, Guinea Bissau and Ascension Island (Dkr15/15.75). Pay phones are coin operated. You'll need a minimum of Dkr2 for a local call and at least Dkr10 to call internationally. Calling to/from satellite phones costs Dkr15/6.90 per minute.

TIME

Most of Greenland is three hours behind GMT, but note that Ittoqqortoormiit is one hour behind GMT, and Pituffik and Qaanaaq are four hours behind GMT. Between early April and late October, daylight-saving time adds one hour.

TOURIST INFORMATION

The national tourist information agency is **Greenland Tourism** (☎ 342820; www.greenland.com; PO Box 1615, Hand Egedesvej, DK-3900 Nuuk). Its superb website is a sensible starting point for all travel planning requirements. Greenland Tourism also publishes several beautiful, glossy brochures and the extremely helpful, free mini-guidebook *Explore Greenland*, which summarises the key practical information and tour options. If you're writing or phoning from abroad you'll generally find it cheaper to deal with the extremely well-organised **Copenhagen office** (☎ 3283 3880; fax 3283 3889; www.greenland.com; PO Box 1139, Strandgade 91, PO Box 1139, DK-1010 Copenhagen K, Denmark). If you're looking for information in your own country, Danish tourist offices (listed on www.visitdenmark.com) can also assist.

Local Tourist Offices

Most towns have their own tourist offices, often with helpful multilingual staff. Levels of efficiency, professionalism and usefulness vary, but several offer organised trips, homestays, free town maps and plenty of local tips. It's well worth emailing questions and tour bookings months ahead of your planned visit. In off-seasons the offices aren't busy, and the most imaginative tourist offices can help individual travellers by pairing up those with similar interests so that both can save on boat-charter expenses. A great deal depends on the manager, however. Technically, the tourist office is not allowed to organise anything on (relatively cheap) boats that aren't officially approved and insured for tourists, but they are allowed to give you contacts for such boats. Whether they will do so is the real question, as tourist offices are currently being semiprivatised and have an increasing incentive to mention only their own official tours.

Most better tourist offices have a decent shop selling regional maps, hiking maps, souvenirs and relevant books.

In a few smaller towns the term 'tourist office' may in fact be a metaphorical hat worn by a distracted employee in the town office. These folks rarely speak English.

Hotels, seamen's homes and certain youth hostels also provide more basic tourist information, and might distribute local maps and brochures.

Weather

Weather forecasts are broadcast in English on KNR radio at 9.10am from Monday to Friday during summer. You can view the fairly reliable weather charts available on http://theyr.net by choosing Grønland. DMI ice maps are available online at www .dmi.dk/dmi/index/gronland/iskort.htm (see p89).

WOMEN TRAVELLERS

Single women travelling in Greenland don't generally encounter any special worries, hassles or funny looks that non-local men wouldn't also have to deal with. There's no need to mention a mythical husband as there might be in certain parts of the world. Staying late at a bar is not advised, however, and you might feel somewhat pestered as the beers chug down.

Tampons are available in even the smallest village stores.

VISAS

The tourist entry requirements for Greenland are similar to the entry requirements for Denmark, but be aware that Greenland is not in the EU or a party to the pan-European Schengen visa agreement. To enter Greenland, citizens of Nordic countries need only a valid identification card. Three-month visa-free stays are available to citizens of EU nations, Australia, New Zealand, Canada, the USA, Japan, South Korea, Singapore, Brunei, Israel and several central-European and Latin American countries. Most ex-Soviet and African nationals require a Danish visa. South Africans should apply at the **Royal Danish Embassy** (☎ 12-430 9340, 342 7620; www.denmark.co.za; Parioli Office Park, Block B2, Ground Fl, 1166 Park St, Hatfield 0028, Pretoria, South Africa) or the Danish consulate in Cape Town.

It is a requirement that all tourists applying for Danish visas must show bank-account details proving 'sufficient funds', a confirmed itinerary with accommodation bookings (or detailed explanations if you plan to camp) and proof of medical insurance coverage of at least €30,000. Before the visa is issued you'll also be expected to show a return ticket, though buying one isn't advised until the visa is approved. Note that you're supposed to apply in your country of residence. The Dkr260-equivalent application fee won't be refunded in case of visa refusal. Full regulations are listed on www.udlst.dk but upon consultation may prove to be somewhat flexible according to specific circumstances. The addresses of Danish embassies are listed on www.um.dk.

Technically, even those tourists who aren't required to have a visa must show that they have 'sufficient funds' for their intended length of stay. However, customs and immigration formalities are normally rudimentary or nonexistent if you're entering Greenland on a standard flight from Denmark or Iceland, unless you look particularly different.

Greenland Transport

GETTING THERE & AWAY

Technically it would be possible to reach Siorapaluk, the northernmost settlement in Greenland, from Canada's Ellesmere Island – either overland across the ice, as Inuit outlaw Qitdlaq did in the 1860s (see p21) – or by kayak, like Jon Turk in the 1990s. Either will be an epic adventure – read Jon Turk's book *Cold Oceans* before you decide to attempt it. Otherwise, unless you're on a cruise, command your own boat or have sledded in from the North Pole, the only practical way to Greenland is by air. Most options are from Copenhagen (Denmark), but in summer there are limited connections from Iceland plus a handful of charter flights from Canada and Germany – at least, in some years.

ENTERING GREENLAND

Arrival in Greenland is remarkably low key. Passports aren't stamped, and you might not even notice that you've passed through customs at all. Before you do so, use the on-arrival duty-free shop to stock up on relatively cheap booze. It will make great presents even if you don't drink yourself. For visa information, see p223.

AIR
Airports & Airlines

Greenland's main international airports are at **Kangerlussuaq** (code SFJ; see p162) and **Narsarsuaq** (code UAK; ☎ 665266; see p97). Departure tax is paid when purchasing tickets.

The only scheduled airlines licensed to serve Greenland:

Air Greenland (code GL; ☎ Greenland 343434, Denmark 3231 4223; www.airgreenland.com) The national carrier.

Air Iceland (code NY; ☎ 570 3030; www.airiceland.is; hub Reykjavík)

SAS (code SK; ☎ Denmark 7010 2000, Greenland 841030, UK 0870-6072 7727, USA 800-221 2350; www.scandinavian .net; hub Copenhagen) Not operating to Greenland at the time of writing, but plans future code-sharing with Air Greenland.

From Denmark

Year-round Air Greenland flies from Copenhagen to Kangerlussuaq four times weekly and to Narsarsuaq weekly. In summer there are two extra services on both routes. Either cost Dkr3607 one way (around €485). Standard return fares cost double. However, various discounts are available for unchangeable advance-purchase returns and for families travelling together. Booking six months ahead can net a considerable discount. It's well worth signing up online for Air Greenland's email bulletins; these sometimes alert you to discounts of up to 70%.

Travelling from Copenhagen to Nuuk involves a change, and costs Dkr4285 via Kangerlussuaq and Dkr4955 via Narsarsuaq.

THINGS CHANGE...

Wherever you travel, exact transport details are vulnerable to change. This is particularly true for Greenland. The details given accurately reflect the connections in 2004, but from year to year the carriers operating to Greenland as well as the timetables they use can vary greatly. Use the information here as a guide to the sorts of possibilities to investigate, but check www.greenland .com to see whether services have been expanded, cancelled or rerouted.

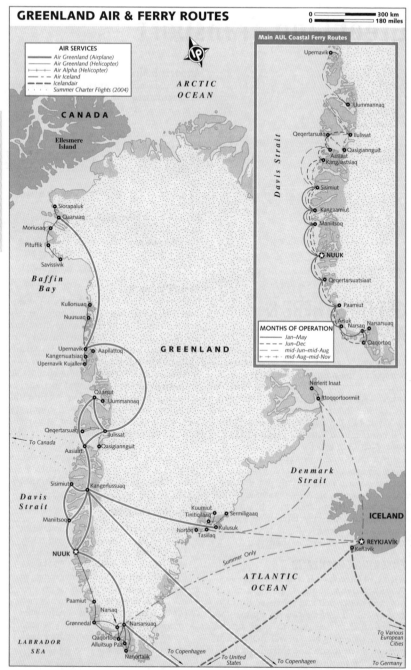

GREENLAND AIR & FERRY ROUTES

GREENLAND TRANSPORT

0 — 300 km
0 — 180 miles

AIR SERVICES
Air Greenland (Airplane)
Air Greenland (Helicopter)
Air Alpha (Helicopter)
Air Iceland
Icelandair
Summer Charter Flights (2004)

Main AUL Coastal Ferry Routes

Upernavik

Uummannaq

Qeqertarsuaq — Ilulissat
Qasigiannguit
Aasiaat
Kangaatsiaq

Sisimiut

Kangaamiut

Maniitsoq

NUUK

Qeqertarsuatsiaat

Paamiut

Arsuk
Narsaq — Narsarsuaq
Qaqortoq

MONTHS OF OPERATION
Jan–May
Jun–Dec
mid-Jun–mid-Aug
mid-Aug–mid-Nov

Davis Strait

ARCTIC OCEAN

CANADA

Ellesmere Island

Siorapaluk
Qaanaaq
Moriusaq
Pituffik
Savissivik

Baffin Bay

Kullorsuaq
Nuusuaq

Upernavik
Kangersuatsiaq
Upernavik Kujalleq
Aapilattoq

GREENLAND

Qaarsut
Uummannaq

Qeqertarsuaq
Ilulissat
Aasiaat
Qasigiannguit

To Canada

Sisimiut
Kangerlussuaq

Davis Strait

Maniitsoq

Nerlerit Inaat
Ittoqqortoormiit

Denmark Strait

Kuummiut
Tiniteqilaaq
Sermiligaaq
Isortoq
Tasiilaq
Kulusuk

ICELAND

REYKJAVÍK
Keflavík

NUUK

Paamiut
Narsaq
Grønnedal
Narsarsuaq
Qaqortoq
Alluitsup Paa
Nanortalik

LABRADOR SEA

Summer Only

ATLANTIC OCEAN

To Copenhagen
To United States
To Copenhagen
To Germany
To Various European Cities

GETTING TO DENMARK
Kastrup Airport (www.cph.dk) is 9km from the centre of Copenhagen. Trains run every 20 minutes to the central station (approximately €3, 13 minutes). Copenhagen is globally well connected, notably by airline **SAS** (www.scandinavian .net), part of the Star Alliance, and throughout Europe by budget airline **Maersk** (☎ 7010 7474; www.maersk-air.com). UK-based **EasyJet** (www .easyjet.com) flies to Copenhagen from London Stansted, Bristol, Newcastle and Berlin. Curiously, Norwegian airline **Wideroe** (www.wideroe .no) has a booking engine which covers several other airlines (including Maersk and SAS) and can sometimes give better prices out of Copenhagen than the airlines themselves.

Another cheap way to reach Copenhagen is by using **Ryanair** (www.ryanair.com) low-cost flights from London Stansted to **Malmö Sturup Airport** (www.lfv.se). Malmö is in Sweden, but it's easily accessed from Copenhagen via the remarkable 16km Øresund tunnel-bridge link. Connecting Flybus 737 (€15, 45 minutes) takes you directly to Copenhagen central train station. **Malmo Aviation** (www.snalsk jutsen.com) has seasonal bargain flights from Malmö to Glasgow, Nice and Stockholm.

SLEEPING IN COPENHAGEN
Many passengers will be effectively forced to spend the night in Copenhagen. In the airport complex itself is a **Hilton hotel** (☎ 3250 1501; fax 3252 8528; www.hilton.com; s/d/tw Dkr1700/1700/1700). If they bed down tidily, ultra-budget travellers with next-day flight tickets are permitted to sleep till 7am in the seating area opposite the airport's main left-luggage office (between terminals 2 and 3).

In Copenhagen city a great room-finding service is available at **Use-It** (☎ 3373 0620; www .useit.dk; 13 Rådhusstraede; ⊙ 9am-7pm mid-Jun–mid-Sep, 11am-4pm Mon-Thu & 11am-2pm Fri rest of yr), which also offers free Internet. The **tourist information office** (☎ 7022 2442; www.visitcopenhagen .dk; 4A Vesterbrogade; ⊙ 9am-4pm Mon-Fri & 9am-2pm Sat Sep-Apr, 9am-6pm Mon-Sat May-Jun, 9am-8pm Mon-Sat & 10am-6pm Sun Jul-Aug) can also help. It charges Dkr60 per booking but is conveniently close to the train station (facing the entrance to Tivoli) and also has an **airport desk** (☎ 3231 2447; terminal 3; ⊙ 6am-midnight).

From Iceland
Twice weekly from mid-June till early September, Air Iceland fly into Narsarsuaq (South Greenland) from Reykjavík (Iceland). Paperless tickets can be booked online, though the website can be somewhat temperamental – if you don't get a confirmation message on the Step 5 page, don't panic. Send an email, and Air Iceland can organise the booking manually. The flights cost Ikr30,000 (around €340) each way, but if you book well ahead and stay less than a month it's possible to get half-price bonus fares. If you wait till June to book a summer trip, there may not be any space left whatsoever, though those prepared to gamble can occasionally find last-minute bargains. Air Iceland also flies from Reykjavík to Kulusuk (see p204), and from Reykjavík to Nerlerit Inaat (Constable Point) once or twice weekly all year. The fare to Nerlerit Inaat is Ikr30,000 one way. From Kulusuk only, it's possible to continue to the rest of Greenland, but only at considerable expense. The summer flights to Kulusuk allow you to make a token day return to Greenland, a possibility offered by many tourist agencies in Iceland.

Air Iceland flights leave from **Reykjavík City Airport** (code RKV; ☎ 569 4100), which is a walkable 1.5km from BSI, Reykjavík's bus terminal, or Ikr500 by taxi. From central Reykjavík or the youth hostel take bus No 5.

Don't confuse Reykjavík City Airport with **Keflavik (Reykjavík International) Airport** (code KEF; www.keflavikairport.com), where virtually all of Iceland's other international flights arrive. That's some 50km to the west. Bus transfers from Keflavik to BSI cost Ikr1100; they depart around 25 minutes after each plane arrives, even late at night.

GETTING TO ICELAND
Generally, the cheapest way to reach Iceland is to fly from London Stansted to Keflavik on low-cost airline **Iceland Express** (☎ 550 0600; www.icelandexpress.com), which has one-way fares as low as UK£68, taxes included. Reaching Stansted from the rest of Europe is easy with a wide variety of low-cost airlines, whose fares are often cheaper than the train from central London. Iceland Express also has fares from Copenhagen to Keflavik for around €100. Iceland's national carrier, **Icelandair** (www.iceland air.net), has much more comprehensive connections to 16 European cities and five American destinations (Minneapolis-St Paul, New York, Boston, Baltimore-Washington

and Orlando). It can prove cost-effective to fly transatlantic on Icelandair, using its Iceland stopover as an opportunity to visit Greenland. Icelandair's London–Keflavik fares have fallen considerably to compete with Iceland Express.

SLEEPING IN REYKJAVÍK

Reykjavík Tourist Information Centre (☎ 590 1500; www.visitReykjavík.is; Adalstraeti 2; 🕙 9am-6pm Mon-Fri, 10am-4pm Sat & 10am-2pm Sun mid-Sep–May, 8.30am-7pm daily Jun–mid-Sep) has a free booking service and an extremely comprehensive accommodation listing on its website. The airport bus from Keflavik will, on request, continue past several town-centre hotels to terminate at the superbly friendly and eco-aware **City Youth Hostel** (☎ 553 8110; www.hostel.is; Sundlaugavegur 34; dm/tw lkr1600/4200).

Keflavik airport stays open all night, but Reykjavík City Airport does not.

From Canada

Great Canadian Travel (☎ 204 949 0199, toll free 0800 661 3830; www.greatcanadiantravel.com) operates a handful of summer charter flights between Canada and Greenland. In 2005 departures are 10 July and 17 July from Iqaluit (airport code YFB) on Nunavut's Baffin Island to Aasiaat (code JEG) on Disko Bay, with returns a week later (one way/return C$650/1440). In August 2004 there were three additional flights from Ottawa to Kangerlussuaq via Iqaluit. Flight-only tickets are sold only as a fallback for seats not filled by the company's tour groups.

From Germany

In 2004 **Troll Tours** (☎ 82 92210; www.trolltours .de, in German) operated direct flights between Frankfurt and Kangerlussuaq (Greenland) for the bargain price of €699 return. Sadly, these were dropped in 2005 but may be re-started in future years. Check the website just in case.

SEA

There are no ferries to Greenland. Royal Arctic Line cargo ships run roughly once a week from Aalborg (Denmark), but will not accept passengers. Yachtsmen should not underestimate the severity of weather conditions. Keep a careful eye on current **DMI ice reports** (www.dmi.dk/dmi/index/gronland /iskort.htm; see p88). **Imray** (www.imray.com) sells

---

Arctic Pilot charts (NP11 for Greenland's east coast, NP12 for the west coast) and the *Faroe, Iceland and Greenland* pilotage publication.

Cruises

Cruises are inevitably expensive, but – when you consider Greenland's often awkward and pricey travel connections – they don't necessarily cost much more than equivalent land-based tours. Options are listed on p65. Prices vary enormously according to comfort levels and the number of stops. Be aware that ice conditions can force disappointing route changes.

TOURS

At least 90 international operators appear to offer such a surprisingly wide range of organised tours that you might imagine Greenland to be swarming with tour groups. In reality, the majority simply get their customers to a Greenland airport, where they are passed on to Arctic Adventure (in the south) or other local agencies further north. Even then you won't necessarily find yourself in a huge group. Indeed, if you choose remote options and less popular dates you might have parts of the tour to yourself. One major advantage of coming on a tour is that (weather permitting) your guaranteed-departure excursions and transfers will be honoured even when there are not enough customers to fill a boat. In similar circumstances independent travellers usually find their trips cancelled. The major tour operators:

Arctic Adventure (www.arctic-adventure.dk) Greenland's biggest private agency. Arctic Adventure offers various Greenland tours, especially in the south. Its excursions and guide services are repackaged and sold by various agents throughout the world. Use the contacts listed on its website to find a relevant tour starting in your home country.

Great Canadian Travel Company (☎ 204 949 0199; www.greatcanadiantravel.com) Charter flights direct from Canada make its tours convenient and cost-effective.

Grønlands Rejserburo (Greenland Travel; ☎ 3313 1011; www.greenland-guide.gl)

Topas Tours (☎ 3311 6922; www.greenland-discoverer .com) Offers specialised hiking and adventure tours with its own team of very knowledgeable guides. These allow you to stay in some of the more remote sheep stations and do the classic treks without the dangers of hiking unsupported.

Troll Tours (☎ 2982-92210; www.trolltours.de) Uses direct charter-flight tours from Germany.

GETTING AROUND

Many tourists mistakenly believe that travelling in Greenland is only possible on a tour. In fact, public helicopters and coastal ferries offer truly splendid ways to see much of the country's great scenery. However, be flexible. Weather conditions mean you simply can't assume that a service will leave on time (or even on the scheduled day). The great Greenlandic word *immaqa* (maybe) is a necessary caveat. Greenland's national airline is commonly nicknamed Immaqa Air.

AIR

Considering its climate, huge size and minuscule population, Greenland is remarkably well served by air links. The main network is operated by **Air Greenland** (☎ 343434; www.airgreenland.com). **Air Alpha** (www .airalpha.com/greenland.aspx) runs a few helicopter connections to the east coast and around Ilulissat, and the Kulusuk – Nerlerit Inaat (Constable Point) route is, curiously, offered by **Air Iceland** (www.airiceland.is).

Unless otherwise stated, fares and flight frequencies quoted in this book are for one-way summer travel. In winter, flights are less frequent, and *immaqa* really comes into its own.

Be aware that, technically, Air Greenland's 20kg baggage allowance includes your hand baggage. Although it's not always strictly enforced, some agents will hit you for even a single excess kilogram. Airport taxes are paid with your ticket purchase, along with an often hefty ticketing charge. Helicopter tickets and all purchases online through Air Greenland's website are presently exempt from this ticketing fee, though a charge is planned eventually. Note that web bookings are not e-tickets: you must pick up the paper tickets at the location you stated when booking online. Hopefully, this silly situation will change.

Helicopter flights in the south are bookable online, but regional village services in the north and east don't appear on general timetables. Village helicopter-shuttle services from Uummannaq, Upernavik and Qaanaaq cost the same flat fee regardless of actual distance flown.

BICYCLE

As long-distance transport a bike is useless. However, some consider it worth hiring one of the somewhat ropy rental bikes available in Narsaq (p109), Qassiarsuk (p104), and particularly Kangerlussuaq (p162), from which a rideable track goes all the way to the inland ice. In Nuuk (p144) there's enough asphalt to keep you pedalling for half a day, and there are some harsh off-road tracks in the surrounding region.

BOAT
Cargo Boat

On a few routes where there is no alternative service, the cargo ships of **Royal Arctic Bygdeservice** (www.ral.gl/royalarctic/dk/rab.htm, in Danish) are permitted to carry a few paying passengers. Tickets are sold through regional AUL offices, but schedules are not widely distributed. Book ahead, as passenger numbers are typically limited to 12.

Cruises

Several companies, including **Scantours** (www .scantours.com) and **Profil Rejser** (www.profil-rejser.dk, in Danish), offer watergoing tours billed as 'cruises', 'coastal steamer rides' or other such romantic names. In fact this usually means that they will simply book you a berth on the regular AUL ferry and add air tickets, a couple of hotels and the odd excursion during longer stops. The budget conscious would be well advised to compare the prices of putting together the same individual elements for themselves.

Ferry

Arctic Umiaq Line (AUL; ☎ 349 900; www.aul.gl) ferries offer an ideal way to meet Greenlanders while you weave between icebergs, sail past majestic soaring peaks and pass through magnificent icescapes. Ice conditions allowing, summer services link west-coast villages from Aappilattoq, near Cape Farewell, to Uummannaq in the north. Note that no single ship does the whole route and that there are no ferries on the east coast. In winter ferries go no further north than Ilulissat. See the map on p226.

The ferries are safe and reasonably comfortable, but they're not always on time. Major delays are announced on Greenland's KNR-TV Teletext page 550, but boats can also arrive (and depart) early, especially at small ports. Always be at the dock at least 45 minutes ahead. Timetables are specific to periods of a few weeks or months, so check carefully that the one you're using is for the exact dates you need. Especially in summer it's worth booking as far ahead as possible, as passenger limits are strictly enforced.

Regular AUL passenger routes are divided into four regional groupings: west coast, south coast, Middle Greenland and Disko Bay.

MAIN WEST-COAST ROUTES

The long-distance west-coast routes are handled by two large ferries, both on weekly loops. The *Sarfaq Ittuk* shuttles between Qaqortoq and Nuuk via Paamiut, extending south to Narsarsuaq and north to Ilulissat in summer. In winter the *Sarpik Ittuk* follows a similar route, but from mid-June to mid-November – when the northern sea ice melts – it runs from Nuuk to Uummannaq via Disko Bay, and even ventures as far as Upernavik till mid-August.

There are various classes. Unless otherwise mentioned, prices given in this book's text are for the cheapest couchette class, which gives you a dormitory bed on a lower deck. By paying some 50% more you'll get a bed in six- or four-bed *kupe* cabin. Plusher three- and two-person cabins cost 70% to 80% more than couchettes, while a single cabin costs almost three times the basic fare and has a private toilet. There are on-board showers and a decent **cafeteria** (sandwiches Dkr38, breakfast Dkr50, lunch buffet Dkr90, dinner mains

Dkr65; ☺ breakfast 7am-9.30am, lunch noon-1.30pm, dinner 5.30-6.30pm). The aft-lounge has nice viewing windows, though a noisy TV makes it less than tranquil. A separate video room screens free movies, and the purser's office has a radio telephone (per minute Dkr10).

SOUTH-COAST ROUTES

Of boats working the south-coast routes, the most useful is the *Najaaraq Ittuk*, which sails between Qaqortoq and Nanortalik three times a week, with varying intermediate stops. May to November it also links Qaqortoq to Narsarsuaq, Narsaq and Itilleq (for Igaliku). December to April the tiny *Aleqa Ittuk* runs fairly sporadically between Qaqortoq and either Igaliku or Nanortalik. Weekly from Nanortalik when ice and sea conditions allow, the 12-seater *Ketil* makes a superbly scenic one-day run through the south's most splendid fjords to reach Aappilattoq.

MIDDLE GREENLAND ROUTES

The most useful of the limited middle Greenland routes is the weekly run between Sisimiut and Itilleq on the *Mima*.

DISKO BAY ROUTES

There are three boats, of which the most useful to tourists is usually the *Aviaq Ittuk*. It hops between Aasiaat, Ilulissat and Qasigiannguit several times a week, stopping at least once weekly in Kitsissuarsuit, Ikkamiut, Ilimanaq, Oqaatsut, Qeqertaq and Saqqaq. The *Nukaraaq Ittuk* makes short trips from Aasiaat to Kangaatsiaq, Niaqornaarsuk and Attu. The *Inuuteq* shuttles between Ilulissat and Qasigiannguit on Wednesdays and Fridays in midsummer.

TICKETS

Note that fares rise around 35% between mid-June and late August. There are discounts for seniors (25% in summer, 50% in the off season), children under 12 (50%), and infants under two (90%).

Where there are no AUL offices, tickets are usually available at the village post office nearest to the port. For a Dkr50 surcharge you can pay once aboard the ferry. However, this depends on space availability. Ship-capacity regulations are strictly adhered to, and it's not uncommon for boats to be fully booked in advance, especially in midsummer. There is a waiting list for places on fully booked boats, so there's still a chance of getting aboard even the fullest ferry if somebody fails to show up. But if you are not flexible with your schedule (ie if waiting an extra week or two would be a problem) it's worth booking tickets as far ahead as is humanly possible.

BOOKING FROM ABROAD

Although the www.aul.gl website has time-tables for each month plus full tables of prices, it is not yet possible to buy tickets online. You can make a reservation by email, but you must pay in full at least two weeks before departure or the reservation will be removed from the system. If you're not likely to be in Greenland a fortnight before departure, the only way to pay is by bank transfer to Bank of Greenland (SWIFT: GRENGLGX, IBAN GL426471 00014 29 59-8). You'll also need to cover the hefty transfer fees. Hopefully, they'll come around to accepting credit-card bookings eventually.

Tour & Charter Boat

Many towns have one or two medium-sized 'tourist boats' that have regular safety in-spections and are expensively licensed for carrying tourists. Day trips organised by tourist offices have to use such boats. Be-cause you can split the cost with up to a dozen others, these tours often prove the cheapest way to reach the popular destina-tions to which there is no regular public transport. In and near Narsarsuaq, Blue Ice (see p99) runs a particularly useful network of tourist-boat transfers in summer.

However, when there are few tourists such tours and transfers are generally cancelled. The cost of chartering a licensed tour boat is exorbitant. Fortunately, nearly every Green-landic family owns a motorised dinghy or powerboat of some description, and finding someone to take you to an out-of-the-way place generally isn't too difficult. The rate you pay depends on negotiation, friendship and luck, and can vary quite extravagantly. Officially, the Hunters & Fishers Associ-ation has fixed fees for chartering; they start at around Dkr1300 per hour for a small speedboat (half price for waiting time). In practice, however, you may be quoted just about anything, including absurdly high or low prices. The best way to charter is gen-erally to be patient: ask around in the vil-lage, and within a day or two you may well find someone who is going where you want to go. If so, reckon on paying Dkr300 to Dkr500 as a token petrol fee. Alternatively, someone may offer to take you for an agreed fare (the cost is much higher if it's a special journey).

Note that unlicensed boat operators aren't insured to carry 'passengers', so they can't advertise for tourist customers even though they may actually do tourist trips unofficially. Such operators cannot be used by tourist of-fices, though a few tourist offices nonetheless pass on names for you to call yourself. Note that not all boatmen are reliable: some un-licensed boats could be dangerous, so a solid recommendation is important.

CAR & MOTORCYCLE

Most of Greenland's 2520 cars and 72 buses are in Nuuk. Nonetheless, even in smaller towns that could be crossed on foot in five minutes, many people seem to jump in a car whenever they set foot outside. By European standards petrol is remarkably cheap (prices are similar to those in the USA), so drivers seem unconcerned at leaving engines run-ning while they shop. Nobody's likely to steal a car, as you simply can't drive far from any town. Indeed, thanks to glaciers and impos-sibly rugged terrain, there are virtually no roads at all beyond city limits. Very minor ex-ceptions include a few tractor tracks around Narsaq and Qassiarsuk, the 5km gravel road from Grønnedal to Ivittuut, and a 70km net-work of rough roads around Kangerlussuaq. None warrants renting a car, though there are a surprising number of taxis even in the small towns. There are only 10 motorcycles registered in the whole country, outnum-bered nine to one by fire engines.

DOGSLED

In the long months of snow and frozen seas, many people in Arctic and East Greenland still get around by dogsled. Greenlandic mushers harness their dogs in a fan forma-tion, as opposed to the more complicated and tangle-prone inline formation used by their counterparts in Alaska and below-the-tree-line Canada.

For visitors a winter sledding tour can be both exciting and memorable. Tourist dogsled trips ranging from one-day samplers to two-week expeditions are offered from Tasiilaq (p206), Uummannaq (p191), Ilulissat (p170), Sisimiut (p158) and several smaller Arctic villages. Typical costs are around Dkr1200 per person per day. The best season is from March to May, when days are longer and temperatures not as extreme as in midwinter. Summer dogsledding is only possible on Disko Island. Except around Tasiilaq, Greenlanders aren't permitted to keep sled dogs south of the Arctic Circle. (Similarly, other dogs cannot be kept north of the Circle; this is to prevent interbreeding that might weaken the genes of highly valued sled dogs.) Accordingly, dogsledding isn't available in Nuuk or elsewhere in southern Greenland.

KAYAK

For information, see p217.

SKI

Before Fridtjof Nansen slapped planks on his feet and set off across Greenland's inland ice in 1888, skis were not well known. Indeed his escapade was widely considered to be reckless and quite potty. Nowadays, however, the icecap crossing is more a race than a world-shattering epic, with surprising numbers making the trip each year. Average crossing time is around 25 days, but the record is a mere week. However, it still requires a lot of planning and written permission (see p216).

Shorter-distance cross-country skiing is possible in many areas.

SNOWMOBILE

From December to March snowmobiles are popular, especially in the south, where dog teams aren't allowed. This is a thrilling but potentially dangerous way to travel, especially if you're not used to the heavy steering and potentially reckless speeds. Don't head out alone, and study carefully the rules of driving to avoid accidents or collisions with cross-country skiers. Insurance problems mean that legally renting a snow mobile is virtually impossible, but if you ask around you can often charter a taxi-style ride.

TOURS

As getting beyond the main hub villages isn't always convenient, even independent visitors may find it easier – and, at times, cheaper – to participate in organised excursions to reach certain destinations. In Ilulissat (p170) there are four tour companies; elsewhere most local tours are organised through tourist offices or organised by outfitters. Departures depend on minimum quotas, and with a group you'll often be better off chartering your own boat. For more information, see Tour & Charter Boat, p231.

Greenland Outfitters

A group of specially qualified guides known as outfitters can provide customised itineraries, possibly including hiking, mountaineering, kayaking, sailing, dogsledding, snowmobiling, fishing and/or bird-watching. Most speak at least some English, and they are licensed and insured to guide travellers. Those in smaller villages usually have only a few tourist visits per year, so their services can be very personal, but you might need to give them considerable warning so they can get time off from their day jobs. **Greenland Tourism** (www.greenland.com) has a town-by-town outfitter listing.

The Arctic

RALPH LEE HOPKINS

Arctic Travel Routes

Travel in the far north is neither cheap nor easy, but it is packed with incredible scenery, wildlife sightings, a vastness of space only dreamed of and a stillness that will calm your soul. In most places you'll have no choice but to fly north, but some regions are accessible by road, and everywhere you'll have the option to raft, canoe and kayak down deserted rivers, hike across kilometres of tundra, climb towering peaks, and dogsled or snowmobile through the long sunny days of spring. You'll need to be prepared, though: a puncture can leave you stranded hundreds of kilometres from the nearest garage, and wilderness trips make the possibility of expensive medical evacuations or encounters with wildlife very real issues.

Travelling across North America you have the choice of two epic road trips taking in fantastic northern peaks, vast national parks and legendary wildlife. Alternatively, fly to remote indigenous communities surrounded by some of the most stunning scenery in all the Arctic and immerse yourself in local culture. In Arctic Scandinavia you can traverse the breadth of Lapland by road, from spectacular coastal fjords and islands across craggy peaks to vast tundra plains; experience the reality of life for modern Sami reindeer herders; or visit the incredible far-flung islands of Svalbard, starting point for many trips to the North Pole. For the adventurous and the thick-skinned, a trip to Arctic Russia brings the prospect of enormous distances across often monotonous territory, difficult access and few facilities, but choose your destinations well and you'll be rewarded by meeting isolated indigenous groups, as well as experiencing incredible fishing and that authentic frontier feel.

The following chapters offer a selection of routes and activities through the vast landscapes of the far north.

Arctic North America Travel Routes

HIGHLIGHTS

▪ Witnessing the migration of the largest caribou herd in the world at Alaska's **Arctic National Wildlife Refuge** (p254)

▪ Flying over Alaska's bizarre **Great Kobuk Sand Dunes** (p262)

▪ Watching a carver conjure spirits out of soapstone in the Inuit art capital, Canada's **Cape Dorset** (p249)

▪ Beating a path to the top of the world and marvelling at the pristine wonders of Canada's **Quttinirpaaq National Park** (p247)

▪ Hiking past a kilometre-high cliff and across the Arctic Circle on Canada's **Akshayuk Pass** (p249).

Big skies, big vistas, big game, big rewards – everything in Arctic North America seems to have succumbed to that supersize effect. In the vast wilderness of the untouched north, wild animals far outnumber people, jagged mountain peaks give way to immense sweeps of desolate tundra, and tiny isolated villages carry on with life through winter's cruel temperatures and perpetual night. It's an area of incredible beauty, engulfing silence and constant awe.

The far north is alien to most North Americans, and although Alaska conjures up an image of year-round ice and snow, most of the state remains firmly below the Arctic Circle. Even the Arctic gateway towns of Fairbanks, Dawson and Iqaluit, isolated frontier towns of the imagination for most southerners, linger well below the 66th parallel. To the tiny population who make their home in the fly-in villages far to the north, the gateway towns are southern cities full of glittering lights, shopping malls, cafés and the cosmopolitan treats of a trip 'out'.

The isolated northern communities range from rough-and-tumble backwaters to tiny traditional villages where the native people still live mainly off the land. Neither will hold your attention for too long, but leaving the settlements behind and making your way into the bush or onto the tundra will leave you smitten by the vast world and hidden drama that lie beyond. It's one of the greatest wilderness experiences on earth.

As you'd expect with all that space and isolation, tourism in Arctic North America isn't especially straightforward. Only two roads cross the Arctic Circle on this vast continent, and travellers will need plenty of time and especially money for their Arctic adventure. Choosing one route, one activity or one area and exploring it properly will vastly improve your experience. Take one trip, though, and we guarantee you'll be back.

GETTING AROUND
Air
Much of the far north of Alaska and Canada is accessible by air only, and many of the most interesting communities are fly-in. Return flights are generally much better value than one-way, and you'll save a bundle with a 14-day advance purchase.

ALASKA
Alaska Airlines (www.alaskaair.com) runs scheduled flights to Fairbanks, Kotzebue and Barrow, and **Air North** (www.flyairnorth.com) flies from Anchorage and Fairbanks to the Yukon, the Northwest Territories (NWT) and British Columbia.

In addition, many smaller regional carriers operate flights to isolated communities, while a large number of charter operators provide 'bush flights' into off-runway locations: river sandbars, wilderness lakes, glaciers and open tundra. Many of these carry outside boat-racks for hauling canoes and kayaks.

Hourly rates for charter services can range from US$300 all the way up to US$1000 per hour. You'll have to pay for the flight time to your destination and the return flight to the plane's home base. If you're not at the designated spot at the designated pick-up time, you'll still have to pay for the flight. If bad weather prevents a pick-up, the pilot will arrive as soon as it's safe to fly in – but be sure you have sufficient supplies to ride out a bad spell of at least several days.

Reliable operators:
Brooks Range Aviation (www.brooksrange.com)
Circle Air (www.circleair.com)
Frontier Flying Service (www.frontierflying.com)
Larry's Flying Service (www.larrysflying.com)
Yukon Air Service (www.yukonair.com)

CANADA

First Air (www.firstair.ca) and **Canadian North** (www
.canadiannorth.com) are the main carriers to Arctic destinations. **Kenn Borek Air** (www.borekair.com)
serves the High Arctic islands from Iqaluit,
First Air covers the Kitikmeot region from
Cambridge Bay, and **Calm Air** (www.calmair.com)
and **Kivalliq Air** (www.kivalliqair.com) cover the
Kivalliq region from Rankin Inlet.

Bus

Bus services in Arctic North America are
severely limited, but where they do exist
they can get you into superb wilderness at
a fraction of the cost of air travel. In Alaska
there is a scheduled van service between
Fairbanks and Prudhoe Bay with **Dalton Highway Express** (www.daltonhighwayexpress.com) from
June to August.

   In Canada services are limited to the Yukon
and the NWT. Whitehorse is the northernmost Yukon terminal for **Greyhound** (www
.greyhound.ca), but from there you can travel
to Dawson and Inuvik along the Dempster
Hwy with **Dawson City Courier** (www.dawsonbus.ca)
from June to September. Greyhound makes
it as far as Hay River in the NWT; from there
you'll need **Frontier Coachlines** (☎ 874 2566),
which runs services to Yellowknife.

Car & Motorcycle

Even with your own transport, road travel is
restricted to a small network, mostly in eastern Alaska and the Yukon. **Arctic Outfitters**
(www.arctic-outfitters.com) in Fairbanks is about
the only hire company willing to let you
travel on the Dalton Hwy (see p250). If you
travel this route, never stop in the middle of
the road to observe wildlife or scenery: huge
trucks travel at high speeds and they have
limited braking ability.

   Driving into the Yukon, the Top of the
World Hwy runs from Tok in Alaska to
Dawson, a 301km (188-mile) jaunt on a wily
but scenic stretch of road. From here you
can start the mother of all road trips up
the Dempster Hwy to the Mackenzie Delta
(see p244). You can rent cars for this trip in
Whitehorse or Dawson (see p238). Headlights are required to be on at all times on
all roads. Make sure you have enough food,
water, warm clothes, blankets and spare tyres
for emergencies. Note that although there
are no specific snow-chain requirements,
governments in both countries recommend

TO THE NORTH POLE

There are no regular flights to the North
Pole from Arctic North America, but you can
get pretty close. Scheduled flights go as far
as Resolute on Cornwallis Island (see p247),
where a chartered Twin Otter can take you
to Ward Hunt Island, just off the northern
tip of Ellesmere Island. From here there's
770km (481 miles) of pack ice between
you and the Pole. Northwinds (see p67)
organises extreme skiing trips (60 days) or
combined skiing and dogsledding trips (52
days) from here to the Pole, but you need
Arctic experience, incredible fitness and
stamina, and a true sense of adventure to
even sign up.

---

that you speak to a tyre specialist to advise
you on which tyres to use. Most local drivers
carry chains in their cars.

   Although petrol is very good value, car
hire is expensive. Check mileage charges
and try to get a deal that includes unlimited
mileage if you're going to tackle one of these
epic routes.

   In much of this area, wildlife such as deer
and moose are potential road hazard. Most
run-ins occur at night, when animals are active and visibility is poor. Always scan the
verges for animals that may bolt out into the
road. Vehicle headlights will often mesmerise
an animal, leaving it frozen in the middle of
the road. Try honking the horn or flashing
the lights to encourage it to move away. In
winter, watch for caribou, which like to amble
down the highways licking off the salt.

ITINERARY 1: CANADA'S DEMPSTER HIGHWAY

**Starting from Dawson, the last remnant of the
Yukon gold rush, the Dempster winds its way
through pristine wilderness flanked by craggy
peaks and rolling tundra before arriving at the
Arctic hub of Inuvik, gateway to the remote communities of the Western Arctic.**

One of the most incredible road trips on
earth, the Dempster Hwy is one of only two
roads in North America that cross the Arctic
Circle (the other, the Dalton Hwy, is outlined
in Itinerary 3).

ARCTIC NORTH AMERICA
TRAVEL ROUTES

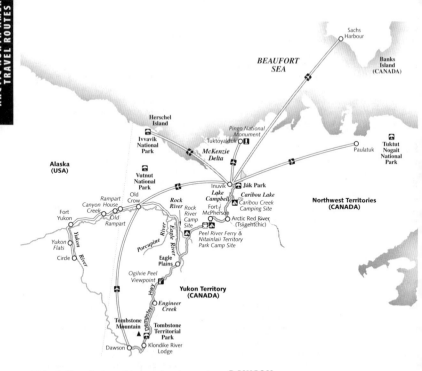

This 747km (467-mile) stretch of gravel winds from the centre of the Klondike gold rush, Dawson, through pristine wilderness, over two mountain ranges and across an expanse of tundra to Inuvik, near the shores of the Beaufort Sea. It's a road deep in history, with stunning scenery and myriad chances to see wildlife. You may catch sight of moose, caribou, bears, Dall sheep, muskoxen and wolves as well as gyrfalcons, peregrine falcons, golden eagles, ptarmigan, Arctic terns, long-tailed jaegers and lesser golden plovers, all without leaving the road.

The highway is open all year, but the crossings of the Peel and Mackenzie Rivers cannot operate during spring thaw and winter freeze (any time from mid-April to June and mid-October to December, respectively). In summer free ferries cross the rivers and in winter there are ice roads. The best time to travel is between June and early September, but you can get daily road reports throughout the year at www.gov.yk.ca/roadreport. Be prepared for plenty of dust in dry weather, slimy mud in wet weather, snow on any day, and tyres that are shredded to ribbons.

DAWSON
☎ 867 / pop 1800

A frontier town that was once nicknamed 'the Paris of the North', Dawson found fame and heady fortune as the centre of the Klondike gold rush. Preserved as a relic of those days, the whole town is a National Historic Site with unpaved roads, boarded paths, no electric wires and a host of historic buildings. You'll also find mounties on horseback, modern-day gold prospectors, and a gambling saloon complete with honky-tonk music and dancing girls. The town gets choked with visitors in midsummer, but it's still well worth a visit for an insight into life on the Klondike and the hardships early prospectors faced. More than a century after the original gold rush, as many as 100 small, often family-owned, enterprises still mine for gold in the surrounding region.

Information
Dawson Medical Clinic (☎ 993 5744; Church St)
Parks Canada (☎ 993 7237; www.parkscanada.ca)
In the VRC Tourist Information office.

Post office (☎ 993 5342; 3rd Ave; ⏰ 8.30am-5.30pm Mon-Fri, 9am-noon Sat)

VRC Tourist Information (☎ 993 5566; www.dawson city.ca; cnr Front & King Sts; ⏰ 8am-8pm)

Western Arctic Information Centre (☎ 993 6167; Front St; ⏰ 9am-8pm) Maps and information on the Dempster Hwy, including road updates.

Sights

Dawson and its environs teem with places of historic interest. If you're planning to see several of Parks Canada's sites then its **pass** (adult/child C$28/14) is a good investment as it allows access to all the sites and tours.

Dawson City Museum (☎ 993 5291; 5th Ave; adult/ child C$7/5; ⏰ 10am-6pm) This is a good place to start any tour of town. It houses a collection of 25,000 gold-rush artefacts, and engaging exhibits walk you through the hardscrabble lives of the miners. The museum is housed in the landmark 1901 Old Territorial Administration Building. Next door is the old locomotive barn, housing historic trains.

Commissioner's Residence (Front St; adult/child C$5/2.50; ⏰ 10am-5pm) Also built in 1901, and aimed to give potential civic investors confidence in the city, the building is noted for being the long-time home of Martha Black. Martha came to the Yukon in 1898, owned a lumberyard and was elected to the Canadian parliament at age 70.

Further north is the **Robert Service Cabin** (cnr 8th Ave & Hanson St; admission free; ⏰ 10am-4pm), a typical gold-rush cabin home to the 'Bard of the Yukon' from 1909 to 1912. Long-time Robert Service re-enactor Tom Byrne gives captivating **readings** (☎ 993 5543; 5th Ave; admission C$10; ⏰ 3pm) of the poet's works at the Westmark Inn.

You can also visit the cabin of Jack London, author of Yukon stories *Call of the Wild* and *White Fang*. Now the **Jack London Interpretive Centre** (8th Ave at Grant St; admission C$2; ⏰ 10am-1pm & 2-6pm), it's a treasure trove of artefacts and information. There are talks about the author at 11.30am and 2.15pm.

On the waterfront you'll find the **SS Keno** (adult/child C$5/2.50; ⏰ 10am-6pm), which plied the perilous white water between Whitehorse and Dawson for more than half a century. Today it features many good displays about travel 100 years ago.

For an insight into the life of the local indigenous people, visit the **Tr'ondëk Hwëch'in Cultural Centre** (☎ 993 6768; www.trondek.com; Front St;

admission C$5; ⏰ 10.30am-6pm). Inside this beautiful wooden building there's a slide show and interpretative talks on the Hän Hwëch'in, or river people, who were the first to inhabit the area. The collection includes traditional artefacts and First Nation regalia. Locally made crafts are for sale.

For culture of an altogether different nature, **Diamond Tooth Gertie's Gambling Hall** (☎ 993 5575; cnr Queen St & 4th Ave; admission C$8; ⏰ 7pm-2am) is a re-creation of an 1898 saloon, complete with small-time gambling, honky-tonk piano and dancing girls. The casino's winnings go toward town restoration, and at weekends it can get packed as locals jostle with tourists to support preservation.

For great views over the Ogilvie Mountains, Klondike Valley, Yukon River and Dawson, head for the **Midnight Dome**, a quarried hill to the north of town. It's accessible by car or a steep footpath from Judge St.

Another good hike goes to the **Ship Graveyard**, where the paddlewheel ferries were abandoned after the completion of the Klondike Hwy. Left to rot on the riverbank just downstream from town, they're overgrown but still fascinating. To get there take the ferry across the river, walk north through the Yukon River camp site for 10 minutes,

---

FAST FACTS

- **Access for independent travellers** Excellent

- **Best time to travel** June to September

- **Difficulty level** Easy to moderate

- **Don't forget** Spare tyres, basic tools, plenty of food and water, blankets, warm clothes, binoculars, first-aid kit, insect repellent

- **Don't miss** Tombstone Mountain, the pingos round Tuktoyaktuk

- **Gateway city** Dawson, Yukon

- **Length of route** 747km (467 miles)

- **Modes of travel** Car, bus

- **Recommended map** International Travel Maps *Yukon Road and Physical Travel Reference Map (1:1,500,000)*; the *Milepost* (see p265)

- **Time needed** 12 hours to a lifetime; one week is a good compromise

and then continue for another 10 minutes north along the beach.

Tours

Excellent walking tours are available with **Parks Canada** (adult/child C$5/2.50) and **Gold City Tours** (☎ 993 5175; Front St), which also runs a trip to the Bonanza Creek gold mine.

Festivals & Events

Trek Over the Top (www.trekoverthetop.com) is the Yukon's premiere snowmobile event, featuring hundreds of snowmobilers travelling from Tok, Alaska, over the Top of the World Hwy to Dawson, takes place in mid-February to mid-March. The town hosts loads of activities for participants and plenty of live music and gambling.

Dawson City Music Festival (www.dcmf.com) is a weekend music festival in July featuring well-known Canadian musicians. Tickets sell out well in advance.

Discovery Days & Yukon Riverside Art Festival is Dawson's premier annual event, celebrating the great discovery of 1896. On the third Monday in August there are parades and picnics, street performances, entertainment, exhibits in local businesses, and a stage show, the Gaslight Follies at the Grand Palace.

Sleeping

Most places are open from May to September and fill up quickly in July and August. Many places will pick you up at the airport if you ask in advance. If you arrive without a booking the VRC will help you find a bed.

Dawson City River Hostel (☎ 993 6823; www.yukon hostels.com; dm member/non-member C$15/19, r C$39; P) This funky hostel is across the river from town and five minutes up the hill from the ferry landing. It's a rustic spot with good views, cabins, a wooded area for tents, a cooking shelter and a communal bathhouse. There's no electricity, and lockers are recommended for your gear.

Bedside Manner B&B (☎ 993 6948; cnr 8th Ave & Princess St; s/d C$79/89; year-round;) This small B&B has simple, comfortable rooms, and the friendly owner can give lots of advice on local events and activities.

5th Ave B&B (☎ 993 5941; www.5thavebandb.com; 702 5th Ave; r C$85-115; year-round;) This is another cosy place in a neighbourhood of historic homes near the museum. It has bright rooms and a large communal sitting area.

Bombay Peggy's (☎ 993 6969; www.bombaypeggys .com; cnr 2nd Ave & Princess St; r C$74-195; year-round;) In a renovated old brothel, Peggy's is the best and most stylish place to stay in town. Rooms range from 'snugs' with shared bath to suites. There's a great pub downstairs.

Aurora Inn (☎ 993 6860; www.aurorainn.ca; 5th Ave; r C$99-190; year-round;) The Aurora has large bright rooms with pine furniture and subtle décor. Service is friendly, and there's a good breakfast (C$10) and an excellent restaurant.

Eating

Klondike Kate's (☎ 993 6527; cnr King St & 3rd Ave; meals C$6-20; breakfast, lunch & dinner) A local favourite, this place dishes up some killer king salmon, and there's a long list of other dishes and great desserts. It's a fun spot out on the covered patio.

Mama Cita's Ristorante (☎ 993 2370; 2nd Ave; meals C$8-22; lunch & dinner) The insanely large portions of excellent pasta draw the crowds, but the pizzas and sandwiches are also popular and the service is good.

Aurora Inn Restaurant (☎ 993 6860; 5th Ave; meals C$9-25; lunch & dinner) This bright and cheery place serves excellent hearty meals. The menu has a German focus, but there's a good choice for all tastes. The steaks at dinner, replete with fresh mushrooms, are tops.

Back Alley (☎ 993 5800; 2nd Ave; meals C$7-14; lunch & dinner) Behind the Westminster Hotel, this top choice serves great souvlaki sandwiches and pizza. There are tables outside to eat at, or you can get free delivery in town.

River West (☎ 993 6339; cnr Front & Queen Sts; snacks C$2-5; 7am-7pm) The best of several places along Front St, this café has excellent coffee, bagels, soup and sandwiches on delicious bread. The tables outside are a local meeting spot.

Drinking

Bombay Peggy's (☎ 993 6969; cnr 2nd Ave & Princess St; 11am-11pm) Peggy's is a delightful place for a drink, with good beers on tap and a fine wine selection. There are some nice quiet tables at the back.

Bars at Westminster Hotel (3rd Ave; noon-late) These two bars are variously known as 'Snakepit', 'Armpit' or simply 'Pit.' The one to your left as you face the pink building has a great old tin roof that matches the age of some of the timeless characters hanging out by the bar. The bar to the right has more of a '70s motif as well as live music many nights. Both get lively.

Getting There & Away

Air North (see p236) serves Whitehorse (1¼ hours, three weekly), Old Crow (1¼ hours, up to three weekly), Inuvik (2½ hours, up to two weekly) and Fairbanks (one hour, three weekly). Flights average between C$130 and C$250 one way.

Dawson City Courier (☎ 993 6688; www.dawsonbus .ca; pick-up cnr 2nd Ave & York St) runs buses to Whitehorse (C$91, eight hours) and Inuvik (C$262, 14 hours). The service runs from Monday to Friday between May and September. Be sure to reserve.

Alaska Trails & Tours (☎ 888-600 6001) has a van service to Dawson from Anchorage, Fairbanks and Tok (C$95, eight hours, three weekly).

Fischer Contracting (☎ 993 6465; www.norcan.yk .ca; km 712 Klondike Hwy) hires out cars and trucks.

DAWSON TO EAGLE PLAINS
363km (227 miles)

Although you could drive straight to Inuvik without a break in 10 to 12 hours, you'd miss the whole reason for travelling this route. Give yourself several days, camp en route and just enjoy the breathtaking scenery along the way.

ACTIVITIES: PADDLING THE PORCUPINE RIVER

If you fancy some true wilderness experience, try an incredible canoe trip from Eagle Plains to Alaska. This unforgettable 1100km (688-mile) trip takes about three weeks and will take you through remote and untouched landscapes with breathtaking scenery and plenty of opportunities for spotting wildlife and meeting the locals.

You'll need to be prepared for true wilderness camping, unpredictable weather, swarms of mosquitoes and little contact with civilisation. You'll have to transport your own canoe to Eagle Plains, where you can launch into the Eagle River. This can be quite shallow in dry periods, so be prepared for some portaging. The trip along the Eagle River and briefly onto the Bell will take about four days, after which you'll join the Porcupine River. The landscape here is full of sweeping vistas of mountains, plateaus and river valleys, and the possibility of spotting moose, caribou, bears, bald eagles and peregrine falcons is high. The 152,000-strong Porcupine caribou herd migrates though this area in spring and autumn on its way to and from birthing grounds in the Arctic National Wildlife Refuge in Alaska (see p254).

After about 10 days of paddling you'll reach the small Gwich'in community of Old Crow (population 300). The tiny community is made up of three rows of traditional log cabins and an airstrip, and most people still rely on seasonal hunting, fishing and trapping for their livelihood. You can stock up on supplies here, hike Crow Mountain or just hang out and meet the locals. So few visitors come to town – it's 560km (350 miles) from the nearest road – that you're sure to get some curious people starting a conversation. Camping on the river banks is free, but there are no facilities. Alternatively, the **Porcupine Bed & Breakfast** (☎ 966 3913; r C$120) has a couple of comfortable rooms. Old Crow has regular flights to Inuvik and Dawson if you wish to take a shorter trip and fly out from here. You can also charter planes to the Vuntut National Park, with its countless kettle lakes and ponds, Porcupine caribou herd and half a million water birds. The park has no services or facilities of any kind.

Downstream from Old Crow the river develops high canyon walls known as the **Ramparts**. In this area you'll see many summer cabins and fishing camps for people from the village. As you cross the Alaskan border you can take a pit stop to wander around the abandoned village of Rampart House. Further on is the older, ghost town Old Rampart. You'll often find some activity going on at the old settlement of Canyon Creek just before you join the Yukon River at Fort Yukon. Many people finish their trip here and fly out, while others continue on and navigate the maze of tributaries on the **Yukon Flats**, one of the most spectacular wildlife havens on the continent, before hitting Circle, Alaska, where there is road access and you can arrange a pick-up.

If you're interested in dogsledding the first portion of this trip from Eagle Plains to Old Crow, visit www.muktuk.com/mushing/oldcrow.html for information.

This is the longest stretch of the Dempster without any services, so be prepared. It'll be 363km (227 miles) before you can buy petrol or food, or get even minor vehicle repairs. Fill your tank at the **Klondike River Lodge** (☎ 993 6892) at the Klondike–Dempster Hwy turnoff. The lodge will hire out jerry cans of gas you can take north and return on the way back.

The first stop en route should be **Tombstone Territorial Park**, the Yukon's newest territorial park, just 73km from the start of the highway. You can't miss stunning Tombstone Mountain, the steep conical massif at the end of the broad sweeping valley. It's a distinctive landmark on First Nation routes and is now an aerial guide for pilots. Here you'll find the **Dempster Highway Interpretive Centre** (◷ 9am-5pm Jun-Sep), which has plenty of information on hiking trails, wildlife and road conditions. There's also a rustic camp site (C$12) with expansive views, pit toilets, river water and firewood. There are several good day hikes leading from the centre; for experienced wilderness hikers there are more rigorous backcountry trips of up to 10 days. The scenery is simply spectacular, even if you never leave the camp site.

Further north, at Engineer Creek (km 194), deposits of iron oxide have turned the river bed and rocks red. The peaks of the **Ogilvie Mountains** to the west are popular with climbers, and if you look closely you'll see flags on the summits. At km 259 the Ogilvie–Peel viewpoint has fantastic views over the mountains and river valley below.

Drive on, taking plenty of time to enjoy the incredible scenery and wildlife before you hit the blink-and-you-miss-it community of Eagle Plains (population 8; km 365.7). This is the only place on the highway with full services. The **Eagle Plains Hotel** (☎ 993 2453; eagle plains@yknet.yk.ca; r C$112-135) has a choice of good but fairly standard rooms, and some decent, reasonably priced food. Book ahead if you want to stay, as tour groups can book the whole place. There's also a garage for fuel, tyre and mechanical repairs, and fantastic views that just seem to go on forever.

EAGLE PLAINS TO FORT MCPHERSON
180km (113 miles)
From Eagle Plains it's only 36km until you cross the Arctic Circle. The point is marked with a large parking area, a wooden sign and a few interpretive displays – ideal for a photo

opportunity but not much more. Further on there's a wonderfully protected camp site at Rock River (km 447; C$12) at the bottom of a wooded valley. It makes a good choice in bad weather, though the mosquitoes will eat you alive in midsummer. Just after the camp site you'll cross the Yukon/NWT border, where you'll need to put your watch back an hour. From here on the road conditions generally deteriorate, but the scenery spreads out before you in a vast stretch of mountains, hills and rolling tundra. The rugged **Richardson Mountains** are part of the migratory route for the Porcupine caribou herd (see p47), and thousands of animals pass this way in spring and autumn. There's also a good chance you'll spot Dall sheep, Arctic foxes and wolves.

At km 539 you'll need to take the **Peel River ferry** (rides free; ◷ 9am-1am late May–Oct) or ice road (open late December to March) to get across to the **Nitainlaii Territorial Park**, just 9km south of Fort McPherson. The park is perched on a cliff overlooking the Peel River, and it's surrounded by a large stand of white birch and white spruce trees. There's a visitor information centre featuring displays on the traditional life of the Gwich'in Dene. The camp site (C$15) has pit toilets, water and firewood. Along the river you'll find several traditional fishing camps.

The small town of **Fort McPherson**, established as a trading post by the Hudson Bay Company in 1840, is home to the Gwich'in people. There's not too much to see other than the cemetery at the Anglican church where the remains of the famous Lost Patrol are buried. These four mounties set off from McPherson on a routine patrol to Dawson just before Christmas 1910. When they still hadn't arrived in late February, a search party led by Corporal Dempster (for whom the highway is named) set out to find them. Their frozen bodies were found just 42km away from town. They had missed the pass out of the delta over the Richardson Mountains and had run out of food.

If you have time, a visit to the **Fort McPherson Tent & Canvas Company** (☎ 867-952 2179; fm tent@netcom.ca) provides an insight for armchair and real-life adventurers. It manufactures prospector tents and tepees used across the north by hunters and trappers.

The only place to stay in town is the **Peel River Inn** (☎ 1-888 866 6784; www.peelriverinn;

r (C$185; **P**), which has rather overpriced but comfortable rooms and a decent restaurant. The hotel can also arrange tours of the area or put you in touch with local outfitters such as **Ch'ii Adventures** (☎ 952 2442; jrossnco@cancom .net) and **Rat River Tours** (☎ 952 2363), which can arrange spectacular wilderness and river tours with a Gwich'in slant. Adventurous canoeists can complete the trip by paddling down the winding Peel River through the Mackenzie Delta.

FORT MCPHERSON TO INUVIK

186km (116 miles)

Soon after leaving McPherson you'll hit the second **ferry crossing** (rides free; ☒ 9am–1am late May–Oct) or the ice road (open from late December to March) at Tsiigehtchic (Arctic Red River; km 615). There's little to see in the community, but the surrounding scenery is stunning.

Eighty-four kilometres (52 miles) north you'll hit the start of the largely undeveloped **Gwich'in Territorial Park Reserve**, a landscape of limestone cliffs and rare Arctic plant communities overlooking Lake Campbell. The park is an unusual example of a reversing delta in the spring and an important migratory-bird staging area in the autumn. It's possible to camp at Vadzaih van Tshik territorial camp site (Caribou Creek; km 717). Facilities are basic, but there's good fishing for trout and cony on Lake Campbell.

Just before you hit Inuvik you'll pass Ják Park, famous for its cranberries, blue berries and cloudberries. The park **camp site** (☎ 777 3613; tent/RV sites C$10/20; ☒ Jun-Sep) has hot showers, firewood, a good view of the delta and a welcome breeze that keeps the mosquitoes down.

INUVIK

☎ 867 / pop 3500

Bustling hub of the Western Arctic, Inuvik has gone from government administrative post to thriving community. The locals are equally divided between Inuit, Dene and non–First Nations people and are incredibly welcoming. Although like most Arctic towns it looks a bit shabby, it's a fascinating place and well worth the effort and expense to visit, especially if you can use it as a jumping-off point for trips to surrounding communities.

For 56 days each year from late May, Inuvik has 24-hour daylight. However, the first snowfalls begin in September, and from early December the sun sets for an eight-week period.

Information

CIBC Bank (☎ 777 2848; 134 Mackenzie Rd) Has an ATM.

Inuvik Regional Hospital (☎ 777 8000; 285 Mackenzie Rd)

Post office (☎ 777 2252; 187 Mackenzie Rd)

Western Arctic Visitors Centre (☎ 777 4727, in winter ☎ 777 7237; www.inuvik.ca; 284 Mackenzie Rd; ☒ 9am–7pm Jun–mid-Sep) Has numerous displays about the area and its ecology.

Sights

The town landmark is **Our Lady of Victory Church** (☎ 777 2236), or Igloo Church, with a lovely interior created by local artists.

Northern Images (☎ 777 2786; 115 Mackenzie Rd; ☒ Mon-Sat) is not just a store but is also a gallery with a huge range of work by northern artists. Many of the works are created in remote aboriginal villages and are quite stunning. Stone carvings are a speciality.

Festivals & Events

The **Sunrise Festival** (☎ 777 2607) brings the locals together in early January for fireworks on the ice to greet the first sunrise after 30 days of darkness.

The Great Northern Arts Festival (☎ 777 3536; www.greatart.nt.ca) is a major show of First Nations art that happens in the third week of July. Most of the more than 100 artists travel from remote villages to display and sell their high-quality work. There are evening dance and drumming performances, as well as workshops and demonstrations during the day.

Sleeping

Happy Valley Campground (☎ 777 3652; Franklin Rd; tent/RV sites C$10/20) This decent camp site is convenient for town, and has hot showers, firewood, RV sites, tent platforms, nice views and a coin laundry.

Arctic Chalet (☎ 777 3535; www.arcticchalet.com; 25 Carn St; cabins C$110) This is the best place to stay, with bright cabin-style rooms in a pretty setting. Each building has a private porch, and there are simple kitchen facilities in each unit. The energetic owners hire out canoes, kayaks and cars, and run dogsledding tours (one day C$98). They're also good sources of local information. There's a rustic cabin

SIDE TRIP: WESTERN ARCTIC

You've come this far, you might as well see the real Arctic. From Inuvik you can access some truly spectacular Arctic wilderness; most tours involve flights over the Mackenzie Delta, a spectacular labyrinth of water, squalls, pingos, wildlife and abandoned trapper's huts on emerald-green banks. Photographers should try for a seat at the rear of the plane.

About 137km (86 miles) northeast of Inuvik is **Tuktoyaktuk**, commonly known as Tuk. Originally the home of the whale-hunting Inuit, it's now a land base for some of the Beaufort Sea oil and gas exploration. There is an **old military base** here dating from the Cold War, as well as **old whaling buildings** and two charming little churches. Pods of beluga whales can be seen in July and early August. The Tuk peninsula has the world's highest concentration of pingos. Some 1400 of the huge mounds of earth and ice made by frost heaves dot the landscape and have been designated the **Pingo National Monument**. Land access is limited to a winter ice road, and most tourists arrive by air in summer as part of half-day trips from Inuvik. The **hamlet office** (☎ 977 2286; www.tuktoyaktuk.com) can provide more information on the area and services.

About 400km (250 miles) east of Inuvik is **Paulatuk** (soot of coal), a 300-strong community whose main claim to fame is the **Smoking Hills**, which contain smouldering sulphide-rich slate and seams of coal. For more information contact the **hamlet office** (☎ 867-580-3531).

Paulatuk is the closest settlement to **Tuktut Nogait National Park**, a wild and untouched place about 45km east that is a major calving ground for bluenose caribou. There are no services or facilities, but a small visitors centre for the park is open in town during the summer. For information, contact **Parks Canada** (☎ 777 8800; inuvik.info@pc.gc.ca; Inuvik).

North of Paulatuk is **Banks Island**, a fantastic place for spotting wildlife and one of the best places to see muskoxen, flocks of snow geese and seabirds in the summer. Only about 150 people live in the island's one community, Sachs Harbour. Contact the **hamlet office** (☎ 690 4351) for information. Prices at **Kuptana's Guest House** (☎ /fax 690 4151; r C$180) include all meals. The guesthouse also organises nature tours of the island.

Aulavik National Park, on the north of the island, covers 12,275 sq km. It has the world's largest concentration of muskoxen, as well as badlands, tundra and archaeological sites. Contact the Parks Canada office in Inuvik (see above) for details on visiting the park.

Ivvavik National Park is another good side trip along the Beaufort Sea. Dominated by the British Mountains, the wild rolling tundra is on the migration route of the Porcupine caribou herd and is also a major waterfowl habitat. Just off the coast is **Herschel Island**, a former whaling station and the Yukon's first territorial park. This desolate and foggy place was once an Inuit settlement, which literally died out after Westerners brought foreign diseases. Today it's rich in birds and other wildlife, and has camping at Pauline Cove's protected harbour during the short summer season. Amenities include fire rings, wind shelters, outhouses and a limited water supply.

without facilities (C$40) for travellers who want a true pioneering experience.

Polar B&B (☎ 777 2554; www.inuvik.net/polar; 75 Mackenzie Rd; r from C$95) This centrally located B&B has four large, comfortable rooms with shared bathroom, common area and kitchen. Prices include free laundry.

The three large hotels in town (see following) are all run by the **Mackenzie Delta Hotel Group** (www.inuvikhotels.com), a local corporation that has enjoyed an unfortunate lack of competition.

Finto Motor Inn (☎ 777 2647; 288 Mackenzie Rd; s/d C$159/174) The best of the trio, the Finto is on the east end of town and has good views. Rooms have enjoyed a revamp and now have large TVs and, most importantly, new furniture. Some have kitchenettes.

Mackenzie Hotel (☎ 777 2861; 185 Mackenzie Rd; s/d C$149/164) and the **Eskimo Inn** (☎ 777 2801; 133 Mackenzie Rd; s/d C$149/164), right in the centre, have little to boast about beyond their typically cheery employees. Rooms are aged, and the hallways will quickly inspire a sense of gloom.

Eating & Drinking

Green Briar Restaurant (☎ 777 4671; 185 Mackenzie Rd; meals C$10-25; 🕑 lunch & dinner) In the Mackenzie Hotel, Green Briar has Arctic foods such as char and muskox and a very popular prime-rib special on Thursday nights, which sells out to locals. There's also a pub, the Brass Rail, and a dance club, the Zoo, in the hotel.

Café Gallery (☎ 777 2888; 90 Mackenzie Rd; meals C$4-10; ☺ 8am-8pm Mon-Fri, noon-8pm Sat & Sun) This pleasant café has espresso, fresh sandwiches, homemade soup and muffins.

Ingamo Hall (☎ 777 2166; 20 Mackenzie Rd) Ingamo Hall serves lunch every other Thursday at 1.30pm for village elders. Visitors are welcome but should call first. There is no charge, and you can hear wonderful stories.

Mad Trapper Pub (☎ 777 3825; 124 Mackenzie Rd; ☺ 11am-2am Mon-Sat) This raucous pub snares locals and visitors alike. Pool tables add to the fun.

Getting There & Around

AIR

Mike Zubko Airport is 14km south of town. **Town Cab** (☎ 777 4777) charges C$25 for the trip to town.

Air North (p236) flies to Dawson, Old Crow and Whitehorse. Canadian North (p237) and First Air (p237) fly daily to Yellowknife, where there are flights throughout the north and to Calgary and Edmonton.

Aklak Air (☎ 777 3777; www.aklakair.ca) has scheduled services to Aklavik, Holman, Tuktoyaktuk, Paulatuk and Sachs Harbour, and runs a free shuttle to the airport for passengers. It also offers charter services to the small Arctic communities and the national parks.

CAR

Arctic Chalet Car Rental (☎ 777 3535; www.arcticchalet.com) hires out a range of vehicles and has a counter in the airport. **NorCan/National Car & Truck Rental** (☎ 777-2346, 800-227-7368; norcan@permafrost.com) also has an airport counter.

ITINERARY 2: FLYING CANADA'S EASTERN ARCTIC

A high-flying odyssey across the eastern Canadian Arctic from Nunavut's buzzing capital, Iqaluit, through tiny isolated communities rimmed by stunning fjords and towering peaks, and on to some of the Arctic's most incredible national parks.

It'll cost you dearly in air fares, but this trip will take you to some of the most stunning areas of all the Arctic and leave you speech-

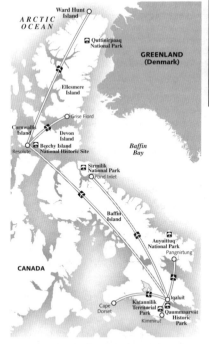

less with awe. From towering rugged peaks dripping in ice to pods of beluga whales and wildlife so unused to humans that it seems tame, this is a pristine Arctic wilderness that few will ever see.

Scheduled flights will take you to most destinations, but as Iqaluit is a hub you'll have to do some backtracking if you want to visit all the communities listed in this itinerary. Alternatively, choose a few destinations that take your fancy or gather a crowd and charter a small plane.

IQALUIT

☎ 867 / pop 6000

Nunavut's capital, Iqaluit (ee-*kal*-oo-eet), is a perversely fascinating place. It has a booming economy but a ramshackle, debris-strewn townscape. The Space Age buildings and prefab houses are hemmed in by a mess of above-ground pipes and seasonally abandoned vehicles, but the young, diverse population gives the town a buzz missing from the more insular villages of the rest of the territory. It's a melting pot of Inuit professionals and politicians, dog mushers and hunters,

FAST FACTS

- **Access for independent travellers** Expensive
- **Best time to travel** April to September
- **Difficulty level** Moderate
- **Don't forget** Camera and plenty of film, lots of warm clothes, credit card
- **Don't miss** Pangnirtung, Cape Dorset artworks
- **Gateway city** Iqaluit, Nunavut
- **Length of complete route** Approximately 8200km (5125 miles) as the crow flies
- **Mode of travel** Air
- **Recommended map** Canada Map Office *Northwest Territories & Nunavut East Arctic* (1:2,000,000)
- **Time needed** Ten days to one month

Ottawa technocrats and Québécois cabbies. Although there aren't too many specific sights to see, there's a choice of restaurants and shops, making it a good hub for a trip to the great white expanse beyond town – the real reason for any visit up north.

Information

Ambulance & Fire (☎ 979 4422)
Baffin Regional Hospital (☎ 979 7300; Niaqunngusiaq Rd)
Bank of Montreal (☎ 979 2901; Queen Elizabeth Way; ☽ 10am-4pm Mon-Thu, 10am-5pm Fri) In the post office building downtown. Nearby are Royal Bank and CIBC.
Police (☎ 979 1111)
Unikkaarvik Visitors Centre (☎ 979 4636; Sinaa St; ☽ 10am-6pm Mon-Fri, 1-4pm Sat & Sun) Has an informative mini-museum and a reference collection of Nunavut books and videos. Topo maps can be purchased here.

Sights

Nunavut's prefab **Legislative Assembly** (☎ 975 5000; Federal Rd; admission free; ☽ 9am-5pm Mon-Fri, tours 1.30pm Mon-Fri Jun-Aug or by appointment) is no marble-columned parliament, but it has nice touches such as sealskin benches and a narwhal-tusk ceremonial mace. You can see impressive local art in the foyer.

Nunatta Sunakkutaangit Museum (☎ 979 5537; Sinaa St; admission free; ☽ 1-5pm Tue-Sun), though itty-bitty, is worth a look. It permanently displays traditional Inuit garments, tools and carvings, and has a more interesting gallery with ever-changing exhibits of contemporary northern art.

The **waterfront** between the breakwater and the Coast Guard station is the focus of traditional Inuit activity. Amid the junked snowmobiles and fuel cans, hunters butcher seals and build boats and sleds. Ask before taking photos.

It's worth taking a walk from downtown along the waterfront to sandy Apex beach, where you'll find the old red-and-white **Hudson Bay Trading Post** (Bill Mackenzie Rd). For longer walks, try **Sylvia Grinnell Territorial Park**, where you'll often see caribou and foxes. There are plenty of paths leading to a waterfall, rapids and escarpments.

Sleeping

Camping at Sylvia Grinnell Territorial Park is the only cheap option. It's pretty basic – there are no facilities except pit toilets – but it is free. For everything else, book ahead and prepare to haemorrhage cash.

Accommodations by the Sea (☎ 979 6074; www .accommodationsbythesea.ca; Bldg 2536, Paurngaq Rd; s/d with breakfast C$120/140) About 2km from downtown, this spacious house has excellent views of the bay. Guests prepare their own breakfasts with food provided.

Crazy Caribou Bed and Breakfast (☎ 979 2449; www.crazycariboubedandbreakfast.com; Bldg 490, Atungauyait St; s/d with breakfast C$120/140) This cosy Inuit-owned place has comfortable rooms, a sauna and free rides from the airport.

Frobisher Inn (☎ 979 2222; www.frobisherinn.com; Astro Hill; r C$210) Up on the hill, the 'Frobe' has modern bayside rooms with marvellous views. There's a good restaurant and the Astro Hill complex has a coffee shop, pool, bar and movie theatre.

Eating

Snack (☎ 979 6767; Nipisa St; breakfasts C$9-11, sandwiches C$6-15; ☽ 6am-8pm) This Francophone-run diner is bedecked with 1950s kitsch and serves cheap, decent, mainstream meals (on paper plates).

Wizard's Bistro (☎ 979 4726; Bldg 1107, Ikaluktuutiak St; lunches C$8-16; ☽ 11am-9pm Mon-Thu, 11am-10pm Fri, 6-10pm Sat) Wizard's conjures up good pastries, wraps and lunch specials, such as Reuben with mulligatawny soup (C$14), but the service is far from magical.

Discovery Lodge Hotel (☎ 979 4433; Niuraivik St; mains C$30-45; ☒ 6am-9am, noon-2pm & 6-9pm) Nunavut's top dining room has an extensive wine list and luscious local cuisine, such as poached Arctic char (C$38) and caribou steak in peppercorn sauce (C$39).

Frobisher Inn (☎ 979 2222; www.frobisherinn.com; Astro Hill; mains C$25-40; ☒ 7am-2pm & 5-9pm Mon-Fri, 8am-2pm & 5-9pm Sat & Sun) A close second to the Discovery, the Frobisher offers caribou, char, pasta and steak.

Drinking

In Iqaluit almost all crimes, as well as the astronomical suicide rate, are linked to drinking. To combat this, the town clamps down on alcohol. Beer and wine can be had with a meal at several restaurants, but there's no liquor store and only one public bar – the Storehouse.

Storehouse Bar & Grill (☎ 979 2222; Astro Hill; ☒ 5pm-12.30am) is a big, new, well-appointed watering hole that is less of a madhouse than the former saloon, but it can still get rough. The pizza and burgers are yummy.

Getting There & Away

Iqaluit is the air hub of the eastern Arctic, with flights to Quebec and Ontario as well as smaller Baffin communities. Iqaluit has nearly daily arrivals from Montréal and Ottawa aboard First Air (p237) and Canadian North (p237) for about C$1300 return. Both airlines serve Iqaluit from Yellowknife for about C$1400 return.

First Air serves all communities on the island, plus Resolute and Rankin Inlet. Kenn Borek Air (p237) has fewer destinations but is often cheaper.

The airport is an easy stroll from downtown, about half a kilometre along Mivvik St. The city is also awash with shared cabs, charging C$5 to go anywhere.

KATANNILIK TERRITORIAL PARK

One of the finest, most accessible parks in Nunavut is just outside the community of Kimmirut (population 433), about 175km (109 miles) from Iqaluit. Katannilik comprises two main features: the Soper River and the Itijjagiaq Trail.

A Canadian Heritage waterway, the aquamarine Soper splashes 50 navigable kilometres through a deep, fertile valley, past cascades, caribou, gemstone deposits and dwarf-willow forests. Paddlers usually spend three days to a week floating and exploring.

Hikers and skiers can opt for the trail, a 120km (75-mile) traditional route over the tablelands of the Meta Incognita Peninsula and through the Soper Valley. The hike usually takes 10 or 12 days. The trailhead is on Frobisher Bay, about 10km west of Iqaluit. For more details, contact **Parks Nunavut** (☎ 975 5900; www.nunavutparks.com).

Most paddlers charter a plane from Iqaluit to the riverside airstrip at Mt Joy. Kenn Borek Air charges C$1634 and can carry over 1000kg of people and gear. If hiking, you can hire an Iqaluit outfitter to boat you to the trailhead; ask for names at the Unikkaarvik Visitors Centre in Iqaluit (opposite).

First Air flies back from Kimmirut to Iqaluit four times weekly (one way C$143).

RESOLUTE

☎ 867 / pop 220

Godforsaken Resolute, on Cornwallis Island, was founded when the federal government lured Inuit here to shore up Canadian sovereignty. The land is downright lunar, with remains of centuries-old villages by the beach. Most visitors are just passing through on their way to Quttinirpaaq National Park (below), the North Pole, or scenic Grise Fjord (p248) – the only Canadian community that's further north.

SIDE TRIP: QUTTINIRPAAQ NATIONAL PARK

If you have a fortune to squander and a penchant for wide-open spaces, head for Quttinirpaaq National Park (formerly Ellesmere Island National Park), right up at the top of the world. It's Canada's second-biggest park and one of the world's most pristine wilderness areas.

Superlatives include numerous High Arctic icecaps and glaciers; **Cape Columbia**, the continent's northernmost point; **Mt Barbeau**, which at 2616m is the highest peak in eastern North America; and **Lake Hazen Basin**, a thermal oasis where, due to their unfamiliarity with humans, animals appear strangely tame. The chartered plane from Resolute costs C$32,000 return for up to six people. For park information, contact Parks Canada in Pangnirtung (p249).

If you have time, try local hiking or fly to **Beechey Island**, about 80km (50 miles) southwest (an air charter for up to 10 people costs C$1660). This desolate place was where the ill-fated Franklin expedition wintered in 1845–6 before vanishing forever. Traces of expedition members and their unsuccessful rescuers remain. Ask at Resolute's hotels for tour and outfitter information.

Qausuittuq Inns North (☎ 252 3900; www.innsnorth .com; s/d C$165/330, with meals C$215/430) is a delightful family-style lodge that has good home cooking. **South Camp Inn** (☎ 252 3737; www.south campinn.com; s/d C$240/480) may be expensive, but it has Internet access in every room, Jacuzzi tubs and free use of snowmobiles.

First Air (p237) has flights to Iqaluit twice a week (C$1793 return), while Kenn Borek Air (p237) serves small High Arctic towns, including Grise Fjord (C$700) and Pond Inlet (C$622), and does charters.

GRISE FJORD
☎ 867 / pop 160

Grise Fjord, at the southern tip of Ellesmere Island, is the northernmost civilian community in Canada and rivals Pangnirtung as the most beautifully located village in Nunavut. Surrounded by spectacular peaks and icebergs, it truly is breathtaking.

Local boat owners can arrange tours to the floe-edge, the spot where the sea ice meets the open water, about 50km east of the village. Here you'll have a good chance of seeing walruses, belugas, seals, polar bears and a variety of sea birds. Along **South Cape Fjord**, 40km west of town, the seas are often choked with icebergs, ensuring stunning photos. Hiking on the area's glaciers and icecaps is also possible. The area is also dotted with **archaeological sites**, including an ancient polar-bear trap, abandoned Inuit camps and the cross erected to a sailor who died on the Otto Sverdrup expedition (see p21).

The **Grise Fjord Lodge** (☎ 980 9913; www.inns north.com) charges C$185 per person, including meals. Alternatively, you can camp free of charge at several inviting streamside sites outside the village. Kenn Borek Air (see p237) flies from Resolute for C$700 return.

POND INLET
☎ 867 / pop 1300

On Baffin Island's north coast, Pond Inlet is in a fabulous setting of rugged mountains,

icy peaks, glaciers and icebergs. Non-Inuit originally arrived here for whaling and trading; now they come to kayak and gaze slack-jawed at the incredible landscape.

You'll get information on local activities and outfitters from the **Nattinnak Centre** (☎ 899 8225; 9am-noon & 1.30-5pm Mon-Fri summer). Some of the best hiking and touring is in nearby **Sirmilik National Park**, a vast haven strewn with spires, glaciers and hoodoos (stone pillars formed by wind and water erosion) that provides breeding grounds for countless sea birds. For details on the park and a list of outfitters organising tours there, contact **Parks Canada** (☎ 899 8092; sirmilik.info@pc.gc.ca; 1-5pm Mon-Fri).

Another ambitious trek is to the summit of 765m **Mt Herodier**, 15km east of town. For something less adventurous, try the short hike out of town to Salmon Creek, where you'll find the remains of an old Inuit village and (in July and August) spots along the coast to fish for Arctic char.

Polar Sea Adventures (☎ 899 8870; www.polarsea adventures.com) hires out kayaks and guides for summer kayaking and whale-watching trips. In late spring, it and other outfitters, including **Tununiq Travel & Adventure** (☎ 899 8194; www.tununiq.com) and **Toonoonik Sahoonik Outfitters** (☎ 899 8928; www.pondtoura.ca), lead wildlife-viewing trips to Sirmilik National Park, Bylot Island and the floe-edge, the biologically rich area where the sea ice meets open water. Whale watching, fjord visits, dogsledding, kayaking, fishing, cross-country skiing and hiking are all possible. Budget on about C$400 per day.

You can camp for free at Qilaluqat Park, though the facilities are basic. Alternatively, the **Sauniq Hotel** (☎ 899 8928; s/d C$185/370, with meals C$260/520) has comfortable rooms, and there's also a guestroom at **Sirmilik Inn B&B** (☎ 899 8688; www.tuniniq.com; s/d with breakfast C$135/220, with all meals C$180/310).

First Air (p237) flies to Iqaluit for C$1130 return, and Kenn Borek Air (p237) serves Resolute for C$622 return.

PANGNIRTUNG
☎ 867 / pop 1364

Among Nunavut's outlying communities, 'Pang' is one of the best destinations to visit, with stunning scenery, art and outdoor opportunities galore. The community, 40km south of the Arctic Circle, hugs a stunning

---

ACTIVITIES: HIKING AUYUITTUQ NATIONAL PARK

Auyuittuq (ah-you-*ee*-tuk) means 'the land that never melts'. Appropriately, there are plenty of glaciers in this 19,500-sq-km park, plus jagged peaks, vertiginous cliffs, deep valleys, fjords and meadows. The most popular activity in the area is the 97km (61-mile) **Akshayuk Pass hiking route** when it's snow-free (between late June and early September). Nearby, intrepid climbers head for Mt Thor, with its incredible 1500m granite cliff face, the earth's tallest wall. You can camp wherever you can find a safe and ecologically responsible spot. Nine emergency shelters dot the pass, but hikers and climbers who get into trouble are responsible for rescue expenses, so make sure you have insurance.

You must register at the Parks Canada office in Pangnirtung (below) and pay the park entry fee – C$15 for a day trip or C$40 for up to three nights – before setting off for the park.

The south end of the pass is 30km from Pangnirtung. In summer you can hike there in two days or have an outfitter take you by boat for C$85 to C$95. For about C$200, through-hikers can arrange to be picked up at the other end by an outfitter from Qikiqtarjuaq (population 519), which is served by First Air and Kenn Borek Air.

---

mountain-flanked fjord and is the gateway to Auyuittuq National Park.

For information on local guides and outfitters, and an insight into Inuit life, visit the **Angmarlik Interpretive Centre** (☎ 473 8737; ☯ 8.30am-9pm Jul & Aug, 8.30am-5pm Mon-Fri Sep-Jun). Next door is the **Parks Canada office** (☎ 473 8828; www.parkscanada.gc.ca; ☯ 8.30am-5pm Jul & Aug, 8.30am-5pm Mon-Fri Sep-Jun).

The town is famous for tapestries, prints and woven hats. You can meet some of the craftspeople and buy their work at the **Uqqurmiut Centre for Arts & Crafts** (☎ 473 8669; inuit art@nunanet.com; ☯ 9am-noon, 1-5pm & 6-9pm Mon-Sat Jul & Aug, 9am-noon & 1-5pm Mon-Fri Sep-Jun).

Hikers should try the 6km **Ukama Trail**, which follows the Duval River and takes about three hours, or the highly recommended 13km **Ikuvik Trail**, which heads for the summit of Mt Duval (671m) and takes about six hours return. Though not always well marked, the Ikuvik Trail hike offers superb views of the town and the fjord. You can pick up a map at the interpretive centre.

You can camp for C$5 at Pitsitunu Tugavik Territorial Park, but don't leave any valuables in your tent. The only hotel is **Auyuittuq Lodge** (☎ 473 8955; s/d C$150/300, with meals C$215/430), which has rudimentary shared rooms and bathrooms. Book early.

It may also be possible to bunk with a local Inuit family if you contact the interpretive centre in advance. Singles/doubles cost C$80/125; with meals they're C$120/175.

First Air (p237) and Kenn Borek Air (p237) fly daily from Iqaluit (return C$288).

CAPE DORSET
☎ 867 / pop 1300

Cape Dorset, on the rocky shore of Baffin Island's Foxe Peninsula, is the epicentre of Inuit art. A half-century ago residents here pioneered modern Arctic carving and printmaking, marketing it to the world with remarkable success. Though many Inuit communities now generate world-class artworks, Cape Dorset's remain the most revered. The **West Baffin Eskimo Cooperative** (☎ 897 8944; ☯ 9am-5pm Mon-Fri winter only) has studios and a gallery, but – in maddening Nunavut fashion – is technically closed in summer. Call ahead, and someone might let you in. The Kingnait Inn also sells sculptures, and you can often find artists carving outside their homes.

You can hike to **Mallikjuaq Historic Park** in about 45 minutes, but only at low tide. Otherwise, hire an outfitter to boat you there. The park features ruins of 1000-year-old pre-Inuit stone houses, hiking trails, wildlife and tundra flowers. Ask at the Kingnait Inn about other hiking routes near town.

Huit Huit Tours (☎ 897 8806; www.capedorsettours .com) offers one-/four-day dogsledding trips (C$75/980) in spring, and week-long fishing, hiking and culture tours (C$1320 to C$3400) in summer. It also operates the waterfront **Beach House** (s/d C$175/350), which has two bedrooms and a kitchen for preparing meals. **Kingnait Inn** (☎ 897 9907; s/d with meals C$250/300) is the local hotel, offering meals and Spartan shared rooms.

First Air and Kenn Borek Air fly to Iqaluit (p245) for about C$450 return.

ITINERARY 3: ALASKA'S DALTON HIGHWAY

Starting from the Arctic frontier town of Fairbanks, the Dalton runs north along the Alaska pipeline before climbing over the Brooks Range, flanked by two of Alaska's most scenic and remote national parks. The route ends on Alaska's North Slope, breeding ground for thousands of caribou and home to a massive oil base.

The 670km (419-mile) Dalton Hwy (better known as the Haul Rd) connects the Elliott Hwy, near Livengood, with Deadhorse, near the Arctic Ocean, with a thin ribbon of gravel. The road was the original truck supply route during the construction of the Trans-Alaska Pipeline, and it's definitely not a trip for the ill-prepared. In summer the 8.5m-wide truck route of coarse gravel is dusty, punctuated with potholes and littered with the carcasses of blown tyres. It's not a question of whether your car will get paint scratches or window chips but of how many, which is the main reason most car-hire companies

in Fairbanks don't allow their vehicles on the highway.

There are few services on the road, and none for the final 360km (225 miles) from Wiseman to Deadhorse. A tow back to Fairbanks can cost US$2000. The road is open year-round, but travellers should only drive it between late May and early September, when there is virtually endless light and the road is usually free of ice. Few people apart from truckers manage to exceed 55mph. Expect a 40mph average and a journey of two hard days to reach the town of Deadhorse, the community that houses the workers of what was once the largest oil reserve in the USA.

If this doesn't make you chicken out you'll be rewarded with some spectacular scenery at Wiseman and the Atigun Pass, access to pristine wilderness and incredible wildlife at Gates of the Arctic National Park and the Arctic National Wildlife Refuge, and a glimpse of real-life Arctic Alaska.

It may seem obvious, but don't feed the bears, don't stop on the road itself and don't drink river water without boiling it for 10 minutes. For trip planning advice, visit http ://aurora.ak.blm.gov/dalton/index.html.

FAIRBANKS
☎ 907 / pop 30,200

A rough-and-tumble northern town, Fairbanks is Alaska's second-largest city and gateway to the Alaskan bush. Downtown Fairbanks has few redeeming features, apart from a cluster of log cabins and sled dogs, and the friendly, hardy and oddball locals who exemplify the Alaskan theme of 'work hard, play hard, drink hard'. The city isn't too interested in providing tourist facilities, and the downtown area has a down-and-out feel, but if you're invited out to the bush or make your own way there you'll have a trip to remember.

Information
Alaska Public Lands Information Centre (☎ 456 0527; www.nps.gov; 250 Cushman St; ⏰ 9am-6pm mid-May–mid-Sep, 10am-6pm Tue-Sat mid-Sep–mid-May) Maps and information on state and national parks, wildlife refuges and recreation areas.

Fairbanks Memorial Hospital (☎ 452 8181; 1650 Cowles St)

Key Bank of Alaska (100 Cushman St) Has an impressive gold nugget display.

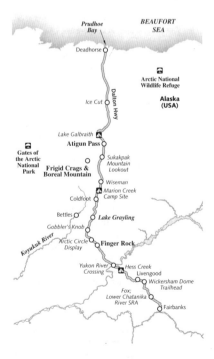

FAST FACTS

- **Access for independent travellers** Good

- **Best time to travel** Late May to early September

- **Difficulty level** Moderate

- **Don't forget** Spare tyres, basic tools, plenty of food and water, blankets, warm clothes, binoculars, first-aid kit, insect repellent

- **Don't miss** Atigun Pass, Gates of the Arctic National Park

- **Gateway city** Fairbanks, Alaska

- **Length of route** 784km (490 miles)

- **Modes of travel** Car, bus

- **Recommended map** International Travel Maps *Alaska* (1:1,500 000), the *Milepost* (p265)

- **Time needed** At least four days

Log Cabin Visitors Centre (☎ 456 5774; www .explorefairbanks.com; 550 1st Ave; ☼ 8am-7pm mid-May–mid-Sep)
Main post office (315 Barnette St)
Wells Fargo bank (613 Cushman St)

Sights & Activities

Start your tour with a visit to the excellent **University of Alaska Museum** (☎ 474 7505; www.uaf .edu/museum; 907 Yukon Dr; adult/child US$5/3; ☼ 9am-7pm Jun-Sep), generally regarded as one of Alaska's best. It's definitely the top attraction in Fairbanks. Inside, the museum is divided into regions of the state, with each section examining the geology, history and unusual aspects of that area. The museum's most famous exhibit is Blue Babe, a fully restored 36,000-year-old bison. Even more impressive, however, is the state's largest public gold display.

Other attractions on the campus include the **Georgeson Botanical Garden** (☎ 474 1944; www .uaf.edu/salrm/gbg; W Tanana Dr; admission US$1; ☼ 8am-10pm May-Sep), a kaleidoscope of flowers, herbs, fruits and gigantic vegetables, and the **Large Animal Research Station** (☎ 474 7207; www.uaf.edu /lars/), which keeps herds of muskoxen, reindeer and caribou. Platforms outside the fenced pastures allow free, all-hours viewing of the herds, but bring binoculars as the

animals aren't always cooperatively grazing nearby. The campus is 6km west of downtown. Take MACS Red Line or Blue Line buses to UAF's Wood Centre.

Back in the centre of town you'll find the incredible **Ice Museum** (☎ 451 8222; 500 2nd Ave; adult/child US$9/6; ☼ 9am-9pm mid-May–mid-Sep). Inside you'll see some 20 tons of ice carved into fabulous sculptures. Also worth a visit is **Fairbanks Community Museum** (☎ 457 3669; 410 Cushman St; admission free; ☼ 10am-6pm mid-May–mid-Sep, Tue-Sat rest of year), which features displays, exhibits and artefacts tracing the city's history.

On 1st Ave there's some old log cabins and several historical buildings, including **St Matthew's Episcopal Church**, a log church originally built in 1905 and reconstructed in 1948. Just across the Chena River Bridge from the visitors centre is the **Immaculate Conception Church** (1904), with its beautiful stained-glass windows.

The city's largest attraction is **Pioneer Park** (☎ 459 1087; Airport Way at Peger Rd; admission free; ☼ 11am-9pm mid-May–mid-Sep), a 44-acre pioneer theme park. It features everything from a gold-rush town to an aviation museum and a native-village museum. There's night-time entertainment at the Palace Theater and Saloon. You can reach the park on a MACS Blue Line bus.

If you're caught by all the tales of gold and glory you can try your own hand at panning at several former gold mines or at selected areas in the bush. **Gold Dredge No 8** (☎ 457 6058; www.golddredgeno8.com; 1755 Old Steese Hwy N; tours adult/child US$23/16), off the Steese Hwy at Goldstream Rd/mile 10, is a good place to start. This five-deck, 76m dredge was built in 1928 and is now a national historical site. The dredge operated until 1959 and still manages to make money – it's probably the most visited dredge in Alaska. Tours are given hourly from 9.30am to 3.30pm every day in summer.

Fairbanks offers a wide variety of canoeing opportunities, from leisurely afternoon paddles to overnight trips into the surrounding area. Several places hire out boats. The most convenient is **7 Bridges Boats & Bikes** (☎ 479 0751; www.7gablesinn.com; 4312 Birch Lane), just off the river at 7 Gables Inn. It provides canoes and a pick-up and drop-off service. Canoes are US$35 a day, and transportation costs US$1.25 a mile (US$10 minimum). You can even arrange to paddle down the Chena River and bike back to the downtown area.

Festivals & Events

Apart from gold, Fairbanks' other claim to fame is as dog-mushing capital of the world, and the city is home to the **North America Sled Dog Championships**, a three-day event in which mushers, some with teams as large as 20 dogs, compete in a series of 32km to 48km (20- to 30-mile) races. Fairbanks is also the start of the **Yukon Quest**, arguably the toughest dogsled race in the world. The 1637km (1023-mile) run between Fairbanks and Whitehorse follows many of the early trails used by trappers, miners and the postal service. Mushers climb four mountains over 900m (3000ft) high and run along 320km (200 miles) of the frozen Yukon River. The race headquarters are at **Yukon Quest Cache** (☎ 451 8985; 410 Cushman St). Inside there's race memorabilia, a few displays and lots of sled-dog souvenirs for sale.

Summer solstice celebrations (www.fairbanks-alaska.com/midnight-sun-events.htm), with footraces, speedboat races, arts and crafts booths and the traditional midnight-sun baseball game, all take place in June.

Fairbanks Summer Arts Festival (www.fsaf.org) has numerous concerts and workshops in the performing and visual arts on the UAF campus in the last two weeks of July.

Golden Days (www.fairbankschamber.org/goldendays), Fairbanks' largest summer festival during the third week of July, celebrates the gold discovery with parades, games, a boat parade and numerous special events, such as the hairy legs contest and the locking up of unsuspecting visitors in the Golden Days Jail.

Tanana Valley State Fair (www.tananavalleyfair.org) is Alaska's oldest fair, held at the fairgrounds on College Rd in early to mid-August and featuring sideshows, a rodeo, entertainment, livestock shows and produce of immense proportions.

Sleeping

Fairbanks has tons of choice when it comes to accommodation. At the visitors centre you can pick up information or use the courtesy phone to check vacancies.

Billie's Backpackers Hostel (☎ 479 2034; www.alaskahostel.com; 2895 Mack Rd; dm US$22; 🖳) Book ahead, as this popular place well deserves your custom. The dorms are fairly standard, but there's free coffee, linen and luggage

storage, a great sundeck, laundry facilities and bike hire at this friendly hostel.

Minnie Street B&B (☎ 456 1802; www.minniestreetbandb.com; 345 Minnie St; s/d US$95/115; 🗶 🖳) This beautifully kept B&B is on the river's north side, a block and a half north of the train station. Rooms have traditional quilts, wooden beds and plenty of floral patterns. Some share bathrooms.

4A Care B&B (☎ 479 2447; www.aaaacare.com; 557 Fairbanks Street; r US$79-149; 🅿 🗶 🖳) This beautiful log home near the university has a selection of bright, comfortable rooms, three wonderful decks and a Jacuzzi.

Pike's Waterfront Lodge (☎ 456 4500; www.pikeslodge.com; 1850 Hoselton Rd; d US$99-205) This large upmarket place on the banks of the Chena River has comfortable modern rooms and plenty of extras, such as a steam room and sauna, exercise facilities and a deck overlooking the river.

Eating

Sam's Sourdough Café (☎ 479 0523; University Ave at Cameron St; breakfast US$4-8; 🕙 6am-10pm) Sourdough specials are available all day at this buzzing place near the university. You can have sourdough pancakes (US$4.75), sourdough omelettes, sourdough sandwiches or a bowl of soup and a mini-loaf of sourdough bread (US$5.75).

Thai House (☎ 452 6123; 526 5th Ave; dinner mains US$9-12) Come here for some of the best Thai dishes in town, including eight vegetarian selections. Don't order anything 'blistering hot' unless you have a cast-iron stomach.

Gambardella's Pasta Bella (☎ 457 4992; 706 2nd Ave; pasta US$10-17, pizzas US$11-13) Homemade pasta dinners and some of the best pizza in the Alaskan interior are the focus at this homey place. It has an outdoor café that is a delight during Fairbanks' long summer days.

Alaska Salmon Bake (☎ 452 7274; Pioneer Park; meals US$26; 🕙 mid-May–mid-Sep) Hungry souls should head for Pioneer Park, where you can choose between grilled salmon, halibut, cod or prime rib. Meals come with salad, sourdough rolls, baked beans, dessert and nonalcoholic beverages (beer and wine are available for an extra charge).

Pump House Restaurant & Saloon (☎ 479 8452; Mile 1.3 Chena Pump Rd; mains US$19-32) The best place to turn dinner into an evening or to enjoy a great Sunday brunch, the Pump House has classic gold-rush atmosphere with a solid mahogany bar and plenty of relics from the city's mining era. Steak and seafood dominate the menu, and you can also enjoy a drink on the outdoor deck while watching the boat traffic on the Chena River. The MACS Blue Line bus goes by here.

Drinking

Rowdy saloons that are throwbacks to the mining days are the area's speciality, though now they're for tourists, not sourdoughs.

Palace Theater & Saloon (☎ 456-5960; www.ak visit.com; Pioneer Park; adult/child US$14/7; ☒ mid-May–mid-Sep) The Palace comes alive at night, with honky-tonk piano, can-can dancers and other acts. Showtime is 8.15pm nightly.

Big I Bar (122 N Turner St) This basic Alaskan bar is the hangout for city workers and reporters from the *Daily News-Miner*. It's a good place to see the locals in action.

Marlin (3412 College Rd) If you fancy some live music, this place simply hops with it six nights a week. It's always busy and has a great atmosphere.

Getting There & Away

AIR

Fairbanks International Airport (☎ 474 2500; Airport Way) serves as the gateway for travellers heading into the Brooks Range and Arctic Alaska. The airport is almost 6km southwest of the city. MACS Yellow Line buses run between the airport and the Transit Park downtown, where you can transfer to any other line.

Alaska Airlines flies daily to Anchorage (US$163), where there are connections to the rest of the state and to Seattle. Air North flies to Dawson (US$110), with a connecting flight to Whitehorse ($163).

For travel into Arctic Alaska, try Frontier Flying Service (p236), Larry's Flying Service (p236) or **Wright Air Service** (☎ 474 0502). All have offices or terminals off University Ave on the airport's eastern side. Regular scheduled flights are available to more than 30 villages, including Bettles, Fort Yukon, Kotzebue, Barrow and Nome.

BUS

Long-distance bus services are available from **Alaska Direct Bus Lines** (☎ 800-770 6652), which runs services to Anchorage (US$70) and Whitehorse (US$140) three times weekly in summer and twice weekly in winter.

Alaska Shuttle (☎ 1-888 600 6001; www.alaska shuttle.com) runs services to Anchorage (US$84, daily in summer, four times weekly in winter) and Dawson (US$160, mid-May to mid-September) three times a week.

CAR

Most people driving to Prudhoe Bay hire a car for five days, but finding somebody in Fairbanks to hire out a vehicle to you for travel on the Dalton Hwy is a major challenge. Drivers generally need to be at least 21 (often 25) and must have their own insurance. Damage to tyres and windscreens is not normally covered by company insurance.

Your best bet is to try **Arctic Outfitters** (☎ 474 3530; www.arctic-outfitters.com; per day US$87) or **Arctic Rent a Car** (☎ 479 8044; www.arcticrentacar.com; 4500 Dale Rd; per day US$60).

Avis (☎ 474 0900), **Budget** (☎ 474 0855) and **National** (☎ 9070 451 7368) may also allow use on the Dalton Hwy.

TRAIN

Alaska Railroad (☎ 458 6025, 800-895 7245; www.alaska railroad.com) has daily departures for Anchorage (US$125) from mid-May to mid-September and four trips a week in winter.

FAIRBANKS TO THE YUKON RIVER
208km (130 miles)

It's 118km (74 miles) up the Steese and Elliott Hwys before you reach the start of the Dalton Hwy. Roadside services are few and far between on this route. Once you leave Fairbanks, your next stop for gas will be at the Yukon River Crossing (mile 56; that's 208km – 130 miles – from Fairbanks), and after that it's Coldfoot (mile 175). You will need to bring extra petrol, a couple of spare tyres, food, water, blankets and insect repellent.

You'll join the Elliott Hwy at Fox and soon pass the **Lower Chatanika River State Recreation Area** (mile 11), a 570-acre park offering fishing, boating and camping opportunities. The area has two camp sites: Whitefish (US$5) and Olnes Pond (US$10).

At mile 28 of the Elliott Hwy are the Wickersham Dome Trailhead parking lot and an information box. From here, trails lead to Bureau of Land Management (BLM) cabins at Borealis-Le Fevre (30km; US$25) and Lee's Cabin (11km; US$25). The hikes have fantastic views overlooking the White Mountains.

SIDE TRIP: ARCTIC NATIONAL WILDLIFE REFUGE

The **Arctic National Wildlife Refuge** (ANWR; http://arctic.fws.gov) is one of the last great wilderness areas in the USA, but oil-company officials and Alaskan politicians are pushing hard to open up this 1.5-million-acre refuge to oil and gas drilling (see p47). For visitors the main attraction here is the profuse wildlife; the sheer numbers have been compared to those of the Serengeti Plains in East Africa. The park is home to wolves, polar bears, grizzlies, muskoxen, Dall sheep, the vast herd of Porcupine caribou and thousands of migratory birds. It's also the habitat of the world's northernmost population of black bears, which makes it the only place where all three North American bear species are present. The landscape stretches from lagoons, beaches and salt marshes to coastal plain, alpine tundra, and the tall spruce, birch, and aspen of the boreal forest.

Wildlife buffs, birdwatchers, rafters, canoers and backpackers who make the effort necessary to get here will be greatly rewarded. You can visit the park yourself or with an organised tour. Visiting the Arctic Refuge on your own requires a great deal of planning, preparation and experience in remote areas. For tips on minimising your impact when hiking and camping, see p255. Air-taxi pilots are very helpful in suggesting routes and itineraries, though most people stick to a few choice locations such as the Sheenjek, Kongakut, the Canning and Hulahula Rivers, the Jago Valley, and the Arctic coast.

Access

Access to the park is by air only. Companies offering air-taxi services include **Brooks Range Aviation** (see p236), **Circle Air** (☎ 907-520 5223; www.circleair.com) and **Yukon Air Service** (☎ 907-479 3993; www.yukonair.com). For a full list, visit http://Arctic.fws.gov/airtaxi.htm. Budget on spending about US$400 to US$1000 per hour for three people.

Tours

A variety of companies offer tours in the ANWR including camping, fishing, wildlife viewing and float trips. Operators include **ABEC's Alaska Adventures** (see p256), **Alaska Alpine Adventures** (☎ 877-525 2577; www.alaskaalpineadventures.com), **Arctic Wild** (☎ 888-577 8203; www.arcticwild.com), **Chilkat Guides** (☎ 907-766 2491; www.raftalaska.com) and **Wilderness Alaska** (☎ 907-345 3567; www.wildernessalaska.com). To see the massive caribou migration you'll need to arrive in mid-June. Budget on spending roughly US$2000 per week. For a full listing of approved companies, visit http://Arctic.fws.gov/recguide.htm.

Reserve through the BLM's **Fairbanks office** (☎ 474 2251, 474 2200; www.ak.blm.gov).

Next up is the service centre, Livengood (mile 71), where you'll find a small general store. At this point, the Elliott Hwy swings west, and in 3km you'll come to the turn-off for the start of your odyssey north. At mile zero of the Dalton Hwy is an information centre that has up-to-date details on road conditions, wildlife sightings and weather reports. The road winds through rolling hills and over small creeks, the largest of which is Hess Creek at mile 25. There's a lookout here with good views of the pipeline. In the trees near the Hess Creek Bridge there are unserviced camp sites, and good fishing for whitefish and grayling.

The highway begins to descend to the Yukon River at mile 47, providing views of kilometres of pipeline. At mile 56 you'll hit the mighty Yukon River, which drains nearly half of Alaska and much of Canada's Yukon. It's the fifth-largest river in North America, beginning in the Yukon and flowing over 3040km (1900 miles) before it reaches the Bering Sea. The 687m (2290ft) wooden-decked bridge is the only one to cross the Yukon in Alaska. Just north of the bridge is the **Yukon Crossing Visitor Centre** (♥ 9am-6pm mid-May–mid-Sep), managed by the BLM. It has interpretive displays on the pipeline and the terrain you're about to enter. On the west side of the highway is **Yukon River Camp** (☎ 665 9001; d US$89), which includes a motel, a restaurant, tyre repair and a phone.

Yukon River Tours (☎ 452 7162; www.mosquitonet.com/~dlacey/yrt.html; adult/child US$25/15) also operates from here and offers boat trips along the Yukon three times a day. The trip takes you to an Athapaskan fish camp and cultural centre, and offers good opportunities to see wildlife.

Six kilometres north of the Yukon River is an old pipeline camp, now a BLM camp site with a pit toilet and a well. Nearby is the turnoff for **Hotspot Café** (☎ 451 7543), which includes rustic accommodation, a restaurant, tyre repair and a phone.

YUKON RIVER TO WISEMAN
211km (132 miles)

At mile 86.5 there is a lookout with a scenic view of granite tors to the northeast, Fort Hamlin Hills to the southeast and the oil pipeline over 150m below. In the next 16km the highway ascends above the tree line into an alpine area where there is good hiking and berry picking. As you reach the summit of Finger Mountain (mile 97.5) you'll see Finger Rock to the east of the highway and panoramic views of the whole area. The road stays in this alpine section for another 8km before the terrain turns rugged.

The **Arctic Circle**, near mile 115 of Dalton Hwy, is the site of an impressive BLM display. The exhibit includes a large, brightly coloured circumpolar map of the imaginary line, and four panels explaining the basis for the seasons and what it means to Arctic plants and animals. There are also picnic tables, a viewing deck, and a road leading a kilometre or so to rustic camp sites.

Keep in mind, however, that you can't really see the midnight sun here, because it ducks behind the mountains on the northern horizon at that magical moment. To view the sun all night long (having driven this far north, you might as well do it), continue on to **Gobbler's Knob**, a hilltop viewpoint at mile 132, where there's a pullover (lay-by) with an outhouse.

From this turnoff the road passes six streams and the small **Lake Grayling** (mile 150) in the next 80km (50 miles), all of which offer superb grayling fishing. At Lake Grayling there's a U-shaped trough gouged out by a glacier 1.5 million years ago. It's a good place to spot water birds and moose.

The next major milestone is Coldfoot (mile 175), a historic mining camp and your halfway point. The lowest temperature in North America (-63°C) was recorded here on 26 January 1989. Originally named Slate Creek, the area was first settled by miners in 1898. When a group of green stampeders got 'cold feet' at the thought of wintering in the district, they headed south and the town was renamed accordingly. In 1981 Iditarod musher Dick Mackey set up an old school bus at Coldfoot and began selling hamburgers to truck drivers heading for Prudhoe Bay. The truckers liked the location so much they helped Mackey build the present truck stop, including raising the centre pole of the building and engraving their names on it.

Services at **Coldfoot Camp** (☎ 866-474 3400; www.coldfootcamp.com; Mile 175 Dalton Hwy; tents/RVs/r US$15/35/165) include petrol, tyre repair, a laundry and the 'furthest north saloon in North America'. The restaurant is open 24 hours,

---

ARCTIC HIKING TIPS

Regardless of where you hike in the Arctic, trekking is a challenge. Hiking across boggy ground and tussock, inevitable on almost any trip, has been described by one guide as 'walking on basketballs'. A good day's hike will see you cover only 8km to 10km. Extended treks require outdoor experience, a good map and excellent compass skills.

If travelling independently, always leave your itinerary with a dependable person and make firm arrangements with an air-taxi operator. Planes can be delayed several days due to bad weather, so carry extra food.

The Arctic ecosystem is very fragile and easily damaged, even by the most sensitive backpackers. It requires years to regenerate, due to the permafrost and the short growing season. For these reasons the National Park Service (NPS) puts a six-person limit on trekking parties.

Camp-site selection is your most important decision when trying to minimise impact. Gravel bars along rivers and creeks are the best choice, due to their durable and well-drained nature. If you must choose a vegetated site, select one with a hardier species such as moss or heath, rather than the more fragile lichens. Avoid building fires at all costs; tree growth in the Arctic is extremely slow, and a spruce which is only inches in diameter may be several hundred years old.

SIDE TRIP: GATES OF THE ARCTIC NATIONAL PARK

One of Alaska's remotest national parks and one of the finest wilderness areas in the world, **Gates of the Arctic National Park** (www.nps.gov/gaar) covers 21,122 sq km (13,125 sq miles) from the southern foothills of the Brooks Range, across the ragged peaks and down onto the North Slope. The park gets its name from the peaks of Boreal Mountain and Frigid Crags that flank the north fork of the Koyukuk River.

The park is home to grizzly bears, wolves, Dall sheep, moose, caribou and wolverines. Fishing is also considered superb, with grayling and Arctic char in the clear streams and lake trout in the larger, deeper lakes.

There are dozens of rivers to run and miles of valleys and tundra slopes to hike. However, there are no maintained trails and the hiking is pretty strenuous. The park is accessible only by chartered aeroplane or on foot from the Dalton Hwy. Prospective backcountry visitors must participate in a mandatory orientation programme at Bettles or Coldfoot.

Hiking

The park has no facilities for visitors. Many backpackers follow the long, open valleys for extended treks, or work their way to higher elevations where open tundra and sparse shrubs provide good hiking terrain. One of the more popular treks is the four- to five-day hike from Lake Summit through the Gates to Lake Redstar. Less experienced backpackers often choose to be dropped off and picked up at the same lake and explore the surrounding region on day hikes from there. Lakes ideal for this include Lake Summit, the Karupa lakes region, Lake Redstar, Lake Hunt Fork and Lake Chimney.

For hiking tips, see p255.

Paddling

Paddlers should head for the John, the north fork of the Koyukuk, the Tinayguk, the Alatna, and the middle fork of the Koyukuk River from Wiseman to Bettles. The headwaters of the Noatak and Kobuk Rivers are in the park. The waterways range from class I to class III in difficulty. Of the various rivers, the north fork of the Koyukuk River is one of the most popular – the float begins in the shadow of the Gates and continues downstream 160km (100 miles) to Bettles through class I and class II waters. Canoes and rafts can be hired in Bettles and then floated downstream back to the village.

However, the best-known river and the most popular for paddlers is the upper portion of the Noatak. This is because of the spectacular scenery as you float through the sharp peaks of the Brooks Range and also because it is a relatively mild river that can be handled by many canoeists on an unguided trip. The most common trip is a 96km (60-mile) float that begins near Portage Creek and ends at a riverside lake near Kacachurak Creek, just outside the park boundary. This float is usually completed in five to seven days. It involves some class II and possible class III stretches of rapids toward the end.

and its photo collection of jackknifed and overturned semitrailers will make you think twice about driving any further. The food is surprisingly good. Fill your tank – the next available services are 390km (244 miles) to the north.

Coldfoot is also a jumping-off point to Gates of the Arctic National Park, which has no road access. The new **Arctic Interagency Visitor Centre** (☎ 678 5209; ⊙ 10am-10pm mid-May–mid-Sep) has interpretive displays, and information on fishing, backpacking, gold panning and camping in the park and surrounding wilderness areas. The park boundary is just to the west of the road.

Beyond Coldfoot, the road enters the **Brooks Range**, a northern spur of the Rocky Mountains with peaks ranging from 1200m to 2700m (4000ft to 9000 feet). Eight kilometres north of Coldfoot, at mile 180, is the Marion Creek camp site (sites US$8), situated in an open spruce forest with stunning views of the Brooks Range. A 3km hike upstream leads to a 6m (20-foot) waterfall.

Bettles

This small village (population 50) serves as the major departure point to the Gates of the Arctic National Park.

The **Bettles Ranger Station** (☎ 692 5494; 8am-5pm Jun-Sep) also serves as a visitor centre, and has displays depicting the flora and fauna of the Brooks Range, a small library, and books and maps for sale.

Camping is allowed behind the Bettles Flight Service building, off the runway at the north edge of the aircraft parking area, where you'll find barbecue grills. It would be just as easy to pitch a tent on the gravel bars along the middle fork of the Koyukuk River.

Bettles Lodge (☎ 692 5111; www.bettleslodge.com; dm/s/d US$15/115/135) has a variety of accommodation available in a classic Alaskan log lodge. There's also a small tavern with bush pilots constantly wandering through in their hip boots.

Sourdough Outfitters (☎ 692 5252; www.sourdoughoutfitters.com; dm/s/d US$30/75/80) has a range of comfy rooms, and there's access to showers (US$4) for campers.

A meal at either hotel will cost US$12 to US$15.

Access

Access to the park's backcountry is by either walking in from the Dalton Hwy or catching a flight from Fairbanks to Bettles ($270) with **Bettles Air Service** (☎ 800-770 5111; www.bettleslodge.com). From Bettles you can charter an air taxi to take you further into the backcountry. Both Bettles Air Service and **Brooks Range Aviation** (☎ 800-692 5444; www.brooksrange.com) run air charters. Sample fares (per plane load, not per person) are US$650 for drop off at the North Fork of the Koyukuk River or US$1216 for drop-off at Lake Summit.

If you're walking, head west at the Wiseman exit just before you reach mile 189 of the Dalton Hwy and continue hiking along the Nolan Rd, which passes through Nolan, a hamlet of a few families, and ends at Nolan Creek. From here you can reach Wiseman Creek and Lake Nolan Creek, at the foot of three passes: Glacier, Pasco and Snowshoes. You can hike from any of these passes to Glacier River, which can be followed to the north fork of the Koyukuk for a more extensive hike.

Otherwise, continue north from Wiseman by hiking along the Hammond Rd, which can be followed for quite a way along the Hammond River. From the river you can further explore the park by following one of several drainage areas, including Vermont, Canyon and Jenny Creeks. The latter heads east to Lake Jenny Creek.

Tours

A number of guide companies run hiking and paddling trips in the park, including **ABEC's Alaska Adventures** (☎ 457-8907; www.abecalaska.com), **Arctic Wild** (☎ 888-577 8203; www.arcticwild.com) and **Sourdough Outfitters** (☎ 692 5252; www.sourdoughoutfitters.com). Typical one-week costs are about US$2000.

After you pass mile 186 there's a lookout where you can view the historical mining community of **Wiseman**, west of the highway across the Koyukuk River, which can now be reached by an improved road at mile 188.6. The town's heyday was in 1910, when it replaced Coldfoot as a service centre for gold miners. Many buildings from that era still stand, including the **Wiseman Trading Company**. The building doubles as the general store and the town's **museum**, with historic photos and mining equipment. Wiseman also has a public phone and a camp site. More comfortable accommodation is available in beautiful log cabins at the **Arctic Getaway** (☎ 678 4456; www.arcticgetaway.com; cabins US$90) or at the **Boreal Lodge** (☎ 678 4566; www.boreallodge.com; s/d US$55/75), which also has a choice of cabins available for US$125 per night.

WISEMAN TO DEADHORSE

362km (226 miles)

More spectacular mountain scenery begins around mile 194, with the first views of Sukakpak Mountain to the north and Wiehl Mountain to the east, both over 1200m (4000ft) in elevation. Poss Mountain (1857m/6189ft) comes into view to the east after another 4km, and the Koyukuk River, a heavily braided stream, is seen near mile 201.

Just before mile 204 is a lookout with an 800m trail leading to Sukakpak Mountain. You'll pass another lookout after mile 206, where there are good views of Snowden Mountain (1733m/5775ft), and reach Disaster Creek after another 10km.

Even if you have no desire to see the North Slope, continue on to **Atigun Pass** and some of the most spectacular scenery of the trip. At an elevation of 1422m (4739ft), this is the highest highway pass in Alaska and marks the continental divide. The steep 3km climb to the pass begins at mile 242.5, and the pullover at the top is an excellent place for spotting Dall sheep and grizzlies. On the north side of the Brooks Range you may spot caribou and muskoxen. To the east are the Phillip Smith Mountains, to the west the Endicott Mountains, and beyond the pass is the flat, treeless coastal plain known as the North Slope.

The Galbraith camp site at mile 275 is located on an old pipeline camp work pad at Lake Galbraith, where both the BLM and the US Fish and Wildlife Service maintain field stations. There is no potable water available at this site, but there are spectacular views of the lake and Brooks Range, and good hiking nearby.

You'll pass three more scenic lookouts on the way to Deadhorse. Ice Cut, at mile 326, is a good place to see peregrine falcons, gyrfalcons and other raptors hunting along the rocky cliffs.

Deadhorse, at mile 414, is the end of the highway, a few kilometres short of the Prudhoe Bay oil fields and the Arctic Ocean. Surprisingly, the town has a population that ranges from 3000 to more than 8000, depending on the season, and three motels, none of which is anything to write home about. Slightly the better of the three is the sprawling **Arctic Caribou Inn** (☎ 877-659 2368; www.arcticcaribouinn.com; r US$125; ☺ Jun-Sep). Other options include the **Prudhoe Bay Hotel** (☎ 659 2449; www.prudhoebayhotel .com) and the **Arctic Oilfield Hotel** (☎ 659 2614). There are also restaurants, fuel, a general store and a post office.

For security reasons, you can't drive into the massive oil complex. If you want to see it, join a commercial tour. Arctic Caribou Inn offers a two-hour bus tour ($37 per person) that includes a brief stop at the Arctic Ocean, where you are allowed to stroll along the beach. On the tour you'll also visit Pump Station 1 and the Oilfield Visitors Center.

Dalton Highway Express (see p237) runs shuttles to the Arctic Ocean for US$39. **Northern Alaska Tour Company** (☎ 474 8600; www.northernalaska .com) offers a three-day trip to Prudhoe Bay from Fairbanks ($749) that includes lodging at Wiseman and Deadhorse, some meals and the flight back to Fairbanks.

ITINERARY 4: NORTHWEST ALASKA

This aerial tour departs from Fairbanks and heads for the traditional Inupiat community of Kotzebue before hitting the incredible wilderness parks of northwest Alaska and Alaska's northernmost town, the whaling community of Barrow.

The vast, flat treeless plains of northwestern Alaska are pitted with mountain ranges, millions of lakes and slow-moving rivers. It's a pristine wilderness with only a handful of settlements and some of the most remote and untouched scenery in the state. Two large indigenous communities, Kotzebue and Barrow, carry on traditional life much as it was in years gone past, and there's fantastic hiking, wildlife watching and canoeing in the Noatak National Preserve and the Kobuk Valley National Park. Incredible desert-like landscapes, thousands of migrating caribou and a real sense of the far north await you if you choose this route. Fairbanks acts as an air hub for the whole area, so you may have to do some backtracking to see all the sights on this itinerary.

FAIRBANKS

For information on Fairbanks, see p250.

KOTZEBUE
☎ 907 / 3600

The traditional Inupiat community of Kotzebue is the transportation and commerce centre for Northwest Alaska. Even so it's extremely difficult for an independent traveller to visit on a limited budget. Most travellers to

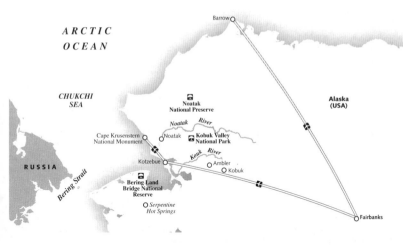

Kotzebue are either part of a tour group on a day trip from Anchorage or are just passing through on their way to a wilderness expedition in the surrounding national parks and reserves. To make the best of a trip you have to get out and explore these remote national parklands and enjoy the warm welcome received by those who want to learn about the local Inupiat culture.

Many residents still depend on subsistence hunting and fishing to survive, but Red Dog Mine, 144km (90 miles) north of town, has boosted the local economy. The mine holds some of the richest zinc deposits in North America and is expected to produce 5% of the world's supply of zinc when it's running at full capacity.

Information
Kotzebue City Hall (☎ 442 3401; 258 3rd Ave) Your best bet for tourist information.
Maniilaq Health Centre (☎ 442 3321; 436 5th Ave)
Post office (Shore Ave)
Wells Fargo Bank (☎ 442 3258; cnr 2nd Ave & Lagoon St)
Western Arctic National Parklands Visitors Centre (☎ 442 3890; cnr 2nd Ave & Lakes St; ☽ 8am-7pm Jun-Sep)

Sights & Activities
Kotzebue is named after Polish explorer Otto von Kotzebue, who stumbled onto the village in 1816 while searching for the Northwest Passage (see p20) on behalf of the Russians. Much of the town's history and culture can be viewed at the **NANA Museum of the Arctic**

(☎ 442 3441; cnr 2nd & 3rd Aves; admission US$20), at the western end of town. The centre is owned and operated by the Northwest Alaska Native Association (NANA), and a two-hour programme of indigenous culture is held at 4pm and 6.30pm daily in summer. The programme includes demonstrations of Inupiat handicrafts and a *nalukataq*, the traditional blanket toss, which historically allowed people to gain enough elevation to observe vast distances of terrain. Although the presentation is scheduled to accommodate day tours from Anchorage, walk-ins are welcome.

FAST FACTS

- **Access for independent travellers** Expensive
- **Best time to travel** June to September
- **Difficulty level** Moderate
- **Don't forget** Camera, plenty of film, plenty of cash, binoculars
- **Don't miss** Paddling the Noatak River, Kobuk's magnificent sand dunes
- **Gateway city** Fairbanks, Alaska
- **Length of route** 1760km (1100 miles)
- **Mode of travel** Air
- **Recommended map** International Travel Maps *Alaska* (1:1,500,000)
- **Time needed** At least one week

Perhaps the most interesting thing to do in Kotzebue is just stroll down Shore Ave (also known as Front St), a narrow gravel road only a few metres from the water at the northern edge of town, and appreciate the historic wooden architecture. Here fishing boats crowd the beach and salmon dries on racks as locals prepare for the long winter ahead. From early June the sun doesn't set for almost six weeks, and this is best place to watch the midnight sun roll along the horizon, painting the sea reddish gold with reflected light.

Also of interest is the large **cemetery** in the centre of town, where spirit houses have been erected over many of the graves.

Sleeping & Eating

Kotzebue does not have a public camp site or hostel. The best bet is to hike south of town well past the airport and pitch your tent on the beach. Much of the beach is narrow and sloping or privately owned, so you may have to scout around for a suitable spot.

Lagoon B&B (☎ 442 3723; 227 Lagoon St; d US$100) This small place has four comfortable rooms

and may feel a little less overrun than the larger hotels.

Nullagvik Hotel (☎ 442 3331; www.nullagvik .com; 308 Shore Ave; d US$149) The Nullagvik is aimed at group tours and offers comfortable corporate-style rooms and decent nosh (mains US$15 to US$25). The hotel is built on pilings to keep the heat and weight of the three-storey building from melting the permafrost.

Bayside Hotel (☎ 442 3600; 303 Shore Ave; d US$115) Just next door to the Nullagvik, this smaller hotel offers slightly cheaper rooms and has a good restaurant (mains US$13 to US$22) serving Chinese and American fare.

Getting There & Away

A return ticket with **Alaska Airlines** (☎ 800-426 0333; www.alaskaair.com) to Kotzebue from Fairbanks usually costs between US$300 and US$400. You can also purchase a return ticket from Anchorage with stopovers in both Nome and Kotzebue.

Tour Arctic (☎ 800-468 2248; www.tour-Arctic.com) offers day trips to Kotzebue from Fairbanks for US$385. You may as well include an

---

ACTIVITIES: PADDLING

Kotzebue provides access to some of the finest river-running in Arctic Alaska. Most trips are self-guided, so you should have plenty of experience and come fully equipped. Popular excursions include those along the Noatak River, the Kobuk River, the Salmon River (which flows into the Kobuk) and the Selawik River.

Trips along the Kobuk National Wild River begin at Lake Walker and travel 224km (140 miles) downstream to the villages of Kobuk or Ambler. From these villages there are scheduled flights to both Kotzebue and Bettles, another departure point for the river. **Bering Air Service** (☎ 442 3943; www.beringair.com) charges US$185 for a one-way flight from either Kobuk or Ambler to Kotzebue. Most of the river is class I, but some lining of boats may be required just below Lake Walker and for 2km or so through Lower Kobuk Canyon. Paddlers usually plan on six to eight days for the float.

The Noatak National Wild River is a 16-day, 560km (350-mile) float from Lake Matcharak to the village of Noatak, where Bering Air has scheduled flights to Kotzebue for US$110 per person one way. However, the numerous access lakes on the river allow it to be broken down into shorter paddles. The entire river is rated from class I to class II. The upper portion, in the Brooks Range, offers much more dramatic scenery and is usually accessed from Bettles (see p256). The lower half, accessed through Kotzebue, flows through a broad, gently sloping valley where hills replace the sharp peaks of the Brooks Range. The most common trip here is to put in at Nimiuktuk River where, within an hour of paddling, you enter the 104km (65-mile) Grand Canyon of the Noatak, followed by the 11km Noatak Canyon. Most paddlers pull out at Kelly River, where there is a ranger station with a radio. Below the confluence with the Kelly River, the Noatak becomes heavily braided.

For more information, contact the National Park Service (www.nps.gov/akso) before you depart for Alaska. Canoes can be hired in Kotzebue through **Arctic Air Guides** (☎ 442 3030; per day US$35), which can also drop you off at remote locations. Air charter costs US$350 per hour.

overnight stay, though, as the cost, including hotel accommodation, is only US$415.

BARROW

☎ 907 / pop 4600

Barrow is the largest Inupiat community in Alaska and retains much of its traditional culture thanks to its isolated location. This is best symbolised by the spring whale hunts and the Nalukataq Festival, staged in June to celebrate a successful hunt.

The scruffy little town, the northernmost community in the USA, lies 528km (330 miles) north of the Arctic Circle and less than 2080km (1300 miles) from the North Pole. Once known as a commercial whaling centre for European and American ships, Barrow is now famous for the midnight sun, and most visitors arrive to set their own farthest-north record. The sun here doesn't set for 82 days from May to early August.

The vast majority of the 8000 tourists who arrive every summer are travelling as part of a package tour. Like Kotzebue, Barrow is an expensive side trip for independent travellers.

Information

Barrow City Tourism (☎ 852 5211; at Momegana & Ahkovak Sts; 2-4pm Mon-Fri Jun-Aug)

Post office (cnr Cunningham & Kongosak Sts)

Samuel Simmonds Memorial Hospital (☎ 852 4611; 1296 Agvik St)

Wells Fargo Bank (☎ 852 6200; cnr Agvik & Kiogak Sts)

Sights & Activities

The main thing to do at the top of the world is to stand on the shore of the Arctic Ocean and look towards the North Pole. You can stroll the gravel road that parallels the sea to view *umiaks* (Inupiat skin boats), giant jawbones of bowhead whales, fish-drying racks, and the jumbled Arctic pack ice that still litters the sandy shoreline in June and can be seen stretched across the horizon even in July.

Within town there's the **Inupiat Heritage Centre** (www.nps.gov/inup; Ahkovak St; admission US$5; 9am-6pm Mon-Fri, noon-6pm Sat Jun-Aug). The nearly 7.5-sq-km (24,000-sq-ft) centre houses a museum, a library and a large room designed for traditional dance performances. The museum features exhibits on the Inupiat culture and commercial whaling, as well as displays

on ice-age animals – mammoths, ancient horses, lions and giant bears – that inhabited the parts of Alaska and Siberia known as Beringia. Each afternoon in summer, local people present a cultural programme that features traditional singing, dancing and drumming.

More Inupiat culture and art is on display in the lobby of the **North Slope Borough Building** (1274 Agvik St). A gift shop here has baleen baskets, sealskin bags and ivory carvings for sale.

Perhaps the biggest attraction in the area is **Point Barrow**, a narrow spit of land about 21km northeast of the city. The spit is the northernmost point of land in mainland North America, dividing the Chukchi Sea to the west from the Beaufort Sea to the east. In winter and spring Point Barrow is where polar bears den; in summer it's the featured stop of organised tours. The buses never actually reach the tip of the point, as the road ends several kilometres short of it. To continue, you must walk or rent an ATV.

East of town, along Gas Well Rd, hikers can observe wildlife such as Arctic foxes, caribou, swans, snowy owls, jaegers, typically testy Arctic terns and numerous other bird species, as well as the untold zillions of mosquitoes that provide nourishment for all the bird life.

Tours

Tundra Tours (☎ 852 3900; www.alaskaone.com/top world) is an Inupiat-owned company offering tours of the town, the Arctic Ocean and the surrounding tundra. A blanket toss and drumming and dance performance is also included in the six-hour tour, which costs US$60 per person and includes lunch.

Arctic Adventure Tours (☎ 852 3800) offers a two-hour wildlife tour to Point Barrow to look for polar bears, marine life such as walruses and a variety of migrating birds (US$60).

Festivals & Events

If you dare to visit off-season, you can experience the dark days of winter at **Kivgiq**, the Messenger Feast, a three-day celebration in January or February that takes place every three years and gathers Inuit from around northern Alaska, Canada and Russia.

Piuraagiaqta is the festival of spring. It's held in April, when the days begin to grow

SIDE TRIP: NORTHWEST ARCTIC NATIONAL PARKLANDS

Kotzebue makes an excellent base to visit the outlying villages of the region and the four national parks and monuments in the area. Eleven small settlements are accessible with Bering Air (see p236), but two of the most interesting are Noatak and Kobuk.

Cape Krusenstern National Monument

The broad coastal plain that makes up Cape Krusenstern National Monument consists of alternating beaches, ice-carved lagoons, and 114 parallel limestone bluffs and ridges that define the changing shorelines of the Chukchi Sea. In autumn migrating waterfowl are drawn to Cape Krusenstern by the watery habitats and rich insect life. Most visitors to the park are on kayaking trips along the coast and through the lagoons, or they come for the hiking, backpacking and wildlife viewing across the wetland landscapes.

Noatak National Preserve

Although stark, the vast open landscapes of the Noatak National Preserve make up what are surely the most beautiful scenes in northern Alaska. This huge, mountain-ringed river basin, bounded by the Baird, De Long and Brooks Ranges, is not only home to the gamut of Arctic wildlife but also straddles the boundary between the *taiga* and tundra ecosystems.

The park has no facilities but makes an excellent destination for canoeists (see p260), who can travel from deep in the Brooks Range to the tidewater of the Chukchi Sea. The park is also popular with wildlife watchers, who come to see the great caribou migrations in late summer and early autumn. The pristine ecosystem here protects some of the Arctic's finest arrays of plants and animals.

Kobuk Valley National Park

Just south of Noatak is the **Kobuk Valley National Park** (www.nps.gov/akso), encircled by the Baird and Waring mountain ranges. The most fascinating aspect of the park landscape is the **Great Kobuk Sand Dunes**, on the southern side of the Kobuk River. This desert-like area of shifting 30m (100ft) dunes is a spectacular sight from the air. Other smaller dune areas exist along the riverside, and older, vegetated dunes cover much of the southern portion of the

longer. There are parades, foot and snow-machine races, dog mushing and *iglo*-building contests.

When the spring whaling hunt has been completed in late June, the whalers celebrate the **Nalukataq Festival** for anything from a few days to more than a week, depending on the success of the hunt. The festival is a rare cultural experience. One Inupiat tradition calls for the whaling crews to share their bounty with the village, and during the festival you'll see families carry off platters and plastic bags full of raw whale meat. The main event of the festival is the blanket toss, in which locals gather around a sealskin tarp and pull it tight to toss people into the air – the effect is much like bouncing on a trampoline. The object is to jump as high as possible, and inevitably there are a number of sprains and fractures at every Nalukataq.

Sleeping & Eating

King Eider Inn (☎ 852 4700; www.kingeider.net; 1752 Ahkovak St; s/d US$175/195; ✕) The newest and nicest hotel in Barrow has bright, comfortable rooms with fairly standard Alaskan décor. The place is so immaculately kept that you must take your shoes off at the door.

Top of the World Hotel (☎ 852 3900; www.topof theworldhotel.com; 1200 Agvik St; d US$175) Outpost for the package tourists, this place can get block-booked during the short summer months. The rooms are decked out in wooden furniture and understated floral patterns, and are pretty spacious.

Barrow Airport Inn (☎ 852 2525; 1815 Momegana St; d US$125) The rooms at this place are fairly functional but include fridges, microwaves and kitchenettes, so you could offset some of your costs by self-catering.

UIC-NARL Hostel (☎ 852 7800; s US$75) The former Naval Arctic Research Lab (NARL) east

valley. The most dramatic dunes are accessible on foot along Kavet Creek, about 5km south of the Kobuk River.

The sand was created by the grinding action of ancient glaciers and has been carried to the Kobuk Valley by wind and water. Sand river bluffs, standing as high as 45m (150ft), hold permafrost ice wedges and the fossils of Ice Age mammals.

The placid Kobuk River, which reaches widths of up to 500m (1640ft), slides along at a negligible gradient of about 6cm per kilometre. An excellent lazy float trip will take you between the villages of Ambler and Kiana. At the Onion Portage archaeological site (where there's a seasonal ranger station), you'll find evidence of the Inupiat cultures that have occupied this area for at least 12,000 years. Caribou migrations pass through between August and October.

Bering Land Bridge National Preserve

It's approximately 90km (56 miles) from the easternmost tip of Russia across the Bering Strait to the North American continent, but in the period from 40,000 to 13,000 years ago so much of the earth's water was locked up as ice that the sea level was considerably lower than it is today. As a result, the two continents were connected by a 1600km (1000-mile) bridge of land that facilitated travel between them. It's generally accepted that this was the crossing point for the Athapaskans and other waves of migrants that would eventually populate much of both American continents.

The bleak and barren landscapes along the northern shore of the Seward Peninsula are now protected in the Bering Land Bridge National Preserve. Evidence of the early human migration can be seen in the area, as well as more than 170 species of birds and relics from the gold rush at the start of the 20th century. Scattered across the reserve are six shelter cabins. The most popular, in a haunting setting at Serpentine Hot Springs, sleeps up to 20 people.

Getting There & Away

The only access to these parks is by air from Kotzebue or, in the case of the Bering Land Bridge National Preserve, from Nome. Bering Air (see p236) has flights to Kobuk and Noatak (US$185). **Cape Smythe Air** (☎ 442 3020; www.capesmythe.com) provides charter flights to villages surrounding the Kobuk National Park (US$141).

of town was transferred to Ukpeagvik Inupiat Corp in the 1980s and is mainly used as the local community college It's the cheapest place to stay, but the rooms are basic and have shared facilities.

Pepe's North of the Border (☎ 852 8200; 1204 Agvik St; dinner US$17-22; 6am-10pm) Barrow's top restaurant is the 'northernmost Mexican restaurant in the world'. Pepe's has good Mexican food, steaks and seafood, and décor that will make you forget you're in Barrow.

Arctic Pizza (☎ 852 4222; 125 Upper Apayauk St; pizzas from US$18; 11.30am-11.30pm) Huge portions of tasty food are dished up at the buzzing pizzeria on the 1st floor, while you'll find something like a fine-dining Italian restaurant upstairs, with wonderful views of the Arctic Ocean.

Brower's Café (☎ 852 5800; 3220 Brower Hill; sandwiches US$8-11, dinner US$17-24; 7am-midnight) A former home for stranded whalers, this late–19th-century building now houses an interesting restaurant that resembles a museum. The food's good, and if the artefacts and photos don't keep you entertained the views over the beach will.

Getting There & Away

The only way to reach Barrow is to fly. An advance-purchase return ticket from Fairbanks to Barrow with Alaska Airlines costs between US$310 and US$350.

Such fares make package tours an attractive option. A one-day trip, including airfare from Fairbanks and a village tour, but not meals, is US$373 through Tundra Tours (see p261). You can stay overnight for US$525. The **Northern Alaska Tour Company** (☎ 800-474 1986; www.northernalaska.com) offers single-day/overnight trips departing from Fairbanks for US$399/450.

ESSENTIAL FACTS

DANGERS & ANNOYANCES

Hypothermia

For information on how to prevent and deal with hypothermia, see p332.

Insects

Insects are the creatures most likely to torture you while you're in the woods. You might hear tales of lost hikers going insane from being incessantly swarmed by blackflies and mosquitoes. Blackflies are at their peskiest from late May through to the end of June, while mosquitoes can be a bother from early spring until early autumn. Ticks are an issue from March to June.

Generally, insect populations are greatest deep in the woods and near water, and they increase the further north you go. You'll be fairly safe in clearings, along shorelines or anywhere there's a breeze. Mosquitoes are at their peskiest around sundown; building a fire will help keep them away. A tent with a zipped screen is pretty much essential while camping.

Minimize skin exposure by wearing long-sleeved shirts tucked into long pants tucked into your socks and/or boots, as well as a close-fitting hat or cap. As a rule, darker clothes attract biting insects more so than lighter ones. Perfume, too, evidently draws the wrong kind of attention. If you're venturing into the backcountry, a bug jacket (essentially a mesh jacket/head-net), available at most camping stores, is recommended.

Take plenty of insect repellent and, to enhance protection, also apply the spray to your clothing, shoes, backpack and tent. For additional information, see p332.

Wildlife

Animals are among the Arctic's greatest assets, but they can also represent serious danger if you invade their turf. Feeding animals or getting too close will make them lose their innate fear of people, which makes it more likely that they'll have to be shot by park rangers.

Bears – always on the lookout for an easy snack – often find camp sites simply irresistible. If you're camping it's wise to cook and eat in one place and sleep well away from it. If you do encounter a bear and it doesn't see you, move a safe distance downwind and make noise to alert it to your presence. If the bear sees you, slowly back out of its path, avoid eye contact, speak softly and wave your hands above your head slowly. Never turn your back to the bear and never kneel down. On all accounts do not come between a female and her cubs.

If a grizzly bear charges, do not run and do not scream (which may frighten the bear and make it more aggressive), because the bear

---

GATEWAY CITIES

Getting to Dawson

Air North (☎ 800-764 0407; www.flyairnorth.com) flies from Whitehorse to Dawson. To get to Whitehorse by air you can pick up an **Air Canada** (☎ 1-888 247 2262; www.aircanada.ca) flight in Vancouver, or an Air North service from Vancouver, Edmonton or Calgary.

Alternatively, bus it to Whitehorse with **Greyhound** (☎ 1-800 661 8747; www.greyhound.ca) and then hop on the **Dawson City Courier** (☎ 1-867 993 6688; www.dawsonbus.ca) to Dawson.

Getting to Iqaluit

Iqaluit has nearly daily arrivals from Montréal and Ottawa aboard **First Air** (☎ 1-800 267 1247; www.firstair.ca) and **Canadian North** (☎ 1-800 661 1505; www.cdn-north.com). Both airlines also serve Iqaluit from Yellowknife.

Getting to Fairbanks

Alaska Airlines (☎ 1-800 252 7522; www.alaskaair.com) flies daily from Anchorage (where there are connections to the rest of the states) and Seattle.

To bus it to Fairbanks you'll need to take the Greyhound service to Whitehorse (see above) and then hop on an **Alaska Direct Bus Lines** (☎ 1-800 770 6652) bus to Fairbanks.

GRAEME CORNWALLIS

The waters around Tasiilaq (p206), Greenland

GRAEME CORNWALLIS

Kulusuk island and surrounds
(p204), Greenland

DEANNA SWANEY

Local paddling a *qajaq* (p86), Kulusuk,
Greenland

Mountaineering, Northeast Greenland National Park (p213), Greenland

GRAEME CORNWALLIS

Polar bear (p56), Alaska, USA

ERNEST MANEWAL

NICHOLAS REUSS

The tundra in bloom (p56),
Canada

LEE FOSTER

Traditional caribou masks, Gates of the Arctic
National Park (p256), USA

Icecap camp, Auyuittuq National Park (p249), Canada

GRANT

may only be charging as a bluff. Drop to the ground, crouch face down in a ball and play dead, covering the back of your neck with your hands and your chest and stomach with your knees. Do not resist the bear's inquisitive pawing – it may get bored and go away. The best way to identify a grizzly is from its large shoulder hump.

If a grizzly attacks you in your tent at night, you're likely dealing with a predatory bear that perceives you as a food source. In this extremely rare scenario, you should fight back aggressively with anything you can find – don't play dead.

Attacks by black bears are extremely rare; they usually occur only if the animal is starving. If a black bear should charge you, make yourself look as big and intimidating as possible, raise your arms or your coat, jump up and down and shout. If the bear attacks, fight back with anything to hand.

Elk, moose and muskoxen are potential dangers whenever you encounter them. Always stay at a safe distance. Females are generally at their fiercest during calving season (mid-May to late June), while bulls are most aggressive during mating season (from mid-September to late October).

The likelihood of being attacked by an animal is extremely slight, and you shouldn't spend too much time thinking about it. It's more important to think about the impact you have on the animal's habitat. Give wildlife respect and space. If you see an animal on the side of the road, consider not stopping. If you do decide to pull over, move on after a few minutes. For comprehensive information on attacks by Arctic animals, visit www.dpc.dk/wildlife.

FURTHER READING

For more in-depth coverage, Lonely Planet publishes individual guides to Alaska and Canada, as well as *Hiking in Alaska*, which discusses hikes around the state.

Another essential companion is the **Milepost** (☎ 1-800 726 4707; www.themilepost.com), which has been through over 50 editions and covers practically every business, service and wide spot in the road along every step of the way. If you're heading beyond the highways, the same publisher also produces the *Alaska Wilderness Guide*, which presents an exhaustive array of possibilities in Alaska's roadless areas.

If you're heading further east in Arctic Canada, be sure to get hold of the comprehensive *Nunavut Handbook*, which can be ordered from **Nunavut Tourism** (www.nunatour.nt.ca).

Anyone hoping to strike off into the Arctic wilderness on their own will thoroughly appreciate a copy of *Planning a Wilderness Trip in Canada & Alaska*, by Keith Morton. It contains information on everything you'll want to know, from chartering a bush flight and surviving bears, insects and inclement weather to gutting fish, cooking a palatable meal and dealing with such wilderness plagues as constipation and flatulence. It focuses on the wilderness areas of Alaska and Canada, but the information is applicable anywhere in the Arctic.

MONEY

At the time of writing US$1 equalled C$1.20. Despite the isolated nature of the communities in Arctic Alaska and Canada, practically every community has an ATM accepting major credit cards.

In restaurants leaving a tip of about 15% of the pretax bill is standard. On the rare occasion that restaurants tack the service charge onto the bill (this is usually done for groups of eight or more), no extra tip is required. When tipping you can either hand the money directly to the server or leave it on the table. Tipping is expected for bar service, too.

Alaska

Alaska uses the American dollar only – if you've just crossed over from the Yukon, don't roll up with Canadian dollars and expect them to be accepted. Changing foreign currency in Alaska – especially Arctic Alaska – is a real headache.

Canada

The Canadian dollar is worth slightly less than the American, so you may feel like you're spending more, but prices in the Arctic regions are pretty much on par across the two countries. Canada's federal goods and services tax (GST) adds 7% to just about every transaction. There's no PST (provincial sales tax) in the Yukon, the NWT or Nunavut.

TELEPHONE

Every Arctic community has a least one payphone, often in the post office or the largest shop. Generally, these accept both coins and prepaid phonecards. Local libraries almost always have Internet access.

Mobile Phones
The only foreign phones that will work in North America are triband models, operating on GSM 1900 as well as other frequencies. If you don't have one your best bet may be to buy a pay-as-you-go phone when you get there. Most cost under $100 (in either the US or Canada), including some prepaid call time. However, the GSM/GPRS network is sparse, and between towns in the far north it's unlikely there will be any reception at all. Most outfitters will hire out radio equipment if you're planning a wilderness trip and want emergency cover.

Phonecards
Prepaid phonecards usually offer the best per-minute rates for long-distance and international calling in North America. They come in denominations of $5, $10 and $20 in both the US and Canada, and are widely sold in shops.

Phone Codes
Area codes Alaska ☎ 907, Yukon/NWT/ Nunavut ☎ 867
Country code ☎ 1 (Long-distance domestic calls must also be preceded by ☎ 1)
Directory assistance ☎ 411
Emergency ☎ 911
International access code ☎ 011
Operator ☎ 0
Toll-free numbers: ☎ 800, ☎ 866, ☎ 877, ☎ 888

TIME
Arctic North America spans five time zones. Alaska Time is one hour earlier than Pacific Daylight Time – the zone in which the Yukon falls. The NWT and Nunavut stretch across three time zones: Mountain Daylight Time, Central Daylight Time and Eastern Daylight Time. When it's noon in Fairbanks, it's 1pm in Dawson, 2pm in Inuvik, 4pm in Iqaluit, 9pm in London and 7am the following day in Melbourne. For more detailed information, see the World Time Zones map on p334.

Both Alaska and Canada observe daylight-saving time, which comes into effect on the first Sunday in April, when clocks are put forward one hour, and ends on the last Sunday in October, when they're put back one hour.

TOURIST INFORMATION
All larger Arctic communities have a tourist office, and information for travellers is generally available from the town council in smaller villages.

Useful planning contacts for a trip north:

Alaska
Alaska Department of Natural Resources (www .alaskastateparks.org) Information on all state parks, including camp sites, cabins for hire and outdoor activities.
Alaska National Park Service (www.nps.gov/akso) Information on national parks, facilities and fees.
Alaska Travel Industry Association (ATIA; www.travel alaska.com) The official tourism marketing arm for the state, with listings of hundreds of B&Bs, motels, camp sites, activities and transport services.

Canada
Canadian Tourism Commission (www.travelcanada.ca) Loads of general information, packages and links.
Northwest Territories (www.nwttravel.nt.ca) NWT Arctic tourism.
Nunavut Tourism (www.nunatour.nt.ca)
Parks Canada (www.parkscanada.ca) Information on all national parks, national historic sites and national marine-conservation areas.
Yukon Department of Tourism (www.touryukon.com)

VISAS
Alaska
Under the US visa-waiver programme, visas are not currently required for citizens of the EU, Australia and New Zealand for visits of up to 90 days, although you must have a valid machine-readable passport. Canadian citizens are exempt from both visa and passport requirements but must show proof of citizenship. Everyone else needs to apply for a US visa in their home country.

Admission requirements to the United States are subject to rapid change. Check with a US consulate in your home country or the **US Department of State** (www.unitedstatesvisas .gov) for the latest requirements. Even those visitors who don't need a visa are subject to a US$6 entry fee at land border crossings.

In 2004 the US Department of Homeland Security introduced a new set of security measures called **US-VISIT** (www.dhs.gov/us-visit). When you arrive by air or sea, you will be photographed and have your two index fingers scanned. This biometric data will be matched when you leave the US. The goals are to ensure that the person who entered the US is the same as the one leaving it, and to catch people who've overstayed the terms of their admission. At the time of writing, this procedure was also being implemented at the busiest land border crossings, including many with Canada, with the goal of extending it to all entry points by the end of 2005. Visitors from visa-waiver countries are currently exempt from being finger-scanned and photographed at land borders, although this may well change at any time.

Canada

Citizens of dozens of countries – including the US, most Western European and Commonwealth countries as well as Mexico, Japan, South Korea and Israel – don't need visas to enter Canada for stays of up to 180 days. US permanent residents are also exempt from obtaining visas, regardless of their nationality.

Nationals of around 150 other countries, including South Africa, Hong Kong and Poland, need to apply for a 'temporary resident visa' (TRV) with the Canadian visa office in their home country (usually at the embassy, high commission or consulate). The website maintained by **Citizenship and Immigration Canada** (CIC; www.cic.gc.ca) has full details, including office addresses and the latest requirements. A separate visa is required if you plan to study or work in Canada.

Arctic Russia Travel Routes

North Pole +

CONTENTS

HIGHLIGHTS

- Catching some of the world's biggest salmon on the **Kola Peninsula** (p275)
- Sledding across the **Yamal Peninsula** (p282) under a flaming aurora borealis to visit a Nenets sacred site
- Spotting whales and walruses on a boat tour of coastal **Chukotka** (p290)
- Marvelling at the survival of the inspiring little Permafrost Museum at **Igarka** (p287)
- Just being granted permission to travel independently in **Chukotka** (p290), **Taymyr** (p289) or **Yamal** (p279)

Many people associate Siberia with cold and jump to the misapprehension that most of Russia is somehow in the Arctic. In fact Vladivostok, the best-known city in Russia's far east, is around the same latitude as Monaco, and most of Siberia is sub-polar. In the genuinely Arctic region, accessible areas are often gruesomely despoiled by Soviet smokestacks and oil fields and their effects. Even some of the mysterious archipelagos off the Arctic coast have been used for nuclear testing or dumping. But there's still a vast area that remains unspoilt and pristine if you have the tenacity to get there. Post-USSR Russia's northern native populations have partially reclaimed some of their traditional culture, and the tundra is once again home to nomadic reindeer herders. There are several large protected areas.

This chapter gets you to main hub towns, but the really interesting part begins once you get beyond them. To do that you'll need to have contacts, make good local friends or join an (inevitably expensive) tailor-made tour. Be aware that Russia's tiresome visa and registration bureaucracy is compounded in several Arctic areas by requirements for very-tough-to-arrange permits. Some stoical visitors consider this hurdle part of the thrill: it certainly means you aren't likely to meet hordes of tourists. In some places you may be one of the first foreign visitors in generations.

GETTING AROUND
Air
Each region tends to have its own 'baby-flot' airline. Since you rarely have a choice you're best not to ponder safety records, though actually the 'Yak' workhorses are very sturdily constructed. Ticket prices tend to be standard at any *aerokassa* (air-ticket office) in Russia, but in some cases you can only book a maximum of two weeks in advance. Seasonal demand can be strong: in early summer many people fly north and in late summer many are leaving. Online air-ticket agents such as www.biletplus.ru rarely handle smaller Arctic destinations.

Be aware that several Arctic airports are across gulfs or rivers from the town they serve, requiring a boat, bus or helicopter transfer according to the state of the ice.

Boat
River steamers are the classic way to cover vast Siberian distances in summer. Those on the Yenisey are the most frequent, but the much rarer service on the Ob offers a more useful chance of making an Arctic loop. Booking ahead is highly advisable but not easy in practice. First-class cabins generally have a private washbasin and only two beds. Third-class cabins have eight bunks. Deck class is just that and rarely offers so much as a seat – tough on a week-long journey, though at least there are restaurants.

Hydrofoils known as *meteor* or *raketa* are much faster. whizzing along at up to 70km per hour. As they're fairly low-lying, though, the views from the windows are limited and often obscured by spray. Hydrofoils can feel somewhat claustrophobic, especially for longer trips.

For shorter local trips you'll probably need to rent motorboats or hitchhike on fishermen's skiffs. (Wooden-framed walrus-skin boats known in Chukotka as *baydar* or *angyaghpik* are reminiscent of Greenlandic *umiaq*, but they're very rarely used these days.)

Roads
Where there's no railway, travelling by land can be virtually impossible in Siberian summers. However, there are a limited number of winter roads where bumps, unbridged rivers and deep bogs become passable once frozen, snowed over and compacted. In winter there's also the possibility of driving along frozen rivers, lakes or even certain bays where routes are carved flat by bulldozers for the purpose. The few 'all-weather roads' are mostly within city limits.

TO THE NORTH POLE

Annual excursions to the top of the world start in April, typically from Khatanga (p289), with a 2½-hour flight to the military/scientific base at **Sredniy Island** (79.5°N), where there's a small museum. Another two hours' flight brings you to ironically named **Borneo Ice Camp** runway, rebuilt annually at around 89°N. From here you can ski or helicopter-hop the last 100km. Recently various alternative routes, notably via Vorkuta and Frans Josef Land, have also been tried.

North Pole Adventures (www.northpole.ru) runs weekend trips to the Pole from Moscow (€6000), with opportunities to attend the North Pole ballooning festival or ice-sculpture festival, or to ski for six days to reach the Pole.

A US$3000 fly-in, fly-out trip from Krasnoyarsk booked through **Dyula Tur** (☎ 3912 591400; Hotel Krasnoyarsk, ul Uritskogo 94) is about the cheapest way to the Pole, but departures are less reliable.

Departing from Germany or Austria and skiing the last sector, you'll pay around US$8000 for an 18-day 'Exnor' adventure with **DAV Summit Club** (☎ 089 642 400; www.dav-summit-club.de, in German), in alternate years. A similar trip starting in Moscow costs $6900 with **Travel Pac** (☎ 095 933 0951; http://old.pac.group.ru).

If just getting to the Pole isn't enough, parachute onto it with **Polar World** (www.skypole.ru) or balloon over it with **Grinex** (www.ec-arctic.ru). Experienced dry-suit divers can even plunge beneath the polar ice with UK-based **Divercity Ltd** (☎ 1908 647300; www.divercityscuba.com), whose two-week expeditions cost around US$12,500 ex Moscow.

It's increasingly popular to cruise to the North Pole by nuclear-powered icebreaker from Murmansk, generally stopping in dramatic Frans Josef Land on the way back. Many agencies sell this tour ex Scandinavia, including Helsinki–Murmansk flights, for US$16,450 to US$27,450. Contact **Quark Expeditions** (www.quarkexpeditions.com), **Journeys International** (www.journeys-intl .com) or **Aurora** (www.auroraexpeditions.com.au). Start in Moscow from US$14,155 with **Condor** (www .condorjourneys-adventures.com).

Perhaps the ultimate icebreaker cruise takes you in 18 days from Murmansk to the North Pole and on through the Northeast Passage. You pass right along Russia's coast via Severnaya Zemlya, the Taymyr Peninsula, the Lena Delta, the New Siberian Islands and Wrangel Island, before arriving at Pevek, on Chukotka's north coast (see p293), to fly on to Alaska. The trip is sold by **Poseidon** (www.northpolevoyages.com) and **Victory** (www.victory-cruises.com) from around US$23,000.

Taking such an icebreaker trip is ethically ambiguous. Some environmental groups are horrified at the potential for nuclear accidents, but a more mundane question surrounds the question of whether the ships' Murmansk-based operating company is obliged to return profits to the state who so expensively had the boats built – originally for strategic icebreaking.

For unsurfaced winter roads a minimum of four-wheel drive is wise; the UAZ minibuses ('Wazzik') are ubiquitous. Six-wheel-drive trucks or Ural buses are more reliable. There are also tank-like transporter vehicles with caterpillar tracks. Very few of the longer 'roads' actually have public transport per se. Arrange rides with local people or hitchhike with a truck driver.

Train

Russia is justifiably proud of its trains, which chug further north than those anywhere else. The wide gauge allows for comfortable sleeping compartments with plenty of legroom. Almost every long-distance ticket includes a numbered fold-down-bed berth with clean sheets provided. Trains are also relatively safe from thieves, as every wagon has at least one *provodnik* (guard and ticket collector) keeping an eye on all who enter. Train rides are so long that they offer a great chance to socialise. Sharing food and the odd gallon of vodka helps to break the ice. In early summer especially you may be surprised to find that a fair proportion of fellow passengers are from the Turkic republics; they're generally seasonal workers earning money in the Arctic oil fields to send home to their families in Baku or Bishkek. These folks are even more effusively hospitable than the initially more guarded Russians.

For Russian railway timetables, www.timetable.tsi.ru is a fabulous resource, but using it takes some learning. Notably it is very unforgiving with spellings, so it helps to know the seven-digit station code of your destination. Useful station codes include Moscow (Moskva) 2000000, Olenegorsk 2004722, Apatity 2004717, Labytnangi 2010180, Yekaterinburg (Sverdlovsk Pass) 2030000, Nyagan 2030528, Priobye 2030295 and Pyt-Yakh 2030607.

ITINERARY 1: THE KOLA PENINSULA

A leisurely wander through European Russia's most accessible Arctic areas, all handily close to Scandinavia.

This route starts off through some of the ugliest, most depressing cities in the Arctic, if not the whole galaxy. That alone has a certain ghoulish fascination and is educational in showing very graphically the effects of environmental carelessness. However, the trip is not intended to be an exercise in masochism, rather a link between various hopping-off points from which you can venture into the contrasting untouched nature of the Kola's lake-dappled tundra and birch-forest *taiga*. Away from the monstrous mining cities lie some of the world's finest salmon rivers, a remarkable geology for mineral collectors, traditional Sami and Pomor cultures, and a few hidden gems such as the brilliant wooden church at Varzuga.

FAST FACTS

- **Access for independent travellers**
  Good for hub towns, expensive for remote fishing areas

- **Best time to travel** June to September for fishing, September to October for reduced midge annoyance, March for skiing

- **Difficulty level** Moderate (permits are less taxing to get here than elsewhere in Russia)

- **Don't forget** Phrasebooks, insect repellent, fishing rod, geological hammer, wads of cash for helicopter rides, mini Geiger counter

- **Don't miss** The bus out of Nikel

- **Gateway city** Murmansk (or Kirkenes, Norway)

- **Length of basic route** 730km

- **Modes of travel** Bus, train, helicopter to reach fishing areas

- **Recommended maps** Download 1:50,000, 1:200,000 and 1:500,000 scales (in Cyrillic) from http://mapr35.narod.ru; buy the (Russian-language) Pti Fyute guidebook for Murmansk Region

- **Time needed** At least a week; add a few days for skiing and two weeks for hiking, fishing or a North Pole icebreaker excursion

- **Time zone** Moscow time (GMT+3)

ARCTIC RUSSIA TRAVEL ROUTES

There's also the Unesco-protected Lapland Biosphere Reserve bordering Finland. In general the scenery improves as you progress southwards and eastwards.

NORWEGIAN BORDER TOWNS

In **Nikel** the land has been poisoned by emissions from metallurgical plants and, although it's often denied, nuclear detonations have been used in places to get at the ore. The result is memorably depressing, like a movie-set vision of post-nuclear apocalypse (see the photo on www.ngu.no /Kola/toc.html). Minerals and cross-border history feature in Nikel's small local museum, a bright-yellow building visible from the very simple **MPPZhKh Hotel** (☎ 81554-20466;

NICKEL-HEADED

The worst devastation in the Kola region (and around Norilsk; see p288) has been caused by the nickel industry pumping noxious emissions into the surrounding environment. In Soviet days the nickel had military uses, but post-USSR its main use is in catalytic converters. That's right – paradoxically, to reduce polluting emissions elsewhere!

Gvardeiskii pr 2; r with shared bath R322). **Zapolyarnye** is a similarly ugly nickel-mining town. Its claim to fame is the world's deepest hole. Some 12km deep but only about 14cm in diameter at its widest point, the hole started as a seismological experiment aiming to investigate conduction of sound waves at deep levels. Sceptical geologists are curious to see if drillers will make it as far as the earth's mantle (16km), which has never been reached. Nearby **Pechenga** has a newly reconstructed monastery and a bandstand-like bell tower.

Getting There & Away

Direct minibuses from Kirkenes (Norway) pass through Nikel and Zapolyarnye. The view from the window is probably enough. If you really want to visit it's possible to join a monthly guided trip from the Norwegian side with **Pasvik Tours** (www.pasvikturist.no). Public buses between Nikel and Murmansk (R140, three hours) are much faster than the train (R60, eight hours, six times weekly), but travelling independently to Nikel from the Norwegian border is complicated by the region's military-border status.

MURMANSK

☎ 8152 / pop 380,000

Halfway between Moscow and the North Pole, Murmansk is the world's largest Arctic city. Russia's main ice-free commercial port, it was founded in 1916 during WWI so that embattled Russia could receive supplies from Britain and France. However, the Bolshevik revolution turned that supportive Franco-British naval presence into a destabilising force. The 'Allies' aided the deposed White Russians and ran Murmansk along with Arkhangelsk as a separatist state until late 1919. Murmansk's strategic importance in WWII resulted in its utter

destruction by German bombers. Today it's home to Russia's nuclear icebreakers. The modern city spreads up surrounding *sopki* (hills) steep enough to make stairs as common as streets in some areas. City-centre façades are now brightly painted and there is a modest cultural life. Most citizens are Russian, but you might meet indigenous Sami during the Festival of the North in late March, when they come to compete in traditional sports.

Orientation

The city occupies three levels: the port, the centre, and the surrounding heights, crowned with dozens of uninspired housing blocks. Dominating the centre is ploshchad Sovietskoy Konstitutsii, also known as Five Corners. To the north of the centre lie Lake Semyonovskoe and a truly immense statue of a soldier, nicknamed Alyosha, who enjoys spectacular views of the city.

Information

There are ATMs and exchange booths in Hotels Polyarnye Zory and Arktika.

Intourist (☎ 454386; Hotel Polyarnye Zory; 🕑 10am-5.30pm Mon-Thu, 10am-5pm Fri) Limited tourist information. Its local tours, cruises and snowmobile trips generally require minimum group numbers, which are rarely attained.

Kola-Tavs (☎ 235510; kolatavs@murmansk.rosmail .com; pr Lenina 19; 🕑 9am-1pm & 2-6pm Mon-Thu, 9am-1pm & 2-5pm Fri) Sells bus, train and air tickets. Branch office in Hotel Polyarnye Zory lobby.

MKTI-Tour (☎ 540390) Organises snowmobiling trips from US$22 to US$106, depending on level of difficulty.

Murmanout (http://murmanout.ru) Very helpful site with copious detail and an interactive city map. See also http://2004.murman.ru for history and www.murman tourism.ru for web-address listings.

Murmansk Maps (http://murmansk.aspol.ru/maps /index.html, in Russian) Download city and bus maps.

Post and telephone office (behind Hotel Arktika)

Teknologi (ul Kolsky 22 & 126; Internet access per hr R16 plus R3 per Mb; 🕑 24 hrs) Internet also available, but more expensive, at Hotels Polyarnye Zory and Arktika.

Sights

The dizzyingly colossal unknown-soldier statue, **Alyosha**, towers above popular swimming place **Lake Semyonovskoe**, where the **Okeanarium** (☎ 315884; pr Geroyev-Severomortsev 4; adult/child R60/40) hosts seal shows. Take trolleybus No 3 up prospekt Lenina. Some 3km further north is the hard-to-find **Military Museum of the Northern Fleet** (Voyenno-marskoy muzey severnogo flota; ☎ 221445; ul Tortseva 15; admission R50; ◷ 9am-1pm & 2-4.30pm Thu-Mon). Many WWII exhibits are complemented by an interesting collection of more modern torpedoes, mines, model ships and chemical-warfare paraphernalia. Get off trolleybus No 4 at the last stop, cross the street, then take bus No 10 for four stops. Walk towards the smokestack and turn left at the shop.

The **Fine Arts Museum** (Khudozhestvenny muzey; ☎ 450385; ul Kominterna 13; admission R10; ◷ 11am-6pm Wed-Sun) occupies Murmansk's oldest stone building, though the collection's only real highlights are prints by Boris Nepomnyashchy. The varied exhibits of the **Krayevyedchesky Museum** (☎ 422617; pr Lenina 90; admission R10, tours in English R450; ◷ 11am-6pm Sat-Wed, ticket office to 5pm) include good features on Sami and Pomor history and the Anglo-American occupation. There's a good souvenir shop, and museum guides can be hired for city tours in English. The **Regional Craft Centre** (City Administration Bldg, 2nd fl, ul Sofi Perovskoy 3; admission free; ◷ 10am-6pm Mon-Wed, 10am-5pm Sat & Sun) shows Kola Peninsula art including Apatity-style canvases 'painted' with mineral powders.

In front of the stadium is a **statue of Anatoly Bredov** (pr Lenina). Finding himself surrounded by Nazi troops, Anatoly detonated a grenade, blowing them and himself to bits. Had he been a Palestinian he'd have been called a terrorist, but as he was a Russian surrounded by WWII Germans he's now a national hero.

In summer you might see one of four **nuclear-powered icebreakers** at the dock, but avoid photography in the port area.

MINERAL EXPORT LICENCES

Getting a mineral export licence is a complex procedure. In Murmansk, first visit the **Sanitary and Epidemiology Inspector** (☎ 72672; ul Kommooni 7) for radioactivity tests. Then go to the **Museum of Local Lore** (☎ 22678; ul Lenina 90) for verification of your export list's accuracy. The **Museum of Arts** (☎ 50385; ul Kominteria 13) will then issue the definitive certificate. Each document can cost around R3000 in fees. See also p276.

Festivals & Events

There's a carnival atmosphere during the 10-day **Festival of the North** (◷ late Mar or early Apr), but Murmansk hotels will be booked solid. Events include ski marathons, a biathlon, ice hockey, 'polar-bear' swimming and curious races in which a reindeer pulls a contestant on skis. Most are held at Dolina Uyuta, a 25-minute ride south of the train station on bus No 12.

Sleeping

69th Parallel Hotel (☎ 565645, 565330; Lyzhny proezd 14; s R400-600, d R640-900, ste R1600) The rooms here have phone and TV, and some have balcony and fridge. The attached nightclub is popular. The hotel is about 10 minutes out of the centre by trolleybus No 1 or 6.

Ogni Murmanska Hotel (☎ 490800; fax 491093; Sankt Peterburg Shosse; r US$40-80) It's 8km out of town, but this place has luxurious rooms (some have two levels) with a private sauna and a great view.

Hotel Polyarnye Zory (☎ 289500, 450282; polar zor@dionis.mels.ru; ul Knipovicha 17; s R930-3565, d R426-4061, ste R4340-5146) This is the most popular choice for Westerners. Large, clean rooms have cable TV, deluxe rooms have sauna, and there's a big, complimentary breakfast buffet. Staff are friendly and speak some English, and there's an excellent *stolovaya* (canteen), a bar, and an upscale restaurant (mains R110 to R320).

Moryak (☎ 45 55 27; ul Knipovicha 23; s R170-750, d R620-1500) Next door to Hotel Polyarnye Zory, this place is simple but adequate.

Meridian (☎ 288600, 288650; www.meridian-hotel .ru; ul Vorovskovo 5/23; s/tw/ste incl breakfast R950-2000/2600/3800) The rooms have been pretty thoroughly renovated here, though pairs of cheaper singles share one bathroom.

Hotel Arktika (☎ 457988; www.hotel.an.ru; pr Lenina 82; standard s R890-1100, d R540-1900, business-class R1490-2200) This three-winged multistorey landmark has remodelled business-class accommodation that approximates Western standards.

Eating

Tsarskaya Okhota (☎ 563709, 255224; Kolsky pr 86; mains R145-250; ◷ noon-midnight) The good-value Russian cuisine here is highly rated by the locals. Furs and hunting trophies are features of the décor, and an angry stuffed bear guards the toilets.

ARCTIC RUSSIA TRAVEL ROUTES

Rvanye Parusa (☎ 478034; ul Egorova 13a; mains R200-350; ⏰ noon-midnight Sun-Thu, noon-3am Fri & Sat) An appealing upmarket complex, this place has Italian, Russian and Japanese sub-restaurants and its own microbrewery (beers R70).

Venskiy Dvorik (☎ 449912; ul Burkova 17a; mains R75-190; ⏰ noon-1am) This cosy pub has good-value Russian food and a R70 lunch menu before 3pm.

Mama-Mia (☎ 455736; ul Egorova 14; pizzas R130; open noon-1am) Popular and well reputed, this pizzeria has a homey, unpretentious interior.

Cyr (☎ 473580; pr Teatralniy 8; fondue R80-130; ⏰ noon-1am) A pleasant if poorly maintained cheese-themed restaurant, Cyr serves sandwiches from R40 and set lunches for R100. There's annoying live music after 8pm.

Dnyom-I-Nochyu (Hotel Arktika; mains R30-60; ⏰ 24hr) A good, cheap cafeteria with bar.

Entertainment

There's a decent **Philharmonic Concert Hall** (Kontsertny zal filharmonii; ul Sofi Perovskoy 3) and a **Puppet Theatre** (☎ 458178; ul Sofi Perovskoy 21A; admission R20-25; ⏰ 11.30am & 2pm Sat & Sun Sep-Jun).

Getting There & Away

Several daily trains run to Apatity (4¼ to five hours) via Olenegorsk (2½ hours). You can buy train tickets online at www.rwza kaz.ru (in Russian) for R120 commission or by phone on ☎ 532626 for R100 commission. Within Murmansk both commission costs include delivery. Daily buses connect with other Kola Peninsula towns, including Monchegorsk (R120, three hours), Nikel

---

ICEBREAKER CRUISES

Murmansk-based nuclear-powered icebreakers were constructed to keep northern Russia's shipping lanes clear but are now frequently used for tourist excursions. However, these can be hard to arrange locally, as most berths are pre sold through Western adventure-tour operators. Most popular are cruises to the North Pole (see p270), but it's arguably more interesting to head for Severnaya Zemlya (two weeks from US$10,500) or Frans Josef Land (12 days from US$6700) with a company such as **Arcturus** (www.arc turusexpeditions.co.uk).

(R140, three hours), Kirovsk (R59, four hours) and Zapolyarnye (R51, 2½ hours). The bus and train stations are next to each other. Both have long, slow ticket queues, so you may prefer to buy through **Kola-Tavs** (☎ 235510; kolatavs@murmansk.rosmail.com; pr Lenina 19; ⏰ 9am-1pm & 2-6pm Mon-Thu, 9am-1pm & 2-5pm Fri).

Getting Around

The city has a relatively efficient trolleybus system. For the airport, bus No 106 and express bus No 106E (R16, 30 minutes) run every 20 to 30 minutes. For Hotels Arktika and Meridian, get off at the train station; use the Detsky Mir stop for the Moryak. **Taxis** (☎ 237770, 262677, 237070) cost around R500 to the airport. In town you'll pay R40 per ride or R140 per hour.

Severomorsk
☎ 81537 / pop 54,000

Just 25km northeast of Murmansk, Severomorsk is the command centre for Russia's northern naval fleet and was the home town of the ill-fated *Kursk* submarine. Like Murmansk, it's overlooked by another immense Soviet statue, this time of a sailor. Severomorsk might be an intriguing place, but it is a completely closed city. Even more secretive is Shtyukozero, 8km beyond, which was the scene of a potential catastrophe in 1984 when a fire swept through silos bristling with nuclear-tipped missiles. Don't attempt to visit!

Lovozero
☎ 81538 / pop 2900

In the peninsula's centre, Lovozero is the concrete-block town to which Stalin forcibly moved many Sami nomads after 1929. This cultural disgrace resulted in the 1938 anticollectivisation rebellion, which was brutally suppressed by the Soviet army and followed by the execution of many Sami chiefs. These days the town has a **Sami history museum** featuring a particularly fine petroglyph. **Lovozero Adventure** organises helicopter trout-fishing trips on the Rova River, sold through www.fishingnorth.com. It can also organise river trips to stay in Sami reindeer camps. In winter the nomad *chum* (see p279) are as close as half an hour's drive from the town.

Hotel Virma (☎ 30169; fax 31094; dm/s/d R450/340/1160) is the only accommodation.

FISHING EXCURSIONS

The Kola Peninsula's wild rivers are teeming with huge salmon and trout. Sport fishers pay handsomely to brave the midges on organised week-long trips, which generally start from Murmansk. Each tour usually includes access by chartered helicopter, transfers to various fishing beats by boat and/or helicopter, and full-board accommodation in dedicated lodges or camps. All demand catch-and-release fishing.

Some consider the Yokanga River to have the world's finest Atlantic salmon runs. There's a real chance of bagging 13kg to 15kg fish. **Kola Co** (www.kolaco.co.uk) tours depart Murmansk on Saturday and include comfortable chalet hotel–style accommodation near the celebrated Lyliok Pool. The tours are sold exclusively through **Frontiers** (☎ UK 20 7493 0798, USA 800-245-1950; www .frontierstravel.com; tours 2200-5390/US$3650-9150; ☺ Jun–mid-Aug), which also organises weeks of similarly world-class fishing on the Ponoi River from the **Ryabaga fishing camp** (www.shackletonint .com/ponoi; tours US$4690-9990) and the new Brevyeni Camp.

You'll get a cheaper if more limited range of boat-access Ponoi beats through Swedish group **Fishing North** (☎ 928 10088; www.fishingnorth.com; tours from US$2950) or **Loop Tackle** (www.looptackle .se/travel), whose **Acha Camp** (tours US$3900-5500) is near tiny Kanyovka village (population 60).

A popular alternative – especially for brown-trout fishing – is **Varzina** (www.varzina.fi), where the owners claim fly fishers can virtually count on catches averaging over 45cm.

There are several daily buses (direct or requiring a change in Revda) from Olenegorsk, where the bus station is just 100m from its train station. Olenegorsk is 2½ hours by rail from Murmansk on the Moscow mainline. Some maps show a rail line to Revda, but this is freight only.

MONCHEGORSK
☎ 81536 / pop 75,000

Lying between three large lakes on what is virtually an island, Monchegorsk has some archetypal early-Soviet architecture, a glorious **Resurrection Cathedral** (1998), and a host of monuments, including a miner on an improbably tall plinth. Although Monchegorsk means 'beautiful tundra', for years it has suffered from the hellhole image created by the ugly nickel plant nearby that was its *raison d'etre*. In recent years, however, the plant has made concerted efforts to clean up its act, and tree-planting schemes have made today's Monchegorsk a relatively green place. It looks best in the red-leafed blush of autumn. The main drag is prospekt Metallurgov.

Information
Galeriya Shopping Centre (Lenin Sq) Has an ATM.
Internet Svyaz-Servis (☎ 58700; ul Lesnaya 10; per hr R40; ☺ 10am-10pm) Take a taxi to find it.
Kola Travel (☎ 57099, mobile 912-287 1311; www .kolatravel.ru; ul Lenina 15/2) Dutch-run local tour agency.
Library (pr Metallurgov 27; ☺ noon-9pm Sat-Thu) Internet access for R30 per hour.

Sberbank (pr Metallurgov 7; ☺ 10am-7pm Mon-Fri, 10am-4pm Sat, closed 2-3pm) Close to the Sever Hotel. Has 24-hour MasterCard ATM.

Sleeping & Eating
Much nicer than the Sever (following), **Hotel Metallurgov** (☎ 74533, 72053; pr Metallurgov 45A; r incl breakfast R600-2400) is supposedly for guests of the nickel plant. It can accept foreign tourists but only those with reservations. The hotel's small restaurant has a good reputation.

The **Sever Hotel** (☎ 72655; pr Metallurgov 4; s/d R570/1140) is tolerable if you don't mind a cockroach or two.

Monchegorsk has an unusually wide variety of good dining alternatives, including Italian, European and Chinese options. **Volshebnitsa** (pr Metallurgov), facing the entrance to the attractive city park, is cosy but unpretentious; **Kofeinya Ani** (pr Metallurgov), handily close to the Sever Hotel, serves good coffee and light meals; and **Rodnichok** (Lenin Sq) is a usefully central restaurant specialising in shashlik (barbecued meat on skewers).

Getting There & Around
Buses run to Murmansk (R101, three hours, five daily) and Kirovsk (R61, 2½ hours, three daily) from a new, central **bus station** (ul Komsomolskaya), where there's also an office for air and rail tickets. The nearest train station is in Olenegorsk, served by regular bus shuttles.

AROUND MONCHEGORSK

Until the mid-1990s the region south of Monchegorsk suffered extensively from appalling levels of air pollution from the nickel works, which produced a black snow of soot. In addition, a catastrophic fire left much of the area's forests looking like skeletons in horribly blackened surroundings. Regrowth is just starting to hide the scars. However, further from town nature becomes much more appealing. Stretching north and west of Monchegorsk towards Norway and Finland is the 2784-sq-km, Unesco-listed **Lapland Biosphere Reserve** (Laplandsky zapovyednik; ☎ 50080). It consists of virgin tundra, alpine grasslands, marshes, lakes, and five small mountain ranges, peaking at 1114m. Photos on www.sll.fi/mpe/laplandski give you the idea. Founded in 1930 to protect local herds, today it holds one of the most concentrated reindeer populations in Europe. Brown bears, elks, wolves and 30 other mammal species also make their home in the reserve. There are several waterfalls on the territory and even a German war plane, resting where it fell during WWII. However, visits to the park are mostly restricted to a few ecological trails around the handful of reasonably comfortable guest cottages at the reserve's main base on the quiet banks of Lake Chuna. You must arrange visits in advance, ideally directly or through travel agencies. The scenery is arguably nicer in the unrestricted areas around Lovozero or on the White Sea coast.

APATITY

☎ 81555 / pop 60,000

Only founded in 1966, Apatity is now the Kola's second-biggest town. It's the world's biggest source of apatite, an industrial source of fertiliser phosphates. Apatite (the name derives from the Greek for deception) is so called because it can be mistaken for much more valuable beryl or olivine. There are literally hundreds of other (rarer) minerals to be found in the nearby Khibiny Mountains, where you can also ski, hike, climb or even search for the Yeti, whose 42cm footprints have supposedly been spotted.

Apatity's main shopping streets are ulitsas Fersmana and Lenina. The train station lies southwest of the centre. Bus stops on ploshchad Lenina are for Monchegorsk and Murmansk, while those along ulitsa Fers-

mana serve Kirovsk. There's a disconnected Akademgorodok (Academic Town).

Information

Econord (☎ 79762; econord@inep.ksc.ru; ul Fersmana 40A; ☺ 10am-5pm Mon-Fri) Good source of information and can arrange trips to the Lapland Biosphere Reserve.

Hotel Ametist Has ATMs and sells regional maps.

Internet salon (pl Lenina; per hr R25; ☺ noon-7pm Mon-Fri, noon-4pm Sat). In the post office. Has a dodgy connection.

Kola-Tavs (ul Lenina 2A) Useful for procuring air, bus or train tickets.

Post office (pl Lenina; ☺ 9am-7pm Mon-Fri, 11am-4pm Sat-Sun)

Sberbank (cnr uls Moskovskaya & Kosmonavtov) Changes money.

South Kola Tours (Yug Kola; ☎ 74178; www.kolaklub .com; Hotel Ametist) Can arrange mineral-export licenses for rock collectors, and stays in Sami tepees, among other things. The company has a helpful Nevada office.

Sights

The 1970s **History Museum** (☎ 79255; admission R15-50; ☺ 2-5pm Mon-Fri) has exhibits on Russian Arctic expeditions, unique drawings of Novaya Zemlya and details of 5000-year-old Sami rock carvings. The user-friendly **Regional Geological Museum** (☎ 37274; ul Fersmana 16; ☺ 9am-6pm Mon-Fri) has fine exhibitions of local rocks and minerals plus some local crafts. Enter from the back. There's an **Open-Air Geological Museum** (ul Fersmana) further west, which is basically a few paths lined with local rock samples. The curious **library**

ACTIVITIES: MINERAL COLLECTING

The Khibiny-Lovozero pluton (a mass of igneous rock that forms underground when a volcano core that has never erupted eventually cools) around Apatity is the world's largest. With over 500 mineral types catalogued, the area is a dreamland for rock collectors. South Kola Tours (see p276) organises geological-based trips and can take care of the complex export-permit arrangements for you if you don't want to spend frustrating days in Murmansk doing them yourself (see the boxed text, p273). The very specialist **Eudialyte Homepage** (www.koeln.netsurf.de/~w.steffens/kola.htm) offers remarkable collated checklists of the samples so far discovered.

building (ul Lenina) resembles the pages of an open book, and hosts exhibitions.

Some Apatity artists 'paint' using coloured dust from crushed local minerals, a style that's catching on all over the Russian north. **Salma Art Salon** (ul Dzerzhinskovo 1; admission R3) is a private cooperative outlet for over 200 Kola Peninsula artists. Prices are low, and the management can arrange the paperwork to expedite customs procedures. **Gallery M** (Polyarnye Bldg, 2nd fl, pl Lenina; admission free; ☯ 2-6pm Mon-Sat) has changing local art exhibitions and a **bar** (☯ noon-midnight Mon-Fri, noon-7pm Sat).

Sleeping & Eating

If the following don't appeal, try one of the hotels in nearby Kirovsk.

Izovela (dom otdykha; ☎ 62666; www.kolaklub.com /isovela/; ul Pobedy 29A; s/d US$19/20) At the eastern edge of town the Izovela sanatorium and spa-cure complex features a nice pool, a sauna/*banya*, a winter garden, massages and two restaurants. Top-end rooms cost US$35. It also runs a **minihotel** (☎ 61452; r R200-700) at Imandra Lake, 13km from town. There are two other minihotels by the lake.

Hotel Ametist (☎ 74501; www.kolaklub.com/amet ist; ul Lenina 3; dm/s/tw/ste dm R190, s R520-650/tw R790, ste R1800) This place has clean if stylistically challenged 'renovated' rooms and cheaper three-bed dorms in a central, eight-storey concrete tower. There's a buffet-bar (mains R60) on the 2nd floor.

Eating options include **Restaurant Zapolyarnye** (ul Lenina 31A; mains R40-50; ☯ noon-midnight Mon-Thu, noon-1am Fri-Sun), which is handy for Izovela, and **Kulinaria** (ul Fersmana 20), which has tasty sweet and savoury pastries. Kiosks near the Open-Air Geological Museum sell snacks and fruit.

Getting There & Away

There are three weekly flights to Moscow Sheremetyevo 1 (R2184, 2¼ hours) on Arkhangelsk Airlines. Trains to Moscow (32 hours) stop in Kandalaksha (two hours). There are several daily trains (*platskart/kupe* R108/194, five to eight hours) and at least three buses (R230, four to five hours) to Murmansk. To Kirovsk it's a quick, 16km hop on bus No 101, 102 or 105 (R10) or by minibus.

Getting Around

Bus Nos 5, 8 and 13 (though not 13K) run between the train station and the town

centre. There's an hourly bus to Khibiny airport, between Apatity and Kirovsk.

KIROVSK

☎ 815231 / pop 40,000

Just half an hour from Apatity, Kirovsk is the Kola Peninsula's ski town. The triangular grid of three- and five-storey Soviet blocks is cupped in an appealing mountain setting that looks rather pretty in winter, when the lake freezes and the three-sided ring of rounded peaks is covered in snow.

Information

Internet Kafé Vechernee (ul Khibinogorskaya 29; ☯ 2-9pm Mon-Sun, 2-11pm Fri & Sat, closed 5-6pm)
Menatep Bank (☯ 9am-1pm & 2-3pm) ATM and exchange booth next to Hotel Ekkos.
Post office (pr Lenina; ☯ 11am-7pm Mon-Fri, 11am-4pm Sat & Sun)

Sights

The fascinating, very decrepit **Kirovsk train station** is a monument to Soviet antilogic. Like many 'Potyomkin villages' it was hastily constructed to impress visiting officials but never finished. Locals joke that its first and last patron was Josef Stalin. It's fun to gingerly climb staircases that drop off into the garbage and ruins below. Don't trust the handrails.

The **Regional Museum** (☯ sporadic) is located in the Kirovsk-25 mikro-rayon (bus No 1, 12 or 105), within an awesome mountain gap. Some experts believe that the neat removal of literally half a mountain here can only have been achieved through a nuclear detonation. On the way you'll pass relatively close to the new orthodox **Kazan Church** (Kazanskaya tserkov) and some attractive **Botanical Gardens** (☎ 51646, 51436; ☯ 9.30am-3pm).

Activities

Kirovsk offers great summer hiking and a long **ski season** (☯ Nov-Jun, best Jan-Apr). Pistes are long and wide, with good gradient variation, some moguls and lots of open space for the less confident. Ski-lift passes cost R200/350/2000 per half day/full day/week. Ski and snowboard rentals (per hour/day R100/250) require your passport as deposit. Buses to the slopes (R5) leave from the post office twice an hour. There are parasailing and ski-jump facilities, too.

Twelve-day guided Khibiny mountain treks out of Kirovsk are organised by **Geographic Bureau** (www.geographicbureau.com; €590; Jul-Aug). Cooks make your food, but you'll need a sleeping bag and a backpack to carry the tent (its hire is included). The single supplement is €80.

Sleeping & Eating

Hotel Ekkos (☎ 32716; www.kolaklub.com/eccos; pr Lenina 12a, 4th fl; s/d/tr R300/600/900) The seven neat rooms on the top floor of this red-turreted new building have TV, private shower and toilet. The place is friendly, but there's no lift.

Hotel Sport (☎ 92650, 91145; www.kolaklub.com /sport; ul Dzerzhinskovo 7A; s R240-390, d R300-450) Each pair of rooms here shares a shower and toilet. Guests get a 25% to 30% discount on ski-lift tickets and enjoy a special ski bus service. The sauna costs R250.

Khibiny Hotel (☎ 58902, 58901; ul Leningradskaya 25; s R425-550, d R780-980) Ideally placed for skiers 200m from the main ski-lift, this large *turbaza* (recreational complex) is about 1km from central Kirovsk. The rooms are merely functional, but they have private bathrooms.

Hotel Severnaya (☎ 54442; pr Lenina 11; s/d US$80/160) This very central hotel has more-or-less Western standards, except for its tiny Russian beds. There's a lobby bar and restaurant (mains R20 to R200) with good food, loud music and cold service.

Eating options include **Kafé Zodiak** (pr Lenina 13; 11am-10pm Mon-Sat, 11am-8pm Sun), which has prepared foods and only one table, and **Internet Kafé Vechernee** (ul Khibinogorskaya 29; 2-9pm Mon-Sun, 2-11pm Fri & Sat, closed 5-6pm). The **market** (pr Lenina; 11am-7pm), opposite the Lenin statue, has a few tables of produce.

Getting There & Away

Return to Apatity (p276) for train services to Kandalaksha. Buses to Murmansk (R240) take around four hours by way of Apatity and Monchegorsk (p275). Bus, train and plane tickets are sold on ulitsa Yubilenaya.

KANDALAKSHA
☎ 81533 / pop 37,200

Set in an area inhabited for millennia by the Sami, Kandalaksha is a White Sea port city that traded with Novgorod from the 11th century. Until it was abolished in 1742

the town's focus was a major monastery whose magical silver bell remains the centre of local legends. Repeatedly sacked by invaders, Kandalaksha was a battleground in the 1919 struggle between the Bolsheviks and British-backed White Russia. Although now noted for its giant aluminium smelter, the area is nonetheless attractively forested, and on the White Sea Islands southwest of town there's a large **sea-bird sanctuary** (permit required). There's a lovely new wooden **church** in the low-rise Nizhnaya Kandalaksha quarter, and the **triple-roofed train station** is rather quaint.

The two hotels in town are the **Spolokhi** (☎ 55768; Nabarezhnaya 130) and the drab, seven-storey **Belo More** (☎ 93100; ul Pervomayskaya 31), behind the central tank monument. Dine at **Restaurant Kanda** (☎ 31418; ul Pervomayskaya 54).

From the **bus station** (☎ 95095), bus No 220 runs every afternoon to Monchegorsk, while No 222 runs to Umba at 8.05am and 5.10pm daily.

Buses to Kemijärvi and thence Rovaniemi (both in Finland) run Monday and Thursday (€35, 4½ hours out, seven hours back) via the recently opened Salla border post. Regular trains run to Murmansk (*platskart/ kupe* R130/235, six to seven hours) via Apatity (two hours). Heading towards Moscow (30 hours) or St Petersburg (23 hours), it's worth stopping at ugly Kem (six hours into the journey) for an excursion to the beautiful **Solovetski Islands** (take a boat from Rabocheostrovsk village). These islands became infamous as the location of Solzhenitsyn's *Gulag Archipelago*, but today they are a contrastingly idyllic archipelago of tranquillity with a splendid church-filled 17th-century Kremlin. Stop again at Petrozavodsk to visit the superb wooden multidomed churches, villages and fortress of **Kizhi Island** (http://kizhi .karelia.ru/). Both places are Unesco World Heritage sites. For full details, see Lonely Planet's *Russia & Belarus* guide.

AROUND KANDALAKSHA
Umba
☎ 81559 / pop 5900

About 80km south of Kirovsk but accessed via Kandalaksha, Umba has a small, attractive old-town area. Its **Museum of Pomor History** displays a traditional *kotch* (see the boxed text, opposite), and in the first week of June the **Pomor Regatta** is a major local boating fes-

POMORS

From a Russian word meaning 'beside the sea', Pomor is a cultural rather than ethnic term for descendants of the medieval Russian pioneers from the Novgorod principality who settled around the White Sea. They were mainly fishing folk who used distinctive timber *kotches* (rowable sailing boats that were designed for ice conditions). Classically, *kotches* were 'sewn' together with wooden grips, moss and tar rather than metal nails. Extensive Pomor trade with Scandinavia led to the development of a distinct Pomor dialect. The Pomor capital was Arkhangelsk, but you'll find a Pomor history museum in Umba (see opposite).

camps are reached by speedboat transfers, which leave from beside the church (R50 to R100 per person). Catch-and-release **fishing licenses** (R160) are available at an inspector's hut in one of the camps and are regularly examined. Fishing packages are available through www.fishing-varzuga.com or all-in from the UK-based **Roxton Bailey Robinson** (☎ 1488 689 701; www.rbrww.com). Other than anglers' lodges there's no hotel, but Apatity's **South Kola Tours** (Yug Kola; ☎ 74178; www.kolaklub .com; Hotel Ametist) offers tailor-made tours, including local homestays.

ITINERARY 2: YAMAL EXPLORER

This is the long, cold way to cross the Asia-Europe divide. Spot gulags (prison camps), oil fields and Nenets herders as you edge closer to the Yamal tundra, then bolt south again towards Moscow.

The rural Yamal region is interesting for its Nenets reindeer-herding culture, although it's well hidden behind a veil of Soviet oil and mining settlements. For independent travellers the basic loop offers an opportunity to explore the Russian Arctic without a lengthy backtrack. Start with multiday steamer or hydrofoil rides down the Ob River between petro-boom towns Khanty-Mansiysk and Salekhard (you could even start further south in delightful Tobolsk). Having visited as much of the Yamal Peninsula as permits

tival. Pomor women put on shows for some tour groups and might dress visitors in rather stylised satin-and-shawl local costumes. **Hotel Zhek** (☎ 50240; ul Sovietskaya 7) is hidden in unit 50 of an apartment block and is unaccustomed to tourists. The **Russian Fishing Club** (☎ 095-916 9154; http://fishing-russ.ru/kolsky/kolsky.htm, in Russian) has a comfortable lodge near Umba that costs around US$100 per day, including three meals and sauna. The area is considered good for pike fishing.

Varzuga

The traditional ex-whaling village of Varzuga is around 140km west of Umba through seemingly endless forest (115km of this is unpaved but driveable). Founded around 1490 by monks from the Solovetski Islands, many of Varzuga's houses are timber cottages with photogenic carved porches. Varzuga's highlight is the stunning **Uspensky Church** (built 1684), an all-wooden structure rising over 30m to a central bulbed spire. Beside it is the quaint **Afansevskaya church** (built 1854) and a delightful log-framed **bell tower**. The latter was built in 2001 but, being rather different in design to a long-lost 17th-century original, it has not be universally well received. Photos and super-detailed historical information (in Russian) are available on www.1553.ru /varzuga/index.htm. A **folklore festival** is held in early June.

Anglers consider the Varzuga River outstanding for Atlantic salmon, and various sport-fishing camps dot the river bank. The

FAST FACTS

- **Access for independent travellers** Good in summer

- **Best time to travel** June to September for the river boats, winter to meet Nenets herders

- **Difficulty level** High, due to permit requirements and linguistic challenges

- **Don't forget** Phrasebook, midge repellent, permits (not needed for Salekhard but very much required for Nadym and the Yamal Peninsula), plenty of patience

- **Don't miss** The attractive north Urals, even if only viewed from the train window

- **Gateway city** Khanty-Mansiysk

- **Length of basic route** 3350km to Moscow (4200km if starting in Tobolsk)

- **Modes of travel** River ferry, plane, train, dogsled in the Yamal

- **Recommended map** Yamal peninsula map downloadable from www.geo cities.com/benselig/, Pti Fyute guidebooks (in Russian) for Yugra, Komi and Nenets AO

- **Time needed** Khanty-Mansiysk to Salekhard, two to three days once the boat finally arrives; Yamal Peninsula, as long as possible; Salekhard to Labytnangi, 1½ hours; Labytnangi to Vorkuta, 12 to 15 hours; Vorkuta to Moscow, two to 2½ days

- **Time zones** Moscow time +2 (GMT +5) Khanty-Mansiysk to Salekhard, Moscow time (GMT +3) Vorkuta, Pechora and Naryan-Mar

and contacts allow, take the train from Labytnangi and wind picturesquely across the northern Urals. The gulag tragedy of Vorkuta makes a moving contrast to the optimism of Salekhard. Direct trains follow the main oil pipeline back to Moscow from both Labytnangi and Vorkuta. With more time you could try a rarely attempted side trip to Naryan-Mar, an alternative reindeer-herding area.

Although the route could be done in reverse, boat journeys are considerably quicker northbound thanks to the Ob Riv-

er's strong currents. Some photos of the loop appear on www.hansrossel.com/fotos /fotografie/rusland.

One obvious problem is that while river boats run only in summer, the Nenets herders are much easier to encounter in winter.

KHANTY-MANSIYSK

☎ 34671 / pop 57,500

Close to the meeting of the Ob and Irtysh Rivers, Khanty-Mansiysk was founded in 1637 as Samarovo, some 5km south of the present city centre. It was so isolated that news of the 1917 revolution passed its trapper population by altogether. Things changed greatly with the discovery of oil, and today it is a bustling city, and unusually pleasant for a modern petroleum town. It's capital of the Khanty-Mansiysk Autonomous Okrug, commonly known as Ugra (Yugra). Originally, Ugra was the ancestral homeland of the Finno-Ugric languages, so a tiny trickle of Hungarian, Finnish and Estonian tourists visit the region to investigate their roots. Today's indigenous inhabitants are the Khanty (formerly known as Ostiyak) and Mansi (formerly Vogul) people. Some are still subsistence hunters and fishers in the *taiga* forest, while some others are engaged in private reindeer herding. Since the 1990s they have been successfully securing land titles to their forest areas and gaining compensation for the extensive damage caused by Soviet-era oil-industry pollution.

Information

Useful websites include www.mubis.ru (indigenous people) and www.admhmao.ru (local affairs), and there's a Pti Fyute regional guide book. Try (Russian only) www.admh mansy.ru for practical info, www.ugra-tv.ru for news and **Ugra Tur-Servis** (☎ 31101; www .ugra-service.ru, in Russian; ul Komsomol 32) for group excursions.

Sights

The regional **museum** (☎ 32754; ul Mira 1) exhibits a mammoth's skeleton. The attached **National Artists' Gallery** features some local Mansi and Khanty exhibitions and an icon collection. The **Geology Museum** (☎ 32776; ul Chekhova 13) concentrates on the oil and gas industries. **Igosheva house-museum** (☎ 20400; Loparev ul 7; ☽ 10am-5pm Wed-Sun) is an eye-catching new building with stylised onion-lobed gable.

Out of town, **Torum-Maa** (☎ 22058; Sobianin ul; 9am-1pm & 2-8pm) is an ethnographic museum showing the seasonal lodgings traditionally used by the local Khanty and Mansi peoples for whom the city is named. Groups are treated to various folkloric shows here. **Shapsha**, 28km northeast, is a 19th-century Old Believers' village. (The Old Believers were the descendents of those who disagreed with Patriarch Nikon's changes to the Russian Orthodox rite in 1653. Continuing to cross themselves with two fingers instead of three, they were oppressed and many fled to Siberia.)

Sleeping

The 'economic' three-star **Hotel Yugra** (☎ 955 54; Komsomolskaya 32; s/d/tw R1430/1800/2440) is well appointed and used by Russian tour groups. Built in 2003, the handily central, six-storey **Hotel Taray** (☎ 20019; ul Lenina 64; tw US$105) is considered the best in town. **Na Syem Kholmakh** (☎ 55692; Sportivnaya 15; tw R1450) is a decent three-star hotel at the top of the city's ski slope. **Tobol Boatel** (dm R100, s R200-408), moored right at the port, is the town's cheapest option.

Getting There & Away

Four weekly flights go to Beryozovo (bookings ☎ 94544, R1065, 50 minutes). From June to September there are crowded but well-maintained Ob–Irtysh river steamers every eight days to Salekhard (first/third class R920/345, two days). The steamers stop at Priobye/Sergino, Beryozovo and the incredibly isolated Oktobrskaya market. Timetables vary every year; request details from **Rosrechflot** (☎ 3812-398521; Omsk). If you have a berth you'll find the boats comfortable; there are passable restaurants on board. Although the scenery is never really dramatic, the curious procession of days and the hypnotic endlessness of the wide riverscapes makes the trip a memorably meditative experience. Reservations are very highly advised. Although it may be possible to get a deck-passage ticket just before departure, there are virtually no seats, let alone anywhere comfortable to lie down.

It's easier to find space on daily midsummer *meteor* to Beryozovo (bookings ☎ 36016, R545) and Priobye.

There's a Khanty-Mansiysk **rail ticket office** (ul Komsomolskaya 28; 8am-1pm & 2-7.30pm Mon-Sat,

to 5pm Sun), but no train station. **Buses** (☎ 334 13) run seven times daily to Pyt-Yakh (four hours) on the Surgut–Tobolsk–Tyumen railway line, and once daily to Surgut. A dramatic 1300m Irtysh bridge was completed in 2004, and buses now run to Nyagan (5½ hours), which is on the Yekaterinburg–Serov–Priobye railway line.

PRIOBYE & SERGINO

☎ 34678 / pop 6900

With little to see, these twin towns are simply an alternative place to join the Ob river boat, thanks to a handy rail connection from Yekaterinburg (train No 338, R480, 21 hours). There's a basic but survivable **hostel** (dm R175) at Sergino dock, which is 6km from the main Priobye train station but closer to Sergino's set-down and pick-up point. There are better hotels in Nyagan (below), 47km south.

AROUND PRIOBYE
Sokord Fortress & Sherkaly

Sizeable mounds on the right bank of the Ob are remnants of the once vast Sokord Fortress mentioned in writings of Ivan the Terrible (1557). Some traditional Khanty buildings here surround a small but informative **ethnographic museum**. The souvenir shop sells local Khanty craftwork. Access is by boat-taxi (R200) from Sherkaly village, which is accessible by ferry from Priobye (R140, 35 minutes, five daily). The fishing is great, but there's no hotel.

NYAGAN

☎ 34672 / pop 36,000

The redeeming feature of this crushingly dull new oil town is the **Nyagan Museum** (admission R50), displaying fascinating archaeological finds from **Emder** (www.hist.usu.ru/urc/english/expeditions.htm), which was the capital of a 12th- to 16th-century Ugrian principality on the Endyr River. Emder's site is 90km southeast of Nyagan, 7km by mud road off the new Nyagan to Khanty-Mansiysk highway. At the time of research archaeologists were still investigating; volunteers keen to join the three-week digs that start each August should contact **Andrey Shpitonkov** (☎ 343-350 7545; uniz@yandex.ru; US$750). Note that, despite claims by some local tour agencies, the plans for a fortress reconstruction remain unattempted as yet.

In Nyagan **Bank Sibirkontakt** (ul Lenina 17) has a 24-hour ATM. Reasonable hotels include the **Sibir** (☎ 33030; ul Uralskaya 7; s/tw R650/1100) and its next-door neighbour **Kedr** (☎ 54674; Uralskaya 5; s R846).

In Yugorsk, 150km southwest of Nyagan on the Serov rail line, there's another fine museum and the surprisingly decent **Hotel Rossia** (☎ 34675-22549; ul Lenina 16; s/tw R950/1450).

BERYOZOVO

☎ 34674 / pop 7500

Beryozovo has a reputation for exile and lawlessness, midges and murder. Founded in 1593, this lonely *taiga* outpost is one of Siberia's oldest, but it never fully recovered from a catastrophic 1808 fire. It was at Beryozovo in 1907 that Trotsky gave his captors the slip while being marched to a Salekhard prison for his role in the 1905 revolution. Trotsky faked sciatica (nerve pains) then, while his guardians enjoyed some amateur dramatics, managed a phenomenal escape: 700km in winter on the back of a deer with a drunken local guide. Beryozovo was the first village in the region to strike oil (in 1953), but it failed to capitalise and it certainly hasn't become wealthy. If you're stuck here and are not afraid of drunken, gun-toting locals, seek out the surprisingly good log-hut **museum** (Sobyanina ul 43) and the **communal grave** of those who failed in a Soviet gulag revolt at Lake Num. At the riverside, in a former Mansi sacrifice site, is a Soviet-era **monument to Prince Aleksander Menshikov**. Menshikov rose from pie seller to confidante of Peter the Great, eventually becoming de facto ruler of all Russia, before being disgraced and exiled to Beryozovo, where he died in 1729.

The new **Grad Berezov** (☎ 21273, 21274, 21625; ul Sobyanina 40; s/d/ste R1300/1600/2400) is the best hotel and has a restaurant. The basic **Hotel Beryozka** (☎ 21800; ul Chkalova 45; dm/s/tw R150/220/350) is much cheaper, and there's also a seedy **dosshouse** (dm R140) at the **dock** (☎ 21332). Opposite the post office, on the main street running from the quay, **Perekryostok Store** (ul Lenina 24; ☺ 11am-10pm) has a café. **Kafé Tsibiryachka** (☎ 21988; ul Sobyanina 35) might have the local culinary delicacy *sosvinskoi* (freshwater herring). The surprisingly well-appointed **airport** (☎ 396171), 1km from the centre, has **Utair** (www.utair.ru) flights to Khanty-Mansiysk (50 minutes), Salekhard

and Moscow. *Meteor* hydrofoils go down the river to Salekhard (R480, eight to 10 hours) every second day.

SALEKHARD

☎ 34591 / pop 35,000

Salekhard is the prosperous capital of the Yamal-Nenets Autonomous Area. It was founded in 1595 after Tsar Fyodor's Cossacks grabbed the region from the Princes of Novgorod. The initial timber stockade-fortress, named Obdorsk, became a famous local fur market and a collection point for *iasak* (tribute tithes paid in animal skins by local hunters and herders). It remained small until the 1930s, when a string of slave-labour camps appeared throughout the region. The most brutal gulags were east of Salekhard along railway-construction project 501. Started in 1949, this was an impractical route that Stalin decided should be built to Igarka regardless of the human cost. It was never finished, though thousands died trying. After Stalin died in 1953 the work stopped, and the tracks have since been largely swallowed by permafrost. See www.yamal.org/501/doc/1_e.htm for much more detail.

Today Salekhard is booming thanks to major gas-field discoveries, and construction is rapidly changing the cityscape beyond recognition. Nonetheless, on clear days there are lovely views towards the Urals between the remaining wooden houses of the **old town**. In the modern Polyarnaya Shopping Mall there's an **internet café** (per hr R50) and two ATMs.

Sights

Salekhard is proud to be the only major town to lie exactly on the Arctic Circle. The **Arctic Circle monument** on the road to the airport is a popular place for sunset photographs. On the same road, the **locomotive-shaped monument** is a new memorial for the victims of the Route 501 gulags.

The oldest of Salekhard's historic **wooden houses** are around the 'gidroport', a former airport for sea-planes. Worth a visit, the main central **church** *(khram)* was planned by a German architect in the early 20th century but was only completed after the USSR collapsed.

The former triangular-fronted wooden **museum** (ul Titova 5) was demolished in 2004, but the brand-new **exhibition complex** has started well, with excellent installations offering detailed (Russian only) insights into Nenets history and the gulag horrors, and a fine collection of WWII propaganda posters. The building itself is an eye-catching if less than functional series of pastel-coloured curves located behind the new market.

Salekhard is the easiest starting point for adventures onto the Yamal Peninsula to meet Nenets herders. If you can't get the relevant permits you can still encounter Nenets and Komi families at Salekhard's outdoor market, especially in winter when some arrive by sled to sell handmade crafts, including reindeer-skin mittens and boots. In summer, market stalls sell essential *komarnik* (antimosquito head-nets).

Sleeping

Geolog (☎ 48442; ul Chapaeva, 22) Take bus No 1 from the airport. The Geolog is on the left, halfway to the city centre. Basic dormitory accommodation is available.

Hotel Sibir (☎ 74696; tw R350) The Sibir's acceptable budget rooms with air-conditioning and wash basin are smaller but newer than those at the Ob (following). It's a white building in a curve of the Labytnangi Hwy near the point where the airport access road turns off. Use the bus stop beside the big Salekhard monument.

Hotel Ob (☎ 74558; airport; dm/s/tw R334/501/868) This place has simple and tidy but overpriced rooms with shared bathrooms, bad mattresses and no curtains.

Hotel Yamal (☎ 46333; ul Respublika 100; tw R2000) The Hotel Yamal offers the most popular compromise between comfort and price.

Hotel Arktika (☎ 40777; ul Respublika 38; tw R3350) Attached to the Polaris shopping mall, this is the best and most central but also the most expensive hotel in town.

Eating

Deva Restaurant (Yamal Hotel, second fl) is reckoned to offer Salekhard's best-value dining. **Restaurant Paris** (river station) is actually a boat. **Piyat Pizz** (Casino bldg, second fl) has real Italian-style pizza. **Paradis** (SOK bldg) is a bar-restaurant in the sports complex, popular with the younger crowd. At the time of research, the restaurant within a glass palace on the new Shaitanka bridge behind the exhibition centre was nearing completion. It should offer diners fine

cross-river panoramas towards Labytnangi and the tundra.

The **Polaris shopping mall** (ul Respublika) has a Turkic bakery offering baklava and a fast-food outlet serving decent shashlik. At the open market seek out *muksun*, frozen white fish that's eaten while only partly thawed; dip in salt or hot mustard.

Getting There & Away

Salekhard's brand-new airport has flights to Moscow (R6000, 3½ hours), Novosibirsk, Nadym, Omsk, St Petersburg, Tyumen and Yekaterinburg. Helicopters serve outlying Yamal villages but are often overcrowded (and you'll need permits; see the boxed text, p284).

Take bus No 1 or 3 to Salekhard's **river station** (rechnoi vokzal; ☎ 34622); from there the main Ob ferries take much longer southbound than downriver. Every eight days in summer they go to Tobolsk (first/third class R1262/371, 4½ days) via Beryozovo (26½ hours) and Khanty-Mansiysk (2½ days). You could continue to Omsk (first/third class R1888/556, one week) via Tara. Occasionally the big ferries venture into the Ob Gulf, supplemented by less comfortable *omik* boats that serve Yar-Sale, Novi Port and beyond. You'll need travel permits for these destinations.

The nearest train station is at Labytnangi, across the Ob River from Salekhard (see p284).

Getting Around

The very handy bus No 1 shuttles between the airport, the Polaris Mall/city centre and the river station.

YAMAL PENINSULA

Yamal means 'end of the earth' in the Nenets language. Dotted with thousands of lakes, its big-sky openness along with the tundra's wealth of life in miniature is a great attraction to some. For others the landscape is simply empty and endlessly monotonous. Spread out across the vast region are 7500 Nenets reindeer herders, many of whom are nomads living in tepee-style *mya* tents (called *chum* in Russian). Their land is still held to be sacred. Key spots are marked with old sleds topped by a pile of reindeer antlers, sometimes surveyed by **totems** that are somewhat reminiscent

---

YAMAL PERMITS

Technically, you'll require a permit to venture into the Yamal Peninsula. Until 2003 several travellers managed a trip without one, but recently authorities have been much stricter, and some visitors have been arrested and deported from Russia for permit violations. Check carefully in Salekhard for the latest information before heading out. The strategic gas-production area Bovanyenkogo is especially sensitive.

---

of the Easter Island *Moai* heads, albeit in miniature wooden form. Other totems have seven notches, representing the seven levels of the Nenets cosmos. Examples are found near the Bovanyenkogo gas and oil fields, to which a remarkable 4000km pipeline from Western Europe is presently under construction.

The discovery of large natural-gas reserves has raised a lot of interest in the area. Anthropologists and archaeologists are regular visitors, often funded by the gas companies. See www.mnh.si.edu/arctic/html/yamal.htm for a trip report. Recent discoveries include some naturally mummified bodies.

Most Yamal access is from Salekhard by oil-company helicopter, though a new railway line and unsealed road are under construction from Obskaya towards Bovanyenko. By ferry you can sail up the Ob Gulf to Novi Port (22 hours, roughly weekly in summer). However you travel you'll need to be self-sufficient, with a tent, all food supplies, good local contacts, permits and loads of time.

Note that in summer most of the Nenets herders head far north towards the Kara Sea coast, where the cold winds reduce the mosquito annoyance. The Nenets come south in winter, and on Sunday from mid-March to early April they organise **winter games**. Notable examples are held in Yar-Sale (the Yamal Peninsula's administrative centre) and most famously in Nadym on the first Sunday in April.

SALEKHARD TO VORKUTA

The nearest train station to Salekhard is in the town of **Labytnangi**, across the wide Ob River. Reaching Labytnangi from Sale-

khard starts with a 10km bus ride to the river ferry from the town centre, running via Hotel Sibir and the airport (R30, last at midnight). The ferry (R20 pedestrians, 15 minutes) runs hourly and leaves you a 3km taxi ride (R50) short of Labytnangi train station. Near Labytnangi the new Gornolyzhnyi Komplex (ski centre) operates a popular if somewhat unchallenging 400m downhill ski run in spring. Costs including equipment rental average R600 per day. In season direct minibuses run from beside Salekhard church.

Daily trains from Labytnangi run at 7am to Moscow (47 hours) and at 9.30am to Vorkuta (12 to 16 hours). Either journey takes you over the nominal **Asia-Europe boundary** after about five hours and is especially scenic through the lovely polar Ural mountains. Several stations en route (Poliarnaya, Sob and Kharp) make good starting points for attractive if challenging mountain walks. Former labour camp Kharp may be an architecturally bland concrete-factory town, but its mountain setting is most attractive and it is rebranding itself as a adventure-tourism centre, with various facilities under construction. From here you could walk or canoe the lovely **Sob River valley**, where there's some chance of meeting reindeer herders in spring or autumn.

At **Obskaya** station the new Yamal railway branches north, paralleled by a rough road. Unofficially, the freight-only trains carry local passengers by arrangement, though there are no stations per se. Some 200km up this line, then a dozen kilometres' sled-ride north, is the hamlet of **Laborovaya** (www.cinetrance.com/faktoria.htm). It's an isolated *faktoriya* (trading post) where lonely shop hunters can exchange their surplus fish and game for basic consumer commodities such as matches and tea. Laborovaya is famous as the home of Nenets activist and writer Anna Pavlovna Nerkagi, who runs a school teaching children the traditional arts of nomad survival.

VORKUTA

☎ 2151 / pop 80,000-116,000

Vorkuta, in the autonomous Komi Republic, is a fascinatingly ugly coal-mining city full of Stalinist buildings on pompously wide avenues. Perhaps the most poignantly interesting part of a visit is that many of the older people you meet will have a personal story about the gulags, 12 of which once ringed the city. A helpful contact is **Georgi Mamulaishvili** (☎ 40933), whose father was president of the gulag victims' support group. The group has erected a **victims' monument** overlooking one former gulag near the river, walkably close to the Hotel Vorkuta. Around 15km out of town, sinking dejectedly into swampy tundra, is the lonely **German and Estonian graveyard** of another former gulag. Take bus No 103 or 104 and ask to be set down at Nemetsky Kladbish stop (R13). En route be awed by the extraordinary ugliness of the old Soviet factories and mines. Note that the city is part of an remarkable programme to very belatedly send 'home' thousands of former gulag victims, though its plans to cut the population by a whopping 36,000 are motivated by the urge to save on pensions as much as the desire to reunite long-shattered families.

The three-room **museum** (opposite ul Lenina 35) has ethnographic displays about the Komi and Nenets peoples, a gulag-history room, and a selection of postcards for sale, including some featuring attractive photos of reindeer herders. In December there's an **ice-carving festival**.

There's an **Internet Klub** (ul Gogolya) hidden on the bottom floor of an apartment block behind a little blue 'castle' building. To change money, find the tiny exchange window in the blue shopping centre beside Hotel Vorkuta (on the first floor, beside the flower shop). Its rates are good.

Polar Travel (☎ 73323; ul Lenina 45) can organise a city tour.

Sleeping & Eating

Lena Hostel (☎ 92670; dm R70) Close to the train station, this neat workers' guesthouse has hot showers and neat, warm rooms. Walk out of the station, then take the second right after a large red building. The hostel (it has no sign) is the second building on the left. It can't register foreigners, so staying more than three nights is not possible.

Hotel Vorkuta (☎ 40609; ul Tsentralnaya 5; dm/s/tw R206/366/412) This is a typical eight-storey Soviet hotel whose 'dorms' are simply one bed in a pot-luck shared twin.

Hotel Gornyak (☎ 70833; fax 34828; ul Mira 3B; s/tw R480/700) Newly renovated in a rather chintzy style, the Gornyak ('miner') is Vorkuta's best

available hotel. A couple of larger apartments cost R1500. Take bus No 5, 7 or 10 to Detsky Mir stop, then walk down ul Mira from pl Mira and you'll find it tucked behind the third and fourth buildings on your right.

The Shangri-la 'Georgian' Restaurant downstairs from the Hotel Vorkuta is reasonably priced, though the portions are small, and not much of the food is really Georgian. The hotel's Bochka pub serves beers. Take bus No 5 to VTVK stop.

Getting There & Away

Two trains daily run to Moscow's Yaroslavlskaya Station: one around midday (No 375, 46 hours) and a faster, more comfortable service in the early evening (No 041; *kupe* R1300, 40½ hours). The daily train back to Labytnangi (*kupe* R260, 12 hours) leaves around 9.40am. There's also a train to Gorkiy (No 039, 40 hours) via Kotlas and Kirov, and every two or three days there's a direct but incredibly slow service to St Petersburg (No 387, 67 hours). A R4 shuttle bus runs the 3km from Vorkuta train station to central ulitsa Lenina.

PECHORA
☎ 82142 / pop 44,000
Pechora, on the Vorkuta–Moscow railway, is the gateway city for the **Yugud-Va National Park** (☎ 52507, 21263; www.sll.fi/mpe/yugudva; Sotsialisticheskaya ul 55). The park is one of the world's 10 largest and is part of the Unesco Komi Virgin Forest reserve, but its most beautiful feature is a spiky comb of mountains at the Urals' northern fringes. Pechora has a **hotel** (☎ 51136; s/tw R350/485) at the airport. Boats to Naryan-Mar run every few days if river levels are high enough. A spur of railway goes to **Usinsk**, which has an attractively renovated, gold-domed **church** (ul Komsomolskaya) and a **hotel** (ul 60let Oktyabrya 14). Plans to construct a new Pechora–Usinsk–Naryan-Mar road were announced in August 2003.

NARYAN-MAR
☎ 81853 / pop 26,000
Administrative centre of the Nenets reindeer herders' autonomous region, Naryan-Mar is now experiencing a mini oil boom. The town sits on the right bank of the Pechora River towards its northern mouth. The only buildings of architectural note are around central Lenin square: a striking new

church and the cutely spired wooden **post office**, which contains a two-computer **internet café** (per hr R40). Behind the wooden exhibition centre, the **museum** has erected a traditional Nenets *chum* showing traditional lifestyle innovations like the moss-bottomed cradles, which are reckoned more hygienic than modern nappies. For photos, see www .nao2000.narod.ru/gallary/G_3.htm. Download a city map from http://narjan.narod .ru/karta.html.

Sleeping & Eating

Three blocks west of Lenin Square, the **Hotel Pechora** (ul Lenina) has decent but expensive rooms aimed at oil businessmen. A cheaper veterinary dormitory is only for those with connections. The hotel has the best-value restaurant (mains R100), with good, cheap breakfasts and a wide menu, including excellent reindeer and wild-mushroom *zharkoye* (hot pot). Further from the centre, **Sibir Restaurant** (mains R140) is also recommended, with strings of Christmas lights on the walls, candles on the tables and some private booths. **Lakomka** is a no-frills café for sandwiches, salads and microwaved lunches. It's downstairs at the rear of the public auditorium next to the kitschy new Lukoil building. Its *kotlet Naryan-Marski* is a ground meat patty served with a dollop of mashed potato. There's a 24-hour supermarket around the corner from the hotel.

Getting There & Away

There are regular flights to Moscow (R5100, three hours) or via Arkhangelsk (70 minutes, twice daily) to many other cities. Helicopters serve outlying tundra districts but cost over €3000 per hour to charter. Cargo boats to Pechora run two or three times weekly when water levels allow. Buses No 4 and 4A run from the airport to the centre, the 4A continuing to the Hotel Pechora and the No 4 going to the river port.

ITINERARY 3: THE ARCTIC YENISEY

Were you permitted to use them, frequent Yenisey steamers would offer the easiest way to cruise a great Arctic river. The wild Taymyr Peninsula and Putorana Plateau are Arctic Russia's adventure treasure troves, and Khatanga has flights almost as far as the North Pole. If only they'd drop those accursed permit regulations...

Summer river transport on the Yenisey runs more frequently than on any other Arctic river. The route described here starts in Igarka, the first ferry stop above the Arctic circle, though it's easy enough to get aboard the same elegant steamers in the old Cossack town of Turukhansk or ride all the way down from Krasnoyarsk (see Lonely Planet's *Russia & Belarus* guide). Indeed the southern section of the river is vastly easier for independent travellers. Those who want to travel the Arctic Yenisey are hamstrung by the fact that key hub cities Dudinka and gruesome Norilsk are officially closed to foreigners. Until you've found someone to get you a permit, this route will be out of bounds for you. Don't underestimate the months of bureaucracy involved in getting these permits. One way to arrange them is to take an expensive full-blown Yenisey cruise (around US$1000 from Krasnoyarsk to Dudinka) with an officially sanctioned travel agency such as **Acris Tour** (☎ 3832 295331; www.acris.ru) or **VIP Tour** (☎ 4152-125444; http://vip-tour.net). The most interesting part of these river trips for many visitors is simply getting hypnotised by the blurring of time while gliding along the vast Yenisey, which can be over 15km wide in places. Read Colin Thubron's *In Siberia* to give you an idea of what happens if you get off alone at a small, random settlement en route.

FAST FACTS

■ **Access for independent travellers** Good as far as Igarka; challenging beyond

■ **Best time to travel** April for the Taymyr and Khatanga, July to September for river boats

■ **Difficulty level** For the main route permits are the top problem, best trumped through expensive but comfortable river cruises. By contrast, exploring the Taymyr and Putorana will prove a physical and mental challenge for even the most hardened adventurer.

■ **Don't forget** Permits (yes, again!), snowshoes and survival gear for the Taymyr, smog-mask for Norilsk, a backup plan in case you can't proceed

■ **Don't miss** Igarka's little Permafrost Museum

■ **Gateway city** Igarka

■ **Length of route** Igarka to Dudinka cruise approximately 350km, Dudinka to Norilsk by road 80km, flight to Khatanga 750km

■ **Modes of travel** River boat, plane, helicopter charter, strenuous hiking to adventure areas

■ **Recommended maps** The comprehensive 1:200,000 regional map sold in Krasnoyarsk, Le Pti Fyute's Taymyr guide (in Russian)

■ **Time needed** One-way cruise to Dudinka, 12 hours from Igarka or around 4½ days from Krasnoyarsk (longer coming back); Taymyr Peninsula, two weeks

■ **Time zone** Moscow time +4 (GMT+7)

If you do manage to get to Norilsk you could venture on towards the beautiful Putorana Plateau and the great Taymyr Peninsula. Both are dramatic total wilderness areas that require an adventurous spirit and a great deal of outdoors self-assurance. You could also fly on to Khatanga, the typical launching point for trips to the North Pole (see the boxed text, p270).

The railway between Norilsk and Dudinka was once touted as the world's most northerly and something of a speciality tourist attraction. However, currently the passenger service has ceased, and permit difficulties have stopped most visitors coming anyway.

IGARKA

☎ 39112 / pop 9000

The ragged timber port of Igarka sulks dejectedly at the Yenisey mouth of the frigid Protoka River, just north of the Arctic Circle. The picture of decay that greets you as you step off the river boat is humblingly pitiful: there's no real port, just a dock hidden away behind a small square of mostly derelict buildings about 5km east of the Hotel Zapolyare. As Gulag 503, Igarka once housed up to 35,000 exiles labouring on a nonsensical, never-to-be-completed train line that Stalin had carelessly doodled across a map to Salekhard. With its dismal climate and hopeless employment prospects, the town appears to be dying. The freeze-thaw moods of the permafrost on which the town is built relentlessly undermine the foundations of those buildings that have survived being burnt down by alcoholics, many of whom have fallen catastrophically unconscious, cigarette in hand. Yet, incredibly, hidden amid the ruins is a museum that beat London's National Portrait Gallery for commendation as European Museum of the Year in 2002. The small but unforgettable **Permafrost Museum** (Vechnoy Merzloty muzey; ☎ 24110; www.museum.ru/M1405; ul Bolshoy Teatr 15A; admission R200; ☺ 9am-12.45pm & 2-5pm Sun-Fri) allows you to descend 10m through the frozen strata into a fairytale world of crystalline condensed breath. It has associated submuseums (separate admission charges) including a gulag memorial and an art gallery displaying mostly the work of local schoolchildren.

Sleeping & Eating

The best accommodation option is a private room (around R400 including three meals) organised through the Permafrost Museum. **Hotel Morskoe Port** (LPK; ☎ 24312; ul Chkalova 3; dm R150), near the museum, is a reasonably cosy house with little rooms off a central heated sitting area. Around 4km away, amid crumbling concrete apartment blocks, the **Hotel Zapolyare** (☎ 21611; 1st Mikro-rayon 7A; s/tw from R425-531/638) is handier for the main shop. It's typical of smaller Soviet concrete hotels, but its deluxe rooms are not bad and have showers attached. On the ground floor, a netting-draped bar-restaurant (open at sporadic hours Friday to Sunday) serves surprisingly passable food. Even in 24-hour midsummer light the town's streets seem deserted. Nonetheless, people materialise from nowhere to fill the minibuses that curl two routes around the town. Bus No 1 goes via the art gallery, and No 2 links the museum and both hotels.

Getting There & Away

Tickets for SIAT flights back to Krasnoyarsk (R3030, 3½ hours, three to four per week) are sold at the bank beside Hotel Zapolyare. The airport is on an island linked to town by boat in summer, bus in winter, and helicopter (R100 per person, five minutes) when the ice is unsuitable for either.

There are ferries (around 12 hours, every two or three days in summer) to Dudinka, but no flights. See the boxed text, p295, for more details.

DUDINKA

☎ 39111 / pop 33,000

Most summer steamers terminate at this closed town of dilapidated pastel-coloured apartment blocks. Cranes hover like rusty vultures over the **port** (☎ 56543; ul Sovietskaya 43), there's a brace of **war memorials** and the **museum** (☎ 24191; ul Shchorsa 13A; ☿ 10am-7pm Tue-Sun) focuses on the geology and natural history of the Taymyr region. Perhaps the most dramatic attraction comes in mid-June, when the Yenisey thaws and vast, car park–sized chunks of ice thrash downriver, making an extraordinary din. Permits for tourists are hard to arrange.

A reasonably priced hotel is the **Severnoe Siyaniye** (☎ 56079; ul Matrasova 14; s R300). Frequent buses run to Norilsk, 80km east.

The *Bliznyak* ferry continues up the Yenisey gulf to Ust Port (six hours) and Karaul (13 hours).

NORILSK

☎ 3919 / pop 290,000

Apocalyptic Norilsk is an improbably large metal-processing city where rivers run a vivid rainbow of evilly polluted colours. Huge nickel, copper and platinum mines make the city wealthy but are responsible for acid rain over a wide area of Siberian tundra.

Yet Norilsk is also the gateway to some of the Arctic's most beautiful wilderness scenery. Permits are required, and Norilsk is only open to foreign visitors who have been specifically invited by a local company. The paperwork can be organised by tour companies but will take at least a month.

The website http://norilsk.net is extensive and has many great photos, but at the time of research the English-language version was under construction. **Rodina Komputer** (Leninskiy pr 7; ☿ 10am-10pm) is one of many *internet klub*s. The city has a distinctive green **mosque** (built 1997) and a **museum** (☎ 460646; Leninskiy pr 14) with exhibits about the city's construction and gulag horrors. The good-value **Hotel Norilsk** (☎ 349930; ul Talnakhskaya 39A; s R280), off ulitsa Sovietskaya, examines permits and visas in minute detail. **Kavkaz Restaurant** (☎ 222815; ul Talnakhskaya 71; mains R80-100) serves inexpensive Georgian food.

Norilsk's Alykel airport is almost 50km west of the centre. It has twice-daily air connections with Krasnoyarsk (R4640), as well as frequent services to Moscow and several Urals cities. A weekly hop serves Khatanga (R4200).

PUTORANA PLATEAU

Starting some 75km east of Norilsk, the ultra-isolated, windswept Putorana Plateau rises magnificently, like a gigantic green-tinged dinosaur dripping with dramatic waterfalls. Russian adventure lovers nickname this the Lost World and rave about the purity of its untouched nature. Beneath lichen-covered rocks, brooks murmur hypnotically, foxberries remain edible beneath carpets of winter snows, and contorted larch trees give the forested areas a mysterious, fairytale atmosphere. Only the top three metres of the Putorana's mesmerising lakes ever thaws, and it's not uncommon to stumble across mammoth tusks. Cross-country skiing treks are best in April, when the lake surfaces are still conveniently frozen. There's a small ranger's hut on Lake Kutaramakan – it looks particularly beautiful ringed with frozen cascades. Wild reindeer herds migrate across it in spring. Kayaking and rafting adventures are possible in July and August. However, visits are only for hardy outdoors adventurers who are wealthy enough to afford the helicopter transfers.

TAYMYR PENINSULA

The gigantic Taymyr (Dolgan-Nenets) Autonomous District spreads north, glistening with lakes and swampy tundra, to mainland Russia's most northerly point at Cape Chelyuskin. The whole region is extremely sparsely populated by humans but is a rich breeding ground for great bird populations, notably Brent geese. There are muskoxen in the Byrranga mountains north of gorgeous Lake Taymyr. Access generally requires a full-scale expedition.

Getting There & Away

With plenty of notice Norilsk-based **Traveller's Club Taymyr** (☎ 423066; alextravel@norcom .ru; ul Ordzhonikidze 2-93) can help you sort out permits for the Taymyr Peninsula and Putorana Plateau, and can organise boats, helicopters, snowmobiling and the various guides that you'll need to explore this wildest frontier of Arctic travel. Trips to the North Pole are also possible. For reliable, English-speaking help in organising trips to this region, contact the ever-obliging **K2** (☎ 3812-693075; www.adventuretravel.ru) in Omsk or **Stan Tours** (info@stantours.com) in Almaty. Although the latter is primarily a Central Asia specialist, the German owner has had some thrilling adventures in the Taymyr. K2 offers a 12-day Putorana trip with fishing, hiking, canyon-rafting and a visit to Lake Kutaramakan. The US$1850 cost out of Norilsk includes helicopter transfers and permits.

KHATANGA

☎ 39176 / pop 5600

Surprisingly large for so isolated an outpost, Khatanga was founded in 1632 but remained little more than six houses and a church until the Soviet era. The local **museum** is well appointed and has an Igarka-style permafrost cave. The village comes alive in April, when locals celebrate a **reindeer festival**, and the town buzzes with an eclectic mix of geologists, explorers and daredevils from all over the globe. That's because flights to Sredniy Island scientific base and thence to the North Pole typically started from **Khatanga airport** (☎ 25417). Consequently, the five-storey **hotel** (s/tw R1200/1500-1900), just 50m from the runway, is comfortable. However, since the well-respected airport managers died in an air crash a few years ago, organisation has become somewhat less reliable. Along with Khatanga's frequently inclement weather, this means that Arctic expeditions are increasingly looking for alternative routes. Khatanga remains the headquarters for the **Taymyr Reserve** (☎ 21097; taimyr@orc.ru), though the disconnected parcels of protected land are very distant.

For details of North Pole trips, see p270.

DIKSON

pop 2900

A few decaying villages are scattered along the ever-widening yawn of the Yenisey Gulf, with ethnic Russians overwhelmingly outnumbering the minuscule population of indigenous Dolgan and Nenets peoples. At the Yenisey's far northern mouth, the incredibly isolated settlement of Dikson was named by explorer Adolf Nordenskjöld for his sponsor, Oskar Dickson, during the 1878 traverse of the Northeast Passage. Dikson's dwindling population remains nervous about potential nuclear pollution from Soviet-era waste that was dumped off the Novaya Zemlya islands, some 500km to the north.

ITINERARY 4: THE ARCTIC LENA RIVER

Flummox even your best-travelled friends by admitting to being one of the first foreigners to cruise this vast yet little-known waterway right to its Arctic delta.

Yakutsk (☎ 41122; pop 200,000), a mineral-rich permafrost city, and the northern Lena River lie within the Sakha Republic (Yakutia). Technically, Yakutia imposes its own visa rules. Though the authors were not asked for special papers, you should check the latest regulations carefully before showing up. The best source of information is the reputable **Sakha Tourist Agency/Tour Service Centre** (☎ 41122-422652; www.yakutiatravel.com; ul Oktyabrskaya 5, Yakutsk), which arranges homestays in villages right across Sakha. It also organises many excursions, including a two-week return Lena River cruise from Yakutsk to Tiksi via Sangar, Zhigansk (originally a 1632 Cossack fortress) and Kyusyur. The cruise includes a diversion to the famous

Lena pillar rock formations on the way back. For full details on Yakutsk, see Lonely Planet's *Russia & Belarus* guide.

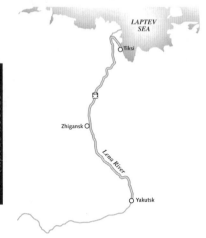

ARCTIC RUSSIA TRAVEL ROUTES

FAST FACTS

- **Access for independent travellers** Difficult (Yakutsk is way off the railway network; going further will require money and tenacity)

- **Best time to travel** Midsummer for river boats

- **Difficulty level** Lack of tourism means you'll be eyed with some surprise if not suspicion; the trips themselves are easy

- **Don't forget** To make good contacts in Yakutsk well before you start, that Sakha has only two (very rough) long-distance 'roads' and that in winter Oimyakon (in Sakha) is the world's coldest spot

- **Don't miss** The Lena pillars (Sakha's greatest attraction, albeit outside the Arctic zone)

- **Gateway city** Yakutsk

- **Length of route** Each way approximately 2200km by boat, 1250km by air

- **Modes of travel** Riverboat, plane

- **Recommended maps** Sakha maps available at Globus bookshop in Yakutsk (pr Lenina 18)

- **Time zone** Moscow time +6 (GMT+9)

TIKSI

☎ 41267 / pop 6100

For years the collapsing settlement of Tiksi, on the Arctic coast east of the Lena delta, was a closed town, a strategic airport for the USSR's air force and nuclear defence. It remains a controlled zone, so all visitors require a border-zone permit. Nonetheless, intrepid foreign travellers who have managed to get such a permit have been allowed to take the weekly flights from Yakutsk (three hours). Some visitors come for *taimen* fishing (from around US$1700 for seven days all in, including helicopter transfers, arranged via www.yakutiatravel.com). Otherwise, once in Tiksi you can stare at the ice cracking on the lugubrious yellow July sea, listen to maudlin tales of how much better life was in the Soviet era or watch scrap metal rust. Weather-ruined Tiksi-3 village nearby is a particularly shocking scene of desolation. Hotels **Moryak** (☎ 54031; tw R315) and **Zapolyare** (☎ 53072; ste R550) are reported to be unexpectedly pleasant.

ITINERARY 5: THE CHUKOTKA PENINSULA

Spot whales and walruses while cruising around Russia's easternmost point visiting ramshackle villages and bizarrely isolated cities en route.

At Asia's easternmost nose, Chukotka offers an end-of-the-world frisson and has a wealth of wild, undisturbed coastline to savour. Although the rather barren, scree-covered fjordsides are not always dramatic, there are good chances to spot whales, walruses and distant coves that very few travellers have ever seen. The itinerary below follows approximately the route of icebreaker cruises like that organised by **Quark Expeditions** (☎ 203 656 0499; www.quarkexpeditions.com; cruises from US$8050 incl flights from Alaska). More limited 12-day whale- and walrus-watching tours with **Circumpolar Expeditions** (☎ 907 272 9299; www.arctictravel.net/tourprovr .htm; Suite 101, 3201 W31st Ave, Anchorage, Alaska 99517, USA) stop off at various villages around the coast and cost from US$3495. The company can also help sort out your visa and permit nightmares and organise bed-and-breakfast accommodation.

ARCTIC RUSSIA TRAVEL ROUTES

FAST FACTS

- **Access for independent travellers** Almost hopeless – as yet almost solely for tours and cruises
- **Best time to travel** July and August
- **Difficulty level** Easy as a tour, very awkward independently
- **Don't forget** Permits, permits, permits
- **Don't miss** walrus-watching boat trips
- **Gateway city** Anadyr or Provideniya
- **Length of route** Approximately 2000km each way, excluding Pevek
- **Modes of travel** Air, cruise ship
- **Time needed** Two weeks for typical cruises
- **Time zone** Moscow time +9 (GMT+12)

Permit requirements make travelling independently awkward; even if you manage it, being on land means you'll miss much of the attraction.

Chukotka undulates between eroded mountains of permafrost rising as high as 1843m in the heart of the peninsula. Some 90% of the region's population is Russian, and there are also around 12,000 Chukchi, 1400 Evenki and Yup'ik, and 1000 Chuvantsi people. The native populations were forced into towns during the Soviet era as the region was exploited for tin, manganese, coal and especially gold mining. However, in purely economic terms mining was never profitable. With the collapse of the Soviet system and its state subsidies, many enterprises became insolvent and roughly half of the population left. Many native people drifted back to their original village settlements, reverting to traditional hunting-based lifestyles. There are some rather folkloric attempts to revive shaman drum dancing. Despite appealing settings, even these settlements are rarely picturesque and they lack the colourful charm of their Greenlandic equivalents. The bigger towns are architecturally miserable.

The region's most prominent personality is Roman Abramovich, who's best known in the west for his free-spending approach to Chelsea Football Club. He has been pouring his money into Chukotka, too.

For a better idea of the region, consult www.chukotka.org and enjoy the excellent photos on www.connexion-dte.dk/mmedia .htm. For wildlife, see http://dinets.travel .ru/chukotka.htm.

ANADYR

☎ 42722 / pop 11,300

Chukotka's main city forms a tatty sprawl across a low-lying tongue of fairly flat land on Anadyr Bay. Functional three- and five-storey concrete blocks line the main thoroughfare, Otke ulitsa, and the town's skyline is dominated by the chimney and cooling towers of the power station. The newly tapped Zapadno-Ozernoe gas field offers Anadyr hopes of economic salvation and has caused a small building boom, with new cinema and shopping complexes recently completed. Near the main post office, the uninspired four-room **regional museum** (☎ 22731; http://mu seum.chukotnet.ru, in Russian; ul Rultytegina 5; admission R10) has a few stuffed auks.

Of three new hotels, the new **Otel Chukotka** (☎ 22661; ul Rultytegina 2) is Anadyr's smartest, with tinkling chandeliers, pseudo-gilt picture frames, a sauna, a business centre and a billiard-bar. **Anadyr Hotel** (☎ 29201; Otke ul 14) is a compact, relatively new grey-and-red building right in the city centre nicknamed Hotel Canada for its builders. its Dolce Vita Restaurant serves supposedly Italian-style food. **Gostinitsa Chukotka** (☎ 22794; ul Energetikov 14) has acceptable but more cramped rooms hidden within a big yellow-fronted apartment complex.

RUSSIA TO ALASKA?

Many dreamers staring at world maps come up with the bright idea of a transcontinental odyssey: crossing between Russia and Alaska. After all, at their nearest points Asia and America are only 89km apart. However, this overlooks a very important detail. The nearest 'road', the Kolyma Hwy, is over 2000km to the southwest. From that road's end in Magadan you could fly to Anchorage, Alaska, with **MAVIAL** (Magadan Airlines; www.magadanair.us), or more complicatedly via Anadyr or Provideniya in Chukotka to Nome (also Alaska). However, there is no land route to the northeast and absolutely no passenger boat to North America. If you're determined to sail the Bering Strait, one option is to join an annual two-week cruise from Anchorage to Provideniya and back to Nome. **CruiseWest** (☎ 206 409 3611; www.cruisewest.com) offers such a trip from US$7799. Sailing your own boat is not impossible, but customs problems are formidable, and you'll be inconveniently limited to entering and leaving Russia via Provideniya like South African adventurer Mike Horn (www.mikehorn.com). For a comprehensive lowdown on who else has crossed and how, see http://members.aol.com/imershein/Page8.html bering.

The **airport** (☎ 56569), across a wide gulf in Ugolnye Kopi, is undergoing a massive re-development, which locals hope will launch Anadyr as more of a tourist hub from 2006. Beluga whales often follow the ferry across.

EGVEKINOT
pop 1900
Low but strikingly abrupt mountains rise directly behind Egvekinot's standard concrete blocks, giving the town a relatively photogenic aspect (see www.egvekinot.ru /gallery for images). Neolithic archaeological finds displayed in the local **museum** suggest that the Kresta Gulf coast has been inhabited for over 5000 years. The first European to visit was Cossack explorer Kurban Ivanov in 1660, followed by Vitus Bering in 1726.

Egvekinot is probably the best starting point for exploring inland Chukotka, thanks to a reasonably serviceable cross-mountain road via the Chukchi settlement of **Amguema** and continuing all the way to the manganese mines at Iultin. The tundra en route houses former gulags as well as nomadic reindeer herders. Continuing overland to Vankarem or Mys Shmidta is only feasible in winter.

There's a reindeer-breeding centre at **Konergino**, across the Kresta Gulf.

Egvekinot has a 50-bed 1970s hotel. An occasional supply ship operates from Anadyr, but most of the very few foreign visitors come on summer tours, such as those offered by **Intourist Ecotours** (www.ecotours -intourist.ru).

PROVIDENIYA
☎ 42735 / pop 2300
On an attractive bay flanked by steep, balding hills, Provideniya is essentially five parallel ranks of decaying Soviet-era apartment blocks behind the deepwater docks. The population was once around 8000, with some 30,000 more housed in nearby military encampments defending the Soviet border. These days many buildings are deserted, giving the town a very eerie atmosphere. In a green 1950s building, the interesting **museum** (☎ 22620; nab Dezhneva 43; admission R10; ⊙ 10am-1pm & 2-6pm Mon-Sat) receives support from the Alaska national parks service. It displays local crafts, including curious wooden snow-goggles and a full-sized *chum*. The director speaks English.

Getting There & Away
Air access is from Anadyr (see p291) or by **Bering Air** (☎ 907-443 5620; info@beringair.com) charters from Nome, Alaska. Guided weekend trips are organised from Alaska by Seattle-based **Worldwise Ecotourism** (☎ 282 0824; www .traveleastrussia.com). The airport is not actually in Provideniya at all but a ferry ride across the bay in Ureliki village.

Novoe Chapalino (p293) can be accessed by UAZ 4WD minibus.

AROUND PROVIDENIYA
The main attraction is visiting the region's coastal waters to observe relatively undisturbed populations of whales, seals and walruses, plus cliffs alive with nesting sea birds. You'll need a boat, of course. If your language skills and permits are up to it

and you have no time constraints, there's a chance to hitch a ride from Provid>eniya to an outlying settlement.

The Chukchi and Yupik people's main occupation is reindeer herding in the gentler tundra valleys. The easiest place to visit them is in **Novoe Chapalino village**, which is connected to Provideniya by a rough road passing a big but deserted former military base. Novoe Chapalino is very pleasantly located on a bay backed by the usual barren valleys. Its anaesthetic box-grid of 1958 houses is being steadily replaced by comfy new stilt-foundationed homes funded by the omnipresent largesse of Roman Abramovich (p290). In spring locals still use dogsleds here. Local dances are performed when day-tripping tour groups arrive from Alaska. **Yanrakynnot** is a whale-hunting village with more attractive wooden houses on gentle grassy undulations. The famous whale graveyard has bones strewn for kilometres along the coast.

CAPE DEZHNEV AREA

The 1200-strong population of **Lavrentia** is roughly 85% Chukchi and Yupik, and traditional hunting is the economic mainstay. The nearby hot springs may soon be used for geothermal power generation. There's a weekly flight to Anadyr and a hotel, but you'll need a special permit to stay. Uninhabited Cape Dezhnev is Asia's easternmost tip. Look for the old Soviet telescopes, which were once used to watch for bourgeois capitalist incursions from Alaska. Now that this lookout station has been abandoned, the closest sizeable village is **Uelen** with its small **craft museum**. *Trekking in Russia & Central Asia*, by Frith Maier, describes a one-week hiking loop of this area, passing through the Valley of Death – very biblical! Further west, in Mys Shmidta, are the **Wrangel Island reserve headquarters** (ul Naberezhnaya 27).

PEVEK

pop 5400

Though the population has halved in the last decade, Pevek remains the main northeastern coastal port and a secondary air hub for airline **Chukotavia** (☎ 22090). Gold mining and border sensitivities make police typically suspicious of visitors. There's a road of sorts to the closed gold-mining town of Bilibino with its nuclear-power station. Extraordinary Northeast Passage icebreaker cruises

from Murmansk disembark here (see the boxed text, p270), and guests are flown by charter flight to Anchorage, Alaska. A 6WD bus can make it to **Komsomolskiy** (population 550), where **Intourist** (www.ecotours-intourist.ru) offers helicopter excursions to the incredible 18km-diameter **Lake Elgygytgyn**, a crater created by a huge meteorite impact 3.4 million years ago. **Tours to Russia** (☎ 095-921 8027; www.tourstorussia.com) runs 350km white-water rafting holidays from here to the Anadyr River.

WRANGEL ISLAND

Often fog- and ice-bound, this gently mountainous nature reserve is considered to have the greatest biodiversity of anywhere in the Arctic. In summer its mosaic of tundra types becomes a carpet of flowers. A Unesco site since 2004, it's a winter hideaway for polar bears. The rich coastal waters are feeding grounds for walruses and grey whales, and there are bird colonies of snow geese and phalarope. The landscape is predictably stark, but longer-term visitors might stumble across bones and tusks of mammoths, which survived here until relatively recent epochs.

The island was named by American whaler Thomas Long for explorer Ferdinand von Wrangel, who had sought but failed to find it in 1820–24. The famous Vilhjalmur Stefansson expedition, sent to claim the island for Britain in 1921, ended in confused disaster. (Sole survivor Ada Blackjack Johnson was rescued in 1923.) In 1926 the USSR created a settlement at Ushakhovskoye to ensure its territorial claim. Today there's a scientific base with huts and a rough helipad. Visitors are only allowed by invitation. **Intourist** (www .ecotours-intourist.ru) organises helicopter visits from Pevek, and every year one or two icebreaker cruises visit from Alaska (see the boxed text, p292) and Anadyr or Provideniya. Various Western agencies, including **Footprint** (www.footprint-adventures.co.uk; cruises from 5750), bring their Chukotka icebreaker cruises here.

ESSENTIAL FACTS

DANGERS & ANNOYANCES

In addition to the usual cautions required for Arctic travel, the main annoyances are bureaucratic, thanks to all the permit requirements. There's also considerable police suspicion towards independent travellers in several of the areas covered. Some small outposts are disintegrating, and one may hear tales of alcohol-fuelled crime, though these are frequently exaggerated. Nonetheless it's wise to have contacts before you arrive.

FURTHER READING

Lonely Planet's *Russia & Belarus* is an essential accompaniment for travels in the rest of Russia and will ideally complement this volume. Regional Russian-language guides by Le Pti Fyute (www.petitfute.ru, in Russian) include *Chukotka*, *Komi* (for Vorkuta), *Nenets AO* (for Naryan Mar), *Murmansk Region* (Kola Peninsula), *Krasnoyarsky Kray* (Arctic Yenisey area) and *Taymyr*. Its *Yugra* is ideal for the Khanty-Mansiysk area (p280), and an English-language edition has supposedly been published, though it's exceedingly hard to find.

Frith Maier's *Trekking in Russia & Central Asia* is a somewhat ageing classic; it's ideal for planning expeditions, though you'll still need local maps. Only a tiny fraction deals with Arctic areas.

Fridtjof Nansen's two-volume *Farthest North* documents his *Fram* expedition from Siberia across the Arctic ice. It's a meticulously detailed yet somewhat tedious read. Much more exciting is *The Land of White Death*, by Valentin Albanov, whose ship attempted to repeat Nansen's exploits – with disastrous consequences. Albanov's truly thrilling escape story is written with pace and style and must rate as one of the greatest classics of Arctic literature.

MONEY

The Russian currency is the rouble abbreviated in this book as R, though in Cyrillic it looks like a P. One rouble equals 100 kopeks. Since the 1997 currency collapse, the rouble has been relatively stable and hovers at around R30 to the US dollar. That currently means R36 to the euro and R52 to the pound sterling. Travellers cheques offer security but generally prove a nightmare to cash. The best buy-sell rate split is always for US dollars (clean, new bills only), though euro rates are not too bad and euro acceptance is now relatively widespread in exchange booths. However, in the Arctic such booths are relatively rare. In many Russian cities ATMs breed like rabbits, but in the Arctic

region you can really only count on them in Salekhard and Murmansk. All in all, up north you'd be well advised to have a good stash of roubles about your person, backed up with greenbacks.

When entering Russia be very sure to fill in *and have stamped* a *deklaratsia* (customs declaration form) stating how much foreign currency you're carrying. At Moscow and St Petersburg you may be told that this is unnecessary, but persist (go through the red lane) if you are likely to leave Russia by a different exit point. Especially when exiting Russia into Mongolia by train, having unstamped or missing *deklaratsia* can result in all your money being confiscated!

TELEPHONE

Russia's country code is ☎ 7. Within Russia, to call any non-local number dial ☎ 8 then wait for a different tone. After that, for an international call tap in 10, the country code, the city code (minus the first zero) and the number. For a Russian intercity call, add the city code (zeros and all) and then the number. Except from call boxes, calling local numbers is generally free, even from hotels. By contrast, calling long distance or international from hotels can be very pricey. You'd be better off with a card phone or, where they don't exist, using a telephone office. Older phone offices still require you to give the number to a counter operator.

Emergency telephone codes:

Ambulance ☎ 03
Fire ☎ 01
Gas leaks ☎ 04
Police ☎ 02

Mobile phones

GSM mobile phones work in most populated areas of Russia using a variety of networks. However, at around US$20 for a local SIM card, it's generally cheaper to buy a Russian telephone number from one of the many local cell-phone stores. As anywhere, the deal varies with the network you select. Inter-network roaming options are possible, but calls on other networks become more expensive. Thus when selecting the SIM card consider where you plan to use the phone – don't buy a SIM card for a Moscow-based network if you'll mostly be visiting eastern Siberia.

GATEWAY CITIES

Getting to Murmansk

Daily flights link Murmansk (p272) with Moscow (R2634, two to three hours), St Petersburg (R2860, two hours) and Arkhangelsk (R2444, two hours). **Arkhangelsk Airlines** (http://avl.aero, in Russian) flies from Tromsø in Norway (two hours, thrice weekly) and Luleå in Sweden (2¾ hours, twice weekly) via Rovaniemi in Finland (1¼ hours). From June to mid-September **Finnair** (www.finnair .com) flies directly from Helsinki, Finland.

Daily trains run from Moscow (*platskart/kupe* R767/1280, 36 hours), St Petersburg (R510/950, 26 to 28 hours), Petrozavodsk (R351/768, 20 hours) and indirectly from Arkhangelsk (R345/606, 30 hours).

Minivans or buses run from Kirkenes, Norway (7am and 8am Monday to Friday, noon Sunday) and Ivalo, Finland (8am Monday to Friday, 7½ hours) with connections to Rovaniemi. In Murmansk services leave from the Hotel Polyarnye Zory (see p273).

Getting to Khanty-Mansiysk

There are daily flights from Moscow (R5100), Tyumen (R3400) and several other cities. Summer steamers coming from Omsk via Tara and Tobolsk call at Khanty-Mansiysk (p280) en route to Salekhard every eight days. From Tobolsk midsummer **meteor** (info ☎ 34511-39467; R706) hydrofoils run once or twice a week. The nearest train station is Pyt-Yakh, which is located on the Surgut–Tobolsk–Tyumen line.

Getting to Igarka

All transport to Igarka (p287) is via the large, pleasant city of Krasnoyarsk, 60 hours east of Moscow along the Trans-Siberian Railway on train No 055 (60 hours). Krasnoyarsk-based airline **SIAT** (Sibaviatrans; www.siat.ru, in Russia; ul Vzlyotnaya 9; ☒ 8am-8pm Mon-Fri, 8am-1pm & 2-6pm Sat & Sun) serves the Yenisey area with several weekly flights to Igarka (R3030, 3½ hours), Turukhansk (R2900), Dudinka (R6200) and Norilsk (R4640).

Every couple of days from June to early October, elegant Dudinka-bound passenger ships with wood panelling and shiny brass fittings depart Krasnoyarsk's spired **river station** (☎ 3912-274446; ☒ 8am-7pm) for Yenisey River odysseys. The ride to Igarka (R1234 to R2974, 74 to 79 hours) includes short stops at Yeniseysk (17 hours) and Turukhansk (38 to 40 hours). There are three to four boats per week. Last-minute tickets are usually available. Note that returning southbound (ie upstream) journeys take about 50% longer.

Getting to Yakutsk

Yakutsk has several weekly air connections to Moscow (R9000), Irkutsk (R3400) and Khabarovsk (R4900), and a twice-monthly river ferry to Ust Kut on the BAM railway, where there are trains to Krasnoyarsk.

Getting to Chukotka

Anadyr (p291) is the main hub, with flights from as far afield as Moscow (Domodedovo) or Khabarovsk, mostly via Magadan on **Chukotavia** (☎ 42722 56569). Chukotka is sporadically accessible from Alaska thanks to charter flights from Anchorage to Anadyr and notably Nome to Provideniya on **Bering Air** (☎ 907-443 5620; info@beringair.com). If you come that way, remember that you'll cross the International Date Line: noon on Monday in Nome is 9am on Tuesday in Chukotka, a 21-hour difference.

Be aware that Chukotka counts as both a closed and a border zone, thus requiring two separate special permits. The exact list of regulations runs to several pages, apparently designed to dissuade any tourist from coming independently. Bering Air and various adventure-tour agencies can help their guests. Permits are notoriously hard to organise individually. At the time of research, a tourism plan due to coincide with the rebuilding of Anadyr airport in 2006 claimed it would simplify visa and permit rules, but don't hold your breath.

TIME

Russia stretches across a phenomenal 10 time zones. Almost all train timetables work on Moscow time (*Maskovski vremya*; GMT+3, GMT+4 in summer), but bus timetables are usually on local time. For air travel check very carefully which time is quoted. See also the World Time Zones chart on p334.

TOURIST INFORMATION

There isn't anything approaching a tourist office anywhere in the region. Local travel agencies might prove helpful. Otherwise, often your best hope for information is joining Internet chat groups (preferably in Russian) with people from the area you wish to visit. Such contacts are likely to give you more reliable information than any other source, but obviously it's very hit and miss.

VISAS

The biggest disincentive to visiting Russia is the miserably complex bureaucracy of visas, permits and registrations. Don't underestimate the cost or irritation involved. Almost all Western nationals require a visa. Application costs generally start at around US$50, assuming you can wait two weeks or so for processing. This rises to $100 or more for quicker service. However, before you can even apply you'll need an officially sanctioned 'invitation'. If you're on a tour the tour operator should provide this. If travelling independently, you'll need to find a 'visa support' company such as www.visa torussia.com to get an invitation. This service can cost tens or hundreds of US dollars, depending on the type and length of visa required and the number of entries. Long-stay and multi-entry visa support can

take weeks, and such visa applications may require you to take an HIV/AIDS test. Good visa support is a topic of endless, useful discussion on Lonely Planet's Thorn Tree site (http://thorntree.lonelyplanet.com/).

Visas come in various types. Independent travellers will find things easier if they can score a 'business visa', even if they have no business to conduct. That's because tourist visas technically limit you to a planned, booked itinerary. Business visas, by contrast, allow you more flexibility.

If money is no object, reputable visa agencies such as the London-based **Thames Consular** (☎ +44-20 8995 2492; www.thamesconsular .com) can organise everything from invitation to visa issuing in one package. For a double-entry business visa, expect to pay around £170 if you can wait a month and £350 to get it the same week. For a single-entry tourist visa, reckon on £120 (15 days' processing) or £210 (next-day service).

Whatever your visa you'll still need to 'register' within three days of arrival. Registration means officially informing the local aliens' bureau (PVU/OVIR) of your presence. If you stay in a better hotel this is generally done for you (keep the proof). If you're staying in budget accommodation you'll have to seek out OVIR yourself. This can be enormously tiresome, even for Russian speakers. You'll save lots of trouble and possibly even money by simply checking in to a good hotel for one night to get registered.

If all this doesn't seem complex enough, many of the Arctic regions are 'closed' or restricted 'border' zones. That means you'll require additional permits. These can be horrendously difficult to procure unless you join an officially sanctioned tour.

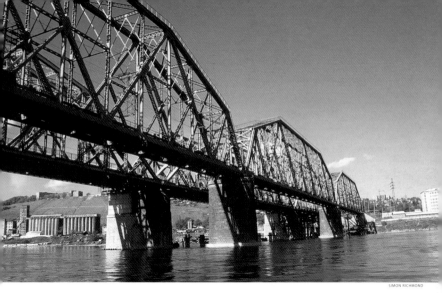

Railway bridge across the Yenisey (p286), Siberia, Russia

SIMON RICHMOND

Lena pillars (p290), Yakutsk, Russia

GRAHAM BELL

Tundra ice, northeastern Siberia (p290), Russia

GRAHAM BELL

ANDERS BL

Snowboarding at Riksgränsen (p309), Sweden

NED FRIARY

Cod tongues and fish soup,
Lofoten (p303), Norway

Napapiiri (p316), Finland's gateway to the
Arctic Circle

DAVID

Rorbu (seaside cottage) with cod drying on racks, Reine (p304), Norway

NED FRIARY

Arctic Scandinavia Travel Routes

North Pole +

ARCTIC SCANDINAVIA
TRAVEL ROUTES

HIGHLIGHTS

- Making it to **Svalbard** (p324), one of the most impressive destinations on earth

- Enjoying a cocktail at the ultra-cool **Ice Hotel** near Kiruna (p309)

- Hiking in **Pallas-Ounastunturi National Park** (p327) or the **Kilpisjärvi** region (p328)

- Looking out over the turquoise seas and fabulous scenery of the **Lofoten islands** (p303)

- Sitting back and admiring the fantastic coastal scenery from the legendary **Hurtigruten steamer** (p298)

★ Svalbard

Hurtigruten Route
Kilpisjärvi ★
Pallas-Ounastunturi ★ National Park
Lofoten ★ Islands
Kiruna ★

The starkly beautiful wilderness of the Scandinavian Arctic makes it a perfect place for the road trip of a lifetime. It's one of Europe's last great wilderness areas and a land of invigorating extremes, but at the same time it's much more accessible than other Arctic regions. A good network of roads, buses and ferries makes travel relatively easy, and the incredible beauty, sense of space and air of serenity that pervade the region are simply unforgettable.

Nature reigns supreme in northern Scandinavia: the scenic coastline, idyllic islands and dramatic fjords dotted with tiny fishing villages give way to majestic mountains, wild forests and the vast windswept stretch of the upland plateau, home to the Sami people, who have herded their reindeer in this area for centuries. Offshore, the Caribbean-coloured seas of Lofoten and the Arctic archipelago of Svalbard are truly an assault on the senses.

The far north of Scandinavia is a land set apart by climate as much as by culture. Long nights of bitter cold and dancing aurora yield to the stark blue skies and crunching snow beloved by skiers, dog-mushers, snowmobilers and ice-fishers. Spring gives way to a fleeting but intense spurt of summer, when you can hike some of Europe's largest and grandest national parks, play midnight golf or hole up in a ramshackle cottage by a lakeshore.

Throw in the towel at work and plan to cover the whole route given here, or bite off a small chunk and explore it in more detail. Dive from a sauna into the snow, sip cocktails in an ice hotel, hike the thousands of kilometres of trails, meander along the coast in search of your own little slice of heaven and enjoy Arctic Scandinavia at its best.

GETTING AROUND

Although most of Arctic Scandinavia is accessible by bus and ferry, it will take you a minor eternity by public transport, as connections only run a couple of times a week on some sections and distances are large. Even for budget travellers, it's worth considering taking the odd flight, or only planning to cover part of the following itineraries. There's a maze of schedules for transport operators, and local tourist offices are invaluable for navigating the region.

Air

The quickest way to get to the far north is by air. **SAS** (www.scandinavian.net) flies to a variety of destinations, including Alta, Bodø, Kirkenes, Kiruna, Narvik and Tromsø. **Braathens** (www.braathens.no) and **Widerøe** (www.wideroe.no) fly to Alta, Bodø, Hammerfest, Kirkenes, Mo i Rana and Tromsø. **Norwegian Air** (www.norwegian.no) flies to Alta, Bodø, Kirkenes, Narvik and Tromsø, and **Finnair** (www.finnair.com) has flights to Ivalo, Kemi, Kittilä and Rovaniemi. Swedish domestic carrier **Skyways** (www.skyways.se) flies to Luleå.

For the best ticket prices book online at least seven days in advance or consider buying an air pass. If you're under 25 it's worth heading to the airport on the off-chance of getting a standby ticket.

Boat

In Norway an extensive network of car ferries and express boats links the country's offshore islands, coastal towns and fjord districts. Most ferries on the road system accommodate vehicles, but express coastal services normally take only foot passengers and cyclists.

The legendary **Hurtigruten** (www.hurtigruten.no) heads north from Bergen every night of the year, pulling into 33 ports on its six-day journey to Kirkenes, where it turns around and heads back south. The return journey takes 11 days and covers a distance of 2500 nautical miles. In agreeable weather, the fjord and mountain scenery along the way is nothing short of spectacular.

Bus

Express buses follow most main highways across the far north, but they may not be frequent. Distances are long and costs can mount up. Generally, there's no price difference between express and regular buses, and discounts are normally available for students, seniors and children. Inter-Rail and ScanRail

TO THE NORTH POLE

Getting to the North Pole from Scandinavia is probably the simplest route around, and a host of companies offer trips and tours. It's not possible to do this trip independently, but you should have no problem finding a package to suit your interests. Many companies can also arrange tailor-made trips if you have special requirements. The jumping-off point of Svalbard (see p324) is not only the world's most accessible bit of the polar north but also one of the most spectacular places imaginable.

For a sedate passage to the Pole, Amazing Cruises & Travel (see p65) offers two-week cruises to the North Pole from Helsinki. If you fancy a simple champagne flight, plenty of companies will help arrange this. Many also offer tours by dogsled, or ski-the-last-degree trips, where you can ski the last geographic degree to the Pole, a trip of six to 10 days. Contact Global Expedition Adventures (p66), Polar Circle Expeditions (p68) or Arcturus Expeditions (p68) for more details.

For extreme marathon runners, **North Pole Marathon** (www.npmarathon.com) organises polar running adventures and provides athletes with return flights from Svalbard, heated tents and food while at the Pole, entry to the official North Pole Marathon, and helicopter flights to the exact Geographic North Pole (US$10,000).

---

passholders get a 50% discount on most long-distance bus routes. All companies offer bus passes, and these generally work out cheaper than buying individual tickets if you're planning plenty of bus travel.

For further information on routes, time-tables, fares and passes, contact the national bus companies:

Connex (www.connex.se, not in English) For routes in Norway and Sweden.

Express Bus (www.expressbus.com) Finnish routes.

Länstrafiken (www.ltnbd.se, in Swedish) For routes in northern Sweden.

Matkahuolto (www.matkahuolto.fi) Finnish routes.

Nor-Way Bussekspress (www.nor-way.no) For Norwegian routes.

Car & Motorcycle

Driving around the far north is one of the best ways to see the region without being confined by irregular timetables and limited public transport on more obscure routes. Expensive car rental is available in all major towns in the far north, but it's generally cheaper to book through an overseas company before you leave home.

Snow and ice can make driving hazardous from September until as late as June, and it's wise to have at least radial snow tyres and, preferably, studded tyres. Petrol is expensive, and in the far north you'd be advised to fill up whenever you can, as stations can be separated by long distances. Rambling reindeer and moose present road hazards, and all incidents involving large animals should be reported to the police.

On long journeys it's a good idea to bring spare tyres and plenty of food and water, as supply posts are limited in some areas.

Train

In Norway **NSB** (Norges Statsbaner or Norwegian State Railways; www.nsb.no, in Norwegian) trains run as far north as Bodø; for destinations further north, there are buses and boats.

There are several dozen train operators in Sweden, although the national network of **Sveriges Järnväg** (www.sj.se) covers all the main lines. **Connex** (www.connex.se, not in English) operates overnight trains to the far north. In summer, most visitors want to take the renowned **Inlandsbanan** (www.inlandsbanan.se) which travels 1000km from Mora to Gällivare via Östersund, Storuman, Arvidsjaur and Jokkmokk, offering a scenic but slow journey north.

The main rail route into the Finnish far north is the Pohjanmaa line, which connects Helsinki with Oulu and continues to Kemijärvi, via Rovaniemi. It's quicker and cheaper than the bus. For more information, visit **VR Ltd Finnish Railways** (www.vr.fi).

ITINERARY 1: THE SCANDINAVIAN NORTH

A winding loop from Mo i Rana (Norway), through the fabulous Lofoten Islands, and the best of Arctic Scandinavia's national parks via the Russian frontier, traditional Sami villages and the northernmost tip of Scandinavia.

ARCTIC SCANDINAVIA TRAVEL ROUTES

This route takes you across the top of Scandinavia in a long, winding journey that features the most spectacular scenery, cultural attractions and pristine wilderness Arctic Scandinavia has to offer. Starting in Norway, it takes in the incredible off-shore islands, dramatic fjords and tiny fishing villages of the coast before heading inland to cross into Sweden, the Abisko National Park and some wonderful hiking opportunities. In Finland the route picks up some strong Sami culture and splendid scenery before crossing back into Norway for a trip to Europe's northernmost tip, and then south through the cosmopolitan towns of Alta and Tromsø.

FAST FACTS

- **Access for independent travellers** Excellent

- **Best time to travel** May to September

- **Difficulty level** Easy to moderate

- **Don't forget** Camera, film, binoculars, insect repellent, head-net; if driving, spare tyres, basic tools, plenty of food and water, blankets, and first-aid kit

- **Don't miss** The dramatic peaks of the Lofoten islands, the Easter Festival at Kautokeino

- **Gateway city** Mo i Rana, Norway

- **Length of route** Approximately 3600km

- **Modes of travel** Car, bus, or a combination of train, bus, boat and air

- **Recommended map** Reise Know-How Verlag *Northern Scandinavia* 1:875,000

- **Time needed** Three weeks to a lifetime

This mammoth route could take a lifetime to do it justice, and you may well want to choose a shorter section to cover. Travelling by public transport can be slow, and it's well worth considering taking some flights or hiring a car if you plan on covering large distances.

The scenery is magnificent and the opportunities for outdoor activities unrivalled elsewhere in Europe. For a traveller looking for a taste of the Arctic, this is one of the most stunning and accessible trips around.

MO I RANA
pop 17,500

Said to be Norway's friendliest town, Mo i Rana is the third largest city in the north, and although it's not the most fascinating place in itself it's a good gateway to the spruce forests, caves and glaciers of the Arctic Circle region. You'll find information at the **Polarsirkelen Reiseliv** (☎ 75 13 92 00; cinfomo@Arctic-circle.no; Ole Tobias Olsensgate 3; ☼ 9am-8pm Mon-Fri, 9am-4pm Sat & 1-7pm Sun mid-Jun–Aug, 10am-3pm Mon-Fri Sep–mid-Jun).

Sights & Activities

Start at the Rana Museum, which has two sections: a **Natural History Museum** (☎ 75 14 61 80; Moholmen 20; admission Nkr15; ☼ 10am-3pm Mon-Fri & 10am-2pm Sat year-round, plus 6-9pm mid-Jun–mid-Aug), which concentrates on the geology, ecology, flora and wildlife of the Arctic Circle region, and the **Museum of Cultural History** (☎ 75 14 61 70; Fridtjof Nansensgata 22; admission Nkr15; ☼ 10am-3pm Mon-Fri & 10am-2pm Sat year-round, plus 6-9pm mid-Jun–mid-Aug), where you'll find exhibits on the local Sami culture and the history of Nordic settlement in southern Nordland.

The limestone-and-marble country northwest of Mo i Rana is riddled with caves and sinkholes. The most accessible cave to visit is **Grønligrotta** (☎ 75 13 25 86; Grønli; adult/child Nkr80/40; ☼ 10am-7pm mid-Jun–mid-Aug), where a 30-minute tour takes you along an underground river, through a rock maze and past a granite block torn off by a glacier.

About 1km closer to town, the trip through **Setergrotta** (☎ 75 16 23 50; Røvassdalen; tours adult/child Nkr175/110; ☼ 11.30am Jun-Aug) is considerably more adventurous. Headlamps, hard hats and coveralls are provided to get you through a couple of extremely tight squeezes and a thrilling shuffle between rock walls while straddling a 15m gorge.

The caves are about 22km from town and there's no public transport.

Mo i Rana is also a convenient base for exploring the **Svartisen glacier** (see p28), the largest ice sheet in northern Scandinavia. Tongues of ice spread down from the ice sheet to form valley glaciers and can be visited in several spots, but the best way to view the massive ice sheet is to take a trip on Lake Svartisvatnet. Boats chug along the lake at least four times daily from late June to August. Ask at the tourist office for details. The ice sheet is 33km north of town.

Sleeping & Eating

Anna's Camping (☎ 75 14 80 74; E6 Røssvoll; caravan/cabin Nkr70/115) About 12km out of town toward the glacier, this riverside camp site has caravans and cabins with shared kitchen and bathroom facilities.

Fammy Leilighetshotell (☎ 75 15 19 99; hotel@fammy.no; Ole Tobias Olsens gate 4; s/d Nkr545/695; P ✗) Rooms at this bright, modern place are fairly functional, and service is casual, but they're good value and have mini-kitchens for self-caterers.

Golden Rainbow Hotel Holmen (☎ 75 15 14 44; holmenho@online.no; TV Westens gate 2; s/d Nkr685/890; P ✗ ▯ ; wheelchair access) Don't be put off by the drab exterior – rooms here are pretty plush and come with minibars and satellite TV. The restaurant (mains Nkr80 to Nkr225) serves a good choice of traditional Norwegian food and has some vegetarian specials.

Abelone Mat og Vinstue (☎ 75 15 38 88; OT Olsensgt 6; mains Nkr70-180) This traditional Norwegian restaurant is a great option if you're travelling with children, and also offers a serious à la carte menu and a pleasant outside dining area.

A Bunnpris supermarket is opposite the tourist office.

Getting There & Away

Mo i Rana's Røssvoll airport, 14km from town, is served by Widerøe and Braathens. You'll get excellent views of the Svartisen icecaps if you arrive by air.

Most visitors arrive at Mo i Rana's unique octagonal train station on one of the two or three daily trains from Trondheim (Nkr625, 6¾ hours) or Bodø (Nkr340, three hours). To go to Bodø by bus you'll have to change at Fauske.

ARCTIC CIRCLE (POLARSIRKELEN)

Along the Arctic Hwy between Mo i Rana and Fauske, the Arctic Circle is made into quite a big deal, with exhibits on Arctic phenomena. The bleak moors on this section of the road are more a result of the 600m altitude than the latitude, however, and northbound travellers quickly descend into the relatively lush, well-vegetated environment that's more typical of northern mainland Norway. At the Polarsirkelsentert, visitors can pay Nkr55 to learn what the Arctic Circle is, peruse a collection of stuffed wildlife specimens and watch an audiovisual presentation on the Arctic regions.

BODØ

pop 42,000

Although set against a wonderful mountain backdrop, Bodø itself has the underwhelming appearance of a town flattened during WWII air raids and completely rebuilt in the not-so-glittering '50s. However, it is the terminus of the northern railway line and a jumping-off point for Lofoten.

Information

There are several banks with ATMs in the central area.

Post office (Havnegata 9)

Tourist office (☎ 75 54 80 00; www.visitbodo.com; Sjøgata 3; ❤ 9am-8pm Mon-Sat & noon-8pm Sun Jun-Aug, shorter hrs rest of year) Internet access is available here for Nkr1 per minute.

Sights & Activities

The **Nordlandsmuseet** (☎ 75 52 16 40; Prinsens gate 116; adult/student Nkr30/15; ❤ 9am-3pm Mon-Fri & noon-3pm Sat & Sun Sep-Apr, shorter hrs May-Aug) covers Nordland history in one of Bodø's oldest buildings. There's also a modern **cathedral** (Kongens gate; ❤ 9am-2.30pm Mon-Fri mid-Jun–Aug).

The **aviation museum** (☎ 75 50 78 50; Olav V gate; adult/student Nkr75/50; ❤ 10am-7pm Sun-Fri & 10am-5pm Sat mid-Jun–mid-Aug, 10am-4pm Mon-Fri & 11am-5pm Sat & Sun mid-Aug–mid-Jun), 2km southeast of town, shouldn't be missed if you have even a passing interest in flight and aviation history. Displays include some scary simulations of jet-fighter flying. About 1km southeast of the aviation museum there's the small **Bodin Kirke** (Gamleriksvei 68; ❤ 10am-3pm Mon-Fri late Jun–mid-Aug), a little onion-domed stone church dating from around 1240.

The lovely 19th-century trading station **Kjerringøy**, 40km north of Bodø, lies on a sleepy peninsula beside luminescent turquoise seas with a backdrop of soaring granite peaks. Most of the timber-built historic district has been preserved as an open-air museum. Buses from Bodø (1½ hours, Nkr65) leave on summer weekdays; fares include the Festvåg–Misten ferry.

The **Saltstraumen Strait** connects Saltenfjord and Skjerstadfjord, where the tides cause one fjord to drain into the other and create a swirling, churning, 20-knot watery chaos that shifts 400 million cubic metres of water every six hours. The maelstrom can be viewed from the Saltstraumbrua bridge.

Sleeping

Bodø HI Hostel & Bodø Gjestegård (guesthouse ☎ 75 52 04 02, hostel ☎ 75 52 11 22; bodo.hostel@vandrerhjem.no; Storgata 90; dm/s/d Nkr150/250/350) This combined hostel and guesthouse uses two buildings. The hostel is newly remodelled and clean, while the simple guesthouse provides homey rooms with separate bath. Breakfast costs Nkr60.

Norrøna Hotel (☎ 75 52 55 50; norrona.hotell@radissonsas.com; Storgata 4B; s/d winter Nkr690/860, summer Nkr490/630; P ✖) This good-value hotel, opposite the bus station, has comfortable rooms with private bath and especially affordable summer (July and August) prices.

Nordlys Hotel (☎ 75 53 19 00; nordlys@rainbow-hotels.no; Moloveien 14; s Nkr495-1120, d Nkr695-1400; P ✖) Scandinavian design touches run throughout this swish hotel, and the harbourside rooms provide great views.

Rooms in private homes (from Nkr200 per person) can be booked through the tourist office.

Eating

Kafé Kafka (☎ 75 52 35 50; Sandgata 5b; sandwiches Nkr68-89; ❤ from 11am Mon-Sat, 3pm-midnight Sun) This cool-kid café-bar serves marinated-vegetable sandwiches, and makes a good place to read. There's live music on some weekends.

Min Plass (☎ 75 52 26 88; Sjøgata 12; dishes Nkr69-124; ❤ 11am-2am Mon-Thu, 11am-3am Fri & Sat, 2pm-midnight Sun) This popular place serves bar snacks such as olives and fish and chips (Nkr49) in addition to burgers, salads and grilled meat. There's a good late-night scene. A freaky trinket-filled plastic man guards the route to the WC.

Løvold's (☎ 75 52 02 61; Tollbugata 9; dishes Nkr35-115; ☺ 9am-6pm Mon-Fri, 9am-3pm Sat) You'll find this place, which has big windows offering a view over the water, above a fisherman's outfitter. It bustles at lunchtime, offering daily specials of traditional Norwegian grub.

Getting There & Around

The airport, 2km away, is served by SAS, Braathens, Widerøe and Norwegian Air. Local buses (Nkr22) marked Sentrumsrunden bring you to town. A taxi costs about Nkr80.

Bodø is the northern terminus of the Norwegian rail network. There is service to Trondheim (Nkr861, 10 hours, three daily). If you're continuing north by bus, be sure to get off 40 minutes before Bodø at Fauske, where the two daily express buses to Narvik (Nkr467, five hours) connect with the train.

The *Hurtigruten* coastal steamer makes its way to and from Lofoten, as do car ferries and express boats. See the tourist office for schedules.

The tourist office rents bikes for Nkr60 per day, plus a deposit. Guests can rent bikes from Norrøna Hostel for Nkr50.

LOFOTEN

The rugged beauty of the Lofoten islands is a highlight of any trip to Arctic Scandinavia. Spectacular glacier-carved mountains soar straight out of the sea, sheer cliffs loom above strikingly picturesque fishing villages, sheltered bays and fjords line the coast, and verdant farmland and sheep pasture fill the gaps in between.

Fishing has dominated the Lofoten economy for years, and although fish stocks have dwindled greatly in recent times the area is still Norway's prime winter fishing ground. Cod is hung out to dry on ubiquitous wooden racks in early summer, shoals of sperm and killer whales ply the waters, and the world's biggest cold-water coral reef lies just offshore, 300m below the surface.

Lofoten is the kind of place you'll be reluctant to leave, not only because of the fabulous scenery but also because of the luxurious accommodation. Many of the fishing community's *rorbuer* (winter shanties) and *sjøhus* (former fishermen's bunkhouses) have been converted into tourist accommodation and provide some of Norway's most atmospheric places to stay.

The four main islands of Austvågøy, Vestvågøy, Flakstadøy and Moskenesøy are all linked by bridge or tunnel, with buses running the entire length of the Lofoten road (E10). This itinerary runs south to north. If you take a ferry from Bodø you'll arrive at Moskenes near Å; take the *Hurtigruten* and you'll arrive in Stamsund.

Tourist information is available at www .lofoten-tourist.no and www.lofoten-info.no.

Å

Å is a wonderfully atmospheric place to start your journey through Lofoten. Red-painted *rorbuer* line the shore of this preserved fishing village, many of them sticking out into the sea, perched on grim rocks connected by wooden footbridges. Racks of drying cod lie nearly everywhere, and picture-postcard scenes occur at almost every turn. In summer visitors enliven the tiny place, while in winter it's stark, haunting and beautiful.

Set in a 1920 cod plant, the **Tørrefiskmuseum** (Stockfish Museum; ☎ 76 09 12 11; adult/student Nkr40/25; ☺ 10am-5pm mid-Jun–mid-Aug, 11am-5pm Mon-Fri rest of Jun & Aug, otherwise by appointment) details the history of the stockfish industry, taking in every step from catching to cooking. Steinar Larson, the gregarious operator, has long family ties to Å, and explains everything about cod (and Å) in fantastic, excited detail.

Many of Å's 19th-century buildings are set aside as the **Norwegian Fishing Village Museum** (☎ 76 09 14 88; admission Nkr40; ☺ 10am-5pm late Jun–late Aug, 11am-3pm Mon-Fri late Aug–late Jun), complete with old boats and boathouses, an 1844 bakery, Europe's oldest cod-liver oil factory, and traditional storehouses.

The camp site at the end of the village has a good hillside view of Værøy island (see p304), which lies on the other side of **Moskenesstraumen**, the swirling maelstrom that inspired the fictional tales by, among others, Jules Verne and Edgar Allen Poe. Just south of Å, you'll find the basic **Moskenesstraumen Camping** (☎ 76 09 13 44; tent sites from Nkr60, huts Nkr300-500; P).

Å HI Hostel (☎ 76 09 11 21; www.lofoten-rorbu.com; dm Nkr175, rorbuer Nkr800-1550; P) offers accommodation in some of the museum's historic seaside buildings. Breakfast is Nkr60 extra. The inviting **Å-Hamna Rorbuer** (☎ 76 09 12 11; aa-hamna@ lofoten-info.no; dm/d Nkr100/350, rorbuer Nkr500-950; P), also at the museum, has pleasant rooms, a pretty communal space in a restored 1860s home, and cosy *rorbuer*, usually with magnificent views, containing four to eight beds each. Off season you can get the best *rorbuer* for around Nkr350, firewood included.

Food choices are limited. The only restaurant is the over-water **Brygga** (☎ 76 09 11 21; mains Nkr115-200), which – predictably – serves good fish. It also operates as the village bar. You can also buy fresh fish from local fishers and pick up other supplies at the small food shop behind the hostel office.

GETTING THERE & AWAY
Nordtrafikk runs up to three daily buses from Å to Leknes (Nkr198, 1¾ hours), Svolvær (Nkr178, 3¼ hours) and Sortland (Nkr320, 5¼ hours).

Ofotens og Vesteraalens Dampskibsselskab (OVDS; ☎ 76 96 76 00; www.ovds.no) runs car ferries from Bodø to Moskenes, 5km north of Å. The trip takes four hours, costs Nkr132 for a passenger and Nkr477 for a car, and operates up to five times daily from 28 June to 11 August (otherwise, it runs once or twice daily except Saturday). Some of these ferries operate via Værøy and Røst.

Reine & Hamnøy

The delightful village of Reine, on the island of Moskenesøy, is another great first-night option if you're straight off the ferry from Bodø. Situated on a calm turquoise bay backed by ranks of mountain cliffs and pinnacles, it has an almost fairytale setting, and it's easy to see why the village has been voted the most scenic place in all of Norway. All buses between Å and Leknes stop in Reine.

Ferries travel from Reine to Vindstad (Nkr21, 40 minutes) through the scenic Reinefjord. From Vindstad, it's a one-hour hike over a ridge to the abandoned settlement of Bunes on the other side of the island, with a magnificent beach, vast quantities of driftwood and the 610m-high

---

SIDE TRIP: VÆRØY & RØST

Lofoten's southern islands of Værøy and Røst have some of the finest bird-watching in Norway, with large colonies of fulmars, guillemots, kittiwakes and terns. There are puffins as well, but the population has dropped by more than 50% in the past decade as a result of dwindling stocks of herring, the main food source for puffin chicks. Although Værøy is mainly high and rugged and Røst is flat as a pancake, both islands offer good hiking, and you'll also find a rare measure of solitude here, considering how well touristed Lofoten generally is.

Craggy Værøy has only 775 people, but 100,000 nesting sea birds. Hiking trails take in some of the more spectacular sea-bird rookeries. The main trail goes along the west coast, beginning about 300m past the island airstrip, and continues south all the way to the virtually deserted fishing village of Mostad. This 10km hike makes for a full day's outing and is not too strenuous, but it is exposed to the elements, so it's best done in fair weather. Other bird-watching outings, including boat tours, can be arranged through the hostel.

Røst, south of Værøy, enjoys one of the mildest climates in northern Norway, thanks to its location in the middle of the Gulf Stream. Access to the best bird-watching requires a boat, as the largest rookeries are on offshore islands. **Kårøy Sjøhus** (☎ 76 09 62 38) can arrange all-day boat trips (Nkr125) that cruise past major sea-bird colonies and stop at an 1887 lighthouse and a vista point. En route it's common to see seals, and there are occasional sightings of orcas (killer whales). Røst itself is flat and, other than the boat trip, there's not much to do.

Atmospheric and authentic *rorbu* accommodation is available at **Værøy HI Hostel** (☎ 76 09 53 75; vaeroy.hostel@vandrerhjem.no; dm/d Nkr150/275; ☀ May–mid-Sep), about an hour's walk north of the ferry landing. A bus can pick you up at the dock. Værøy's only nightlife option, **Kornelius Kro** (☎ 76 09 52 99; korn-kro@online.no; Sørland; r Nkr350-700), also has a restaurant, a pub and a few simple but clean cottages out the back.

From 29 June to 12 August there's at least one ferry daily between Bodø and Værøy (Nkr121, four to six hours) and six days a week between Moskenes and Værøy (Nkr53, 1½ hours). There's a boat service from Værøy to Røst (Nkr65, two hours, five days a week) and from Røst to Bodø (Nkr145, 4¼ hours, once or twice daily). Sailing durations given are for direct ferries, but note that not every boat is direct. If your trip begins and ends in Bodø, ask about discounted return fares. Detailed schedules are available at boat terminals and tourist offices.

cliff of Helvetestind. Every weekday except Tuesday you can take a morning ferry from Reine and then catch an afternoon ferry back – call ☎ 76 09 12 78 or ☎ 94 89 43 05 for the current schedule.

The quiet and scenic little fishing islet of Hamnøy, 4.5km north of central Reine, has the pretty **Eliassan Rorbuer** (☎ 76 09 23 05; rorbuer@online.no; Hamnøy; 2-/4-person rorbuer Nkr550/750; **P**), right on the water. Linen costs Nkr80 extra. The highly regarded **Hamnøy Mat og Vinbu** (☎ 76 09 21 45; Hamnøy; mains Nkr130-165; ☺ closed winter) restaurant serves stellar local specialities, including *bacalao* (dried and salted cod) and cod tongues. There's a deck with picnic tables and a cosy dining room.

There's a Coop supermarket in Reine.

Stamsund
pop 1000

The traditional fishing village of Stamsund makes a fine destination largely because of its dockside hostel, a magnet for travellers, who sometimes stay for weeks on end. Here, as elsewhere on Lofoten, highlights include hiking, fishing and feeling overwhelmed. A popular town activity is to stare at the *Hurtigruten*'s approach.

The wonderful old beach house **Justad HI Hostel/Rorbuer** (☎ 76 08 93 34; fax 76 08 97 39; dm/s/d Nkr115/250/300, cabins Nkr600-800; ☺ mid-Dec–mid-Oct; **P**), 1km from the centre, is a haven for independent travellers and very difficult to leave. Rowing-boat rental is free, and if the aurora borealis is out, the host might pound on your door to let you know.

The village centre contains a bakery and the fine Skæbrygga bar and restaurant (fishy mains are Nkr150 to Nkr175). A Joker supermarket, post office and bus stop are a couple of minutes uphill from the hostel, and there's a Hansen bakery by the main road at the southern end of the village.

The *Hurtigruten* coastal steamer stops en route between Bodø (Nkr325) and Svolvær (Nkr116). From 20 August to 24 June, buses from Leknes to Stamsund (Nkr29, 25 minutes) run up to eight times daily, less often on Saturday and Sunday, with the last bus departing from Leknes at 8.50pm.

Henningsvær
pop 500

Henningsvær's nickname, 'The Venice of Lofoten', is a tad overblown, but few people

would disagree that this bohemian enclave and active fishing village is the brightest and trendiest place in the archipelago. The outdoor seating at the waterside bars and restaurants is ideal for observing the lively scene, especially at weekends. There's also a couple of **art galleries** and a climbing school, **Nord Norske Klatreskole** (☎ 76 07 49 11; www.nordnorsk klatreskole.no, in Norwegian; N-8330 Henningsvær), which offers a wide range of technical climbing, kayaking and skiing courses all around Arctic Norway. If you want to tackle Svolværgeita or any other Lofoten peak, climbing with an experienced guide, including equipment, costs Nkr900/1000 per day for one/two people.

Accommodation at the climbing school's **Den Siste Viking** (☎ 76 07 49 11; Misværveien 10; dm Nkr175) crosses a Lofoten *rorbu* with an English pub and a Himalayan trekkers' lodge. Its **Klatrekafeen** (☺ 11am-1am) has a small selection of homemade light meals (Nkr75 to Nkr130) and snacks, as well as coffee and desserts.

Buses shuttle from Henningsvær to Svolvær (Nkr39, 35 minutes) and Kabelvåg (Nkr36, 25 minutes) two to eight times daily.

Lofotr Vikingmuseum

This 83m-long chieftain's house, Norway's largest Viking building, has been excavated at Borg, near the centre of Vestvågøy. The site's **Lofotr Vikingmuseum** (☎ 76 08 49 00; adult/student/child Nkr90/70/45; ☺ 10am-7pm mid-May–Aug, 1-3pm Fri Sep-Apr) offers an insight into life in Viking times, complete with a scale-model reconstruction of the building, guides in Viking costume and a replica Viking ship, which you can row at 2pm (Nkr20).

Kabelvåg

Kabelvåg presents a more intimate face than its larger neighbour, Svolvær. A few old timber buildings remain, and the small town square wraps around the harbour and has an informal outdoor market. The road into the village passes Norway's second-largest **wooden church**. Built a century ago to minister to the influx of seasonal fisherfolk, the church has 1200 seats – far more than are needed for the village's current population.

Behind the old prison, a trail leads uphill to the **statue of King Øystein**, who in 1120 ordered the first *rorbu* to be built to house fishermen who had been sleeping under their overturned rowing boats. This was not just a touch of kindness, as the tax on the exported dried fish was the main source of the king's revenue.

Some of these original *rorbuer* have been excavated as part of the **Lofotmuseet** (☎ 76 06 97 90; www.lofotmuseet.no; Storvågan; adult/student Nkr45/35; ☒ 9am-6pm mid-Jun–mid-Aug, 9am-3pm mid-Aug–mid-Jun), a regional history museum on the site of the first town in the polar regions.

Nearby, the seafront **Lofoten Aquarium** (☎ 76 07 86 65; Storvågan; adult/student/child Nkr80/60/40; ☒ 10am-7pm mid-Jun–mid-Aug, 11am-3pm mid-Aug–Jun & Feb–mid-Jun) shows you some of the faces that made Lofoten great, including the heroic cod and some harbour seals in an outdoor tank. You can eat their relatives (the cod, not the seals) in the museum café.

Ørsvågvær Camping (☎ 76 07 81 80; www.orsvag .no, in Norwegian; Ørsvågvær; tent sites Nkr100, cabins Nkr300-940; ☒ P), located 3km and two inlets west of Kabelvåg, has basic cabins. The **Kabelvåg HI Hostel** (☎ 76 06 98 98; kabelvaag.hostel@vandrerhjem .no; dm/s/d Nkr245/405/605; ☒ Jun–mid-Aug; P) is at a school 10 minutes north of the village centre; breakfast is included. The hostel has a cafeteria with sporadic hours, and the charming fish, sandwich and pizza pub **Præstenbrygga** (☎ 76 07 80 60; Torget; mains Nkr35-140; ☒ from 11am), affiliated with an outdoor school for college types and other students, is in the village centre.

You can walk the 5km to Svolvær or catch one of the roughly hourly buses (Nkr18, 10 minutes).

Svolvær
pop 4100
By Lofoten standards the main port town of Svolvær is busy and modern. On the square facing the harbour you'll find a couple of banks, a taxi stand and the helpful regional tourist office, **Destination Lofoten** (☎ 76 06 98 00; Torget; ☒ 9am-9.30pm Mon-Fri & 9am-8pm Sat, 10am-9.30pm Sun mid-Jun–mid-Aug, shorter hrs rest of year).

Daredevils, or just plain crazy mountaineers, like to scale **Svolværgeita** (The Svolvær Goat), a distinctive two-pronged peak visible from the harbour, and then jump the 1.5m from one horn to the other – a graveyard at the bottom awaits those who miss. For phenomenal views, hikers can ascend the steep path to the base of the Goat and up the slopes behind it. There's also a rough route from the Goat over to the extraordinary **Devil's Gate**; ask the tourist office for details.

A fun trip from Svolvær is a boat trip into the spectacularly steep and narrow **Trollfjord**. Tours run five times daily between about 10 June and 20 August, and cost Nkr300 per person; the tourist office has details.

For 83km of breathtaking cycling, take the Narvik ferry to Holandshamn and make your way back to Svolvær along the **Kaiser Route**. Along the way, lonely shore, jagged mountains and abandoned farms will be your constant companions. Unlike trips to the west side of Lofoten, this trip takes in parts of the islands largely undiscovered by tourists. A long stretch runs parallel to the **Trollfjord**. The Danish site www.digermulen.de outlines the journey (click on Kaiserroute), and provides a glimpse of the scenery. Do your planning at the tourist office, where you can pick up the handy *Sykkel Guide* (Nkr120), containing detailed topographic maps.

The tourist office can also help you book world-class fishing trips (Nkr400) in the bountiful waters.

SLEEPING & EATING
Svolvær Sjøhuscamping (☎ 76 07 03 36; www.svolver -sjohuscamp.no; Parkgata 12; d per person Nkr390) This rustic red beach house has a dockside location: turn right onto the first road past the library, and it's a five-minute walk east of the harbour.

Rica Hotel Svolvær (☎ 76 07 22 22; rica.hotel .svolvar@rica.no; Lamholmen; s Nkr795-1345, d Nkr995-1345; P ☒) This flamboyant contemporary hotel juts right out over the water and combines modern comforts with nifty *rorbu* styling. The hotel has even cut a hole in the floor of one suite to accommodate jig fishing.

Bacalao (☎ 76 07 94 00; Kirkegata; mains Nkr70-125; ☒ 10.30am-1am Mon-Thu, 10am-2.30am Fri & Sat, noon-1am Sun) A hangout for fishers and students, this large, minimalist café in a room feels like a retrofitted garage, and dishes up cakes, salads, club sandwiches and reindeer with pasta.

Kjøkkenet (☎ 76 06 84 80; Lamholmen; small dishes Nkr90-95, mains Nkr225-250) Down on the harbourside, this restaurant looks like an old-time Scandinavian kitchen (it serves the traditional staple: fish) and has a bar made from a WWII Polish troop ship lifeboat. Whale tartar anyone?

GETTING THERE & AWAY
Svolvær has a small airport where you can catch Widerøe flights to Bodø.

Buses to and from Vesterålen (below) travel between Svolvær and Sortland (Nkr136, 2½ hours) three to four times daily, crossing the dramatically scenic waters of the Fiskebøl–Melbu ferry (Nkr68 for car and driver). Buses to Leknes (Nkr98, 1½ hours), with connections to Å (Nkr178, 3½ hours), leave Svolvær four to six times daily. The Narvik–Lofoten Ekspressen runs between Svolvær and Narvik (Nkr436, eight to 9¼ hours, one to two daily).

Express boats ply the waters between Svolvær and Bodø (Nkr246, 3½ hours), and Svolvær and Narvik (Nkr350, 3½ hours), daily except Saturday (but there's no Monday sailing from Svolvær to Narvik).

Svolvær is also a stop for the *Hurtigruten* coastal steamer.

VESTERÅLEN

The islands of Vesterålen aren't quite as dramatic as those of Lofoten, but they're still very attractive to visitors. For tourist information, consult **Vesterålen Reiseliv** (☎ 76 11 14 80; Kjøpmannsgata 2, Sortland).

Vesterålen is connected by ferry from Fiskebøl on Austvågøy (Lofoten) to **Melbu** on Hadseløya. Melbu has a couple of **museums** and a famous **music festival**, featuring classical, jazz and blues, every July. The other main town, **Stokmarknes**, is a quiet market community best known as the birthplace of the *Hurtigruten* coastal steamer.

Nyksund (www.nyksund-info.com), on Langøya, is a former abandoned fishing village that's now re-emerging as an artists' colony. From the crumbling and collapsing old structures to the faithfully renovated commercial buildings, every scene is a photo opportunity, and the lively youthful atmosphere belies the fact that only recently Nyksund was considered a ghost village. There's a great walk over the headland from Nyksund to Stø (three hours return), at the northernmost tip of Langøya. Ask the tourist office for details of **whale-watching tours** from Stø.

Andenes, on Andøy, seems a long way from anywhere, but there's whale-watching, a whale centre, a natural history centre, a lighthouse and a couple of museums. **Whale Safari** (☎ 76 11 56 00; www.whalesafari.no) runs popular three- to five-hour whale-watching cruises from the whale centre between late May and mid-September. Trips depart at least once daily (at 10.30am) and cost Nkr695. Sightings of

sperm whales are guaranteed, or your next trip is free. Dress warmly.

Sleeping & Eating

Holmvik Brygge (☎ 76 13 47 96; www.nyksund.com; s/d Nkr250/350) In Nyksund, this cosy place offers irregular rooms done up like those in an old fisherman's house. The facilities are shared.

Andenes HI Hostel (☎ 76 14 28 50; andenes.hostel@ vandrerhjem.no; Havnegata 31, Andenes; dm/s/d Nkr150/ 215/325; ☺ Jun–Aug; **P**) This timber-built hostel, which includes the Lankanholmen Sjøhus, is a wonderful old building by the sea; breakfast is Nkr60 extra.

Den Gamle Fyrmesterbolig (☎ 76 14 10 27; Richard Withs gate 11, Andenes; s Nkr250-350, d Nkr300-400; **P**) The rooms here in the charming lighthouse-keeper's cottage are another great option.

A bakery and an informal café can be found at the Andenes whale centre, while the restaurant at the Norlandia Hotel serves a good Arctic menu.

Getting There & Away

Sortland is the main transport hub in Vesterålen. Both Sortland and Stokmarknes are stops for the *Hurtigruten* coastal steamer. Buses between Melbu and Stokmarknes (Nkr45, 45 minutes) run several times daily on weekdays and twice daily at weekends. Bus No 8 runs between Sortland and Svolvær (Nkr136, 2½ hours) three to four times daily. Buses to Leknes (Nkr98, 1½ hours), with connections to Å (Nkr178, 3½ hours), leave Svolvær four to six times daily.

NARVIK

pop 14,100

Narvik was established a century ago as an ice-free port for the rich Kiruna iron-ore mines in Swedish Lappland (spelt Lapland in Norway and Finland). The town is bisected by a monstrous transshipment facility, where the ore is offloaded from rail cars onto ships bound for distant smelters. In April and May 1940, during WWII, fierce land and naval battles took place around the town as the Germans and the Allies fought to control the iron-ore trade.

Ask the helpful Narvik **tourist office** (☎ 76 94 33 09; www.narvikinfo.no; Kongens gate 26; 9am-7pm Mon-Fri, 11am-7pm Sat & Sun mid-Jun–mid-Aug, shorter hrs rest of year) for details of local hiking routes. The post office is 300m south on Kongens gate, the train station is at the north end of town, and the Lofoten express boat dock is on Havnegata, just over 1km south of the centre, down Kongens gate.

Sights

The impressive **Red Cross War Museum** (☎ 76 94 44 26; Kongens gate; adult/child Nkr40/10; ☷ 10am-10pm Mon-Sat & 11am-5pm Sun mid-Jun–mid-Sep, 11am-3pm Mar-Jun) displays WWII equipment and tells the tale of the Nazi occupation of Narvik, coveted for its ore production. The presentation isn't flash, but you're still likely to leave feeling rather stunned.

The town's **Ofoten Museum** (☎ 76 96 00 50; Administrasjonsveien 2; adult/child Nkr25/5; ☷ 11am-3.30pm Mon-Fri & noon-3pm Sat & Sun Jul, 10.30am-3pm Mon-Fri Aug-Jun) occupies a wonderful building dating from 1902, and tells of Narvik's farming, railway-building and ore-transshipment heritage.

Weather permitting, the Fjellheisen **cable car** (☎ 76 96 04 94; Mårveien; return adult/child Nkr80/45; ☷ 10am-1am mid-Jun–Jul, 1-9pm early Jun & Aug) soars up 656m for breathtaking views of the midnight sun and the surrounding peaks and fjords.

The tourist office can arrange sightseeing, fishing and whale-watching tours. In October and November, **Tysfjord Turistsenter** (☎ 75 77 53 70; Storjord; www.tysfjord-turistsenter.no /safari; cruises Nkr700) runs extraordinary orca-watching cruises from Storjord, about 85km south of Narvik on the E6. The Nor-Way Bussekspress bus to and from Fauske passes less than 1km from Storjord.

Sleeping & Eating

Narvik Camping (☎ 76 94 58 10; Rombaksveien 75; tent sites Nkr75, cabins Nkr500-750) The nearest camp site to Narvik, this place is 2km northeast of town on the E6.

Spor 1 Gjestegård (☎ 76 94 60 20; post@spor1.no; Brugata 2; dm/s/d Nkr160/400/500) This place made for backpackers is located in former rail cabins by the tracks. It has well-kept dorm rooms, charming hosts, a sauna, and a well-equipped, clean kitchen.

Narvik HI Hostel (☎ 76 96 22 00; narvik.hostel@ vandrerhjem.no; Dronningensgate 58; dm/s/d Nkr195/375/ 475; ☷ 24 Jun–17 Aug) Recently moved to a central downtown location, this bright, modern place has good rooms. Breakfast is Nkr60 extra.

Breidablikk Gjesthus (☎ 76 94 14 18; www.breid ablikk.no; Tore Hunds gate 41; dm/s/d Nkr185/425/550) Another central option, this pleasant guesthouse, with a hillside fjord view, is a good bet. Ask for a room on the higher floors. Breakfast costs Nkr50.

There are several places to eat within easy walking distance of the tourist office, most of which aren't very nice. Rising above the rest is **Astrup Kjeller'n** (☎ 76 96 04 02; Kinobakken 1; mains Nkr85-225; ☷ from 11am), with an old-time feel and huge servings of pasta, steak and local specialties. The **Narvik Storsenter shopping centre** (Kongens gata 66) 300m west of the train station has one of Norway's many Peppe's Pizza outlets and a Rimi supermarket.

Getting There & Away

Narvik's airport is served by Widerøe from Bodø and Tromsø. Norwegian Air flies from Oslo.

Some express bus connections between Fauske and Tromsø require an overnight break in Narvik. Nor-Way Bussekspress buses run to and from Fauske (Nkr381, five hours, twice daily), and to and from Tromsø (Nkr315, four to five hours, two or three daily). The Narvik–Lofoten Ekspressen runs daily between Narvik and Svolvær (Nkr501, eight to 9¼ hours).

The spectacular mountain-hugging **Ofotbanen railway** spans a range of landscapes –

SIDE TRIP: ØVRE DIVIDAL NATIONAL PARK

A wild, roadless and lake-studded 750-sq-km chunk of Norway between Setermoen and the Swedish and Finnish borders comprises Øvre Dividal National Park. While it lacks the spectacular steep-walled scenery of coastal Norway, this remote semi-forested upland wilderness still enjoys lots of alpine peaks and views. The most popular hike is the eight-day Troms Border Trail, which links seven unstaffed Den Norske Turistforening (Norwegian Mountain Touring Association) huts. The map to use on the Troms Border Trail and the Abisko Link is Statens Kartverk's *Turkart Indre Troms*, at a scale of 1:100,000. In summer, hikers cannot underestimate the mosquito nuisance in this area; use a head-net and carry plenty of repellent. Access to the park is difficult and by private vehicle only.

fjord-side cliffs, birch forests and rocky plateaus – all within the 55 minutes between Narvik and the Swedish border. Riksgränsen (Nkr88, 55 minutes) is the first stop inside Sweden, and you'll pass through some 50 tunnels and snowsheds to get there. Trains continue on to Kiruna (Nkr155, three hours) with overnight connections to Stockholm. For information on the express boat to Svolvær, see p306.

RIKSGRÄNSEN

☎ 0980 / pop 50

Your first stop in Sweden is tiny Riksgränsen village, set in rugged countryside and promoted as 'the most northerly ski resort in the world'. The craggy mountains provide dramatic descents, and you can even ski under the midnight sun in June. Rental of downhill gear/snowboards costs from Skr280/317 per day, and a daily lift pass is Skr294; the ski season can run until midsummer.

There's not much to the tiny settlement here, but you can visit Sven Hörnell's **wilderness photography exhibition** (☎ 43111; www.sven -hornell.se; 9am-6pm Feb-Sep) at his gallery and shop. The exhibition itself is free, and there's an **audiovisual show** (Skr70; 3pm daily mid-Jun–Aug, call for other times). Commentary is in Swedish only, but you don't have to understand it to appreciate the stunning photography of Norrland (several provinces in the northern half of Sweden).

Riksgränsen Ski & Spa Resort (☎ 40080; www.riks gransen.nu; r per person summer/winter from Skr436/601; mid-Feb–Sep) is a large resort popular with skiers, and offers lots of organised wilderness activities in both the skiing and summer seasons. Rooms and apartments are available.

Bus No 91 runs from Riksgränsen via Abisko to Kiruna (Skr117, two or three a day). Three daily trains run on the Narvik–Kiruna–Luleå route.

KIRUNA

☎ 0980 / pop 23,900

Kiruna, the northernmost town and largest *kommun* (municipality) in Sweden, takes in the country's highest peak, Kebnekaise (2111m), and several fine national parks and trekking routes, making it an excellent base for wilderness tours. It's also home to Sweden's most famous ice hotel.

The helpful **tourist office** (☎ 18880; www .kiruna.se; Lars Janssonvägen 17; 8.30am-8pm Mon-Fri

---

THE ICE HOTEL

The highlight of a trip this far north is a visit to the fabulous **Ice Hotel** (☎ 66800; www.icehotel.com; Marknadsvägen, Jukkasjärvi; day visit adult/child Skr120/60), a truly unique experience.

Every winter at Jukkasjärvi, 18km east of Kiruna, an amazing structure is built from tonnes of ice taken from the frozen local river. This huge, custom-built *iglo* has a chapel, a bar – where you can drink from a glass made of ice – and exhibitions of ice sculpture by international artists. It also has more than 60 rooms where guests can sleep on beds covered with reindeer skins and sub-zero sleeping bags. Temperatures inside the structure remain a balmy -5°C to -8°C (outside it can be as low as -30°C). The hotel is normally open from mid-December to late April (weather permitting), and there are numerous activities for guests to pursue, from snowmobile safaris and skiing to ice fishing and dogsledding.

Bus No 510 goes to the hotel. See the Sleeping and Eating sections (below and p311) for further details of accommodation prices.

& 8.30am-6pm Sat & Sun summer, Mon-Sat rest of year) has loads of detailed brochures, and staff can arrange various activities, including year-round Sami experiences; rafting, hiking, horse-riding, rock-climbing and fishing in warmer weather; and ice fishing, dogsledding and snowmobile safaris in winter. The **library** (Biblioteksgatan), behind the bus station, offers free Internet access.

A visit to the Ice Hotel (see boxed text above) is a must. Also worthwhile is a visit to **Kiruna kyrka** (Kyrkogatan), the town church, which looks like a gigantic Sami tent; it's particularly pretty against a snowy backdrop. You can also visit the depths of the **LKAB iron-ore mine** (☎ 18880; tours adult/child Skr195/50), 540m underground. Two-hour English-language tours depart from the tourist office regularly from June to August, although they operate during other months if there's enough interest.

Sleeping

STF Vandrarhem Kiruna (☎ 17195; www.kirunahostel .com; Bergmästaregatan 7; dm/s/d Skr150/270/360) The central location, good facilities (including

SIDE TRIP: ABISKO NATIONAL PARK

Less rugged and more accessible than other parks in Arctic Sweden, the 77-sq-km **Abisko National Park** lies on the southern shore of scenic Lake Torneträsk and is full of excellent day hikes. The park is well served by buses, trains and the scenic mountain highway between Kiruna and Narvik.

The **Naturum** (☎ 40177; www.abisko-naturum.nu), next to the Svenska Vandrarhem i Förening (STF; Swedish Tourist Association) lodge in Abisko, provides good information on the region. For breathtaking views, take the **Linbana chairlift** (return Skr110; ☉ 9.30am-4pm), 900m up to the mountain top of **Njulla** (1169m).

Hiking

The popular **Kungsleden** ('King's Trail') follows the Abiskojåkka Valley 450km south from Abisko to Hemavan; there are huts and lodges along most of the route. From Absiko village you can opt for day trips of 10km or 20km along the route. For longer hikes you can try diversions to the summit of **Kebnekaise** (2111m), the country's highest peak, or the magical national park of **Sarek** (which has no huts and few bridges).

A good alternative to the Kungsleden is a trek to **Sjangeli**, southwest of Abisko. It was an unsuccessful mine in the 17th century but is now a Sami-run wilderness centre. A 70km loop route connects Sjangeli with both Abisko and Riksgränsen.

In Björkliden, 8km northwest of Abisko, the **Björkliden Fjällby resort** (☎ 64100; www.bjorkliden .com) offers a full range of summer and winter activities and even has a nine-hole golf course. Tours are also organised by STF at Abisko Turiststation (see Sleeping & Eating, following); both places offer outdoor gear for hire.

July, August and September are recommended months for hiking, but be aware that the boggy ground nurses zillions of mosquitoes. You'll need waterproof (preferably rubber) boots at any time of the year, and warm clothes; despite the midnight sun, it can still get cold very quickly. Winter escapades are too risky for the uninitiated, due to blizzards, extreme cold and avalanches.

Sleeping & Eating

Abisko Fjällturer (☎ 40103; www.abisko.net; dm Skr150) This small hostel is a backpacker's delight. It has comfortable accommodation and a lovely wooden sauna, but the treat is in the activities on offer. The friendly owners keep a large team of sled dogs, and for Skr600 in winter you get a night's hostel accommodation and the chance to drive your own sled. There are also half-/full-day sled trips (Skr900/1500), and popular week-long sled trips from late February to early April (Skr8800, including meals and accommodation). You'll need to book very early for the longer trips. In summer you can take mountain walks with the dogs (Skr300, including one night in a dorm).

Abisko Turiststation (☎ 40200; www.abisko.nu; dm/s/d Skr290/510/700; ☉ Mar-Apr & mid-Jun–mid-Sep) This is another excellent choice, with a variety of accommodation options, all kept to the usual high STF standards. Trekking gear can be hired here, and there are guided tours, a shop with basic groceries, a pub, and a restaurant (breakfast/lunch/dinner Skr75/75/195). Accommodation prices here are reduced by Skr100 for HI/STF members.

There's a supermarket in Abisko village for self-caterers, and a café-restaurant nearby.

Self-service **STF huts** (dm members Skr185-275, nonmembers Skr285-375) along Kungsleden are spread at 10km to 20km intervals between Abisko and Kvikkjokk; you'll need a sleeping bag. Member/nonmember day visitors are charged Skr40/50; campers pay Skr60/80. The excellent 100km trek from Abisko to Nikkaluokta runs via the STF lodge **Kebnekaise Fjällstation** (☎ 55000; info@kebnekaise .st.se; dm/s/d from Skr320/850/1000; ☉ Mar-Apr & mid-Jun–mid-Sep). Meals are available here, and guided tours to the summit of Kebnekaise are offered.

Getting There & Away

In addition to trains (stations are at Abisko Östra and Abisko Turiststation) between Luleå and Narvik, bus No 91 runs from Kiruna to Abisko (Skr94). Bus No 92 travels from Kiruna to Nikkaluokta (Skr69, two to three a day), at the Kebnekaise trail heads. Kvikkjokk is served by bus No 47, which runs twice daily on weekdays to and from Jokkmokk (Skr117).

sauna) and adjacent Chinese restaurant make this hostel a basic but good bet. Breakfast is Skr60.

Hotell City (☎ 66655; www.hotellcity.se, in Swedish; Bergmästaregatan 7; s/d Skr750/850) In the same building as the hostel, this new hotel has pleasant, modern rooms and affordable rates. Prices include breakfast and access to the hostel's kitchen.

Gullriset Lägenhetshotellet (☎ 10937; www .fabmf.se/gullriset, in Swedish; Bromsgatan 12; apartments Skr400-700) About 1.5km from the tourist office is this bargain option, perfect for self-caterers and those who fancy more space than a hotel room offers. You can rent an apartment sleeping up to four people, with kitchen, bathroom and cable TV.

Ice Hotel (☎ 66800; www.icehotel.com; Marknadsvägen, Jukkasjärvi; d from Skr2800) Staying at the Ice Hotel is a unique experience, and if you have the cash it shouldn't be missed. There are other options, including stylish hotel rooms (heated and *not* made of ice; doubles in winter/summer are Skr2800/1330), or three-bed cabins with skylights enabling you to watch the northern lights from your bed in winter (single, double or triple Skr2800).

Eating

Kiruna is not particularly well endowed with great eateries.

Café Safari (☎ 17460; Geologsgatan 4; light meals Skr20-60) Easily the nicest in town, this café has good coffee, cakes, and light meals such as sandwiches, quiche and baked potatoes.

Restaurant Winter City (☎ 10900; Bergmästaregatan 7; lunch buffet Skr55, meals Skr92-140) Adjacent to the STF hostel, this cosy place offers classic Chinese dishes, cheap lunches, takeaway meals and kids' options.

3nd Baren (☎ 66380; Föreningsgatan 11; lunch Skr65, dinner mains Skr69-189) This popular, moderately priced restaurant serves local specialties like reindeer, or you can play safe with steak or pasta. It's a lively drinking spot in the evening.

Ice Hotel Restaurant (☎ 66884; Marknadsvägen, Jukkasjärvi; mains Skr190-280) Opposite the accommodation complex in Jukkasjärvi is this high-quality restaurant specialising in local produce. Try the Arctic char or reindeer and, for dessert, cloudberry mousse or moose cheese parfait. Some meals even come on plates made of ice. The lunch buffet (available in summer) costs Skr95.

There's an **ICA supermarket** (Föreningsgatan; ⏰ 9am-7pm Mon-Fri, 10am-4pm Sat, 11am-4pm Sun), next to 3nd Baren.

Getting There & Away

The small **airport** (☎ 68000; www.lfv.se), 9km east of the town, has direct daily flights to Stockholm with SAS. An airport bus (Skr50) connects with most flights.

Regional buses in this vast region are operated by **Länstrafiken Norrbotten** (☎ 020-470047; www.ltnbd.se, in Swedish). Buses operate from the bus station on Hjalmar Lundbohmsvägen, opposite the Stadshus (town hall), and serve all major settlements. Bus No 91 runs two or three times daily to Riksgränsen (Skr117) via Abisko (Skr94); bus Nos 10 and 52 go to Gällivare (Skr117).

Regular trains connect Kiruna with Stockholm (overnight) and Narvik (Norway). Trains going to Narvik call at Abisko and Riksgränsen.

GÄLLIVARE
☎ 0970 / pop 19,700

The town of Gällivare and its northern twin Malmberget are surrounded by forest and dwarfed by the bald Dundret hill. It's not the world's most interesting place, but is important as the northern terminus for Inlandsbanan, and there are good opportunities for summer and winter activities.

The **tourist office** (☎ 16660; www.gellivare.se; Centralplan; ⏰ 8am-5pm Mon-Fri), by the train station, hires bicycles and can organise wilderness excursions.

Dundret (821m) is a nature reserve with superb views; you can view the midnight sun here from 2 June to 12 July. In winter there are four Nordic courses and 10 ski runs of varying difficulty. The mountaintop resort also organises numerous activities including snowmobile safaris and northern lights tours.

Kåkstan (Malmberget; admission free; ⏰ 9am-5pm) is a historical 'shanty town' museum village dating from the 1888 iron-ore rush. Bus No 1 to Malmberget (5km north of Gällivare) departs from opposite the Gällivare church.

STF Vandrarhem Gällivare (☎ 14380; www.explore lapland.com; Barnhemsvägen 2; dm member/non-member Skr160/195) is across the footbridge from the train station. Accommodation is in well-equipped cabins, bikes can be hired, and a variety of activities can be organised.

Quality Hotel Lapland (☎ 55020; www.qualityhotel
.gellivare.se; Lasarettsgatan 1; s/d Skr1195/1490, discounted
to Skr690/890; **P** ✕ ; wheelchair access) Opposite
the train station is a more expensive option,
with large comfortable rooms. Your best bets
for dining in Gällivare are the restaurant
(lunch Skr68) and the pub (mains Skr95 to
Skr230) here. It also has a decent menu of
cheaper dishes such as pasta and burgers,
and local specialities such as elk fillet and
Arctic char.

Getting There & Away

Regional buses depart from the train station. Bus No 45 runs daily to Östersund
(Skr410) via Jokkmokk and Arvidsjaur, bus
No 93 serves Kungsleden (from mid-June to
mid-September only), bus Nos 10 and 52 go
to Kiruna (Skr117), and bus No 44 runs to
Jokkmokk (Skr94).

Connex trains come from Luleå and
Stockholm (sometimes changing at Boden),
and from Narvik in Norway. More exotic is
Inlandsbanan (see p299), which terminates
at Gällivare; the train journey from Östersund costs Skr697.

JOKKMOKK

☎ 0971 / pop 5900

The small town of Jokkmokk, also on Inlandsbanan, is just north of the Arctic Circle
and started as a Sami market and mission.
Since 1605 the **Jokkmokk Winter Market** (www
.jokkmokksmarknad.com) has taken place here; the
three-day event attracts some 30,000 people
and starts on the first Thursday in February.
If you're interested in Sami handicrafts this
is *the* place to go.

The **tourist office** (☎ 22250; www.turism.jokkmokk
.se; Stortorget 4; ☺ 8am-5pm mid-Jun–mid-Aug, Mon-Fri
rest of year) can help with visitor information.

The **Ájtte museum** (☎ 17070; Kyrkogatan 3; adult/
child Skr50/free; ☺ 9am-5pm May-Sep, Sun-Fri Oct-Apr)
is the highlight of a visit to Jokkmokk; it
gives the most thorough introduction to
Sami culture anywhere in Sweden. It also
offers exhaustive information on Lappland's
mountain areas, with a full set of maps,
slides and videos, and a library. A research
visit is recommended for planning wilderness trips.

Naturfoto (☎ 55765; ☺ 9am-5.30pm Jun-Aug), at
the main Klockartorget intersection, exhibits
and sells work by a local wilderness photog-
rapher, Edvin Nilsson. There are a number of

Sami handicraft studios around town – ask at
the tourist office.

About 7km south of Jokkmokk you'll cross
the **Arctic Circle**; you'll find a summertime café
and camp site here on road No 45.

Sleeping & Eating

STF Vandrarhem Jokkmokk (☎ 55977; www.jokkmokk
hostel.com; Åsgatan 20; dm/d Skr165/410; 🖳) This comfortable hostel behind the tourist office has
laundry, sauna, Internet facilities and bikes
for rent. It's a favourite with Inlandsbanan
travellers and worth booking in advance in
summer.

Hotell Gästis (☎ 10012; www.hotell-gastis.com, in
Swedish; Herrevägen 1; s/d/tr Skr850/995/1200, discounted
to Skr650/750/900) It doesn't look too promising
from the outside, but this hotel offers decent value with pleasant but unremarkable
rooms, sauna, and a good restaurant with
lunch specials and à la carte dinners. The
hotel has discounted rates from mid-June
to mid-October.

Ájtte museum restaurant (Kyrkogatan 3; lunch Skr65)
Here you can try local and Sami specialities,
including fresh local fish or a sandwich with
reindeer meat.

Café Piano (☎ 10400; Porjusvägen 4; lunch Skr60, dinner mains Skr50-120; ☺ Mon-Sat) This is one of the
town's best options, with a grand piano inside, a large garden outside, and an extensive
menu, including inexpensive pizza, pasta and
wok meals.

Getting There & Away

Buses arrive and leave from the bus station
on Klockarvägen. Bus Nos 44 and 45 run
daily to and from Gällivare (Skr94). Inlandsbanan trains stop in Jokkmokk; for mainline
trains, take bus No 43 to Murjek (up to six
a day) or bus No 44 to Boden (Skr126) and
Luleå (Skr157).

LULEÅ

☎ 0920 / pop 72,000

The capital of Norrbotten, Sweden's largest
county, Luleå is a major transport hub with
some interesting diversions and good-value
accommodation. The **tourist office** (☎ 293500;
www.lulea.se; Storgatan 43; ☺ 9am-7pm Mon-Fri & 10am-
4pm Sat & Sun Jun-Aug, 10am-6pm Mon-Fri & 10am-2pm Sat
Sep-May) will help with inquiries, and the **library**
(Kyrkogatan) has free Internet access.

The most famous sight in Luleå is the
Unesco World Heritage–listed **Gammelstad**,

or Old Town, which was the medieval centre of northern Sweden. The stone church dates from 1492 and is surrounded by 424 wooden houses where the faithful from outlying villages would stay in order to attend church on Sunday or religious festivals. Six church stables also remain. The open-air museum **Hägnan** (🕑 Jun-Aug) and a nature reserve are nearby.

Norbottens Museum (☎ 243500; Storgatan 2; admission free; 🕑 10am-5pm Tue-Sun) is worth a visit for the Sami section and some very interesting short films on the northern lights and Sami identity. In summer there are a number of boat trips to the surrounding archipelago.

If you'd like to stay, the **Comfort Hotel Max** (☎ 220220; www.choicehotels.se; Storgatan 59; s/d Skr1125/1325, discounted to Skr490/690) is a huge bargain at weekends and in summer, as discounted rates at this well-equipped business hotel include breakfast and a dinner buffet.

For food, head to **Roasters** (☎ 88840; Storgatan 43; lunch Skr67, snacks Skr28-59), a stylish spot with extensive lunch options, grilled foccacia and ciabatta, strong coffee, and outdoor seating.

Getting There & Away

The **airport** (☎ 244900; www.lfv.se) is 9km southwest of the town centre. There are about a dozen flights daily between Stockholm and Luleå with SAS and **Nordic Airlink** (☎ 08-528 06820; www.flynordic.com). An airport bus (Skr50) and **Skyways** (www.skyways.se) will get you directly to and from Gothenburg. Take the airport bus from the bus station (Skr45).

Länstrafiken Norrbotten buses cover the 100,000-sq-km county. The maximum fare is Skr280, a 30-day pass covering the entire county costs Skr1475 and bicycles are carried for Skr50. Bus No 100 runs to Haparanda (Skr117) four times daily. Bus No 44 goes to Jokkmokk (Skr157) and on to Gällivare (Skr245) once daily.

Direct Connex trains from Stockholm and Gothenburg run at night only. Most trains from Narvik and Kiruna terminate at Luleå.

HAPARANDA & TORNIO

Haparanda ☎ 0922 / pop 10,400
Tornio ☎ 016 / pop 23,200
Haparanda was founded in 1821 as a trading town to replace Tornio (spelt Torneå in Swedish), which Sweden had lost to Russia. Now the two border towns almost function

as one entity and are most famous for their 18-hole golf course.

Both the krona and the euro are accepted at most places. Tornio is one hour ahead of Haparanda.

Green Line Centre (☎ Sweden 12010, Finland 432 733; http://infokiosk.haparanda.se, or www.tornio.fi, in Finnish; 🕑 8am-8pm Mon-Fri & 10am-8pm Sat & Sun Jun–mid-Aug, 8-11.30am & 12.30-4pm Mon-Fri mid-Aug–May) is the joint Haparanda–Tornio tourist centre.

Sights & Activities

There are few sights in Haparanda but Tornio has a pair of lovely churches worth visiting: the beautiful wooden **Tornio Church** (built 1686) on Seminaarinkatu and the tiny **Orthodox Church** on Lukiokatuthe, built by order of Tsar Alexander I. Also worth a visit are the **Lapin Kulta Brewery** (☎ 43366; Lapinkullankatu 1; 🕑 free tours 2pm Tue & Thu Jun-Aug) and the **Aine Art Museum** (☎ 432 438; Torikatu 2; adult/child €2/1; 🕑 11am-6pm Tue-Thu, 11am-3pm Fri-Sun), which has a big collection of Finnish art from the 19th and 20th centuries.

The biggest attraction, however, is the unique **Green Zone Golf Course** (Finland ☎ 431 711; Näräntie 1; green fees 18 holes €33, par 3 course €8, club hire €10). Not only can you play midnight golf (with the sun shining), but the course actually straddles the border. You can tee off in Finland and hit the ball into Sweden; this means that if you start at, say, 12.30am, the ball will remain in the air for an hour and land in yesterday. All this novelty, and a round on a pretty good course, can be yours when the snow melts away between late May and late August. To play after 10pm you need to book in advance.

The scenic **Kukkolaforsen rapids**, on the Torne älv 15km north of town, are also well worth a visit (take bus No 53 or 54). There's a **tourist village** (🕑 midsummer to mid-August) that includes a camp site and cabins, a restaurant, a café, a fish smokehouse, saunas, and a museum. For rafting trips, contact **Lapland Connection** (☎ 253 405; www.safarisunlimited.fi).

Sleeping & Eating

Camping Tornio (☎ 445 945; sirkka.hyry@pp.inet.fi; Matkailijantie; tent sites €18, cabins per double €54) This place is about 3km from town on the road to Kemi.

STF Vandrarhem Haparanda (☎ 61171; www.haparandavandrarhem.net; Strandgatan 26; dm/s/d Skr160/250/320) This excellent hostel isn't far from

ARCTIC SCANDINAVIA TRAVEL ROUTES

Haparanda town centre. Some rooms have private bathroom, plus there's a sauna, a laundry and self-catering facilities. You can also opt for a meal at the decent onsite restaurant.

Stadshotellet (☎ 61490; www.haparandastadshotell.se; Torget 7; s/d Skr1090/1390, discounted to Skr650/850) This large, once grand hotel is the focus of Haparanda, and its pub-restaurant, the Gulasch Baronen (mains Skr70 to Skr120) offers reasonably priced meals in a convivial atmosphere. Some beds are as little as Skr295 in summer.

Matkakotti Heta (☎ 480 897; Saarenpäänkatu 39; s/d/tr €27/42/60) Located in a pretty part of Tornio, this guesthouse has slightly eccentric owners, who add to the character of the place. There's a cosy lounge with art gallery and sauna. Breakfast is available (€5).

Umpitunneli (☎ 430 360; Hallituskatu 15; ⊙ 11am-2am, to 4am Fri & Sat) For entertainment Finnish-style, head to this classic open-air dance pub and restaurant where you can see the *humppa* (traditional dance and music) in full swing from Wednesday to Saturday. Year-round it's a rollicking bar and nightclub.

Getting There & Away
Regular buses connect Haparanda and Tornio (Skr15). There are regional buses from Luleå (Skr117) and towns further south. Daily, bus No 53 travels north along the border via the Kukkolaforsen rapids, Övertorneå and Pajala, and then continues west to Kiruna (Skr270). Buses to Rovaniemi (€17.50, 2½ hours) run via Kemi.

ROVANIEMI
☎ 016 / pop 35,400
Rovaniemi is the capital of and gateway to Lapland, though there's not much Lappish about the town. It was razed by retreating Germans in WWII, and rebuilt with the main streets radiating out from Hallituskatu in the shape of reindeer antlers – obvious only from the air. Despite its lack of architectural appeal, it still makes a good base for activities such as dog or reindeer sledding, white-water rafting, skiing, and touring by snowmobile. It's also a friendly place for the budget traveller.

Information
Etiäinen (☎ 647 820; ⊙ 10am-5pm) At Napapiiri (the Arctic Circle), this is the information centre for the national

parks and trekking regions, with information on hiking and fishing in Lapland.
Main post office (Postikatu 1; ⊙ 9am-8pm Mon-Fri)
Rovaniemi Health Centre (☎ Sweden 32241, Finland 322 4900; Sairaalakatu 1)
Santa Claus Tourist Centre (☎ 346 270; www.rovaniemi.fi; Koskikatu 1; ⊙ 8am-6pm Mon-Fri & 10am-4pm Sat & Sun Jun–late Aug, 8am-4pm Mon-Fri late Aug–May) It has a corny name, but this is an excellent source of information for all of Lapland. It also has Internet access (per 15 minutes €2).

Sights & Activities
With its beautifully designed glass tunnel stretching out to the Kemijoki River, spacious layout, and engrossing, well-presented exhibitions, **Arktikum** (☎ 317 830; www.arktikum.fi; Pohjoisranta 4; adult/child €11/5; ⊙ 9am-7pm mid-Jun–mid-Aug, 10am-6pm early Jun & late Aug, 10am-6pm Tue-Sun Sep-May) is one of Finland's premier museums. Superb displays focus on Arctic flora and fauna as well as the Sami and other people of the Arctic. Give yourself at least a couple of hours to get around it. It's a pleasant walk from the centre if you follow the path along the river.

The smaller **Rovaniemi Art Museum** (☎ 322 2822; Lapinkävijäntie 4; adult/child €4/2, admission free Sat; ⊙ noon-5pm Tue-Sat) has changing exhibitions of Finnish modern art. Across the Ounasjoki River and 3km above the town, the **Ounasvaara Ski Centre** (☎ 369 045; www.ounasvaara.net) has six downhill ski slopes and three ski jumps, plus a summer tobogganing run. It's a good spot for hiking in summer. Two-hour **boat cruises** (☎ 0400-292 132; adult/child €10/5; ⊙ 2pm, 5pm & 8pm) on the Kemijoki River are another good summer activity.

Tours
Several tour companies in town specialise in the 'Lapland experience'. In winter and early spring the most popular activities include snowmobiling (from €88), and husky and reindeer safaris (from €100). Summer tours include river cruises from €20, and white-water rafting and fishing expeditions from €45 to €115 per person. Ask at the tourist office for details.

Festivals & Events
Rovaniemi hosts a bursting calendar of festivals and events all year round. For more details, visit www.rovaniemi.fi. Some of the best:

FEBRUARY
Northern Lights Festival A variety of sports and arts events.

MARCH
Reindeer City Race Skiers fly through the town centre behind their charges.
Ounasvaara Winter Games Skiing and ski-jumping competitions.

JUNE
Jutajaiset Showcase of folk music, dance and other Sami traditions.

JULY
Kemijoki Rock Festival The best of local and smaller international rock acts.

AUGUST
Roots & River Blues Festival A northern festival for the blues enthusiast.

Sleeping

Matka Borealis (☎ /fax 342 0130; www.matkaborealis .com; Asemieskatu 1; s/d €45/58; ✗ P) Rovaniemi's cosiest and best-value guesthouse is just about opposite the train station. It's a friendly place with clean, simple rooms, all with attached bathroom. Breakfast is included.

Hotel Aakenus (☎ 342 2051; www.hotelliaakenus .net; Koskikatu 47; s/d €65/75, d summer €50; ✗) This simple but welcoming private hotel is a short walk north of the centre. It has a sauna, a restaurant and nonsmoking rooms, and the local swimming hall is around the corner.

Hotel Santa Claus (☎ 321 321; www.hotelsantaclaus .fi; Korkalonkatu 29; s/d €110/132; ✗ ▣) Rovaniemi's newest hotel has unusually large rooms with modern trimmings and some strange '70s touches involving red velour. Some fifth-floor rooms have balconies overlooking Koskikatu. Breakfast and sauna are included.

City Hotel (☎ 330 0111; www.cityhotel.fi; Pekankatu 9; s/d €91/115). This stylish boutique hotel with piano bar and chesterfield couches in the lobby has neat, compact rooms with satellite TV and minibar.

Rantasipi Pohjanhovi (☎ 33711; www.rantasipi.fi; Pohjanpuistikko 2; s/d €113/133) Rovaniemi's oldest hotel (rebuilt in 1947 after the WWII destruction) retains some charm and has the legendary restaurant and dance club Nite Life (see right).

Eating

Mariza (☎ 319 616; Ruokasenkatu 2; lunch buffet €5.90-6.50; ❨ 10am-3pm Mon-Fri) This simple diner offers a fabulous lunch buffet of home-cooked Finnish food, including hot dishes, soup and salad.

Cómico (☎ 344 433; Koskikatu 25; nachos €3.50, mains €7.80-16.60; ❨ 11am-midnight Mon-Wed, 11am-2am Thu & Fri, noon-2am Sat & Sun) A colourful bar and restaurant just below street level with American-diner seating, this place shows old movies and serves Tex-Mex (nachos and burritos), burgers, steaks, and salads.

Hai Long (☎ 313133; Valtakatu 35; lunch €7.50, dinner mains €6-12; ❨ 11am-10pm) For inexpensive Chinese food and good lunch buffets (11am to 3pm) you can't go too far wrong here.

Fransmanni (☎ 0201-234695; Koskikatu 4; mains €8.50-20; ❨ 11am-midnight Mon-Thu, 11am-1am Fri, 1pm-1am Sat, 1pm-midnight Sun) A casual atmosphere and tempting menu make this French-Finnish fusion chain with booth seating a good option. It's one of several Rovaniemi restaurants to add a 'Lapland menu' to its usual fare – try the whitefish, sautéed reindeer or breadcheese with cloudberry cream.

Puolukka (☎ 310 222; Valtakatu; mains €16-25; ❨ 11am-3pm & 5-11pm Mon-Fri, 4-11pm Sat, 5-10pm Sun) This is arguably Rovaniemi's best restaurant when it comes to traditional Lappish cuisine. It's not cheap, and the restaurant itself is unassuming, but the food is delicious and includes reindeer, whitefish, and cloudberry desserts.

Entertainment

Rovaniemi has loads of bars and nightclubs in the town centre.

In summer **Oluthuone** (Koskikatu) is a great place to kick back under the midnight sun in the open-air beer terrace.

A tiny, eccentric pub with no seats, **Pub Ylityö** (Koskikatu 5) was voted one of the world's best bars by *Newsweek* in 1996.

Irish Times (☎ 319 925; Valtakatu 35; ❨ 11am-2am Mon-Sat, noon-2am Sun) is Rovaniemi's best Irish pub. It has a great heated terrace at the back, international beers, pool tables downstairs and a relaxed vibe.

Nite Life (☎ 33711; Pohjanpuistikko 2; ❨ to 4am Fri & Sat) is the place for some real Finnish-style partying; head to the dance club (*humppa* and tango) at Rantasipi Pohjanhovi, then cram into the nightclub (€8).

Getting There & Away

Finnair has daily flights to Rovaniemi from Helsinki, Kemi and Oulu. An airport bus (€5) meets all flights; it leaves the central bus station one hour before flight departures.

Frequent buses travel to Kemi (€15.20, 1½ hours), Hetta (in Enontekiö, five hours), Sodankylä (€17.50, two hours), Ivalo (4½ hours) and Inari (five hours).

The train is the best way to travel between Helsinki and Rovaniemi (€70.20, 10 to 12 hours) – it's quicker and cheaper than the bus. There are eight daily trains (via Oulu), including four overnight services.

Major car-hire companies have offices in Rovaniemi or at the airport. Rates are highest from February to April and June to August. Try **Europcar** (☎ 0400-433507; Koskikatu 6) or **Budget** (☎ 312 266; Koskikatu 9).

NAPAPIIRI (THE ARCTIC CIRCLE)

The official **Arctic Circle marker** is in Napapiiri, 8km north of Rovaniemi. Built on top of it is the 'official' **Santa Claus village**. The **Santa Claus post office** receives close to a million letters each year – he and his helpers actually reply to almost 50,000. As tacky as it sounds, it's all good fun. You can send a postcard home with an official Santa stamp (you can arrange to have it delivered at Christmas) and meet the bearded man in red in his grotto (that's free, but signs warn that Santa is a registered trademark and can only be photographed by his elves – the cost is €17). There are also some excellent souvenir and handicraft shops here. You can visit the dogs in **Husky Park** and, in winter, take short husky sled rides. Bus No 8 goes hourly from Rovaniemi train station (€5.20 return).

SODANKYLÄ

☎ 016 / pop 9900

The busy market town of Sodankylä is a reasonable place to break the journey between Rovaniemi and northern Lapland, and is renowned for the **Midnight Sun Film Festival** (www .msfilmfestival.fi), held in mid-June. Tickets and programs are available from the **tourist office** (☎ 618 168; www.sodankyla.fi; Jäämerentie 3; 9am-5pm Mon-Fri).

The **old wooden church** (10am-6pm Jun-Aug), near the town centre, is worth a look. It was built in 1689, making it one of the oldest in Lapland. Mummified bodies of local priests and their families are buried beneath the church floor.

In the same building as the tourist office, the **Andraes Alariesto Gallery** (☎ 618 643; adult/child €5/2) displays Sami art by famous Lapp painter Alariesto, who favoured a primitive style to depict traditional Sami life.

If you plan to stay, **Majatalo Kolme Veljestä** (☎ 611 216; Ivalontie 1; s/d/tr €38/54/65) is a lovely guesthouse with tidy rooms (shared bathroom), a guest lounge with open fire, sauna, kitchen, and breakfast included. For food, head to **Café Kerttuli** (☎ 624 383; Jäämerentie 11; snacks €2-5, mains €5.50-16; 10am-8pm Mon-Thu, 10am-10pm Fri & Sat, noon-6pm Sun), where the lunchtime buffet (€9) and sunny terrace facing the main street make this Sodankylä's top choice.

There are daily buses to and from Rovaniemi (€17.90, 1¾ hours) and Ivalo (€19.70, two hours).

SIDE TRIP: PYHÄ-LUOSTO REGION

The area between the fells of Luosto (514m) and Pyhä (540m) forms a popular winter-sports centre midway between Kemijärvi and Sodankylä. The high season extends from February to May, but in summer it's also excellent for trekking, particularly in the 43-sq-km **Pyhätunturi National Park** that surrounds **Pyhä Fell**. The most notable sight is the steep **Pyhäkuru Gorge** between the Kultakero and Ukonhattu peaks. According to local legend, **Lake Pyhänkasteenlampi** (Lake of Holy Baptism), in the gorge, was where EM Fellman, the 'Apostle of Lapland', forcibly baptised the Sompio Sami in the 17th century to convert them to Christianity. Pyhä and Luosto each have resort 'villages' packed with hotels and restaurants. For information on the area, accommodation, weather and slope conditions visit www.luosto.fi or www.pyha.fi.

You can also try **Pyhä-Luosto Matkailu** (☎ 020-838 4248; Pyhä- Luostontie 2) in Luosto or the **Pyhähippu Reservation Centre** (☎ 882 820) in Pyhä for tourist information.

Pyhätunturi Nature Centre (☎ 882 773) has information on Pyhätunturi National Park, as well as summer activities. It's adjacent to the Pyhä downhill ski centre; follow the signs from the main Kemijarvi–Sodankylä road (road No 5).

URHO KEKKONEN NATIONAL PARK

The 255,000-hectare **Urho Kekkonen National Park** (www.metsa.fi/natural/nationalparks/urhokekkonen nationalpark) is a highly rated trekking area, partly because of the large network of wilderness huts, but also because of the unspoilt beauty of the low *tunturi* (hills). The northern part of the park is a barren wilderness area of fells crossed by ravines, steep slopes and scree. Further south, treeless tundra gives way to forest wilderness.

The three main entry points to the park have information centres:

Saariselkä Information Cabin (☎ 668 122)

Savukoski National Park Visitor Centre (☎ 841 401; Samperintie 32)

Tankavaara National Park Visitor Centre (☎ 626 251)

Hiking

The park is divided into four zones, each with different rules; you'll get details from the visitor centres. Hikers need to carry all their food, as wilderness huts in the park are not stocked with supplies. Note that hiking can be challenging, as many marked trails are either faint or almost nonexistent. A map and compass are essential for much of the park. The three maps to have are the 1:50,000 *Sompio–Kiilopää* map, which will do for short hikes from Saariselkä; the 1:50,000 *Sokosti–Suomujoki* map, which takes in Lake Luirojärvi; and the 1:100,000 *Koilliskaira* map, which shows the entire park.

There are lots of possible walking routes around Saariselkä using wilderness huts as bases. The main attractions are the **Rumakuru Gorge**; **Lake Luirojärvi**, including a climb up nearby **Sokosti** (718m); **Paratiisikuru**; and **Lumikuru**. There are also two historical **Scolt fields**, with restored old houses, 2km south of Raja-Jooseppi and 2km west of Snelmanninmaja hut, respectively.

The four- to six-day loop from the main road to Lake Luirojärvi is the most popular route, and can be extended beyond the lake. To reach more remote areas you can take the week-long trek from Kiilopää to Kemihaara, but the least crowded option follows old roads and walking routes all the way from Raja-Jooseppi in the north to Kemihaara or Tulppio in the southeast.

Within the park are 200 designated free camp sites and 30 free wilderness huts; a handful of other huts carry a €9 nightly charge and must be booked in advance through any of the park visitor centres. More distant huts usually have mattresses, gas or wood-burning stoves and sometimes telephones or saunas. Almost all are near water. The visitor centres can supply maps and details of the huts.

Buses run to Saariselkä from Sodankylä daily.

INARI

☎ 016 / pop 550

As unprepossessing as it seems at first, the tiny village of Inari is the most interesting point of civilisation in far northern Lapland. This is the main Sami community in the region and a centre for genuine Sami handicrafts under the name 'Sami Duodji'.

Inari Info (☎ 661 666; www.inarilapland.org; ☼ 9am-7pm Jun-Aug, 10am-4pm Mon-Fri rest of year) doubles as the post office and Alko store.

Don't miss **Siida** (☎ 665 212; www.samimuseum .fi; adult/child €7/3; ☼ 9am-8pm Jun-Sep, 10am-5pm Tue-Sun Oct-May), one of the finest conceptual and open-air museums in Finland. The exhibition successfully brings to life Sami origins, culture, lifestyle and present-day struggles. Outside is a fine open-air museum featuring Sami buildings, handicrafts and artefacts (open summer only).

There's a marked 7.5km walking track (starting from the Siida parking area) to the 18th-century **Pielpajärvi wilderness church**. If you have a vehicle, there's another parking area 3km closer. In winter or spring you'll need snowshoes and a keen attitude to tackle this walk.

In summer, boat trips leave for the prominent **Ukko Island** on Lake Inarijärvi, an ancient sacred site for the Inari Sami. The two-hour cruises are run by **Lake & Snow** (☎ 0400-295 731; adult/child €12/6; ☼ tours 2pm Jun, Aug & Sep, 2pm & 6pm Jul). From November to late April, when the lake is frozen over, you can take a snowmobile out to the island (€60 to €100 per person).

Inarin Porofarmi (☎ 673 912) is a reindeer farm run by a Sami family. You can meet reindeer, try lassoing, see Sami shows, and take reindeer safaris in winter. The farm is 14km from Inari on the back road to Kittila.

Reindeer races are held on the lake in the first week of April, and a big **ice-fishing competition** draws the crowds two weeks later.

SIDE TRIP: LEMMENJOKI NATIONAL PARK

Slush through desolate wilderness rivers, explore the rough Arctic landscape and bump into isolated gold panners in the middle of nowhere in 2855-sq-km **Lemmenjoki** (www.metsa.fi/natural/nationalparks/lemmenjoki/first.htm), Finland's largest national park. One of the country's most diverse parks, its hiking trails extend for over 70km through the vast reserve, and there are several free wilderness huts.

Lemmenjoki Nature Centre (☎ 0205-647 793; ☒ 9am-9pm Jun-Sep) is just before the village of Njurgulahti, about 50km southwest of Inari. It has a small interpretive exhibition and a powerful set of binoculars, and sells maps and fishing permits. Accommodation at Njurgulahti includes two camp sites.

Almost all trails start from Njurgulahti, including a 4km marked nature trail suitable for families with children. The majority of the trekking routes lie within the relatively small area between the Lemmenjoki and the Vaskojoki Rivers. A 18km loop between Kultala and Ravadasjärvi huts takes you to some of the most interesting gold-panning areas. As you can do this in two days, many trekkers head over Ladnjoaivi Fell to Vaskojoki hut and back, which extends the trek to four or five days. For any serious trekking you will need the 1:100,000 *Lemmenjoki* map.

As well as hiking trails and opportunities for gold panning, there's a **boat cruise** along the Lemmenjoki valley in summer, from Njurgulahti village to the Kultahamina wilderness hut at Gold Harbour. A 20km marked trail also follows the course of the river, so you can take the boat one way, then hike back.

The **Sallivaara Reindeer Roundup site**, 70km south of Inari, was used by Sami reindeer herders twice yearly until 1964. Roundups were an important social event for the people of northern Lapland, usually lasting several weeks and involving hundreds of people and animals. The Sallivaara reindeer corrals and cabins were reconstructed in 1997, and there are plans to stage roundups here in autumn and spring. Park at Repojoki, then follow the marked trail, 6km one way.

In summer, Gold Line buses run at least once a day from Inari to Lemmenjoki (two hours).

Sleeping & Eating

Uruniemi Camping (☎ 671 331; tent sites €11, 2-person cottages €17-23, 4-person cottages €30-70; ☒ Jun–late Sep) About 2km south of town, this is a well-equipped lakeside camp site with cottages, a café, a sauna, and boats and bikes for hire.

Hostel Jokitörmä (☎ 672 725; www.jokitorma.com; dm/s/d €16/26/38; P ☒) This great place has cosy two- and four-person rooms, and a separate set of cottages, each with their own kitchen and bathroom facilities. The hostel is on the Arctic Hwy about 27km north of Inari. All buses will stop here on request.

Hotel Inari (☎ 671 026; hotelli.inari@luukku.com; s/d/tr €38/45/60; ☒ year-round) The local hotel is also the hub of the village – pub, restaurant, Saturday night disco and general local hangout. Upstairs there are small simple rooms with attached bath. The restaurant (mains €8 to €11, pizzas €5 to €9) offers Lappish dishes and interesting pizzas such as the one with sautéed reindeer, peach and onion. The terrace at the front is a great place to sit in summer and meet the locals.

Getting There & Away

The Arctic Hwy runs through Inari, so buses from Rovaniemi ply the route right through to Nordkapp, Tana Bru and Kirkenes (all in Norway) in summer. Buses stop outside the tourist office. Although you can't make reservations or buy tickets here, you can pick up timetables, and there are no problems getting a seat (pay the driver). Gold Line buses run daily to and from Ivalo (€6, 40 minutes), with connections south to Rovaniemi.

KARIGASNIEMI

The small village of Karigasniemi is a crossing point from Finland to Norway along the popular Nordkapp route. It has services such as a bank and a post office. Fell Sami, the language of the local people of Karigasniemi, is also the main dialect spoken across the border in Norway.

Camping Tenorinne (☎ 676 113; tent/cabin €14/30; ☒ Jun–mid-Sep) has rustic log cabins and a pleasant location away from the main road.

Two buses a day travel from Ivalo to Karigasniemi, continuing on to the Norwegian town of Karasjok. A shared taxi travels to

Sami villages north of Karigasniemi along the Teno River on Tuesday and Friday.

KARASJOK

pop 2900

While Kautokeino is the most Sami settlement in Norway, Karasjok (Kárásjvjohka in Sami) is the undisputed capital of Sami Norway and home of the Sametinget, the Sami parliament. It also has Finnmark's oldest **church** (1807), the only building left standing in Karasjok after WWII. The Nazis' burnings mean that the centre of today's Karasjok consists of a couple of strip malls connected by the E6 and Rv92. But, this being Finnmark, the settlement area doesn't extend very far before vast and empty wilderness returns.

The **tourist office** (☎ 78 46 88 10; www.koas.no; Porsangerveien 1; ⊙ 9am-7pm Jun–mid-Aug, 9am-4pm Mon-Fri rest of year), at the junction of E6 and route Rv92, can book winter dogsled rides, and arrange salmon fishing, riverboat trips and other summer activities.

The **Sami Museum** (☎ 78 46 99 50; Museumsgata 17; adult/child Nkr25/5; ⊙ 9am-6pm Mon-Sat, 10am-6pm Sun 9 Jun–19 Aug, shorter hrs rest of year), just 500m northeast of the town centre, covers Sami history. For something flasher and much more superficial, try the **Sami Park** (☎ 78 46 88 10; Porsangerveien 1; adult/child Nkr95/60; ⊙ 9am-7pm mid-Jun–late Aug, shorter hrs rest of year) – a theme park and reindeer farm.

The wonderful **Karasjok HI Hostel** (☎ 78 46 71 66; karasjok.hostel@vandrerhjem.no; dm/s/d Nkr150/300/375; [P]) is 6km west of town; breakfast costs Nkr60, dinner is available, and staff can organise a variety of summer and winter tours. At **Engholm's Husky** (☎ 78 46 71 66; www.engholm.no; Rv92; cabins Nkr150-300 plus per guest Nrk100; [P]), dog lovers will enjoy the rustic, well-furnished cabins near where owner Sven keeps his sled dogs and pups. Most cabins have a kitchen but no bathroom. Breakfast costs Nkr50, and there is a free sauna. Sven also offers excellent winter dogsled and cross-country skiing tours (Nkr7400 to Nkr13,200), as well as summer dog-packing tours.

Gammen (☎ 78 46 74 00; Porsangerveien 1; mains Nkr190-250; ⊙ 11am-11pm mid-May–mid-Aug), at Sami Park, offers traditional dishes in a 'Sami-inspired' dining room. The place consists of four squat, turf-covered huts with a central hearth – very hobbit. In the central shopping centre, **Márkan Kafé** (Markangeaidnu 1; dishes Nkr25-95; ⊙ 10am-6pm Mon-Fri, 10am-3pm Sat) sells sandwiches and omelettes at bargain prices, and there's a nearby supermarket.

Getting There & Away

Buses connect Karasjok with Hammerfest (Nkr308, 4¾ hours, daily except Saturday), Kirkenes (Nkr452, 5½ hours) and Nordkapp (Nkr435, five hours, summer only). The Finnish Lapin Linjat buses to Ivalo (Nkr180, 3¾ hours) and Rovaniemi (Nkr450, 5½ hours) also pass through Karasjok. Bus No 405 runs from Karasjok to Kautokeino (Nkr189, two hours, twice a week).

NORDKAPP

Nordkapp, a high rugged coastal plateau at 71°10'21"N latitude, claims to be the northernmost point in Europe (Knivskjelodden is actually the northernmost point; see following), and it's the main destination for most visitors to the far north. The sun never drops below the horizon from mid-May to the end of July, and to many visitors Nordkapp's steep cliffs and stark scenery emanate a certain spiritual aura. Indeed, long before other Europeans took an interest in the area, Nordkapp was considered a power centre by the Sami people.

Nowadays there's a rip-off Nkr175 entrance fee and a touristy complex with exhibits, eateries, souvenir shops and a post office. The 180-degree theatre runs a rather

---

SIDE TRIP: KEVO NATURE RESERVE

Some of the most breathtaking scenery in Finland is protected by the 712-sq-km Kevo Nature Reserve. Within its boundaries you'll find the splendid gorge of the Kevo River, which features some spectacular waterfalls.

The main trail runs through the canyon from the Utsjoki–Kaamanen road to the Karigasniemi–Kaamanen road and is 63km long. The trek is rough and takes about four days one way. You'll need the 1:100,000 *Kevo* topographical sheet to tackle it.

Rules for visiting the Kevo reserve are stricter than those concerning national parks: hikers cannot hunt, fish or collect plants and berries, *must* stay on marked trails, and can only overnight at designated camp sites. The gorge area is off limits from April to mid-June.

SIDE TRIP: KIRKENES

The former mining town of Kirkenes (population 4500) was Norway's most bombed place during WWII, with over 1000 air-raid alarms. The town is not a major tourist destination, but it does get some visitors, since it's the end of the line for the *Hurtigruten* coastal steamer and a jumping-off point into Russia. To find the small town centre, head west (make a right) from the dock and follow the signs. It's about 1.5km. Or just take the waiting shuttle bus.

The **tourist office** (☎ 78 99 25 44; www.kirkenesinfo.no, not in English; Presteveien 1; ☯ 8.30am-6pm Mon-Fri & 8.30am-5.30pm Sat & Sun Jun–mid-Aug, 8.30am-4pm Mon-Fri mid-Aug–May) can help you plan winter activities, such as king crab safaris (Nkr750), snowmobile trips along the border (Nkr950), and night-time dogsled rides (Nkr1075).

A good first stop is the **Sør-Varanger Grenselandmuseet** (☎ 78 99 48 80; Førstevannslia; adult/student/child Nkr30/15/free; ☯ 10am-6pm mid-Jun–Aug, 10am-3.30pm Sep–mid-Jun), which has displays on WWII history, local geography, culture, religion and Sami crafts. It details the history of the region as a border area, where Russian, Norwegian, Finnish and Sami culture collide. Another WWII interest is a cold **cave** (cnr Presteveien & Tellef Dahls gate; tours adult/child Nkr100/50; ☯ mid-Jun–mid-Aug), which was used as an air-raid shelter. Tours are held at noon, 3pm, 6.15pm and 9pm. Up on a nearby hill, there's a **statue** dedicated to the Soviet soldiers who liberated the town.

Barbara's B&B (☎ 78 99 32 07; barbara@ trollnet.no; Henrik Lunds gate 13; s/d Nkr300/450; **P**) has two rooms, free Internet and a friendly dog. **Rica Arctic Hotel** (☎ 78 99 29 29; Kongensgate 1-3; s Nkr705-1195, d Nkr895-1325; **P**) offers the usual amenities, but rooms are worn and contain ugly furniture.

Culinary delights aren't plentiful. Your best bet is the **Ritz** (☎ 78 99 34 81; Dr Wesselsgata 17; mains Nkr59-203; ☯ 3-11.30pm Mon & Tue, noon-12.30am Wed & Thu, noon-2.30am Fri & Sat, 1-11.30pm Sun) pizza restaurant and bar. The **Sentrum Kafé** (☎ 78 99 63 00; Dr Wesselsgata 18; sandwiches Nkr25-60; ☯ 9am-11pm) serves open-face sandwiches and marzipan cake to a roomful of people sitting on cheaply upholstered couches. Self-caters should try the **Coop Mega** (☎ 78 97 06 66; Solheimsveien).

SAS, Braathens, Norwegian Air and Widerøe fly into Kirkenes' airport, a 20-minute drive from town; flying in and out of Ivolo, Finland, some 250km away, may be cheaper. The airport bus costs Nkr64/32 per adult/child, and a taxi is about Nkr275. Kirkenes is also the terminus of the *Hurtigruten* coastal steamer.

By land, buses serve Karasjok (Nkr452, 5½ hours), Hammerfest (Nkr744, 10¼ hours) and Alta (Nkr784, 12¾ hours) and many points in between.

Visiting Russia

Day and weekend bus tours from Kirkenes to Murmansk in summer are arranged by **Sovjetrejser** (☎ 78 99 25 01; polarscout@grenseland.no; Kongensgate 1-3). The guided bus tour, including lunch and sightseeing, costs Nkr1090/1290 per day/weekend but you'll have to add on the cost of a Russian visa, typically Nkr450 to Nkr1300, depending upon your nationality. For longer tours, try Pasvik Tours (p68). Travellers interested in visiting Russia on their own can take the bus to Murmansk (4½ hours, Nkr350/700 one way/return), and pay the visa fee, but you'll need an 'official invitation'. Contact the **Russian Consulate** (☎ 78 99 37 37; Kirkegata) for details. Visa processing takes around 16 days, so make sure you contact Sovjetreiser or the consulate well in advance.

Visiting Ovre Pasvik National Park

Even when the diabolical mosquito swarms make life hell for warm-blooded creatures, the lakes, tundra bogs and Norway's largest stand of virgin *taiga* forest lend a strange appeal to odd little Øvre Pasvik National Park. This is the last corner of Norway where wolves, wolverines, lynx and brown bears still roam freely, and it seems more like Finland or Siberia than anywhere else in Norway. The park is also home to moose and a host of birds that are rare elsewhere in Norway.

Hikers can douse themselves in repellent and follow the poor road that turns southwest 1.5km south of Vaggatem, where there's a coffee shop and camp site, and ends 9km later at the car park near the northeastern end of Lake Sortbrysttjørna. There, a marked track leads southwest for 5km, passing scenic lakes, marshes and bogs to end at the Ellenvannskoia hikers' hut beside the large Lake Ellenvatn. The best map is Statens Kartverk's *Krokfjellet 2333-I*, which, conveniently, covers the entire park.

There is no public transport to the park.

repetitious short film, but if you want to really appreciate Nordkapp take a walk out along the cliffs. If the weather is fair you can perch yourself on the edge of the continent and watch the polar mist roll in.

The continent's real northernmost point, **Knivskjelodden** (71°11'08"N latitude) is inaccessible to vehicles, but you can hike 9km to this lovely promontory from a marked car park about 9km south of Nordkapp. It takes about five hours to walk there and back.

An asphalt road winds across a rocky plateau and past herds of grazing reindeer up to Nordkapp. Depending on snow conditions, it's usually open from May to mid-October; the **Road User Information Centre** (☎ 177) gives opening dates.

From mid-May to the end of August, local buses run daily at 12.15pm and 9pm between Honningsvåg and Nordkapp (Nkr66, one hour). There is an additional service at 8.20pm between 2 June and 16 August, and another at 10.55pm between 2 June and 9 August. Between 2 June and 9 August the last bus departs Nordkapp at 1.10am, allowing views of the midnight sun. Avoid so-called tours, which charge considerably more for similar services.

HAMMERFEST
pop 9200

Most visitors to Hammerfest arrive by the *Hurtigruten* coastal steamer and have an hour or two to poke around. Unless you have unusual interests, that's about as much time you'll need. The fishing town's oddest experience can be had at the Royal & Ancient Polar Bear Society (see Sights, following). Those who spend more time here usually have a car, though they should take heed that ongoing natural-gas exploration off the coast has brought a lot of energy types to town, which in turn has caused hotel rates to rise prohibitively.

The **tourist office** (☎ 78 41 21 85; Rådhuset) operates out of the Polar Bear Society.

Sights

The small, well-done **Gjenreisningsmuseet** (Reconstruction Museum; ☎ 78 42 26 30; Kirkegata 21; adult/child Nkr40/15; ☼ 10am-6pm mid-Jun–Aug, 11am-2pm Sep–mid-Jun) details the rebuilding of Hammerfest after WWII. Nearby, the bizarre **Royal & Ancient Polar Bear Society** (☎ 78 41 31 00; Rådhuset; admission Nkr20; ☼ 6am-5.30pm 24 Jun–10 Aug, shorter hrs

rest of year) is dedicated to preserving northern culture, and has exhibits on Arctic hunting and local history. Any visitor can take out membership (Nkr150); members get a certificate, a champagne toast and their admission fee waived for life. The bone they use to 'knight' you – something a male walrus misses dearly – is a real crowd-pleaser.

Just west of the Reconstruction Museum on Kirkegata is Hammerfest's contemporary **church**, where you can often find reindeer grazing in the graveyard. For lovely views of the town, coast and mountains, climb the 86m-high **Salen Hill**; the 10-minute trail begins behind the small park directly up from the town hall.

Sleeping & Eating

AF Camping Storvannet (☎ 78 41 10 10; Storvannsveien; cabins Nkr320-340; ☼ late May–late Sep; **P**) Just 2km east of the town centre, this basic place offers simple rooms and cooking facilities.

Quality Hotel Hammerfest (☎ 78 42 96 00; hammerfest@quality.choice.no; Strandgata 2; s/d from Nkr645/795; **P**) Rooms at this chain hotel have loads of character – some resemble cabins on ocean liners.

Kafé RettVest (Sjøgata 10; mains Nkr65-130; ☼ 10am-5pm Mon-Fri, 10.30am-3pm Sat) This bustling café sits a block from the coastal streamer's dock and serves lasagne, tortellini, reindeer and omelettes. It isn't pretty, but the crowds lend it a good feel.

Sandberg bakery (☎ 78 41 18 08; Strandgate 19; sandwiches Nkr36; ☼ 9am-4pm Mon-Fri, 10am-3pm Sat) Serving painfully good pastries and coffee, this town favourite will give you reason to return.

Self-caterers can find a big **Coop supermarket** (9am-8pm Mon-Fri, 9am-6pm Sat) just east of the town hall.

Getting There & Away

The *Hurtigruten* coastal steamer stops here. Once or twice daily (four days weekly from mid-August to late June), buses run between Hammerfest and Alta (Nkr183, 2¾ hours). There's also a bus between Hammerfest and Kirkenes (Nkr744, 10¼ hours), via Karasjok (Nkr305, 4¾ hours).

ALTA
pop 17,350

If anything in Finnmark can be called cosmopolitan, Alta is it. It's easily Finnmark's largest town and, thanks to the Finnmark Municipal University, it's home to 2000 students. It's a sprawling place, however, stretching for at least 15km along the E6. The town's two main centres, Sentrum and Bossekop, are 3km apart. The biggest attraction in town is a collection of Unesco-protected rock carvings, which date from 4000 BC. If this doesn't grab your fancy, wilderness surrounds the city, as do opportunities to go ice fishing or dogsledding. Inquire at the **tourist office** (☎ 78 45 50 00; Sandfallveien 1; ⏱ 8am-3.30pm), 1km northwest of Sentrum off the E6.

Sights & Activities

Alta's main sight is the impressive, World Heritage–protected, **prehistoric rock art** (☎ 78 45 63 30; www.alta.museum.no; Altaveien 19; adult/child Nkr70/free; ⏱ 8am-11pm mid-Jun–mid-Aug, 8am-8pm early Jun & late Aug, 9am-6pm May & Sep) at Hjemmeluft, on the E6, 4km southwest of Bossekop. A 3km-long network of boardwalks leads past many of the 3000 rock carvings of hunting scenes, boats, fertility symbols, bears and reindeer that date back as far as 4000 BC. Wait for the snow to melt before visiting, otherwise the rocks will be covered. The admission charge includes guiding, and admission to the adjacent **Alta Museum**, with regional exhibits.

The Altaelva River rushes through the scenic 400m-deep **Sautso**, northern Europe's grandest canyon. It's best seen as part of a tour, which includes access to the Alta Power Station dam and a snack in a traditional Sami *lavvo* (tent). Contact the tourist office for more information.

Alta is also renowned for its salmon run; several local companies provide fishing tours. Again, the tourist office has details.

Sleeping & Eating

Wisløff Camping (☎ 78 43 43 03; www.wisloeff.no, in Norwegian; Øvre Alta; tent sites from Nkr70, cabins Nkr300-400; **P**) This award-winning place has happy

---

SIDE TRIP: KAUTOKEINO

Kautokeino remains emphatically Sami, and it resembles no other town in Norway. Around 85% of the townspeople have Sami as their first language, and it's not uncommon to see locals in traditional dress. Around one third of the population earn their living working in some aspect of reindeer herding.

Because the tourist industry isn't as developed (or as plastic) as that in Karasjok, there isn't as much to do. While this is problematic for some, others seek out the more authentic culture that can be enjoyed here.

The **tourist office** (☎ 78 48 65 00; ⏱ 10am-4pm Mon-Fri May-Aug) is in a kiosk by the main road through town. It's best to call ahead to make sure someone is there.

The best time to visit is during the **Easter Festival** (www.saami-easterfestival.org), when thousands of costumed Sami participate in championship reindeer racing, theatre and cultural events, and the little town busts at the seams.

The **Kautokeino Hamlet & Museum** (☎ 78 48 71 00; Boavonjarga 23; adult/child Nkr20/free; ⏱ 9am-7pm Mon-Sat & noon-7pm Sun mid-Jun–mid-Aug, 9am-3pm Mon-Fri mid-Aug–mid-Jun) presents a traditional Sami settlement, complete with an early home, temporary dwellings, a trapping exhibit, and several agricultural and pastoral outbuildings.

The very friendly **Kautokeino Camping** (☎ 78 48 54 00; Suomalvodda 16; tent sites Nkr100, cabins Nkr280-1000, motel rooms Nkr480-850; **P**) south of the river, has a Sami *lavvo* with an open fire.

Alfred's Kro (☎ 78 48 61; 18 Hannoluohkka 4; mains Nkr60-135; ⏱ 11am-6pm Mon-Fri, noon-6pm Sat & Sun) offers traditional dishes involving reindeer. For an unusual experience, visit **Madam Bongos** (☎ 78 48 61 60; dinner Nkr160) in the middle of nowhere, about 11km out of town. The dinner, always the same, features coffee, *bidus* (a vegetable and reindeer soup), reindeer steak, and berries with cream. You must call first to make an appointment and to get directions.

The town's bar, **Mara's Pub** (⏱ from 8pm Tue-Fri, from 1pm Sat & Sun) occasionally books small bands. Its rough wooden floors, booths and benches mark a town institution (it's the main nightlife spot), and costumed revellers shoehorn themselves in whenever a wedding occurs. It's beneath Alfred's Kro.

Buses connect Kautokeino with Alta (Nkr193, 2½ hours).

little beige and red cabins, 4km south of Bossekop on highway Rv93.

Alta HI Hostel (☎ 78 43 44 09; alta.hostel@van drerhjem.no; Midtbakkveien 52; dm/s/d Nkr180/270/300; ☾ late Jun–late Aug; **P**) Just a short walk from the Sentrum bus stop, this bright-red place has simple, good-value accommodation.

Hotel Aurora Borealis (☎ 78 45 78 00; www.hotel aurora.no; Saga; s/d Nkr750/850; **P**) This cosy, art-filled place is tucked away about 6km east of Bossekop on the E6. Staff will help plan snowmobile trips (including the option of spending a night in a Sami tent), dog-sledding excursions and fishing trips (the kitchen will even prepare what you catch).

Vica Hotell (☎ 78 43 47 11; www.vica.no; Fogde-bakken 6; s Nkr1020-1285, d Nkr1120-1485; **P**) In a wooden former farmhouse in Bossekop, this place offers free sauna, Internet access, and outdoor hot tub (perfect in winter). The rooms have character, and the public spaces are filled with stuffed creatures. The attached Henrik Restaurant (mains Nkr167 to Nkr299) serves huge portions from an Arctic menu that includes reindeer, elk, cod, and a warm soup of cloudberries served with homemade ice cream.

Omega (☎ 78 44 54 00; Markedsgata 14-16; lunch Nkr64-104, dinner Nkr89-229; ☾ 11am-midnight Mon-Wed, 11am-1am Thu-Sat) This popular joint serves excellent tapas and salads. One of these involves a filling piece of salmon baked under a layer of chevre and accompanied with fried onions, mushrooms and greens (Nkr89). Head next door to Alpha, a small red bar, for drinks with the Nordland cool crowd.

Getting There & Away

Norwegian Air and Braathens service the Alta airport, 3.5km east of Sentrum. A Nor-Way Bussekspress service runs between Tromsø and Alta (Nkr380, 6¾ hours, once daily). FFR buses run to and from Kautokeino (Nkr193, 2½ hours), Hammerfest (Nkr180, 2¾ hours), and Nordkapp (Nkr290, 5¾ hours) once or twice a day.

TROMSØ

pop 47,100

In contrast to some of the more sober communities dotting the north coast of Norway, Tromsø is a spirited place with street music, cultural happenings and more pubs per capita than any other Norwegian town – it even has its own brewery.

A backdrop of snowcapped peaks provides spectacular scenery, excellent hiking in summer, and great skiing and dogsledding from September to April. Many polar expeditions have departed from Tromsø, earning the city the nickname 'Gateway to the Arctic'. A statue of explorer Roald Amundsen (see p20 and p22), who headed some of the expeditions, stands in a little square down by the harbour.

Information

Main post office (Strandgata 41)

Tourist office (☎ 77 61 00 00; www.destinasjontromso.no; Storgata 61; ☾ 8.30am-6pm Mon-Fri & 10.30am-5pm Sat & Sun Jun–mid-Aug, 8.30am-4pm Mon-Fri mid-Aug–Jun)

Sights & Activities

The city centre has many period buildings, including the old cathedral, **Tromsø Domkirke** (Storgata 25) – one of Norway's largest wooden churches – and a **Catholic church** (Storgata 94), both built in 1861. Tromsø's most striking church, however, is the **Arctic Cathedral** (☎ 77 64 76 11; Hans Nilsensvei 41; adult/child Nkr22/free; ☾ 10am-8pm Jun-Aug, shorter hrs rest of year), on the mainland over the bridge. It's a freaky '60s building that looks like a lot of triangles stuck together.

Also worth a visit is the **Tromsø Museum** (☎ 77 64 50 00; www.imv.uit.no; Lars Thøringsvei 10; adult/child Nkr30/15; ☾ 9am-8pm Jun-Aug, shorter hrs Sep-May), at the southern end of Tromsøya. It's northern Norway's largest museum and has some well-presented displays on Arctic wildlife, Sami culture and regional history. Take bus No 28 from Stortorget. Nearby, the restored WWII fort at the **Tromsø Military Museum** (☎ 77 62 88 36; Solstrandveien; adult/child Nkr30/15; ☾ noon-5pm Wed-Sun Jun-Aug, noon-5pm Sun May & Sep) includes a former ammunition store with an exhibition on the 52,600-tonne German battleship *Tirpitz*, which was sunk by British air forces at Tromsø on 12 November 1944.

Modern and well executed, **Polaria** (☎ 77 75 01 00; Hjalmar Johansens gate 12; adult/child Nkr75/40; ☾ 10am-7pm mid-May–mid-Aug, noon-5pm mid-Aug–mid-Jun) features extensive displays on polar topics ranging from exploration to natural history, a 180-degree cinema showing an interesting film about Svalbard, and an aquarium with Arctic fish and four bearded seals.

The **Polar Museum** (☎ 77 68 43 73; www.polar museum.no; Søndre Tollbugata 11; adult/child Nkr43/10; ☾ 10am-7pm mid-June–mid-Aug, shorter hrs mid-Aug–mid-Jun) has exhibits on the Arctic frontier.

ARCTIC SCANDINAVIA TRAVEL ROUTES

Some are interesting, while others – such as those on hunting furry Arctic creatures – are of less universal appeal.

Established in 1877, the **Mack Brewery** (☎ 77 62 45 00; www.mack.no, in Norwegian; Storgata 5; tours Nkr100; ⏱ tours noon-4pm Mon-Thu) produces Mack's Pilsner, Isbjørn, Haakon and several dark beers; the tour fee includes beer stein, beer and souvenir. You can smell the brewery from a block away.

On sleepless nights you can stroll by the light of the midnight sun through the 1.6-hectare **botanical garden** (☎ 77 64 50 78; Breivika; admission free; ⏱ 24 hrs), which blooms brightly despite its northern locale. Take bus No 20. You can get a fine city view by taking the **cable car** (☎ 77 63 87 37; Solliveien 12; return adult/child Nkr70/30; ⏱ 10am-5pm Apr-Sep, to 1am clear nights when midnight sun in view) 420m

up Mt Storsteinen. Take bus No 26 from Stortorget harbour.

Festivals & Events

Tromsø International Film Festival (☎ 77 75 30 90; www.tiff.no) is held in mid-January. Perhaps the most exciting of Norway's film festivals, it shows forgotten classics, weird shorts, American independents and films from Northern Norway, the Baltic States, and elsewhere.

Sleeping

Tromsø Camping (☎ 77 63 80 37; www.tromsocamping .no; tent sites/cabins Nkr150/400-900; ℗) This place on the mainland, 2km east of the Arctic Cathedral, has some spots next to a small river; others are less spectacular. Cabins have cooking facilities. Take bus 26.

SVALBARD

Svalbard is *the* destination for an unforgettable holiday. This wondrous archipelago is the world's most readily accessible piece of the polar north and one of the most spectacular places imaginable. Vast icebergs and floes choke the seas, and ice fields and glaciers frost the lonely heights, but Svalbard also hosts a surprising variety of flora and fauna, including seals, walruses, Arctic foxes and polar bears.

Trips to Svalbard are best planned. When you arrive you'll almost certainly want to participate in some kind of organised trek or tour, and many need to be booked early. To learn more, visit the tourist board's excellent website, www.svalbard.net.

Longyearbyen, the largest settlement on Svalbard, has an airport with flights to and from Tromsø. You'll find all the usual facilities, including a post office, a bank (with an ATM), and a library. Barentsburg, the Russian settlement, is about 40km west, while Ny Ålesund, a Norwegian research station with an airstrip, is about 100km northwest. Apart from in the immediate vicinity of the settlements, there are no roads.

Dozens of exciting tour options are listed on the tourist board website. Accommodation, transport and meals are usually included in longer tours, but day tours are also available (see under Longyearbyen, following). The most popular tour operators:

- **Spitsbergen Travel** (☎ 79 02 61 00; www.spitsbergentravel.no) Offers week-long cruises, multi-day snowmobile safaris, five-day dogsledding trips (Nkr10,300) and 12-day trekking tours (Nkr16,600).

- **Basecamp Spitsbergen** (☎ 79 02 46 00; www.basecampexplorer.com) Offers unique lodging options, including rooms on an ice-locked ship. It arranges short ski trips, five-day dogsled and snowmobile expeditions (Nkr9000), and more.

- **Svalbard Wildlife Service** (☎ 79 02 56 60; www.wildlife.no) Offers varied tours, including camping, kayaking, glacier exploration and seven-day summer ski trips to Ny Åesund (Nkr10,950).

Longyearbyen

This frontier-like community with a population of 1700 is strewn with coal-mining detritus and enjoys a superb backdrop, including two glacier tongues: Longyearbreen and Lars Hjertabreen.

At the **Svalbard Museum** (☎ 79 02 13 84; Skjæringa; admission Nkr30; ⏱ 11am-7pm Mon-Fri, noon-4pm Sat, 1-7pm Sun Jul & Aug, shorter hrs rest of year), west of the centre, exhibits cover mining, 17th-century whaling, and the history, climate, geology, wildlife and exploration of the archipelago.

Tromsø HI Hostel (☎ 77 65 76 28; tromso.hostel@ vandrerhjem.no; Åsgårdveien 9; dm/s/d Nkr175/275/405; ☽ mid-Jun–mid-Aug; P) This clean and tidy basic hostel sits 1.5km west of the city centre. Phone for directions.

Hotell Nord (☎ 77 68 31 59; www.hotellnord.no; Parkgata 4; s Nkr450-540, d Nkr590-695; P) This friendly place, up on the hillside just west of the centre, feels like an informal guesthouse. The cosy rooms are available with or without private bathroom, and rates include breakfast.

Comfort Hotel With (☎ 77 68 70 00; www.with .no; Sjøgata 35-37; s/d Nkr1290/1490, summer & weekend Nkr805/970; P) Waterside, amenity-filled rooms along with fine (and complimentary) dinner buffets make this place a good option for a more upmarket experience.

The tourist office books rooms in private homes for around Nkr250/450 for a single/ double. Most are within a 10-minute walk of the centre.

Eating

Meieriet (☎ 77 61 36 39; Grønnegata 37; mains Nkr56-136; ☽ 8am-1.30am Mon-Thu, 8am-3am Fri, noon-3am Sat, noon-1.30am Sun) This characterful place adorned with red leather sofas, antique radios and a pool table serves mostly stirfried dishes. There's also a weekend DJ.

Amtmandens Datter (☎ 77 68 49 06; Grønnegata 81; mains Nkr88-135; ☽ noon-2.30am Mon-Sat, 3pm-3am Sun) Pub-like and student-friendly, this place serves beer, salads and vegetarian sandwiches. It's a great place to hang out, with Internet access and plenty of newspapers and board games.

Svertshuset Skarven (☎ 77 60 07 25; Strandtorget 1; mains Nkr125-250; ☽ from 4pm) Near the harbour

---

Many short trips and day tours that vary with the season are on offer, including fossil hunting (Nkr290), mine tours (Nkr590), boat trips to Barentsburg and Pyramidien (Nkr920), dogsledding (from Nkr750), dogsledding on *wheels* (Nkr550), diving trips (Nkr1200), glacier hiking (Nkr490), ice-caving (from Nkr520), kayaking (from Nkr550), mountain biking (Nkr420), horse-riding (Nkr420), and snowmobiling (from Nkr1250). Contact the tourist board for more details.

Accommodation options include the popular **Longyearbyen Camping** (☎ 79 02 10 68; info@ terrapolaris.com; per person Nkr80; ☽ late Jun–early Sep), next to the airport and about an hour's walk from town; **Mary-Ann's Polar Rigg** (☎ 79 02 37 02; riggen@longyearbyen.net; s/d Nkr395/550), a simple guesthouse with kitchenette and hot tub (linen is Nkr100 extra and breakfast is Nkr95); **Spitsbergen Nybyen Gjestehus** (☎ 79 02 63 00; spitsbergen.guesthouse@spitsbergentravel.no; s Nkr495-650, d Nkr840-990), a large, functional building south of the centre; and **Basecamp Spitsbergen** (☎ 79 02 46 00; www .basecampexplorer.com; s Nkr800-1550, d Nkr950-1750), a top-notch establishment featuring rooms with a seal hunter's cabin look and a common space with a glass roof for polar night viewing.

For food, **Huset** (☎ 79 02 25 00; mains Nkr195-255), west of the centre, remains a popular choice for both Arctic- and French-style meals. The good food becomes even more impressive if you remember where exactly you are eating it. In the central shopping mall you'll find the Svalbardbutikken supermarket and **Kafé Busen** (mains under Nkr100), which serves daily specials as well as typical cafeteria fare.

SAS and Braathens fly regularly from Tromsø to Longyearbyen. A taxi to town costs Nkr100 to Nkr120. The airport bus (Nkr35) serves the various accommodation options.

Around Svalbard

Independent travel around Svalbard is heavily regulated in order to protect both the virgin landscape and you. Because of this, travel to the very few settlements is usually done as part of a tour. One of these settlements is **Barentsburg** (pop ulation 900), a Soviet-era relic. Simultaneously depressing and fascinating, this tiny Russian town still mines and exports coal. A statue of Lenin stares over the bleak human-made landscape and the impressive natural landscape that surrounds it.

Tourist cruises might also bring you to **Ny Ålesund** which, at latitude 79°N, is a wild place with none-too-friendly scientists and downright hostile Arctic terns (you may have to beat the latter off with a stick). Remnants of past glories include a **stranded locomotive**, previously used for transporting coal, and an **airship pylon**, used by Amundsen and Nobile on their successful crossing of the North Pole in 1926.

ARCTIC SCANDINAVIA TRAVEL ROUTES

and festooned with nautical instruments, this local favourite serves an Arctic menu that includes a delicious whale soup (Nkr79), fish burgers and reindeer steaks.

You can buy fresh boiled shrimp from fishing boats at Stortorget harbour. The harbourside **Coop Mega supermarket** (Stortorget 1) has a cheap 2nd-floor cafeteria and a nice view over the water.

Entertainment

Tromsø enjoys a thriving nightlife. On Friday and Saturday most nightspots stay open past 4am. Many also serve light meals. The following recommendations merely scratch the surface.

Blå Rock Café (☎ 77 61 00 20; Strandgata 14; 🕒 11.30am-2am Sun-Thu, 11.30am-3am Fri & Sat) This place attracts a young, cool crowd. Instruments and pictures hang from the rafters, 75 types of beer spill on the ground, and live bands and DJs (playing rock, naturally) rattle the rafters.

Strøket (☎ 77 68 44 00; Storgata 46; 🕒 4pm-1.30am Tue-Thu, 4pm-3am Fri, noon-3am Sat, 7pm-midnight Sun) The three floors of restaurant, bar, and disco pull in the hipsters like pollen to insects.

Getting There & Away

Tromsø is the main airport hub for northern Norway, with direct flights to Oslo, Bergen, Bodø, Trondheim, Alta, Hammerfest, Kirkenes and Longyearbyen. Airport buses (Nkr40) depart from the Radisson SAS Hotel Tromsø. A taxi costs Nkr100 to Nkr200.

There are two or three daily express buses between Tromsø and Narvik (Nkr315, four to five hours). Buses to and from Alta (Nkr355, 6¾ hours) run once daily.

The *Hurtigruten* coastal steamer stops here and is the best route south to Bodø, where you can get a train back to Mo i Rana.

ITINERARY 2: NORTHWEST FINLAND

A trip through the wilds of northwest Finland from Rovaniemi, the gateway to Lapland, though some of Scandinavia's remotest national parks and across the border into Norway.

Northwestern Lapland is best known for its downhill ski resorts, superb summer hiking, and rafting and canoeing on the mighty

FAST FACTS

▪ **Access for independent travellers** Excellent

▪ **Best time to travel** May to September

▪ **Difficulty level** Easy to moderate

▪ **Don't forget** Camera, film, binoculars, insect repellent, head-net and, if driving, spare tyres, basic tools, plenty of food and water, blankets, and first-aid kit

▪ **Don't miss** Skiing in Levi, hiking In Pallas-Ounastunturi National Park

▪ **Gateway city** Rovaniemi, Finland

▪ **Length of route** Approximately 580km

▪ **Modes of travel** Car, bus

▪ **Recommended map** Eurokarte *Finland* 1:750,000

▪ **Time needed** Three to 10 days

Muoionjoki and Tornionjoki Rivers, which form the border between Finland and Sweden. The region is sparsely populated and offers some of the best-preserved wilderness in Europe. Whether you just pass through on a road trip or set off on an extensive trek, allow enough time to get a real sense of this wide-open wilderness country.

Getting Around

See p298 for details on travel options in the Scandinavian far north.

ROVANIEMI

For details on Rovaniemi, see p314.

KITTILÄ

☎ 016 / pop 3000

According to legend, Kittilä was named after Kitti, daughter of the mighty witch Päiviö, who appears in local fairytales. Although the town is the main service centre for north-western Lapland, Kittilä has little to recommend it to travellers except as a jumping-off point for ski resort Levi, 20km to the north.

The few sights include the old wooden **church**, designed by CL Engel and completed in 1831, and the **Taidemuseo Einari Junttila** (☷ Mon-Sat), which commemorates a local artist who once lived in the building.

The **Kittilä open-air museum** (☷ 9am-6pm Tue-Sun Jun-Aug), 3km south of the village, features a collection of traditional buildings. In early July, Kittilä hosts a traditional **market** that attracts folks from all over Lapland.

If you do decide to stay, **Hotelli Kittilä** (☎ 643 201; www.levi.fi/hotellikittila, in Finnish; Valtatie 49; s/d €75/110; P ✗ ☒), at the northern end of the village, is the town's only real hotel. The restaurant serves a decent buffet lunch (€8 to €14).

There are daily flights between Helsinki and Kittilä. The airport is 4km north of town. There are seven buses a day from Rovaniemi to Kittilä (€22, 2½ hours) and on to Levi (€25, three hours).

LEVI & SIRKKA

☎ 016

Levi is a major skiing centre built around the village of Sirkka, and is one of the most popular ski resorts in Lapland, particularly with the party crowd. The ski season usually runs from November to May. In summer and autumn, trekking and mountain biking are the main outdoor activities.

The **tourist office** (☎ 639 3300; www.levi.fi; Myllyojoentie 2; ☷ 9am-4.30pm Mon-Fri, 11am-5.30pm Sat & Sun) handles accommodation bookings as well as snowmobile safaris, dogsledding treks and reindeer rides.

The ski resort has 45 downhill slopes and 19 lifts. Two lifts operate in summer, and mountain bikes can be hired from the ski-hire shop. Ice-fishing on the frozen lake is popular in spring.

Accommodation prices go through the roof in the peak seasons: February to May, and December. From May to September, though, you can get a comfortable cabin sleeping up to five people for as little as €45 a night, and hotel prices drop to rates comparable to those anywhere else in Finland.

The best budget choice in Levi is **Levin Matkailumaja** (☎ 641 126; www.levi.fi/matkailumaja, in Finnish; Levintie 1625; cottages €50-135), which has a group of cosy, self-contained cottages in the middle of the village.

There are seven buses a day from Rovaniemi to Levi (€25, three hours) via Kittilä.

SIDE TRIP: HETTA & PALLAS-OUNASTUNTURI NATIONAL PARK

The village of Hetta is a good base for treks into the surrounding area. There's a municipal **tourist office** (☎ 556 211) at the junction of the Hetta main road and the route toward Karasjok (Norway).

The nearby **Pallas-Ounastunturi National Park** (www.metsa.fi/natural/nationalparks/pallas-ouna stunturi/index.htm) protects the area surrounding **Pallastunturi Fell**. The main summer attraction is the excellent 60km trekking route from Hetta to **Hotel Pallastunturi** (☎ 016-532 441) inside the park, but the area also offers excellent winter skiing. The route is one of the easiest long-distance walks in Lapland and can easily be completed in four days. There are seven free wilderness huts, but they can be packed with people in summer, so it's wise to carry a tent.

The **Fell Lapland Nature Centre** (☎ 647950; www.enontekio.fi; Peuratie) is the local tourist office and a visitor centre for the Pallas-Ounastunturi National Park. Hetta has lots of accommodation, including summer camping and cabins. **Hetan Majatalo** (☎ 554 0400; hetan-majatalo@co.inet.fi; s/d €57/76; ☷ year-round) is a fine guesthouse with country-style rooms, all with TV and bathroom.

The long Ounasjoki, one of the best canoeing rivers in Lapland, runs from Hetta in the north to Rovaniemi in the south, and passes Sirkka and Kittilä. Canoes and equipment can be hired at **Pole Star Safaris** (☎ 641 688, 049-391 090) at the Levin Portti tourist centre in Levi. Companies in Kittilä also offer equipment hire.

There is one bus a week direct from Rovaniemi to Pallas. Buses to Hetta run daily from Rovaniemi (€36.60, five hours) via Kittilä.

ARCTIC SCANDINAVIA
TRAVEL ROUTES

KILPISJÄRVI
☎ 016
The remote 'left arm' of Finland is home to some of Finland's highest mountains (which aren't very high), but this scenic outpost on the shores of Lake Kilpisjärvi is really the preserve of serious trekkers or travellers with private transport.

The area offers fantastic trekking. Most people climb **Saana Fell** (1029m), or walk (or take a boat taxi, €13) to the **Malla Nature Park**, where you can stand on the joint border of Sweden, Norway and Finland. Serious hikers can walk to **Halti Fell** (1328m), the highest in Finland. There are wilderness huts en route, but a map is essential. Information and accommodation are available at the hiking centre, **Kilpisjärven Retkeilykeskus** (☎ 537 771; retkeilykeskus@sunpoint.net; ☺ early Aug–late Sep), also the best place to find advice on routes.

There's a daily bus between Rovaniemi and Kilpisjärvi (€47.50, eight hours) via Kittilä. From early June to mid-September **Eskelisen** (www.eskelisen-lapinlinjat.com) runs daily buses to Tromsø (€27.60, 3½ hours).

ESSENTIAL FACTS

DANGERS & ANNOYANCES
For information on dangers posed by insects and wildlife, see p264. For information on how to prevent and deal with hypothermia, see p332.

FURTHER READING
For more in-depth coverage, Lonely Planet publishes individual guides to Finland, Norway and Sweden. Another useful publication is Lonely Planet's *Scandinavian Phrasebook* (with language background and phrases in Danish, Finnish, Icelandic, Norwegian and Swedish).

The Svalbard boxed text (p324) in this chapter is intended to provide information for tourists and casual independent travellers only. Those who want more background information or wish to mount a longer expedition should look for *Svalbard: Spitsbergen, Franz Josef Land, Jan Mayen*, by long-time Svalbard resident Andreas Umbreit.

If you're planning any multiday hikes *Walking in Norway*, by Connie Roos, includes several routes in Arctic Norway that are accessible by public transport.

MONEY
Finland is the only Nordic country to adopt the euro. In Norway the currency is the Norwegian krone (Nkr); in Sweden it is the Swedish krona (Skr). ATMs are available in the larger Arctic towns and accept Visa, Plus, EC, Cirrus, Eurocard or MasterCard.

Most currencies can be easily exchanged in Scandinavia, but US dollars, pounds sterling and euros are the best to carry. *Bureaux de change* such as Forex and post offices tend to offer better rates, and they charge lower fees or commissions than banks.

For the most part, tipping isn't required in Scandinavia, although if you round up the bill or leave a little something in recognition of good service, it won't be refused.

TELEPHONE
You can ring abroad from almost any phone box in Scandinavia, though with the popularity of mobile phones there are fewer and fewer of them. Often they accept phonecards or credit cards only. Reverse-charge (collect) calls are usually possible, and communicating with the local operator in English should not be much of a problem. Local libraries almost always have Internet access.

Mobile Phones
Most populated parts of Scandinavia use GSM 900/1800, compatible with the system in the rest of Europe and Australasia but not with the North American GSM 1900 or the totally different system in Japan. You can hire mobile phones everywhere except Norway, and it's particularly easy in mobile-centric Finland. Another option is to buy a local SIM card with a rechargeable account. This is particularly good value in Sweden and Finland.

Coverage across the north is patchy, though, and may not be worth the cost. Local telephone companies and national tourist offices can advise on coverage.

Phone Codes
Norway has no domestic telephone codes.
Country code Norway ☎ 47, Sweden ☎ 46, Finland ☎ 358
Directory assistance ☎ 411
Emergency ☎ 112
International access code ☎ 00
National/international operator Norway ☎ 180/181, Sweden ☎ 118118/118119, Finland ☎ 020202/020208

Phonecards

Public telephones that accept stored-value phonecards are the norm, and in some places coin-operated phones are almost impossible to find. Phonecards are available from post offices and shops. More and more public telephone kiosks are giving callers the opportunity to pay by credit card.

TIME

Time in Norway and Sweden is one hour ahead of GMT/UTC, the same as most of Western Europe. Finland is two hours ahead of GMT/UTC. When it's noon in Tromsø or Kiruna, it's 1pm in Finland, 11am in London, 6am in New York and 9pm in Sydney.

Norway, Sweden and Finland all observe daylight-saving time. Clocks are set ahead one hour on the last Sunday in March and are set back one hour on the last Sunday in October.

TOURIST INFORMATION

All larger Arctic communities have a tourist office with English brochures, free maps and helpful multilingual staff. Most are open long hours in summer and short hours (or not at all) in winter. They will book hotels and make reservations for transport and tours; a small charge may apply. In smaller villages information for travellers is generally available from the town council.

Some useful contacts for pre-departure planning:

Finnish Tourist Board (www.visitfinland.com)
Finnmark Tourist Board (www.visitnorthcape.com)
Norwegian Tourist Board (www.visitnorway.com)
Swedish Tourism Associated (www.turism.se) Lists Sweden's tourist information offices and their contact details.
Swedish Travel and Tourism Council (www.visit-sweden.com)
Virtual Finland (virtual.finland.fi)

VISAS

Citizens of the UK, the USA, Canada, Ireland, Australia and New Zealand don't need visas if visiting a Scandinavian country for less than three months; the same is true for citizens of EU and European Economic Area countries and most Commonwealth countries (except South Africa and several other African and Pacific countries). Citizens of South Africa and other African, Asian and some Eastern European coun-

---

GATEWAY CITIES

Getting to Mo i Rana

If you want to fly to Mo i Rana you'll have to fly with **SAS** (☎ 81 52 04 00; www.scandinavian.net) to Trondheim and then hop on a **Braathens** (☎ 81 52 00 00; www.braathens.no) or **Widerøe** (☎ 81 00 12 00; www.wideroe.no) flight to Mo i Rana.

Alternatively, **NSB** (Norges Statsbaner or Norwegian State Railways; ☎ 81 50 08 88; www.nsb.no) runs trains from Oslo, and **Nor-Way Bussekspress** (☎ 82 02 13 00; www.nor-way.no) runs buses on the same route.

Getting to Tromsø

Tromsø is the main airport hub for northern Norway, with direct flights to Oslo, Bergen and Trondheim with SAS, Braathens, Widerøe and discount airline **Norwegian Air** (☎ 81 52 18 15; www.norwegian.no).

Tromsø is also served by **Hurtigruten ferries** (☎ 81 03 00 00; www.hurtigruten.no) and Nor-Way Bussekspress coaches.

Getting to Rovaniemi

Finnair (☎ 600-140 140; www.finnair.com) has daily flights to Rovaniemi from Helsinki, Kemi and Oulu.

VR Ltd Finnish Railways (☎ 600-4192; www.vr.fi) trains are the best way to travel overland between Helsinki and Rovaniemi as they're quicker and cheaper than the bus. There are eight daily trains (via Oulu), including four overnight services.

---

tries need tourist visas for entry to Scandinavian countries; these are only available in advance.

With a valid passport most travellers will be able to visit Scandinavian countries for up to three (sometimes even six) months, provided they have some sort of onward or return ticket and/or 'sufficient means of support' (money). Except at international airports, it's unlikely that immigration officials will give you and your passport more than a cursory glance – if that.

Websites with useful information for visitors with visa questions:

Finnish Directorate of Immigration (www.uvi.fi)
Norwegian Directorate of Immigration (www.udi.no)
Swedish Migration Board (www.migrationsverket.se)

HEALTH

Health

CONTENTS

BEFORE YOU GO

Prevention is key to staying healthy while abroad. A little planning before departure, particularly for pre-existing illnesses, will save trouble later. See your dentist before a long trip, carry a spare pair of contact lenses and glasses, and take your optical prescription with you. Bring medications in their original, clearly labelled containers. A signed and dated letter from your doctor describing your medical conditions and medications, including generic names, is also a good idea. If carrying syringes or needles, be sure to have a doctor's letter documenting their medical necessity.

INSURANCE

If you're an EU citizen or from Switzerland, Iceland, Norway or Liechtenstein, the European Health Insurance Card will cover you for emergency health care or in the case of accident while in European Economic Area (EEA) countries, which include Denmark, Finland, Norway and Sweden.

The card will not cover you for non-emergencies or emergency repatriation. It is being phased in from mid-2004 and will be fully operational by the end of 2005. Old documentation (such as the previously used

E111) will be available in the interim. Every family member will need a separate card. In the UK, application forms are available from post offices or can be downloaded from the Department of Health website (www.dh.gov.uk). Note that Greenland isn't part of the EEA but is covered by a separate reciprocal health-care agreement with the UK.

Citizens of other countries should find out if there is a reciprocal arrangement for free medical care between their country and the country visited. For travel to Arctic North America or Arctic Russia you should take out health insurance. If you do need health insurance, strongly consider a policy that covers you for the worst possible scenario, such as an accident requiring emergency evacuation. Find out in advance if your insurance plan will make payments directly to providers or reimburse you later for overseas health expenditures. The former option is generally preferable, as it doesn't require you to pay out of pocket in a foreign country.

RECOMMENDED VACCINATIONS

The World Health Organization (WHO) recommends that all travellers should be covered for diphtheria, tetanus, measles, mumps, rubella and polio, regardless of their destination. Since most vaccines don't produce immunity until at least two weeks after they're given, visit a physician at least six weeks before departure.

ONLINE RESOURCES

The WHO's publication *International Travel and Health* is revised annually and is available online at www.who.int/ith. Other useful

---

CHECK BEFORE YOU GO

It's usually a good idea to consult your government's travel-health website (if available) before departure:

- **Australia** www.dfat.gov.au/travel
- **Canada** www.travelhealth.gc.ca
- **United Kingdom** www.doh.gov.uk /traveladvice
- **United States** www.cdc.gov/travel

websites include www.mdtravelhealth.com (travel-health recommendations for every country, updated daily), www.fitfortravel.scot .nhs.uk (general travel advice), www.agecon cern.org.uk (advice on travel for the elderly) and www.mariestopes.org.uk (information on women's health and contraception).

FURTHER READING
Health Advice for Travellers (currently called the 'T6' leaflet) is an annually updated leaflet by the Department of Health in the UK available free in post offices. It contains some general information, legally required and recommended vaccines for different countries, and reciprocal health agreements. Lonely Planet's *Travel with Children* includes advice on travel health for younger children. Other recommended references include *Traveller's Health,* by Dr Richard Dawood (Oxford University Press), and *The Traveller's Good Health Guide,* by Ted Lankester (Sheldon Press).

IN TRANSIT

DEEP VEIN THROMBOSIS (DVT)
Blood clots may form in the legs during plane flights, chiefly because of prolonged immobility – the longer the flight, the greater the risk. The chief symptom of DVT is swelling or pain of the foot, ankle or calf, usually but not always on just one side. When a blood clot travels to the lungs, it may cause chest pain and breathing difficulties. Travellers with any of these symptoms should immediately seek medical attention.

To prevent the development of DVT on long flights you should walk about the cabin, contract leg muscles while sitting, drink plenty of fluids, and avoid alcohol and tobacco.

JET LAG & MOTION SICKNESS
To avoid jet lag (common when crossing more than five time zones), try drinking plenty of nonalcoholic fluids and eating light meals. Upon arrival, get exposure to natural sunlight and readjust your schedule (for meals, sleep and so on) as soon as possible.

Antihistamines such as dimenhydrinate (Dramamine) and meclizine (Antivert, Bonine) are usually the first choice for treating motion sickness. A herbal alternative is ginger.

IN GREENLAND & THE ARCTIC

AVAILABILITY & COST OF HEALTH CARE
Good health care is readily available, and for minor, self-limiting illnesses pharmacists can dispense valuable advice and over-the-counter medication. They can also advise when more specialised help is required. The standard of dental care is usually good; however, it is sensible to have a dental checkup before a long trip.

In all Arctic communities you will find some sort of medical care. In Greenland and Arctic Scandinavia health care is excellent and in Scandinavia it's generally free to those carrying a European Health Insurance Card (see p220). Note that in Sweden travellers still have to pay some treatment costs. Facilities in Arctic North America are also modern and well equipped, but treatment can be expensive so you'd be well advised to take out comprehensive travel insurance. In Arctic Russia facilities are generally older and below Western standards, and there's often a shortage of basic supplies and equipment. Access to medical treatment is generally by cash payment at Western rates. Travellers in remote regions should bring their own syringes with them.

In all Arctic communities there will be some medical facilities available, but many smaller settlements do not have a resident doctor. Local nursing stations are, however, generally very well equipped and staffed with specially trained nurses qualified to deal with most problems. For serious illness or emergencies a medical evacuation is generally necessary and can be exorbitantly expensive. Make sure your insurance covers you for this.

INFECTIOUS DISEASES
Tick-borne encephalitis is spread by tick bites. It is a serious infection of the brain, and vaccination is advised for those in risk areas who are unable to avoid tick bites (such as campers, forestry workers and ramblers). Two doses of vaccine will give a year's protection; three doses up to three years.

Rabies is a viral infection of the brain and spinal cord that is almost always fatal. Rabid dogs and foxes are found in Arctic areas, and you should be very wary of any animal acting strangely. The rabies virus is carried in the saliva of infected animals; if an animal bites or scratches you, clean the wound with large amounts of soap and water and contact local health authorities immediately.

Although tuberculosis is increasingly common in Arctic communities the disease is only spread through prolonged close contact with an infected individual.

TRAVELLER'S DIARRHOEA

In most Arctic areas tap water is safe, but it's best to always check with a local. If you're unsure you should boil, filter or chemically disinfect (with iodine tablets) any water you drink. Eat fresh fruits or vegetables only if cooked or peeled; be wary of dairy products that might contain unpasteurized milk. Make sure meats are properly cooked, and avoid buffet-style meals. If a restaurant is full of locals the food is probably safe.

If you develop diarrhoea, be sure to drink plenty of fluids, preferably an oral rehydration solution such as dioralyte. A few loose stools don't require treatment, but if you start having more than four or five stools a day you should start taking an antibiotic (usually a quinoline drug) and an antidiarrhoeal agent (such as loperamide). If diarrhoea is bloody, persists for more than 72 hours or is accompanied by fever, shaking, chills or severe abdominal pain, you should seek medical attention.

ENVIRONMENTAL HAZARDS
Giardia

Giardia is an intestinal parasite that lives in the faeces of humans and animals and is normally contracted through drinking water. It is one of the most common parasitic infections in humans in Arctic regions. Problems can start several weeks after you've been exposed to the parasite, and symptoms may sometimes remit for a few days and then return; this can go on for several weeks or even longer.

The earliest signs are a swelling of the stomach, followed by pale faeces, diarrhoea, frequent gas and possibly headache, nausea and depression. If you exhibit these symptoms you should visit a doctor for treatment.

Hypothermia & Frostbite

Proper preparation will reduce the risks of getting hypothermia. Even on a warm day in the Arctic the weather can change rapidly. Take waterproof garments and warm layers, and inform others of your route.

Acute hypothermia follows a sudden drop of temperature over a short time. Chronic hypothermia is caused by a gradual loss of temperature over hours.

Hypothermia starts with shivering, loss of judgement and clumsiness. Unless rewarming occurs, the sufferer deteriorates into apathy, confusion and coma. Prevent further heat loss by seeking shelter, wearing warm, dry clothing, drinking hot, sweet drinks and sharing body warmth.

Frostbite is caused by freezing of and subsequent damage to bodily extremities. It is dependent on wind-chill, temperature and length of exposure. Frostbite starts as frostnip (white, numb areas of skin) from which complete recovery is expected with rewarming. As frostbite develops, the skin blisters and becomes black. Loss of damaged tissue eventually occurs. Wear adequate clothing, stay dry, keep well hydrated and ensure you have adequate calorie intake to prevent frostbite. Treatment involves rapid rewarming. Avoid refreezing and rubbing the affected areas.

Insect Bites & Stings

As the surface of the Arctic tundra melts it becomes waterlogged as the permafrost prevents water from draining. Couple this with the warmer temperatures of summer, and you've got a perfect breeding ground for insects. Arctic mosquitoes can be ferocious and can be the bane of your existence on a summer trip up north. Bring strong DEET-based insect repellent and a head-net, and wear long-sleeved shirts and long trousers.

Bees and wasps cause real problems only to those with a severe allergy (anaphylaxis). If you have such an allergy, carry EpiPen or similar adrenaline injections.

TRAVELLING WITH CHILDREN

All travellers with children should know how to treat minor ailments and when to seek medical treatment. Make sure the children are up to date with routine vaccinations, and discuss possible travel vaccines well before departure, as some vaccines are not suitable for children under a year old.

Remember to avoid contaminated food and water. If your child has vomiting or diarrhoea, lost fluid and salts must be replaced. It may be helpful to take rehydration powders for reconstituting with boiled water.

Children should be encouraged to avoid and mistrust any dogs or other mammals because of the risk of rabies (see opposite) and other diseases.

SEXUAL HEALTH

Condoms are widely available across the Arctic. When buying condoms, look for a European CE mark, which means they have been rigorously tested. Keep them in a cool, dry place or they may crack and perish.

Emergency contraception is most effective if taken within the next 24 hours after unprotected sex. The International Planned Parent Federation (www.ippf.org) can advise on the availability of contraception in different countries.

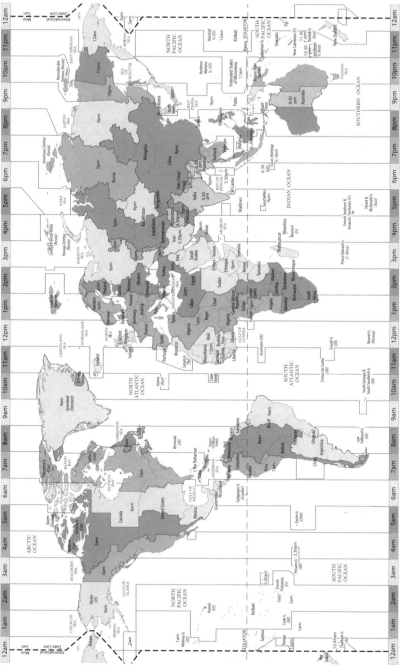

Language

CONTENTS

The official language of Greenland is Greenlandic (see p339 for some useful words and phrases), one of many Inuit dialects spoken in the Arctic. Regional variations do occur – West Greenlanders can understand variations of West Greenlandic, but their dialect and East Greenlandic are not mutually intelligible.

The second language of Greenland is Danish, which is spoken by nearly everyone. Only a small percentage of Greenlanders speak a language other than Greenlandic and Danish.

DANISH

PRONUNCIATION

You may find Danish pronunciation difficult. Consonants can be drawled, swallowed and even omitted completely, creating, in conjunction with vowels, the peculiarity of the glottal stop or *stød*. Its sound is rather as a Cockney would say the 'tt' in 'bottle'. Stress usually falls on the first syllable. As a general rule, the best advice is to listen and learn. Good luck!

Vowels

Danish	Pronunciation	Guide
a	a	as in 'act'
	aa	as the 'a' in 'father'
e/æ	e	a short, flat 'e' as in 'met'
eg	ai	as in 'aisle'
i	i	as in 'hit'
	ee	as the 'ee' in 'bee'
o	o	a short 'o' as in 'pot'
ov	ow	as the 'ow' in 'growl', but shorter
u	oo	as in 'book'
	a	before 'n', as the 'a' in 'walk'
y	ew	a long, sharp 'u' – purse your lips and say 'ee'
ø	er	as the 'er' in 'fern', but shorter
øj	oy	as in 'toy'
å	or	as the 'a' in 'walk'

Consonants

Consonants are pronounced as in English with the exception of the following:

Danish	Pronunciation	Guide
d	d	as in 'dog'
	th	as in 'these'
g	g	before vowels, a hard 'g' as in 'get'
j	y	as in 'yet'
r	r	a rolling 'r' in the throat, abruptly cut short
ch	sh	as in 'ship'

ACCOMMODATION

I'm looking for a ...
Jeg leder efter ...
yai *li·*thaa *ef·*daa ...

camp site
en campingplads   in *kam·*ping·plas
guesthouse
et pensionat   it pang·sho·*naat*
hotel
et hotel   it ho·tel

LANGUAGE

youth hostel
et vandrehjem it *van*·dra·yem

What is the address?
Hvad er adressen?
va er a·*draa*·sen
Could you write it down, please?
Kunne De/du skrive adressen ned? (pol/inf)
koo·ne dee/doo *sgree*·ve a·*draa*·sen nith
Do you have any rooms available?
Har I ledige værelser?
haa ee *li*·thee·e *verl*·saa

I'd like (a) ...
Jeg vil gerne have ...
yai vi *ger*·ne ha ...
  bed
  en seng in seng
  single room
  et enkeltværelse it *eng*·geld·verl·se
  double bed
  en dobbeltseng in *do*·beld·seng
  room
  et værelse it *verl*·se
  double room
  et dobbeltværelse it *do*·beld·verl·se
  room with a bathroom
  et værelse med bad it *verl*·se me bath
  to share a dorm
  plads i en sovesal plas ee in *sow*·saal

How much is it ...?
Hvor meget koster det ...?
vor *ma*·eth *kos*·daa di ...
  per night
  per nat per naad
  per person
  per person per per·*son*

May I see the room?
Må jeg se værelset?
mor yai si *verl*·seth
Where is the toilet?
Hvor er toilettet?
vor er toy·*le*·deth
I'm/we're leaving now/tomorrow.
Jeg/Vi rejser nu/i morgen.
yai/vee *rai*·sa noo/i morn

CONVERSATION & ESSENTIALS
Hello.
Goddag/Hej. go·*daa*/hai
Goodbye.
Farvel. faa·*vel*
Yes.
Ja. ya

No.
Nej. nai
Thank you.
Tak. taag
You're welcome.
Selv tak. sel taag
Excuse me.
Undskyld. orn·sgewl
Sorry.
Beklager. bi·*kla*·aa
What's your name?
Hvad hedder De/du? va *hi*·thaa dee/doo (pol/inf)
My name is ...
Mit navn er ... mit naa·oon er ...
Where are you from?
Hvor kommer De/ vor *kom*·aa dee/
du fra? doo fraa (pol/inf)
I'm from ...
Jeg er fra ... yai er fraa ...
I like ...
Jeg kan lide ... yai kan lee ...
I don't like ...
Jeg kan ikke lide ... yai kan ig lee ...
Just a minute.
Et øjeblik. it *oy*·e·blig

SIGNS

Indgang	Entrance
Udgang	Exit
Information	Information
Åben	Open
Lukket	Closed
Forbudt	Prohibited
Politi	Police
Toilet	Toilet/WC
Herrer	Men
Damer	Women

DIRECTIONS
Where is ...?
Hvor er ...? vor er ...
Go straight ahead.
Gå lige ud. gor *lee*·e ooth
Turn left.
Drej til venstre. drai ti *vens*·draa
Turn right.
Drej til højre. drai ti *hoy*·yaa
at the next corner
ved næste hjørne vi *nes*·de *yer*·ne
at the traffic lights
ved trafiklyset vi traa·*feeg*·lew·seth

behind *bag* baa
in front of *foran* *for*·an

far (from)	*langt (fra)*	laangd (fraa)
near (to)	*nær (ved)*	ner (vi)
opposite	*modsat*	moth·sat

EMERGENCIES

It's an emergency!
Det er en nødsituation!   di er in *nerth*·si·too·a·shon
Help!
Hjælp!   yelb
There's been an accident!
Der er sket en ulykke!   daa er skit in *oo*·ler·ge
I'm lost.
Jeg er faret vild.   yai er *faa*·aeth vil
Go away!
Forsvind!   for·*svin*

Call ...!
Ring efter...!
ring *ef*·daa ...
  a doctor
  en læge   in *le*·e
  the police
  politiet   po·li·*tee*·eth

HEALTH

I'm ill.
Jeg er syg.   yai er sew

I'm ...
Jeg har ...
yai haa ...
  asthmatic   *astma*   *asd*·ma
  diabetic   *diabetes*   dee·a·*bi*·tes
  epileptic   *epilepsi*   e·pee·leb·*see*

I'm allergic to ...
Jeg er allergisk over for ...
yai er a·*ler*·geesg *ow*·aa for ...
  antibiotics   *antibiotika*   an·tee·bee·o·tee·ka
  aspirin   *aspirin*   as·bee·*reen*
  penicillin   *penicillin*   pin·ee·see·*leen*
  bees   *bier*   *bee*·aa
  nuts   *nødder*   *nerth*·aa
  peanuts   *peanuts*   *pee*·nuts

antiseptic	*antiseptisk*	an·tee·*seb*·tisg
condoms	*kondomer*	kon·*do*·maa
diarrhoea	*diarré*	dee·a·*re*
medicine	*medicin*	mi·dee·*seen*
nausea	*kvalme*	*kval*·me
sunblock cream	*solcreme*	*sol*·krem
tampons	*tamponer*	taam·*pong*·aa

LANGUAGE DIFFICULTIES

Do you speak English?
Taler De engelsk?
ta·laa dee *eng*·elsg
How do you say ... in Danish?
Hvordan siger man ... på dansk?
vor·*dan* see·aa man ... por dansg
I understand.
Jeg forstår.
yai for·*sdor*
I don't understand.
Jeg forstår ikke.
yai for·*sdor* ig
Can you show me (on the map)?
Kunne De/du vise mig det (på kortet)? (pol/inf)
koo·ne dee/doo *vee*·se mai di (por *kor*·deth)

NUMBERS

0	*nul*	norl
1	*en*	in
2	*to*	tor
3	*tre*	tre
4	*fire*	feer
5	*fem*	fem
6	*seks*	segs
7	*syv*	see·ew
8	*otte*	o·de
9	*ni*	nee
10	*ti*	tee
11	*elve*	*el*·ve
12	*tolv*	tol
13	*tretten*	tra·den
14	*fjorten*	*fyor*·den
15	*femten*	*fem*·den
16	*seksten*	*sais*·den
17	*sytten*	*ser*·den
18	*atten*	*a*·den
19	*nitten*	*ni*·den
20	*tyve*	*tew*·ve
21	*enogtyve*	in·o·tew·we
30	*tredive*	*trath*·ve
40	*fyrre*	*fer*·e
50	*halvtreds*	haal·*tres*
60	*tres*	tres
70	*halvfjerds*	haal·*fyers*
80	*firs*	feers
90	*halvfems*	haal·*fems*
100	*hundrede*	*hoo*·naath
1000	*tusind*	*too*·sen

SHOPPING & SERVICES

I'd like to buy ...
Jeg vil gerne have ...   yai vi *ger*·ne ha ...
How much is it?
Hvor meget koster det?   vo *maa*·eth *kos*·daa di

LANGUAGE

GLOSSARY

Abbreviations in this glossary are: D (Danish), F (Finnish), G (Greenlandic), N (Norwegian), R (Russian), S (Sami), Sw (Swedish).

brædtet (D) – food market
chum (R) – a Nenets yurt
dovekies – penguin-like small birds
Finnmark – Norway's largest, least populated and northernmost county
kaffemik (G) – coffee party
kivioq (G) – dovekies stuffed in hollowed-out seal carcasses and left to rot
komarnik (R) – head-net
Kommunia (D) – local government office
humppa (F) – traditional dance and music
kupe (R) – train class with four berths in a closed compartment
lavvo (S) – tent

Norrland (Sw) – Sweden's northern provinces, beginning about two hours north of Stockholm and continuing to the north coast
nunatak (G) – a rocky peak that emerges from or is surrounded by glacier ice
outfitter – guide with the necessary insurance to lead tourist trips
platskart (R) – train class with sleeping berths in an open carriage
qajaq (G) – hunting boat traditionally used by men
rorbu (N) – winter shanty
sjøhus (N) – former fishermen's bunkhouse
sourdough – originally meaning a settler or prospector in Alaska or the Yukon, but now used to describe anyone who has spent a few winters in the region
taiga – the transitional zone between subarctic boreal forests and High Arctic tundra
tunturi (F) – hills
umiak (G) – skin boat traditionally used by women

Do you accept ...?
Tager I ...? plur
taa ee ...
  credit cards
  kreditkort   kre·*deed*·kort
  travellers cheques
  rejsechecks   rai·se·shegs

I'm looking for ...
Jeg leder efter ...
yai *li*·thaa *ef*·daa ...
  a bank
  en bank   in bank
  the hospital
  hospitalet   hors·bi·*ta*·leth
  the market
  et marked   it *maa*·geth
  the museum
  museet   moo·*se*·eth
  the police
  politiet   po·lee·*tee*·eth
  the post office
  postkontoret   *post*·kon·tor·eth
  a public toilet
  et offentligt toilet   it *o*·fend·leed toy·*let*
  the tourist office
  turistinformationen   too·*reest*·in·for·ma·sho·nen

TIME & DATES
What time is it?
  Hvad er klokken?   va er *klo*·gen
It's ... o'clock.
  Klokken er ...   *klo*·gen er ...
in the morning
  om morgenen   om *mor*·nen

in the evening
  om aftenen   om *aafd*·nen

When?	*Hvornår?*	vo·*nor*
today	*i dag*	ee da
tomorrow	*i morgen*	ee morn
yesterday	*i går*	ee gor
Monday	*mandag*	*man*·da
Tuesday	*tirsdag*	*teers*·da
Wednesday	*onsdag*	*ons*·da
Thursday	*torsdag*	*tors*·da
Friday	*fredag*	*fre*·da
Saturday	*lørdag*	*ler*·da
Sunday	*søndag*	*sern*·da
January	*januar*	*yan*·oo·aa
February	*februar*	*feb*·oo·aa
March	*marts*	maards
April	*april*	a·*preel*
May	*maj*	mai
June	*juni*	*yoo*·nee
July	*juli*	*yoo*·lee
August	*august*	aa·oo·*gorsd*
September	*september*	sib·*tem*·baa
October	*oktober*	og·*to*·baa
November	*november*	no·*vem*·baa
December	*december*	di·*sem*·baa

TRANSPORT
Public Transport
What time does the ... leave/arrive?
  Hvornår går/ankommer ...
  vor·*nor* gor/*an*·kom·aa ...

boat	båden	bor·then
bus	bussen	boo·sen
plane	flyet	flew·eth

the first	første	fers·de
the last	sidste	sees·de
ticket	billet	bi·let
ticket office	billetkontor	bi·let·kon·tor
timetable	køreplan	ker·plan

Private Transport

Where can I rent a ...?
Hvor kan jeg leje en ...?
vor kan yai *lai*·e in ...

car	bil	beel
4WD	firehjulstrækker	fee·ya·yools·trer·gaa
motorbike	motorcykel	mo·tor·sew·gel
bicycle	cykel	sew·gel

Is this the road to ...?
Fører denne vej til ...?
fer·aa *den*·ne vai ti ...

Where's the next service station?
Hvor er næste benzinstation?
vor er *nes*·de ben·seen·sda·shon

I'd like ... litres.
Jeg vil gerne have ... liter.
yai vi *ger*·ne ha ... *lee*·ta

diesel/petrol
diesel/benzin
dee·sel/ben·seen

GREENLANDIC

PRONUNCIATION

Greenlandic pronunciation is difficult. Consonants come from deep in the throat and some vowels are scarcely pronounced. Your best bet is to listen and learn, but if it all seems too much, you can always fall back on Danish.

Vowels

a	as the 'u' in 'hut'
aa	as the 'a' in 'father'
e	as the 'a' in 'ago'
i	as in 'marine'
o	as in 'hot'
u	as the 'oo' in 'cool'

Consonants

Consonants are pronounced as in English with the exception of the following:

g	as in 'goose'
j	as in 'jaw'
k	as in 'key'
l	as in 'leg'
ng	as in 'sing'
q	pronounced as a 'k' from deep in the back of the throat
v	as in 'van'

ACCOMMODATION

hotel	hoteli
guesthouse	unnuisarfik
youth hostel	angallatsinut unnuisarfik
camp site	tupertarfik

Do you have any rooms available?
Inimik attartungasaateqarpise?
Does it include breakfast?
Ullaakkoorsioneq ilaareerpa?

I'd like ...	... piumavunga.
a single room	Kisimiittariamik
a double room	Marluuttariamik

How much is it ...?	... qanoq akeqarpa?
per night	Unuinnarmut
per person	Inummut ataatsimut

CONVERSATION & ESSENTIALS

Hello.	Inuugujoq, kutaa/Haluu.
Goodbye, best wishes. (long-term parting)	Inuulluarit. (sg)/ Inuulluaritse (pl) Ajunnginniarna (sg)/ Ajunnginniarise (pl)
Bye/See you soon. (short-term parting)	Takuss'.
Yes.	Aap.
No.	Naagga/Naamik.
Thank you (very much).	Qujanaq (qujanarsuaq).
Do you speak English?	Tuluttut oqalusinnaavit?
What's your name?	Qanoq ateqarpit?
My name is ...	...-imik ateqarpunga.

NUMBERS

Numbers in Greenlandic only go up to 12 – after 12 there is only *amerlasoorpassuit*, 'many'. From 12 onwards you have to use Danish numbers (see p337).

1		ataaseq
2		marluk
3		pingasut
4		sisamat
5		tallimat

6	arfinillit
7	arfineq marluk
8	arfineq pingasut
9	qulingiluat
10	qulit
11	arqanillit
12	arqaneq marluk

SHOPPING & SERVICES

Where is a/the ...?	... sumiippa?/Naak ...?
bank	banki
market	kalaalimineerniarfik
police	politeeqarfik
post office	allakkerivik
public toilet	anartarfik
telephone centre	oqarasuaat/telefooni
tourist office	takornarissanut allaffik

Is it far from here?	Maanngaanit ungasippa?
Go straight ahead.	Siumuinnaq.
Turn left.	Saamimmut sangulluni.
Turn right.	Talerpimmut sangulluni.
How much is it?	Qanoq akeqarpa?
What time does it open/close?	Qaqugu ammassarpat/matusarpat?

TIME & DATES

What time is it?	Qassinngorpa?
today	ullumi
tomorrow	aqagu
morning	ullaaq
afternoon	ualeq

Monday	Ataasinngorneq
Tuesday	Marlunngorneq
Wednesday	Pingasunngorneq
Thursday	Sisamanngorneq
Friday	Tallimanngorneq
Saturday	Arfininngorneq
Sunday	Sapaat

TRANSPORT

What time does the ... leave/arrive?
Qaqugu ... aallartarpa/tikkiuttarpa?

boat	ilaasortaat
bus	bussi
plane	timmisartoq

I'd like a ... ticket.	... bilitsimik pisorusuppunga.
one-way	Siumuinnaq
return	Siumut-utimut

EAT YOUR WORDS

The Greenlandic and Danish words and phrases below should help you decode menus and communicate with local people about food.

USEFUL PHRASES

The Greenlandic translation is given first, followed by the Danish.

Can I have some more please?
| Aammalu suli? | Må jeg få lidt mere, tak? |

It tastes good.
| Amaq. | Det smager godt. |

I don't like it.
| Mamarinngilara. | Det kan jeg ikke li'. |

That's enough, thanks.
| Naammappoq. | Det er nok, tak. |

What is it?
| Sunaana? | Hva' er det? |

FOOD GLOSSARY

Greenlandic – Danish – English

aalisakkaq – fisk – fish
aarrup neqaa – hvalroskød – walrus meat
ammassat panertut – tørret lodde – dried capelin
aqisseq – fjeldrype – ptarmigan
arferup neqaa – hvalkød – whale meat
eqaluk pujogaq – røget ørred – smoked trout
mattak – hvalfedt – whale blubber
neqi – kød – meat
neqi suaasalik puisi – (klar) sælsuppe – seal broth soup
nikkut – tørret kød – dried meat
nilaap ernga – isvand – icewater
panertut – tørret fisk – dried fish
puisip neqaa – sælkød – seal meat
qaleralik – Grønlands helleflynder – Greenland halibut
saarullik panertoq – tørret torsk – dried cod
tikaagulliup neqaa siataq – minkhvalsbøf – minke whale steak
tuttup neqaa – karibu kød – caribou meat

Behind the Scenes

THIS BOOK

This is the 2nd edition of *Greenland & the Arctic* (formerly the two titles *The Arctic* and *Iceland, Greenland & the Faroe Islands*). The 1st edition of *The Arctic* was written by Deanna Swaney, who also wrote the 1st edition of *Iceland, Greenland & the Faroe Islands* and updated that book's 2nd edition. The 3rd edition was updated by Graeme Cornwallis and Deanna Swaney, and the 4th edition by Graeme Cornwallis. *Greenland & the Arctic* 2 was written by Etain O'Carroll and Mark Elliott, and co-ordinated by Etain. Dr Caroline Evans contributed to the Health chapter.

THANKS from the Authors

Etain O'Carroll Special thanks to Don Irving and Frontiers, who started my love affair with the north. *Quana* to all in Cambridge Bay who made me so welcome, and particularly to Donna and George Hakongak for their friendship and generosity, and to Sandra Card for taking me into her home and being so generous with her time and knowledge on those numerous land trips. *Massi-cho* to all in Old Crow for their generosity of spirit and sharing of local knowledge. Thanks also to Siw Møller Kristensen at Greenland Tourism; Robert Peroni and Inge Weber in Tasiilaq; Jens Laursen and Jørgen Laursen in Kangerlussuaq; Kai AB Drastrup in Mani-itsoq; Jane Nielsen in Sisimiut; Fredrick Lundblad in Aasiaat; Silver, Poul Therkelsen and Ole Gamst Pedersen in Ilulissat; Hanne Andersen in Uummannaq; Saki Daorana in Qaanaaq; and Bo Albrechtsen in Upernavik. On the home front, thanks to BF&M for all the support and hefty tomes on Arctic history, to

Mark B for the crackly phone calls and virtual smiles, to Miles Roddis, Paul Harding and Carolyn Bain for help on travel routes, to Mark Elliott for all the tips and suggestions, and to Amanda, Alan and Imogen for their good humour and patient replies.

Mark Elliott Without the remarkable help, hospitality and wisdom of many wonderful people, my job would have been far less interesting and vastly more difficult. Enormous thanks to Annette Lindmardtsen, Henning Stehr Nielsen, Knud Holmsgaard, Sonja Peary, Rasmus Lohse, Niels Taekker Jepsen, Finn Lynge and Rie Oldenburg, Kirsten Løgstrup, Karen and Eigil Kjaer, Jaspur Midjord, Themo Benjaminsen, Anton, Lars Isaksen and the hunters of Aappilattok, Heidi Møller and family, Jes ('Yes') Burghardt, Sigridur 'Sirra' Olafsdottir, Siw Møller Kristensen, Chris McCully, Tony and Sarah Whitehouse, Birger Knudsen, Mirella and Sergio Passuello, Marc and Sue Seidenberg, Hardtmut Finke, Soren Thalund, Thor Hjarsen, Gunnar in Narsarsuaq, Christopher Tautermann, Georg Nyegaard and Aleqa, Florian Stammler, Gerhardt in Qaqortoq, Pilu Nielsen, Mini at Kangerluarsorujuk Qinngua, Christie and Isabelle, Grenville Byford and Yosi Ya'ari, Sarah Johnstone, Arnaud Ramina, Wieland de Hoon, Debbie Chase, Igor Fedyaev, Rainer Rontti, Peter McCleod, Irina Chirkova, Gavin Menzies, Hans Rossel, Folke Von Knobloch, Bent Nielsen, Bruce Forbes, Monica Schou, Carsten Egevang, Anders Nilsson, Anne-Marie Malchow, Olivier and Katrine Colleau, Svetlana Sapanovich, Klaus Martinsen, Ingebo, George Gogolev, Stuart Lyon, Nina Collins, various tourist offices and all

---

THE LONELY PLANET STORY

The story begins with a classic travel adventure: Tony and Maureen Wheeler's 1972 journey across Europe and Asia to Australia. There was no useful information about the overland trail then, so Tony and Maureen published the first Lonely Planet guidebook to meet a growing need.

From a kitchen table, Lonely Planet has grown to become the largest independent travel publisher in the world, with offices in Melbourne (Australia), Oakland (USA) and London (UK). Today Lonely Planet guidebooks cover the globe. There is an ever-growing list of books and information in a variety of media. Some things haven't changed. The main aim is still to make it possible for adventurous travellers to get out there – to explore and better understand the world.

At Lonely Planet we believe travellers can make a positive contribution to the countries they visit – if they respect their host communities and spend their money wisely. Every year 5% of company profit is donated to charities around the world.

at LP, especially Etain, Alan, Amanda and Imogen. Love and endless gratitude to Dani Systermans and my beloved parents.

CREDITS

Greenland & the Arctic 2 was commissioned and developed in Lonely Planet's London office by Alan Murphy, Imogen Franks and Amanda Canning, and assessed by Sam Trafford. The book was coordinated by Sarah Bailey (editorial), and Jolyon Philcox and Bonnie Wintle (cartography). Kate James and Lucy Monie assisted with editing and proofing. Hunor Csutoros, Csanad Csutoros, James Ellis, Owen Eszeki, Jacqueline Nguyen and Jacqui Saunders assisted with cartography. Katherine Marsh laid the book out, and Laura Jane designed and laid out the colour content. Jane Hart designed the cover. Kate Evans assisted with editorial layout checks, and David Kemp and Wibowo Rusli assisted with cross-referencing. Jacqui Saunders, Michael Ruff and John Shippick assisted with indexing. Quentin Frayne, Jodie Martire and Karin Vidstrup Monk prepared the Language chapter. Overseeing production were Charles Rawlings-Way (Project Manager), Yvonne Byron and Bruce Evans (Managing Editors), and Anthony Phelan, Corinne Waddell and Mark Griffiths (Managing Cartographers).

The series was designed by James Hardy, with mapping development by Paul Piaia.

THANKS from Lonely Planet

Many thanks to the following travellers who used the last edition and wrote to us with helpful hints, useful advice and interesting anecdotes.

Laure Arnold, Michele Beltrame, Karina Bernlow, Roger Bielec, Sara Bjornsdottir, Vanessa Burgess, Donnie Campbell, Gordon Campbell, Debbie Chapman, David Connah, Edward Coppola, Geert De Coninck, Rod Dalitz, Allan Edelsparre, Sascha Frenzel, Laura Galimberti, Nathan Girdner, Lars Gyllenhaal, Sigurður Hjartarson, Bob & Jo Hunter, Brett Jackson, Edward Jones, Joel Kaplan, Toby Kenyon, Kou Kusunoki, Frank Laan, Andrew Leung, Paul Logman, Michael Loungo, John Mason, Babis Mitsonis, Richard Morris, Nicole Mueller, Gerry Murphy, Margo Orlando, Angeliki Partiniotaki, Juhasz Peter, Marie Peyre, Steinunn Ragnarsdóttir, Rieke Raphael, Lorelei & Pete Redding, Birthe Rossel, Don Rosso, Svanhvit Helga Runarsdottir, Claudia Schwabl, Remy Swaab, Ben Van Heest, Melinda Viksne

ACKNOWLEDGMENTS

Many thanks to the following for the use of their content:

Globe on back cover © Mountain High Maps 1993 Digital Wisdom, Inc.

BEHIND THE SCENES

SEND US YOUR FEEDBACK

We love to hear from travellers – your comments keep us on our toes and help make our books better. Our well-travelled team reads every word on what you loved or loathed about this book. Although we cannot reply individually to postal submissions, we always guarantee that your feedback goes straight to the appropriate authors, in time for the next edition. Each person who sends us information is thanked in the next edition – and the most useful submissions are rewarded with a free book.

To send us your updates – and find out about Lonely Planet events, newsletters and travel news – visit our award-winning website: **www.lonelyplanet.com/feedback**

Note: We may edit, reproduce and incorporate your comments in Lonely Planet products such as guidebooks, websites and digital products, so let us know if you don't want your comments reproduced or your name acknowledged. For a copy of our privacy policy visit www .lonelyplanet.com/privacy

Index

INDEX